Available for the first time in English, Bogdanovich's *Russian History of the War of 1813* continues where the *History of the War of 1812* left off. In describing the events of 1813, the author strives to give an accurate portrayal of one of the most important years in European history and pays tribute to the service of the Russian army in the liberation of Germany. Russia, of course, could not defeat Napoleon alone. But the Russians, having begun the war in Prussia and the Duchy of Warsaw without the assistance of allies, managed to draw Prussia into their cause, and eventually Austria, Sweden and Britain.

This book will appeal to those interested in Napoleonic military history, as well as to wargamers and gives a fascinating insight into the surprisingly cosmopolitan Russian army officers of that era. Although Bogdanovich had access to Russian state archives and private papers, he also makes extensive use of published German and French memoirs and histories in order to provide additional context and balance. Volume 1 covered the period from the Russian invasion of the Duchy of Warsaw up to the Armistice of June 1813. Volume 2 covers from the resumption of hostilities in August 1813 until the Coalition advance to the Rhine by December 1813, from the Battle on the Katzbach to the climactic Battle of Leipzig and on to the Battle of Hanau.

Born in Sumy, Ukraine, in 1805, Bogdanovich was initially educated in the Noble Regiment, being commissioned into the artillery in 1823. Bogdanovich saw combat in the Polish campaign of 1831 and upon his return in 1833, he entered the Imperial Military Academy, becoming its Director of Operations until 1839. Thereafter, he served on committees of the General Staff. He died in August, 1882 in Oranienbaum. General Bogdanovich is famed for a number of major works, making an invaluable contribution to Russian military historiography. His *History of the Patriotic War of 1812* won the Demidov Prize for History in 1861.

Peter G.A. Phillips is a veteran of 27 years in the British Army Intelligence Corps, including working as a Russian, German, and Serbo-Croat linguist, thereafter spending five years as part of a Civil Service team training British Armed Forces personnel to serve in UK diplomatic missions. He is now retired and spends his time translating Russian military histories of the Coalition Wars. His published translations include: Mikhailovsky-Danilevsky's histories of the wars of 1805 and 1806-1807; a collaboration with renowned Napoleonic historian Dr Alexander Mikaberidze of Ilya Radozhitskii's trilogy of memoirs covering 1812-1814; and numerous articles for The Waterloo Association's website www.napoleon-series.org. Peter now lives in the Philippines with his Filipina wife of 34 years. They have two adult daughters.

The Russian History of the War of 1813 Volume 2

The War to Liberate Germany

Modest Ivanovich Bogdanovich

Translated by Peter G.A. Phillips

Helion & Company

Helion & Company Limited
Unit 8 Amherst Business Centre
Budbrooke Road
Warwick
CV34 5WE
England
Tel. 01926 499619
Email: info@helion.co.uk
Website: www.helion.co.uk
Twitter: @helionbooks
Visit our blog at http://blog.helion.co.uk/

Published by Helion & Company 2026
Designed and typeset by Mach 3 Solutions Ltd (www.mach3solutions.co.uk)
Cover designed by Paul Hewitt, Battlefield Design (www.battlefield-design.co.uk)

Original text published as *History Of The War Of 1813 For The Liberation Of Germany According To Reliable Sources. Compiled in accordance with Supreme orders*, St Petersburg, 1863
Translation © Peter Philips 2025
Maps and diagrams adapted from the originals © Helion & Company 2025

Cover: Battle of Kulm, the 17th of August, 1813, by Alexander von Kotzebue (Public domain)

Every reasonable effort has been made to trace copyright holders and to obtain their permission for the use of copyright material. The author and publisher apologise for any errors or omissions in this work, and would be grateful if notified of any corrections that should be incorporated in future reprints or editions of this book.

ISBN 978-1-804518-21-2

British Library Cataloguing-in-Publication Data.
A catalogue record for this book is available from the British Library.

All rights reserved. No part of this publication may be reproduced, stored in a retrieval system, or transmitted, in any form, or by any means, electronic, mechanical, photocopying, recording or otherwise, without the express written consent of Helion & Company Limited.

For details of other military history titles published by Helion & Company Limited, contact the above address, or visit our website: http://www.helion.co.uk

We always welcome receiving book proposals from prospective authors.

Contents

List of Maps		v
Translator's Foreword		vi
21	Resupply and reconstitution of the forces upon the conclusion of the armistice	7
22	Initial operations by the Army of Silesia following the end of the armistice	16
23	The battle on the Katzbach	40
24	The Battle of Großbeeren	69
25	Action at Hagelberg	91
26	The offensive by the main Coalition Army from Bohemia into Saxony	107
27	The Battle of Dresden	126
28	The Battle of Dresden (continued)	147
29	The Coalition retreat from Dresden into Bohemia. Actions at Berggießhübel and Hellendorf	167
30	The action at Kulm on 17 (29) August	181
31	The Battle of Kulm, 18 (30) August	201
32	The Battle of Dennewitz	223
33	Napoleon's Operations against the main army and Army of Silesia from after the Battle of Kulm until the unification of French forces around Dresden	240
34	Measures taken by the Coalition in order to concentrate their forces	273
35	Partisan operations since the ending of the armistice	286
36	Operations by Graf Wallmoden's Corps. The action at Göhrde and capture of Bremen	302
37	Blücher's flank-march from Bautzen to the Elbe. The Battle of Wartenburg. The Crown Prince of Sweden crosses the Elbe	308
38	The concentration of forces by both sides at Leipzig. Cavalry action at Liebertwolkwitz	327
39	The Battle of Leipzig. The actions at Wachau and Lindenau on 4 (16) October	363
40	The Battle of Leipzig (continued)	392
41	The Battle of Leipzig, 6 (18) October 1813 (continued)	412
42	The Battle of Leipzig (conclusion)	434
43	The Coalition pursuit of Napoleon's army from the Elster to the Main	450
44	The Battle of Hanau	463
45	Operations against the Danes and the liberation of the Netherlands	490
46	Sieges of the fortresses to the rear of the Coalition Army	501
47	Conclusions	520

Chapter numbering runs sequentially on from the previous volume

Appendices

I	Disposition issued by Blücher on the morning of 11 (23) August	37
II	General Yorck's letter to King Friedrich Wilhelm III, dated 25 August, new style	38
III	The calculation of Coalition troop strength in the fighting on the Katzbach	64
IV	Disposition issued by Blücher on the morning of 14 (26) August	65
V	Alexander I's rescript to Blücher and Sacken's dispatch to Volkonsky, regarding the Battle on the Katzbach	66
VI	The composition of Bülow's corps	89
VII	The composition of Hirschfeld's and Putlitz's detachments	101
VIII	Disposition issued by General Hirschfeld on 27 August [new style]	102
IX	Differences between Plotho's and Vaudoncourt's accounts of the Battle of Hagelsberg	105
X	Davout's corps and the Danish contingent at Hamburg	106
XI	The composition of Vandamme's force	125
XII	The composition of Prinz Eugen von Württemberg's force	143
XIII	Extracts from the War Diary of II Corps and Lieutenant General Wachten's notes	144
XIV	Note submitted to Emperor Alexander by General Moreau a week before the Battle of Dresden	162
XV	Emperor Alexander's letter to General Moreau's widow	165
XVI	Oberst Schöler's liaison with Kleist at Kulm	192
XVII	Yermolov's reluctance to commit the Russian Lifeguard at Kulm	193
XVIII	Yermolov's succession to command of Osterman's force at Kulm	194
XIX	Supreme Orders dated August 1814 for the former Committee for the Wounded	195
XX	General Yermolov's report on the action at Kulm	196
XXI	Listing of the Coalition forces assembled against Vandamme on 18 (30) August	218
XXII	Austrian reluctance to fight at Kulm	219
XXIII	German reaction to Vandamme as a prisoner of war	220
XXIV	General Bülow's letter to the Tsar after the Battle of Dennewitz	239
XXV	Composition of the Austrian army from 22 August (3 September)	263
XXVI	The composition of General Bennigsen's Army of Poland	268
XXVII	Bernadotte's letter to Blücher, dated 6 October, 1813, new style	324
XXVIII	Composition of Yorck's force, dated 21 September (3 October)	325
XXIX	Berthier's letter to Murat, dated 12 October, new style	357
XXX	Comparison of estimates of Murat's troop strength before Leipzig	359
XXXI	Bernadotte's letter to Emperor Alexander, dated 15 October 1813, new style	360
XXXII	Comparison of estimates of Napoleon's troop strengths at Leipzig	388
XXXIII	Coalition forces at the actions at Wachau and Connewitz on 4 (16) October 1813	389
XXXIV	Composition and deployment of Coalition forces at Möckern	409
XXXV	Planned march-routes for the Army of Bohemia and Army of Silesia after Leipzig	461
XXXVI	Movements by the Army of Poland and Army of the North after Leipzig	462
XXXVII	Emperor Alexander's letter to the King of Bavaria, dated 11 (23) September 1813	485
XXXVIII	Composition of Graf Wrede's Austro-Bavarian army	488
XXXIX	Composition of the Coalition blockade corps at Danzig	518

Sources For The History of the War Of 1813   523
Index   531

List of Maps

Map showing Blücher's operations following the expiry of the Armistice.	20
The battle on the Katzbach, 14 (26) August 1813).	44
Map to follow operations by the Main Army and Army of the North in August and September 1813.	73
Plan of the Battle of Großbeeren, 11 (23) August 1913).	79
Action at Hagelberg, 15 (27) August 1813.	90
Plan of the Battle of Dresden.	122
Plan of the Battle of Dresden, 15 (27) August 1813.	145
Map of troop movements from Dresden to Kulm.	166
Plan of the Battle of Kulm.	180
Plan of the Battle of Kulm.	199
Plan of the Battle of Dennewitz.	221
Map of General Chernyshev's march on Kassel in September 1813.	291
Plan of the Battle of Wartenburg.	314
Plan of the action at Wachau, 4 (16) October 1813.	362
Plan of the Battle of Möckern, 4 (16) October 1813.	391
Plan of the Battle of Leipzig, 6 (18) October 1813.	410
Plan of the Battle of Hanau.	468
Plan of the Danzig Area.	511
Plan of the Siege of Danzig.	515

Translator's Foreword

When I set out on the epic task of translating Bogdanovich's histories of the wars of 1812–1814, I had the naive desire to present the finished books as close to the originals as possible. A lot has changed in publishing since the 1860s, however, and the cost of reproducing (and hand-packing) hard-copy versions of the enormous and highly detailed maps would have placed the price of these books beyond the budgets of all but the most dedicated bibliophile. Consequently, compromises have had to be made, but modern technology has also offered a rather neat solution: to place the maps on the Helion website such that the digital versions may be viewed in a 'zoomable' version, making all the delicious detail of the originals accessible to readers. The maps for this volume are available at https://www.helion.co.uk/military-history-books/the-russian-history-of-the-war-of-1813-volume-2-the-war-to-liberate-germany.php.

21

Resupply and reconstitution of the forces upon the conclusion of the armistice

The situation with regard to ration supplies for the army. – Measures taken upon the conclusion of the armistice for the delivery of provisions and fodder from the Duchy of Warsaw. – The purchase of supplies in Silesia. – The procurement of fodder, livestock and wine in Bohemia. The difficulty of feeding the army in this country. – Measures taken by the Austrian government. – Requisitioning methods upon the resumption of hostilities. – Regarding the impossibility of effectively and efficiently supplying rations to the army. Supplying the troops with essential supplies, exclusively in kind. – The factors behind this. – Ration supply for independent formations of the army. – Conventions regarding the provisioning of troops, concluded between the Russian government, Prussia and Austria.

Measures taken by the commissariat department. – Purchase of cloth and linen and tailoring of uniform items in the Duchy of Warsaw and Prussia. – Distribution of cloth and linen to troops against receipts from factories in Silesia. – Requisitions in Saxony. – The delivery of cloth to Silesia from Russia during the armistice. – Clothing the troops; the establishment of significant warehouses in Grodno and Brest. – Preparation of short, sheepskin coats. – Purchase of waistcoats in Bohemia and 100,000 pairs of boots in Leipzig. – Difficulties in procuring, delivering and sewing clothes, etcetera. Difficulties in the efficient distribution of supplies in wartime. Hospitals abroad. – Agreements with deputies from Old Prussia regarding the subsistence for Russian patients following the battles of Lützen and Bautzen. – The establishment of medical departments in Bohemia, Saxony and during the march to the Rhine. – Supplying the troops with combat stores.

Provisioning for Napoleon's army being exclusively by requisition. – The desolation of Saxony. – The decline of discipline among the troops. – Conditions in the medical department.

When describing military events, it is a most difficult matter to present administrative instructions regarding provisioning for the army and, in general, the resupply of the troops with every necessity. The order and strict reporting which exists in peacetime for the issue and receipt of items, and in the procurement and expenditure of supplies, become completely impossible during wartime: unanticipated situations, encountered at every step, force changes to the regular methods; the incessant arrival and departure of units obstructs rigorous accounting. Military historians find insufficient information in official documents, none of which satisfactorily explain either the merits or the consequences of administrative decisions, while in memoirs there are only general notes on the state of the troops, provisioning, commissariat, medical and other departments, the movements of parks and mobile magazines and so on. All this leads to many military events being explained inaccurately, due to a lack of data relating to the administration of the army. And therefore, no matter how scarce the sources may be that might shed light on the administrative activities in the army, they will always be precious in the eyes of those who are dissatisfied with conclusions drawn on the eventual outcome of their movements and operations.

Upon the conclusion of the armistice, the significant numbers of the Russo-Prussian force assembled in Silesia had exhausted this country and forced the Coalition monarchs to establish a temporary military administration in the Duchy of Warsaw,[1] whose main duties were the distribution of requisitions and the delivery of supplies collected for the army. At the beginning of the armistice, the situation seemed hopeless: there was no hard-tack in the regimental trains, while the mobile magazines lagged far behind the army. In the first instance, provisions were being delivered from warehouses located in nearby Prussian fortresses, and in the meantime, requisitions were being collected in significant amounts throughout the entire territory of Poland from the Silesian border as far as Bromberg [Bydgoszcz], Warsaw and Krakau [Kraków], from where rations were being delivered to the Oder. Resupply from Thorn [Toruń] had been arranged in a similar fashion. The troops found great resources in Silesia itself; but since the delivery of hay turned out to be problematic, the troops acquired grass instead through foraging. Many life-sustaining supplies were acquired by purchase; in particular, covertly from Austrian territory. Quite a significant amount of flour was brought in from upper Silesia. Residents of the central zone between the belligerent armies, Breslau [Wrocław] citizens for the most part, delivered a lot of grain to Schweidnitz [Świdnica] and other Coalition Army locations. Mobile magazines were also used for the delivery of provisions: one of them, made up of 3,000 peasant carts, originally assigned to the former Army of Moldavia, arrived on the Vistula in very poor condition, but after wintering in the Duchy of Warsaw, set off and arrived in Silesia with 25,000 *Centner* (more than 60,000 *Pud* [over 2,000,000 pounds]) of hard-tack, which, having a long shelf-life, was used to feed the troops not only in 1813, but also into the subsequent campaign.[2]

---

1   Report No. 7 by Chief of Staff, Major General Toll, to Adjutant-General Prince Volkonsky, dated 26 September (8 October) 1813 (Log of incoming documents, No. 1,560).
2   Georg Graf von Cancrin, *Ueber die Militairökonomie im Frieden und Krieg und ihr Wechselverhältniss zu den Operationen*, I, 87-88.

Even prior to setting off for Bohemia from Silesia, a significant amount of fodder, livestock and wine were purchased in the former country for the Russian army.[3]

Upon arrival in Bohemia on the left bank of the Elbe, the Russian army had with it 24 days' worth of hard-tack in a mobile magazine (which Barclay [Mikhail Bogdanovich Barklay de Tolli or Michael Andreas Barclay de Tolly] stated: 'I furtively smuggled in with me'), in addition to the ten days' of provisions on the man and in regimental transport. Some of these supplies were expended during their stay in the vicinity of Teplitz [Teplice], because the Austrian commissariat, although it had undertaken to deliver everything needed by their allies, and notwithstanding the huge preparations they had made, could not satisfy the needs of the Main Army, and, moreover, the panic caused by the Coalition retreat following the battle of Dresden forced the Austrians to suspend ration resupply. This was an extremely difficult period in relation to ration supply for the forces. Forage was obtained in the Ore Mountains and on their northern slopes in Saxony. Cancrin wrote: 'While remaining in place, one should stockpile as much as possible, because efforts made subsequently to replenish supplies may prove to be untimely.' The Austrian commissariat very prudently took care of the delivery of supplies from remote areas of their Empire. The baking of flour into bread and hard-tack was carried out partly in camp ovens, hastily set up by the troops, and partly in the towns by the population. The main difficulty lay in the organisation of mobile magazines.[4]

With the opening of hostilities, the main source for the resupply of essential stores for the army was through requisitioning, which was decided upon on the following grounds:

When moving out of contact with the enemy, in sparsely populated areas, at each stage, or at least at each of the locations where the troops had rest-days, a large store of provisions and fodder, or just of hay, was to be prepared; in more populous areas, ready-prepared rations were to be obtained from land-owners, who, as a reward for this, were to be given money from the local government in the country, or they were to be resupplied from magazines. Even in Saxony, until coming into contact with the enemy, most of the army were to be fed in quarters, and the troops were to bivouac only occasionally. During overnight halts, and especially on rest-days, supplementary magazines were to be used to provide support to the troops and to provide rations for the headquarters. When advancing to contact with the enemy, or in the event that it was impossible to rely on the assistance of local government, commissioning agents were to be sent forward with the Cossack patrols in order to encourage the population to provide supplies. These patrols were also used to prevent the disorder often caused by the trains and detachments, and to that end, was adopted as a permanent regulation that the population should not give anything to the troops without it being allocated by commissioning agents.

---

3 Account of the activities of the Quartermaster's Department in the war against the French in 1812, 1813 and 1814, submitted to Emperor Alexander I by General Barclay de Tolly (manuscript).
4 Graf Cancrin, I, 88-89; Barclay de Tolly's Account of the activities of the Quartermaster's Department.

Once the troops were in contact with the enemy, then the men, having a four-day supply of hard-tack and herding livestock behind them, were to be fed from the ten-day supply of provisions, on the man and in regimental transport, replenished from mobile magazines. These magazines, with the exception of some located at the headquarters, were to be located several echelons behind the army; the closest at a distance of one or two stages. Necessity sometimes forced the troops to resort to foraging, not only in Saxony, but even in Bohemia, and the population of the country suffered a great deal, not only from the Russians and Prussians, but also from their own Austrian forces. The honest Barclay wrote: 'We can safely say that ours were better than many others.' Experience itself had shown that with swift and sudden movements, with troops located in bivouacs, it was impossible to feed each of the independent detachments from their trains alone. Organic transport was frequently insufficient, and even if there was enough, they could not be pre-positioned with an army whose rear was already congested with light baggage and reserve artillery. It was a common occurrence for the hard-tack wagons to lag behind the formations, the four-day rations held on the man would be depleted, and essential supplies would have to be obtained by force if necessary. Barclay de Tolly stated that under the contemporaneous system of military operations, regular provisioning of the army with supplies was impossible, and should anyone decide to strive for rigorous correctness in this regard, they would be forced to revert to the previous system of a five-day march supply of rations for the army, in which the delivery of supplies was not coordinated with the movements of the forces, and the troop movements themselves were dependent on magazines. Yet it would be necessary to abandon decisive operations in this event.

During the second campaign of 1813, and in general during the campaigns abroad in 1813-1814, the troops were to receive rations in kind, while funds were not to be issued to regiments for local purchase. In 1807, during operations in Old Prussia, the issue of cash-in-lieu had been permitted. If this method had been resorted to during the armistice of 1813 in Silesia, the army would have been subjected to starvation, because the country could not provide the required amount of supplies. This forced us to resort to requisitioning in the Duchy of Warsaw, throughout the entire region between the Oder and the Vistula, and to the purchase of grain in Austrian Silesia. All of this notwithstanding, Russian forces would have suffered an extreme shortage of provisions and fodder had it not been permitted to release some of the supplies from Prussian magazines located in the fortresses, with repayment in cash.

With the exception of Prussia, where some of the levied requisitions were repaid immediately, in every other country, most particularly in enemy territory, receipts were ordered to be issued; yet this order was very often not carried out by regimental commanders and other commanders of military formations.

The above-stated system of feeding the troops was followed not only in the Main Army, but also in the others. The use of requisitioning methods turned out to be especially convenient in independent corps and detachments, which, being smaller in numbers, could obtain everything they needed without difficulty from the local population. The siege corps at Danzig [Gdańsk] was satisfied in the main with supplies delivered by sea from Russia. They also received some provisions and fodder from Prussia and the Duchy of Warsaw. Initially, grain reserves sent from

Russian ports to Pillau [Baltiysk] and Swinemünde [Świnoujście] were intended to feed the main body of the active army, but subsequently the Russian army, due to its distance from the delivery points, could not use these reserves, and they were used by the troops blockading Danzig. Some of the provisions were transported to Thorn, for the reserves, or were given to the Prussian government, as replacement for that expended by Russian forces in Silesia during the armistice. Barclay noted: 'Thus, every prudent measure was of benefit, although they did not always achieve the objective for which they were adopted.'

In order to facilitate the means of acquiring supplies in the theatre of war, conventions were concluded between the Russian government and the Coalition Powers of Prussia, and Austria for the supply of rations to the troops, at prices determined through a dedicated tariff, which, being calculated by averaging aggregate prices in the various provinces, were generally lower than those existing at the locations where the vast armies were concentrated. These conventions prevented price rises, postponed repayment terms and denied the possibility of feigned shortages, which were as harmful as the shortages themselves. The tariffs determined for rations supplied to Russian forces were not entirely consistent with the provisions existing in Russia. Thus, for example, on occasion the ratio of bread supplied decreased while the proportion of meat increased, rations might be decreased, and so on. Having said that, the troops were satisfied with the subsistence they received, while the population were not subjected to extortionate demands. In general, during this entire campaign, up until the Coalition arrived on the Main, the Russian army fed itself on the basis of what became known as the Kutuzov tariff, approved once the borders of the Empire were crossed. In the army under Count Wittgenstein [Pëtr Khristianovich Vitgenshtein or Ludwig Adolf Peter zu Sayn-Wittgenstein], during their stay in Old Prussia, as well as in the corps blockading Danzig, the troops received provisions according to a special tariff, in foreign measures, where the proportion of bread was reduced.

With regard to uniforms for the troops, purchases of cloth and linen were made at the beginning of the year in the Duchy of Warsaw and Prussia, but the tailoring of uniform items entrusted to General Count Sievers [Karl Karlovich Sivers or Carl Gustav von Sievers] required a great deal of time, and therefore the finished clothing could not be delivered quickly to the army. Some of the items were sent by sea to Königsberg [Kaliningrad]. A special commission was established in Kalisz. The troops, having received the most essential items there, then moved beyond the Elbe. In Saxony, the regiments commanded by generals Count Miloradovich [Mikhael Andreevich Miloradovich] and Wintzingerode [Ferdinand Fëdorovich Vintsingerode or Ferdinand von Wintzingerode] obtained clothing through requisitions. The Grenadier Corps were allowed to acquire the necessary amount of cloth and linen against receipts from local factories on the march through Silesia. But the outfitting of the troops was not a great success. According to Barclay de Tolly: 'In general, the commissariat department demanded great regularity, and therefore could not get this organised as abruptly as the ration supply for the troops.' The small amount of enemy stocks found by Coalition forces were used to their advantage, but could never meet their needs. In addition, some items were not suitable at all, such as boots, which turned out to be too close-fitting for Russian soldiers.

Throughout the duration of the armistice, the troops were resupplied with clothing and footwear. The Lifeguard, having received cloth from the Duchy of Warsaw, managed to tailor theirs. The items manufactured under Count Sievers in Königsberg were delivered to Brieg [Brzeg]. Linen for summer breeches was purchased in Silesia. The woollen cloth purchased for the army by the Kherson police chief Konstantinov was also sent to Brieg. Thanks to these orders, the troops set off on the new campaign in uniforms and footwear of decent quality. At the same time, measures had been taken to ensure the resupply of the army with these items in the future. According to returns from the intendant-general, significant stores of items had been established in Grodno and Brest. Orders were issued to collect all the old short sheepskin coats left by the troops in various locations with the onset of summer, and to buy some 100,000 new ones and deliver them to Bohemia. Following the retreat from Dresden, while stationed in the vicinity of Teplitz, the troops received some munitions items from Brieg.

During the second offensive from Bohemia, orders were issued to buy waistcoats for the soldiers, but they did not arrive in time and were delivered later. Following the battle of Leipzig, the materials for 100,000 pairs of shoes were purchased in this city, at one thaler and six groschen each, while the overall cost of a pair of boots was five paper roubles 16½ kopecks. This footwear was delivered to the army after the Rhine crossing, but despite this, Russian soldiers never went barefoot during their campaigns abroad.

In general, the acquisition of commissariat items turned out to be more difficult than obtaining provisions and fodder, while even greater concerns and consumption of time were associated with clothing and footwear. Tailoring and the manufacture of items through foreign contractors was very expensive and slow. Working with our own artisans in the regiments turned out to be unfeasible, because the administrative echelon is typically in disarray in wartime. The delivery of finished goods from Russia across the considerable distance to the theatre of war was almost impossible, also due to the scarcity of resources following the devastation of many provinces in the war of 1812. According to Barclay de Tolly, in wartime it is essential to establish mobile tailoring workshops in advance. He believed that

> every administrative instruction in our army was hampered by the lack of common sense in the auditing of military accounts. As a result of this, everyone thought more about protecting themselves than about improving the process itself, because the most honest and efficient of men could get into trouble if they cared more about the effective execution of the matter rather than observing the formalities established in the regulations. This formality is necessary for the prevention of wilful abuse, but the excess and ambiguity of the forms and processes could have disastrous consequences.

Barclay de Tolly noted that not only was the extraction, production and delivery of provisions and commissariat supplies extremely difficult in wartime, equally so was their effective distribution to the troops. He remarked:

This may be judged by anyone who actually witnessed the distribution of provisions to the headquarters and a hundred regiments in a single night: no one was willing to wait their turn; many tried to obtain supplies by force. The correct issue of hay was particularly difficult, which made foraging inevitable even in countries where they could be resupplied through requisitioning.[5]

With regard to medical services in the Russian army, throughout the war of 1813, they were guided by the Regulations for Hospitals Abroad drafted in Plock [Płock] by the Intendant-General, the Director of Hospitals and the Staff Doctor. An agreement was concluded with deputies sent from the administration of Old Prussia during the headquarters of the Russian armies' stay in Plock regarding the care of Russian and French patients, of whom there were over 18,000 in this area at that time. It was agreed to pay 20 Prussian groschen (about 70 silver kopecks) for each of them who received Rhine wine, and 15 groschen (about 52 kopecks) without wine. Some supplies were issued free of charge by the locals. This resolution existed until the end of the war, and although the Russian government was obliged on the basis of the Kalisz Convention to establish its own administration in other hospitals, or bring them under their own administration with some local allowances, the Prussians continued to provide food for remote Russian hospitals and received the due amount for this later, during the general settlement of accounts.

Once the army moved from the Duchy of Warsaw to the Elbe, there were almost no sick men left anywhere, and upon arrival in Saxony, a hospital was immediately set up at local expense. Despite the defeat at the battle of Lützen, very few wounded remained on the battlefield; all those remaining were transported in *Vorspann* [carriages] to Dresden. Their onward transportation would have encountered no particular difficulties had many of these carts not been hijacked in the chaos by marauders with looted property, or had the troops proceeded with minimal regimental baggage. Often, the transport of a worthless saddle by local residents would cost 100 times its value. The sick and wounded, after the battles of Lützen and Bautzen, were sent to Silesia and the Duchy of Warsaw.

During the armistice, very few men fell sick, while, in contrast, many recovered men returned to the army from hospital. Those who did fall ill were admitted to Silesian hospitals and sent from there to the Duchy of Warsaw on carts on which requisitioned supplies had been delivered from this country.

Upon the arrival of Russian forces in Bohemia, the sick were initially sent to Austrian hospitals; subsequently, the Russian government undertook to establish its own medical administration. But although a Chief Superintendent was appointed for Russian hospitals in Bohemia as well as the institution of several small hospitals, the timely organisation of this department, without officials, without orderlies and so forth, turned out to be impossible, and therefore Russian patients in Bohemia remained under the care of the Austrian government until the very end of the war, which received compensation during the general settlement of accounts.

---

5   Barclay de Tolly's Account of the activities of the Quartermaster's Department.

Following the second offensive by the Main Coalition Army into Saxony, hospitals were established at local expense in Zwickau, Altenburg, and eventually in Leipzig. Despite the many patients who were laid up in this city or were admitted to hospital after the fighting in October 1813, the medical department was in a decent state there and the mortality rate was not significant.

Throughout the ongoing campaign to the Rhine, hospitals were maintained at the expense of those territories in which they had been established, but with the entry of every German state into the general coalition of European powers, along with the resolution of their duties regarding the provisioning department, it was decided that all members of the coalition should participate proportionately in the maintenance of hospitals. Austria alone did not consent to this, wishing to take their sick under their own care. Nevertheless, many sick Austrians were maintained at the expense of the territories in which the hospitals were located. Russia and Prussia together paid 474,000 silver roubles to the *Zentral Verwaltungs Rat* [Central Committee] for the maintenance of their sick.[6]

The supply of projectiles and cartridges for the forces, thanks to the activities of the Russian Chief of Artillery, Prince Iashvili [Levan Mikhailovich Iashvili], and his Chief of Staff, General Sukhozanet [Ivan Onufrievich Sukhozanet], was very successful. At the beginning of the armistice, artillery officers were sent to every infantry regiment in order to calibrate their firearms.[7] The movement of the reserve parks, which had fallen far behind the army during its advance, was hastened, and in general the Russian artillery, both in terms of mobility and operation in combat, was not inferior to either the enemy or coalition artillery.

The provisioning of the French army was obtained through requisitions while stationed on the Elbe and in surrounding localities, which was facilitated by the prosperity of Saxony where Napoleon's troops were mainly concentrated. The constant presence of significant bodies of troops in this country was very onerous for the population. The French military administration were famous for their skill at extracting resources from conquered or allied territory for their forces' subsistence, and in this regard served as the model on the basis of which every European state organised the logistics departments of their armies in wartime. But this system could only be implemented in very wealthy countries, and even those would be completely exhausted through excessive exploitation. It was especially painful for the population upon whom the huge multinational army were stationed, who were accustomed to looting and had a sense of entitlement. Barns, and even domestic housing located in the vicinity of the bivouacs, were dismantled by soldiers, sometimes unnecessarily. Not even the cemeteries of Dresden Neustadt and others in the vicinity of the French camps were spared. Crosses over the graves were torn down, coffins were dug up. Having robbed the living, they also stole from the dead. Soldiers sold shrouds taken from corpses in the markets, and wreaths of silk flowers, stolen by sacrilegious hands.

---

6   Barclay de Tolly's Account of the activities of the Quartermaster's Department.
7   Ilya Timofeyevich Radozhitskii, The German Liberation War of 1813, The Memoirs of a Russian Artilleryman, 83-84 (English translation by Alexander Mikaberidze and Peter G.A. Phillips).

The devastation of the region had disastrous consequences for the French army, which was gradually constrained by the coalition armies advancing from several directions and was eventually limited to the surroundings of Dresden. The French commissariat were forced to reduce the ration allowances; meat was rarely provided; the soldiers starved or looted, stealing the villagers' last morsels. Orders were issued to take marauders and shoot every tenth man [decimation], but the execution of this order turned out to be impossible, because the entire army had turned into an assembly of marauders. The delivery of life-support and combat supplies from the Rhine was hampered by raids by coalition partisans. Back in early [mid] September, the population of the country had received strict orders to hand over all reserves of gunpowder and lead in their possession.[8]

Thus, the much lauded French commissariat could not meet the needs of the army. The French medical services were also in poor condition. According to Marshal Marmont [Auguste Frédéric Louis Viesse de Marmont], had the supplies necessary for the troops been collected in Dresden and if the hospitals there had been supplied with everything necessary, then the French army could have been stronger by 50,000 men. In a conversation with Napoleon, not to mention the importance of saving so many men, Marmont told him that preserving this many veteran soldiers would cost half as much as recruiting, arming and marching up 50,000 conscripts: consequently, through the efficient expenditure of 25,000,000 francs to improve the troops' subsistence and the hospitals, another 25,000,000 and 50,000 men could have been saved. Napoleon, reluctant to admit the infallibility of the marshal's conclusions, replied: 'even if I had released these funds, they would have been stolen and everything would have remained the same.'[9] We find similar opinions regarding the French commissariat in all the memoirs of the era we are describing.

> Human life was considered as nothing, and while it cannot be proven that some of their doctors and guards hastened the death of any sick who had money, then at least it is reliably known that those dying were searched and robbed of their last threads in their terminal delirium. The immorality in the hospital and provisioning departments reached such an extent that any of the officials of these departments who showed any sense of conscience or compassion for humanity was considered an outright imbecile by their comrades.[10]

---

8   Ernst Otto Innocenz von Odeleben, *Relation circonstanciée de la campagne de 1813 en Saxe*, II, 196-198.
9   Marmont, *Mémoires du maréchal Marmont, duc de Raguse*, V, 171.
10 Karl August Weinhold, *Dresden und seine Schicksale im Jahr 1813*, 58-59.

22

Initial operations by the Army of Silesia following the end of the armistice

Instructions issued to Blücher. – Amendments to them. – Composition and strength of the Army of Silesia. – Corps commanders: Langéron, Sacken, Yorck. – The factors that prompted Blücher to forestall the enemy by occupying the neutral zone. – The advance of the Army of Silesia. – Retreat of Ney's force beyond the Katzbach and Bober. – The actions on 7 and 8 (19 and 20) August: at Kaiserswaldau and Thomaswaldau; at Plagwitz; at Siebeneichen.

Napoleon's advance from Dresden to Görlitz and on to the Bober river. – The actions on 9 [21] August at Plagwitz and Bunzlau; the retreat of the Army of Silesia behind the river Schnelle Deichsa. – Blücher's orders in the event of a further retreat. – The Coalition retreat behind the Katzbach.

Napoleon's departure. – Blücher's thoughts. – The Coalition deployment at Goldberg. – The action at Goldberg on 11 (23) August. – The retreat of the Army of Silesia towards Jauer; the state of the Coalition forces. – Measures taken by Blücher. – Disagreements among the coalition commanders. – Yorck's letter to King Friedrich Wilhelm III.

Based on the general plan of operations drawn up in Trachenberg [Żmigród], the Army of Bohemia and Army of the North were to operate aggressively, while the Army of Silesia was to avoid a general battle unless there was an undoubted superiority in strength on its side. The Army of the North was tasked with crossing the Elbe between Torgau and Magdeburg and to move towards Leipzig without delay. The Army of Bohemia, although it did not receive a definitive indication of its operational mission when the plan was being drafted, nevertheless, following its concentration at Budin [Budyně nad Ohří], was also directed towards Leipzig via the Ore Mountains. Thus, it might have been expected that the opening of offensive operations on the part of the Coalition would initially be by the Army of the North and subsequently by the Army of Bohemia, and finally by the Army of Silesia. Instead the opening moves were initiated by Blücher [Gebhard Leberecht von Blücher], then the

Main Army slowly set out from Bohemia towards Saxony, while the Crown Prince of Sweden [Jean-Baptiste Jules Bernadotte] limited himself to defensive operations.

On 30 July (11 August), Blücher received secret instructions in Reichenbach [Dzierżoniów] from Barclay de Tolly, on the basis of which the Army of Silesia was to advance and stay in contact with the enemy, and to attack them as soon as they turned against the Coalition Main Army, but to avoid a decisive clash. This *modus operandi* was incompatible with the character of the passionate Prussian commander; Blücher responded directly that he, not having the qualities necessary to conduct an exclusively defensive war, would rather resign the honorary title of commander-in-chief. Whereupon Barclay de Tolly and Quartermaster-General, Lieutenant General Diebitsch [Ivan Ivanovich Dibich or Hans Karl Friedrich Anton von Diebitsch und Narten], who was accompanying him, pointed out to Blücher that a commander leading an army of 100,000 cannot be bound by any instructions to such an extent that, while remaining undoubtedly on the defensive, they miss any favourable opportunities to operate offensively and cause damage to the enemy. Blücher, satisfied with this clarification of the instructions, announced to Barclay that he would be taking command of the army upon the condition that he be permitted to attack the enemy should he consider it necessary. Should his opinions not receive the approval of the Coalition Monarchs, then he requested to be given some other assignment. Since there was no response to this proposal, Blücher granted himself the right to operate independently, in accordance with the situation.[1]

The army entrusted to Blücher consisted of two Russian corps, comte Langéron's [Alexander Fëdorovich Lanzheron or Louis Alexandre Andrault de Langéron] and Sacken's [Fabian Vilhelmovich Osten-Saken or Fabian Gottlieb von der Osten-Sacken], and a Prussian corps under Yorck [Johann David Ludwig von Yorck]. The corps under General-of-Infantry comte Langéron numbered 40,000 men in its ranks, including some 9,000 regular and irregular cavalry with 176 guns. The number of men present in Lieutenant General Sacken's corps reached some 16,000, of whom more than 7,000 were cavalrymen, with 60 guns. In *Generalleutnant* Yorck's corps there were a total of some 38,000 men present, and these included 6,000 regular cavalry, and 104 guns. Thus, the active strength of Blücher's army was 94,000 men: 66,000 infantry, 22,000 cavalry and 6,000 artillerymen with 340 guns.[2]

Comte Langéron, who had participated in many wars and temporarily commanded a Russian army during the war with the Turks and gained renown as a valiant and well-organised commander, considered himself slighted at being subordinate to Blücher. To crown their mutual animosity, Langéron knew the contents of the instructions received by Blücher, but did not know about their amendments as a result Barclay's discussions with Blücher. This emboldened comte Langéron to

---

1 Carl von Weiß (Müffling), *Zur Kriegsgeschichte der Jahre 1813 und 1814 – Die Feldzüge der Schlesischen Armee Unter dem Feldmarschall Blücher von der Beendigung des Waffenstillstandes bis zur Eroberung von Paris*, second edition, 1-3.
2 Returns on the status of forces, signed by generals Langéron and Sacken; Theodor von Bernhardi, *Denkwürdigkeiten aus dem Leben Carl Friedrich Grafen von Toll*, III, Beilagen, 513-516; Müffling, 4-5.

take on the role of chief of operations as soon as he noticed Blücher's deviation from the above-mentioned instructions, which could and did in fact lead to his wilful re-interpretation of orders from the Commander-in-Chief. The commander of the other Russian corps, Baron Sacken, in contrast, distinguished himself through the precise execution of Blücher's instructions, but his harsh and irritable nature would make it difficult for the Commander-in-Chief to communicate with him, having not yet managed to earn the respect of the Russian troops and their commanders.[3] As for General Yorck, he had learned of the assignment of his corps to Blücher's army with great displeasure, whom he considered a 'cowboy' who had gained popularity beyond his merits and abilities. In Yorck's opinion, Blücher was completely dependent on the men around him, and especially on General Gneisenau [August Wilhelm Anton Neidhardt von Gneisenau], who, in Yorck's opinion, was nothing more than a pompous bluffer and theorist. Müffling's [Philipp Friedrich Carl Ferdinand von Müffling, also known as Weiß] discretion and social status seemed to Yorck to be suitable only for the complete ensnaring of the veteran Blücher. Under the influence of such thoughts, Yorck, for fear of becoming dependent on his staff, personally issued even the most trifling of orders. While Blücher trusted his faithful associates Gneisenau and Müffling completely, who, in turn, also permitted the junior officers an independent range of actions, this is what one of Yorck's aides-de-camp wrote about him. 'Yorck ordered, managed and administered everything himself; he demanded only obedience and diligence from his subordinates. None of them had the slightest influence on his operations.' Despite such differences between Blücher's and Yorck's *Hauptquartier*, perhaps even thanks to such differences between them, everything worked out as well as could be expected subsequently. The concepts of 'strategists and enthusiasts' were executed by 'tacticians, assertive men' and, when drafting bold plans, should the former often get carried away beyond the extent of the possible, losing track of time and space, then the latter would take care 'of the soldiers' feet and stomachs, of musket flints and horseshoes' in a word, of everything without which the most brilliant ideas cannot be crowned with success. According to one of the officers on Yorck's staff: 'the lofty ideas of the masters in the *Hauptquartier* could hardly have been realised had their executor not been Yorck, who was engaged in the moulding of his corps with conscientious diligence and strict perseverance and operated just as coolly and courageously on the battlefield.'[4]

In anticipation of the resumption of hostilities, Sacken's corps was located near Breslau, Yorck's corps at Wernersdorf [Pakoszów, seven miles west of Hirschberg], Langéron's corps were assembled partly at the Zobtenberg [Ślęża, 11 miles east of Schweidnitz], partly at Landeshut [Kamienna Góra]. In general, the entire countryside occupied by the armies of both sides had been stripped bare from upper Silesia to the Elbe except for the neutral zone including Breslau, which could still provide resources for sustaining the troops. It was easy to foresee that if the enemy had managed to forestall the Coalition by occupying this territory and foraging for supplies located there, then the Army of Silesia would have to march for two

---

3   Müffling, 4-5.
4   Johann Gustav Droysen, *Das Leben des Feldmarschalls Grafen Yorck von Wartenburg*, III, 8-10.

additional days to cross this devastated area. Moreover, there was every probability that Napoleon, having received intelligence on the offensive against him from Bohemia by the Main Coalition Army, would immediately concentrate his forces towards Dresden. This situation under which he could take advantage of the six days, from the time of the announcement of the end of the truce until the opening of hostilities, would enable him to add the corps facing the Army of Silesia and Army of the North to his reserves stationed in Saxony. Thus, forestalling the enemy by occupying the neutral zone was very important for Blücher, giving him the opportunity, firstly, to deceive the enemy in the calculation of their strength and intentions through an offensive by the Army of Silesia, and secondly, in the event of a concentration of Napoleon's forces towards the Elbe, would stay in contact with them and steal two marches.

The French themselves gave Blücher an excuse for violating the terms, according to which neither side was to send troops into the neutral zone until 5 (17) August. As early as 1 (13) August, enemy patrols and foraging detachments had appeared in Jauer [Jawor] and Schönau [Świerzawa]. As soon as the report arrived at the *Hauptquartier*, he issued orders to his corps commanders – to move forward and push the enemy back, but not to cross the far limit of the neutral zone (the river Katzbach [Kaczawa]) before the expiration of the agreed period.[5] The next day [14 August new style], the formations set off in the directions assigned to them. Sacken's corps, having occupied Breslau, moved through Lissa [Wrocław-Leśnica], and onwards to Neumarkt [Środa Śląska] towards Liegnitz [Legnica]; Yorck, moved on Jauer, and on towards Goldberg [Złotoryja]; Langéron, to Bolkenhain [Bolków], towards Schönau; Lieutenant General Count Pahlen [Pëtr Petrovich Palen or Paul Carl Ernst Wilhelm Philipp von der Pahlen], with Saint-Priest's VIII Corps [Emmanuil Frantsevich Sen-Pri or Guillaume-Emmanuel Guignard de Saint-Priest], Borozdin's 1st Dragoon Division [Nikolai Mikhailovich Borozdin 2nd], Emmanuel's Dragoon Brigade [Georgi (Yegor) Arsenievich Emmanuel or Djordje Manojlovic] and three Cossack regiments, moved along the mountains, from Landeshut, through Schmiedeberg [Kowary], towards Hirschberg [Jelenia Góra]. The enemy forces, who had not anticipated the Coalition attack at all, withdrew almost without resistance across the Katzbach on 5 (17) August, and began to retreat to the river Bober [Bóbr] after dark: the corps under Lauriston [Jacques Jean Alexandre Bernard Law de Lauriston] and Macdonald [Étienne (Jacques-Joseph-Alexandre) Macdonald] corps along the road from Goldberg towards Löwenberg [Lwówek Śląski], while the corps under Ney [Michel Ney] and Marmont and Sébastiani's cavalry [Horace François Bastien Sébastiani] went from Liegnitz, through Haynau [Chojnów], towards Bunzlau [Bolesławiec].[6] The French were extremely irritated by the Coalition incursion into the neutral zone, and with good reason. For their part, the Coalition commissars at Neumarkt, insisting on strict compliance with the terms of the armistice, insisted that the Army of Silesia return behind the demarcation line. Taking offence at this demand, Blücher wrote to the Prussian commissar, General Krusemark: 'Foolish

---

5 Blücher's dispositions dated 14 August, new style.
6 See Map No. 1: Map Showing Blücher's Operations Following the Expiry of the Armistice.

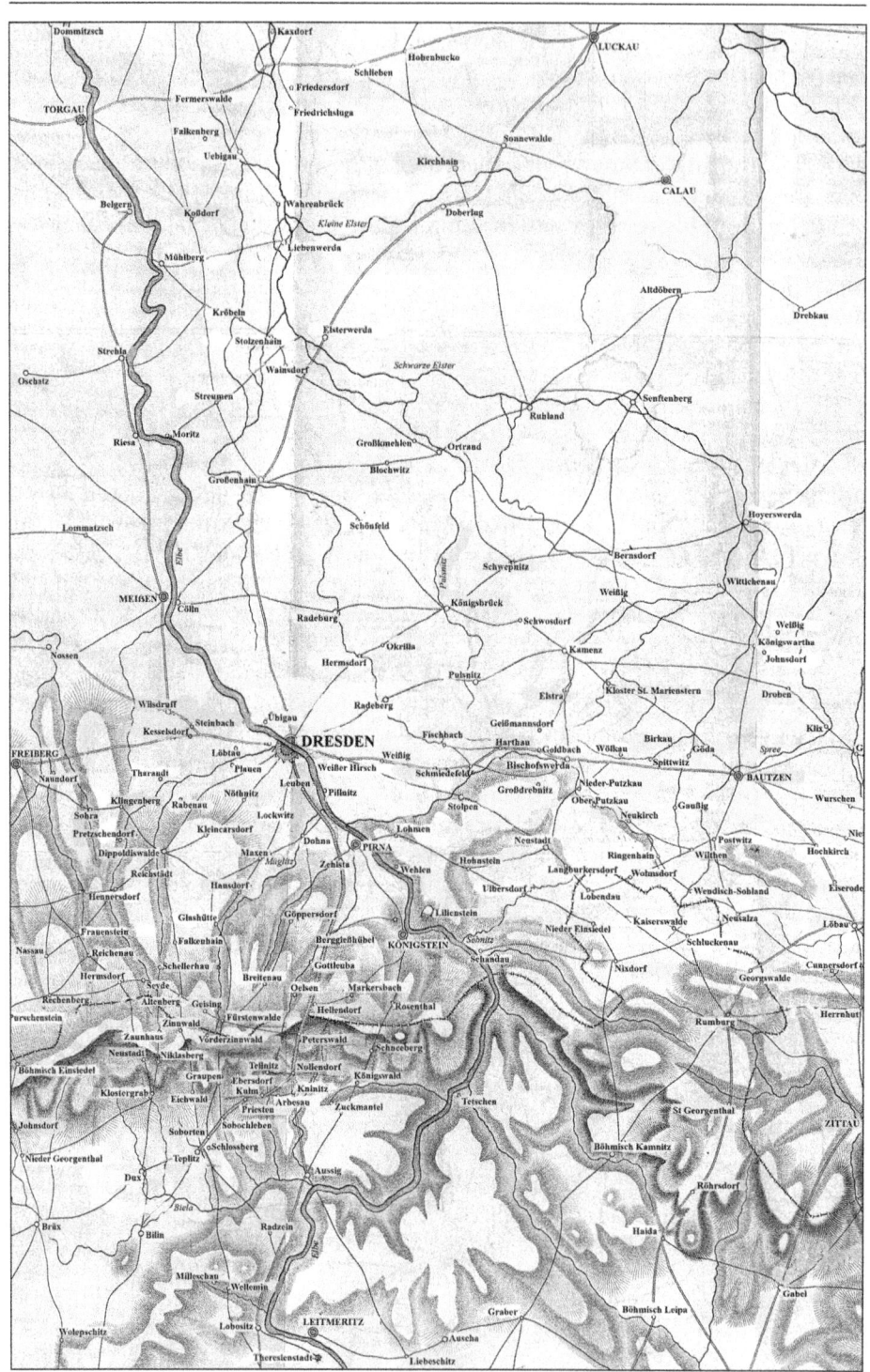

Map showing Blücher's operations following the expiry of the Armistice.

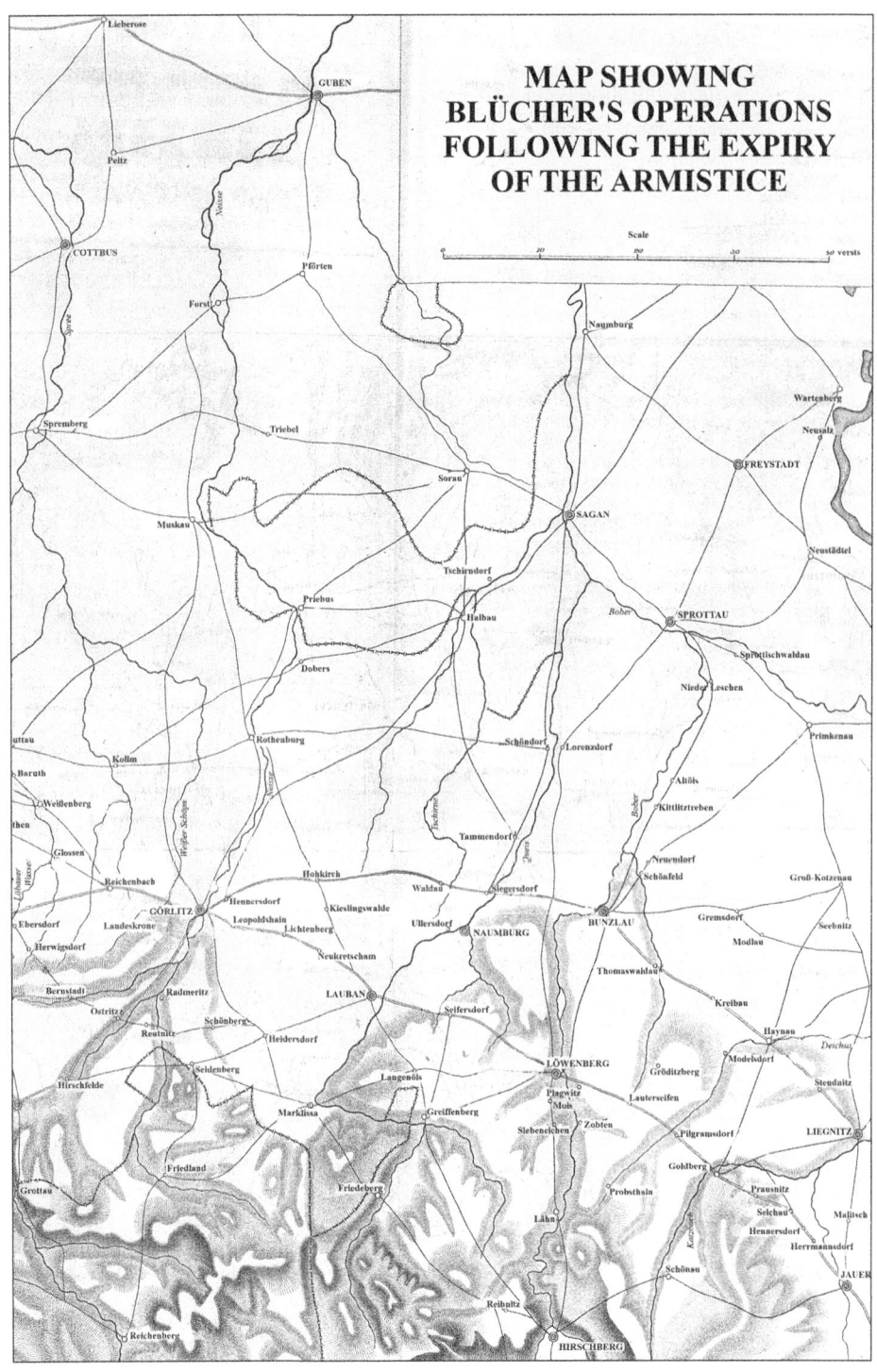

diplomatic antics and the writing of notes must now come to an end. I shall set the pace without notes.'[7]

On 6 (18) August, intelligence was received that the French had abandoned their position on the Katzbach. The Coalition forces immediately received orders to advance after the enemy up to the Bober: Sacken to Haynau and on towards Bunzlau, Yorck to Goldberg and on towards Löwenberg; Langéron was to move somewhat to the left, in the direction of Zobten [Sobota]; Pahlen was to move further to the left, to Hirschberg; the partisan detachment under Major General Kaisarov [Paisy Sergeevich Kaisarov] proceeded ahead of him to occupy Lähn [Wleń] on the Bober. Macdonald, who was stationed south of Löwenberg with *11e Corps*, seeing the need to protect the French army positions from being outflanked on their right, attacked Kaisarov with troops from Zucchi's Italian Brigade [Carlo Zucchi] and forced the Russian detachment to retreat to Hirschberg.[8] This French show of force, which had the appearance of a committed attack, prompted comte Langéron to pause at Schönau, which slowed down the advance of the other Coalition corps. The following day, 7 (19) August, Blücher held Yorck's corps at Goldberg until noon, sending the Prussian vanguard under *Oberstleutnant* Lobenthal [Karl Friedrich Ludwig von Lobenthal] towards Gröditzberg [Burg Grodziec] independently with the entire reserve cavalry commanded by Jürgaß [Georg Ludwig Alexander von Wahlen-Jürgaß]; Sacken received orders to advance on Bunzlau.[9] On the part of the French, Marmont's corps was sent from Bunzlau to engage Sacken in order to support Ney's corps, which was retreating towards the Bober. At two o'clock in the afternoon, a very bitter action began at Kreibau [Krzelów] and Kaiserswaldau [Okmiany, three miles south-west of Kreibau]; Vasilchikov's cavalry [Illarion Vasilievich Vasilchikov], supported by all the jäger regiments commanded by Major General Voeikov [Alexei Vasilievich Voeikov], advanced frontally, while General Neverovsky [Dmitry Petrovich Neverovsky], moving to the left with the 27th Division, outflanked the enemy on their right; following this, the 8th Jägers and 9th Jägers, protecting their flank, assisted Colonel Novak [P.I. Novak 2nd] in seizing very advantageous high ground with the guns of 18th Horse Artillery Company and silenced a French battery. The enemy, having withdrawn from their position, were pursued to Thomaswaldau [Tomaszów Bolesławiecki] (less than one *Meile* from Bunzlau), under the thunder of an incessant cannonade.[10]

---

7 '*Die diplomatischen Narrenpossen und das Notenschreiben müsse nun eine ende haben. Ich werde den Takt ohne Noten schlagen.*' Müffling, 12; Carl von Plotho, *Der Krieg in Deutschland und Frankreich in den Jahren 1813 und 1814*, II, 89-92; Frédéric Guillaume de Vaudoncourt, *Histoire de la guerre soutenue par les Français en Allemagne*, 141.
8 *Le Moniteur*, 6 September 1813, new style.
9 Infantry: fusilier battalions from *1. Ostpreußisches Infanterie and 2. Ostpreußisches Infanterie, Leib-Regiment*, and *Brandenburgisches Infanterie*; Landwehr regiments: *5. Schlesisches* and *15. Schlesisches*; cavalry: one squadron each of *2. Leib-Husaren* and *Schlesisches Landwehr Kavalerie*; four squadrons of *Brandenburgisches Ulanen*; artillery: *2. Batterie zu Fuß* and *3. Batterie zu Pferde* (both with six-pounders), six battalions, six squadrons and 16 guns in total. Plotho, II, 89.
10 Log of outgoing documents, General Sacken's Corps (Archive of the Military Topographic Depot (M.T.D.) No. 44,585); General Sacken's dispatch No. 247 to Adjutant General Volkonsky, dated 27 August (M.T.D. No. 16,644); Vaudoncourt, 141.

On the following day, 8 (20) August, Sacken attacked the enemy at Thomaswaldau and forced them to retreat to Bunzlau. The town of Bunzlau, strongly fortified by the French, was abandoned by the enemy as soon as the corps under Ney and Marmont had reached the bridge over the Bober, at four o'clock in the afternoon. Sacken's force could have immediately seized the town; but, fortunately, their advance was delayed by order of the corps commander who, in all likelihood, had received intelligence from the population about the trap that was being set for them. Hardly half an hour had passed after the departure of the enemy when several explosions were heard and finally a large powder magazine was blown sky-high; the entire town was showered with a hail of shell, canister shot and masonry and caught fire in many places. Every building was either destroyed, or significantly damaged, but none of the inhabitants died. Sacken's troops had occupied Bunzlau by evening but the French held the bridge over the Bober and had emplaced strong batteries on the high ground on the left bank in order to defend the crossing.[11] In the Coalition army's centre, *Oberstleutnant* Lobenthal's vanguard and the reserve cavalry attacked the rearguard of Lauriston's Corps at Plagwitz [Płakowice] on 8 (20) August. After a very heated battle, the French were forced to retreat into the night beyond the Bober towards Löwenberg, destroying the bridges behind them.[12] The success of this attack was greatly facilitated through operations by the leading elements of Langéron's corps: on 7 (19) August, while his main body was making the short march to Probsthain [Proboszczów] (15 *versts* south-east of Löwenberg [one *verst* equals ⅔ miles]), the vanguard, commanded by Major General Rudzevich [Alexander Yakovlevich Rudzevich], had reached the village of Zobten on the Bober (five *versts* upstream of Löwenberg) early in the morning. The bridge there had been destroyed; but the Cossacks found a ford and, crossing the river, formed up on the high ground of the left bank. The cavalry followed them across, and thereafter the infantry and artillery. At ten o'clock in the morning, Rudzevich ejected the enemy detachment holding the village of Siebeneichen [Dębowy Gaj]; General Emmanuel, with the Kiev Dragoons and Livland Mounted-Jägers, pursued the beaten enemy as far as Ober-Mois [Mojesz Górny], while his Cossacks attacked a convoy moving from Lähn towards Löwenberg, taking 260 prisoners, a significant sum of money and Macdonald's own carriage. Even more important was the fact that, as a result of Rudzevich's bold advance, the French forces on their right wing had been divided in two. Ney's corps, at Gröditzberg, were in danger of being cut off from the Bober crossings at Bunzlau and Löwenberg, on the one hand by Sacken's corps, which had already taken Thomaswaldau, and on the other, by Langéron's 30,000 men who had arrived in the vicinity of Zobten. Blücher, wanting to take advantage of Ney's mistake (who remained isolated ahead of the other French troops with his corps), ordered Yorck to fix him frontally for as long as possible, while Sacken was ordered to block him between Gröditzberg and Bunzlau, and Langéron was to move to Lauterseiffen [Bielanka] and Deutmannsdorf [Zbylutów, three miles north-west of Lauterseiffen], behind the enemy. But Langéron did not carry out this order, under

---

11 Friedrich Richter, *Geschichte des Deutschen Freiheitskrieges vom Jahre 1813 bis zum Jahre 1815*, I, 344-346.
12 Plotho, II, 94-96; Vaudoncourt, 141.

the pretext of the exhaustion of his troops, which not only made it possible for Ney to retreat behind the Bober at Bunzlau on 8 (20) August, as mentioned above, but also contributed to Macdonald counter-attacking Rudzevich's vanguard with superior forces. The Russian force formed up in several squares and managed to retreat across the ford back over the Bober towards Zobten with all the trophies they had captured. The losses in Langéron's force on 7 (19) August, overall, reached 68 officers and 1,573 lower ranks; the enemy casualties are not known precisely but in all likelihood were significant.[13]

Napoleon, although he had intelligence on the plan of action drawn up in Trachenberg, nevertheless believed that the Coalition would not dare to weaken the defences of Silesia by detaching a significant part of their forces from there to Bohemia. He was mostly expecting an offensive by the Coalition from Silesia towards the Bober, or from Bohemia, along the right bank of the Elbe, towards Lusatia [Lausitz]. He remained unconcerned about an attack on the left bank of the Elbe, especially since, throughout the duration of the armistice, Dresden had been prepared to hold out for some time against an enemy superior in numbers. Based on these assessments, Napoleon left Dresden on 3 (15) August, his birthday, for Görlitz, whence the *Garde* and cavalry corps under Latour-Maubourg [Marie Victor Nicolas de Faÿ de Latour-Maubourg] had set out on the same day. Having examined the surroundings of Königstein and halting in Bautzen on 5 (17) August, awaiting the arrival of his reserves, he proceeded to Görlitz on 6 (18) August, at the same time as the Coalition forces under Barclay de Tolly, moving from Silesia to Bohemia, had almost completed their flanking movement. Had Napoleon found out about this ahead of time and attacked the Coalition on the march with his superior numbers, he could have disrupted their operational plan. But by the time he arrived in Görlitz, it was no longer possible to prevent the concentration of Coalition forces on the river Eger [Ohře]. Wishing to collect definitive intelligence on the Army of Bohemia, on 7 (19) August, Napoleon pushed the corps under Prince Poniatowski [Joseph-Antoine Poniatowski or Józef Antoni Poniatowski], stationed in Zittau, forwards to Rumburg [Rumburk], Gabel [Jablonné v Podještědí] and Kratzau [Chrastava, six miles northwest of Reichenberg], while he hastened to Zittau himself, with two divisions of the *Jeune Garde*. The weak Austrian *2. leichte Division* under Graf Bubna [Ferdinand von Bubna und Littitz], having been engaged by Poniatowski's force, immediately retreated into Bohemia, and the French learned from prisoners they had taken about the concentration of the Army of Bohemia on the left bank of the Elbe, which clearly revealed the Coalition's intentions of moving their main force across Napoleon's lines of communications in the direction of Dresden, or towards Leipzig. On the other hand, couriers were constantly arriving from Ney with reports of the advance by Blücher's forces in strength. In order to avoid the danger of being attacked simultaneously by both Coalition armies, Napoleon decided to march against Blücher with the reserves and, having pushed him back, return for the defence of Dresden. In undertaking this movement, he was very much reliant on the methodical slowness of the Austrian staff and on the inevitable difficulties of conducting operations

---

13 Plotho, II, 94-97; Müffling, 13-15; Heinrich Beitzke, *Geschichte der deutschen Freiheitskriege in den Jahren 1813 und 1814*, II, 152-158.

with a huge army composed of troops from three nations.¹⁴ Hoping to conceal his intentions, Napoleon ordered Poniatowski to go even further into Bohemia with his corps and Lefebvre-Desnouettes [Charles Lefebvre-Desnouettes] with two divisions of *Jeune Garde*, leaving Vandamme's corps [Dominique Joseph René Vandamme] at Rumburg and Victor [Claude-Victor Perrin] at Zittau either to support them or move towards Dresden, as necessary. While on 8 (20) August, he moved to Lauban [Lubań] himself, with the rest of the *Garde* together with *1er corps de cavalerie* under Latour-Maubourg, numbering some 40,000 men, and the next day [21 August new style] linked up with the troops retreating behind the Bober near Löwenberg.¹⁵

The arrival of Napoleon with the reserves gave his force numerical superiority, taking advantage of which, at nine o'clock in the morning on 9 (21) August, he set off towards Löwenberg. Lauriston's *5e Corps* were in the lead, followed by Macdonald's *11e Corps* and Latour-Maubourg's cavalry. The *Garde* proceeded as the reserve. Marshal Ney had received orders to advance through Bunzlau with his *3e Corps*, Marmont's *6e Corps* and Sébastiani's cavalry. The concentration of enemy forces at Löwenberg, their switch to an offensive posture and the enthusiastic cheers of '*Vive l'empereur!*': everything indicated the arrival of Napoleon himself and significant reinforcements for the French army. Indeed, at this very moment, the *Empereur des Français* was solemnly distributing Eagles to his newly raised regiments. Some of his warriors were seeing him for the first time; others had not seen him for a long time. As the regiments paraded past, Napoleon roused them for the imminent battle with staccato shouts of: 'Come, come, my boys; we must advance!'¹⁶ His every movement revealed anxious impatience. By the corner of the stables of the inn *Zum weißen Roß* in Löwenberg, leaning against a high bench on which two maps had been laid out, he stood, now rocking the bench, now repeatedly unbuttoning and buttoning his gray overcoat.

Blücher was also preparing for an offensive at the same time as Napoleon's arrival. The location of strong enemy batteries on the high ground of the left bank of the river was interpreted by him as a show of force, intended to secure the continuing French retreat. Once the enemy, having built bridges, began to cross the Bober, Blücher reinforced the leading elements of Yorck's corps, commanded by *Oberstleutnant* Lobenthal, with *2. Brigade* under Prinz Karl zu Mecklenburg [Karl Friedrich August zu Mecklenburg-Strelitz].

There are two hills near the village of Plagwitz, opposite Löwenberg, one *verst* from the Bober, on either side of the village, parallel to the course of the river. The slopes of both hills closest to Plagwitz are quite steep: the northern one, called the Weinberg [Winna Góra], extends about two *versts* in length, while the width of its crest is no more than 300 or 400 paces. The southern hill, the Steinberg, is much longer and near the village of Höfel [Dworek] it extends over a considerable distance. The former, together with the village of Plagwitz, was occupied by the troops of Yorck's corps, while on the latter there were only outposts from Langéron's corps.¹⁷

---

14 Vaudoncourt, 139-140; Beitzke, II, 12-14.
15 Vaudoncourt, 140; Beitzke, II, 14-15.
16 '*Allons, allons, mes enfans; il faut avancer!*'
17 Müffling, 17-18.

At around noon, Maison's division [Nicolas-Joseph Maison], having crossed the bridge, attacked the Prussian force occupying the Weinberg. The Prussians defended themselves very stubbornly until five o'clock and at the end of the action were reinforced by the 7th Jägers and 37th Jägers from Kaptsevich's X Corps [Pëtr Mikhailovich Kaptsevich], located between Höfel and Zobten, and then retreated to Gröditzberg under the protection of the Seversk Mounted-Jägers and several squadrons of Ukrainian Cossacks. Langéron's corps retreated to Pilgramsdorf [Pielgrzymka] behind the Schnelle Deichsa [Skorą], while Sacken's corps, after a rather heated action at Bunzlau, retreated towards Modelsdorf [Modlikowice], shielded by Major General Ushakov's [Sergei Nikolaevich Ushakov 2nd] counter-attacks with the Smolensk Dragoons and Courland Dragoons. The losses in Blücher's force on 9 (21) August overall reached 30 officers and 1,600 lower ranks. That night the entire Army of Silesia retreated beyond the Deichsa, and settled in the area from Pilgramsdorf to Adelsdorf [Zagrodno, 6½ miles north-east of Pilgramsdorf].[18]

The French pursued the Coalition rather weakly with the corps under Ney and Lauriston. The rest of the force settled down for the night on the left bank of the Bober. Napoleon's *quartier général* [headquarters] and the *Garde* were located in Löwenberg. The enemy troops, not content with plundering the countryside they now held, devastated it completely: crops were trampled; avenues and orchards felled; in Schloss Plagwitz [Zamek w Płakowicach] the contents of the library were either looted, trampled into the mud or ditched in the local ponds; precious works of art, paintings by the Teniers [Abraham and David Teniers], Lucas Cranach and other famous artists, were ripped apart; documents were scattered; the cold-frames were shattered; rare and exotic plants in the orangery were uprooted. There was no mercy either for the houses of God or the hospitals: Catholic churches, along with Lutheran ones, were defiled in an orgy of insanity; tombs were excavated, bodies were exhumed, the most sacred objects of worship were desecrated; the sick and dying were robbed of their last possessions and thrown from their beds into the streets. Of all the enemy formations, only Macdonald's corps alone, thanks to the humanitarian nature of its commander, did not indulge in violence and observed the strictest discipline.[19]

The commander-in-chief of the Army of Silesia displayed foresight and caution most appropriate to the situation in which Napoleon's offensive in superior strength placed him. Anticipating that the force entrusted to him might be forced to retreat deep into Silesia, Blücher notified the Silesian *Generalgouverneur*, General Gaudi [Friedrich Wilhelm Leopold von Gaudi], and demanded that he immediately begin building a fortified camp by the fortress at Neiße [Nysa]. But at the same time, wanting to reassure the troops regarding the continuing retreat, he announced in orders to the army that it had not been forced upon them by the superiority of

---

18 Blücher's report to King Friedrich Wilhelm III, dated 21 August new style (there is also a copy in the Log of incoming documents, No. 1,232); Richter, I, 348-352; Beitzke, II, 169-173; Vaudoncourt, 142-143; Carl von Weiß (Müffling), 17-20, according to his statements, the casualties in the Army of Silesia were over 2,000 men, while the enemy, whose skirmishers worked most skilfully, lost slightly fewer.
19 Richter, I, 353-355.

enemy numbers, but had been undertaken with the intent of distracting them from the Elbe, while the Main Coalition Army invaded Saxony: on Blücher's orders, this notice was read out to every company and squadron. The corps commanders of the Army of Silesia were informed that the Commander-in-Chief proposed to avoid a pitched battle, but would not leave the positions held on the Deichsa until the enemy had deployed superior numbers along the left bank of this river. Thus, having concentrated his corps over one *Meile*, from Adelsdorf to Pilgramsdorf, determining lines of retreat for each of them and monitoring the side roads with dedicated detachments,[20] Blücher intended to wait until the situation became clearer.

But when the enemy attacked Langéron's vanguard at ten o'clock in the morning, this general went to Goldberg without Blücher's permission and reported to the Commander-in-Chief about the retreat of his corps. Having received this information, Blücher ordered the other corps to retreat. Yet because the enemy pursued the Coalition very slowly, Yorck was ordered to halt at Gröditz and repulse the advancing columns. Meanwhile, Blücher, wanting to keep Langéron at Goldberg, rode there himself, but found no Russian troops there, who by that time were already retreating along the road to Jauer. Several officers were sent to Langéron with insistent demands to return and take up positions on the Katzbach at Goldberg. Comte Langéron had already managed to retreat to Seichau [Sichów], more than a *Meile* (seven *versts*) from Goldberg, but he fulfilled the orders issued to him and moved back to Goldberg, where his troops arrived during the night of 10 to 11 (22 to 23) August.

In anticipation of his arrival, Blücher issued orders for the defence of the position at Goldberg: the town and high ground of the Flensberg (to the south-east of Goldberg) were occupied by six Prussian battalions, from Yorck's corps, with 14 guns. In the second echelon were six squadrons under *Oberst* Katzler [Andreas Georg Friedrich von Katzler]. Upon the arrival of General Kaptsevich, with the 7th Jägers and 37th Jägers and some of the cavalry, he took command of all the troops assembled at Goldberg. As soon as preparations for the defence of the position had been completed, the enemy, having occupied the high ground at Wolfsberg [Wilcza Góra], opened a strong cannonade on the town and threw the Landwehr infantry and cavalry into confusion, who had never been under fire before, but the presence of mind of the commanders helped the troops to hold on to the positions they occupied. On that same day, Count Pahlen's detachment set off from Hirschberg towards Schmiedeberg.[21]

Yorck's corps, which had remained to delay the enemy at Gröditz (as has already been mentioned), at four o'clock in the afternoon, received orders to continue the retreat and, leaving six battalions at Goldberg commanded by Major Goltz

---

20 Langéron's corps was to follow the highway, from Pilgramsdorf to a position behind Goldberg; Yorck's corps from Ulbersdorf [Wojcieszyn] to Kosendau [Kozów] across the Katzbach; Sacken's corps from Adelsdorf and Seifersdorf [Łukaszów] to Giersdorf [Gierałtowiec], also on the right bank of the Katzbach. Lanskoy's detachment were on the road from Bunzlau to Haynau, while Lieutenant General Count Pahlen's detachment were on the road from Hirschberg to Goldberg. Müffling, 21; Beitzke, II, 173-174.
21 Military daily notes from Lieutenant General Prince Shcherbatov's VI Infantry Corps (M.T.D. No. 44,585); Beitzke, II, 174-176.

[Ferdinand Friedrich von der Goltz], and the cavalry under *Oberst* Katzler, withdrew after dark behind the Katzbach to Dohnau [Dunino, five miles south-west of Liegnitz] and Nieder Krayn [Krajów, six miles west of Malitsch]. Yorck's force, having marched for several days in succession and having covered the last three stages without having chance to cook a meal anywhere, were extremely exhausted.[22] Sacken's corps withdrew to Schmochwitz [Smokowice, four miles south-west of Liegnitz] and set up camp there.[23]

Napoleon, having forced the Coalition to retreat behind the Katzbach, returned to Löwenberg and spent the night of 10 to 11 (22 to 23) August there. Having received confirmatory intelligence regarding the advance of the Army of Bohemia into Saxony, that night he ordered his *Garde* to march towards Dresden and the next morning he proceeded there himself with the King of Naples [Joachim Murat]. Marmont's *6e Corps* and Latour-Maubourg's *1er corps de cavalerie* also set off for Saxony. Command of the forces remaining in Silesia was entrusted to Marshal Macdonald (*3e Corps, 5e Corps, 11e Corps* and *2e corps de cavalerie*). Marshal Ney, on the march to Rothkirch [Czerwony Kościół, five miles west of Liegnitz], received orders to go to Dresden. Because it had not been made clear whether he was supposed to arrive there with or without his corps, Ney's force moved towards Saxony, and it was only once they were already on the march that they received orders to return. In the absence of Ney, command over them was entrusted to *général de division* Souham [Joseph Souham].[24]

Blücher knew about neither Napoleon's departure nor about the weakening of the enemy army facing him, but nevertheless decided to give battle at Goldberg. Believing the enemy to be incomparably stronger than they actually were, Blücher did not want to engage in a general battle, but had the intention of limiting himself to a determined rearguard action, in fact, in order to prevent the decline in morale of his troops, who, seeing the country given over to looting and violence by the French with every backwards step, were openly showing distrust in the Commander-in-Chief.[25] Blücher's intentions were further buttressed by a letter from Emperor Alexander, received at the headquarters of the Army of Silesia on the evening of 11 (23) August, in which the Tsar, notifying the Prussian commander of the offensive by the Army of Bohemia, insisted that Blücher contribute to the overall success by remaining in contact with the enemy and harassing them with incessant attacks.[26]

The terrain around Goldberg, where the Coalition decided to block the enemy advance, is less hilly than the area around Löwenberg. To the north of Goldberg lie the undulating plains of Silesia and rocky outcrops are only formed along the deep valley of the Katzbach and its tributaries. There are dominant peaks and elevated areas (plateaus) in some places. The forested Wolfsberg peak and the village of Wolfsdorf [Wilków], south of Goldberg, on the left wing of the position, were occupied during the morning of 11 (23) August by an infantry formation, consisting

---

22 Droysen, III, 36-37.
23 Richter, I, 356.
24 Richter, I, 356; Vaudoncourt, 143.
25 Richter, I, 357.
26 Emperor Alexander I's letter from Jungfernteinitz dated 7 (19) August.

of four battalions with 18 guns, commanded by Major General Rudzevich.[27] The 2nd Ukrainian Cossack Regiment were stationed to the right of the Wolfsberg in echelon behind the infantry, while six squadrons were to the left of the village of Wolfsdorf also in echelon behind the infantry.[28] Goldberg lay in the centre of the position and was occupied by four Prussian battalions commanded by Major Goltz. The remaining regiments of X Corps, consisting of eight battalions with 18 guns commanded of Lieutenant General Kaptsevich, were stationed on the high ground to the right of the town in support.[29] The high ground of the Flensberg, south-east of the town, was held by two Prussian battalions with ten guns.[30] Behind them, to the left of the Flensberg, were Korff's cavalry [Fëdor Karlovich Korf or Friedrich Nikolai Georg von Korff], and even further back, VI Corps and IX Corps formed the main reserve of the centre and left wing under Prince Shcherbatov [Alexei Grigorievich Shcherbatov] and Olsufiev [Zakhar Dmitrievich Olsufiev 1st] respectively. On the right wing of the position, on the far bank of the Katzbach, there is a small elevated plain and the villages of Niederau and Hohberg [Wyskok]. Blücher, having received intelligence on the morning of 11 (23) August of the movement of enemy troops from the Bober towards Görlitz, and assessing that weak forces had been left facing him with the sole purpose of concealing a general retreat by the French army, at eight o'clock in the morning, issued the dispositions for an attack.[31] The Prussian *2. Brigade* under Prinz Karl zu Mecklenburg, moving forwards at the head of Yorck's corps, occupied Röchlitz [Rokitnica, three miles east of Goldberg] and crossed the Katzbach.

But at this very moment the French army attacked the Coalition positions at Goldberg. Blücher, being forced to switch to the defensive, and concerned that the enemy might outflank him on the right, ordered Prinz Karl to seize the plateau on the left bank of the Katzbach as quickly as possible, fixing his left flank on the village of Niederau and extending the right to Hohberg. The remainder of Yorck's force, with the exception of those stationed at Goldberg and on the Flensberg, were sent to assist the right wing. The consequence of these deployments were three actions happening simultaneously on 11 (23) August: on the right wing of the Army of Silesia on the left bank of the Katzbach; in the centre at Goldberg, and on the left wing at the Wolfsberg.

The Prinz zu Mecklenburg, having crossed the Katzbach at Röchlitz and leaving one of his battalions there, moved hastily to the positions assigned to him, but he

---

27 29th Jägers and 45th Jägers were in the front line with the Arkhangelogorod Infantry and Staro Ingermanland Infantry in the second line, covered by a half-company from 34th Battery Artillery Company and 28th Light Artillery Company (Plan of the battle of Goldberg, 11 (23) August, M.T.D. No. 20,021).
28 Two squadrons of Livland Mounted-Jägers and four squadrons of Kiev Dragoons (Plan of the battle of Goldberg).
29 The units in X Corps were: 7th Jägers, 37th Jägers, Schlüsselburg Infantry, Olonets Infantry, Staroskol Infantry and Vyatka Infantry, a half-company of 34th Battery Artillery Company and 3rd Light Artillery Company (Plan of the battle of Goldberg).
30 One battalion from the *Leib-Regiment* and one battalion of Silesian *Landwehr*, six three-pounder and four six-pounder cannon.
31 For the contents of this disposition, see Appendix I at the end of this chapter.

encountered the enemy before reaching them and deployed his brigade into battle formation: four battalions in the front line, three in the second, the remaining two were behind the left flank in the Katzbach valley. There were four guns on each flank of the front line. The two cavalry regiments were on the extreme right flank. The remaining three squadrons of cavalry were deployed behind the infantry on the left flank: overall, the brigade commanded by the Prinz zu Mecklenburg had nine battalions, 11 squadrons and one battery, numbering 6,400 men.[32] These troops came under attack from Macdonald himself with *11e Corps* and some of Sébastiani's cavalry, numbering some 20,000 men with 30 guns, while Lauriston crossed at Seiffenau [part of Jerzmanice-Zdrój] with *5e Corps* and the remaining cavalry and led an attack on Goldberg and the Wolfsberg.

At about nine o'clock in the morning, the enemy, having opened a strong cannonade on the light half-battery located on the right flank of the Prinz zu Mecklenburg's position, directed Gérard's division [Étienne Maurice Gérard] against the centre. Within a few minutes, three Prussian guns had been knocked out, while the fourth was dragged back from its position. Whereupon, the French batteries turned their fire on the infantry formed up in battalion columns and inflicted severe casualties on them. The commander of the other Prussian half-battery, on the left flank of the brigade, having witnessed the superiority of the enemy artillery, held his fire until Macdonald's infantry had closed to a range of about 400 paces. Several rounds of canister halted the enemy and forced them to retreat, but after that the Prussian guns were pelted with a hail of shells and round shot. The first shell to hit one of the *Landwehr* battalions stationed 30 paces behind the half-battery, caused such a mindless panic in the inexperienced warriors that the entire battalion fled. The guns, left without immediate protection, were withdrawn. On the left flank of the brigade, the battle was limited to efforts by the *Landwehr* to capture a temporary barracks set up by the enemy during the armistice. These very solidly built barracks, provided the French with sound cover from the Prussian skirmishers' bullets but, despite this, the *Landwehr*, supported by fusiliers, fought at the barracks for some time. Unfortunately, the poorly armed *Landwehr* battalions, in action for the first time, had all been placed together on the left wing, one of the most threatened locations of the position. The loss of many officers, including the commander of the *Landwehr* battalions, *Obersleutnant* Grumbkow, left his young soldiers horror-stricken. At this very moment, the French cavalry, consisting of 12 squadrons, charged at the disordered battalions. All the efforts of the officers to restore order in the ranks were fruitless but, fortunately, the enemy, counterattacked by the *Brandenburgisches Ulanen* and two Cossack regiments from Langéron's corps, paused and were finally checked by the fusiliers of the *2. Ostpreußisches Infanterie*, who came to the rescue

---

32 Prinz Karl zu Mecklenburg's force consisted of: both musketeer battalions of *2. Ostpreußisches Infanterie* and two battalions of *Schlesisches Landwehr* in the front line. Both battalions of *1. Ostpreußisches Infanterie* and one battalion of *Schlesisches Landwehr* in the second line. The fusilier battalions from both Ostpreußisches *Infanterie Regimenter* behind the left flank. Four guns were on each flank from *Hauptmann* Huet's six-pounder foot battery. In reserve were the *Brandenburgisches Ulanen* and *2. Leib Husaren*, two squadrons of *Mecklenburgisches Husaren* and one squadron of *Landwehr*. Richter, I, 358; Beitzke, II, 179; Friedrich Förster, *Geschichte der Befreiungskriege, 1813, 1814, 1815*, I, 650.

of the *Landwehr*. Taking advantage of this, one of the *Landwehr* battalions, under the command of Major Rostken, managed to rally and struck with fixed bayonets, but were forced to yield to the superior enemy and, together with the rest of Major Kempski's battalion, retreated towards the Katzbach. Their retreat forced the line battalions of both Ostpreußisches *Infanterie Regimenter* to move to the left in order to hold the line with the fusiliers. Two French battalions, racing towards the right wing of the position, were driven back by the second battalion of *1. Ostpreußisches Infanterie* and retreated to the barracks near the village of Hohberg. But at that very moment the French cavalry, consisting of 24 squadrons, raced to attack the line regiments and surrounded them on every side. Prinz Karl, together with *Oberstleutnant* Lobenthal, who was trying to restore order to the troops disrupted in the fighting, barely managed to escape into the square of the second battalion of *1. Ostpreußisches Infanterie*. With this battalion's colours in his hands, Prinz Karl shouted out: 'Now East Prussia, make this count!'[33] The battalion, delighted at the example set by the brother of their unforgettable *Königin* Luise [Luise von Mecklenburg-Strelitz], engaged the enemy at very short range with several volleys and drove them back with a shout of 'Hurrah!' The French cavalry, having managed to reform, raced back to attack the second battalion of *2. Ostpreußisches Infanterie*, which, having allowed them right up to their square, opened rapid fire: at the same time, the four light guns dragged away at the beginning of the action, engaged the French with canister at a range of 200 paces and inflicted huge casualties on them. Having driven the enemy off, Prinz Karl ordered the troops to withdraw from their positions. The retreat was all the more difficult because both of Katzler's cavalry regiments,[34] due to a misunderstanding, had been recalled from the battlefield to Goldberg. The enemy pursued the Prussian force with all their cavalry, but were held back by the infantry with the assistance of the valiant *Mecklenburgisches Husaren*. Prinz Karl, having retired one and a half *versts* to the high ground facing the Bricken-Kretscham [Bricken Inn], took up new positions in the Katzbach valley and, being supported by the 7th Jägers and 37th Jägers and Isaev 2nd's Cossacks detached from Kaptsevich's X Corps, remained in place until two o'clock in the afternoon, and then, by order of the Commander-in-Chief continued to retreat further. The Prussian brigade's overall losses reached 28 officers and 1,747 lower ranks, including some 500 taken prisoner. In the evening, having gone to meet the hero of that day, the Prinz zu Mecklenburg, General Yorck said to him: 'Thus far, Your Highness has worn the Order of the Black Eagle as the King's brother-in-law; today you have earned it.'[35]

The actions in the centre and left wing of the general Coalition position began at half past eight o'clock in the morning. Lauriston's corps, having crossed the Katzbach at Seiffenau and downstream of this point, attacked Goldberg, the Wolfsberg heights and the village of Wolfsdorf simultaneously. Major Goltz, holding the town with four battalions, defended stubbornly for fully five hours. Having received orders to evacuate Goldberg at two o'clock in the afternoon, he set out from there, but when,

---

33 '*jetzt Ostpreußen, gilt's.*'
34 *Brandenburgisches Ulanen* and *2. Leib-Husaren*.
35 '*Bisher trugen Eure Durchlaucht den schwarzen Adler Orden als Schwager des Königs; heute haben Sie ihn Sich verdient.*'

after that, they were ordered to reoccupy the town, the Prussian troops turned back and drove the French into the open with loud shouts of 'Hurrah!' Soon after, the enemy managed to establish a foothold on the left wing of the Coalition position, and the troops occupying the town received orders to retreat for a second time, which was carried out in the best order. The losses of the detachment occupying Goldberg were ten officers and 487 lower ranks.[36]

The enemy attack on the left wing was more successful. Rochambeau's division [Donatien-Marie-Joseph de Vimeur de Rochambeau], at the head of Lauriston's corps, ejected Rudzevich's vanguard from the village of Wolfsdorf and seized the Wolfsberg. At the same time, the majority of Sébastiani's cavalry moved to their right, around the left flank of the position. In order to shore up the vanguard, 15th Division were sent forward, consisting of four battalions, with 15th Battery Company, commanded by Major General Kornilov [Pëtr Yakovlevich Kornilov]. The Russian troops fought most bravely, but the French held on to the Wolfsberg.[37] Having no chance of pushing the enemy back, the regiments under Rudzevich and Kornilov fell back and deployed their right flank towards the Flensberg. The French force moved further forward, protecting themselves on their left flank with one of the infantry regiments formed in square, and on their right with cavalry, but the Russian cavalry checked the enemy through successful counterattacks: the 2nd Ukrainian Cossack Regiment cut through the skirmisher screen spread out in front of the square, while General Emmanuel successfully attacked the French cavalry several times with the Kiev Dragoons and Livland Mounted-Jägers.[38] Taking advantage of this, the Russians moved forward in turn. The high ground of the Wolfsberg changed hands three times. Eventually, the French held on to it in the end. The troops under Rudzevich and Goltz, having received orders to retreat, headed along the highway towards Jauer, shielded by Adjutant General Korff's cavalry, who repelled the pursuing enemy several times.[39] Olsufiev's IX Corps were positioned in front of the Prausnitz [Prusice] defile in order to cover the retreat of Rudzevich's and Kornilov's troops. By nightfall, comte Langéron's entire corps were assembled on the position at Hennersdorf [Chroślice], with the exception of the force under the comte de Saint-Priest (formerly commanded by Lieutenant General Count Pahlen, who was retreating from Schmiedeberg towards Landeshut). The losses to the Russian force in the action around the Wolfsberg reached 1,500, and 400 to the Prussians. Consequently, the losses to the Army of Silesia in the actions around Goldberg were more than 4,000 men overall.[40] Blücher intended to immediately concentrate his

---

36 Droysen, III, 39-40; Beitzke, II, 183.
37 '... Hier zeichneten sich das 29ste und 45ste Jäger-Regiment, die Regimenter Archangel und Ingermanland und die 15te russische Division vortheilhaft aus, indem sie mehrere Angriffe zurück schlugen und den Feind am weiteren Vordringen hinderten...' Richter, I, 363.
38 '... la cavalerie ennemie fit plusieurs belles charges et le combat se soutint pendant assez longtems avec opiniâtreté...' Vaudoncourt, 144.
39 Korff's cavalry consisted of: the Tver Dragoons, Chernigov Mounted-Jägers, Seversk Mounted-Jägers, 1st Ukrainian Cossacks and 3rd Ukrainian Cossacks (diary of the movements of Adjutant General Baron Korff's corps).
40 Plan of the action at Goldberg, 11 [23] August 1813 (Archive of the M.T.D. No. 20,021); Richter, I, 363.

entire army at Jauer, but Langéron pointed out to the Commander-in-Chief that his corps, which had been on the march the previous night, was in urgent need of a rest, and remained in Hennersdorf.

While the fighting at Goldberg was underway, Sacken's corps, having received orders to retreat to Jauer, moved away from Schmochwitz via Hochkirch [Babin Kościelec] and Malitsch [Małuszów] to Profen [Mściwojów, four miles east of Jauer].[41]

General Yorck, having received the disposition issued by the Commander-in-Chief in the morning, moved forward with the *1. Brigade, 7. Brigade* and *8. Brigade* and elements of the reserve cavalry, but had barely managed to move about four *versts* away from Goldberg when he was ordered to return across the Wütende Neiße [Nysa Szalona] river. Yorck left Hünerbein's *8. Brigade* [Friedrich Heinrich Karl Georg von Hünerbein] at Laasnig [Łaźniki, five miles east of Goldberg] as a backstop in support of Goltz's detachment holding Goldberg, while he retreated himself beyond the Wütende Neiße with the brigades under Steinmetz [Karl Friedrich Franciscus von Steinmetz] and Horn [Heinrich Wilhelm von Horn] and with the reserve cavalry. At dusk, another order was received – to retreat to Jauer: thus Yorck's force, having travelled about 30 *versts* that day, had to make a night march of more than ten *versts* in pouring rain, without having chance either to light fires or to revitalise themselves with a meal. As if to crown the disasters that had befallen the hungry, exhausted soldiers, they had to march along a muddy road congested with the trains from Sacken's and Langéron's corps. The soldiers, losing patience, forced their way through with musket butts but, despite such forceful measures, two *Landwehr* battalions and one of line infantry fell behind the other infantry, lost their way and wandered all night. The troops, arriving in the dark at the camp site where no firewood or straw had been kept for them, were in a pitiful state. Yorck sent orderlies off in every direction to round up his scattered soldiers. Without bothering to mask his displeasure, he publicly denounced the Commander-in-Chief, saying: 'The Prussian army will be destroyed through exhausting marches and hardship before it even comes to battle.' Indeed, the Army of Silesia was in a precarious situation: the unit commanders were fractious, the soldiers had lost heart and there were no food supplies. Orders from the Commander-in-Chief, which contradicted one another, seemed a clear sign of his indecision. Under these circumstances, he decided to give battle on the open undulating ground beyond Jauer, and if the enemy stopped the pursuit, Blücher intended to go looking for a fight. His situation could not get worse even if he lost the battle, while a more likely victory would facilitate all his subsequent operations.[42]

Having been unable to concentrate on 11 (23) August, the day of the battle of Goldberg, the Army of Silesia continued to retreat on 12 (24) August. A new rearguard was formed to replace the completely disordered rearguard of Yorck's Corps, commanded by *Oberst* Katzler,[43] who, together with the reserve cavalry under *Oberst*

---

41 Plotho, II, 105.
42 Müffling, 25-26.
43 The rearguard infantry, commanded by Major Hiller, included Silesian grenadier and Seidlitz *Landwehr* battalions from *1. Brigade*; Brandenburg grenadiers and Kempski *Landwehr*

Jürgaß, were positioned at the village of Alt Jauer [Stary Jawor, two miles north of Jauer]. Yorck's main body retreated to Kohlhöhe [Goczałków Górny] and Groß Rosen [Rogoźnica], one *Meile* (seven *versts*) from the city of Jauer, Sacken's corps were deployed to the right of the Prussian forces at Kohlhöhe, while Langéron's corps, together with Blücher's Hauptquartier, were at Striegau [Strzegom], two *Meilen* (about 15 *versts*) behind Jauer. The French army did not pursue the Coalition and settled along the Katzbach: Souham's division from Ney's *3e Corps* were stationed at Rothkirch, with two battalions holding Liegnitz;[44] Lauriston's *5e Corps* were forwards of Goldberg, with a vanguard pushed up to Prausnitz; *11e Corps* and Sébastiani's cavalry were behind Goldberg.[45]

The Commander-in-Chief of the Army of Silesia, not knowing for definite of the weakening of the enemy forces facing him and finding it necessary to take measures in case of further retreat into Silesia, on the night of 11 to 12 (23 to 24) August wrote to General Bennigsen [Leonty Leontievich Bennigsen or Levin August Gottlieb Theophil von Bennigsen], who had arrived in the Duchy of Warsaw with the Reserve Army (the so-called Army of Poland), asking him to send some of the troops entrusted to him to assist the Army of Silesia. Having informed the Silesian *Generalgouverneur*, General Gaudi, about the current state of affairs, Blücher repeated the demand for the immediate military occupation and supply of provisions to the fortresses, and – most importantly – asked for the *Landsturm* to be called up in all districts lying to the rear or on the flanks of the enemy army. Finally, on that same night of 11 to 12 (23 to 24) August, he sent a report to the King regarding all the orders he had issued.[46]

But what made things more difficult for Blücher was the ill will towards him from his main associates, the corps commanders. Langéron, as we have already seen, sometimes permitted himself to ignore the orders of the Commander-in-Chief. Yorck, having received the disposition to attack the next day and not yet having chance to reassemble his scattered force, sent Major Diedrich to Blücher to report to him how much rest the corps would need. Indeed, Yorck's troops, having made four night marches over the course of six days, eating only bread and resting in the mud, were in a pitiful condition. The clothing and footwear of the *Landwehr* warriors were worn out. The cartridges had been dampened from the heavy rain. Of the 30,000 infantrymen, barely 25,000 remained present. Blücher did not pay any attention to Yorck's representations and the next morning the Prussian troops, at the given signal, set off on the march. Yet no sooner had the main body of the corps reached Jauer, than an order was received to halt. Yorck, having lost patience, went

---

battalions from *8. Brigade*; Thüringian grenadier battalion and a company of Guard Jäger from *7. Brigade*. The cavalry consisted of: four squadrons of *Litauisches Ulanen*, four squadrons of Neumark *Landwehr* and four squadrons of *Brandenburgisches Ulanen*. The artillery consisted of one battery each of foot and horse artillery. Richter, I, 365-366.

44 At this point, the remaining troops from *3e Corps* were still on the return march from the Bober to the Katzbach.
45 PlothoCarl von Plotho, *Der Krieg in Deutschland und Frankreich in den Jahren 1813 und 1814*, II, 89-92; Frédéric Guillaume de Vaudoncourt, *Histoire de la guerre soutenue par les Français en Allemagne*, 141., II, 105; Vaudoncourt, 144.
46 Beitzke, II, 187.

to the Commander-in-Chief for an explanation, which resulted in a very heated argument between them in the presence of many Russian officers. The irritated Blücher insulted Yorck to such an extent that he decided to ask the King to accept his resignation from service.[47]

> Your Majesty, my aim has been to serve the supreme interests and to promote the good of the state to the best of my ability throughout my 43 years of service. May Your Majesty therefore deign to graciously accept it as the purest expression of my convictions when I freely confess that I can no longer be of any use to Your Majesty in command of First Army Corps, which has been most graciously entrusted to me. Perhaps my imagination is too limited to understand the brilliant intentions that guide General von Blücher's overall command. However, first-hand experience shows me that continuous marches and counter-marches in the eight days of the reopened campaign have already put the troops entrusted to me in a state that would not allow us to expect a favourable outcome in the event of a vigorous enemy offensive. The fact that they have not yet taken such action is a blessing that has protected the combined army here from events similar to those of 1806. Precipitate and inconsequential operations, unverified intelligence and grasping at every apparent enemy movement, while being ignorant of the practical elements which, over and above lofty opinions, are necessary for the leadership of a large army are the causes, unfortunately known from experience, which can destroy an army before it can achieve its main purpose, to strike when it is appropriate. My duty as a subordinate general demands blind obedience from me. My duty as a loyal subject, on the other hand, requires me to strive against the malign, and this collision has the natural consequence that I am an obstruction to the commanding general and become more harmful than useful on the whole. Therefore, I turn to Your Majesty with the most humble request to release me from command of First Army Corps and to place me in another position, no matter how subordinate, where I can serve Your Majesty to advantage. However, I dare to suggest to Your Majesty most humbly that approaching old age and weakened health will soon make it difficult for me to be able to serve Your Majesty with the strength and diligence that I myself demand of me. I would therefore also regard it as a particular grace and favour from Your Majesty if the Sovereign decides to order me to retire and even in quiet seclusion I would keep in my heart the loyalty and submissiveness to my King that I have striven to maintain throughout my entire service.
>
> I most humbly ask Your Majesty to decide on my most humble request as soon as possible; the good of Your Majesty's service requires it. I remain Yours in deepest respect…[48]

---

47 Droysen, *Das Leben des Feldmarschalls Grafen Yorck von Wartenburg*, III, 8-10, III, 42-44.
48 For the full text of this letter (in German) see Appendix II at the end of this chapter.

As for General Sacken, the Commander-in-Chief was completely satisfied with his operations, but did not meet him in person until 13 (25) August. Wanting to express his approval and consult with him about the proposed offensive, Blücher went to his quarters and talked with him for a long time. This meeting established a mutual respect between the old warriors.[49]

---

49 Müffling, 27.

Appendix I

Disposition issued by Blücher on the morning of 11 (23) August

Dispositions for an attack, issued by Blücher at eight o'clock on the morning of 11 (23) August:

> The light cavalry under General Baron Sacken are to head from Schmochwitz via Adelsdorf to Gröditzberg, and halt there in order to fix the enemy while Yorck's force move into their rear via Neudorf [Nowa Wieś Złotoryjska] towards Gröditzberg.
>
> General Yorck's corps are to move to Ulbersdorf, sending cavalry with horse artillery to Neuwiese [Nowa Wieś Grodziska] in order to fix the enemy, and get around their left flank and into their rear, such that the right wing of Yorck's corps is forwards of Pilgramsdorf. The 12-pounder battery is to remain in reserve on the high ground on this side of Pilgramsdorf; the troops, without going into a prolonged cannonade, are to attack the enemy with all their might; the reserve cavalry are to remain on the right wing.
>
> As soon as the sound direction of the cannonade indicates that Yorck's corps has seized this high ground, Langéron's corps are to attack the enemy right flank.

I shall be on the promontory forwards of Goldberg, next to Langéron's corps.

> The Katzbach remains the base of operations. All wounded and prisoners are to be sent to Jauer, whence *Oberstleutnant* Krauseneck [Johann Wilhelm von Krauseneck] is to set off immediately from Liegnitz with eight battalions, 12 squadrons and two batteries.

Appendix II

General Yorck's letter to King Friedrich Wilhelm III, dated 25 August, new style

General Yorck's letter to King Friedrich Wilhelm III, dated 25 August, new style, from Jauer

Ew. K.M. Allerhöchstes Interesse und des Staates Beste nach Kräften zu befördern, ist durch 43-jahrige Dienstzeit mein Bestreben gewesen. Geruhen also Ew. K.M. es als den reinsten Ausdruck meiner Ueberzeigung huldreichst entgegenzunehmen, wenn ich freimüthig das Bekenntniss ablege, dass ich Ew. K.M. bei dem mir allergnädigst anvertrauten Commando des esten Armeecorps nicht ferner nützlich sein kann. Vielleicht ist meine Einbildungskraft zu beschränkt, um die genialen Absichten, welche das Oberkommando des General von Blücher leiten, begreifen zu können. Der Augenschein lehrt mich aber, dass fortwährende Märsche und Contremärsche in den acht Tagen des wiedereröffneten Feldzüges die mir anvertrauten Truppen bereits in einen Zustand verstzt haben, der bei einer kräftigen Offensive de Feindes kein günstiges Resultat erwarten lässt. Dass er solche bisher noch nicht ergriffen hat, ist ein Glück, das die hier vereinte Armee noch bisher vor Ereignissen denen von 1806 ähnlich geschützt hat. Uebereilungen und Inconsequenzen bei den Operationen, unrichtige Nachrichten und das Greifen nach jeder Scheinbewegung des Feindes, dabei Unkunde in den praktischen Elementen, welche zur Führung einer grossen Armee mehr als sublime Ansichten nöthig sind, sind die leider durch die Erfahrung bekannten Ursachen, welche eine Armee zu Grunde richten können, bevor sie zu ihrer Hauptbestimmung gelangen kann, wenn es sich gebührt, zu schlagen. Meine Pflicht als Untergeneral fordert von mir blinden Gehorsam. Meine Pflicht als treuer Unterthan fordert mich dagegen auf, dem Uebel entgegenzustreben, und diese Collision hat die natürliche Folge, das ich dem commandirenden General im Wege bin und dem Ganzen mehr schädlich als nützlich werde. Daher wende ich mich zu Ew. K.M. mit der allerunterthänigsten Bitte, mich von dem Commando des ersten Armeecorps zu entlassen, und mich in ein anderes, wäre es auch ein noch so subalternes Verhältnis setzen zu wollen, wo ich Ew. K.M. mit Nutzen dienen kann. Dabei wage ich es aber Ew. K.M. allerunterthänigst vorzustellen, dass herannahendes Alter und geschwächte Gesundheit es mir bald schwer machen werden Ew. K.M. mit der Kraft und Thätigkeit, die ich selbst von mir fordere, dienen zu können. Ich würde daher auch das als eine besondere Huld und Gnade von Ew. K.M. ansehen, wenn Allerhöchst dieselben deschliessen würden, mir den Ruhestand anzuweisen und auch in der stillen Zurückgezogenheit würde ich Treue und Unterwürfigkeit gegen meinen König im Herzen bewahren, die durch meine ganze Dienstzeit ich mich bestrebt.

Tiefunterthänigst bitte ich Ew. K.M. über meine allerunterthänigste Bitte des allerbaldigsten zu entscheiden; das Beste Ew. K.M. Dienstes erfordert es. In tiefster Ehrerbietung ersterbe ich.

23

The battle on the Katzbach

Blücher's situation upon retreating to Jauer. – The advances by the armies under Blücher and Macdonald. – Description of the area where the battle on the Katzbach took place. – Force strengths for both sides. – Artillery strengths.

The battle on the Katzbach. Locations of Sacken's and Yorck's corps for combat. Location of Langéron's corps. – The retreat of the Prussian vanguard and the French crossing of the Katzbach and Wütende-Neiße. – The occupation of the Taubenberg by Coalition artillery. – Close-quarter combat in the Wahlstatt valley. – Prussian cavalry operations. – Vasilchikov's attack. – The general advance by Sacken and Yorck. – The defeat of *11e Corps* (Macdonald's). – Operations by (Souham's) *3e Corps*. – The state of the forces under Sacken and Yorck. – The retreat of Rudzevich's vanguards to the main position. – Russian cavalry operations. – The French attack on the main position. – Langéron's co-operation with Prussian forces. – The combat losses of both sides. – Blücher's orders.

Measures taken by Blücher in order to pursue the defeated enemy. – Difficulties encountered by the Coalition. – The forces allocated for the initial pursuit. – The situation of the retreating enemy; their losses. – Blücher's principles of war.

The retreat by Puthod's division; its destruction by Russian forces at Pilgramsdorf. – The Coalition liberation of Bunzlau. – The advance of the Army of Silesia to the river Queis. – The outcome of the battle on the Katzbach. – Blücher and his colleagues. – Awards.

Upon retreating to Jauer, Blücher's army had been significantly weakened by combat losses and many men falling sick from forced marches made in inclement weather, along bad roads, with very unsatisfactory rations for the troops. The corps commanders were reluctant to carry out the orders of the Commander-in-Chief. The troops, exhausted by labour and hardship, not understanding the reason for the incessant movements, first forwards, then back, had lost confidence in their commander: Blücher's situation was such that the only means of improving it was to gain a victory in a pitched battle, and had Napoleon continued to pursue the Army of Silesia instead of returning to Saxony, then Blücher, having reached Jauer, in all likelihood would have given battle, which, given French numerical superiority, led by a brilliant commander, would have had disastrous consequences for the Coalition. But Napoleon, who valued Dresden very highly as the focus (*pivot*) of his operations, was forced to be content with pushing Blücher back, although it had not changed the state of affairs in Lusatia and Silesia at all. The Coalition's casualties in the actions on 9, 10 and 11 (21, 22 and 23) August were significant, yet the French losses were hardly fewer.[1] According to General Jomini [Antoine-Henri de Jomini], Napoleon, upon leaving for Saxony, had ordered the *chef d'état-major* Berthier [Louis-Alexandre Berthier] to write to Macdonald:

> that, due to the state of morale among our troops, there was nothing better than to march on the enemy as soon as he wished to take the offensive: in this case, the Coalition would undoubtedly move on several points, while Macdonald, in contrast, would have to concentrate his forces at a single location, in order to attack them in force and immediately regain the initiative. He has been warned of plans to debouch from Zittau towards Prague in the event that the enemy has not yet seriously threatened the entrenched camp at Dresden, or to emerge in front of this camp should the enemy present themselves there with the bulk of their forces. It has been recommended to him, in the event that he is attacked by a superior enemy, to fall back behind the Queis [Kwisa], to hold Görlitz, and to constantly maintain communications with the Emperor in order to reunite if necessary. Should he come under pressure… he should retreat, in the worst case, to the entrenched camp at Dresden.[2]

Yet no one had mentioned this order from Napoleon except General Jomini, who was no longer in the French army by the end of the armistice. Indeed, there was no great need to give such instructions to a commander who had already commanded independent armies more than once.

---

1 '*Les trois journées des 21, 22 et 23 coutèrent à l'ennemi six à sept mille hommes tués, blessés ou prisonniers; notre perte, depuis le 17, s'éleva à près de six mille hommes…*' Vaudoncourt, 144. In reality, the losses in the actions on 9, 10 and 11 (21, 22 and 23) August reached 8,000 men on each side.

2 '*Berthier reçut, le 23 août, l'ordre de lui écrire: que, dans l'étât moral de nos troupes, il n'y avait rien de mieux à faire que de marcher à l'ennemi aussitôt qu'il voudroit prendre l'offensive: dans ce cas, les alliés se porteraient sans doute sur plusieurs points, et Macdonald, au contraire, devrait réunir ses troupes sur un seul, àfin de déboucher en forces sur eux et de reprendre sur-le-champ l'initiative. On le prévint de projet de déboucher de Zittau sur Prague, dans le cas ou l'ennemi ne menacerait pas encore sérieusement le camp retranché de Dresde, ou de déboucher par ce camp, si l'ennemi s'y présentait avec le gros de ses forces. On lui recommanda, dans la supposition qu'il fût attaqué par un ennemi superieur, de se replier derrière la Queisse, de tenir Goerlitz, et de se maintenir sans cesse en communication avec l'empereur pour se reunir au besoin. S'il était pressé… il se retirerait, au pis aller, jusque dans le camp retranché de Dresde.*' Jomini, *Vie politique et militaire de Napoléon*, VI, 18-19.

After retreating to the vicinity of Jauer, Blücher ordered some of the cavalry to be sent on a reconnaissance in the direction of the Katzbach, from which it emerged out that the enemy, having occupied Goldberg and Liegnitz, remained static. Major General Pahlen 2nd's detachment, sent to Konradswaldau [Kondratów, five miles north-east of Schönau] in order to guard the left flank of the army, reported that the enemy, who had appeared near the town of Schönau, had also not undertaken any further advances.[3] The inaction of the French troops gave Blücher cause to conclude that Napoleon had departed with a significant part of the army, and intelligence provided by informants confirmed his suspicions. Resolutely deciding to engage in a general battle, Blücher intended to take advantage of the weakening of the enemy and attack them before they had time to evade a clash.

To that end, on the night of 12 to 13 (24 to 25) August, the following disposition was issued to the army.

> At dawn on 25 August [new style], a reconnaissance is to be carried out by the reserve and vanguard cavalry from all three corps, with horse artillery: the cavalry from Sacken's corps are directed from Liegnitz towards Bunzlau; from Yorck's corps along the axis from Liegnitz to Goldberg; from Langéron's corps towards Goldberg and Schönau.
>
> The troops are to cook their meals such that they are ready to move out by eight o'clock in the morning.
>
> If the enemy have reached the mountains in order to enter Bohemia, then the army should head into the mountains. Should they begin to retreat towards Saxony, the army are to follow them there.
>
> I shall await the reconnaissance reports in Jauer, which should be delivered to me via the orderlies by eight o'clock in the morning. Each corps is to assign an orderly officer who is to report to General Gneisenau to receive orders.
>
> The entire infantry component are to move towards Jauer not before eight o'clock and not later than upon a signal of three cannon shots from Jauer.[4]

At around noon on 13 (25) August, the signal shots were heard. The infantry of the Army of Silesia, having set out from their camps, passed through Jauer and settled down in bivouacs in the evening as follows: Sacken's corps at Malitsch; Yorck's corps at Jauer (where they halted by order of the Commander-in-Chief); Langéron's corps at Hennersdorf; Saint-Priest's detachment at Schönau; Major General Count Pahlen 2nd at Konradswaldau; with forward elements at Liegnitz, Kroitsch [Krotoszyce] and Seichau. It rained almost incessantly for three days, beginning on 12 (24)

---

3   Major General Count Pahlen 2nd, having set out from Jauer to Herrmannsdorf and on to Konradswaldau on 11 (23) August with the Dorpat Mounted Jägers, one infantry brigade and a half-company of light artillery, added General Umanets' Kinburn Dragoon Regiment [Andrey Semënovich Umanets] to his detachment. Diary of the movements of Adjutant-General Korff's corps.

4   Disposition signed by Blücher.

August. All the mountain rivers and streams burst their banks. The roads had mostly become impassable, and water crossings were extremely difficult.

On Macdonald's part, Ney's corps, mistakenly sent to Lusatia, had managed to return to the army on the Katzbach but not before 13 (25) August, which prevented the French commander from leaving the vicinity of Goldberg before 14 (26) August. On the morning of that day, his troops reoccupied their previous locations, namely: Souham's *3e Corps* were at Rothkirch, having detached part of the force towards Liegnitz; one of the divisions of this corps was on the march from Haynau to Liegnitz; Sébastiani's cavalry were at Hohendorf [Wysocko, four miles east of Goldberg]; Lauriston's *5e Corps* were at Goldberg; his vanguard was at Prausnitz; Macdonald's 11th Corps were behind Goldberg and at Schönau.[5] Having concentrated some of his forces, Marshal Macdonald undertook to push Blücher's army deeper into Silesia. He believed that he would find the Coalition in the positions they had taken up at Jauer and hoped that his mere appearance would be enough to expel the Coalition. The French forces were ordered to move forward on 14 (26) August in the following directions: *3e Corps* towards Neudorf [Nowa Wieś Legnicka] and Malitsch, having crossed the Katzbach at Liegnitz; *11e Corps* towards Weinberg [Winnica] and Brechelshof [Brachów] after fording the river at Schmochwitz; Sébastiani's cavalry up the left bank of the Neiße having crossed at Kroitsch; *5e Corps* from Seichau towards Hennersdorf; Puthod's division [Jacques Pierre Louis Marie Joseph Puthod] towards Schönau.[6]

Thus, both military commanders, neither aware of the other's intentions, planned to operate offensively: both Blücher and Macdonald thought they could transfer their armies across the Katzbach without any interference from the enemy. The ignorance of both sides about the intentions and movements of the enemy was facilitated by bad weather, which prevented observations being made over any significant distance.[7]

The consequence of the offensives by both armies was their unexpected encounter with each other on the Katzbach River.[8]

The area in which this battle took place is formed by the triangle between Goldberg, Liegnitz and Jauer. The Katzbach river, which forms one side of the triangle, flows across an open plain, except in the vicinity of Hohendorf and Rimberg [Rzymówka], where the left bank forms a cliff close to the river channel. The main crossing points between Goldberg and Liegnitz are at: Goldberg, Niederau, Röchlitz, Kroitsch, Schmochwitz, the Teichmann manor and Liegnitz. Halfway between Goldberg and Liegnitz, a mountain torrent, the Wütende Neiße flows into the Katzbach, dividing the battlefield into two parts. The main crossing points over this river are at: Brechelshof, Schlaup [Słup], Schlauphof and Nieder Krayn. The banks of the Neiße are generally steep, the right bank in particular dominates the left and towers above

---

5 Plotho, *Der Krieg in Deutschland und Frankreich in den Jahren 1813 und 1814*, II, 107; Vaudoncourt, *Histoire de la guerre soutenue par les Français en Allemagne*, 144; Diary of Korff's corps.
6 Vaudoncourt, 145.
7 Beitzke, *Geschichte der deutschen Freiheitskriege in den Jahren 1813 und 1814*, II, 193.
8 See Map No. 2, The battle on the Katzbach, 14 (26) August 1813.

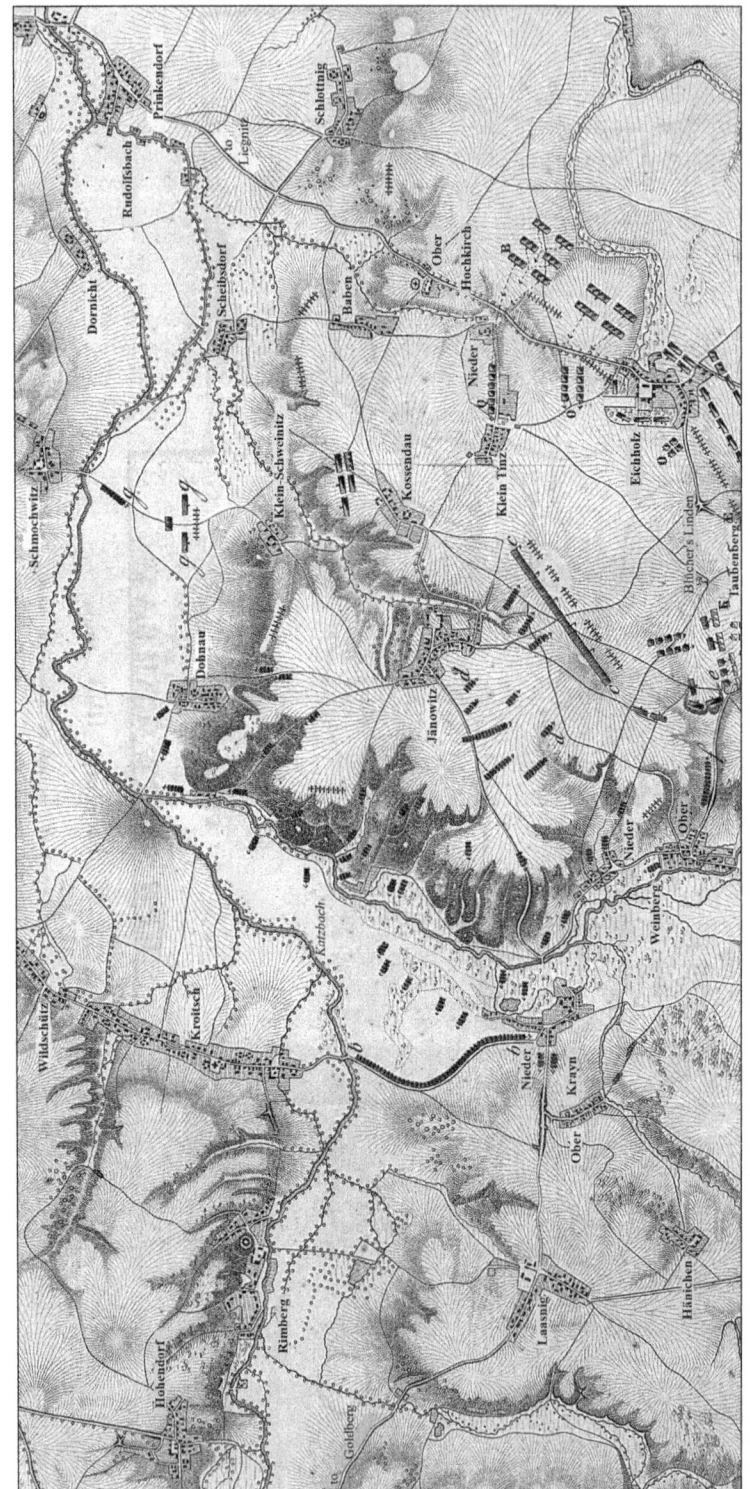

The battle on the Katzbach, 14 (26) August 1813).

Legend to the Plan of the Battle on the Katzbach

Coalition Forces

A.A. Deployment of Yorck's corps the night before the battle.
B.B. Deployment of Sacken's corps into positions.
C.C. Deployment of the vanguard of Langéron's corps.
D.D. Initial deployment of Langéron's corps.
E. Russian battery artillery company.
F. Prussian battery.
G. Major Hiller's four battalions.
H.H. Prussian *7. Brigade*.
K. Prussian reserve cavalry moving to engage the enemy emerging from the Weinberg ravine.
L.L. Prussian *2. Brigade* advance.
M.M.N.N. battalions of *2. Brigade*.
O.O. Advance of Vasilchikov's cavalry.
P.P. Advance of the Prussian cavalry.
Q. Cossacks.
R.R. Prussian *1. Brigade* advance.
S. Attack and capture of the Weinberg by Olsufiev's force.
T. Attack and capture of the Steinberg by Prince Shcherbatov's force.
U. Lieutenant Colonel Nesterovsky's battery.

French Forces

a.a. Deployment of Lauriston's *5e Corps* before the battle.
b.b. Advance of Macdonald's *11e Corps*.
c.c. Sébastiani's cavalry.
d.d. Infantry advance.
e.e. Three battalions attacked and driven off by troops from Prussian *8. Brigade*.
f. French troops emerging from the Weinberg ravine.
g.g. Elements of Souham's *3e Corps*.
h.h. Advance of Lauriston's *5e Corps*.
k.k. Two French battalions marching to seize the high ground at Buschmühle.
l.l. Lauriston's advance.
m.m. Attack on the left flank of the Russian forces.
n.n. The French take Hennersdorf and seize the Steinberg.
o.o. French batteries behind Hennersdorf.
p.p. French seizure of the Weinberg.

the river channel downstream of Nieder Krayn. In dry seasons, the Katzbach and Neiße are fordable at many points, while conversely, in rainy seasons they burst their customary banks, sweep away bridges and become significant obstacles. The Wütende Neiße has a very steep gradient and being fed by many mountain streams during the floods, is especially distinguished by these characteristics. The soil across the entire area of the battlefield is clay, and therefore, after heavy rains, it caused inconvenience for the movement of troops, and especially guns, which bogged down in it right up to the axles.

The area on the right bank of the Neiße, on which Sacken and Yorck fought, is a plateau with gentle undulations that do not in any way impede the movement of troops. On one of these knolls between the village of Eichholz [Warmątowice Sienkiewiczowskie] and the Bellwitzhof Manor stands a distinctive linden tree, named for Blücher (*Blücherlinde*), because the Prussian hero was located here for most of the duration of the battle. The main roads in the area on the right bank of the Neiße were: firstly, from Jauer through Brechelshof, Weinberg, Nieder Krayn (where it crosses the Neiße) and forks – through Kroitsch towards Bunzlau, and through Röchlitz towards Goldberg; secondly, from Jauer through Malitsch towards Liegnitz.

On the left bank of the Wütende Neiße, the ground has a completely different character. Here, half a *Meile* (about three and a half *versts*) from this river, rises the forest-covered spur of the Sudeten- Mönchswald [Bober-Katzbach-Vorgebirge or Pogórze Kaczawskie]. The road passing from Jauer, through Hennersdorf and Seichau, towards Goldberg, along the valley between the Mönchswald and the Neiße, crosses the river Plinsa [Błotnica] at right angles and a series of hills in front of Hennersdorf. At this location there is a very advantageous position for a corps of 15,000 to 20,000, protected frontally by the Silberflüschen stream, and on the flanks by the Neiße channel and the mountains. There is another position forwards of this, facing the village of Seichau, covered from the front by the Plinsa, requiring fewer troops, but having said that, being overlooked by the dominant high ground on the left bank of this river.[9]

It is quite difficult to determine the precise number of troops on each side that participated in the fighting on the Katzbach. The Army of Silesia, less some 12,000 men killed, wounded and sick who had left the ranks since the reopening of hostilities, overall would have consisted of approximately some 85,000 men, while with the exclusion of the corps under the comte de Saint-Priest and the detachment under Count Pahlen, the number of men would not have exceeded 75,000. Macdonald, minus those lost from the ranks in the action at Goldberg, would have had some 75,000 men, but from this number the following should be excluded: firstly, Puthod's division of *5e Corps* detached to Schönau; secondly, Ledru's division [François Roch Ledru des Essarts] (formerly Gérard's) of *11e Corps* directed towards Hirschberg on 14 (26) August; thirdly, Charpentier's division [Henri François Marie Charpentier] of that same corps also did not take part in the fighting; fourthly, two divisions from *3e Corps* that did not manage to participate in the action: thus, it is easy to explain why some painstaking historians show the actual number of French troops who fought at the Katzbach to be no more than 48,000 men. Yet there were overall some 65,000 on the battlefield.[10] With regard to the artillery of both sides in the fighting on the Katzbach, the data is even less reliable. The total number of guns of the Army of Silesia reached some 340, but from this total we must exclude: firstly, the artillery with the forces under the comte de Saint-Priest and Major General Count Pahlen 2nd, a total of 40 to 50 guns; and secondly the artillery left behind in Jauer by comte Langéron, before his advance towards Hennersdorf; according to Müffling, at the battle on the Katzbach, Langéron had just 30 light guns,[11] but since, in all likelihood, he had left only the heavy companies (six in total) in Jauer, he would have had some 50 light and horse artillery pieces with his corps. From these figures it can be concluded that there would have been some 200 guns with the Army of Silesia during in the battle. Macdonald's total number of guns reached some 300, but since the artillery

---

9   Peter von Sporschill, *Die große Chronik. Geschichte des Krieges des verbündeten Europa's gegen Napoleon Bonaparte in den Jahren 1813, 1814 und 1815*, I, 501-502; Weiß (Müffling), 28.
10 For a breakdown of these numbers, see Appendix III at the end of this chapter.
11 For a breakdown of these numbers, see Appendix III at the end of this chapter.

from several divisions would not participate in the battle at all, it is unlikely that the French could face the Coalition with more than 180 or 200 guns.

At dawn on 14 (26) August, Yorck's corps set off from the camp at Jauer in two echelons, towards Bellwitzhof, and deployed in closed columns concealed on the reverse slopes between Brechelshof and Bellwitzhof. The forward elements, commanded by *Oberst* Katzler, were sent towards Nieder Krayn. Blücher's Hauptquartier were in Brechelshof that same morning. At 11 o'clock, a disposition was issued for the onward movements by the army, in the conclusion to which Blücher wrote: 'I have faith that once the enemy retreats, the cavalry will show valour. Let the enemy know that they cannot escape from our hands with impunity.'[12] The disposition ordered all corps to move at two o'clock in the afternoon, but at noon precisely the outposts informed him that the enemy were advancing in numerous columns.[13]

Indeed, Macdonald, unaware of the movements of the Army of Silesia back towards the Katzbach, believed he would find them beyond Jauer, or even further, and set out from the vicinity of Goldberg, without taking proper precautions in the event of unexpected contact with the enemy. It has already been mentioned above that one of his divisions had been sent towards Schönau, and another to Hirschberg. A third division (from Souham's corps) was still on the march from Haynau to Liegnitz. The remaining eight infantry divisions and the cavalry, numbering some 60,000 men, had set off from their locations without any coordination with each other: Lauriston's *5e Corps* set off at nine o'clock; *11e Corps* one hour later, while Souham's *3e Corps* were so late that they barely made it to the end of the battle. Macdonald was himself with Lauriston's force, and therefore was not in a position to directly control the course of the battle at the decisive point, in the centre.[14] *5e Corps* was heading via Prausnitz towards Hennersdorf, on the left bank of the Wütende Neiße; *11e Corps* via Kroitsch; *3e Corps* much later, via Rothkirch towards Liegnitz.

The weather was still stormy; it was raining heavily; the troops of both sides got stuck in the mud; many *Landwehr* warriors lost their footwear and were marching barefoot. It was so overcast all day that any visibility beyond 200 paces became impossible. Both armies moved towards each other, unable to see the enemy with whom they were about to fight.

As soon as intelligence on the French advance arrived, the Coalition sent batteries to the most advantageous points for artillery operations and hastily formed up for battle. General Sacken, who had previously advanced the troops from his corps to keep level with Yorck's corps, positioned their right flank on the village of Eichholz, and their left flank on the Christianshöhe manor: General Neverovsky's 27th Division were stationed in the front line, Count Lieven 3rd's 10th Division [Ivan Andreevich Liven or Johann Georg von Lieven] were in the second; the Courland Dragoons and Smolensk Dragoons, commanded by Major General Ushakov, were on the right flank of the second line, behind the village of Eichholz, which was held by 8th Jägers and 39th Jägers, and in whose support the Okhotsk Infantry and Kamchatka Infantry formed an extension on the right of the front line. Adjutant-General Vasilchikov

---

12 For the text of this disposition, see Appendix IV at the end of this chapter.
13 Plotho, II, 109.
14 Beitzke, II, 195-196.

1st, commanding the 2nd Hussar Division, was stationed to the right of Eichholz, while Karpov 2nd's six Cossack regiments [Akim Akimovich Karpov] were on the extreme right flank.[15]

Yorck's corps deployed to the left of Sacken's force. Horn's *7. Brigade* formed the right wing of the front line, while Hünerbein's *8. Brigade* formed the left. Three battalions of *Brandenburgisches Infanterie* together with the Russian 11th Jägers and 36th Jägers held the village of Schlaup in order for Yorck's corps to maintain communications with comte Langéron's. To that same end, the following were stationed near this village: a battalion of Briesen *Landwehr* and two squadrons of *Brandenburgisches Husaren* from *8. Brigade*; a Silesian grenadier battalion from *1. Brigade*, and two squadrons of *Ostpreußisches National Kavallerie* from the reserve cavalry. *Oberst* Hünerbein took command of all the troops stationed at Schlaup, while *Oberstleutnant* Borcke [Karl August Ferdinand von Borcke] took command of the remaining six battalions of *8. Brigade*. The remaining two infantry brigades, *1. Brigade* under *Oberst* Steinmetz and *2. Brigade* under Prinz Karl zu Mecklenburg. Initially they were stationed about 1,200 paces behind the front line, but later *2. Brigade* entered the centre of the front line between *7. Brigade* and *8. Brigade*, while *1. Brigade* remained behind the left flank in reserve. The reserve cavalry, commanded by *Oberst* Jürgaß, were stationed behind the infantry of *2. Brigade*.[16] Yorck's front line infantry were initially deployed in line, but were subsequently reformed into attack columns.[17]

Langéron's corps were stationed on the left bank of the Wütende Neiße, in positions near Hennersdorf, while his vanguard force were on the high ground in front of this village, facing the Plinsa river, the banks of which were held by the 45th Jägers. The 29th Jägers were to the right of the highway, while the Arkhangelogorod Infantry and Staro Ingermanland Infantry were to its left. The 2nd Ukraine Cossacks were on the extreme right wing, while the Livland Mounted-Jägers and Kiev Dragoons were on the extreme left. The 3rd Ukraine Cossacks were behind the left flank. The 2nd Don Cossack Artillery Company were emplaced on a rise forward of the left wing vanguard infantry. Comte Langéron's main body was located on the reverse slopes of the Weinberg and Kirchberg: Prince Shcherbatov's VI Corps extended their right wing (7th Division) towards the Breiteberg [Bazaltowa Góra], while their left (18th Division) extended towards the Kirchberg. The 11th Jägers and 36th Jägers (as mentioned above) occupied Schlaup, while the 28th Jägers and 32nd Jägers were deployed on the high ground between this village and the Kirchberg. The 9th Division and 15th Division of General Olsufiev's IX Corps were stationed behind the Weinberg in two lines, holding Hennersdorf with 10th Jägers and 38th Jägers, with 12th Jägers holding the course of the stream to the left of Hennersdorf (from where this regiment was subsequently transferred to the second line), and 22nd Jägers were in Herrmannsdorf [Męcinka]. The cavalry were in reserve. X

---

15 General Sacken's dispatch No. 252 to Prince Volkonsky, dated 3 [15] September (Archive of the M.T.D. No. 44,585; Log of outgoing documents, Sacken's corps).
16 Plotho, II, 110.
17 Beitzke, II, 202; August Wagner, *Plane der Schlachten und Treffen, welche von der preussischen Armee in den Feldzügen der Jahre 1813, 14 und 15 geliefert worden*, II, 26-27.

Corps (less the regiments stationed in the vanguard behind the Plinsa) were initially located in reserve behind the right wing of this position, and were subsequently sent to Peterwitz [Piotrowice], in order to protect the army from being enveloped from Schönau.[18]

As soon as the leading Prussian troops, sent to the left bank of Katzbach, encountered enemy cavalry, they quickly began to retreat across the river, holding the villages of Rimberg, Kroitsch and Wildschütz [Wilczyce] with infantry. The French pressed them persistently, barely giving them chance to retreat. Sébastiani crossed the Katzbach via a ford. Both of Macdonald's divisions proceeded behind them across bridges laid near the villages. The Prussian troops were in a rush to cross the Wütende Neiße. Some of the infantry held the village of Nieder Krayn, but since it was impossible to fire muskets soaked by the rain, resistance by the weak vanguard would not last long. These troops, driven out of the village, hurriedly began to climb the forested cliffs on the right bank of the Neiße in order to redeploy there and hold off the enemy. The French were in pursuit: the infantry across the bridge at Nieder Krayn; the cavalry and guns via a ford. The water level was rising by the minute, yet somehow it was still possible to cross. Most of the French infantry, having crossed the river, turned to their left. The remainder headed towards Weinberg. The cavalry, trying to overtake the infantry in order to protect their transition into battle formation, disordered them. The battalions became intermixed with each other. Directing the troops became impossible. Seeing the enemy in disarray prompted the commander of the Prussian vanguard, Major Hiller [Johann August Friedrich Hiller von Gaertringen], to reform the force entrusted to him on the plateau, in two lines:[19] the infantry on the left, with the cavalry on the right wing. Fahrenkamp's six-pounder battery unlimbered and held the enemy up using the ground very skilfully. Upon arrival at Christianshöhe, the vanguard were supported by the entire reserve cavalry under *Oberst* Jürgaß and retreated with it to the main body of the corps.[20]

Thus the enemy blocked the Coalition advance, and the disposition issued shortly before could not be carried out. But this unexpected turn of events did not unsettle Blücher. He tried to show that he had taken everything that was happening into account, and, having allowed some of Macdonald's army onto the plateau, that he had decided on his own accord to attack the French with the corps under Sacken and Yorck and to eject the enemy from the steep banks of the Neiße. The officer he sent with orders for Yorck, a brave but clumsy man, conveyed to him the will of the Commander-in-Chief, saying: 'General Blücher wants you to attack the enemy, after allowing them to cross in such strength as you would be able to defeat.' Yorck, who was constantly at odds with Blücher, replied: 'Go forwards and count them. One can barely see to count one's own fingers in this rain.'[21] Meanwhile, enemy round shot were already reaching the Prussian troops, Yorck ordered the infantry, formed in columns, to deploy into line, both to maintain proper intervals between the

---

18 Wagner, II, 25-26.
19 The Prussian vanguard consisted of two grenadier battalions, two of *Landwehr* and one of Thuringians, two of *Ostpreußisches Jäger*, eight squadrons and two batteries. Plotho, II, 105.
20 Beitzke, II, 197-199; Vaudoncourt, 145.
21 Droysen, *Das Leben des Feldmarschalls Grafen Yorck von Wartenburg*, III, 53.

battalions and to reduce casualties caused by shelling. At the same time, he instructed *Oberstleutnant* Schmidt to drag the artillery up the sloping high ground forwards of the Christianshöhe manor (the Taubenberg). But even before Schmidt had chance to carry out this order, fire was opened from the Taubenberg from the guns of the Russian 13th Battery Company under Colonel Brahms, placed there on Sacken's orders. The commander of the reserve artillery of Yorck's corps, *Oberstleutnant* Schmidt, placed three Prussian batteries to the left of them. Under cover of the cannonade from these guns, the Prussian infantry moved forward.[22]

Having received orders to attack the enemy, Sacken answered the officer sent by Blücher: 'Tell him my answer is simply Hurrah!' The troops of both corps stationed on the right bank of the Neiße, went on the attack almost simultaneously, at three o'clock in the afternoon, and Yorck's front line, at the insistence of Blücher, reformed into columns. At the same time, the Coalition incrementally deployed 92 guns, which the French, due to the difficulty of ascending onto the plateau and moving across the very sticky ground, could counter with only 40 guns.[23]

The Prussians of *8. Brigade* entered a close-quarter battle ahead of all the other troops. The French were stationed in three battalion squares with four guns at the entrance to the ravine leading to the village of Ober Weinberg, in the Wahlstatt valley [Legnickie Pole]. The Brandenburg battalion under Major Othegraven [Karl Thomas von Othegraven], which had not yet managed to reform into column, was pelted with canister shot from very close range and, having unexpectedly stumbled upon the leading central square, charged with fixed bayonets, enveloping the enemy on all sides and destroyed most of the French battalion, resorting to bayonets and rifle butts. The few French survivors were taken prisoner. This brilliant attack was facilitated by the *Landwehr* battalion under Major von Thiele. The remaining two squares were driven off by two battalions of *12. Reserve-Regiment* with the loss of all four guns. The enemy *Chasseurs à cheval*, sent to the rescue of the infantry, were engaged by the reserve cavalry under *Oberst* Jürgaß. The *National-Kavallerie*, *1. Westpreußisches Dragoner* and *Litauisches Dragoner* went on the attack, put the *Chasseurs à cheval* to flight, took several guns and scattered one square. Behind them, in the second line, were the following regiments: *1. Neumärkischen Landwehr-Kavallerie* and *Brandenburgischen Ulanen*. Three *National-Kavallerie* squadrons charged at the enemy cavalry moving along the ravine from Weinberg, put them to flight and forced them to abandon in haste the guns that were with them, but were held up at Weinberg by fire from the skirmishers holding this village. The *Litauisches Dragoner*, having been sent up to the vanguard even before the battle and remained on the left bank of Katzbach even as the French were already crossing to the right bank, also distinguished themselves in no lesser fashion. The valiant

---

22 Sacken's dispatch to Prince Volkonsky, dated 3 [15] September; Droysen, III, 53; Wagner, II, 28. In his report to Emperor Alexander I, dated 16 (28) August, from Goldberg, Blücher wrote: 'Ich verdanke diesen wichtigen Sieg vorzüglich dem General Sacken, der die Höhe zwischen Bellwitzhof und Eichholz schnell und unaufgefordert durch eine 12-pfündige Batterie besetzen liess, wodurch es mir möglich wurde sogleich den förmlichen Angriff auf den feindlichen rechten Flügel zu dirigiren.'

23 Vaudoncourt, 28; Sporschill, I, 507-508; Beitzke, II, 203.

dragoons, completely isolated by the enemy, not only forced their way through the line of French squares and batteries under a hail of round shot and canister, they also charged the artillery, cut down many infantry and gun crews and rendered a significant number of guns unserviceable. At that very moment, the French cavalry charged at the dragoons, but they escaped due to the attacks by all the other regiments from Jürgaß's reserve.

However, this attack by the Prussian cavalry had no significant outcome, because the Prussians, having thrown the enemy back, did not occupy the Kreuzberg high ground with a howitzer battery in order to destroy the columns emerging from Ober Weinberg with shellfire, and did not place one or two cannon to enfilade the exit from the ravine. This negligence cost the Prussian troops dearly. Three enemy battalions climbed up onto the Kuhberg [Krowa Góra] from the direction of Weinberg, taking refuge in the scrub there from the rain with their guns, and at the same time as the cavalry of both sides were intermixed in close-quarter combat, they opened fire on the Prussian horsemen. At the same time, almost all of Sébastiani's cavalry deployed in sight of the fighting troops. Bogged down in the mud, in the pouring rain, the Prussian cavalry could not maintain order in their ranks and were forced to retreat. *Rittmeister* Novelli found himself among the French cavalry with one of the *National-Kavallerie* squadrons but managed to escape by ordering his soldiers to shout: *Vive l'empereur*! which deceived the enemy *lancier* regiment standing next to them. Four guns of *1. Reitende Batterie*, which accompanied the Prussian cavalry during the attack, were captured by the French, who, hotly pursuing the retreating regiments, burst into the gap between Borcke's and Horn's battalions and drove off the cavalry stationed there behind the second line. Yorck, annoyed by this failure, showered Jürgaß with reproaches, saying to him: 'You have completely broken your cavalry up.' He hastened to the batteries himself with Major Bülow's Brandenburg battalion. At the same time, Hiller's infantry engaged the enemy horsemen with bayonets fixed, while four battalions of Prinz Karl zu Mecklenburg's *2. Brigade* moved forward with drums beating and with a deafening shout of Hurrah! and, passing through the interval between *7. Brigade* and *8. Brigade*, burst into the midst of the French cavalry. The other four battalions of *2. Brigade* formed up to the left of Bellwitzhof in order to protect the left flank of the corps. Jürgaß's cavalry were positioned behind the infantry. Katzler's advance with the Neumark *Landwehr* cavalry and the Russian hussars forced the enemy to fall back. The time had come to decide the outcome of the battle. Blücher himself, remembering the youthful exploits of his younger years, drew his sabre and, together with his faithful companions, Katzler and Jürgaß, with trumpets sounding and shouts of *Vorwärts*! raced into the attack and after repeated efforts forced the French to turn their backs.[24]

During these actions on the left wing of Yorck's corps, operations on his right wing and Sacken's corps were almost entirely limited to a cannonade. Meanwhile, Sacken, seeing that the left flank of the enemy force was completely open, was preparing to outflank them with the majority of the cavalry from his corps. The commander of 2nd Hussar Division, Adjutant General Vasilchikov ordered Major General Karpov

---

24 Wagner, II, 28-30; Beitzke, II, 203-206; Förster, *Geschichte der Befreiungskriege, 1813, 1814, 1815*, I, 670-672.

to find out whether the villages on their left flank were occupied by the French, and having learned that there were no enemy troops in them, he issued orders for a general attack. At around five o'clock in the afternoon, the attack was launched from three directions: Major General Yurkovsky [Anastasy Antonovich Yurkovsky] was directed straight ahead with the Alexandriya Hussars and Mariupol Hussars; Major General Lanskoy [Sergei Nikolaevich Lanskoy] passed between Eichholz and Klein Tinz [Tyńczyk Legnicki] with the Akhtyrka Hussars and Belorussia Hussars, striking into the enemy flank, while Major General Karpov proceeded through Klein Tinz with six Cossack regiments and moved to get behind the French. Neverovsky's 27th Division followed behind the hussars, while Lieven's 10th Division remained in place. The Prussian cavalry, having managed to rally and reform, contributed to the attack by the Russian hussars. More than 8,000 horsemen from both sides were sent into action between Klein Tinz and Jänowitz [Janowice]. Macdonald was relying on Souham's *3e Corps* to protect *11e Corps* from being outflanked by reaching the battlefield from Rothkirch via Prinkendorf [Przybków] but, in order to avoid a lengthy detour, Souham's force had been directed to Kroitsch and Nieder Krayn and due to the congestion of cavalry there, could not arrive in time to assist the corps under attack. The enemy cavalry, surrounded by superior numbers, were driven back through their own infantry and threw them into disarray. Blücher, taking advantage of this, ordered the entire infantry component of both corps to advance. The French, forming battalion squares, tried to halt the Coalition, but were driven off the plateau into the Wütende Neiße and Katzbach, with the loss of 30 guns.[25] Eventually, once one of the divisions from *3e Corps* managed to push through Dohnau onto the plateau along with three regiments of light cavalry, the battle resumed with renewed vigour, but these troops could no longer save the situation and were also pushed back to the Katzbach. The French fled, trying to get back across the rivers that had burst their banks, but by then the fords had already become too deep, and the bridges had been swept away, except for one, built specifically in case of flooding at Nieder Krayn. All the men, horses and carts that suddenly congested the river bank could not possibly cross this single bridge. To complete the disastrous fate of Macdonald's forces, the artillery under Sacken and Yorck, having approached the edge of the plateau, smashed the enemy crowds. Many threw themselves into the water and drowned in the deluge, swept away by the swift mountain torrent. The two French battalions that remained on the high ground at Weinberg were also driven back to Nieder Krayn by Prinz Karl zu Mecklenburg with two battalions of Ostpreußisches Infanterie, which occupied the village and, in driving the enemy across the river, captured the last bridge on the Neiße. This was the last action by Yorck's corps.[26]

On the right wing of the Coalition army, Sacken's corps closed up to Schweinitz and lined the towering bluffs near the Neiße's confluence with the Katzbach with their batteries. At seven o'clock (at nine o'clock in the evening according to other sources),

---

25 Diary of military operations by Baron Sacken's corps (Archive of the M.T.D. No. 16,643); In Sacken's dispatch to Prince Volkonsky it states that 50 guns were taken in this action (Archive of the M.T.D. No. 44,585; Log of Sacken's outgoing documents).
26 Sacken's dispatch to Prince Volkonsky dated 3 [15] September; Wagner, II, 30-32; Beitzke, II, 206-208.

two divisions from *3e Corps*, with two cavalry regiments and 12 guns, commanded by the corps' *chef d'état-major*, General Tarayre [Jean-Joseph Tarayre], crossed the Katzbach via a ford at Schmochwitz, waist-deep in water, and began to ascend the fairly steep bluffs near Schweinitz. But being engaged by a strong cannonade from Sacken's batteries, they were forced to withdraw beyond the Katzbach, and suffered very significant casualties.[27] The darkness of the night ended the fighting.[28] Despite the elation roused in the Coalition forces by their victory, they were exhausted, having stood all night in the mud, with the rain falling in streams and extinguishing their fires. Many of the soldiers, and especially the *Landwehr* warriors, had lost their footwear. Everyone, without exception, was soaked to the skin. The trains had no chance of reaching the troops.[29]

During the course of the events described, a stubborn battle was taking place on the left bank of the Wütende Neiße between the corps under Langéron and Lauriston. Due to the bad weather preventing him from being able to observe operations by the left wing of his army and not receiving any news from there, Blücher assessed from the direction of the cannonade that Langéron was retreating, being unable to hold the enemy back. Indeed, the French had been marching against Rudzevich's forward position in numerous columns from nine o'clock in the morning, having sent two battalions with two guns to get around their left flank, which, passing along a ravine through the forest, seized the high ground in front of Buschmühle [Bogaczów, 1½ miles west of Herrmannsdorf]. The Russian vanguard, despite this, held out stubbornly. But concerned about being outflanked, Langéron ordered Rudzevich to withdraw the force entrusted to him to the left wing of the main position, where they were repositioned between Herrmannsdorf and the Mönchswald. At the same time, Major General Count Pahlen 2nd was ordered to withdraw behind Konradswaldau in order to shield the road leading to Jauer.

The position held by the main force under comte Langéron was highly advantageous: its front was covered by the Silberflüschen stream. The right flank rested on the Wütende Neiße near the village of Schlaup, where elements of Hünerbein's brigade were located, while the left flank adjoined the wooded mountains and was defended by two battalions from Rudzevich's vanguard. The villages of Hennersdorf and Herrmannsdorf, held by infantry, were the strong-points of the position, while the high ground was lined with artillery and should have presented an insurmountable barrier to the enemy efforts. But Langéron, who was not at all minded to fight a decisive battle, had been exclusively preoccupied with securing his line of retreat into Silesia, and therefore had left all his heavy artillery in Jauer, which, in his opinion, would be more of a hindrance than a help when moving along the poor roads. These orders, issued without the knowledge of the Commander-in-Chief, deprived Langéron of the means to defend the position he had duly occupied and would have placed him in a very dangerous situation had Sacken and Yorck not won a brilliant victory.

---

27 Souham's corps included *10e régiment de hussards* and a dragoon regiment from Baden.
28 Sacken's dispatch to Prince Volkonsky dated 3 [15] September.
29 Beitzke, II, 208.

After Rudzevich had retreated into the main position, the French crossed the Plinsa and at noon launched an attack on Hennersdorf in several columns. The 10th Jägers and 38th Jägers stubbornly held out in this village and, meanwhile, a cannonade ensued in which the larger calibre French artillery, numbering some 40 guns, worked to advantage against the lighter Russian batteries. Comte Langéron, having at the same time received news from General Yuzefovich [Dmitry Mikhailovich Yuzefovich] regarding a strong enemy column attacking Schönau, sent most of X Corps (which had been stationed behind the right wing of the position, commanded by General Kaptsevich) to Peterwitz and instructed him to transfer the force entrusted to him to Moisdorf [Myślibórz, four miles west of Jauer], if this proved necessary in order to deny the route to Jauer to the enemy.

At two o'clock in the afternoon, Lauriston, having attempted to envelope the Russian position from the left flank, directed three columns against the left wing of Langeron's force: one on Herrmannsdorf, the others on the sector between this village and the mountains. The former was repelled by General Count de Witt [Ivan Osipovich de Witt] with the 4th Ukrainian Cossacks, and the other two were driven back by General Emmanuel with the Kiev Dragoons and Colonel Paradovsky [Philip Osipovich Paradovsky] with the Livland Mounted-Jägers. The courageous Paradovsky, seriously wounded in the action at Goldberg on 11 (23) August, nevertheless, fought at the head of his regiment and was killed.[30]

At around four o'clock in the afternoon, Lauriston, probably already having heard of the failure of the other French corps and wanting to launch a diversion in their favour, decided to launch a reinforced attack. Having opened heavy fire from all the batteries emplaced against the Russian position, the enemy captured Hennersdorf and occupied the high ground of the Steinberg (between this village and Schlaup). The 28th Jägers and 32nd Jägers were forced to retreat behind the Schlaup ravine, while the 10th Jägers, 12th Jägers and 38th Jägers retreated to the second line, on the reverse slopes of the Weinberg. The enemy were quick to exploit their success and concentrated the fire of the guns located on the high ground near Hennersdorf against the Weinberg and, silencing the Russian battery stationed there, took possession of this dominant high ground. General Olsufiev, having received orders from comte Langéron to take this important point from the enemy, committed the Nasheburg Infantry, Ryazhsk Infantry and Yakutsk Infantry into the fire, which, commanded by Major General Udom 2nd, [Yevstafy Yevstafievich Udom], raced up the slopes and beat back the French. As all the muskets had been misfiring due to the pouring rain and it was impossible to shoot, a fierce hand-to-hand fight ensued. The troops fought with bayonets and musket butts.

Prince Shcherbatov's VI Corps, having also received orders to move forwards in order to maintain the links to the Prussian forces, carried out this movement quickly and in good order. His left wing reoccupied part of the village of Hennersdorf, while Major General Meshcherinov [Vasily Dmitrievich Meshcherinov] recaptured the Steinberg with the 28th Jägers and 32nd Jägers.

---

30 Military memoirs (diary) of General-of-Infantry comte Langéron; Wagner, II, 32-33; Richter, *Geschichte des Deutschen Freiheitskrieges vom Jahre 1813 bis zum Jahre 1815*, I, 381-383.

Prince Shcherbatov immediately ordered Lieutenant Colonel Nesterovsky's 34th Light Artillery Company to occupy this high ground. The actions of this artillery on the enemy flank silenced the nearest French battery. The Prussian troops greatly contributed to the success of the defence by Langéron's corps. Having learned of his retreat, Blücher sent Steinmetz's brigade, which was in reserve, to Schlauphof in order to assist him and directed *Oberst* Müffling to conduct a thorough reconnaissance of the progress of the battle on the left bank of the Neiße.

Oberst Steinmetz, having received orders to cross the Wütende Neisse and outflank Lauriston's force, sent three battalions to Schlaup, four to Schlauphof, while he forded the river downstream of Schlaup himself, with a battalion each of *Leibgrenadiers* and Rakau's *Landwehr*. The battery, which was attached to the brigade, protected by an Ostpreußisches grenadier battalion, was positioned on the high ground on the right bank, in order to operate against enemy troops holding the opposite river bank. *Oberst* Steinmetz pushed them back. But the cannonade and firefight at Hennersdorf continued until 11 o'clock at night.

Comte Langéron, having received information from *Oberst* Müffling regarding the successes achieved by the other Coalition corps and about Sacken's important participation in it, took measures to compensate for his own lapses. The troops of X Corps and the artillery stationed at Jauer were ordered to rejoin the main body immediately, while the detachment under Major General Count Pahlen 2nd was ordered to advance towards Konradswaldau.[31]

The enemy casualties at the battle on the Katzbach were very significant, but there is no way to determine them precisely. A differing number of trophies are also presented in various official communiques: in Blücher's report to the King: 36 guns, 110 ammunition caissons, between 1,200 to 1,400 prisoners of war; in comte Langéron's diary: 40 guns and several thousand prisoners. On the Coalition side, the overall losses reached some 2,875 men, namely: 575 from Sacken's corps, 900 from Yorck's, 1,400 men from Langéron's.[32] But the Army of Silesia suffered incomparably greater losses from extreme exhaustion, hardship and inclement weather. The *Landwehr* suffered in particular. Only men gifted with a strong physical constitution could endure the forced marches without footwear, without greatcoats, in canvas overalls. During the night of 14 to 15 (26 to 27) August, in one *Landwehr* battalion, only 271 men remained present from the 577 enrolled. In another, there were 407 out of 625. These losses were similar in the others.[33]

In the dark of night, under heavy rain, the victorious commander returned to the village of Brechelshof with his retinue, where his Hauptquartier were located. Gneisenau rode with him. The bad weather blocked all thoughts of anything except the hard work endured during this day. Everyone was silent. Blücher alone, turning to his comrade, spoke: 'Well, Gneisenau, we won the battle, and no one on the planet can challenge us on that. Now we must think about working out, in a coherent

---

31 Comte Langéron's military memoirs; War Diary of Shcherbatov's VI Corps; Wagner, 33-35; Richter, I, 383-384; Beitzke, II, 210-211.
32 General Sacken's dispatch to Prince Volkonsky dated 3 [15] September; comte Langéron's military memoirs; Beitzke, II, 211.
33 Droysen, III, 61.

manner, how it was that we won it.' These few words are enough to demonstrate the completely straightforward nature and modesty of the Prussian hero, who, fully comprehending the importance of the victory he had won, was no less aware that he owed this success more to Providence from above than to his own orders. As soon as he got into shelter from the rain, Blücher began drafting reports for the main headquarters of the Army of Bohemia, immediately issued dispositions for operations on the following day and that same evening addressed the population of Breslau in his own handwriting, notifying them of the victory, asking them to take care of the wounded and promising to show considerable gratitude should they consider it possible to send some sort of food supplies for his valiant comrades.[34]

Blücher's attention was drawn in particular to the pursuit of the enemy.[35] General Yorck received orders to cross the Katzbach at Kroitsch at two o'clock in the morning and advance towards Pilgramsdorf and Ulbersdorf [Wojcieszyn, 2½ miles north of Pilgramsdorf] on the Schnelle Deichsa, with Horn's brigade and Jürgaß's reserve cavalry. Sacken's cavalry, commanded by Adjutant General Vasilchikov, were to cross the Katzbach, at Schmochwitz, and advance on Liegnitz and Haynau, while General Rudzevich was to move to Goldberg with the vanguard of Langéron's corps. The main bodies were assigned to follow these leading elements as soon as the soldiers had cooked themselves a hot meal. The detachments directed through the mountains were ordered to head as quickly as possible towards the Bober, while the corps under the comte de Saint-Priest was to move by forced marches towards Greiffenberg [Gryfów Śląski].[36]

Blücher's orders to cross the deep, fast-flowing river in the dark of night could not be carried out. In Yorck's corps Hauptquartier it was decided that 'Messrs. Gneisenau and Müffling had no understanding of the movements of an army' and postponed the crossing until dawn. It continued to rain all night, and on through 15, and even 16 (27 to 28) August. The water level in the Katzbach was constantly rising and swamped the bridge at Kroitsch. The ravines along which they had to move were cluttered with carts and debris from the enemy trains. At six o'clock in the morning on 15 (27) August, Horn's *7. Brigade* crossed together with three regiments of reserve cavalry and two batteries: the infantry forded chest-deep in water, the cavalry swam, the guns crossed the bridge awash with floodwater. The enemy were completely driven out of Kroitsch. But as the flood waters continued to rise, General Horn, concerned at being isolated from the other elements of the corps, not only halted the advance of his brigade at Kroitsch and Wildschütz, but also sent the artillery back across the Katzbach. The cavalry were sent forward and captured many guns and ammunition caissons. Yorck attempted to cross after Horn, but was forced to abandon his efforts and reported this to the Commander-in-Chief, who, paying no heed to his protestations, ordered him to cross the Katzbach wherever and however he could.[37] Blücher was dissatisfied that the leading formations, who had already crossed the rivers, and the cavalry especially, were lagging behind the

---

34 Karl August Varnhagen von Ense, *Leben des Fürsten Blücher von Wahlstadt*, 190-191.
35 See Map No. 1: Map Showing Blücher's Operations Following the Expiry of the Armistice.
36 Beitzke, II, 214.
37 Beitzke, II, 214; Droysen, III, 65.

enemy, and ordered Yorck to continue the pursuit relentlessly with all his might. At the end of his instructions, he made the remark that 'it is not enough to win, but, in addition, one must exploit the victory. If we leave the enemy unmolested, they will recover once more and we will be forced to give battle again in order simply to maintain the gains that have already been achieved.' Despite the energetic persistence of the Commander-in-Chief and the efforts of Yorck himself, the crossing at Kroitsch turned out to be impossible, and the whole of 15 (27) August was lost in fruitless attempts. Eventually it was decided to head to Goldberg, where there was a strong bridge and the crossing would be less problematic. On the morning of 16 (28) August, the remaining brigades of Yorck's corps forded the Wütende Neiße and moved over the muddy, completely sodden ground, through Goldberg, to Leisersdorf [Uniejowice, four miles north-east of Pilgramsdorf] on the Deichsa, where the vanguard arrived in the evening at dusk together with Yorck's corps Hauptquartier, while the rearmost elements had arrived in Goldberg by ten o'clock at night. There were crowds of straggling soldiers on the road to Goldberg who were unable to catch up again until 17 (29) August.

Sacken's corps, also finding themselves unable to cross at Schmochwitz, were forced to detour to Liegnitz, crossed the river there via a bridge on 16 (28) August and reached Haynau the next day [29 August], sending the vanguard on to Wolfshayn [Wilczy Las, 2½ miles west of Kreibau].

Comte Langéron was able to cross the Katzbach at Goldberg on 15 (27) August, over the very convenient bridge, but halted his main body near this town and gave them a rest day on 16 (28) August, awaiting the arrival of his heavy artillery from Jauer. A vanguard was formed in order to pursue the enemy, supported by regiments from Kaptsevich's X Corps, which had not participated in the battle on the Katzbach.

Thus, the French were initially pursued only by the leading elements that had managed to cross the Katzbach: Vasilchikov's cavalry and Karpov's Cossack detachment from Sacken's corps; Horn's brigade, Katzler's vanguard and Jürgaß's reserve cavalry from Yorck's corps; Rudzevich's vanguard, Grekov's Cossack detachment and Kaptsevich's corps from Langéron's corps. The sluggishness of the main forces irritated Blücher all the more because on 15 (27) August, news of the victory won by the Allies at Großbeeren arrived at his *Hauptquartier*. In trying to encourage his exhausted soldiers to speed up the march, he repeated numerous times: 'Keep moving forwards, boys! If you push hard, you can save yourself another battle.' In response, shouts were heard of: 'Long live Papa Blücher!'[38]

While the victorious Army of Silesia may have been losing men at every step, then it may be easily understood how much greater were the losses of the defeated army retreating in bad weather along impassable roads. Even while the battle was still underway, those who fled the battlefield were going to Goldberg, first individually, then in whole crowds and eventually, once darkness had fallen, Macdonald's force passed through the town in complete disorder, muddled up with one another. The disorder increased even more when Lauriston's corps violently began to force their

---

38 'Nur vorwärts, Kinder! Wenn ihr tüchtig darauf losgeht, könnt' ihr eine neue Schlacht sparen.' 'Vater Blücher lebe!' Beitzke, II, 214-217; Varnhagen von Ense, 191-192.

way across the only bridge on the Katzbach. Due to the bad weather, cold and hunger, the soldiers' senses became so dulled that the officers only managed to drive them out of their billets and induce them to further retreat with great difficulty. The last of them left at around noon. Almost everyone headed along the road towards Löwenberg.[39]

Despite the haste of this retreat, which gradually turned into a complete rout, the leading elements of the Army of Silesia inflicted significant damage on the enemy.

Rudzevich was on the move towards Prausnitz and the Wolfsberg even before dawn on 15 (27) August with the vanguard of Langéron's corps. With every step they took, they encountered the dead, the dying, the wounded, the exhausted. Horses, ammunition caissons and guns were scattered everywhere on the road and along the verges. The enemy were surrendering in droves. Grekov's Cossacks attacked a French detachment assembling at Prausnitz, scattered it and took 700 prisoners and five guns. Another detachment of 1,500 men was cut off from Goldberg at the Wolfsberg by Cossacks who had managed to seize the town, and was then attacked by Major General Panchulidzev 1st [Ivan Davydovich Panchulidzev or Panchulidze] with the Tver Dragoons, Seversk Mounted-Jägers and Chernigov Mounted-Jägers. The Tver Dragoons rode the enemy down from the left flank and completely cut them off from the town. Major General Denisyev [Luka Alexeevich Denisyev] enveloped them from the right flank with the Seversk Mounted-Jägers and cut them off from the forest, while the Chernigov Mounted-Jägers drove them back frontally. Panchulidzev launched an attack from three sides after the enemy had fired their muskets at a Russian *parlementaire* sent to demand their surrender, and despite a valiant defence by the French, he scattered them and captured about 1,000 men, including Colonel Morand and 17 officers.[40] 1,200 wounded were found in Goldberg's hospitals, including 200 Russians and 400 Prussians. On that same day [27 August], General Emmanuel caught up with the enemy rearguard near Pilgramsdorf with the Kharkov Dragoons and Kiev Dragoons, scattered them and took six guns and 1,200 prisoners. Overall, on 15 (27) August, 18 guns were taken in battle or were found by Langéron's force.[41]

The pursuit of the enemy by the detachments under Yorck and Sacken was not so successful, because Souham's *3e Corps* retreated in good order, having suffered less in battle and was being shielded by the majority of Sébastiani's cavalry. In addition, Horn, concerned lest he be cut off from the army by the constantly rising waters of the Katzbach, sent almost all his guns back to the right bank of this river, and thereby lost the opportunity to pursue the enemy relentlessly. At the same time, the tireless and enterprising Katzler fell ill. It was not until 16 (28) August that Prussian troops advanced from Röchlitz to Haynau, and continued to pursue the defeated army onwards towards Bunzlau. Sacken's leading troops, having detoured to Liegnitz, passed through Hayanu that same day [28 August], also en route to Bunzlau.[42]

---

39 Beitzke, II, 217.
40 War Diary of Adjutant General Korff's corps. In comte Langéron's diary the defeat of this column is attributed to Lieutenant General Kaptsevich.
41 Comte Langéron's military memoirs (diary); Sporschill, I, 511.
42 Plotho, II, 115-116; Beitzke, II, 218-219.

The Commander-in-Chief was extremely dissatisfied with the slowness of the advance. The corps commanders listed the difficulties encountered by the troops every step of the way in their reports: flood waters, impassable roads; they reported on the exhaustion of the soldiers, the disorder in the *Landwehr*, and the lack of provisions and fodder. Blücher, paying no attention to all these complaints, repeated his orders for a speedy offensive, and eventually sent Yorck a rather harsh memorandum, concluding with the following admonition: 'when pursuing a fleeing enemy, there is no need to attack *en masse* with entire brigades, or even entire battalions and squadrons. Everything that falls behind must be left behind and follow the troops.

No heed should be paid to the complaints of cavalry commanders: keep in mind only the all-important objective – the destruction of the enemy army, the sacrifice of several hundred horses, which will die from exhaustion, is acceptable.

By missing the opportunity to exploit the victory, we would have to fight another battle, when one should have been enough to resolve the matter…'[43]

The Commander-in-Chief then demanded an explanation from the governor of Silesia as to why the *Landsturm*, which was supposed to take part in the destruction of the defeated enemy, had not been deployed. The answer to this was that the assembling of the *Landsturm* had been hampered by the flooding, making it difficult to deliver orders, that the proximity of enemy troops prevented the post offices from sending out dispatch riders, and so on.[44]

Despite all the obstacles encountered, through Blücher's iron will, the Coalition managed to cut off a significant part of the enemy army. On 17 (29) August, after the long period of stormy weather, clear weather arrived, but at the same time the water levels in the mountain rivers reached their highest point. The most important of them, the Bober, presented a huge obstacle to the retreating enemy. The French troops raced towards the bridges at Löwenberg and Bunzlau, but the former had been deeply submerged by rising water on 17 (29) August, and therefore the enemy columns, having no hope of crossing there, turned towards Bunzlau. Nevertheless, those who were upstream of Löwenberg faced inevitable destruction. The troops of Puthod's division, sent to outflank Schönau and moving through the mountains, were forced to fight under even worse conditions than Macdonald's other formations. The infantry had to cross many mountain streams, waist-deep in water. On the evening of the same day as the battle [26 August], Puthod was closing in on Schönau with his disordered regiments, but could not cross the Katzbach. The next day, 15 (27) August, he managed to move his division across the river, albeit weakened by many stragglers. Afterwards, having engaged some of Langéron's cavalry, he was forced to move back to the left bank of the Katzbach, which was achieved with heavy losses to the troops and the trains. Having received news of the loss of the battle, General Puthod began to retreat, but instead of heading towards Zobten (as Macdonald had advised), he went to Hirschberg, where he hoped to cross the Bober more easily and rejoin Ledru's division detached from *11e Corps*. He was constantly attacked On the march there by Yuzefovich's cavalry, which took 1,200 prisoners. Most of his soldiers scattered through the villages and forests.

---

43 Blücher's letter to General Yorck, dated 31 August, new style from Hohlstein [Skała] (north of Löwenberg).
44 Beitzke, II, 219.

All the efforts of the commanders to restore order among troops wracked by suffering beyond their endurance, were wasted. Late at night on 15 (27) August, the French arrived in Hirschberg, but Ledru's division were not there, and the crossing turned out to be impossible.[45] It was claimed at the time that there was a somewhat passable ford a little upstream of Hirschberg, at Eichberg [Dąbrowica (Mysłakowice), 3½ miles upstream of Hirschberg] but Puthod did not know that and moved downstream on 16 (28) August and, being unable to cross at Lähn, proceeded down towards Zobten and camped near this village during the night of 16 to 17 (28 to 29) August. The next day, 17 (29) August, at eight o'clock in the morning, the French division arrived at Plagwitz. The enemy tried unsuccessfully to dump masonry from the shore to the bridge awash with water. The strength of the river current rendered every effort by the French in vain, and meanwhile, at about ten o'clock, Langéron's leading troops were approaching. General Puthod immediately ordered the burning of all his remaining baggage and formed his division up in battle order on the high ground at Plagwitz. Whereupon the Russians attacked him from several directions: General Emmanuel enveloped the enemy left flank with the Kharkov Dragoons and Kiev Dragoons, supported by Rudzevich's vanguard, and cut the road to Bunzlau, while General Korff advanced from Lauterseiffen to Zobten with five cavalry regiments and a Don artillery company, and from there, having enveloped the enemy right flank, moved down the course of the Bober; Prince Shcherbatov arrived from Pilgramsdorf via Petersdorf [Pieszków, 3½ miles east of Plagwitz], in support with VI Corps.[46] Having placed six guns from Lieutenant Colonel Nesterovsky's 34th Light Artillery Company on high ground overlooking the enemy position and, following several successful salvos, had created confusion in the French ranks, whereupon Shcherbatov ordered his jägers to attack. Colonel Dietrich [Andrey Bogdanovich Dietrich or Diedrich], with 11th Jägers and 36th Jägers, and Major General Meshcherinov, with 28th Jägers and 32nd Jägers struck with bayonets fixed and drove the enemy back. On the far side, Rudzevich's regiments inflicted an equally severe defeat on the French. The cavalry followed the infantry. The enemy force, despite their very brave resistance, were defeated and driven back into the river, where many drowned, others were cut down or laid down their weapons. Among those killed in the Bober's torrent were: général de brigade Sibuet [Benoît Prosper Sibuet], several officers and 400 lower ranks. Those taken prisoner included: général de division Puthod, 13 battalion commanders, up to 100 officers and up to 3,000 lower ranks. The trophies of a victory that cost the Russian force no more than 80 men were: 16 guns and two Eagles captured by officers of the 28th Jägers, Lieutenant Kalinin and Ensign Bogdanov. Thus, Puthod's division, which had numbered more than 10,000 men in its ranks when operations resumed, had been completely destroyed.[47]

---

45 Ledru's (Fressinet's) division were retreating towards Greiffenberg by this time.
46 The regiments in Korff's command were: Tver Dragoons, Kinburn Dragoons, Chernigov Mounted-Jägers, Seversk Mounted-Jägers and Dorpat Mounted-Jägers (War Diary of Adjutant General Korff).
47 Comte Langéron's report on the action at Plagwitz, dated 18 (30) August; comte Langéron's military memoirs (diary); War Diary of Adjutant General Korff's corps; War Diary of Prince Shcherbatov's VI Infantry Corps; Richter, I, 385-386; Beitzke, II, 219-222; Vaudoncourt, 147-148.

Langéron's corps, might have quickly caught up with the retreating enemy if they could have immediately crossed the Bober. But every attempt by comte Langéron to cross the river at Löwenberg over the course of two days, 17 and 18 (29 and 30) August, was unsuccessful. Eventually, on the morning of 19 (31) August, once the water levels had dropped somewhat, he managed to build pontoon bridges at Löwenberg and 1½ *Meilen* upstream at Dippelsdorf [Przeździedza, three miles south of Zobten]. Langéron's force, having crossed the Bober, arrived at Lauban in the evening.[48]

Yorck's and Sacken's leading formations, directed towards Bunzlau, took many prisoners and wagons, but were unable to cut off any significant elements of the French force. On 18 (30) August, the Coalition caught up with the enemy rearguard at Bunzlau and attacked them in the presence of Sacken himself. The French defended themselves stubbornly in the town, and then set fire to the bridges over both branches of the Bober. But *Oberst* Katzler advanced to the left of the town with his vanguard and placed *Leutnant* Borowski's *2. Reitende Batterie* on the Kesselberg and, having opened a cannonade across the bridges, forced the enemy to quit the town.[49] The enemy attempts to destroy the bridges failed. The Prussian battery, with the assistance of 12 Russian heavy guns, also dragged up onto the Kesselberg, smashed the French on the bridges and on the opposite bank, while the Prussian vanguard, reinforced by elements of Horn's brigade and two battalions from the Okhotsk Infantry and Kamchatka Infantry, repelled the enemy several times as they emerged from the village of Tillendorf [Bolesławice, 1½ miles north-west of Bunzlau] towards the bridges. This bitter action continued until nightfall and cost Yorck's corps eight officers and 350 lower ranks. On the morning of the following day, 19 (31) August, the enemy withdrew from the banks of the Bober, retreated towards Lauban, Naumburg [Nowogrodziec] and Siegersdorf [Zebrzydowa], behind the river Queis, and destroyed the bridges. The Coalition forces, crossing immediately at Bunzlau, advanced further in two directions: Sacken's corps towards Siegersdorf, while Yorck's corps went towards Naumburg. At the same time, Langéron had been directed towards Lauban (as already mentioned). The *Hauptquartier* was relocated to Löwenberg. By nightfall that same day, Blücher's entire army was already on the Queis. The Commander-in-Chief, having ordered an immediate start to the rebuilding of bridges destroyed by the French, decided to give the army a rest day on 20 August (1 September). On this day, a service of thanksgiving was held for all units of the force with cannon salutes. At the same time, orders were issued to the army, in which Blücher, thanking the troops for their courage and steadfastness in enduring toil and hardship, calculated the spoils of victory.[50]

Indeed, the importance of the success achieved was greater than was believed immediately after the battle. More than 100 guns, 250 ammunition caissons, many other wagons, two Eagles and 18,000 prisoners fell into the hands of the victors.

---

48 Plotho, II, 120.
49 *Oberst* Katzler's vanguard consisted of: the *Brandenburgisches Ulanen*, one *Reitende Batterie*, one *Batterie zu Fuß*, three *Abtheilungen* of skirmishers from the *Leib-Regiment* and the *Schützen Zuge* of the *Leib-Füsilieren*; Plotho, II, 118; Beitzke, II, 223.
50 Richter, I, 390-391.

Overall, the had enemy lost some 30,000 men.⁵¹ The casualties in the Army of Silesia were also very significant. Blücher himself believed them to be no more than 1,000 men, probably meaning only those killed or wounded in combat. In reality the losses were incomparably greater. From the opening of hostilities after the armistice until 20 August (1 September), Yorck's corps lost about 13,000 men. Less than half of the available number of men remained in the *Landwehr* infantry (only 6,277 out of 13,369). Some battalions had just 100 men in the ranks. Since the reopening of hostilities, Sacken's corps had lost 2,800 men, while Langéron's corps had lost more than 6,000 men. Overall, losses in the Army of Silesia extended to over 22,000 men. Yet of these, several thousand stragglers rejoined the army, in which there were 81,000 men, including the corps under Saint-Priest, according to returns dated 20 August (1 September).⁵²

The victory on the Katzbach strengthened the confidence of the Army of Silesia in their worthy commander: although Langéron and Yorck, even subsequently occasionally allowed themselves to criticise the orders from headquarters, they nevertheless became their diligent executors, while Sacken, who had earned the general respect of the Prussian forces through his actions on the Katzbach, was completely loyal to Blücher, who, for his part, also had complete faith in him. The day after the battle, the Commander-in-Chief, in the presence of several officers and soldiers, stated:

> We owe a lot to General Sacken. His 12-pounder guns on the high ground at Eichholz made our work easier, while the cavalry, striking Sébastiani from the rear, completed the victory. We must give him his due.

As soon as Blücher had uttered these words, they became famous throughout the Prussian forces. Soon after this, General Sacken happened to be riding past Yorck's corps. Having recognised him, the Prussian officers expressed their deep respect for him, while the Prussian soldiers announced him to the surrounding area with loud shouts of Hurrah! This form of greeting, inspired by the awareness of many thousands of warriors in Sacken's talents, was a worthy reward for the feats he had accomplished.⁵³

The news of the Katzbach victory was received by the Coalition Monarchs on the battlefield of Kulm [Chlumec], following the defeat of Vandamme, and produced general delight. King Friedrich Wilhelm rewarded Blücher with the *Eisernes Kreuz* [Iron Cross]; Kaiser Franz awarded him the *Kommandeurkreutz* of the *Maria-Theresien-Orden*; Emperor Alexander I, having taken off his own insignia of the

---

51 Varnhagen von Ense gives the French losses in the fighting on the Katzbach as 30,000 men overall, with the number of prisoners as 20,000, with the Coalition taking 105 guns and more than 300 ammunition caissons (*Leben des Fürsten Blücher von Wahlstadt*, 195). In the Army Order of the Day issued by Blücher, the numbers given are 18,000 prisoners, 103 guns, 250 ammunition caissons, two Eagles, and so on.
52 Reports on the composition of forces, signed by Blücher, Langéron and Sacken; Beitzke, II, 228; Droysen, III, 74-75.
53 Carl von Weiß (Müffling), 32.

Order of St. Andrew the First-Called, sent it to the Prussian general, honouring him with the following rescript:

> General! I count among the most beautiful moments of the campaign those where I am able to give you proof of the particular satisfaction that I have experienced, by doing justice to your brilliant valour, to the pace of your operations, to the energy of your movements. I have removed from my coat, at this moment as we are pursuing a brilliant victory on our side, the symbols of the Order of Saint Andrew, with which I decorate you. I do not believe that this circumstance adds anything to the testimony of my satisfaction, but it will prove to you that I have not lost a moment to grant you, and the brave men under your command, the assurance of the pleasure with which I have learned of your success. The soldier is nourished by the glory of their commander, just as the commander by that of their soldiers. Tell them, General, how much I appreciate their actions and receive assurance of all my sentiments.[54]

Blücher's main accomplices, Sacken and Yorck, received the *Schwarzer Adlerorden* [Order of the Black Eagle], and the former was awarded, in addition, the Order of St. George, 2nd class, and promoted to general-of-infantry. Emperor Alexander granted comte Langéron a monogram of His name on his epaulettes and 30,000 roubles. The Akhtyrka Hussars, Belorussia Hussars, Alexandria Hussars and Mariupol Hussars received shako badges with the inscription 'За отличие 14 августа 1813 года' [for distinction on 14 August, 1813], and so on.

The blows inflicted on the enemy by the troops of the Army of Silesia on the Katzbach were hard, but their most important consequence was the collapse of morale in Macdonald's army. The disorder among the French troops increased with every backwards step they took, while the lack of food supplies completed their pitiful situation. Just as the French commissariat in the era of the Napoleonic wars was not distinguished by foresight, so the troops were forced to take care of themselves. It is easy to imagine to what extent the difficulties of such methods of supplying the army reached after a battle lost, during a hasty retreat through a devastated country whose population detested the French. Under such circumstances, the only way to feed the troops was to acquire supplies through robbery, which led to looting and the complete collapse of discipline.

---

54 For the full details of awards and reports, see Appendix V at the end of this chapter.

Appendix III

The calculation of Coalition troop strength in the fighting on the Katzbach

The number of Coalition troops in the fighting on the Katzbach has been calculated variously as follows:

> In Plotho: 117 battalions, 78 squadrons, 31 batteries and 19 Cossack regiments, for a total of 65,000 to 70,000 men with 320 guns.

In the periodical *Zeitschrift für Kunst, Wissenshaft und Geschichte des Krieges*, 1830: 109¾ battalions, 86 squadrons, 26 batteries and 17 Cossack regiments, for a total of 81,500 men with 260 guns.

The latter calculation is also found in the works by Sporschill and Förster, but it is hardly entirely reliable. Not least of which is the erroneous depiction of the composition by troop types in the corps under Sacken and Yorck, namely:

With Sacken: 20 battalions, 20 squadrons 9 Cossack regiments and five batteries (instead of 19 battalions, 30 squadrons, 12 Cossack regiments and five batteries).

With Yorck: 44¾ battalions, 48 squadrons and 13 batteries (instead of 45 battalions, 44 squadrons and 13 batteries).

It should also be noted that in Langéron's corps, following the detachment of the forces under the comte de Saint-Priest and Major General Count Pahlen 2nd, there were 35 battalions remaining, not 45.

The numbers in Macdonald's force are shown in the *Zeitschrift* as:

> In *3e Corps*: 15 battalions and six squadrons for a total of 6,000 men.
> In *5e Corps*: 34 battalions for a total of 15,000 men.
> In *11e Corps*: 26 battalions and eight squadrons for a total of 21,000 men.
> In *2e corps de cavalerie*: 67 squadrons for a total of 6,000 men.
> In total: 75 battalions and 81 squadrons for a total of 48,000 men.

But this data is also inaccurate: in *5e Corps*, following the detachment of Puthod's division towards Schönau, there could not have been more than 27 battalions; in *11e Corps* following the detachment of a division to Hirschberg, there were 18 battalions rather than 20; while in *2e corps de cavalerie* there were a total of 52 squadrons. Consequently, Macdonald may have had from 60 to 62 battalions and from 66 to 70 squadrons on the battlefield; and if we take a battalion as having 600 men and a squadron 100, in reality there were 44,000, while with artillery personnel 48,000 men.

Appendix IV

Disposition issued by Blücher on the morning of 14 (26) August

The detachments under General comte Langéron, located at Schönau and Konradswaldau, upon receipt of this order, are immediately to set off along the road to Goldberg and attack the enemy in order to divert their attention.

Comte Langéron's vanguard are to remain in place, while his corps is to move to their right, cross the Katzbach downstream of Weinberg [*sic*], and thereafter, should the opportunity present itself, downstream of Röchlitz, and deploy into battle formation between Kosendau [Kozów] and Hohendorf, while the cavalry are to push the enemy back to the Deichsa (*gegen die schnelle Deichsel*).

Yorck's corps are to cross the Katzbach at Kroitsch and Dohnau and move to the left of Rothkirch, towards Steudnitz, in order to cut the enemy forces stationed at Liegnitz off from Haynau, and to attack them from the rear.

Sacken's corps are to fix the enemy corps at Liegnitz frontally, and then follow Yorck over the Katzbach and attack the enemy on their right flank. If possible, General Sacken is to detach light cavalry beyond the Katzbach, downstream of Liegnitz, towards Rüstern [Rzeszotary, three miles north of Liegnitz] in order to envelope the enemy on their left flank and to cut them off from Glogau [Głogów].

I shall be with the leading column of Yorck's corps.

I have faith that once the enemy retreats, the cavalry will show valour. Let the enemy know that they cannot escape from our hands with impunity.

Hauptquartier at Brechelshof, 26 August 1813, 11 o'clock in the morning. Blücher.

All columns are to move at two o'clock precisely.

Appendix V

Alexander I's rescript to Blücher and Sacken's dispatch to Volkonsky, regarding the Battle on the Katzbach

Emperor Alexander I's rescript to Blücher:

> *Général! Je compte parmi les beaux momens de la campagne ceux, où Je puis vous donner des preuves de la satisfaction particulière qu J'éprouve, en rendant justice à votre brillante valeur, à l'activité de vos opérations, à l'energie de vos mouvemens. J'ai détaché de mon habit, au moment où nous poursuivions de notre côté une brillante victoire, les marques de l'ordre de Saint André, dont je vous ai décoré. Je ne crois pas que cette circonstance ajoute quelque chose au témoignages de ma satisfaction, mais elle vous prouvera que je n'ai pas perdu un instant pour vous donner, à vous et aux braves sous vos ordres, l'assurance du plaisir avec le quel j'ai appris vos succès. Le soldat se nourrit de la gloire du chef, comme le chef de celle de ses soldats. Dites leur, général, combien j'apprécie leurs actions et recevez l'assurance de tous mes sentimens.*

General Baron Sacken's dispatch to Adjutant General Prince Volkonsky, regarding the battle on the Katzbach:

> The corps advanced from Malitsch at one o'clock in the afternoon. The leading troops met and rejoined them. The enemy were firing a strong cannonade. The crest, the key to the whole position, was occupied by Colonel Brahms' artillery. He was joined by *Oberstleutnant* Werbowski and the Prussian artillery. Lieutenant General Vasilchikov 1st, who commanded the entire cavalry component, and Major General Ushakov, who commanded the reserves, were stationed between this crest and the village of Eichholz facing the enemy front. The village of Eichholz was held by the 8th Jägers and 39th Jägers, supported by the Okhotsk Infantry and Kamchatka Infantry.
>
> Lieutenant General Neverovsky was stationed in the front line, on the reverse slope. Major General Count Lieven was in the second line. The Prussian cavalry had this high ground partly to their front, partly to their right.

Once it was noticed that the enemy left wing could be outflanked, major generals Lanskoy, Karpov and Vasilchikov [Dmitry Vasilievich Vasilchikov 2nd] took to the right, leaving the village of Eichholz to their left. Lieutenant General Neverovsky supported them with all his infantry. Major General Count Lieven replaced him in the first line.

Upon the arrival of all the troops on their locations, they launched a decisive attack from all sides. Major Generals Karpov, Lanskoy and Vasilchikov 2nd suddenly advanced from the flank, Lieutenant General Vasilchikov 1st from the front, the Prussian cavalry behind them. The enemy were instantly driven back, and in less than an hour they found themselves with their artillery in our hands and themselves in the Katzbach and 'the Russians inherited their bones.' Night overtook us here. The enemy also sent an infantry division and artillery from Liegnitz in order to save those fleeing. Lieutenant General Neverovsky and Major General Count Lieven drove them off with bayonets fixed. Thus ended the glorious day. The rain was torrential. The river Katzbach, which had been passable everywhere on foot, had become a torrent and the enemy's grave. The consequences of the victory are that we are here, and with regard to the success of the corps, we took 50 cannon and captured: one general, two field officers, 61 subalterns, and 4,916 lower ranks. The losses on our side were: seven non-commissioned officers and 81 privates killed; one general, three field officers, 13 subalterns, 29 non-commissioned officers, four musicians and 343 privates wounded; one subaltern taken prisoner; five non-commissioned officers, two musicians and 86 privates missing in action.

Blücher's appeal to the troops of the Army of Silesia, dated 1 (13) September:

Silesia has been cleared of the enemy. To your courage, valiant warriors of the Russo-Prussian Army, which is under my command, to your efforts and patience in enduring toil and hardship, I owe the happiness of wresting a flourishing region from the hands of an avaricious enemy.

At the battle on the Katzbach, the enemy advanced boldly towards you. Courageously, with the speed of lightning, you rushed at them, stopped them with musketry and drove them back with fixed bayonets to the rocky banks of the Wütende Neiße and the Katzbach.

You have crossed rivers and mountain streams in flood. You have spent entire nights in the mud. You have suffered a want of rations, which could not be delivered to the army along the bad roads, by insufficiently mobile trains. You have endured hunger, cold, bad weather, and even in some measure a lack of decent clothing and footwear: and despite all this, you did not grumble and relentlessly pursued the enemy you had defeated. I thank you for your very dignified behaviour. Only those who combine these qualities may be called a true warrior.

You have taken 103 guns, 250 ammunition caissons, mobile hospitals and magazines, captured three generals, a large number of officers and 18,000 lower ranks, took two Eagles and other trophies from this battle.

The remnants of the force that fought against you on the Katzbach, stricken with terror, cannot bear the sight of your bayonets. You have seen the roads and fields between the Katzbach and the Bober. At every step you have encountered the signature of the confusion of your enemies.

Let us sing a hymn of thanksgiving to the God of hosts, with whose help you have overthrown the enemy. Let the threefold thunder of our guns conclude the time dedicated to prayer. And then chase down the enemy once more.

24

The Battle of Großbeeren

The Army of the North and its Commander-in-Chief, the Crown Prince of Sweden. – The deployment of the formations of the Army of the North at the reopening of hostilities after the armistice. – Composition and strength of Oudinot's army; the formations directed to operated with him.

The proclamation by the Crown Prince. – The conference regarding imminent operations. – Guerilla warfare. – Oudinot's offensive. – The actions at Trebbin, Wilmersdorf and Wietstock. – The Prince's intention to retreat behind the Spree. – The deployment of the Army of the North on 10 (22) August.

The advance by Oudinot's force on 11 (23) August. – Bertrand's movements towards Blankenfelde. – The ground at Blankenfelde. – The deployment of Tauentzien's force. – The action at Blankenfelde.

The deployment of Bülow's force at Heinersdorf. – Reynier's advance on Großbeeren. – The ground at Großbeeren. – The seizure of the village by the Saxons. – Bülow's advance from Heinersdorf towards Großbeeren. – The battle of Großbeeren. – The casualties on both sides. – The sluggish pursuit. – The consequences of the battle.

On the basis of the general plan of action drawn up at Schloss Trachenberg (see Chapter 19), it had been decided that the Army of the North under the Crown Prince of Sweden, having left 15,000 to 20,000 men facing Hamburg and Lübeck in order to monitor the French and Danes, should concentrate in the vicinity of Treuenbrietzen, in order to cross the Elbe between Torgau and Magdeburg and advance towards Leipzig. The Commander-in-Chief of the Army of the North aroused high hopes as one of the former colleagues of the great military genius. He was also rumoured to have drafted the general plan of action for all the armies of the coalition formed during the armistice. The population of Prussia regarded this warrior with curiosity and support, who had come from distant Sweden with their valiant sons in order to help oppressed Germany against the French, his own countrymen.[1]

---

1 Beitzke, *Geschichte der deutschen Freiheitskriege in den Jahren 1813 und 1814*, II, 235.

Despite such favourable public opinion, however, the Crown Prince's situation was very delicate. The army entrusted to him had a multi-national composition. Its administration was extremely complex and, it was said, eluded the prince, who knew only the language of his native country, and therefore struggled to address the troops entrusted to him directly. The execution of operations planned on the basis of the general plan required an extraordinary combination of courage balanced with prudence and caution: their mission, while denying the enemy access to Berlin, was to cross a major river upon which all the fortresses were occupied by strong enemy garrisons. In addition, once they were advancing on the left bank of the Elbe, the axis of operations for the Army of the North was threatened; from one side by Davout's corps [Louis-Nicholas Davout] stationed at Hamburg, and from the other, by Napoleon's main force concentrated at Dresden. Finally, to his rear were the fortresses on the Oder, Stettin [Szczecin], Küstrin [Kostrzyn] and Glogau, still held by French troops, which had to be kept under observation.[2]

The army entrusted to the Crown Prince consisted of around 156,000 men with 369 guns, namely: 24,018 Swedes with 62 guns; 31,954 Russians with 120 guns; 81,580 Prussians with 144 guns, and 18,922 others with 43 guns.

The Crown Prince, having arrived in Berlin on 12 (24) July, began inspecting the troops of the Army or the North as they were gathering in the vicinity of this capital. Of these, the Swedish corps, according to Sir Charles Stewart [Charles William Stewart], who was serving as the British military commissioner to the Crown Prince, was inferior to the Russian and Prussian forces in equipment, tactical training and combat experience. Wintzingerode's corps consisted of soldiers already familiar with the toil and hardship of war. The successes they had achieved in the first campaign, under the command of the outstanding partisans, Chernyshev [Alexander Ivanovich Chernyshev], Tettenborn [Friedrich Karl von Tettenborn], Dörnberg [Wilhelm Caspar Ferdinand von Dörnberg], Vorontsov [Mikhail Semënovich Vorontsov] and Benckendorff [Alexander Khristoforovich Benkendorf or Konstantin Alexander Karl Wilhelm Christoph von Benckendorff], greatly raised the morale of these troops. The same may be said of Bülow's corps [Friedrich Wilhelm von Bülow], enthused to perform great deeds by the successes achieved at Halle and Lukau and by the responsibility that lay upon them – protecting the Prussian capital. Of the force under Graf Tauentzien [Bogislav Friedrich Emanuel von Tauentzien], only 20 battalions and 28 squadrons with 28 guns were assigned to operate in the field, commanded by General Dobschütz [Leopold Wilhelm von Dobschütz]. The rest were to be used to invest and monitor the fortresses on the Oder and Elbe. The *Landwehr* battalions and squadrons of both Prussian corps were better composed than the *Landwehr* in the other Coalition armies: Tauentzien's corps, which, with the exception of one infantry regiment, consisted of national militia, subsequently performed as well as the line troops at Großbeeren and Dennewitz. Thus, to the chagrin of Napoleon, who referred to the *Landwehr* as scum (*canaille*), they defeated the justly renowned French forces led by famous military commanders.[3]

---

2 Förster, *Geschichte der Befreiungskriege, 1813, 1814, 1815*, I, 753-754.
3 Beitzke, II, 238-239.

Even before taking command of the army, the Crown Prince aroused the displeasure of Prussian military personnel by criticising operations by the gifted and aged-in-service Bülow. Subsequently, the prince further armed popular opinion in Prussia against himself by not committing the weak Swedish force into battle and often expressing preference for Russian soldiers over Prussians. Under such circumstances, Bülow and Tauentzien, commanding most of the forces concentrated in front of Berlin, considered themselves to have the right to deploy at their own discretion, which quite naturally did not please the prince and put him under strained relations with the Prussian generals subordinate to him.

Upon the reopening of hostilities, on 4 (16) August, the formations of the Army of the North were positioned as follows.[4]

The headquarters of the Crown Prince of Sweden was in Charlottenburg [4½ miles west of Berlin]; Wintzingerode's Russian corps were camped at Spandau [14 miles north of Potsdam] (less the detachments under Count O'Rourke [Iosif Kornilovich Orurk or Joseph Cornelius O'Rourke] and Adjutant General Chernyshev numbering 8,000 men, advanced forwards of the right flank in the sector from Gommern [ten miles south-east of Magdeburg] to Belzig); Stedingk's Swedish corps [Curt Bogislaw Ludwig Christoph von Stedingk] were camped at Charlottenburg; Bülow's Prussian *III. Korps* were in Berlin and forwards of the city, having pushed the brigades under Thümen [Heinrich Ludwig August von Thümen] and Borstell [Karl Leopold Heinrich Ludwig von Borstell] forwards in order to hold the fortified positions on the Nuthe and the Notte; of the troops from Tauentzien's Prussian *IV. Korps*, the reserves under General Dobschütz were stationed behind the Spree, at Altlandsberg [15 miles east of Berlin] and Müncheberg [33 miles east of Berlin], the corps under General Hirschfeld [Karl Friedrich von Hirschfeld] was at Brandenburg [25 miles west of Potsdam]; the remaining troops, consisting of 23 battalions, 16 squadrons and 2½ batteries, in total some 16,000 men with 18 guns, were monitoring the fortresses of Stettin, Küstrin and Magdeburg. Finally, Graf Wallmoden's Russo-Prussian Corps [Ludwig Georg Thedel von Wallmoden-Gimborn], assigned to guard the army on the right flank, was located at Gadebusch, forwards of Schwerin. With the exception of this corps, which had a completely independent sphere of operations, as well as the observation, partisan and other independent detachments, the Crown Prince had about 100,000 men and some 270 guns assembled forwards of Berlin.[5]

On Napoleon's part, the following were assigned for operations towards Berlin, commanded by Marshal Oudinot [Nicolas Charles Marie Oudinot]: his own *12e Corps*, *7e Corps* under *général de division* Reynier [Jean-Louis-Ébénézer Reynier], *4e*

---

4 See Map No. 3, to follow operations by the Main Army and Army of the North in August and September 1813.

5 The formations of the Army of the North, assembled forwards of Berlin, when operations resumed after the armistice, consisted of: 20,000 men and 62 guns in the Swedish corps; 20,000 men and 80 guns in Wintzingerode's Russian corps; 40,000 men and 102 guns in Bülow's Prussian corps, and 14,000 men with 28 guns in Tauentzien's Prussian corps, for a total of 94,000 men with 272 guns. Plotho, *Der Krieg in Deutschland und Frankreich in den Jahren 1813 und 1814*, II, 122-125; Richter, *Geschichte des Deutschen Freiheitskrieges vom Jahre 1813 bis zum Jahre 1815*, I, 393; Bernhardi, *Denkwürdigkeiten aus dem Leben Carl Friedrich Grafen von Toll*, III, *Beilagen*, 517-519.

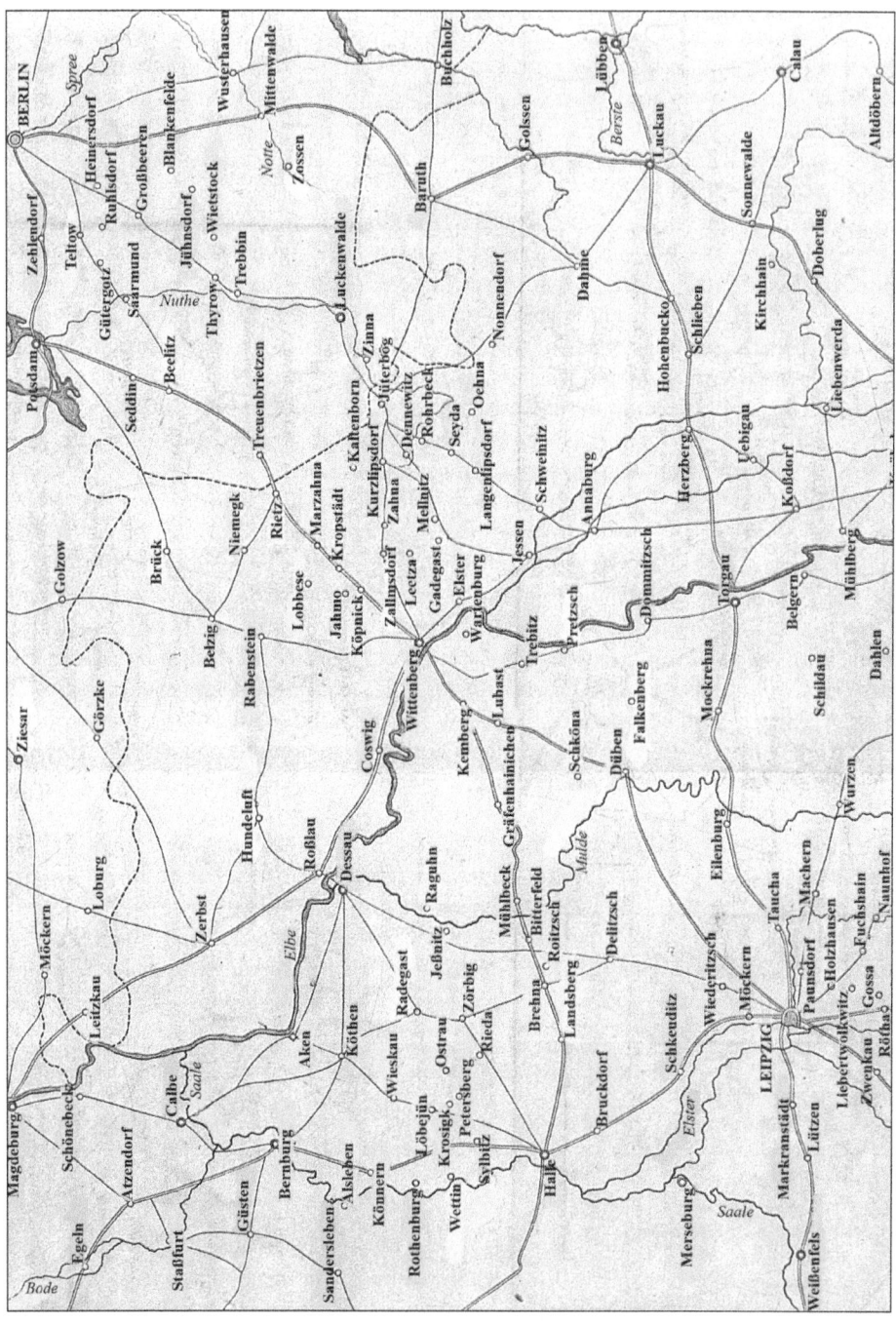

THE BATTLE OF GROSSBEEREN

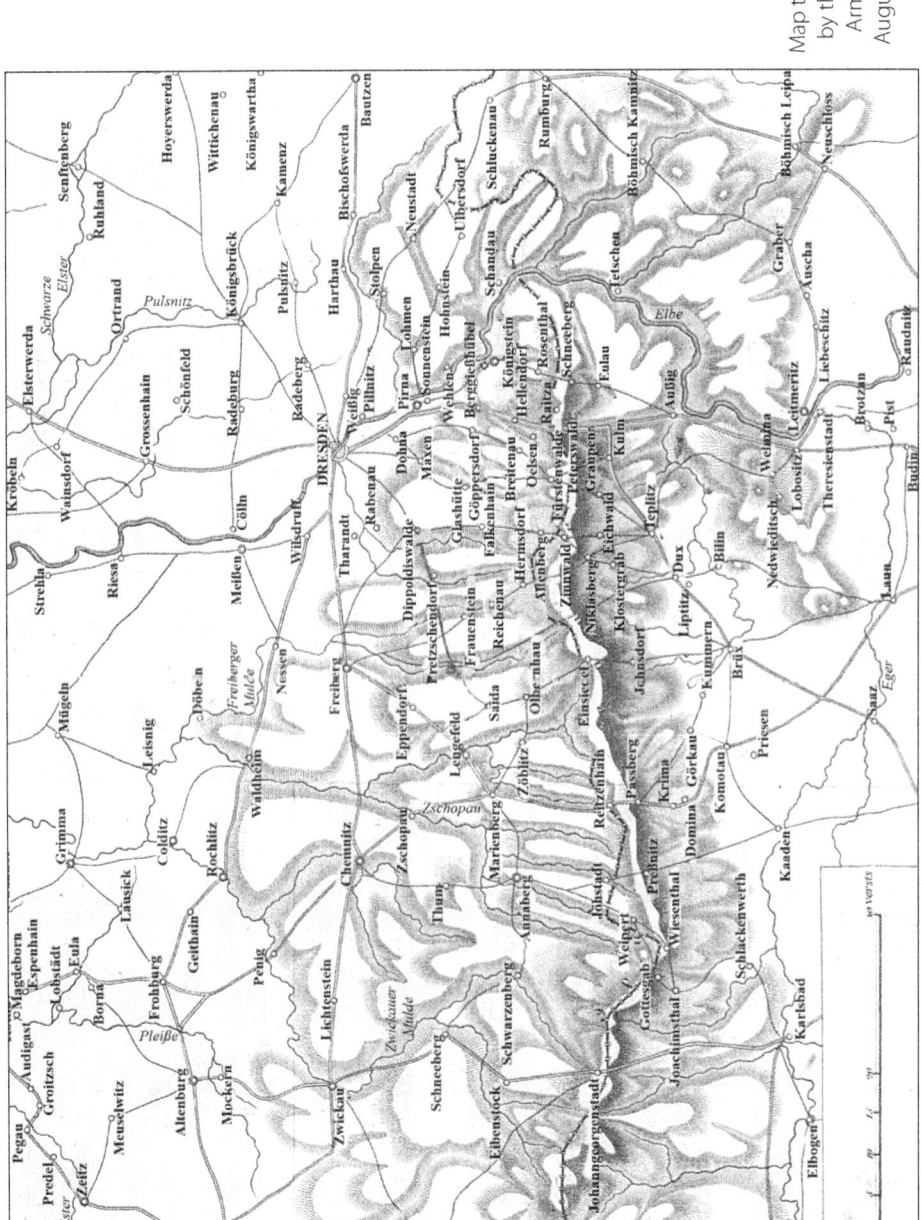

Map to follow operations by the Main Army and Army of the North in August and September 1813.

Corps under général de division Bertrand [Henri-Gatien Bertrand] and *3e Corps de cavalerie* under général de division, duc de Padoue (Arrighi [Jean-Thomas Arrighi de Casanova]), numbering 73,000 men with 200 guns,[6] of whom 36,000, almost half, were foreigners.[7] The unreliability of these troops became apparent over the duration of the armistice: the Italians were deserting to the Coalition in droves in order to make their way through Austrian territory to their homeland, while the troops of the *Confédération du Rhin* remained with the hated French colours solely out of fear of Napoleonic [martial] law that had oppressed them for many years.[8] Despite the patchy composition of this army, Napoleon considered it quite sufficient to defeat the defenders of Berlin. It was known that Tauentzien's corps and significant elements of Bülow's corps consisted of *Landwehr* who, in his opinion, were nothing more than a rabble of poorly armed and untrained men who could not compete against regular troops. He was no less contemptuous of the Commander-in-Chief of the Army of the North – the former *maréchal* Bernadotte. In conversation with Graf Bubna, Napoleon said of him: 'As for this one, he is only good for pawing the ground.' The Crown Prince of Sweden, for his part, showed his disdain for Napoleon, announcing to the partisans that whoever managed to capture him would receive 500,000 roubles and a special award for their detachment.[9]

Having ordered Marshal Oudinot to capture Berlin, Napoleon assigned Girard's division [Jean-Baptiste Girard] to operate in support of him, numbering 12,000 men with 18 guns, assembled at Magdeburg.[10] In addition, Marshal Davout, stationed at Hamburg, received orders to march on Berlin via Mecklenburg territory with all the troops that could be spared from the lower Elbe: thus Napoleon, hoping to concentrate more than 100,000 men for operations against the Army of the North, had no doubt of their success.[11] As for Marshal Oudinot, he was a veteran warrior from the days of the Republic, covered with scars – evidence of his fearlessness: at the Berezina he had been wounded for a twentieth time. His unsuccessful operations against Wittgenstein in 1812 dimmed his fame, yet at the crossing of the Berezina,

---

6   Plotho, II, Beilagen, 79-87; Bernhardi, III, Beilagen, 497-503. In Vaudoncourt (*Histoire de la guerre soutenue par les Français en Allemagne*, 128-129) Oudinot's army is presented as having 71,000 men. In Wagner (*Plane der Schlachten und Treffen, welche von der preussischen Armee in den Feldzügen der Jahre 1813, 14 und 15 geliefert worden*, I, 32-33) 77,000 men are shown.

7   The national contingents of Oudinot's army were: in *4e Corps* (36 battalions and eight squadrons), ten French battalions, 14 Italian battalions, 12 Württemberg battalions and eight Württemberg squadrons; in *7e Corps* (29¼ battalions and 13 squadrons), eight French battalions, 19¼ Saxon battalions, two Württemberg battalions and 13 Saxon squadrons; in *12e Corps* (34 battalions and 14 squadrons), 22 French battalions, ten Bavarian battalions, two Illyrian battalions, six Bavarian squadrons, four Westphalian squadrons and four Hessian squadrons; in *3e corps de cavalerie*, 87 French squadrons, giving a total of 40 French battalions, 87 French squadrons, 59¼ foreign battalions and 35 foreign squadrons, numbering 24,000 French infantry, 10,800 French cavalry, 32,000 foreign infantry and 3,200 foreign cavalry. In total, Oudinot's army had: 34,900 Frenchmen and 35,200 foreigners or, including artillerymen: 36,800 Frenchmen and 36,200 foreigners.

8   Wagner, I, 34.

9   '*Pour celui-la, il ne fera que piaffer.*' Bernhardi, III, 519-520; Woldemar von Löwenstern, *Denkwürdigkeiten eines Livländers*, II, 80-81.

10 Plotho, II, 130.

11 Adolphe Thiers, *Histoire du Consulat et de l'Empire*, XVI, Edit de Brux, 426.

the remnants of the French army owed their salvation to his command and presence of mind, while at the battle of Bautzen, Napoleon entrusted him with the attack on the Coalition right wing, and the marshal directed it with all the resoluteness necessary in order to achieve success. Nevertheless, Oudinot did not show his usual determination in his operations against the Army of the North: the multi-national composition of his force raised doubts in his mind, while the corps commanders subordinate to him did not inspire confidence in their abilities: Bertrand was known more for his knowledge of engineering rather than his military achievements, while Reynier considered himself slighted in comparison with his peers who had reached the rank of marshal and he carried out their orders grudgingly, moreover, despite all of Reynier's commendable qualities, he lacked that which was most valued by Napoleon himself, namely, good luck.

In proceeding with the opening of hostilities, the Crown Prince expressed his views in an appeal to his troops on 3 (15) August. He proclaimed:

> Soldiers! With weapons in hand we must defend the security and independence of Europe. Motivated by feelings similar to those that roused the French people to a concerted effort in 1792 and contributed to them repelling invasion from enemy armies, we must valiantly endure the struggle against an enemy whose domination weighs heavily on your brothers and families. Soldiers! The future ahead of you is enviable – the fruits of your efforts will be the salvation of Europe, the restoration of political balance, which should put an end to 20 years of subjugation, and at last, a general peace. May you be found worthy of this glorious destiny through your single-mindedness, observance of discipline and courage.

Two days later, on 5 (17) August, the Crown Prince, having invited General Bülow to his headquarters, asked him to give his opinion on impending operations, because 'in this war, which principally concerns Prussia, the casting vote belongs to the Prussian military commanders.' As in the first campaign of 1813, every Prussian general wanted to immediately march on Saxony due to the already meagre Brandenburg territories having been completely depleted by the forces quartered there: this was also Bülow's opinion. The Swedish generals Adlercreutz [Carl Johan Adlercreutz] and Löwenhielm [Gustaf Carl Fredrik Löwenhielm] expressed agreement with his assessment, but the Crown Prince replied in a tone inferring that he would not permit anyone to seek an engagement with superior enemy forces, that he considered an offensive to be reckless.[12] Eventually, it was found to be necessary to carry out reconnaissances in order to collect intelligence on the enemy. Colonel Löwenstern [Woldemar Hermann von Löwenstern], having been detached from Wintzingerode's corps with Popov 13th's and Rebrikov's two weak Cossack regiments, was ordered to make his way via Baruth into the French army rear area in order to capture Napoleon, who, according to intelligence received in the Crown Prince's headquarters, was on his way to join Oudinot's force in order to take over command,

---

12 Förster, I, 756-757.

under escort of two squadrons. Other light detachments had been sent forwards: from Thümen's and Borstell's Prussian brigades stationed on the rivers Nuthe and Notte, towards Trebbin and Baruth; from Wobeser's force [Karl Georg Friedrich von Wobeser] (Tauentzien's corps) stationed at Beeskow [37 miles east of Baruth], towards Guben [27 miles south-east of Beeskow] and so on. Colonel Löwenstern, wanting to cross the French army's line of operations as discreetly as possible, led them by a roundabout route to Jüterbog and Schweinitz, towards Herzberg. Having scattered an enemy battalion in the vicinity of Oehna and captured 300 prisoners, Löwenstern sent them to Beelitz with a small escort, to Count O'Rourke, thereafter, having captured 130 unarmed infantrymen and reaching Herzberg, he learned from the dispatches of an intercepted courier that Napoleon had moved suddenly towards Silesia against Blücher: their hopes of capturing Napoleon thus dashed, the Russian partisans turned back towards Sonnewalde on 12 (24) August, where the Cossacks discovered an infantry column, surrounded it and attacked with Popov 13th's Cossacks, scattering the enemy detachment and captured more than 500 men. The entire baggage train that was with this force and their military treasury of 700,000 francs fell into the hands of the victors, who then returned to Beelitz with all their booty.[13]

As a result of the nearby reconnaissances made by Coalition light detachments, it had become apparent that enemy forces assembled at Lukau and Dahme had pushed their vanguards towards Baruth and Jüterbog. On 7 (19) August, the French army crossed the border of Mark Brandenburg province, and two days later [21 August new style], continuing their advance in three columns, approached the defensive line formed between the Nuthe and Notte rivers. Bertrand's corps was moving from Sperenberg [10½ miles north-west of Baruth] and Saalow [7½ miles east of Trebbin], towards Nunsdorf [four miles south of Wietstock]. Reynier's corps were somewhat to their left, from Christinendorf [3½ miles east of Trebbin] towards Wilmersdorf [2½ miles south-east of Thyrow], while Oudinot himself was heading for Trebbin with *12e Corps*. The Crown Prince, for his part, made some movements on that same day, 9 (21) August, but his army was still spread out over a considerable area: Hirschfeld's detachment remained at Brandenburg. Wintzingerode's corps were stationed at Beelitz, holding the town of Brück [11 miles south-west of Beelitz] with a special detachment, and had sent cavalry and Cossacks towards Jüterbog in order to threaten the enemy flank. General Bülow positioned himself to the left of Saarmund with *3. Brigade* and *6. Brigade*, between this place and Sputendorf [six miles east of Saarmund]. The Prussian *4. Brigade* and *5. Brigade* remained at Trebbin and Mittenwalde. The Swedish corps were at Potsdam. Tauentzien was forwards of Berlin on the high ground at Tempelhof [four miles south of Berlin] with Dobschütz's force as the army's general reserve. Finally, Wobeser's detachment were at Müllrose [47 miles east of Zossen] and Beeskow along the right bank of the Spree.[14]

At about two o'clock in the afternoon, Oudinot's force advanced in three columns: Bertrand's *4e Corps* towards Nunsdorf, General Reynier's *7e Corps* towards Wilmersdorf; Oudinot himself attacked Trebbin with *12e Corps*, where

---

13 Plotho, II, 125-126; Löwenstern, *Denkwürdigkeiten eines Livländers*, II, 81-91.
14 Plotho, II, 126-129; Beitzke, II, 248.

three Prussian companies, without artillery, defended themselves for a full four hours and retreated only once the enemy had got around their left flank.[15] On that same day (21 August new style), Bertrand's force captured Nunsdorf. The leading elements under Thümen, having retreated to Thyrow, left six companies from *5. Reserve Infanterie* forwards of the canal in an unfinished lunette near Wilmersdorf. On the following day, 10 (22) August, the enemy, having spent several hours monitoring this weak outpost, attacked it with two divisions, Saxons under Le Coq [Karl Christian Erdmann von Le Coq] and Italians under Fontanelli [Achille Fontanelli], consisting of 24 battalions. Oudinot's force, supported by a bombardment from two 12-pounder batteries, advanced in seven columns and forced the incomparably weaker Prussian detachment to retreat behind the canal. Somewhat earlier, the divisions under Durutte [Pierre François Joseph Durutte] and Sahr [Otto Sahrer von Sahr] had attacked Thümen stationed at Wietstock with three battalions and here the Prussian troops also held the enemy up for several hours but General Thümen, concerned at being cut off from Bülow's corps (which had meanwhile moved to Heinersdorf) in the event of a rapid enemy advance on Kerzendorf [two miles west of Wietstock], retreated and rejoined the main body of the corps with his infantry. General Oppen [Adolf Friedrich von Oppen] was left with five cavalry regiments and 16 guns in order to defend the defile at Wietstock.[16] The French, having heavily garrisoned the village of Wietstock, attempted to cross the causeway and canal, but were engaged with canister and forced to retreat in complete disarray. A second enemy attempt was equally unsuccessful. General Oppen, wanting to resolve the matter as quickly as possible, withdrew his batteries and, allowing several of Durutte's battalions to cross the swampy defile, counter-attacked them initially with 12 squadrons, and then with another eight. But the French quickly formed up into several squares and repelled the Prussian cavalry that swept around them on all sides. Both Prussian regiments, the *Königin Dragoner* and *2es Westpreussisches Dragoner*, were met with a hail of bullets and having lost many men and horses, were completely disordered. The valiant Oppen, driven to despair, lost heart, stating: 'this is the most miserable day of my life.' But *Oberst* Boyen [Ludwig Leopold Gottlieb Hermann von Boyen] managed to placate him somewhat. The Prussian cavalry retreated to Heinersdorf, while Oudinot's force, having captured the defiles on the route to Berlin, on the night of 10 to 11 (22 to 23) August, positioned themselves as follows: *12e Corps* at Thyrow with Arrighi's cavalry; Reynier's *7e Corps* forwards of Kerzendorf; Bertrand's *4e Corps* at Jühnsdorf: the French were thus no more than three *Meilen* (about 20 *versts*) from the Prussian capital. At the same time, Girard's division was approaching Ziesar.[17]

---

15 The town of Trebbin was held by one company from *4es Ostpreussisches Infanterie*, commanded by Major Clausewitz, and two companies from *5es Reserve Infanterie*, commanded by Major Meyer. Wagner, I, 37.
16 General Oppen's cavalry detachment consisted of: *Pommersches National-Kavallerie, 1. Dragoner (Königin), 2es Westpreussisches Dragoner*, two regiments of reserve cavalry, *5. Reitende Batterie* and *6. Reitende Batterie*, for a total of 20 squadrons with 16 guns. Other sources show just four regiments with Oppen.
17 Plotho, II, 135-136; Beitzke, II, 252-255; Förster, I, 760.

The location of the enemy army just a short march from Berlin aroused great fears in the country. It was easy to foresee what the population of Prussia might expect from a conqueror embittered by their heroic resistance. The Crown Prince thought it vital to gather the corps commanders for a conference in his headquarters, located in Philippsthal, [2½ miles] north of Saarmund at the time. He repeated several times that he had every intention of giving battle, but at the same time he expressed all sorts of doubts about its success, speaking of the unreliable composition of the army, about the significant numbers of *Landwehr* who had never been in action, and about the likelihood of Napoleon himself arriving in overwhelming strength. In this case, according to the prince, he would have to retreat beyond the Spree and sacrifice Berlin. When Bülow expressed the opinion that under no circumstances should Berlin be conceded without a battle, then the prince stated:

'What is Berlin? A city!'

Bülow replied 'Allow me to note, Your Highness, that for us Berlin is the capital of the state, and that I and my troops are ready to die with weapons in hand rather than retreat beyond Berlin.'

The Crown Prince, convinced of the selflessness of his companions, told them that he himself had been persuaded of the need to give battle, and that he intended to retreat only if Napoleon arrived with the main body of his army.[18]

On 10 (22) August, the Coalition army took up the following positions: Hirschfeld's detachment conducted a forced march of five *Meilen* (35 *versts*) from Brandenburg towards Saarmund; Wintzingerode's corps were stationed at Gütergotz [Güterfelde]; the Swedish corps were at Ruhlsdorf; Tauentzien was at Blankenfelde; Wobeser's detachment was en route to Buchholz; General Chernyshev's cavalry were at Beelitz and Treuenbrietzen, having sent strong patrols out towards Trebbin, Luckenwalde and Jüterbog: thus, the Army of the North blocked enemy access to Berlin, while maintaining the opportunity to operate on their lines of communications with light forces.[19] Despite the Coalition forces being more concentrated than before, the main body under the Crown Prince still held a line from Gütergotz to Blankenfelde of two *Meilen* (about 15 *versts*), and besides, their position was vulnerable to being enveloped on both flanks. Such terrain offered no defensive advantages, and therefore the Coalition had no choice but to wait for the emergence of enemy columns from the Großbeeren forest and to attack them before they could deploy. But time was passing, and still no orders had been issued in the event of the French army emerging and, according to statements by Prussian military historians, Tauentzien had even received orders to retreat to Berlin. Yet in the meantime, even before this order could be executed, the French had attacked Tauentzien at Blankenfelde.[20]

---

18 Beitzke, II, 256-257.
19 Dispatch regarding the battle of Großbeeren, submitted by the Crown Prince of Sweden to Emperor Alexander's headquarters.
20 Beitzke, II, 258-259. According to Förster (I, 764), Tauentzien had been ordered to retreat behind Berlin.

THE BATTLE OF GROSSBEEREN 79

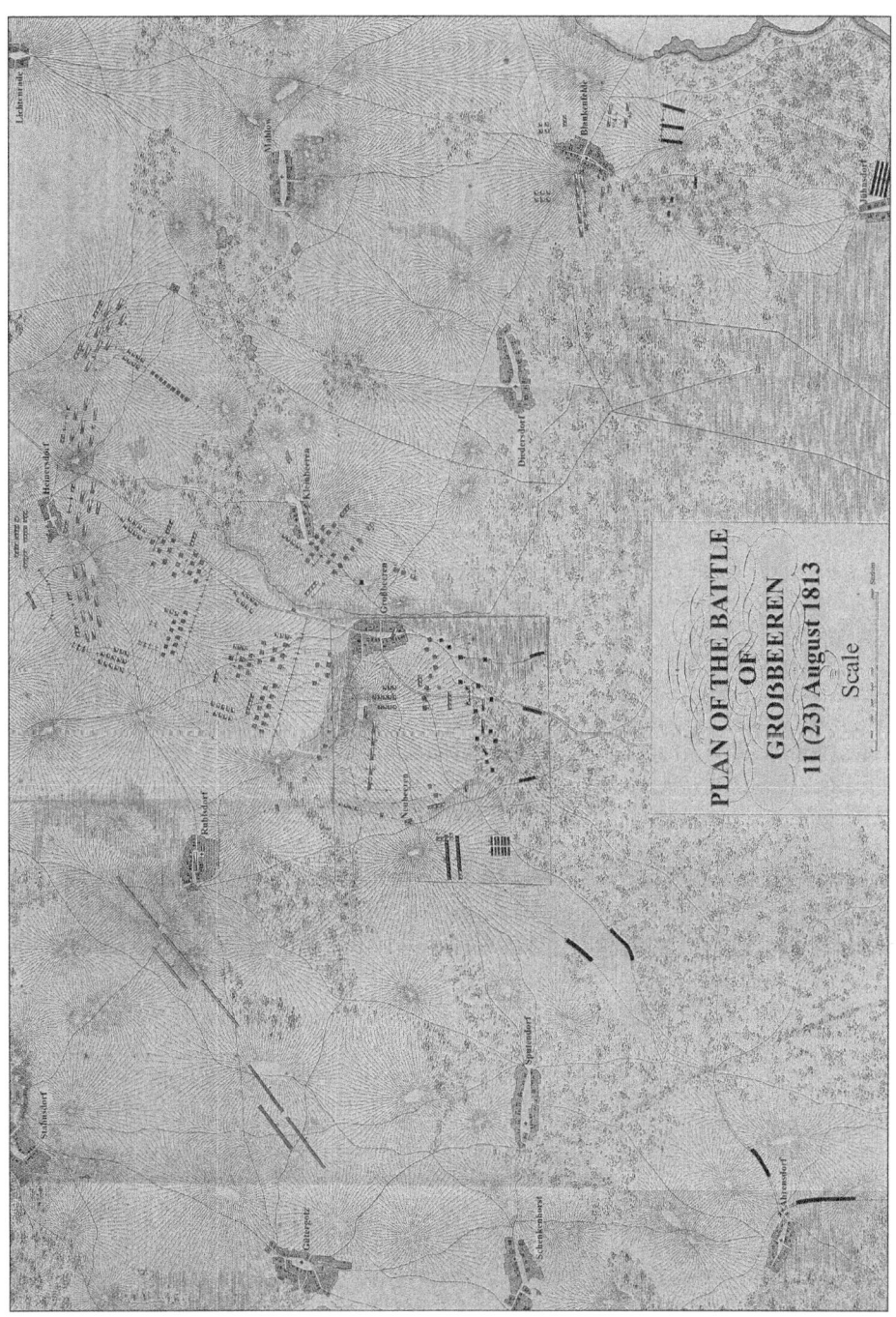

Plan of the Battle of Großbeeren, 11 (23) August 1913).

The ground between the armies of the opposing sides was mostly covered with forest and swamps. There were three roads leading in the direction of Berlin: from Jühnsdorf through Blankenfelde; from Wietstock through Großbeeren, and from Trebbin through Ahrensdorf and Sputendorf. Large sandy hills along these roads made the movement of artillery and cavalry extremely difficult.[21]

On 11 (23) August, the army set out from their overnight halt in three columns: Bertrand's corps towards Blankenfelde; Reynier's towards Großbeeren; *12e Corps* towards Ahrensdorf with Arrighi's cavalry; Oudinot himself remained in Trebbin. The latter two columns set off later than the first, despite the fact that they had more ground to cover. By operating in this way, Oudinot wanted to divert the attention of the Coalition to their left flank and then lead a decisive attack on their centre and right wing; but he lost sight of the fact that the French columns could be defeated in detail, separated, as they were, by swamps and forests over a frontage of 15 *versts*, and deprived of the opportunity to maintain proper liaison with each other due to a lack of lateral communications.[22]

General Bertrand was far ahead of the rest of the French army with his corps numbering 20,000 men and attacked Tauentzien, who could oppose him with no more than 16 battalions and 16 squadrons with 28 guns, numbering 12,000 men.[23] Of the entire infantry component of the Prussian corps, only the four battalions of *5. Reserve Infanterie* were trained to operate in loose formation. All other infantry and all the cavalry consisted of *Landwehr* who had received grossly insufficient combat training. Fortunately for the Coalition, the ground around Blankenfelde was conducive to defensive operations: the village of Blankenfelde lies at the exit of a vast area covered with thick scrub (Jühnsdorfer Heide); to the right of the village is a large swamp, while to the left is a branch of the Rangsdorfer See; the position between the swamp and the lake, a frontage of no more than 2,000 paces, could be comfortably defended, at least for a time, by Tauentzien's small corps. His force, in anticipation of the enemy, were positioned as follows: skirmishers and the entire fusilier battalion of *3. Reserve Infanterieregiment* were spread across the forest forwards of the position; the other battalions of this regiment were stationed facing the exits of the forest with two squadrons of *2. Neumärkische Landwehr Kavallerie*, to the right of the village of Blankenfelde; the remaining infantry were formed up in column along either side of the village, in two waves, with the cavalry to their rear in reserve; two guns guarded the exits

---

21 See Map No. 4 Plan of the Battle of Großbeeren.
22 Beitzke, II, 259-260, 263.
23 Tauentzien's force at Blankenfelde consisted of: *Schlesisches Infanterie* (three battalions); *3. Reserve Infanterieregiment* (four battalions – three according to some sources); *1. Kurmärkische Landwehr* (two battalions); *5. Kurmärkische Landwehr* (four battalions); *2. Neumärkische Landwehr* (three battalions); *2. Neumärkische Landwehr Kavallerie* (two squadrons); *Westpreussische Landwehr Kavallerie* (four squadrons); *1. Kurmärkische Landwehr Kavallerie* and *7. Kurmärkische Landwehr Kavallerie* (four squadrons); *3. Pommersche Landwehr Kavallerie* (four squadrons); *Berliner Landwehr Kavallerie* (two squadrons); *17. Batterie zu Fuß, 20. Batterie zu Fuß*, half of *27. Batterie zu Fuß*, and one horse artillery battery. Wagner, I, 30, 43; Richter, I, 409. In Bernhardi (III, *beilagen*, 518), this part of Tauentzien's corps is shown as consisting of 20 battalions, 28 squadrons and four batteries.

to the village; while all the remaining artillery was allocated to the infantry in the fighting line.[24]

At about ten o'clock in the morning, Bertrand's French force, having driven the Prussian skirmishers out of the forest, emerged from there in three strong columns. Artillery advanced in between them. It seemed that the enemy had the intention of attacking the position on its left flank, but as they closed to cannon range, they halted, advanced two batteries and began a cannonade. Tauentzien responded with fire from six guns, brought elements of his force closer to the left flank and waited for the assault from the stronger French corps. But instead, Bertrand, at one o'clock in the afternoon, fell back towards Jühnsdorf. Tauentzien pursued them through the forest, captured 11 officers and 200 lower ranks and returned to his position. By two o'clock in the afternoon, the fighting had completely died down and the forces from both sides were simply standing undisturbed: Bertrand at Jühnsdorf, while Tauentzien was at Blankenfelde.[25]

Throughout the duration of this action, Bülow, not being attacked himself, believed that the enemy intended to envelope the army from the left flank and break out towards Berlin. With the cannonade thundering on the left wing intensifying at around noon, Bülow therefore decided to go to the aid of the attacked force, and reported this to the Crown Prince immediately as he set off for Diedersdorf. But when he arrived there, the action at Blankenfelde was already ending. Bülow's force halted, and after that, moved back to Heinersdorf, where they formed up for battle in front of this village.[26] Prinz Hessen-Homburg's *3. Brigade* [Ludwig Wilhelm von Hessen-Homburg] were to the right of Heinersdorf stretching towards Ruhlsdorf. *Oberst* Krafft's *6. Brigade* [Karl August Adolf von Krafft] and General Thümen's *4. Brigade* were either side of the Berlin road. The *5. Brigade* under General Borstell was on the left wing. The cavalry reserve under General Oppen and reserve artillery were behind the village. The vanguard of Bülow's corps, consisting of three battalions, four squadrons and a half-battery, commanded by Major Sandrart [Karl Wilhelm Emanuel von Sandrart], held Großbeeren.[27]

---

24 The deployment of the Prussian *IV. Korps* in the position at Blankendelde was as follows: *3. Reserve Infanterieregiment* and two squadrons of *2. Neumärkische Landwehr Kavallerie* were forwards of the village, at the exits to the forest; two guns from *20. Batterie* were at the exits to the village with a small infantry escort; to the right of the village, in two waves, were: *2. Neumärkische Landwehr* and *5. Neumärkische Landwehr* and one battalion of *Schlesisches Infanterie*, for a total of eight battalions, with 12 guns of *17. Batterie* and half of *27. Batterie*, while to the left of the village were: two battalions of *1. Kurmärkische Landwehr* and two battalions of *Schlesisches Infanterie*, with six guns from *20. Batterie*, with *3. Westpreussische Landwehr Kavallerie* a little to their rear. *1. Kurmärkische Landwehr Kavallerie* and *3. Pommersche Landwehr Kavallerie* (six squadrons) were stationed behind the infantry of the right wing, while two squadrons of *7. Kurmärkische Landwehr Kavallerie* and two squadrons of *Berliner Landwehr Kavallerie* were behind the infantry of the left wing. The location of the horse artillery allocated to Tauentzien's corps is not mentioned. Wagner, I, 43-44; Richter, I, 409.
25 According to Plotho (II, 137-138), the enemy lost between 500 to 800 men taken prisoner alone. Beitzke, II, 260-262. Vaudoncourt wrote that Bertrand's corps were in combat all day (*Histoire de la guerre soutenue par les Français en Allemagne*, 167).
26 Plotho, II, 138.
27 For details of Bülow's corps, see Appendix VI at the end of this chapter.

General Reynier, having set out at around noon from his overnight halt at Wietstock with *7e Corps*, numbering 20,000 men with 70 guns, approached the exits from the forest facing the village of Großbeeren at four o'clock.[28] Despite the soldiers only having marched no more than a *Meile* (seven *versts*), they were weary from moving along bad roads in inclement weather. Sahr's Saxon division marched at the head of the column, followed by the French division under Durutte, and finally the Saxon cavalry brigade made its way along the verges keeping level with the infantry. The baggage train of the entire corps, stretching between the divisions under Durutte and Le Coq, greatly hindered the movements of the troops proceeding in the tail of the column. Oudinot, for some unknown reason, believed that there would be no significant engagements that day, and remained in Trebbin, issuing orders for an offensive by the left column (*12e Corps* and Arrighi's cavalry) along with the centre column, but his orders were not precisely carried out, and the troops on the left wing, which had to cover a greater distance than the Saxons, were late and therefore could not assist them.

The village of Großbeeren lies on the route along which Reynier's corps were advancing, at a distance of about a *verst* from the exits from the forest. A depression stretches along the eastern side of the village with a deep drainage ditch (the Lilograben) leading to a marshy swamp, while beyond this ditch, 2,000 paces away, lies the village of Kleinbeeren. To the west of Großbeeren, two *versts* away, is the Neubeeren manor.

At about four o'clock in the afternoon, Reynier's corps attacked the Prussian vanguard force located at Großbeeren. Sahr's Saxon division, emerging from the forest, formed up for battle: Bose's brigade [Karl August Joseph Friedrich von Bose] were stationed on the right wing, while Ryssel's brigade [Gustav Xaver Reinhold von Ryssel] formed the left. Twelve guns were advanced against the Prussian half-battery stationed on the Windmühlenberg, lobbing several shells into the village, setting it on fire. Thereafter, Sperl's Saxon grenadier battalion, supported by a battalion of the *Linien Regiment König*, drove the Prussian troops out of the village and by five o'clock in the afternoon had forced them to retreat to the main body of the corps around Heinersdorf. Sahr's division moved onto the Windmühlenberg, with their right flank extended towards Großbeeren, holding this village with one battalion. Durutte's French division and the Saxon cavalry under Gablenz [Heinrich Adolph von Gablenz] were stationed in the support line, at the exits from the forest, while Le Coq's Saxon division, arriving a little later, extended to their left towards Neubeeren. It was raining heavily. Visibility was almost zero, and Reynier, unaware of the location of a strong Prussian corps at a distance of less than two *versts* from him at Heinersdorf, considered operations to be over for that day. It seemed as if his corps were completely secure from attack: on the right – a swampy depression and a drainage ditch, across which it was possible to move only at Großbeeren, while on the left, the troops of *12e Corps* and Arrighi's cavalry, according to the timings, should already be close. Thus, Reynier, not considering himself as being in any kind

---

28 Reynier's corps consisted of: Sahrer von Sahr's division of nine battalions; Le Coq's division of 10¼ battalions; Gablenz's cavalry brigade of 13 squadrons and 52 Saxon artillery pieces. The number of French guns is not mentioned. *Feldzüge der Sachsen*, 198-202; Wagner, I, 32-33.

of danger, wanted to spend the night in Großbeeren and ordered quarters to be found for himself. His entire staff concerned themselves solely with finding shelter from the bad weather as quickly as possible.[29]

In contrast, Bülow, having received intelligence from his vanguard on the enemy positions at Großbeeren, and knowing that an entire French corps was facing Tauentzien, decided to take advantage of the dislocation of Oudinot's forces and attack the troops closest to him. To that end, the following hastily drawn up disposition was issued:

> It is ordered that the enemy right wing be attacked, Großbeeren is to be captured and the enemy flank columns are to be induced to retreat by driving the centre of the French army into the defiles. Prinz Hessen-Homburg's *3. Brigade* are to form the right wing, *Oberst* Krafft's *6. Brigade* the left, General Thümen's *4. Brigade* are to proceed as the reserve behind the left wing. The brigades are each to form two waves. The cavalry attached to the infantry are to move behind the second wave, while the reserve cavalry are to be behind the flanks of the general battle formation. General Borstell is to advance through Kleinbeeren towards Großbeeren with *5. Brigade*, in order to envelope the enemy on their right flank, but primarily in order to shield the left flank of the corps.[30]

It has been claimed that at the very time that he was dictating this disposition, he received orders from the Crown Prince to retreat towards Berlin, and that instead, he marched towards Großbeeren with his corps and reported this to the prince.[31] There is at least no doubt that the Crown Prince, having received Bülow's report, sent his Adjutant-General Graf Löwenhielm to him with orders to seize Großbeeren.[32]

Despite the pouring rain and the fatigue of the troops, who had very meagre supplies with them, Bülow's orders to take up arms and march against the enemy were met with general shouts of joy (Hurrah!) from the entire corps. At about five o'clock in the afternoon, the force, having formed up in battle formation in accordance with the disposition, moved to attack: the reserve cavalry proceeded behind the infantry, namely: Tresckow's brigade [Karl Alexander Wilhelm von Treskow or Tresckow] (*Königin Dragoner* and *2. Westpreussishes Dragoner*) on the right, while Sydow's brigade [Hans Joachim Friedrich von Sydow] (*2. Kurmärkische Landwehr Kavallerie, 4. Kurmärkische Landwehr Kavallerie* and elements of *Pommersche Landwehr Kavallerie*) were behind the left wing of the battle formation with the *Schlesisches Husaren*. The *Westpreussisches Ulanen* had been detached to Borstell's brigade.[33] The commander of the corps artillery, *Oberstleutnant* Holtzendorff [Karl

---

29 Reynier's corps consisted of: Sahrer von Sahr's division of nine battalions; Le Coq's division of 10¼ battalions; Gablenz's cavalry brigade of 13 squadrons and 52 Saxon artillery pieces. The number of French guns is not mentioned. *Feldzüge der Sachsen*, 198-202; Wagner, I, 32-33.
30 Plotho, II, 139.
31 Beitzke, II, 266, 267.
32 Beitzke, II, 266.
33 Wagner, I, 47-48.

Friedrich von Holtzendorff], on Bülow's orders, pushed 5½ batteries 300 paces forwards of the first wave, including the Russians under Colonel Dietrichs.[34] A Russian battery and 2½ Prussian batteries proceeded in reserve, behind the infantry.[35] All this artillery, numbering 78 guns, was put into action almost from the very beginning of the battle. The enemy responded with a cannonade from six batteries, numbering 44 guns, leaving three batteries (24 guns) in reserve. *Leutnant* Neindorff's Prussian *5. Reitende Batterie* [Friedrich Ludwig Wilhelm von Neindorff], sent to their right, escorted by a dragoon squadron, worked on the enemy flank, but were engaged by fire from two batteries, which managed to knock out four Prussian guns. A little later, *Överste* [colonel] Cardell [Carl von Cardell] reinforced them with four Swedish guns. Overall, 82 guns were put into action by the Coalition.[36]

Simultaneously with Bülow's advance, Borstell moved towards Kleinbeeren with *5. Brigade* and sent Major Knobloch to hold this village with a small detachment.[37] Once it had become apparent that there were no enemy there, Borstell realigned his force with the other Prussian brigades, facing towards Großbeeren: the infantry were formed in two waves, cavalry on the flanks, artillery at the tip of the right wing, on the Lilograben.[38]

General Reynier, having received word of the emergence of the enemy from Kleinbeeren, sent two battalions from the Saxon *König Regiment* and *Prinz Anton Regiment*, with a half-battery, to the far side of the Lilograben, but no sooner had they had chance to debouch on the other side of the ditch, than they were subjected to enfilade fire from Borstell's battery and were forced to retreat back to Großbeeren.[39]

As soon as Borstell's brigade had formed up facing Großbeeren and the fire of the enemy batteries became noticeably weaker, Bülow led the infantry with bayonets fixed, en echelon from their left flank. At about six o'clock in the afternoon, *Oberst* Krafft, having received orders to seize Großbeeren, attacked the enemy in this village with the first battalion of *Kolbergische Landwehr*, supporting them on the left with the second battalion of this regiment, while to their right was the second battalion of *5. Reserve Infanterie* (Thümen's brigade). An attack was also launched on Großbeeren from the direction of Kleinbeeren by two battalions of *2. Reserve Infanterie* (Borstell's brigade). The Prussian force advanced at a quick pace, with drums beating and loud cheering, and drove the enemy out of the flaming village. General Borstell quickly passing through Großbeeren with the first

---

34 The artillery in Bülow's battle formation consisted of: Lieutenant Colonel Dietrichs' Battery Company with 12 guns; Prussian *4. Batterie* (eight 12-pounders); *5. Batterie, 6. Batterie* and *16. Batterie* (24 six-pounders); *19. Batterie* (four six-pounders), for a total of 48 guns.
35 Bülow's artillery reserve consisted of: a Russian heavy company (ten guns); *5. Reitende Batterie, 6. Reitende Batterie* (16 guns); *19. Batterie* (four six-pounders), for a total of 30 guns (Wagner, I, 49).
36 Richter, I, 413.
37 Borstell's force consisted of: the *Pommersches Grenadier Bataillon*; three battalion of *Pommersches Infanterie*; three battalions of *2. Reserve Infanterie*; four battalions of *2. Kurmärkisches Infanterie* (only two battalions were committed to action); *Pommersches Husaren* (five squadrons); *Westpreussisches Ulanen* (four squadrons from the cavalry reserve); *10. Batterie* (six-pounders); *11. Reitende Batterie*, for a total of 12 guns. Wagner, I, 50.
38 Wagner, I, 50.
39 Plotho, II, 140.

battalion of *2. Reserve Infanterie* drove a battalion from the *Prinz Anton Regiment* and Sperl's grenadiers, stationed to the right of the village, into the swamp, where many Saxons were drowned, stabbed with bayonets or beaten with musket butts, or were captured. *Hauptmann* Röhl, with one of the companies from this battalion, captured two guns stationed to the left of the village, while Major Gagern [Hans Karl Adam von Gagern], with second battalion of *5. Reserve Infanterie*, captured three guns.[40] Borstell's cavalry (four squadrons of *Westpreussisches Ulanen* and one squadron of *Pommersches Husaren*) caught the enemy infantry moving towards the forest, broke into a square and took two guns, capturing more than 100 crew and escort personnel.[41]

After capturing Großbeeren, Bülow pushed Prinz Hessen-Homburg's *3. Brigade*, which had remained behind, and brought Thümen's *4. Brigade* into the line. The reserve cavalry on the right wing outflanked the enemy in order to complete their defeat. Sahr's division was pushed back from the Windmühlenberg towards the forest. He himself, wanting to defend the artillery, rushed towards the Prussian force with two battalions from *Linien Regiment von Low*, but being attacked by two battalions from *5. Reserve Infanterie*, commanded by Major Gagern, lost many men in close-quarter combat and received several wounds, and barely escaped capture. The *Pommersches Husaren* attacked the retreating infantry, which, however, were rescued by a successful counter-attack by Saxon lancers, who drove the Prussian regiment back and recaptured the three guns they had taken. But after that, *1. Pommersche Kavallerie* made several successful attacks on the Saxon lancers, captured their regimental commander and overran a battery.

General Reynier had intended to restore the battle with Durutte's force, but this division was swept away by the retreating Saxons. Le Coq's division, which was to the left of the others, covered the retreat of the defeated troops and followed them towards Löwenbruch [2½ miles north of Wietstock], leaving *Oberst* Brause [Friedrich August Wilhelm von Brause] as the rearguard, with three battalions, one jäger company, two squadrons and four guns. At dusk, once the outcome of the battle had already been decided, Fournier's cavalry division [François Louis Fournier-Sarlovèze] appeared near Neubeeren together with Guilleminot's infantry division [Armand Charles Guilleminot] from the direction of Ahrensdorf, moving in the direction of the thundering cannonade from Großbeeren, in order to assist Reynier's corps. As it was already completely dark by this time, the French cavalry, emerging from the forest, halted and deployed in two waves, each of 12 squadrons, while the infantry remained in the forest. Major Sandrart, with his *Leib-Husaren*, supported by the *Westpreussisches Ulanen* coming up from the left wing, decided to attack the enemy, struck their flank, and exploiting the shock of the charge and the darkness which prevented the French from noticing the small numbers in his detachment, scattered the entire enemy division and took many prisoners.[42]

---

40 Plotho, II, 140-141; Wagner, I, 52.
41 Wagner, I, 52-53; Richter, I, 415-416.
42 Wagner, I, 54; Richter, I, 416-417; Beitzke, II, 271.

At eight o'clock in the evening, the fighting was completely over. The darkness of the night did not allow Bülow to pursue further than the edge of the forest. Some of his force returned to bivouacs near Heinersdorf.[43]

The casualties in the Saxon force reached some 2,124 men, including 28 field officers and subalterns and 2,096 lower ranks. The trophies of this day consisted of 26 guns, of which 14 were captured from *7e Corps*, 60 ammunition caissons and between 1,500 and 2,000 prisoners. In addition, the victors recovered some 2,000 muskets from the battlefield, abandoned by the fleeing enemy, which encouraged the *Landwehr* to replace their pikes with firearms.[44] The Prussian force lost more than 2,000 men killed and wounded in all actions on 9, 10 and 11 (21, 22 and 23) August, namely: 51 officers and some 1,600 lower ranks in Bülow's corps, while Tauentzien's corps lost more than 500 men. Six Prussian guns had been knocked out.[45]

The Crown Prince pursued the enemy very feebly. Had he set out early the next day with his entire force, he could have caught the corps under Reynier, Oudinot and Arrighi before they could pass the choke-points at Wietstock and Thyrow. Yet instead, he gave his troops a rest day for the entirety of 12 (24) August, and having only set off the following day, he advanced by short stages: Bülow's corps spent the night of 13 (25) August at Thyrow, Tauentzien at Zossen, the Russian and Swedish corps remained in place about two *Meilen* (15 *versts*) away from the battlefield, while the prince's headquarters were located at Teltow. The onward advance continued just as slowly, moreover, the Coalition force became extended over a considerable area, namely: Wobeser's detachment received orders to move from Baruth towards Luckau in order to seize this fortified location, which was crowned with brilliant success on 16 (28) August;[46] Tauentzien's corps advanced to Baruth; Bülow's corps reached Elsholz ([three miles south] from Beelitz); Wintzingerode was at Beelitz; the Swedish corps and headquarters relocated to Saarmund on 14 (26) August. The Crown Prince, thinking more of self-defence than about an offensive, ordered the fortifications at Trebbin to be strengthened. The French army, taking advantage of the sluggish Coalition operations, retreated in short stages across the Zahnabach to Wittenberg, while the Crown Prince, deploying part of his army to face the enemy, moved to Zeiden, near Rabenstein on 25 August (1 September). Thus, in the 11 days

---

43 Wagner, I, 55.
44 At Großbeeren, Sahr's division lost: 116 men killed; 250 wounded, including General Sahr and 11 officers; 1,564 missing in action, including nine officers; for a total of 20 officers and 1,910 lower ranks. Le Coq's division lost eight officers and 185 lower ranks. There is no precise data on the losses to Oudinot's other formations. Durutte's division lost six guns. Plotho, II, 142; *Feldzügen der Sachsen*, 129-131. According to Vaudoncourt, the overall losses to Oudinot's force amounted to 1,500 men taken prisoner alone and 30 guns, *Histoire de la guerre soutenue par les Français en Allemagne*, 167.
45 Plotho, II, 142 and *Beilagen* XXI. According to Beitzke (II, 276), Prussian casualties from the battle of Großbeeren reached some 150 men killed and some 900 wounded. Richter (I, 418) gives the losses to the Prussian force as: 159 killed, 662 wounded and 228 men missing in action.
46 General Wobeser, approaching Lukau on 16 (28) August, forced the garrison of this town to capitulate. The prisoners amounted to 16 officers and 670 lower ranks (an Italian battalion and a Saxon battalion of the *Prinz Maximilian Regiment*), together with another 150 sick and wounded. Nine guns and a great deal of stores went to the victors. Plotho, II, 155-156.

that elapsed after the Großbeeren victory, the Army of the Northern Army advanced only 11 *Meilen* (about 80 *versts*).[47] Neither the lust for battle of the Coalition troops, nor their superiority in cavalry, which offered the Coalition the opportunity to operate decisively without being exposed to unexpected danger: nothing would induce the prince to increased activity.

Notwithstanding the hesitancy of operations by the Commander-in-Chief of the Army of the North allowing the enemy time to recover, draw in reinforcements and soon launch another offensive towards Berlin, the victory at Großbeeren had very important consequences. As the battle continued, every shot heard from the battlefield aroused the sympathy of Berlin's population. The residents of the Prussian capital waited in trepidation for a decision on their fate. Just as in 1812 when Muscovites had rushed to Poklonnaya Gora to face Napoleon, many of the *Landsturm* soldiers went to the Kreuzberg [two miles south of the city]. Among them were Professor Fichte [Johann Gottlieb Fichte] with two pairs of pistols, [the actor] Iffland [August Wilhelm Iffland] in armour from 'The Maid of Orleans' and other civilians. In the night, news came of the victory and flight of the enemy, who had considered the country their prey, and everyone breathed freely. The delight and joy of the population were expressed as the heartfelt sentiments of a great nation ought to be expressed. Thousands of people of every class went to Heinersdorf, greeting the defenders of their fatherland, offering them all kinds of life support, trying to ease the suffering of the wounded. The most noble of ladies and maidens, along with all the women who arrived from Berlin, bandaged the wounded, took care of their needs and thanked the dying in their final moments for their sacrifice.[48] The victory at Großbeeren, instilling self-confidence in the troops of the Army of the North, made them feel unbeatable and was the beginning of a series of successes that distinguished the operations of this army in the second campaign of 1813.

The defeat of Napoleon's forces at Großbeeren had very detrimental consequences for him, sowing the seeds of discord between the French and their allies – the Saxons. Despite the courageous resistance of the Saxon warriors in the unequal struggle at Großbeeren, the French attributed the loss of the battle to them, while they criticised the French for having put the Saxon force up against an incomparably stronger foe, and not only failing to support them, but also seeking salvation in flight. The stationing of Napoleon's *Grande Armée* in Saxony throughout the duration of the armistice had completely depleted the country, whose population, deprived of the last of their possessions, no longer viewed Napoleon as their defender, nor the powerful ally of their Sovereign, but as an ambitious man who would sacrifice them in order to achieve his objectives. The displeasure of the Saxons against the French, which increased with every new disaster of the war, was demonstrated by the entry of almost all the prisoners captured in the Battle of Großbeeren into the service of the Coalition.[49]

Napoleon was quite rightly dissatisfied with Oudinot's operations, and especially with the fact that, having lost the battle, he retreated to Wittenberg rather than

---

47 Plotho, II, 160-162; Beitzke, II, 276-277.
48 Beitzke, II, 272-273; Förster, I, 774-775.
49 *Feldzüge der Sachsen*, 227; Vaudoncourt, 167.

towards Torgau, in a direction that, by moving him away from French reserves stationed in Dresden, overextended the weakened formations of the French army. Having the intention of relaunching the offensive on Berlin, Napoleon entrusted command of the forces that had been led by Oudinot to a military commander known for his decisiveness, Marshal Ney, and promised to significantly strengthen his army.

Appendix VI

The composition of Bülow's corps

Bülow's corps consisted of:

Prinz Hessen-Homburg's *3. Brigade* – 11 battalions and one battery deployed at Heinersdorf; five squadrons of *1. Leib-Husaren* detached to the vanguard.

Generalmajor Thümen's *4. Brigade* – eight battalions, three squadrons and one battery at Heinersdorf; first battalion of the *Elbe Landwehr* in Saarmund with Hirschfeld's detachment; two companies of *Westpreussische Jäger* left at Heinersdorf during the advance of the corps.

Borstell's *5. Brigade* – 11 battalions, five squadrons and one battery at Heinersdorf.

Oberst Krafft's *6. Brigade* – six battalions, four squadrons and one battery at Heinersdorf; third battalion of *1. Neumärkische Landwehr* at Stettin; third battalion of *Kolbergische Landwehr*, first battalion of *9. Reserve Infanterie* and first battalion of *Neumärkische Landwehr* detached to the vanguard.

Generalmajor Oppen's cavalry reserve – 26 squadrons and two batteries at Heinersdorf; two squadrons of *Brandenburgisches Dragoner* at Stettin; there was just one squadron from the *Königin Dragoner* attached to the corps.

Oberst Holzendorf's reserve artillery – 3½ batteries; four guns from 19. Batterie were detached to the vanguard.

Colonel Dietrichs' Russian artillery – two batteries.

Prussian pioneers – two companies.

In total, including the vanguard, in this corps there were: 40 battalions, 43 squadrons, ten Prussian batteries (80 guns) and two Russian artillery companies (22 guns), numbering around 40,000 men with 102 guns. Extracted from returns presented in Wagner (I, 27-29) and Bernhardi (III, 518).

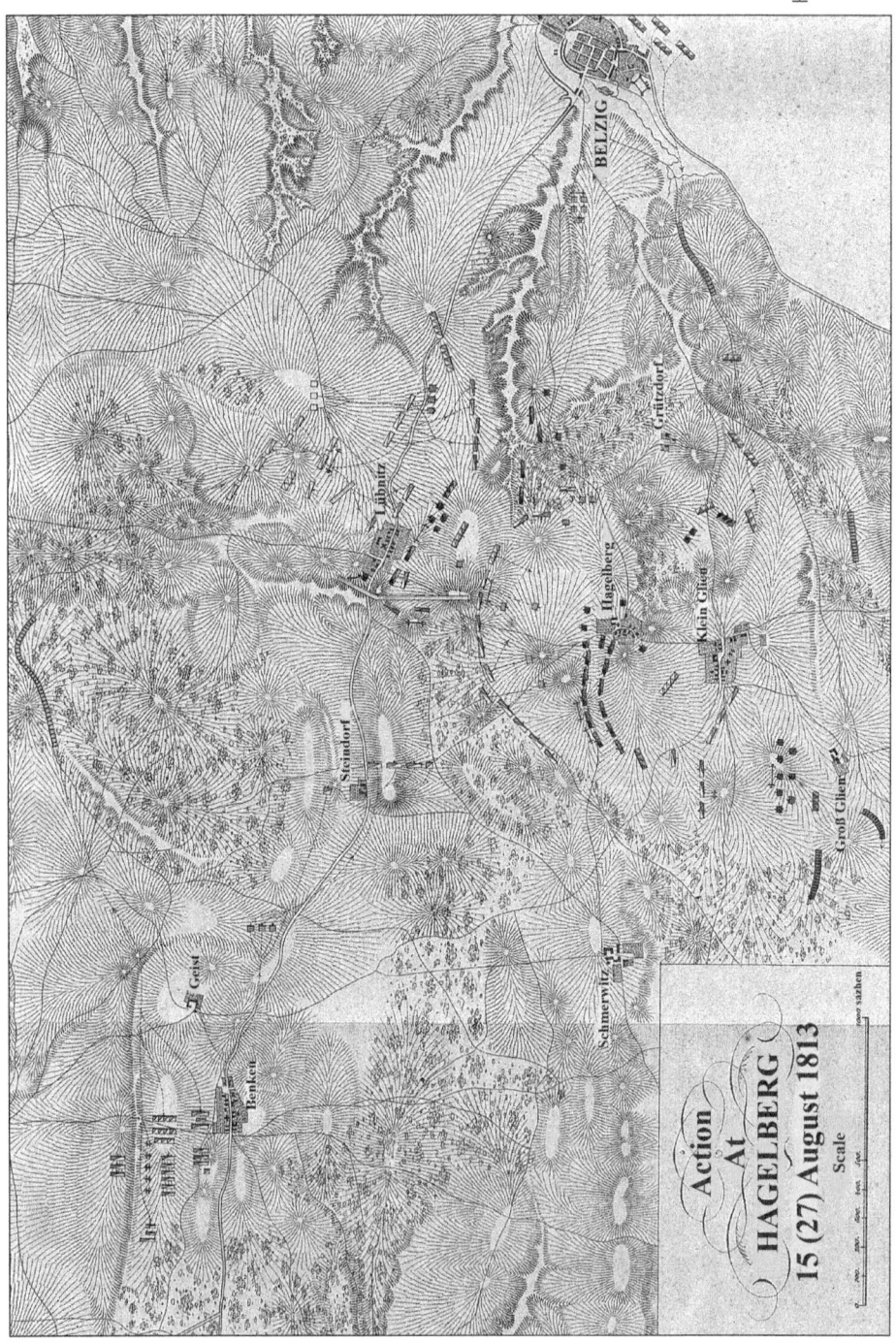

Action at Hagelberg, 15 (27) August 1813.

25

Action at Hagelberg

The mission of General Hirschfeld's detachment. – Girard's advance. – The arrival of Adjutant-General Chernyshev's detachment at Belzig. – The deployment of Girard's force. – Hirschfeld's flanking movement. – The action at Hagelberg.

Davout's departure from Hamburg. – The strength, composition and deployment of Graf Wallmoden's independent corps; vanguard; Lützow's detachment. – The action at Lauenburg. – The Coalition retreat towards Hagenow and Wismar. – The advance of Davout's force towards Schwerin and Wismar. – Lützow's movements behind enemy lines; the raid on the transport at Rosenhagen; the death of Theodor Kerner. – Davout's retreat back to the Hamburg area. – The deployment of Wallmoden's force.

One of the immediate consequences of the Battle of Großbeeren was the victory scored by Coalition forces at Hagelberg.

When hostilities resumed after the armistice, General Hirschfeld's detachment, numbering 12,800 men, was tasked with covering the right flank of the Army of the North and monitoring the garrison of Magdeburg. General Putlitz [Friedrich Ludwig Wilhelm Otto Gans zu Putlitz] was tasked with the latter mission, with 4,000 men, being advanced to Königsborn [six miles east of Magdeburg], while Hirschfeld himself was initially stationed at Brandenburg, with the main body of his detachment and later moved to Saarmund.[1] The majority of Hirschfeld's force were *Kurmärkische Landwehr* infantry or cavalry, almost all of them middle-aged men who had spent their lives in agricultural work, or were tradesmen engaged in various crafts. The weapons and training of these hastily raised troops were very poor.[2]

Simultaneously with the advance by Oudinot's army towards Berlin, the Magdeburg commandant, General Le Marois [Jean Léonor François Le Marois], sent a detachment of about 12,000 men with 22 guns to assist him, commanded by General Girard. Only eight battalions (about 5,000 men) and the artillery in this

---

1 For the details of Hirschfeld's and Putlitz's detachments, see Appendix VII at the end of this chapter.
2 Förster, *Geschichte der Befreiungskriege, 1813, 1814, 1815*, I, 782.

detachment were made up of Frenchmen. The rest of the infantry and all the cavalry were from foreign contingents, Girard's force consisted almost entirely of recruits.[3] As the enemy detachment advanced, General Putlitz, being unable to stop them, retreated to Brandenburg and occupied the local fortifications upon arrival there on 11 (23) August. Two days later, on 13 (25) August, Hirschfeld's main force joined him, reinforced by the first battalion of *Elbe Landwehr* and one six-pounder gun from *6. Batterie*. Meanwhile, having reached Ziesar on 10 (22) August, Girard turned from there towards Belzig in order to close the gap to Oudinot's army, and arrived in the vicinity of this location on 13 (25) August, at the same time as Hirschfeld's detachment were moving towards Golzow and as the arrival in Belzig of Chernyshev's raiding detachment, consisting of five Cossacks regiments, numbering about 2,000 men.[4] The following day [26 August, new style], Girard conducted a reconnaissance in force against the Cossacks occupying Belzig, but being unable to dislodge them, he deployed with four battalions, two squadrons and four guns on the high ground by the town. His remaining troops were stationed at Lübnitz, in line forwards of this village, on both sides of the road leading to Benken. On that same day, 14 (26) August, Hirschfeld arrived in the vicinity of Görzke: thus, Girard's detachment were between the forces under Chernyshev and Hirschfeld, but, having turned his attention exclusively in the direction of Belzig, he did not know about the appearance of the Prussian detachment to his rear. In contrast, Hirschfeld knew both the enemy strength and their locations, but he did not have any accurate information regarding Chernyshev's detachment.[5]

At dawn on 15 (27) August, the Cossacks provoked an alarm at the enemy camp at Lübnitz and then withdrew to Belzig. General Hirschfeld, taking advantage of the French negligence in guarding the position they occupied only from the direction of Belzig, led his detachment towards Benken in two columns, and, having reached the Windmühlenberg near this village, set off along the road from Lübnitz to Steindorf with a small patrol in order to monitor the enemy.[6] This reconnaissance confirmed to him that the French were unaware of the presence of the Prussian detachment in their rear, at a distance of no more than half a *Meile* (around 3½ *versts*): under such circumstances, it was vital to move forward as quickly as possible and attack the enemy, who, not expecting an attack from Benken at all, were holding ground unsuitable for a stubborn defence. Yet General Hirschfeld, was of the old school, trained in the tactics of the Seven Years' War when an attack from the flank was

---

3 Girard's detachment consisted of: *18e Ligne*; *19e Ligne*; *26e Légère* (eight battalions in all); Westphalian *4. Infanterie*; Westphalian *9. Infanterie* (four battalions in all); three battalions from the Saxon duchies; *Régiment d'Illyrie* (two battalions); one *bataillon de marche*; six squadrons, for the most part from the Saxon duchies (some sources show three squadrons). Wagner, I, 34; Beitzke, *Geschichte der deutschen Freiheitskriege in den Jahren 1813 und 1814*, II, 278.
4 See Map No. 5, Action at Hagelberg. Chernyshev's detachment consisted of: Sysoev 3rd's Cossacks; Grekov 18th's Cossacks; Vlasov 3rd's Cossacks, Ilovaisky 11th's Cossacks and Zhirov's Cossacks, numbering 55 officers and 1,993 lower ranks. Report on force composition, signed by Adjutant-General Wintzingerode on 1 [13] August.
5 Plotho, II, 144-148; Wagner, I, 96-97; Beitzke, II, 279.
6 Plotho, II, 150.

considered the surest means of achieving success, and preferred to go left-flanking in order to attack the enemy. To that end, a very complex disposition was issued.[7] Leaving *Oberstleutnant* von Reuss at Benken with three battalions, one squadron and one Prussian cannon,[8] and ordering him to take 'a route close to the edge of the forest as far as Steindorf... in order to threaten the enemy flank and rear, especially if the enemy should retreat towards Glien and Wiesenburg [6½ miles west of Belzig],' Hirschfeld led the rest his force (15 battalions, 11 squadrons and ten Russian guns) to the left through the forest which lay on the flank of Girard's detachment.[9] The *1. Reserve Infanterie* (three battalions) led followed by the cavalry and artillery protected on their right by skirmishers from the first battalion of the reserve infantry. Thereafter, came the brigades under Boguslawski [Carl Anton Andreas von Boguslawski], Putlitz and finally, Marwitz [Friedrich August Ludwig von der Marwitz] (numbering 12 *Landwehr* battalions).[10] It has been claimed that Hirschfeld gave a speech to his *Landwehr*, concluding it with the words: 'with bayonets fixed, attack and fight valiantly, like the Romans [sic] at Thermopylae.'[11]

General Girard, located in very broken terrain and having little cavalry, could not carry out continuous clearance patrols around the positions he occupied, and besides, the cloudy rainy weather made visibility very poor. These circumstances contributed to Hirschfeld completing the flanking movement unnoticed by the enemy. At about one o'clock in the afternoon, the Prussian vanguard, having reached the forest edge facing Lübnitz, debouched from there and formed up in front of the forest. But for the untrained *Landwehr* following the vanguard, deploying for battle required so much time that only some of them managed to get out into the open before Girard's force, having refused their left wing, repositioned themselves facing the forest. The right wing of the French infantry moved forward to the right of the village with artillery. Several guns had also been placed to its left. Thus, Hirschfeld's outflanking movement did not achieve its objective – to attack the enemy in the flank.

Despite this, however, the Prussian cavalry, commanded by *Oberst* Bismarck [Friedrich Adolf Ludwig von Bismarck], emerging from the forest, charged at the enemy's cavalry taking them by surprise and drove them off behind Girard's infantry, but being engaged with canister shot, they were forced to fall back. Meanwhile, the Russian battery opened fire on Lübnitz. Behind them was

---

7   For the full text of this disposition, see Appendix VIII (in the original German, and in English translation) at the end of this chapter.
8   *Oberstleutnant* von Reuss' detachment consisted of: a battalion each of *4. Kurmärkische Landwehr, 7. Kurmärkische Landwehr* and *Elbe Landwehr*; one squadron of *3. Kurmärkische Landwehr Kavallerie* and one cannon.
9   Hirschfeld's force outflanking the French consisted of: four battalions of *1. Reserve Infanterie (Ostpreussisches)*; four battalions of *3. Kurmärkische Landwehr*; two battalions of *4. Kurmärkische Landwehr*; four battalions of *6. Kurmärkische Landwehr*; one battalion of *7. Kurmärkische Landwehr*; three squadrons of *3. Kurmärkische Landwehr Kavallerie*; and four squadrons each of *5. Kurmärkische Landwehr Kavallerie* and *6. Kurmärkische Landwehr Kavallerie* and ten Russian guns. Wagner, I, 97-98.
10 Wagner, I, 99.
11 'mit gefälltem Bajonet greift an und fechtet tapfer, wie die Römer bei Thermopilä.' Förster, I, 784.

Boguslawski's brigade (three battalions). The vanguard (three battalions) was moved forward en echelon to the left of the artillery, while even further to the left was Bismarck with the *3. Kurmärkische Landwehr Kavallerie* and *5. Kurmärkische Landwehr Kavallerie*, leaving *3. Kurmärkische Landwehr Kavallerie* to protect the battery. The detachment under *Oberstleutnant* von Reuss, having passed through a birch grove (Schmerwitzer Thiergarten), positioned themselves in front of it: the cavalry squadron on the extreme right wing; the three battalions with the Prussian cannon to the left. Meanwhile, Hirschfeld's leading four battalions (two battalions of *1. Reserve Infanterie* and two of *4. Kurmärkische Landwehr*), having managed to form up in front of the forest, went on the attack, while Bornstädt's battalion (second battalion, *3. Kurmärkische Landwehr*) burst into the village set ablaze by shellfire and seized it, capturing one gun. General Girard, having retreated to Hagelberg, took up new positions here and, in order to secure his right flank and to threaten the rear of the Prussian force advancing against him with envelopment, he occupied the Belzig woods with the troops that had been facing Chernyshev and placed two guns on the high ground of the Gutenberg [north of Grützdorf]. General Hirschfeld, noticing this movement, sent the brigades under Putlitz and Marwitz to the woods, as they gradually emerged from the forest.[12]

Following the occupation of Lübnitz by Prussian troops, the second battalion of *3. Kurmärkische Landwehr* under Major Bornstädt, moved along the road to Hagelberg after the retreating enemy. As he reached the edge of the Belzig woods, he was joined on the left by two battalions from *1. Reserve Infanterie*, commanded by Major Langen, and on the right by three battalions with one cannon under *Oberstleutnant* von Reuss. The *3. Kurmärkische Landwehr Kavallerie*, having been rejoined by the squadron detached to Reuss' brigade, was stationed on their extreme right flank. Major Bornstädt, hoping to drive the enemy from this position, moved to the attack. The other battalions, stationed either side of him, supported the attack. But Girard, having placed all his artillery on the high ground near Hagelberg, greeted the Prussian force with a powerful cannonade. Hirschfeld could counter them with only half this number of guns. The infantry, in the pouring rain, could not fire and were forced to retreat into a birch grove under the protection of *3. Kurmärkische Landwehr Kavallerie*. Two battalions of *6. Kurmärkische Landwehr*, which had joined the left flank of this force, were carried back along with them.[13]

Matters had also taken an unfavourable turn on the left wing of the Prussian corps, despite the fact that Hirschfeld had twice as many troops there.[14] The Prussian infantry, approaching the woods, deployed and delivered rapid volleys, to which the enemy skirmishing screen occupying the edge of the woods responded

---

12 Plotho, II, 152-153; Wagner, I, 99-102.
13 Wagner, I, 102; Beitzke, II, 281.
14 There were eight battalions facing the Belzig woods: second and third battalions of *4. Kurmärkische Landwehr* from Boguslawski's brigade; Marwitz's reserve brigade to their left with first, third and fourth battalions of *3. Kurmärkische Landwehr*; while Putlitz's brigade were to their right with third and fourth battalions of *6. Kurmärkische Landwehr* and second battalion of *7. Kurmärkische Landwehr*. Putlitz's remaining units: first and second battalions of *6. Kurmärkische Landwehr* were stationed to the right of the woods, while fourth battalion *1. Reserve Infanterie* were escorting the guns. Wagner, I, 102-103.15.

with less frequent, but incomparably more lethal fire. The pouring rain, which soaked the muskets, disrupted their fire. One of the Prussian battalions, negligently approaching the high ground behind which some of the enemy infantry were stationed, was unexpectedly greeted with a volley (another source states that it was an exploding shell). The *Landwehr* fighters, overwhelmed by uncontrollable fear, fled in such disorder that they knocked their commander, General Putlitz, from his horse, who, having broken his collarbone in the fall, barely managed to escape capture.[15] But as soon as the *Landwehr* got out of range of the enemy fire, they rallied and reformed. Meanwhile, the movement of a cavalry column was noticed from Belzig towards Groß Glien, and at the same time the two French guns stationed on the right flank at the edge of the Belzig woods were falling back along with the battalion escorting them. *Oberstleutnant* Marwitz, noticing the retreat of this force, moved forwards once more and attacked the enemy in the woods with the skirmishers from his brigade, but having received orders from Hirschfeld to go to the aid of the defeated right wing, he headed there behind the five battalions that were to remain and which, together with his skirmishers, continued to advance through the Belzig woods. Marwitz's brigade, having passed the woods, turned towards the left and joined the right wing of the detachment.[16] The situation of the Prussian force was very unfavourable: they were stretched out in a single wave and had no reserves following up. There is no doubt that Girard would have taken advantage of what for him were favourable circumstances, had the appearance of Chernyshev's Cossack detachment to his rear not forced the French to pay attention exclusively to their own defence. To that end, Girard began to concentrate his force around Hagelberg, which made it easier for the left wing of the Prussian force to secure the Belzig woods. The marksmen from Marwitz's brigade, having passed through the woods, spread out behind enemy lines and took a howitzer. In the centre, Major von Rohr [Otto Christian Albrecht Ludwig von Rohr], having rallied and reformed his infantry, rushed into the village of Gagelberg with two battalions (other sources say three) and captured it,[17] but the enemy, setting up a battery on the windmill hill, engaged the advancing troops with canister, forced them to abandon the village and pursued them with two battalions, which, however, soon turned to their right towards Grützdorf. Three squadrons were also sent there with several guns on Girard's orders, in order to hold off the Cossacks and Marwitz's skirmishers. At this moment, second battalion 4. *Kurmärkische Landwehr* left the Belzig woods and moved towards Hagelberg, but halted when they encountered the two battalions sent there by Girard. Thereafter, several hundred skirmishers drove these [French] battalions out of the scrub around Grützdorf and into the open, whereupon the French, in a deep ravine surrounded on all sides by Prussian infantry, laid down

---

15 Wagner, I, 102; Beitzke, II, 280-281; Förster, I, 784.
16 According to Wagner (I, 103), two guns were sent to support Marwitz.
17 Major von Rohr seized Hagelberg with second battalion 7. *Kurmärkische Landwehr* and fourth battalion 6. *Kurmärkische Landwehr* who had fled during the attack on the woods. Richter *Geschichte des Deutschen Freiheitskrieges vom Jahre 1813 bis zum Jahre 1815*, I, 428-429.

their weapons, numbering 33 officers and 1,320 lower ranks.[18] The success of this attack was facilitated by Adjutant General Chernyshev, who charged at the enemy cavalry with two Cossack regiments and completely scattered three squadrons and some of their infantry, taking 500 prisoners and one gun.[19]

The defeat of Girard's right wing created confusion among the other French units and forced him to take measures for a further retreat. General Hirschfeld, for his part, concerned with the correct alignment of his infantry for an attack en echelon, hesitated, and the enemy might have been able to evade further combat had the inexperienced but courageous Prussian troops not gone into action without orders. The precedent was set by the first battalion of *4. Kurmärkische Landwehr* under Major Grolman [Wilhelm Heinrich von Grolman], who charged at the enemy without firing a shot. Following this, the fourth battalion of *1. Reserve Infanterie*, under Major Rembow, went on the attack. Marwitz's brigade (three battalions) and *3. Kurmärkische Landwehr Kavallerie* followed them. The enemy engaged the advancing troops with musket fire but after the heavy rain, many weapons misfired and therefore the matter was decided with bayonets and musket butts. Grolman's and Rembow's battalions took the high ground at Hagelberg. The former broke into the village behind the enemy, while the latter consolidated on the high ground. Major Zschüssen captured two guns with the first battalion of *3. Kurmärkische Landwehr* and, trapping one of the battalions of the French *19e Ligne* against a masonry wall, laid them low for the most part with musket butts. Another battalion of this same *19e Ligne* was almost completely wiped out or captured by the fourth battalion of *3. Kurmärkische Landwehr*, under the command of Major Schönholz. The entire Prussian line moved forwards towards Hagelberg, partly from the direction of Lübnitz, partly from Belzig wood. The French, attacked from the front and outflanked, defended themselves stubbornly in the village, where they lost about 4,000 men in close-quarter combat. Girard himself was severely wounded.[20] The enemy tried to check the Coalition advance, initially at Klein Glien, and then at Groß Glien, but being unable to hold on to these positions, they retreated in two columns, towards Magdeburg and Wittenberg. The Cossacks pursued them until nightfall and captured several hundred more prisoners. Overall, the losses to Girard's detachment in the action at Hagelberg reached more than 4,000 men killed and some 5,000 prisoners; seven guns, 20 ammunition caissons and the entire train went to the victors. The Prussian force took between 70 and 80 officers and more than 3,000 lower ranks prisoner and captured six guns and 17 ammunition caissons, while Chernyshev's Cossacks took 60 officers, 1,700 lower ranks, one gun and three ammunition caissons. Hirschfeld's force lost a total of 39 officers and about 1,700 lower ranks.[21]

---

18   Wagner, I, 105; Richter, I, 429-430. Among those who particularly distinguished themselves here was *Leutnant* Hergass.
19   Plotho, II, 154; Wagner, I, 105-106; Beitzke, II, 282.
20   Wagner, I, 106-107; Richter, I, 430; Beitzke, II, 282-283.
21   Adjutant General Wintzingerode's report to Emperor Alexander dated 22 August (3 September), Archive of the M.T.D. No. 29,182; Log of outgoing documents, No. 1,301; The Crown Prince of Sweden's dispatch on military operations, No. 3, dated 28 August new style;

Barely a third of the men from Girard's entire detachment returned to the Elbe, with 15 guns.

Davout's offensive against the Army of the North had no effect on the course of hostilities.

The number of troops in the French *13e Corps*, commanded by Marshal Davout, ranged from 27,000 to 30,000 men, while the number of troops in the Danish contingent assigned to assist the French on the lower Elbe ranged from 10,000 to 12,000: therefore, Davout had in total some 40,000 men at his disposal. Having detached around 12,000 men to garrison Hamburg, the marshal could go into the field with a 27,000 strong corps.[22] Facing him stood the combined corps under Graf Wallmoden, consisting of 22,500 men with 53 guns.[23] Thus, the French force had superiority in numbers. In addition, Wallmoden's situation was unfavourable in that his corps contained troops of a very multi-national nature: Tettenborn's Cossacks, the Russo-German Legion under Arentschildt [Wilhelm Daniel von Arentschildt], the Prussian partisan detachments under Lützow [Ludwig Adolf Wilhelm von Lützow] and Reiche [Ludwig von Reiche], two Mecklenburg detachments under Vegesack [Eberhard Ernst Gotthard von Vegesack] and the Erbprinz zu Mecklenburg-Schwerin [Friedrich Ludwig zu Mecklenburg-Schwerin], Engelbrechten's Swedish-Pomeranian force [Herman Fredrik Christian von Engelbrechten], the *Hanseatische Legion/Bürgergarde* and King's German Legion [Hanoverian] troops under Dörnberg and a detachment of British troops. The assistance of Engelbrechten's division, which consisted of more than 4,000 men, could not be counted upon because, in the event of a retreat by the corps, its mission was to withdraw to Stralsund, while the rest of Wallmoden's force were to head for Berlin. The tactical training and equipment of the troops were most unsatisfactory: they had neither workshops nor mobile hospitals, no general staff and no logistics department. Graf Wallmoden had received instructions from the Crown Prince: to limit himself to observation, and in the event of an attack by superior enemy numbers, to withdraw the force in the indicated directions.[24]

The river Stecknitz separated the Coalition from the French and would serve as Graf Wallmoden's first line of defence. This river, which has its source near Lübeck and flows into the Elbe at Lauenburg, is connected via a canal with the river Trave, flowing into the Baltic, therefore serving as a link between this sea and the Elbe.

Wagner, I, 108; Richter, I, 431; Beitzke, II, 284. For details of Plotho's and Vaudoncourt's accounts of losses from this action, see Appendix IX at the end of this chapter.

22 Beitzke, II, 285-286. For a breakdown of these forces, see Appendix X at the end of this chapter.
23 Wallmoden's combined corps consisted of: 16,000 infantry, 5,500 cavalry and 1,000 artillerymen. Richter, I, 464; See also Vol. 1 of this work, Chapter 20, Appendix XXXIII. Plotho (II, *Beilagen*, 63) shows: 19,635 infantrymen; 3,850 cavalrymen; 1,350 Cossacks; 561 artillerymen, for a total of 25,396 men. In the *Oestereichische Militärische Zeitschrift, 1827*, IV, it shows: 18,000 infantrymen; 6,400 cavalrymen; 1,351 artillerymen, for a total of 25,751 men with 60 guns, of which only 36 were fully equipped for operatons. Bernhardi (*Denkwürdigkeiten aus dem Leben Carl Friedrich Grafen von Toll*, III, 519) shows: 17,772 infantrymen; 3,880 cavalrymen; 1,415 Cossacks; 1,500 artillerymen, for a total of 24,567 men with 60 guns.
24 Richter, I, 464; Beitzke, II, 286.

The defensive line along the Stecknitz, stretching for some nine *Meilen* (about 60 *versts*), constituted a barrier over which it was possible to cross only at locations in Lauenburg, Mölln [12½ miles north-east of Schwarzenbek], Krummesse [seven miles south of Lübeck], and so on. A second defensive line between Zarrentin [eight miles west of Wittenburg] and Lübeck is formed by the Ratzeburger See and Schallsee. Further to the east the ground is completely open over a vast area.

Because the most convenient crossing over the Stecknitz was located at Lauenburg, the Coalition considered it essential to build three entrenchments on the high ground forwards of this town but, due to lack of time, their construction had not been completed. All the other bridges had been dismantled. The defensive line from Mölln to Lauenburg was guarded by the forward detachment of Wallmoden's corps, namely four Cossack regiments and the volunteer detachment under Major Lützow, some 2,000 infantry (other sources give 3,000) and about 2,000 cavalry in total, under the overall command of General Tettenborn. Lützow's infantry, with three two-pounder cannon, which constituted the entire artillery of the vanguard, occupied Lauenburg and the entrenchments. One of the Cossack regiments was stationed behind Mölln. The rest of Wallmoden's force was deployed as follows: the Swedish-Pomeranian force at Grevesmühlen; the Russo-German Legion between Schwerin and Wittenburg; most of the King's German Legion and *Hanseatische Legion/ Bürgergarde* were at Grabow; Dörnberg's cavalry were at Zarrentin in order to support the vanguard, while Graf Kielmansegg [Friedrich Otto Gebhard von Kielmansegg] was monitoring the sector between Boizenburg and Dömitz with a battalion of Hanoverian jägers [*Kielmannseggeschen Jäger*] and five squadrons of hussars. Wallmoden's headquarters were at Hagenow [7½ miles south-east of Wittenburg].[25]

Although the force composition of Wallmoden's corps, due to its diversity, presented significant difficulties and although liaison between its various units sometimes resembled the pandemonium, of the Tower of Babel, then at least the composition of the vanguard was completely consistent with its mission – to monitor the enemy and delay, where possible, the advance of their superior forces. The Cossacks, were literally the eyes of the corps and vigilantly observed every movement by the French, while Lützow's detachment were the concept incarnate of the rising of Europe against its common oppressor. Soldiers served in this detachment from all the German *Länder*, from the distant Tyrol, from those subject to Napoleon, like Saxony, Westphalia and Holland, and even from Spain. All classes were represented in the *schwarzen Schaar*: The Prinz von Carolath, Graf Hardenberg, Steffens [Heinrich Steffens], Dr. Jahn [Johann Friedrich Ludwig Christoph Jahn] and Theodor Körner served in it and, under cover of the deepest secrecy, several women even fought in the ranks of the defenders of their fatherland.[26]

Davout began operations immediately after the ending of the armistice. On 5 (17) August, the French, having crossed the demarcation line, moved towards Mölln and Lauenburg in two columns. Each of them had about 3,000 men with six guns. The Cossack regiment stationed in Mölln was taken by surprise, but retreated with

---

25 Sporschill, *Die große Chronik*, I, 599; Förster, I, 837.
26 Richter, I, 466-467.

minor losses. The action at Lauenburg was much more stubborn. The unfinished fortifications located there were defended by two battalions from Lützow's group and Riedl's Tyrolean sharpshooters [Jakob Riedl] with one Cossack regiment. Due to a lack of officers, both battalions were commanded by *Leutnant* Heyde [Detloff Gustav Friedrich Wilhelm von der Heyde], while the guns, located singly in each of the flèches, were commanded by *Feuerwerker* Gärtner. Since none of the crew knew how to lay the guns, Gärtner had to run from one fortification to another. The deep ditch in front of the earthworks served as cover for the skirmisher screen. The French, having occupied the forest on the opposing high ground, emerged from there in significant strength with four guns, but did not assault the Coalition force, rather positioning themselves in front of the forest to face them. Lützow's jägers, losing patience with the enemy inaction, abandoned their positions and boldly advanced to engage them. Two guns attached themselves to support the attack. The French fell back into the forest, but engaged the jägers from there with heavy canister and musket fire and forced them to retreat to the fortifications.

The following day, 6 (18) August, the enemy again attacked Lützow's positions with five battalions and three guns. Yet despite the small calibre of the Coalition artillery, Gärtner managed to knock out two French guns. The Prussian jägers and Tyrolean sharpshooters, having repelled the enemy, advanced and forced them to abandon the high ground they had been holding. A few hours later, Davout's force launched another attack with two fresh battalions, but were repulsed with casualties. On this day the Coalition lost 11 officers and 400 lower ranks. Just before dawn on 7 (19) August, the enemy attacked the fortifications and captured them. General Tettenborn, leaving *Rittmeister* Graf Bothmer with 50 Cossacks at the destroyed bridge near Büchen [nine miles north of Lauenburg] in order to detain the enemy at the crossing of the Stecknitz, retreated by short stages towards Hagenow and deployed near the village of Vellahn [ten miles south-west of Wittenburg], having retreated a distance of three *Meilen* (about 20 *versts*) over three days, by 9 (21) August. The Russo-German legion and Dörnberg's cavalry were also concentrated there by Graf Wallmoden, together with the vanguard of 6,000 infantry and 3,000 cavalry with 12 guns. At noon on 9 (21) August, Davout attacked Wallmoden at Camin [six miles south-west of Wittenburg] and Vellahn with 20,000 men, driving towards Wittenburg and Hagenow but all their attacks were repulsed by the Coalition force. Nevertheless, the superiority of enemy numbers forced Wallmoden to retreat to Hagenow the next day [22 August new style]. General Vegesack received orders to withdraw from Grevesmühlen towards Wismar.[27]

Davout did not pursue the Coalition corps but turning to the left, moved his headquarters to Wittenburg on 11 (23) August and to Schwerin on 12 (24) August, where he remained until 21 August (2 September). Loison's division [Louis Henri Loison], having been sent to Wismar, forced Vegesack to retreat towards Rostock.[28]

---

27 Plotho, II, 319-320; Förster, I, 837-840; *Oestereichische Militärische Zeitschrift, 1827*, IV, 22-25.
28 Vaudoncourt, 186-187. Having described the operations against Wallmoden by Davout in a very prejudicial manner, Vaudoncourt nevertheless drew the following conclusions: 'It would be difficult to explain the inaction of the latter, unless we admit that he had orders not to advance further until he received word that the duc de Reggio's expedition to Berlin

General Tettenborn, heading from Wartenburg [*sic*, Wittenburg?] to Warsow [ten miles south-west of Schwerin], positioned himself across the enemy line of communications and deprived Marshal Davout of the opportunity to receive news from Dresden or other locations on the Elbe, which forced the French to remain inactive at Schwerin, while Oudinot was defeated at Großbeeren, and Girard at Belzig.[29] Major Lützow, sent to cut the road from Gadebusch to Schwerin with 200 hussars and Cossacks and a small detachment of jägers and Tyrolean sharpshooters, deployed covertly in the forest near Rosenhagen [seven miles south-east of Gadebusch] on the night of 13 to 14 (25 to 26) August. At dawn, his outposts gave warning of the approach of an enemy convoy escorted by a strong infantry detachment. Major Lützow immediately gave orders for an attack: the Cossacks were ordered to charge into the convoy and halt it, while Lützow would attack the escort himself with the hussars. Some of the drivers cut their traces and left with their horses, leaving their carts as booty for the Cossacks, but the French infantry, sheltering in the ditches at the sides of the road, fired at Lützow's hussars, who, although they captured the convoy and dragged it away, nevertheless suffered quite significant casualties. The loss of Theodor Körner was particularly painful, 'the Tyrtaeus of Germany,' bard of the struggle for the independence of his fatherland. Being Lützow's aide de camp and closest comrade, he had charged at the French taking refuge in the forest and fell, mortally wounded by a bullet. He fell in the prime of his life, his memory living on in his songs, in the legends of his homeland, in the hearts of his friends. His remains were laid to rest at the village of Wöbbelin [4½ miles west of Neustadt], one *Meile* [five miles] north of Ludwigslust [4½ miles north of Grabow]. A small monument was erected over his grave, with a sword and lyre, shaded by an oak tree and with a short inscription.[30]

Graf Wallmoden, realising that Davout had no intention of moving decisively against him, wanted to move to Warin in order to link up with Vegesack's detachment and attack Loison, and on 21 August [2 September] he had already reached the outskirts of Crivitz [12½ miles east of Schwerin], but having learned of the French withdrawal, he proceeded behind them towards Schwerin. Indeed, Marshal Davout, having in all probability received news of the failures of Oudinot and Girard, had set off from Schwerin on 16 (28) August and withdrew to Ratzburg behind the lakes and swamps, while the Danish detachment fell back on Lübeck. The Coalition pursued the enemy with light troops and captured many prisoners. Wallmoden's corps redeployed across the sector from Grevesmühlen to Dömitz, limiting themselves to the monitoring of their powerful foe.[31]

---

had succeeded. It seems, however, that even in this case, he could have pushed General Wallmoden a little further and continued to threaten the movements of the Prince of Sweden...' (*Il serait difficile d'expliquer l'inaction de ce dernier, à moins qu'on n'admette qu'il avait l'ordre de n'avancer plus loin, que lorsqu'il aurait reçu la nouvelle que l'expédition du duc de Reggio sur Berlin avait réussi. Il parait cependant, que même dans ce cas, il aurait pu pousser le général Walmoden u peu plus loin et menacer davantage les mouvemens du prince de Suède...*)

29 Plotho, II, 320-321.
30 Richter, I, 471-472; Förster, I, 843-845. The final swan song of this national poet was the famous *Schwerdtlied*, written by him a few hours before his death.
31 Plotho, II, 322; Sporschill, I, 604-605.

Appendix VII

The composition of Hirschfeld's and Putlitz's detachments

Hirschfeld's detachment consisted of: *1. Reserve Infanterie* (four battalions); *3. Kurmärkische Landwehr* (four battalions; *4. Kurmärkische Landwehr* (three battalions); *6. Kurmärkische Landwehr* (four battalions); *7. Kurmärkische Landwehr* (three battalions); *3. Kurmärkische Landwehr Kavallerie*; *5. Kurmärkische Landwehr Kavallerie*; *6. Kurmärkische Landwehr Kavallerie* (each of four squadrons); ten Russian artillery pieces under Captain comte Chamborant, numbering: infantry – 378 officers and 11,200 lower ranks; cavalry – 42 officers and 880 lower ranks; artillerymen – six officers and 190 lower ranks, for a total of 426 officers and 12,270 lower ranks (Wagner, I, 31).

Putlitz's detachment consisted of: fourth battalion of *1. Reserve Infanterie*; *6. Kurmärkische Landwehr* (four battalions); fourth battalion of *3. Kurmärkische Landwehr*; one squadron each from *3. Kurmärkische Landwehr Kavallerie*; *5. Kurmärkische Landwehr*; *6. Kurmärkische Landwehr Kavallerie*; three Prussian artillery pieces, numbering: infantry – 120 officers and 3,700 lower ranks; cavalry – 10 officers and 220 lower ranks (artillerymen strength is not known), for a total of 130 officers and 3,920 lower ranks (Wagner, I, 93; Plotho, *Der Krieg in Deutschland und Frankreich in den Jahren 1813 und 1814*, II, 125).

Appendix VIII

Disposition issued by General Hirschfeld on 27 August [new style]

[The entire cavalry, with the exception of one squadron (von Bornstädt's), are to march to the left, under the direction of *Oberst* von Bismarck. The fusilier battalion is to lead, followed by the two musketeer battalions of *1. Reserve Infanterie*. The fusilier battalion is to march in the centre, the two musketeer battalions to the left, followed by 11 squadrons of cavalry, then ten artillery pieces commanded by Captain comte Chamborant. The skirmishers from the first battalion of *1. Reserve Infanterie* are to shield the artillery from the right; then the three battalions of Boguslawski's Brigade are to proceed, followed by the six battalions commanded by General von Putlitz, then the two battalions under *Oberstleutnant* von Marwitz.

The march is to be conducted in the greatest and most silent and calm manner possible, and any readying of muskets is to be forbidden on pain of six weeks close arrest, such that there will be no negligent discharge of muskets, all these battalions are to march off to the left. When ordered, the fusilier battalion is to advance, the two musketeer battalions turn in, the cavalry moves off behind the two musketeer battalions and the fusilier battalion at the trot, and advances as the ground dictates, and is immediately to seek to launch an assault on the enemy.

The artillery is to remain limbered and is to move as the ground dictates. The two battalions under von Liewen and von Schwerin are to march behind the artillery, are to turn in once they come level with the two musketeer battalions of *1. Reserve Infanterie*, and support their assault. Von Bornstädt's battalion and the other battalions are all to turn in once von Bornstädt's battalion reaches the artillery. The two battalions of *1. Reserve Infanterie* are to form up for the advance, followed at 200 paces by von Liewen and von Schwerin, and at the same time by von Bornstädt, von Held and the artillery, thereafter the battalions are to proceed *en echelon* at 150 paces. The enemy locations and the ground will indicate the correct time for the battalions to lower their muskets. The battalions under *Oberstleutnant* von Marwitz are to turn to face the enemy centre and remain in reserve.

Oberstleutnant von Reuss, with the battalions under von Ozerowsky, von Stutterheim, von Grollman and the squadron under von Bornstädt, are to march off to the right, taking a route close to the edge of the forest as far as

Steindorf, where *Oberstleutnant* von Reuss may position his artillery and his battalions to advantage in order to threaten the enemy flank and rear, especially if the enemy should retreat towards Glien and Wiesenburg.

Oberstleutnant von Reuss must not begin his attack until the cavalry has marched off. Further changes to the disposition, just as with the use of the ground, must be made in accordance with the situation, and I recommend calm and order. The attacks must not descend into a firefight, but must be decided by lowering the musket and using the bayonet, as our brave comrades did at Großbeeren. If, contrary to expectations, the attacks do not succeed, the retreat will be via Verlorenwasser [3½ miles north of Benken], Klein and Groß Briesen [6½ miles south-west of Golzow], to the area of Wollin [eight miles east of Ziesar] and Gräben [5½ miles north-east of Görzke], where Major von Diczelsky is stationed.

All are to march off by sections, the fusilier battalion is not to take part in the assault, but is to stay in the scrub, covering the left flank of the entire formation].

Die sämmtliche Kavallerie, mit Ausnahme einer Esquadron (der von Bornstädt), marschirt links ab, unter Führung des Obersten von Bismark. Das Füsilier-Bataillon hat die Tete, dann folgen die 2 Musquetier-Bataillons vom 1sten Reserve-Regiment. Das Füsilier-Bataillon aus der Mitte, die beiden Musquetier-Bataillons links abmarschirt, hierauf folgen die 11 Esquadrons Kavallerie, dann 10 Stück Geschützt unter dem Capitan Grafen Chamborant. Die Tirailleurs vom 1sten Bataillon des 1sten Reserve-Regiments decken rechter Hand die Artillerie; hierauf folgen die 3 Bataillons der Brigade von Boguslawsky, dann die 6 Bataillons unter Kommando des Generals von Puttlitz, darauf die 2 Bataillons des Oberst-Lieutenants von Marwitz.

Es wird in der grössten und möglichsten Stille und Ruhe der Marsch fortgestetzt, und alles Maddern an den Gesehren wird bei 6 Wochen strengem Arrest verboten, damit kein Gewehr losgehe, diese sämmtlichen Bataillons links abmarchirt. Wenn es befohlen wird, marschirt das Fusilier-Bataillon auf, die beiden Musquetier-Bataillons schwenken ein, die Kavallerie trabt hinter den beiden Musquetier und Füsilier-Bataillons weg, und marschirt dem Terrain gemäss auf, und sucht sofort einen Angriff auf den Feind zu machen.

Die Artillerie bleibt im Marsch, und fährt dem Terrain gemäss auf. Die beiden Bataillons von Liewen und von Schwerin marschiren hinter der Artillerie, schwenken, wenn sie gegen die beiden Musquetier-Bataillons des 1sten Reserve-Regiments kommen, ein, und unterstützen deren Attaque. Das Bataillon von Bornstädt und die übrigen Bataillons schwenken sämmtlich ein, wenn das Bataillon von Bornstädt an die Artillerie stösst. Die beiden Bataillons des 1sten Reserve-Regiments treten zum Avanciren an, auf 200 Schritt folgt von Liewen und von Schwerin, und zugleich von Bornstädt, von Held und die Artillerie, so folgen die Echellons, zu Bataillons auf 150 Schritt. Die Stellung des Feindes und das Terrain wird zeigen, wenn die Bataillons zur rechten Zeit das Gewehr fällen sollen. Die Bataillons unter dem Oberst-Lieutenant von Marwitz schwenken gegen die Mitte des Feindes ein und bleiben zur Reserve.

Der Oberstlieutenant von Reuss, mit den Bataillons von Ozerowsky, von Stutterheim, von Grollman, der Esquadron von Bornstädt, marschiren rechts ab, nehmen den Weg dicht am Saume des Waldes bis gegen Steinsdorf, woselbst der Oberstlieutenant von Reuss sein Geschütz und seine Bataillons vortheilhaft placiren kann, um des Feindes Flanke und Rücken zu beunruhigen, vorzüglich aber wenn des Feindes Rückzug nach Glien und Wiesenburg geschehen sollte.

Der Oberstlieutenant von Reuss muss mit seiner Attaque durchaus nicht eher anfangen, als bis die Kavallerie aumarschirt ist. Das Weitere und die vorkommenden Abänderungen in der Disposition, wie auch der Gebrauch des Terrains, müssen die Umstände geben, und empfehle ich Ruhe und Ordnung. Die Attaquen müssen sich nicht mit Schiessen abgeben, sondern das Gewehr fällen und mit dem Bajonett entschieden, wie unsere braven Kameraden bei Gross-Beeren; sollten wider Verhoffen die Attaquen nicht reüssiren, so ist der Rückzug über Verloner-Wasser, Klein und Gross-Briesen, nach der Gegend von Wallin und Gröben, wo der Major von Diczelsky stehet.

Es marschirt alles in Sections ab, das Füselier-Bataillon macht die Attaque nicht mit, sondern bleibt im Busch, und deckt die linke Flanke der ganzen Aufstellung. [original spelling has been retained].

Appendix IX

Differences between Plotho's and Vaudoncourt's accounts of the Battle of Hagelsberg

According to Plotho (II, 154), Hirschfeld's detachment took seven guns along with many ammunition caissons, more than 140 officers and 2,000 lower ranks, while Chernyshev's Cossacks took one gun, three ammunition caissons and more than 1,300 prisoners. In Plotho (II, 155), the casualties in Hirschfeld's detachment are given as: nine officers and 232 lower ranks killed; 30 officers and 748 lower ranks wounded.

Vaudoncourt wrote (*Histoire de la guerre soutenue par les Français en Allemagne*, 168):

> On 27 August, Hirschfeld's Prussian division, which had retraced its steps following the battle of Großbeeren, attacked General Girard. The action was to our advantage at first, but General Chernyshev having arrived during the fighting with a cavalry corps, attacked the French division from behind and the matter was decided against us. General Girard, wounded, was driven back towards Magdeburg, having lost a thousand prisoners and six cannon...

> *Le 27, la division prussienne de Hirschfeld qui après le combat de Gross-Beeren était revenue sur ses pas, attaqua le général Girard; le combat fut d'abord à notre avantage, mais le général Czerniszeff étant venu pendant l'action avec un corps de cavalerie, attaquer la division française à dos, l'affaire fut décidée contre nous. Le général Girard blessé, fut repoussé vers Magdebourg, ayant perdu un millier de prisonniers et six canons...*

Appendix X

Davout's corps and the Danish contingent at Hamburg

In the *Oestereichische Militärische Zeitschrift, 1827*, IV, 13-14, Davout's corps is shown as follows:

Formation	Men
13e Division – 14 battalions	8,000
40e Division – 14 battalions	9,000
50e Division – 12 battalions	9,000
28e Chasseurs à cheval & *Lanciers lituaniens*	1,600
Provisional/march regiments – dragoons & cuirassiers	1,250
Cuirassier brigade (dismounted)	2,400
Gendarmes & mounted *Douaniers*	758
Crews for nine batteries	500
Sailors, labour companies	1,300
Sappers, invalids and depot troops	1,000
Douaniers (on foot)	400

For a total of 32,358 infantrymen and 2,850 cavalrymen with 68 guns.

The Danish contingent consisted of: an infantry division of 10,000 men; 2,500 cavalry and 40 guns.

26

The offensive by the main Coalition Army from Bohemia into Saxony

---

The slowness of preparations for the campaign. – A breif description of the ground in the theatre of operations. – The composition of the columns of the Army of Bohemia. – The strength of Saint-Cyr's force left in Saxony by Napoleon. – The Coalition offensive, initially towards Leipzig, and then towards Dresden. – The factors that delayed the advance of the Army of Bohemia. – The arrival of the Coalition outside Dresden. – The conference regarding imminent operations. – Measures taken to protect the army's lines of communications to Bohemia.

The strength, composition and deployment of Saint-Cyr's force assigned to the defence of Dresden. – The deployment of the Coalition force on the eve of the Battle of Dresden.

The plan of operations drafted by Napoleon. – The movement of French forces towards Stolpen. – The news of Saint-Cyr's dangerous situation in Dresden. – The detachment of Vandamme to Königstein and advance of Napoleon's main force towards Dresden. – The inaction of the Coalition. – Schwarzenberg's dispositions for 14 (26) August. – Operations in front of Dresden on the morning of 14 (26) August.

Based on the operational plan drawn up in Trachenberg, it had been decided to advance the main Coalition army from Bohemia into Saxony and, leaving an observation corps at Dresden, send the other formations towards Leipzig. Never before, neither in ancient times nor in the modern era, has a commander-in-chief of a huge army begun to execute the difficult mission assigned to him with such ignorance of everything that he ought to have known. *Feldmarschall* Schwarzenberg [Karl Philipp Johann Nepomuk Joseph zu Schwarzenberg] had no intelligence – neither about the ground features of the area that was going to serve as the theatre of operations, nor about the fortifications of Dresden and the enemy forces gathered there, nor about the condition of the troops entrusted to him. The staff of the commander-in-chief were unconcerned about reconnoitring the roads along which they were supposed to move, or about supplying their own troops with clothing and footwear, or ensuring the supply of vital necessities. Despite the advantage of having informants on the ground hostile to the French, there was no accurate intelligence on the enemy, and therefore everything was done in the dark. Instead of beginning hostilities immediately after the end of the armistice on 5 (17) August, the Austrian government continued to pursue fruitless negotiations with Napoleon until 9 (21) August. It was not until 7 (19) August that a meeting regarding imminent operations was held at the headquarters located in Melnik [Mělník, 23 miles south-east of Leitmeritz]. An immediate invasion would prove impossible because the Russo-Prussian force under Barclay de Tolly had not yet had time to concentrate in the camp at Budin. It had been intended to set off on 9 (21) August, and thus four days were lost at the very opening of hostilities: this waste of time was all the more unforgivable because the enemy corps under Saint-Cyr [Laurent de Gouvion-Saint-Cyr], which was all that stood in the way of the Coalition operations, could not offer effective resistance.[1]

In order to invade Saxony, it was necessary to cross the Ore Mountains (Erzgebirge). This mountain range rises between 2,000 and 2,500 feet and runs parallel to the Eger river valley. Its slopes facing Bohemia are very steep and mostly wooded. The crest is relatively level, in the form of a plateau, upon which peaks rise here and there, and there are open clearings. The northern slopes of the range, towards the Saxon side, are very steep and are intersected by many river valleys, which present even more obstacles to the movement of troops than the steep slopes bordering Bohemia. These difficulties are increased by the lack of suitable routes. Even nowadays there are only a few very good roads through the Ore Mountains, while in 1813 there were only two highways: one from Teplitz to Dresden, on which there were some very steep gradients, and the other from Komotau [Chomutov] via Marienberg and Chemnitz to Leipzig. In addition, the following roads lay in this sector:[2]

1. From Aussig [Ústí nad Labem] via the Schneeberg [Sněžník] to Königstein and Pirna.
2. From Teplitz, the old road to Geiersburg [Kyšperk, two miles east of Graupen], Fürstenwalde, Breitenau, Göppersdorf to Dohna or from Fürstenwalde to Maxen and Lockwitz to Dresden.
3. From Teplitz to Zinnwald, Altenberg, Falkenhain and Dippoldiswalde to Dresden.
4. From Teplitz to Niklasberg and Frauenstein, to Freiberg.
5. From Dux [Duchcov] to Rechenberg and Freiberg.
6. From Brüx [Most] to Johnsdorf [Janov u Litvínova], Einsiedel and Sayda [6½ miles west of Rechenberg], to Freiberg.

---

1 Saint-Cyr, *Mémoires pour servir à l' histoire militaire sous le Directoire, le Consulat et l'Empire, Campagne de 1813, en Saxe*, 53-55. 'Had the enemy attacked on 18 August, our troops would have arrived on the positions they were intended to occupy at the same time as them, and the engagement would have taken place before any infantry soldier of *14e Corps* could fire a single shot.' (*Si l'ennemi avait attaqué le 18, nos troupes pouvaient arriver en même temps que lui sur les positions qu'elles étaient destinées à occuper, et la rencontre aurait eu lieu avant qu'aucun soldat d'infanterie du 14e corps eût brulé une seule amorce de sa vie*).
2 See Map No. 1: Map Showing Blücher's Operations Following the Expiry of the Armistice.

7. The main road that runs from the Leipzig highway to Marienberg and Freiberg.

The units of the main army had concentrated in the area between Teplitz and Kaaden [Kadaň, 23 miles south-west of Brüx] by 9 (21) August, and the next day, 10 (22) August, entered Saxony in four columns:

The first column, commanded by Count Wittgenstein, consisting of I Corps and II Corps, along the highway from Teplitz towards Dresden;

The second column, of Kleist's Prussian corps [Friedrich Emil Ferdinand Heinrich von Kleist], from Brüx via Johnsdorf and Sayda, in the direction of Freiberg; the formations under Count Wittgenstein and Kleist were followed by the Russo-Prussian reserves, namely: the Guard, Grenadier Corps and reserve cavalry;

The third column, commanded by the Erbprinz zu Hessen-Homburg [Friedrich Joseph Ludwig Carl August zu Hessen-Homburg], consisting of infantry divisions under: Moritz Liechtenstein [Moritz Joseph Johann Baptist von und zu Liechtenstein], Colloredo [Hieronymus Karl von Colloredo-Mansfeld], Civalart [Karl Leopold Civalart d'Happoncourt], Chasteler [(Johann) Gabriel Chasteler de Courcelles], Bianchi [(Vincenz Ferrer) Friedrich von Bianchi], and cavalry divisions under: Nostitz [Johann Nepomuk Nostitz-Rieneck] and Schneller [Andreas von Schneller], from Komotau to Marienberg, in the direction of Chemnitz; Emperor Alexander and *Feldmarschall* Schwarzenberg were with this column;

The fourth column, under *Feldmarschall* Gyulay [Ignác (Ignaz) Gyulay von Maros-Németh und Nádaska], consisting of infantry divisions under: Alois Liechtenstein [Alois Gonzaga Joseph von und zu Liechtenstein], Crenneville [Ludwig Karl Folliot de Crenneville(-Poutet)], Weissenwolf [Nikolaus Joseph Rochus von Weissenwolf], and Lederer's cavalry division [Ignaz Ludwig Paul von Lederer], from Kaaden to Preßnitz [Přísečnice] and on towards Marienberg; behind this column, under the command of Graf Klenau [Johann Joseph Cajetan von Klenau und Janowitz], came the *3. leichte Division* under Mesko [Joseph Mesko de Felsö-Kubiny] and the infantry divisions under Hohenlohe [Ludwig Alois Joachim zu Hohenlohe-Bartenstein] and Mayer [Anton Mayer von Heldensfeld]. In addition, a strong raiding detachment under *Oberst* Graf Mensdorff [Emmanuel von Mensdorff-Pouilly] of the Austrian service was sent from Eger [Cheb] towards Plauen.[3]

By the time the general offensive by the Army of Bohemia was launched, it was mistakenly believed in the headquarters that Napoleon was on the left bank of the Elbe in a strong position near Leipzig with the greater mass of his forces, having advanced his leading formations to the Bohemian mountains. Based on this erroneous assessment, the Coalition intended to push the right hand column to Königstein, Pirna and Dresden, in order to seize the closest Elbe crossings, while at the same time attacking Napoleon with the troops from the remaining three columns. Emperor Alexander, disagreeing with the Commander-in-Chief, believed that they should be expecting an enemy offensive from Lusatia into Bohemia, and therefore,

---

3   Hofmann, *Zur Geschichte des Feldzuges von 1813, Zweite Auflage*, 121-123; Karl Heinrich Aster, *Schilderung der Kriegsereignisse in und vor Dresden, vom 7. März bis 28. August 1813*, 114-117.

in order to guard the Elbe crossing at Melnik, the 2nd Grenadier Division and the Chuguev Uhlans were sent there and to that same end, the Russo-Prussian Guard remained in the Teplitz valley until 12 and 13 (24 to 25) August, and then moved slowly towards Saxony.[4] Count Wittgenstein received orders: during the advance towards Dresden, to leave strong observation detachments at Königstein and Pirna, and in the event of pressure from an enemy superior in numbers, to retreat to a position at Nollendorf [Nakléřov] and hold out there until the last possible moment, and then to retreat across the Eger river towards Budin.[5] In order to provide security for the main army from the direction of Zittau, Blücher was ordered to send VIII Corps under the comte de Saint-Priest to Bohemia, via Trautenau [Trutnov, 29 miles south of Hirschberg] and also Langéron's entire force, if they were not needed for the pursuit of the enemy.[6]

On 10 (22) August, all four columns of the Army of Bohemia crossed the Saxon border. Only Count Wittgenstein's right hand column came into contact with the enemy. The remaining formations did not encounter any obstacles on the march, but were forced to move along bad roads and suffered a shortage of rations.[7]

Napoleon, believing that the Coalition main force assembled in Bohemia would head into Lusatia along the right bank of the Elbe, had entrusted the defence of Dresden, and the left bank of the Elbe in general, to Marshal Gouvion-Saint-Cyr, with *14e Corps*, in which, according to the rolls, there were 26,000 men, yet in reality there were 22,000 conscripts who had not received any military training.[8] These troops were deployed in order to monitor the exits from Bohemia as follows: *42e Division* at Lilienstein opposite Königstein, in the fortifications on the right bank of the Elbe; *43e Division* on the Teplitz highway; *44e Division* near Borna [two miles north of Göppersdorf] on the old Teplitz road passing through Geiersburg; *45e Division* near Dippoldiswalde, on the road to Altenberg; a cavalry brigade of ten squadrons guarded the exits from the mountains in the sector from Marienberg to Hof. In addition, General Lhéritier's dragoon division [Samuel François Lhéritier de Chézelles], consisting of 18 squadrons attached to Saint-Cyr's corps, was divided between *42e Division* and *43e Division*.[9]

On 10 (22) August, the force under Claparède [Michel Marie Claparède] and Lhéritier retreated to Zehista and further beyond Dohna after being attacked in positions near Berggießhübel by Count Wittgenstein's vanguard, commanded

---

4   '… by taking up a central position between Zittau and Prague, Napoleon intends to separate the main army from the Army of Silesia…' Emperor Alexander I's letter to the Crown Prince of Sweden, dated 21 August, new style.
5   Extracted from the disposition for 22 August new style, signed by Prinz Schwarzenberg.
6   Barclay de Tolly's dispatch No. 576 to Blücher, dated 6 [18] August, from Elbekosteletz [Kostelec nad Labem].
7   Beitzke, *Geschichte der deutschen Freiheitskriege in den Jahren 1813 und 1814*, II, 19-20.
8   Such was the strength of *14e Corps*, according to Saint-Cyr. But Thiers believed that there were at least 28,000 or 29,000 men in this corps. *Histoire du Consulat et de l'Empire, XVI, Edit. de Brux.* 313-314.
9   Saint-Cyr, *Mémoires*, 63-64, 80.

by Major General Roth [Loggin Osipovich Roth].[10] General Mouton-Duvernet [Régis Barthélemy Mouton-Duvernet], who was stationed at Lilienstein with the *42e Division*, crossed to the left bank of the Elbe and moved past the Königstein fortress towards Krietzschwitz [three miles south-east of Pirna]. General Helffreich [Bogdan Borisovich Gelfreich 1st or Gotthard August von Helffreich] was detached against them, with five battalions and six guns from I Corps, two squadrons of Lubny Hussars and Ilovaisky 12th's Cossacks [Vasily Dmitrievich Ilovaisky].[11] After Mouton-Duvernet retreated back to Lilienstein, Helffreich's detachment were left at Cotta [2½ miles north of Berggießhübel] in order to monitor Königstein. Count Wittgenstein moved his headquarters to Pirna, and deployed the units of II Corps at Dohma [1½ miles] south of Zehista. The following day, 11 (23) August, Wittgenstein's force relocated to Großsedlitz [1½ miles east of Dohna], while Saint-Cyr recalled all his divisions to Dresden, except for the *42e Division* left at Lilienstein. On that same day, Kleist's corps were positioned at Reichenau, pushing their vanguard to Hennersdorf; the Austrians were at Rechenberg and Sayda; 1st Grenadier Division were at Nassau; 2nd Lifeguard Division were at Hermsdorf; the Russo-Prussian reserve cavalry were at Neuhausen [six miles south-west of Rechenberg]; 1st Lifeguard Division and the Prussian *Garde* were en route from Brüx to Teplitz. The headquarters of Emperor Alexander and Schwarzenberg were at Mittelsaida [11½ miles south of Freiberg]; that of the King of Prussia was at Brüx; the Austrian Kaiser's *Hoflager* was at Postelberg [Postoloprty, 5½ miles south of Wolepschitz] on the river Eger.[12] The Coalition, having no enemy contacts in the direction of Leipzig, began to doubt the veracity of their assessments. Fortunately, the day before, one of Marshal Saint-Cyr's aides-de-camp had been captured with dispatches, from which it was learned that Napoleon was on the Silesian border, and that Dresden was held by Saint-Cyr's corps alone. Under such circumstances, onward movement towards Leipzig was pointless. Instead, by taking advantage of Napoleon's absence, the Coalition could capture Dresden, the most important stronghold of the French army. Yet in the headquarters, any unanticipated change to the operational plan was greeted with disbelief and, in all likelihood, the Coalition army would have continued to move towards Leipzig, had accurate intelligence about the location of enemy forces not subsequently been received: on the night of 10 to 11 (22 to 23) August, two regiments of Westphalian hussars defected from the French camp at Reichenberg [Liberec] to the Austrian detachment under Graf Neipperg [Adam Albert von Neipperg]. They confirmed the previous intelligence on Napoleon's advance into Silesia, about the weakness of Poniatowski's force pushed forwards from Lusatia across the Bohemian border, and so forth. On the evening of

---

10 Major General Roth's vanguard consisted of: 20th Jägers, 25th Jägers, 26th Jägers, 34th Jägers (eight battalions in total; the Grodno Hussars; 3rd Battery Artillery Company, 34th Battery Artillery Company, 7th Horse Artillery Company under Major General Nikitin, and Rodionov 2nd's Cossacks. Count Wittgenstein's report on operations by his force, dated 10 (22) August.

11 The Tenginsk Infantry and Estland Infantry from 14th Division, with Grand Duchess Yekaterina Pavlovna's Battalion from 5th Division were under Major General Helffreich's command.

12 Plotho, *Der Krieg in Deutschland und Frankreich in den Jahren 1813 und 1814*, II, 33-34.

11 (23) August, this intelligence was quickly transmitted via couriers established in advance, through Theresienstadt [Terezín], to Mittelsaida, where the headquarters were located at the time. The Coalition monarchs met at Komotau on 12 (24) August in order to confer on a change of direction. Here it was eventually decided to march on Dresden.

Such a change of direction by a large army, with a huge number of guns and with immense baggage trains, presented extreme difficulties. In heading towards Leipzig, the troops, for the most part, had descended alongside the rivers, and as the valleys opened out they encountered ever fewer obstacles. In contrast, after changing the original direction, the columns, having made a rather sharp wheel to the right, had to cross the river valleys along very poor roads.[13] Wishing to avoid a too roundabout route, Schwarzenberg sent Kleist's corps and all the Austrian formations (second, third and fourth columns), with the exception of Klenau's corps and Mesko's division, towards Dippoldiswalde, a consequence of which was the congestion of troops, artillery and trains at this point, which, having converged onto a single road, could not arrive at Dresden simultaneously. The force under Klenau and his vanguard under Mesko, moving along a diversionary route to Freiberg, lagged behind all the others and arrived even later. On 13 (25) August, barely half the army had managed to assemble at Dresden, and all the other formations were still on the march, despite the advance over a distance of eight to ten *Meilen* (60 to 70 *versts*) being completed in four stages. Without any doubt, half of the Coalition army was more than enough to capture Dresden, for the defence of which Saint-Cyr had, together with the city garrison, less than 30,000 men. But (as has already been mentioned) the Coalition were completely unaware of the fortifications of Dresden and the number of its defenders. They did not even have good mapping of the surroundings of this city, and therefore in Schwarzenberg's headquarters they were planning from a poor quality, outdated Petrie map.[14]

At around noon, Emperor Alexander and the King of Prussia, with the Commander-in-Chief and their entire retinue, including the generals Moreau [Jean Victor Marie Moreau] and Jomini, arrived at the high ground near Räcknitz [two miles south of Dresden] in order to survey the city. Moreau, who had spent many years in exile from his fatherland, was deeply moved to see the French forces so famous for their achievements, saying: 'These are the soldiers whom I so often led to victory.' At four o'clock in the afternoon, Count Wittgenstein's corps (with the exception of Helffreich's detachment which remained near Königstein, and II Corps at Pirna) wheeled to face the Großer Garten. The Grodno Hussars and Sumy Hussars, marching at the head of the vanguard of the first Coalition column, attacked Lhéritier's cavalry, which was under Murat's personal command, near Reick [1½ miles north-west of Leuben], and drove the enemy back to the Großer Garten with the loss of three guns.[15] Kleist's corps was located at Strehlen [3½ miles north-west of Lockwitz] and Maxen. Two divisions from the third column, Moritz Liechtenstein's and Colloredo's, were stationed at Räcknitz. Chasteler's division

---

13 Beitzke, II, 20-21.
14 Beitzke, II, 22.
15 Saint-Cyr, 90; Hofmann, 128.

from the fourth column was facing Plauen. The remaining Austrian formations were located at Kleincarsdorf, Dippoldiswalde and Freiberg. The headquarters of Emperor Alexander and *Feldmarschall* Schwarzenberg were at Nöthnitz. That of the King of Prussia was at Zehista. The Austrian Kaiser's was at Teplitz.[16]

As Emperor Alexander was surveying Dresden, General Jomini proposed taking advantage of the weakness of the enemy force and storming the city. Moreau expressed doubts about the success of an assault and said: 'Sire! We would sacrifice 20,000 men and get our noses bloodied. We must not demoralise our troops.'[17] In Toll's opinion [Karl Fëdorovich Tol or Karl Wilhelm von Toll], it was vital to take a central defensive position, from where the Coalition could block enemy attacks on both Franconia and Bohemia. It should be noted that even earlier, Toll had advised not approaching Dresden, rather to halt at Dippoldiswalde. Emperor Alexander remained undecided for some time, but, eventually, having been convinced by the arguments of Moreau and Toll, he not only expressed his views opposing an immediate assault on Dresden, but also would not agree to such an attempt at all. Schwarzenberg considered it better to storm the city, but, as a sophisticated courtier, he accepted the opinion of the Tsar. As the meeting continued, night fell. The Commander-in-Chief, having encountered strong opposition to his views, but not abandoning his proposed assault, postponed it for almost 24 hours.[18] Since the delay to the decisive offensive had very harmful consequences, no one wanted to take responsibility for it before the court of public opinion: the Russians and Prussians blamed Schwarzenberg for this. The Austrians blamed Barclay de Tolly. It is possible that the cautious Barclay had actually decided to storm the fortified city, being completely unaware of the resources at the enemy's disposal, due to the unforgivable negligence of the Commander-in-Chief. But eventually the darkness in which the headquarters had been stumbling, little by little began to dissipate. One of the Prussian volunteers was sent into Dresden disguised as a peasant and, having safely returned, reported that five lunettes had been built in front of the Altstadt and that the city was occupied by just 20,000 French and a small detachment of multi-national troops.[19] But this news did not galvanise the Coalition into increased activity. All their attention was focused on protecting the army from an attack in the back from the direction of Königstein, where the enemy had a fortified crossing point. It has already been mentioned that General Helffreich had been sent there to monitor it directly, with five battalions from I Corps, two squadrons of Lubny Hussars, one Cossack regiment and six guns. For their support, if necessary, II Corps under Prinz Eugen von Württemberg [Friedrich Eugen Karl Paul Ludwig von Württemberg] was at Cotta:[20] thus, Count Wittgenstein had only the 5th Division under Major General Mezentsov [Vladimir Petrovich Mezentsov] from I Corps, the jäger brigade from 14th Division and Major General Melissino's cavalry [Alexey Petrovich Melissino], for a total of 10,000 men.[21]

---

16 Hofmann, 128-129; Plotho, II, 41.
17 'Sire! Nous sacrifierons vingt mille hommes et nous nous casserons le nez. Ji ne faut pas démoraliser nos trouppes.'
18 Alexander Andreevich Shcherbinin's notes from his service in the headquarters of the Army of Bohemia.
19 Beitzke, II, 37.
20 Hofmann, 143.
21 Plotho, II, 39-40.

Saint-Cyr had the following troops for the defence of Dresden: three French divisions, numbering 15,000 to 20,000 men; three Westphalian regiments numbering 4,500 men with eight guns, and several thousand allied troops (Dutch, Polish, Saxon and Badenese). Saint-Cyr's corps consisted of conscripts, some of whom had not reached legal age. It goes without saying that these soldiers, not only lacking military experience, but also not having received proper combat training, did not know how to use the ground, and therefore lost many men in combat to no purpose. But although their training and physical strength were lacking, they often compensated for this deficit with natural dexterity, a sense of national pride and devotion to their Emperor, which was passed down the generations from veteran *grognards* to the young soldiers.[22]

The troops defending Dresden were deployed as follows: Claparède's *43e Division* in the sector from the left bank of the Elbe to the Freiberger Tor, holding the Großer Garten with four battalions; Berthezène's *44e Division* [Pierre Berthezène] were to defend the Pirnaische Vorstadt [one mile east of Dresden], while Razout's *45e Division* [Louis-Nicolas de Razout] were to defend Friedrichstadt [1½ miles northwest of Dresden]. The fortifications erected forwards of Dresden were occupied as follows: No. I at the Ziegelschlag, 60 infantrymen with one gun; No. II (also known as No. 3) at the Pirnaischer Schlag, 120 men with three guns; No. III (also known as No. 5) at the Moczinskis Garten, 120 men with four guns; No. IV (also known as No. 7), forwards of the Falkenschlag, 120 men with three guns; No. V (also known as No. 8), 120 men with three guns.[23] The gap between lunette No. I and the bank of the Elbe was blocked by a palisade. The protruding corner of the Moczinskis Garten was fortified in a similar manner. The suburbs, surrounded by masonry walls, would serve as redoubts for the outlying fortifications. Forwards of the Prinz Antons Garten between the Pirnaischer Schlag and the Dohnaischer Schlag, a ditch had been dug along the wall. All the entrances were barricaded with palisades. Abatis had been arranged in the Großer Garten. The Hopfgarten manor, which consisted of sturdy buildings, was surrounded by a masonry wall. The weakest part of the city, besides Friedrichstadt, which had not been put into any kind of defensive state, was the sector between the Moczinskis Garten and the Falkenschlag: following the destruction of redoubts No. III and No. IV (No. 5 and No. 7), nothing could have prevented the advance of a battery of 20 heavy guns and, having made a breach in the city wall, rushed troops there, which, while waiting for the best moment for the assault, could be conveniently concealed in the vicinity of the assault point.[24]

---

22 Saint-Cyr's force consisted of: the French *42e Division* under General Mouton-Duvernet (in Königstein), *43e Division* under General Claparède, *44e Division* under General Berthezène, *45e Division* under General Razout; cavalry under General Milhaud of: two squadrons of *7e chevau-légers lanciers*, four squadrons of *2e chasseurs à cheval d'Italie*, four squadrons of *14e hussards*, part of Lhéritier's division; a Westphalian contingent of: three infantry regiments commanded by *Oberst* Hille, eight guns from *Oberst* Pfuel's battery; a Saxon contingent of: the Leibgrenadiergarde Bataillon, *Artillerieschule, Artillerie und Ingenieur Depot, Sappeure Abteilung*. There is no information on the composition of other allied contingents. Aster, 100-111, 123.
23 The number of guns and infantry defending the Dresden fortifications were subsequently increased.
24 Wagner *Plane der Schlachten und Treffen, welche von der preussischen Armee in den Feldzügen der Jahre 1813, 14 und 15 geliefert worden, Anhang*, 7-8.

During the night of 13 to 14 (25 to 26) August, the Coalition army was deployed at Dresden as follows: Count Wittgenstein's force, numbering 10,000 men, was on the right from Striesen to Gruna; their corps headquarters were at Dobritz; Kleist's force, 35,000 men in total, was at Leubnitz and Maxen; their corps headquarters were at Torna; Graf Colloredo was behind Räcknitz with his division and that of Moritz Liechtenstein, numbering 15,000 men; Chasteler's division of 10,000 men was on the high ground facing Plauen; Bianchi's division and Schneller's cavalry, numbering some 13,000 men, were at Kleincarsdorf; Mesko's division, 4,000 men, were en route from Tharandt to Löbtau. Overall, there were 87,000 men concentrated at Dresden. The remaining Austrian troops (Crenneville's, Civalart's, Alois Liechtenstein's and Weissenwolf's infantry divisions, and the cavalry divisions under Nostitz and Lederer) and the Russian reserves (2nd Lifeguard Division, 1st Grenadier Division, Lifeguard Light Cavalry Division and two cuirassier divisions), numbering some 80,000 men, were located at Dippoldiswalde. Klenau's corps, numbering 22,000 men, were approaching Freiberg. The Prussian *Garde-Brigade* were stationed at Kulm. The headquarters were deployed as follows: Emperor Alexander's and *Feldmarschall* Prinz Schwarzenberg's at Nöthnitz; the King of Prussia's at Zehista; Barclay de Tolly's at Leubnitz; the Austrian Kaiser's *Hoflager* at Teplitz. A raiding detachment under Major General Prince Kudashev [Nikolai Danilovich Kudashev] was sent to reconnoitre the enemy and to establish communications with the Army of the North under the Crown Prince of Sweden, who had been tasked with crossing the Elbe downstream of Dresden, and invading Lusatia.[25]

Despite the assault on the city being postponed, there was constant skirmishing between the forward elements of both sides, stationed within sight of one another, and the cannonade did not stop. Meanwhile, as the Coalition were wasting time, Napoleon was taking steps in order to drive them from Dresden.

It has already been stated in our description of operations in Silesia before the battle on the Katzbach that, having learned of the offensive by the Army of Bohemia into Saxony, Napoleon entrusted the pursuit of the retreating Blücher to Macdonald, while he set off for Saxony himself on 11 (23) August, ordering his reserves and Marmont's corps to head there by forced marches. Upon arrival in Görlitz on the evening of that same day, Napoleon received intelligence on the advance of significant enemy forces towards Dresden, and although at that time the Coalition were still moving the bulk of their force towards Leipzig, it was known that the right hand column of their army was headed along the highway through Peterswald [Petrovice u Chabařovic]. Napoleon would be able to move to Dresden with units coming from Silesia and those left in Lusatia, cross the Elbe there and push the Coalition back into the mountains. Yet with his customary faith in his military intuition, he preferred to exploit the advantages on his side in order to inflict a decisive blow on his enemies. By possessing a bridge on the Elbe connecting Lilienstein to Königstein, he intended crossing at this location, cutting the Teplitz highway with an 100,000 strong army and, getting behind the Coalition, push them back against the Elbe, across which they did not hold a single crossing point. Yet in order for this brilliant concept to

---

25 Plan of the battle of Dresden, 14 (26) August, signed by General Harting, Archive of the M.T.D. No. 20,011; Plotho, II, 40-41; Hofmann, 136-137.

succeed, it was vital that the Coalition were denied the chance to capture Dresden and the bridges located there. On the morning of 12 (24) August, having arrived in Bautzen, Napoleon learned from dispatches received from Saint-Cyr that the threat to Dresden was increasing hourly and that French forces were being pushed back towards the city. Thereafter, intelligence was received on the movement of the Coalition headquarters from Mittelsaida to Reichstädt, near Dippoldiswalde, from which it could be concluded that the Army of Bohemia was heading for Dresden. This convinced Napoleon of his original intention – to march to Pirna. Vandamme received orders to move there with his corps, reinforced to over 40,000 men.[26] The units marching from Silesia, having covered six *Meilen* (more than 40 *versts*) to Görlitz the day before, made a march of 5½ *Meilen* (about 40 *versts*) to Bautzen on 12 (24) August, and four *Meilen* (30 *versts*) to Stolpen on 13 (25) August, where on that same day Victor's corps arrived from Zittau and Napoleon arrived himself. The movement from the river Bober to Stolpen was very tiring for the troops. The artillery and cavalry moved along the main road, the infantry made their way along the edges of the fields. While on the short stage from Königstein, Napoleon gave his troops a few hours of rest. Vandamme received orders to cross on the evening of 13 (25) August at Königstein. The other corps were to follow: thus, some 120,000 men were preparing to get behind the Coalition army stationed near Dresden.[27]

Because it was absolutely essential for the success of Napoleon's planned operations that Saint-Cyr remain in Dresden at least until 16 (28) August, and wanting to have correct information on the situation of his corps, upon his departure from Bautzen Napoleon sent his *officier d'ordonnance* Gourgaud [Gaspard Gourgaud] to Dresden, telling him:

> I shall be on the march to Pirna tomorrow, but I shall halt in Stolpen – ride to Dresden; be there tonight. Visit Durosnel [Antoine Jean Auguste Durosnel], the duc de Bassano [Hugues-Bernard Maret], Marshal Saint-Cyr, the King of Naples that night and reassure them all. See the Saxon minister Gersdorff [Karl Friedrich Wilhelm von Gersdorff] also. Tell him that you cannot present yourself to the King because you are leaving immediately but that tomorrow I will be able to lead 40,000 men to Dresden, and that I have taken measures to bring up the entire army. At dawn, you are to go with the chief of engineers, go around the redoubts and the city perimeter, and after examining everything carefully, return to me as quickly as possible. I want to know the actual state of affairs and Marshal Saint-Cyr's and the duc de Bassano's thoughts on things. Go!

Upon arriving in Stolpen, Napoleon received intelligence that increased his anxiety: 'Dresden could fall to the enemy at any minute.' Such were the content of the dispatches sent. At the same time, Oudinot's report on the defeat of his army at Großbeeren was delivered. This unexpected setback somewhat shook Napoleon's resolute plans. At 11 o'clock at night Gourgaud arrived. In his own words:

---

26 For details of Vandamme's force, see Appendix XI at the end of this chapter.
27 Thiers, XVI, 315-319.

in Dresden they hoped only for the arrival of the Emperor. The enemy had already attempted to attack the fortifications, and if this assault had been more determined, they would have captured the city. Fortunately, their columns were halted, but enemy troops are constraining Saint-Cyr's deployment, throughout the entire sector from Gruna to Plauen. Upon the arrival of Klenau's corps, Dresden will be completely surrounded and its fate will be sealed. Saint-Cyr's situation is very grave. The abandonment of the Großer Garten has already been proposed.

Napoleon commented: 'Yet, in the end, what does the duc de Bassano think?'
'Sire! He replied that the city cannot hold out for longer than 24 hours.'
'And you?'
'From everything I have seen, I am convinced that Dresden will fall tomorrow if Your Majesty does not arrive there.'
'You are forcing me to change my course of action,' said Napoleon. 'I am absolutely sure of the truth of your words.'
Gourgaud replied, 'Sire! I would swear it on my life.'[28]
Gourgaud's report, made under the influence of the terror imbued in Dresden by the appearance of the Coalition army, indeed prompted Napoleon to abandon his intended plan, the execution of which would have had the most decisive consequences. Instead of marching to Königstein with the entire army threatening the enemy lines of communications, he intended to go to Dresden, to the aid of his ally, the King of Saxony, while operations in the rear of Schwarzenberg's force would be left to Vandamme, who, having cut the Pinsk highway, would be able to drive the Coalition onto awkward routes and block their retreat into Bohemia.[29] Knowing the passionate, courageous character of Vandamme, Napoleon considered it necessary to give him, as an adviser and director, the prudent, comprehensively educated engineer, General Haxo [François Nicolas Benoît Haxo]. In sending him, Napoleon ordered him to tell Vandamme to advance from Pirna to Berggießhübel, position himself on the high ground at Peterswald, hold all the mountain defiles and await the outcome of the battle of Dresden, furthermore, that it was left to him to complete the victory, maintaining his composure and paying no heed to the size of the crowds (*cohue*) of fleeing enemy. Napoleon concluded his instructions by saying: 'Explain my concept to Vandamme precisely and tell him everything I expect from him. He will never have a better opportunity to earn a marshal's baton.'[30] Whereupon, Gourgaud was sent to Dresden once more, with instructions to encourage the defenders of the city and notify them of Napoleon's imminent arrival on the following morning. He was also ordered to send Teste's division [François Antoine Teste] to Dresden and to tell Lefebvre-Desnouettes that his cavalry must be at immediate readiness for onward movement. The *Vieille Garde* were also to march at dawn from Stolpen.

At dawn on 14 (26) August, Napoleon's formations set off along their respective routes towards Dresden. The *Garde* were in the lead; behind them came

---

28 Agathon Jean François Fain, *Manuscrit de 1813*, 256-259.
29 Thiers, XVI, 323-324.
30 Fain, II, 259-260.

Latour-Maubourg's cavalry, Victor's *2e Corps* and Kellermann's cavalry [François Étienne Kellermann]; Marmont's corps had also been directed towards Dresden along the Bautzen road. At about nine o'clock in the morning Napoleon, riding on horseback towards Dresden himself, ordered the batteries placed on the high ground on the near bank of the Elbe to be strengthened and to fire on the approaches to Saint-Cyr's left flank units. Then, having entered the city together with Latour-Maubourg's cuirassiers, Napoleon went to King Friedrich August, accompanied by cheers from the troops and the population. Even the wounded crowded the streets on crutches, greeting him with shouts of: *vive l'empereur*! After a short meeting with the King of Saxony, Napoleon went to the suburbs through the Pillnitz gate [Rampischer Schlag] and, having reached its outer limits, walked or rode around the line of fortifications to the Freiberger Schlag, and then returned to the main bridge and remained there for several hours, greeting the troops and pointing out the exits behind which they were to position themselves in anticipation of debouching from the city.[31]

At this time as Napoleon, with his usual efficiency, was taking steps to defend Dresden, the Coalition, as before, not only remained inactive but had not yet even managed to decide on a course of action. It is true that the strength of the Army of Bohemia in the vicinity of Dresden had increased but, for the most part, the Coalition forces did not close up to the city before nightfall. Miloradovich had arrived at Dippoldiswalde just the day before, on 13 (25) August, with the 2nd Lifeguard Division, 1st Grenadier Division, Lifeguard Light Cavalry Division, 2nd Cuirassier Division and 3rd Cuirassier Division, while Grand Duke Konstantin Pavlovich had reached Glashütte with 1st Cuirassier Division. It was obvious that both the Russian reserves and the Austrian and Prussian troops who had arrived at Dippoldiswalde and Maxen that same day, could have joined the Coalition army stationed at Dresden in a timely manner the following morning. Yet instead, only part of the Austrian and Prussian force arrived in good time. Still others arrived in the evening, or at night, and even the next morning. The orders for the troops to march to Dresden were, in all likelihood, issued late. At the very least, there is no doubt that Klenau, who was supposed to arrive at Tharandt, had received orders to move there so late that he only managed to set off at four o'clock in the afternoon, and as he had to pass along extremely bad roads, having reached Grillenburg [4½ miles south-west of Tharandt] he was forced to camp for the night in the Tharandt forest.[32]

The disposition for operations on 14 (26) August, issued by the Commander-in-Chief, included the following instructions:

> Upon the arrival of Civalart's division and both divisions of the left wing, they are to ensure that the village of Löbtau and the environs of Schusterhaus all the way to the Elbe are cleared of enemy troops.

Thereafter, in order to assault the city, the troops will form up in five columns, namely:

---

31 Fain, II, 264-266; Thiers, XVI, 326-327.
32 Bernhardi, *Denkwürdigkeiten aus dem Leben Carl Friedrich Grafen von Toll*, 157-158.

First Column – under General Count Wittgenstein, is to hold the villages of Blasewitz and Striesen. This column, having been assigned to make a demonstration, is to advance as far as possible, attempting to exploit any favourable situation, and even, in the event of a great success, may break into the Dresden suburbs.[33]

Second Column – or that part of Kleist's corps which reached Strehlen yesterday, is to mount a demonstration attack on the Großer Garten and is to distract enemy attention (if the Großer Garten has, in the meantime, been seized by our troops, the demonstration is to proceed against the city).[34] The troops should be encouraged to break into the suburbs at any favourable opportunity.

Both of these columns are to advance their heavy artillery and bombard the city.

Third Column – Austrian *1. leichte Division*, is to advance as far as possible without needlessly losing men and is to protect the batteries positioned to bombard the city. This column is also to operate as a demonstration force, but is to take advantage of any favourable opportunity and may even seize the suburbs. During this advance there must be demonstrations against the Schloss Garten.[35] Colloredo's division are to support the attacking force, advancing in columns as far as the high ground forwards of Kaitz.

In order to bombard the city, four 12-pounder position batteries are to be placed between Plauen and Räcknitz.

Fourth Column – Austrian third reserve division, having occupied Plauen, is to shield the advance of the Fifth Column. Four 12-pounder position batteries are to be advanced in order to support the assault by the Fifth Column.

Fifth Column – Bianchi's division, having formed up in column on the site of their current location, are to occupy the village of Löbtau and clear the enemy from Schusterhaus to the Elbe. Schneller's division is to be attached to this column. As soon as this force has taken Löbtau, four 12-pounder position batteries are to be deployed to bombard Friedrichstadt.

Chasteler's grenadier division, having lined up in column, is located in reserve to support, if necessary, the force that is holding Plauen.

Nostitz's and Lederer's divisions are to be stationed in reserve between Coschütz and Kaitz, extending their right wing to the left of the latter village.

Overall, all troops must be ready for action.

One Cossack regiment is to head towards Bautzen. Another raiding detachment, commanded by Colonel Seslavin [Alexander Nikitich Seslavin], having crossed the Elbe at Briesnitz, is to raid towards Radeberg.

---

33 '... *und kann im glücklichsten Fall selbst in Vorstädte von Dresden eindringen.*'
34 '... *greift als Demonstration den Grossen Garten an...*'
35 There was no such garden at all; from this it may be concluded that the Commander-in-Chief did not have entirely accurate information about placenames around the city.

The bombardment of the city and the advance of the left wing are to begin at four o'clock in the afternoon precisely. The Sovereigns and the Commander-in-Chief (Prinz Schwarzenberg) will be located on the high ground between Plauen and Räcknitz.

From the headquarters at Nöthnitz, 25 August 1813.

Thus, orders were issued for a general attack on Dresden, but there was no mention of seizing the city. Every attack was limited to a demonstration, while the Commander-in-Chief had not seen to the actual assault, and did not even explain at which location the main attack was intended to be carried out. The Russian and Prussian forces were permitted to break into the suburbs, yet they remained completely unaware of their further missions. The Third Column under Graf Colloredo was ordered: to exploit every favourable opportunity, and 'may even seize the suburbs,' as if such success were the ultimate objective of the attack. The Fourth Column and Fifth Column were to limit themselves to occupying the villages and manor houses in the vicinity of the outer limits of the city suburbs. It was as if the Commander-in-Chief, being unable to give a clear account of his intentions himself, hoped to shake the enemy's resolve with a strong cannonade, push them back into the city, and then, depending on the circumstances, continue the offensive, or limit himself to the initial objectives. These indecisive orders were destined to neutralise the energy of unit commanders and have harmful consequences.

The enormous width of the front of the advancing force made it very difficult to control their operations: it being at least 15 *versts* from Blasewitz (on the Elbe upstream of Dresden) to Briesnitz (on the Elbe downstream of Dresden). In addition, the Coalition forces, being located on both sides of the rocky Plauenscher Grund (Weißeritz ravine), were divided into two parts, unable to support one another. It is true that the significant superiority of Coalition numbers facilitated independent operations by each of these individual formations, yet the measures taken by Schwarzenberg in this regard were also erroneous. Klenau's rather significant corps, advancing from Freiberg, had been assigned to support the formations located on the left side of the ravine and, had it gone directly along the Freiberg highway towards Dresden, it would have arrived there on 14 (26) August, or on the morning of 15 (27) August at the latest. But the Commander-in-Chief, completely unfamiliar with the lay of the land, sent Klenau's force to Tharandt along the Weißeritz valley, probably intending to bring this corps closer to the other columns on the march to Dresden. As a result, Klenau had to move along a very awkward route, which did not allow him to reach Dresden in a timely manner. Meanwhile, in anticipation of Klenau's arrival, Schwarzenberg left part of the force assigned to occupy the sector on the left side of the Plauenscher Grund on the right side and thereby weakened the left wing of the army.[36]

On the morning of 14 (26) August, fighting broke out between the advanced elements of both sides. At around five o'clock, Kleist's vanguard attacked the Großer Garten. At seven o'clock, the Austrians advanced, while at eight o'clock the Russians

---

36 Beitzke, II, 40-42.

THE OFFENSIVE BY THE MAIN COALITION ARMY FROM BOHEMIA INTO SAXONY   121

advanced to contact between the Großer Garten and the Elbe: thus, in anticipation of a general offensive, several actions broke out that had almost no coordination with each other.

The troops of the vanguard under General Zieten [Hans Ernst Karl von Zieten] moved into Strehlen at dawn, found this village clear of enemy and immediately attacked the Großer Garten. Behind them Pirch's *10. Brigade* [Georg Dubislav Ludwig von Pirch] were in reserve. The French, having occupied the palace in the middle of the garden, defended themselves very stubbornly, but were driven out of there. By eight o'clock in the morning, Prussian troops had captured the entire south-eastern part of the garden and thereby contributed to the success of Count Wittgenstein's attack. But all their efforts to seize the abatis erected in the western part of the garden were in vain, and at nine o'clock the order came to halt the offensive. Thereafter, lively fire from skirmishers continued until noon, supported by a cannonade, while the Prussian force stationed at Maxsen assembled (*9. Brigade, 12. Brigade* and the reserve cavalry). While in the afternoon, in anticipation of a general assault, the firing became less frequent and eventually died out altogether.[37]

The advance of Count Wittgenstein's small Russian corps was delayed by the need to take several manor houses by force forwards of the Pirnaische Vorstadt. Even more difficult for the Russians were operations by strong enemy batteries pushed forwards of the Ziegelschlag on both sides of the Hopfgarten manor, as well as those stationed on the far bank of the Elbe along the Bautzen road, which put the Russian batteries and the advancing columns under crossfire. All this notwithstanding, however, the men of Mezentsov's 5th Division resolutely attacked the manor, supported by the Sumy Hussars and Lubny Hussars, commanded by General Melissino. The bloody battle raged for several hours with varying success, but the Russians captured the Engelhardt manor and held on to it. On the left wing of Wittgenstein's force, adjacent to the Großer Garten, the men of the 25th Jägers and 26th Jägers, under Roth's command, took the north-eastern part of the gardens in combat and moved along the plain between the Großer Garten and the Pillnitz road. The French, having evacuated the manor houses, with the exception of Hopfgarten, and retreating to the Pirnaische Vorstadt, repelled all subsequent attacks by the Russian force. At around noon, Count Wittgenstein received orders to cease operations in anticipation of a general advance by the Coalition army.[38]

On the Austrian side, the entire morning was spent positioning the troops and artillery on the high ground at Räcknitz and facing Plauen. Only a few rounds were fired at lunettes No. III and No. IV. Behind Räcknitz was the *1. leichte Division* under Moritz Liechtenstein (two battalions and 12 squadrons with a horse artillery battery), and behind them, somewhat to the left, was the division under Colloredo (12 battalions with a 12-pounder battery). While opposite Plauen was Chasteler's reserve division (eight battalions with a battery).[39]

At 11 o'clock, Emperor Alexander arrived on the high ground behind Räcknitz from Nöthnitz. From this location the movements of French troops along the

---

37 Aster *Schilderung der Kriegsereignisse in und vor Dresden*, 175-178.
38 Aster 171-175.
39 Austrian batteries had six guns each.

Plan of the Battle of Dresden.

Legend to Map No. 6

Coalition Forces

A.A.	Count Wittgenstein's force
B.B.	Roth's vanguard
C.C.	Zieten's vanguard
D.D.	Pirch's 10. Brigade
E.E.	Jagow's 11. Brigade
F.F.	Prinz August's 12. Brigade
G.G.	Braun's reserve artillery
H.H.	Röder's reserve cavalry
I.I.	Klüx's 9. Brigade
K.K.	Moritz Liechtenstein's 1. leichte Division
L.L.	Colloredo's division
M.M.	Chasteler's division
N.N.	Mesko's division
O.O.	Greth's brigade
P.	Mumb's brigade
R.R.	Schneller's cavalry
S.S.	Weissenwolf's division
T.T.	Bianchi's division
X.	Lukov's advance
Y.	Melissino's advance
Z.	Vlastov's advance

French Forces

a.a.	Roguet's division
b.b.	Decouz's division
c.c.	Barrois' & Dumoustier's divisions
d.d.	Teste's force
e.e.	Latour-Maubourg's & Pajol's cavalry
f.f.	Doumerc's cavalry
g.g.	General Gros' attack

Bautzen road to Dresden were visible and the cannonade between Wittgenstein's batteries stationed on the left bank of the Elbe and the enemy's operating from the right bank could be heard. As at this point, the arrival of Napoleon with his reserves in Dresden was already known,[40] General Jomini advised a retreat to Dippoldiswalde and taking up strong positions there on the enemy line of communications, to accept a defensive battle, which, with the significant numerical superiority of the Coalition and with the terrain advantages of the position, presented a high probability of success. Meanwhile, the Prussian King and *Feldmarschall* Schwarzenberg, who had arrived at this meeting, insisted on the need to fight on. And indeed, it seemed quite strange, having got to Dresden with a huge army, to fall back without a fight. But, on the other hand, this course of action would be completely consistent with the general plan drawn up in Trachenberg: the Coalition, by avoiding a decisive denouement until their armies were close enough for mutual support, would put Napoleon in a more difficult situation than by entrusting the outcome of the war to the fortunes of battle. The enemy army, possessing many strongholds on the Elbe, had secure supplies of rations and, having been defeated, could always retain

---

40 The news of the arrival of the *Empereur des Français* in Dresden was brought to the Coalition by the spy Schneider, who was sent by Napoleon himself, hoping to delay the attack by the Coalition army and gain time until the arrival of the expected reinforcements. Ferdinand Lecomte, *Le général Jomini: sa vie et ses écrits*, 171.

the option to retreat to the far side of the river. In contrast, the Coalition army was already suffering from a shortage of vital supplies and, in the event of a lost battle, would have to retreat along awkward routes, through the Ore Mountains, to Bohemia. All these factors forced the Commander-in-Chief to hesitate with his intentions, and he even gave his word to the Coalition Sovereigns that he would cancel the dispositions for the assault on Dresden, but time was passing, and the troops never received new orders to replace the existing ones. In any case, if the *Feldmarschall* did not consider it beneficial to retreat without a fight, it would be necessary, at least, as General Jomini suggested, to concentrate the frontage for the assault on the sector to the right side of the Plauenscher Grund: by operating in this way, the Coalition would avoid splitting their forces with a difficult terrain barrier and preserve the shortest and most convenient of all links with Bohemia along the Pirna highway.[41]

The Austrian troops located to the right of the Plauenscher Grund, having lost several hours in pointless movements, advanced to attack. Chasteler's infantry captured Plauen and contributed to the seizure of the Reisewitzscher Garten, on the left bank of the Weißeritz, by troops from Bianchi's division. Thereafter, the Austrians drove the enemy out of every building as far as the Freiberg road, occupied Feldschlößchen, 600 paces from the Seevorstadt, and pushed strong batteries forwards to bombard lunettes No. IV and No. V. But every attempt to capture these fortifications and break into the suburbs was repelled by fire from the lunettes, from the suburbs and from the main ramparts.[42]

At the same time as the Austrian forces stationed to the right of the Plauenscher Grund were forming up for battle, the other divisions, under Gyulay's overall command, were located on the left side of the Weißeritz, as follows: Bianchi's division, consisting of 12 battalions with one battery, were in the bivouacs between the villages of Dölzschen and Roßthal; Weissenwolf's, also of 12 battalions, had advanced towards Wölfnitz; Schneller's cavalry division, of 20 squadrons with one battery, were located forwards of Burgstädtel, maintaining liaison between Weissenwolf's and Mesko's divisions; Mesko's *3. leichte Division*, consisting of three battalions and 12 squadrons, had moved up towards Cotta. After a short rest, the divisions under Bianchi and Weissenwolf advanced on Löbtau, captured this village, and upon the arrival of Greth's brigade [Carl Joseph Franz von Greth] (from Crenneville's division), they seized the manors of Klein Hamburg, Altona, and others abandoned by the French.[43] Mesko's division drove the enemy out of Cotta and Schusterhaus and, together with Greth's brigade, occupied the sector as far as the Elbe.[44]

Overall, the Coalition limited themselves to their minor successes and halted in anticipation of a general assault, as if gifting the enemy the chance to reinforce themselves with troops coming from Lusatia and Silesia and to take steps to defend Dresden. Napoleon would skilfully exploit their mistake.

---

41 Aster, 178-180.
42 Aster, 180-184; Beitzke, II, 45-46.
43 See Map No. 6 Plan of the Battle of Dresden, 14 (26) August.
44 Aster, 185-188; Beitzke, II, 48-50.

Appendix XI

The composition of Vandamme's force

Vandamme's force consisted of:

Formation	Unit	Battalions	Squadrons
1er Division General Philippon [Armand Philippon]	7e léger	4	
	12e ligne	4	
	17e ligne	4	
	36e ligne	2	
2e Division General Dumonceau [Jean-Baptiste Dumonceau de Bergendal]	13e léger	4	
	25e ligne	4	
	51e ligne	4	
	57e ligne	2	
General Quiot's brigade [Joachim Jérôme Quiot du Passage] from *23e Division*	55e ligne	2	
	85e ligne	4	
21e Brigade de cavalerie légère General Gobrecht [Martin Charles Gobrecht]	9e chevaulégers lanciers		2
	Anhalt *Chevaulegers*		2
	Total (24,000 men):	34	4

Assigned in addition: 7,000 infantry and 500 cavalry from *42e Division* of *14e Corps*; six battalions from Erbprinz Reuß's brigade [Heinrich LXI. Reuß zu Köstritz] of *2e Corps*, numbering 4,500 men; 22 squadrons from General Corbineau's light cavalry division [Jean-Baptiste Juvénal Corbineau], numbering 3,600 men.

In total: 52 battalions of infantry – 35,000 men, 30 squadrons of cavalry – 4,600 men, giving a grand total, including artillerymen, of 42,000 men with 80 guns.

Heinrich Aster, *Die Kriegsereignisse zwischen Peterswalde, Pirna, Königstein und Priesten im August 1813 und die Schlacht bei Kulm*, 59-60; Thiers, *Histoire du Consulat et de l'Empire*, XVI, *Edit de Brux*, 317.

27

The Battle of Dresden

The concentration of Napoleon's forces towards Dresden. Their composition and strength. – Napoleon's plan of operations. – The Coalition proposal to call off the assault.

The fighting on 14 (26) August. Preliminary dispositions of the Coalition forces and their advance to contact. – Operations by Count Wittgenstein, Kleist, Colloredo, Chasteler and Gyulay prior to the French counter-attack. – The advance of the French forces. – The Coalition are repulsed at all points. – Napoleon's and Prinz Schwarzenberg's orders for operations for the following day.

The fighting on 14 (26) August in the vicinity of Pirna. The composition and strength of the force under Prinz Eugen von Württemberg. – His plan of operations. – The deployment of his force in the position at Krietzschwitz. – The arrival of Count Osterman-Tolstoy. – The action at Krietzschwitz. Prinz Eugen's retreat towards Zehista. – The detachment of the 1st Lifeguard Division to assist him. – Osterman assumes command of all forces assembled at Pirna.

On the morning of 14 (26) August, returning to the great Dresden bridge after his reconnaissance, Napoleon took measures to repel the Coalition army. In anticipation of the concentration of his forces in Dresden, he ordered the Westphalians, who were performing security duties within the city, to reposition themselves in front of the Wilsdruffer Vorstadt. As the arriving troops marched through the city, they were given a ration of wine. The regiments proceeded with bands playing and went into action as if they were going to a festival. The soldiers took off their backpacks and, brushing the dirt and dust from their greatcoats and trousers, changed into their dress uniforms.[1] Arriving at around noon, the *3e Division* of the *Jeune Garde* under General Decouz [Pierre Decouz], consisting of ten battalions, was sent to the Rampischer Schlag (today's Pillnitzer Straße), in addition, the *10e Voltigeurs de la garde*, were sent to the Pirnaischer Schlag, in support of *44e Division*.[2] At about

---

1   Förster, *Geschichte der Befreiungskriege, 1813, 1814, 1815*, I, 545-546.
2   The *3e Division* of the *Jeune Garde* consisted of: *4e, 5e, 8e, 9e* and *10e voltigeurs de la garde*.

one o'clock in the afternoon, Napoleon surveyed the area between the Ziegelschlag and the Pirnaischer Schlag once more. At the third hour the *1er corps de cavalerie* under Latour-Maubourg arrived, consisting of 56 squadrons and numbering 10,000 to 12,000 men. This cavalry, together with 5,000 horsemen commanded by General Pajol [Pierre Claude Pajol], was sent across the lower floating bridge to the meadows of Ostrawiese near Friedrichstadt.³ The other three divisions of the *Jeune Garde* arrived in Dresden throughout the duration of the general action and were directed as follows: Roguet's *4e Division* [François Roguet] to the Pirnaischer Schlag; Barrois' *2e Division* [Pierre Barrois] to the Dippoldiswalder Schlag; while Dumoustier's *1er Division* [Pierre Dumoustier] went to the Falkenschlag.⁴ Command of the *3e Division* and *4e Division* was entrusted to Marshal Mortier [Adolphe Édouard Casimir Joseph Mortier], and over the *1er Division* and *2e Division* to Ney. Eight battalions from Teste's division were sent across the lower floating bridge to Friedrichstadt in order to support the cavalry.⁵ Of the regiments of the *Vieille Garde*, three were detached as follows: *2e grenadiers à pied de la garde* to the Pirnaischer Schlag, the *fusiliers-chasseurs de la Garde* to the Falkenschlag and *2e chasseurs à pied de la Garde* to the Freiberger Schlag. The other units of the *Vieille Garde* remained in the Altstadt, at the Residenzschloss, forming the general reserve (nine battalions with 30 guns), commanded by generals Friant [Louis Friant] and Curial [Philibert Jean-Baptiste Curial].⁶ The strength of the entire French force defending Dresden on this day reached 70,000 men. Napoleon remained at the masonry bridge in the Altstadt himself. From here he controlled the course of the battle, sending out orders via the officers of his suite. In addition, he had direct reports on the battlefield through the Saxon *Oberst* von Haak, who monitored the movement of the Coalition forces from a bell tower and conveyed his observations to the Emperor via mounted orderlies stationed at the foot of the bell tower.⁷

Napoleon's operational plan was based on accurate information on the Dresden area and the routes leading from there to Bohemia. Taking advantage of the complete dislocation of the Austrian force into two parts by the deep Plauenscher Grund, after waiting for the arrival of his troops, he undertook to attack the Coalition left wing and drive them back into the ravine. Napoleon intended to attack the right

---

3   Aster states (*Schilderung der Kriegsereignisse in und vor Dresden*, 191-192) that Pajol commanded *5e corps de cavalerie*, consisting of 46 squadrons, and that in both corps, his and Latour-Maubourg's, there were 23,000 men. Yet from statements by French historians it is clear that *5e corps de cavalerie* had not yet been activated.
4   The composition of these *Jeune Garde* divisions were: Roguet's – two battalions of *flanqueurs-chasseurs* and two battalions of *flanqueurs-grenadiers*; *4e, 5e, 8e, 9e* and *10e tirailleurs de la garde*, for a total of 14 battalions with one battery. Barrois' – *1er, 2e, 3e, 6e* and *7e tirailleurs de la garde*, for a total of ten battalions with one battery. Dumoustier's – *1er, 2e, 3e, 6e* and *7e voltigeurs de la garde, 11e tirailleurs de la garde*, for a total of 12 battalions.
5   The composition of the brigade from Teste's division detached to Friedrichstadt was: *21e ligne* and *33e ligne*.
6   The composition of this *Vieille Garde* reserve was: *1er grenadiers à pied de la garde*; *1er chasseurs à pied de la garde*; a battalion of *fusiliers-grenadiers de la garde*; *Velites de Turin*; *Velites de Florence*; Saxon *Leibgrenadiergarde* and *grenadiers polonais*, for a total of nine battalions with five batteries.
7   Beitzke, *Geschichte der deutschen Freiheitskriege*, II, 53.

wing of the Army of Bohemia at the same time, to seize the best route of all those leading through the Ore Mountains (the Teplitz highway) and push the Coalition onto very awkward routes that led through country that could not provide any resources for the army. Consequently, the French forces were, as already indicated, mainly concentrated on the flanks. The weakening of their centre posed no significant disadvantage, because the units located there were fighting behind fortifications which enabled the French to hold out awaiting the success of their flanking attacks, moreover, Napoleon had a reserve made up of select units from his *Vieille Garde* just in case.[8]

Having received word of the advance by the Army of Bohemia towards Dresden at four o'clock in the afternoon, Napoleon addressed the large retinue surrounding him, saying: 'good. Mount up!'[9] While he remained on horseback himself, as before, by the ramp of the masonry bridge, meeting the arriving regiments and constantly sending aides-de-camp and orderlies along the Bautzen road to hurry on the march of the troops. The regiments, for the most part, crossed the Elbe via the masonry bridge from where Napoleon gave them directions to their positions, encouraging the soldiers with a few words that evoked enthusiastic cheers.[10] This brilliant commander, completely confident of victory, turned to the Saxon *Militärberater* [Minister of War], General Gersdorff, who was in his retinue, saying:

> Although the enemy has commenced operations quite well, they have nevertheless strayed from their role (he believed that the Coalition had deviated from the plan drawn up at Trachenberg). If they attack me, they will endanger the outcome of their campaign.[11]

Indeed, the indecisiveness of the measures taken by the Coalition commander would make the victory easier for Napoleon. Having finally realised that an assault on a fortified city defended by an entire army under the command of Napoleon himself did not guarantee a positive outcome, Schwarzenberg went to look for his *Chef des Stabes* [chief of staff] in order to issue new orders cancelling the original disposition. It would have been much easier to issue the necessary instructions to the formation commanders via the orderlies stationed at the main headquarters, but Schwarzenberg could not make this decision without consulting Radetzky [Johann Josef Wenzel Anton Franz Karl Radetzky von Radetz] and Langenau [Friedrich Karl Gustav August von Langenau]. However, taking into account that with the cancellation of the issued disposition there would be no agreement on a course of action, one cannot help but admit that the field marshal's hesitations and doubts were quite reasonable: it was essential to decide whether the army should remain in its position near Dresden, or retreat to another position, to Dippoldiswalde, or finally to retreat back to Bohemia with 200,000 men, avoiding a decisive engagement with the enemy once Napoleon had appeared, as if out of fear inspired by his name. And

---

8 Beitzke, II, 52.
9 *'eh bien, à cheval!'*
10 Aster, 192.
11 Beitzke, II, 53.

so Schwarzenberg, who had never been distinguished by either strength of will or quick thinking, went to look for his advisers. It has been claimed that he could not find them, but it seems much more likely that Radetzky and Langenau convinced the field marshal once more of the need for the proposed assault, and that his disposition should deliberately not be cancelled.[12]

At around four o'clock in the afternoon, the signal for the general assault on Dresden came – three cannon shots from the high ground at Räcknitz. On this signal, fire was opened from all the Coalition batteries stationed on the front line and the columns assigned to assault the city moved forward. At this point, the Coalition forces near Dresden were positioned as follows: Count Wittgenstein's corps were partly between the Blasewitz forest and Striesen (5th Division, the Sumy Hussars and Lubny Hussars), and partly between Striesen and the Großer Garten (the vanguard commanded by Roth, supported by the Grodno Hussars). Of Kleist's force, Zieten's vanguard were holding the Großer Garten; Pirch's *10. Brigade* were in reserve behind the Großer Garten; *Oberstleutnant* Jagow's *11. Brigade* [Friedrich Wilhelm Christian Ludwig von Jagow] were behind and inside Strehlen; *Generalmajor* Klüx's *9. Brigade* [Joseph Friedrich Karl von Klüx] were between Strehlen and Grünewiese; Prinz August von Preußen's *12. Brigade* [Friedrich Wilhelm Heinrich August von Preußen] were to the left of Strehlen; *Oberstleutnant* Braun's artillery reserve [Johann Carl Ludwig Braun] were further left behind the high ground at Zschertnitz; *Generalmajor* Röder's cavalry reserve [Friedrich Erhard Leopold von Röder] were forwards of the village of Torna; the rest of the cavalry were near Gruna and forwards of Zschertnitz. Moritz Liechtenstein's and Colloredo's Austrian divisions were behind Räcknitz; Chasteler's division was behind Plauen. Mesko's *3. leichte Division* was on the left side of the Plauenscher Grund at Cotta with Greth's brigade (from Crenneville's division); Mumb's brigade [Franz Mumb] (from the same division) and Schneller's cavalry were further back in reserve; Graf Ignác Gyulay was at Roßthal with Bianchi's and Weissenwolf's divisions. The strength of the Coalition forces on the field of battle on 14 (26) August, overall, reached more than 100,000 men, but only half of them were sent into action. The battle began with a cannonade from 124 guns, of which four were from 6th Horse Artillery Company assigned to Melissino's force. There were two Russian heavy companies with Count Wittgenstein, numbering 24 guns, stationed forwards of Striesen on the Windmühlenberg. Kleist had three eight-gun batteries on the Dohna road, forwards of Rothen Haus. Four Austrian position batteries, numbering 24 guns, were forwards of Räcknitz facing lunette No. III. Another four Austrian batteries, numbering 24 guns, were facing lunette No. IV, and a similar number were on the left bank of the Weißeritz near Löbtau.[13]

---

12 Alexander Andreevich Shcherbinin's manuscript notes; Bernhardi, *Denkwürdigkeiten aus dem Leben Carl Friedrich Grafen von Toll*, III, 159-160.
13 Plotho, *Der Krieg in Deutschland und Frankreich in den Jahren 1813 und 1814*, II, 43-45; Wagner, *Plane der Schlachten und Treffen, welche von der preussischen Armee in den Feldzügen der Jahre 1813, 14 und 15 geliefert worden*, II, 32-35; Sporschill, *Die große Chronik*, I, 425; Aster, 194.

On this signal, the Coalition forces assigned to the assault moved towards the city simultaneously, but for the most convenient presentation of events of this battle, the operations by each of the five formations of the army (Wittgenstein's, Kleist's, Colloredo's, Chasteler's and Gyulay's) will be described separately.

The attack by Count Wittgenstein's force

At about four o'clock in the afternoon, the attack was launched on Hopfgarten by six battalions of the Sevsk Infantry, Kaluga Infantry and 23rd Jäger regiments: from this force, the 23rd Jägers, with two horse artillery pieces, commanded by Major General Lukov [Fëdor Alexeevich Lukov], moved to the right of Engelhardt's hotel, while the Sevsk Infantry and Kaluga Infantry, with two more horse artillery pieces, commanded by Major General Melissino, headed to the left of the hotel. At the same time, General Roth moved along the Großer Garten with ten battalions from 20th Jägers, 21st Jägers, 25th Jägers, 26th Jägers and 34th Jägers and six guns, in order to support the attack by the Prussian force under General Zieten. Wittgenstein's remaining troops, consisting of six battalions of Perm Infantry, Mogilev Infantry, and 24th Jägers, were directed towards the Windmühlenberg.

The enemy detachment occupying the hotel was driven out by the Sevsk Infantry, which also forced the French sheltering in the Sandgrube pit to retreat. Exploiting this success, General Melissino opened a cannonade on Hopfgarten and the foundry yard, supported by the fire of a battery located on the Windmühlenberg. The enemy, for their part, having placed a strong battery to the right of Hopfgarten, hit the Russian columns with a crossfire from this artillery in conjunction with the batteries located on the far bank of the Elbe at Linkschesbad and the Marcolini manor. Under the covering fire of this cannonade, Marshal Mortier initially formed Decouz's division up (ten battalions) between lunettes I and II, and then Roguet's division (12 battalions) forwards of the Ziegelschlag. At the same time, the French set up a battery at Antons manor, which inflicted a heavy loss on the Russian force, killing General Lukov. Count Wittgenstein sent Major General Vlastov [Yegor Ivanovich Vlastov or George Vlastos] to assist the troops in combat, with the 24th Jägers.[14] Vlastov moved along the deep Landgraben drain, but, upon passing the Windmühlenberg, he was halted by fire from the guns in lunette No. I, as well as from a battery of *artillerie à cheval de la garde* placed to the right of the lunette, and another battery on the high ground forwards of the Rampischer Schlag. At six o'clock, the remaining regiments from 5th Division, under the personal command of Count Wittgenstein, moved up to the Windmühlenberg.[15]

Roth's operations on the left flank of the Russian troops were undistinguished. The men of the 25th Jägers and 26th Jägers, having lined the wall of the Großer Garten,

---

14 This manor, lying on the banks of the Elbe upstream of Dresden, should not be confused with the Prinz Antons Garten, in the Pirnaische Vorstadt.
15 Plotho, II, 45; Wagner, 35; Aster, 195-197; Hofmann, *Zur Geschichte des Feldzuges von 1813*, 141-142; Plan of the Battle of Dresden, signed by General Harting (Archive of the M.T.D. No. 20,011).

facing lunette No. II, began a lively firefight with the enemy and attempted to close up to the fortification, but were repelled by the French. At five o'clock, together with Prussian forces, they launched an attack along the Pirna highway.[16]

The attack by Kleist's force

The Prussian force was given the mission to direct an assault between the Dohnaer Schlag and Pirnaischer Schlag and to capture lunette No. II. General Zieten attacked the abatis in the Großer Garten as early as two hours before the signal for the general offensive, with three battalions from his vanguard: third battalion of *6. Reserve Infanterie (9. Brigade)* tore down the abatis under enemy canister fire, while the fusilier battalions of *1. Schlesisches Infanterie, 3. Reserve Infanterieregiment* and *10. Reserve Infanterie* simultaneously attacked the French defending the abatis. But, despite the efforts of the battalion commanders, Lettow and Offenau, the latter of whom was seriously wounded, the Prussian troops were unable to take possession of the abatis. General Zieten committed his entire vanguard to action and was subsequently supported by *10. Brigade* under *Generalmajor* Pirch, who, relieving the most disordered battalions of the vanguard with fresh troops, and with the assistance of General Roth, captured the rest of the Großer Garten. After lining the extreme edge of this garden with a skirmishing screen, the Prussian troops launched an attack on lunette No. II and on the Prinz Antons Garten. This operation presented extreme difficulties: the lunette, 300 paces from the Großer Garten, was strongly held by infantry and bristled with guns. At the exit to the Pirnaischer Vorstadt, facing the Großer Garten, there was another garden (Antons Garten), surrounded by a masonry wall, behind which a strong battery was emplaced, and the wall itself was defended by a dense screen of skirmishers. The remainder of the suburb's perimeter was surrounded by palisades and a ditch. In addition, outside the suburb in the vicinity of the lunette, the French had occupied every ditch, fence and hedge with a screen of skirmishers. Overall, the entire edge of the Großer Garten on which the Prussian troops were stationed, was being lashed with canister and even musket fire from the suburb. Despite all these difficulties, the columns under Zieten and Pirch nevertheless tried to break into the suburb, but were repulsed with enormous casualties. Having no sapper squads with them and not being equipped with either planks for crossing ditches or ladders for scaling walls, the brave Prussian soldiers died in vain, and were finally forced to retreat.

At the same time as the above action was taking place, General Kleist directed another assault on the Dohnaer Schlag. Having concentrated Jagow's entire *11. Brigade* at Rothen Haus, he brought up from the reserve *3. Batterie* and *6. Batterie* armed with 12-pounders, and *1. Batterie* with seven-pounder howitzers, protected by two battalions of *10. Reserve Infanterie*. This artillery, passing to the left of Rothen Haus, unleashed a heavy bombardment of the Dohnaer Schlag and on lunette No. III. The remaining troops of *11. Brigade*, consisting of six battalions with one

---

16 Aster, 205; Hofmann, 142.

six-pounder battery, were left behind the village of Strehlen. Once the Austrians had captured lunette No. III, and Zieten's and Pirch's troops had driven the enemy out of the Großer Garten, then Kleist, wanting to exploit these successes by capturing the Dohnaer Schlag, sent both battalions of *10. Reserve Infanterie* and Graf Dohna's *Schlesisches Landwehr* battalion against the suburb. Borcke's other *Schlesisches Landwehr* battalion occupied Rothen Haus, while the rest of the troops from *11. Brigade* were stationed behind this village in reserve. The columns advancing towards the city were shielded from the direction of Antons Garten by the embankment along the Kaitzbach, and did not take any casualties, while the screen of skirmishers covering them had already got to within ten paces of the gates, but at that very moment the French suddenly opened a fierce cannonade from batteries located at the entrances to the suburbs and engaged them with musket fire, which forced the Prussian troops to retreat.[17]

Colloredo's attack

Fire was opened from the guns positioned on the front line of the right wing as soon as the signal was given, whereupon the Austrian batteries moved forward: the artillery located to the right of Räcknitz was moved forward to bombard lunette No. III; while Chasteler's batteries fired on lunettes No. IV and No. V. Several large calibre howitzers were used to lob shells into the city. The actions of the Austrian artillery were very successful: many of the French guns stationed within and outside the fortifications were knocked out and their crews suffered heavy casualties. The columns directed through Räcknitz towards lunette No. III were successful. These troops, consisting of the *1. Jäger-Bataillon* and *2. Jäger-Bataillon*, supported by four battalions of the *Infanterieregiment Froon* and *Infanterieregiment De Vaux*, under the personal command of Graf Colloredo, advanced beside embankments that shielded them from the fire of lunette No. III from the front, from lunette No. IV from the left flank and from the battery stationed at the Dippoldiswalder Schlag, and closed in on lunette No. III. The French engaged the attackers with canister fire, but they ran out of this ammunition at the very moment when they could do have done most damage to the assaulting columns. The Austrians, despite the losses they had suffered, closed up to the lunette. At their head were the brave commanders of the jäger battalions, *Oberst* Lutz and *Oberstleutnant* Schneider. The jägers quickly dropped into the ditch, pulled down several palisades and climbed onto the parapet along with the leading *Froon* and *De Vaux* divisions [pairs of companies]. The French fought back with bayonets and musket butts, but were driven out of the lunette with the loss of six guns located within it. Following this, one of the position batteries was brought very close to the city ramparts. The jägers assaulted the Mosczinski Garten, while the *Infanterieregiment Froon* and *Infanterieregiment De Vaux*, secured the lunette. But every Austrian effort to take possession of this garden, surrounded by a high wall, was repulsed with losses and the valiant *Oberstleutnant* Schneider was killed.

---

17 Wagner, 36-37; Richter, *Geschichte des Deutschen Freiheitskrieges*, II, 38-39; Aster, 209-213; Hofmann, 141; Plan of the Battle of Dresden, signed by General Harting.

Chasteler's division, holding Plauen, shielded the advance of the Gyulay's force on the left bank of the Weißeritz. The batteries from this division operated successfully against the Freiberger Schlag and knocked out several guns.[18]

Gyulay's attack

At five o'clock in the morning, Mesko's division, after reaching Gorbitz, had captured Schusterhaus and Cotta. Eight companies and two squadrons from this division, commanded by *Generalmajor* Paumgartten [Maximilian Sigmund Joseph von Paumgartten], were sent to Meißen to destroy the bridge there. Bianchi's division advanced along both banks of the Weißeritz to Löbtau and captured this village and the manors of Altona and Klein Hamburg to its front. Weissenwolf's division advanced between Naußlitz and Gorbitz. Schneller's cavalry, turning to the left, maintained liaison between the divisions under Weissenwolf and Mesko, while Crenneville's division proceeded in reserve.

After occupying Löbtau and the manors in front of this village, as well as Schusterhaus, Austrian troops attempted to break into the outskirts of Friedrichstadt, but all their attempts, made in inadequate strength, were unsuccessful.[19]

Thus, although the Coalition was gaining success at every point, and had even captured one of the French fortifications, they had not achieved any decisive results. Meanwhile, Napoleon, having concentrated some 70,000 men in the Dresden suburbs, was preparing unexpected blows for the Coalition. At six o'clock in the afternoon, as the suburbs and the Altstadt itself, pelted with a hail of shells, were burning at many points, and as fear and confusion gripped the inhabitants of the city, the French forces, assembled at its outer perimeter, quickly debouched into the open and counter-attacked the Coalition: Roguet's and Decouz's divisions of the *Jeune Garde*, under Marshal Mortier's overall command, emerged from the Ziegelschlag and Rampischer Schlag and raced on, from the former towards Antons manor, and from the latter towards the Engelhardt hotel. Some of the cavalry set out from the Pirnaischer Schlag in order to shield their right flank. Barrois' and Dumoustier's other two divisions of the *Jeune Garde*, under Marshal Ney's command, emerging from the Freiberger Schlag, Falkenschlag and Dippoldiswalder Schlag, moved forwards across the area between the Mosczinski Garten and the Plauenscher Grund. Murat quickly exited Friedrichstadt with Latour-Maubourg's and Pajol's cavalry, supported by eight battalions from Teste's force, and deployed his regiments on the plain with their right flank resting on the Elbe. Berthezène's division, defending the Pirnaischer Vorstadt, also advanced to attack.[20] Napoleon

---

18 Aster, 221-233; Wagner, 38-39; Sporschill, I, 426; Richter, II, 40-42; Plotho, II, 48.
19 Aster 246-249; Plotho, II, 48-49.
20 Military historians agree among themselves about the directions taken by Roguet's and Decouz's divisions. Regarding the directions of Barrois' and Dumoustier's divisions, (in Thiers – Parmentier's), Saint-Cyr and Thiers write that they debouched from the Pirnaischer Schlag. Vaudoncourt states from the Plauischer Schlag (Freiberger Schlag?). Plotho from Friedrichstadt. Hofmann and Wagner from the Falkenschlag, Freiberger Schlag and

galloped to the battlefield himself and was at the head of Barrois' division. One of the officers of his suite was killed, many were wounded.[21]

The counter-attack by French forces

At the same time as the departure from the Pirnaischer Vorstadt of two divisions of *Jeune Garde* under Mortier's command, and Doumerc's cavalry [Jean-Pierre Doumerc] (21 squadrons) stationed to the right of the Pillnitz road, Murat set off from there to Friedrichstadt in order to take command of the right wing of the French army. On the right wing of the Coalition army, the troops under Count Wittgenstein, weakened by the losses they had suffered, were forced to retreat, but at the very moment that the enemy were emerging from the Ziegelschlag, and as all the streets leading there from the city were congested with troops, guns and ammunition caissons, one of the Russian shells lobbed into the suburb hit a large wagon full of ammunition. Several shells that exploded as a result killed two of the four horses harnessed to the wagon and the drivers scattered. The remaining two horses, in terror of the detonations, turned back and raced through the suburbs and into the city with the flaming wagon, from which projectiles were constantly cooking-off. The infantry moving towards the exits, having encountered this hellish vehicle, turned aside, which caused extraordinary chaos. Had the Russians taken advantage of this opportunity and resumed their assault, then, in all likelihood, they would have driven the enemy back. But the favourable moment was lost, and the French generals managed to restore order. Outnumbered by the enemy, Wittgenstein's force evacuated the Engelhardt hotel and retreated to the Windmühlenberg. The enemy, not content with this success, attacked this hill, captured it at dusk and attempted to break into the village of Striesen, but, on being repulsed, set it on fire with shellfire and turned it to ruins. General Klüx, who had arrived with the Prussian 9. *Brigade*, on the orders of Barclay de Tolly, to assist the Russian force, positioned himself behind Striesen. Night put an end to the fighting in which both sides suffered significant casualties. Among the wounded were the French generals Decouz and Combelle [Jean Antoine François Combelle]. The Russian troops had completely evacuated Striesen by one o'clock in the morning and moved into bivouacs between Gruna, Seidnitz and Tolkewitz. Klüx's brigade retreated through Gruna towards Leubnitz. The French divisions under Decouz and Roguet halted at Striesen. They were followed by Doumerc's cavalry and Nansouty's *cavalerie de la garde* [Étienne Marie Antoine Champion de Nansouty], which had arrived in the evening.[22]

Roth's force, having been engaged by superior enemy forces directed towards the Großer Garten and along the highway, retreated step by step to the northeastern part of the garden and held out there during the night of 14 to 15 (26 to 27) August, moving, at the same time, into Gruna, Grünewiese, and setting up a screen

---

Wilsdruffer Schlag. Richter has Barrois exiting the Falkenschlag, while Dumoustier left via the Freiberger Schlag and Wilsdruffer Schlag.
21 Fain, *Manuscrit de 1813*, II, 273.
22 Wagner, 35-36; Aster, 198-204; Richter, II, 35-36.

of outposts, indirectly aligned from the middle gate of the Großer Garten to the Landgraben at Striesen. The French outposts were located within sight of those of the Russians.[23]

It has already been mentioned above that Kleist's force, having been repulsed by the enemy from the Dohnaer Schlag outpost, had fallen back. At that time, the Austrians had lost their hold on lunette No. III, which allowed the French *44e Division* under General Berthezène to exit the suburb and launch a surprise attack on the Prussian skirmishers. The enemy, having forced Jagow's troops to retreat, quickly pursued them and cut off Dohna's and Borcke's battalions. Surrounded on all sides by French infantry, the Prussians lost many men, but managed to break out. By the end of the fighting on the night of 14 to 15 (26 to 27) August, Kleist's corps had redeployed as follows: the vanguard were in Strehlen, holding the palace in the Großer Garten with two battalions from *1. Westpreussisches Infanterie*; *10. Brigade* were around Grünewiese; *11. Brigade* (with three batteries attached from the artillery reserve) and *12. Brigade* were behind Strehlen; the reserve cavalry were between Leubnitz and Torna; General Kleist and the Prussian Kronprinz (later King Friedrich Wilhelm IV) spent the night in Strehlen.[24]

After repelling Graf Colloredo's attacks on the Mosczinski Garten, the French went on the offensive here too. At the same time as Marshal Mortier's attack, Ney debouched from the Falkenschlag with the divisions under Barrois and Dumoustier and led the assault on Feldschlößchen. Napoleon, during his morning reconnaissance of this built up area held by Austrian troops, had stated: 'This location will not be easy to take; I shall leave its capture to the *Vieille Garde*.' These few words, spreading like lightning through the ranks of the *Jeune Garde*, were enough to incite these brave warriors to heroic feats. Ney's force captured Feldschlößchen, while General Gros [Jean Louis Gros] drove the Austrians out of lunette No. III. Gros himself was among the wounded.[25]

Murat's attacks, with Latour-Maubourg's and Pajol's cavalry, supported by infantry from Teste's force and part of Dumoustier's division, numbering 12,000 men, were carried out somewhat earlier than the offensive by Ney's force. The French infantry commanded by General Teste, exiting the Löbtauer Schlag, attacked the Altona and Klein Hamburg manors with the assistance of Pajol's cavalry, but Prinz Hessen-Homburg, with the Hungarian *Hieronymus Colloredo Infanterie* and *Hiller Infanterie*, repelled the enemy and held out for a long time in these buildings, while Mariássy's [Andreas Mariássy de Márkus et Batiszfálva] and Quallenberg's [Karl von Quallenberg] other two brigades enveloped Teste from the right flank.[26] The Austrians were eventually driven out of Altona, but continued to hold out in Klein Hamburg and only evacuated this manor after midnight. General Csollich [Markus Csollich], with the *Kaiser Infanterie* and *Kottulinsky Infanterie* (Weissenwolf's

---

23 Aster, 205-206; Hofmann, 142.
24 Wagner, 37-38; Aster, 213-218; Richter, II, 39.
25 Wagner, 39; Aster, 237-240.
26 *Infanterieregiment Hieronymus Colloredo* and *Infanterieregiment Hiller*, were part of Bianchi's division. Aster shows *Infanterie-Regiment Kaiser Alexander* instead of *Hieronymus Colloredo* (*Schilderung der Kriegsereignisse in und vor Dresden*, 250).

division), supported and relieved a battalion of the *Simbschen Infanterie* (Bianchi's division), which was holding the village of Löbtau. The brigades under Grimmer [Anton Grimmer von Riesenburg] and Herzogenberg [August (Picot de Peccaduc) von Herzogenberg] were positioned on both sides of Naußlitz, while Schneller's cavalry were on the left flank of the latter brigade, in order to maintain liaison with Mesko's division. No sooner had the Austrian forces occupied these positions, than Murat launched a general attack: Teste's infantry assaulted Löbtau, while Latour-Maubourg's cavalry swept around to the right of Friedrichstadt and launched an attack on Mesko's division. The assault on Löbtau was repulsed by General Csollich. Just then, Murat sent the *1er chasseurs à cheval du royaume d'Italie* into the gap between Cotta and Drescherhäuser, aiming to isolate the left wing of the Austrian army from the divisions under Bianchi and Weissenwolf. However, the *Kienmayer Husaren*, stationed partly in the village of Cotta, partly outside the village, hidden in a ravine overgrown with bushes, sprung an ambush, striking the enemy in the flank and captured almost all the *chasseurs à cheval*. Exploiting this success, the Austrians moved several guns forward, but the strong enemy cannonade forced them to retreat behind Cotta. The Austrian batteries stationed to the left of Drescherhäuser and firing successfully at Murat's cavalry, were also forced into silence by the successful actions of a French *artillerie à cheval de la garde* battery. At dusk, the Saxon *Kürassier-Regiment Zastrow* launched a very successful attack on the *Manfredini Infanterie* (Mesko's division) and took many prisoners. Despite all this, however, the Austrians held on to the locations they occupied. Among the Austrian wounded were: *Feldzeugmeister* Gyulay, *Feldmarschallleutnant* Schneller, Prinz Philipp Hessen-Homburg and *Generalmajor* Mariássy. On the French side, the wounded included: général de division Dumoustier and *généraux de brigade* Boyeldieu [Louis-Léger Boyeldieu], Tindal [Ralph Dundas Tindal] (both of the *Garde*), Godart [Roch Godart], Bertrand and Paliard [Nicolas Augustin Paliard or Paillard] (*14e Corps*). The conscripts of the *Jeune Garde* and from Saint-Cyr's corps particularly distinguished themselves. These 'brave children,' as General Pelet [Jean-Jacques Germain Pelet-Clozeau] called them, were no less courageous or fearless than their veteran comrades.[27] Yet there were few voluntarily attracted to military life, which required consistency as much as passion. Eyewitnesses of the Battle of Dresden testify that many of the recruits deserted the following night, and that in one of the regiments of the *Jeune Garde*, which suffered very few combat casualties, on the morning of 15 (27) August, out of 3,000 men, barely 1,000 remained.[28] Many Austrian soldiers, hungry, barefoot and exhausted, also abandoned their Colours and surrendered to the leading French units the next morning.[29]

Thus, on the first day of the battle of Dresden, the Coalition had been repulsed at all points by the French, while the troops under Count Wittgenstein had been pushed back about two *versts*. The inhabitants of Dresden, fearfully awaiting an assault and all the disasters associated with it, considered themselves indebted to Napoleon for

---

27 Wagner, 39-40; Aster, 247-250; Richter, II, 42-44; Sproschill, I, 429.
28 *Darstellung der Ereignisse in Dresden, im Jahr 1813. Von einem Augenzeugen*, 120; F. v. D. [Louis Amanley de Guehery?], *Napoleon in Dresden und auf Elba, Zweites Heft*, 74.
29 Aster, 251.

their salvation, but their fate had not yet been finally decided. A huge army still stood under the ramparts of their city. After the terrible day, a tumultuous, restless night followed. Almost no one slept a wink. Troops, guns, carts, infantry from the corps under Victor and Marmont, and Nansouty's *cavalerie de la garde* constantly passed along the streets.

Napoleon, having travelled around the positions of his left wing himself, from the Elbe to the Dohnaer Schlag by the light of torches and camp fires, returned to the Residenzschloss. At ten o'clock, one of the battalions of the *Jeune Garde* arrived there with 700 Austrian prisoners, one Colour and four guns captured at the Dippoldiswalder Schlag. Napoleon left the Schloss to see the battalion, expressed his pleasure to the *Garde* and distributed many crosses of the *Légion d'honneur* to them. Believing that the Coalition would retreat from Dresden in the night, he said: 'I shall pursue them hot on their heels. Vandamme should already be across the Elbe. I shall get to Bohemia before the enemy.'[30]

The French troops, both those already in Dresden and those that were supposed to assemble there during the night, were ordered to position themselves outside the Altstadt by dawn, as follows: Latour-Maubourg's and Pajol's cavalry, commanded by Murat, and Victor's *2e Corps* in Friedrichstadt; Marmont's *6e Corps*, the *Vieille Garde* and reserve artillery in the centre between the Dippoldiswalder Schlag and Dohnaer Schlag; Saint-Cyr's *14e Corps* in the Großer Garten; the *Jeune Garde*, commanded by Ney and Mortier, and Nansouty's *cavalerie de la garde* in the Pirnaische Vorstadt.[31]

As darkness came, cold rain began to fall heavily. The troops were soaked to the skin and got stuck in the mud whenever they moved. No less uncomfortable for the large Army of Bohemia was the almost complete lack of essential supplies. The physical suffering was aggravated by falling morale – a consequence of a failed assault: the Coalition forces spent a terrible night under the influence of all these unfavourable circumstances. Following forced marches and heated combat, the French were exhausted in the extreme, but being protected during the battle by natural and man-made obstacles, they lost fewer men and repelled the attack at all points, which somewhat increased their moral resilience. In addition, they could shelter from the bad weather in city buildings, while the Coalition forces were stuck in the open, in the mud, in bivouacs. Rations for the French were supplied from resources that the city and the extensive suburbs were able to provide. Napoleon himself took care, throughout the duration of the battle and the subsequent night, to supply the troops not only with food but with wine, spirits and beer. As the night progressed, Victor's corps, the rest of Marmont's corps and other reinforcements arrived in Dresden, swelling the French army to 120,000 men.[32]

---

30 Beitzke, II, 66-67.
31 Dispositions for 27 August. Jacques Mar Norvins, *Portefeuille de 1813*, II, 308-309.
32 When operations resumed after the armistice, the corps assembled by Napoleon for the defence of Dresden numbered some 150,000 men. Of these troops, some had not yet been in action at all, namely: the *Vieille Garde, cavalerie de la garde* and Victor's corps. The combat losses of the others could not have been more than 15,000 men. Calculating troop losses from disease and forced marches at 15,000 men, by 15 (27) August the available number of men reached 120,000.

On the Coalition side, it was decided to remain in their current positions until joined by Klenau's corps, and then to resume the attack on Dresden.

Late in the evening, Emperor Alexander went to Nöthnitz, where his headquarters were located, while the King of Prussia went to the village of Kausche. The Commander-in-Chief remained on the battlefield until ten o'clock, drafting orders for the next operations. Justice demands that it be said that the measures he took were most erroneous: as early as the first day of the battle of Dresden, Napoleon's intentions were clear – to envelope the Coalition on both flanks and push them back both from the Pirna highway and from the Freiberg road, and therefore Schwarzenberg should have paid attention to holding these routes open in adequate strength. But in the Austrian headquarters it was believed that Count Wittgenstein's corps, located on the plain formed by one of the loops of the Elbe, was in danger of being isolated from other formations. In addition, intelligence was received on the appearance of a significant enemy corps from the direction of Königstein: all this forced Schwarzenberg to pull the right wing back (the corps under Wittgenstein and Kleist) and place them on the high ground between the Dohna and Dippoldiswalde roads. All that remained on the plain to the right of Gruna was the weak vanguard of the Russian corps commanded by Major General Roth. The left wing of the Coalition army was still beyond the Plauensche Grund, and the position, just as on the previous day, was stretched out over two *Meilen*. Yet even as Graf Klenau was reporting the imminent arrival of his force the next morning, the Commander-in-Chief considered it necessary to transfer the divisions under Bianchi and Weissenwolf (with the exception of Csollich's brigade), together with the majority of their cavalry, to the right bank of the ravine during the night. The following remained on the left bank: Mesko's division, Csollich's brigade, two regiments of light cavalry, two squadrons of cuirassiers and an insignificant number of guns: in anticipation of the arrival of Graf Klenau, these units entrusted to *Feldmarschallleutnant* Graf Weissenwolf were reinforced only by the division under Alois Liechtenstein. The remainder of Klenau's force, delayed by bad weather that had ruined the roads, were unable to get into action, which had disastrous consequences for the left wing of the Coalition army. The Austrian divisions under Colloredo and Chasteler were in the centre, between the Dippoldiswalde road and the Plauensche Grund, with Lederer's cavalry division arriving at night. Behind them, in the second line, were the divisions that had arrived from Dippoldiswalde: Civalart's infantry division and Moritz Liechtenstein's cavalry division, and Nostitz's cavalry were in the third line. The divisions under Bianchi, Weissenwolf and Schneller were located in reserve at Gittersee, commanded of Ignác Gyulay. The number of Coalition troops assembled at Dresden, together with the Russo-Prussian reserves that arrived in the night, overall, according to the most conservative estimates, reached 160,000 men.[33]

Vandamme opened his operations against the line of communications of the Army of Bohemia at the same time as the battle of Dresden.

II Corps and part of I Corps had been left to monitor this force, consisting of 20 battalions, two squadrons and one Cossack regiment, numbering some 11,000 men

---

33 Aster, 265-268; Bernhardi, III, 169-170; Beitzke, II 67-69.

with 24 guns.[34] Having received intelligence on the crossing of Vandamme's corps at Königstein on 13 (25) August, the prince decided, despite the enormous enemy numerical superiority, to advance from Zehista in order to engage them so that he might take advantage of the very rough terrain to delay them and slow down the deployment of the French force.

To that end, Major General Prince Shakhovskoy [Ivan Leontievich Shakhovskoy] and Colonel Wolfe [Ivan Pavlovich Wolf or Peter Johann Paul Wilhelm Wolfe] were sent to Struppen [3½ miles north-west of Königstein] with the Chernigov Infantry and Murom Infantry, two squadrons of Lubny Hussars and two guns. The remaining elements of II Corps were left at Rottwerndorf [2½ miles south-east of Zehista] in case of any moves towards Dresden. The leading troops were stationed in the Königstein forest and on the high ground at Nonenstein [*sic*, Sonnenstein?] near the Elbe. At six o'clock in the morning on 14 (26) August, during a skirmish between the Russian and enemy outposts, several prisoners were captured who revealed that Vandamme had crossed at Königstein on the previous night with 50,000 men. Prinz Eugen immediately sent a report on this to Count Wittgenstein, and thereafter decided to occupy the plateau with the main body of his corps in order to block enemy access to the Pirna highway. At eight o'clock in the morning, the force entrusted to him took up positions between Krietzschwitz and Struppen. In the front line were: Wolfe's brigade, from Thürmsdorf [two miles north-west of Königstein] to Nickolsdorf, and Helffreich's detachment were at Leupoldishain [2½ miles west of Königstein]. All in all, having detached three jäger regiments to Roth's vanguard and the Reval Infantry to monitor in the direction of Pirna, 15 battalions remained to II Corps, numbering about 7,000 men, while Helffreich's detachment consisted of five battalions, numbering 2,000 men. At around noon, Grand Duke Konstantin Pavlovich passed through Cotta on the way to Dresden with the Russo-Prussian reserves. The Prinz von Württemberg sent Colonel Wachten [Otto Ivanovich Vakhten or Hans Otto von Wachten] to him with a request for reinforcements, but the Grand Duke, having received orders to join the army, limited himself to assisting the prince by detaching Her Majesty's Leib-Cuirassiers, commanded by Prinz Leopold von Sachsen-Coburg [Leopold Georg Christian Friedrich von Sachsen-Coburg-Saalfeld], who, upon reaching Krietzschwitz, formed the reserves of II Corps along with the Lubny Hussars. At four o'clock in the afternoon (other sources state five o'clock), Count Osterman-Tolstoy [Alexander Ivanovich Osterman-Tolstoy] arrived from the headquarters in order to take command of the assembled forces facing Königstein on the right wing of the army. German historians, somewhat biased towards Prinz Eugen, considered it inappropriate to appoint Count Osterman to replace him, but they have lost sight of one very important factor: up to this point, the prince had never commanded an independent formation; in contrast, Osterman had operated completely independently at the battle of Ostrovno.[35]

---

34 For details of Prinz Eugen's force, see Appendix XII at the end of this chapter.
35 In the action at Gedeonovo, in 1812, the prince directed operations in the presence of Barclay de Tolly. War Diary of II Corps, Archive of the M.T.D. No. 47,344; Lieutenant Wachten's notes, Archive of the M.T.D. No. 47,353; Bernhardi, III, 163-166.

Count Osterman, who had become famous for his fearlessness in the Patriotic War of 1812, was a man of wilful and irritable character, but, despite being placed in extraordinary circumstances, he showed himself worthy of his renown. According to the words of Prinz Eugen himself, Osterman, although voluntarily giving him control of the ongoing course of action, nevertheless, did not concede the place of honour when advancing to engage the threat.[36]

The positions taken up by the prince on the Pirna plateau offered important advantages: they were protected frontally by a ravine; the right wing, strengthened by the village of Krietzschwitz, rested on the steep bank of the Gottleuba river, while the left wing rested on the village of Struppen and the Elbe. The enemy, in advancing against this position, would be forced to fight their way out of the forest and deploy under Russian artillery fire.

At four o'clock in the afternoon, Colonel Wolfe's skirmishers were driven out of the forest by the enemy. At the same time, General Helffreich moved off from Leupoldishain towards Rottwerndorf, having sent General Ilovaisky 12th to Berggießhübel with his Cossacks and the Grand Duchess' Battalion. The Prinz von Württemberg ordered Colonel Wolfe to retreat to the high ground between Struppen and the Elbe with the Chernigov Infantry and two guns and join the left wing of the corps, while sending the Murom Infantry to the village of Krietzschwitz, already held by a battalion of Minsk Infantry. The 4th Jägers were ordered to defend the village of Groß-Struppen; the Kremenchug Infantry, Volhynia Infantry and Tobolsk Infantry were stationed in two lines in column of attack between Struppen and Krietzschwitz, and a little behind these villages; 16 guns from 14th Light Company and 27th Light Company, commanded by Colonel Baykov [Ivan Ivanovich Baykov], were deployed behind the ravine, ahead of the front line; the hussars and cuirassiers were in reserve. Prince Shakhovskoy was entrusted with direct command of the left flank, while the prince himself was on the right, behind the village of Krietzschwitz.

No sooner had Wolfe's force managed to fall back to their position, than the enemy, emerging from the forest, moved forward in several columns, but were engaged and checked by the fire of the Russian battery, to which the enemy could not reply due to the absence of their artillery. The French columns, for the most part, headed along the road known as the Burgstraße, and along the edge of the forest, towards Krietzschwitz, which obliged the prince to reinforce this location with the Volhynia Infantry. A very lively firefight broke out here. The commander of the Murom Infantry, Lieutenant Colonel Vietinghoff [Andrei Karlovich Fitingof or Vietinghoff], was killed. Count Osterman suffered a contusion to the arm, but would not leave the battlefield. General Pyshnitsky [Dmitry Ilyich Pyshnitsky] moved to reinforce the left wing with the Kremenchug Infantry, leaving only the Tobolsk Infantry in the second line. Whereupon the enemy cavalry deployed facing Baykov's battery. Observing this, the prince pushed the Tobolsk Infantry forward to protect the guns, and ordered the cuirassiers to move into the front line to the left of the infantry. The enemy launched an attack on the left wing of II Corps in several columns covered by a dense screen of skirmishers, but still without artillery support.

---

36 For details of this decision, see Appendix XIII at the end of this chapter.

The losses to the Russian force, and especially the 4th Jägers, were very serious, but Prince Shakhovskoy managed to hold out in the village of Groß-Struppen until nightfall. The French deployed several guns against Baykov's battery at dusk and opened a cannonade, which, however, did not last long. The casualties in II Corps ranged from 1,500 to 1,800 men. In advancing against the Russians benefitting from natural obstacles and with artillery support, in all likelihood, the French lost more.[37]

After the action at Krietzschwitz, the enemy, having deployed strong batteries facing the Russian position during the night, would be able to attack them in overwhelming strength and envelope the troops of II Corps, weakened by the losses suffered, on both flanks. Prinz Eugen clearly saw the impossibility of maintaining his position. It remained to be decided whether he should protect the route to Bohemia, or provide support from the rear for the army stationed at Dresden. The simultaneous fulfilment of these two objectives was impossible, due to the small number of troops at the prince's disposal. The protection of the Pirna highway, in the event of the army retreating to Bohemia, promised success only once positions had been occupied at Nollendorf, and even then, there was nothing preventing Vandamme from outflanking the Russians by using side roads, or, by leaving one division facing them at Berggießhübel, moving into the rear of the Coalition army. In contrast, by retreating towards Dresden, II Corps would be strengthened by significant reinforcements, and besides, Prinz Eugen believed that Schwarzenberg had launched an offensive in the sure hope of success, and that the capture of Dresden by the Coalition forces made the protection of the lines of communications with Bohemia less important than was the case with this city and the bridges on the Elbe located there under Napoleon's control.

Based on this assessment, the Prinz von Württemberg withdrew the troops of II Corps and the cavalry attached to them to the high ground behind Zehista, leaving as a rearguard: General Pyshnitsky on the Pirna plateau near the Himmelreich manor with the Volhynia Infantry and Kremenchug Infantry; while 4th Jägers were on the Kohlberg [two miles south of Pirna]. Helffreich's detachment were located at Cotta, and Ilovaisky's detachment at Berggießhübel. Thus, although the Pirna highway was not adequately protected, it remained under observation by Russian forces.[38]

As it was very important to convey the outcome of the action at Krietzschwitz to headquarters and about the measures taken to secure the lines of communications for the army, the Prinz von Württemberg sent his Chief of Staff, Colonel Hofmann [Georg Wilhelm von Hofmann], there on the evening of 14 (26) August with instructions to expedite the dispatch of reinforcements to assist II Corps.

Colonel Hofmann called on Count Wittgenstein, who sent him to Barclay de Tolly, while Barclay sent him to Schwarzenberg. The commander-in-chief was surprised and dissatisfied in equal measure at the weakness of the detachment left at Königstein. Just as the Austrian general staff were concerned with protecting the shortest and easiest lines of communication with Bohemia, Schwarzenberg, greatly concerned by Hofmann's report, summoned Radetzky and Prince Volkonsky [Pëtr Mikhailovich Volkonsky?] to a meeting. Both of them expressed their conviction of the need to

---

37 War Diary of II Corps.
38 War Diary of II Corps.

protect the highway, and therefore the Commander-in-Chief repeated to Hofmann several times that holding this route open was the Prinz von Württemberg's primary operational objective. This same opinion was expressed once again by Radetzky as he escorted Hofmann out of the door to the room in which the meeting had taken place. At the same time, they directed him back to Barclay de Tolly, with orders to strengthen the detachment at Königstein. Barclay, who was not as convinced of the importance of holding the Pirna highway as were the Austrian staff, limited himself to detaching the 1st Lifeguard Division, commanded by General Yermolov [Alexei Petrovich Yermolov] to assist the Prinz von Württemberg, and on the march from Ottendorf [three miles south of Zehista] to Dresden at the time.[39]

In the meantime, Prinz Eugen had withdrawn the troops of II Corps from the Gottleuba river and repositioned them between Pirna and Zehista. Despite the darkness of the night and the pouring rain, the crossing of the deep ravine through which this river flows was carried out in good order, and the Russian troops redeployed in the positions indicated for them, where at dawn they were joined by the 1st Lifeguard Division, the Lifeguard Hussars and the Tatar Ulans, as well as General Pyshnitsky's rearguard. Count Osterman took command of the entire force assembled at Pirna, numbering some 16,000 men with 40 guns, not including the detachments under Helffreich and Ilovaisky.[40]

---

39 Hofmann, 147; Bernhardi, III, 167.
40 War Diary of II Corps.

Appendix XII

The composition of Prinz Eugen von Württemberg's force

Prinz Eugen von Württemberg's force consisted of:

> Units from II Corps: Murom Infantry, Reval Infantry, Chernigov Infantry, Selenginsk Infantry, Tobolsk Infantry, Volhynia Infantry, Kremenchug Infantry, Minsk Infantry, 4th Jägers, two squadrons of Lubny Hussars, 14th Light Artillery Company and 27th Light Artillery Company; for a total of 15 battalions,[1] two squadrons and 18 guns (six guns had been detached to Count Wittgenstein's vanguard.
>
> Units from I Corps, commanded by Major General Helffreich: Tenginsk Infantry, Estland Infantry and Grand Duchess Yekaterina Pavlovna's Battalion (five battalions), Ilovaisky 12th's Cossacks and six foot artillery pieces.

According to the Prinz von Württemberg's own account, the Selenginsk Infantry were detached to Count Wittgenstein's vanguard, but the presence of this regiment at Dresden is not mentioned anywhere (War Diary of II Corps, Archive of the M.T.D. No. 47,344).

---

1 Three of these regiments were only able to field a single battalion.

Appendix XIII

Extracts from the War Diary of II Corps and Lieutenant General Wachten's notes

> ... One must know the loyal nature of Count Ostermann in order to understand that a few observations on my part were enough to induce him to surrender the care of this action to me, which was about to begin and whose outcome was also important to us. This compromise on his part, dictated by the conviction that it is dangerous to replace one commander with another during combat and thus muddling the views of two people on the execution of arrangements of which only one may be precisely aware, effectively saved me from a disaster, prevented the consequences of the misunderstanding whose real cause I still do not know to this day, and thus brought about the victory on 17 (29) August – a triumph due to two reasons: to the virtue and courage of one who, in ceding his right of seniority here, never shied away from leading in the place of honour and in the face of danger...

Archive of the M.T.D. No. 47,344.

> ... *Il faut connaitre le caractère loyal du comte Ostermann pour comprendre que quelques observations de ma part suffirent pour l'engager à m'abandonner les soins de l'affaire, qui allait commencer et dont l'issue nous tenat également à coeur. Cette condescendance de sa part, dictée par la conviction qu'il est dangereux de remplacer un chef par l'autre au moment du combat et de confondre ainsi les vues de deux personnes dans l'exécution de dispositions dont un seul peut être au fait éxactement, me sauva effectivement d'un abume, prévint les suites d'un quiproquo dont j'ignore encore aujourd'hui la cause réelle, et achemina ainsi la victoire du 17 (29) – un triomphe dû par double raison à la vertu et au courage de celui qui en cedant ici son droit d'ancienneté, ne ceda cependant jamais le pas pour aller au dévant du danger et de l'honneur...*

In contrast, Wachten wrote in his notes:

> The prince announced to him (Osterman) that he had issued all the orders necessary to engage the enemy, and that he, in such an important and critical situation for the force he commanded, could not and would not hand over command of them.

APPENDIX XIII 145

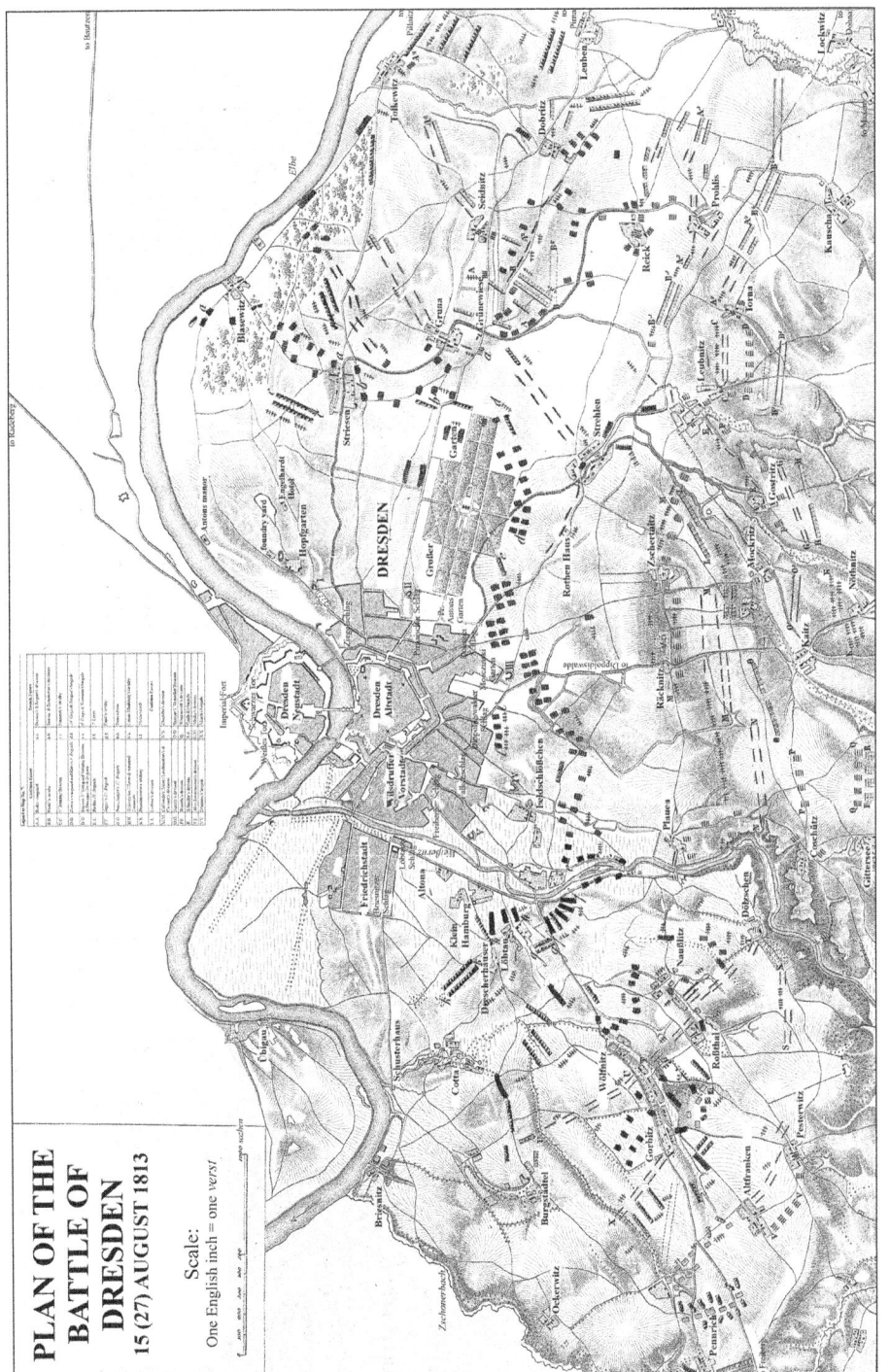

Plan of the Battle of Dresden, 15 (27) August 1813.

Legend to Map No. 7

Coalition Forces

A.A.	Roth's vanguard	
B.B.	Röder's cavalry	
C.C.	5th Infantry Division	
D.D.	Zieten's vanguard and Klüx's *9. Brigade*	
D'D'	Russian 2nd Lifeguard Infantry Division & Prussian *Garde Brigade*	
E.E.	Pirch's *10. Brigade*	
F.F.	Jagow's *11. Brigade*	
G.G.	Prinz August's *12. Brigade*	
H.H.	*Schlesisches Ulanen* & mounted *Landwehr*	
K.K.	Prussian reserve artillery	
L.L.	Lederer's division	
M.M.	Colloredo's, Moritz Liechtenstein's & Civalart's divisions	
N.N.	Chasteler's division	
O.O.	Nostitz's division	
O'O'	Russian 1st Grenadier Division	
P.P.	Bianchi's division	
Q.	Weissenwolf's division	
R.	Schneller's division	
S.S.	Csollich's brigade	
T.T.	Alois Liechtenstein's division	
U.U.	Mesko's division	
V.V.	Mariássy's brigade	
X.X.	Mumb's brigade	

French Forces

a.a.	Decouz's & Roguet's divisions
b.b.	Barrois' & Dumoustier's divisions
c.c.	Nansouty's cavalry
d.d.	*14e Corps* & Jacquet's brigade
e.e.	*6e Corps* & Normann's brigade
f.f.	*2e Corps*
g.g.	Pajol's cavalry
h.h.	Teste's force
k.k.	Latour-Maubourg's cavalry
l.l.	*Vieille Garde*

28

The Battle of Dresden (continued)

The deployment of both sides on the morning of 15 (27) August. The fighting on 15 (27) August. The cannonade. Operations on the Kaitzbach and in the centre. – Operations on the right wing of the Coalition army: the advance by the *Jeune Garde* and Nansouty's cavalry; the gradual retreat by Roth's vanguard and Röder's cavalry; their subsequent redeployment. The proposal by Moreau and Jomini to attack the enemy left wing with Barclay de Tolly's forces. – Moreau is severely wounded. – Operations on the Coalition left wing: a comparison of the strength of both sides at this location; Murat's advance and the defeat of the Austrians. – The Coalition are forced to retreat. – Dispositions for the retreat. – Napoleon's return to Dresden.

The situation at Pirna on 15 (27) August. The deployment of Russian forces at Zehista. – Vandamme's inaction.

Napoleon prepares for battle once more; his orders. – He has doubts about a successful end to the war.

On the morning of 15 (27) August, the Coalition forces concentrated around Dresden were deployed as follows:[1] the vanguard of Count Wittgenstein's corps, commanded by Major General Roth, were stationed from the Pirna highway at Grünewiese, to the Pillnitz road, near the Tolkewitz forest, holding the village of Blasewitz with a small outpost of infantry and Cossacks; 5th Division, commanded by Prince Gorchakov [Andrei Ivanovich Gorchakov], were deployed in the sector between Torna and Leubnitz. Röder's cavalry were stationed behind Gruna in support of the Russian contingent, while Zieten's Prussian vanguard and Klüx's *9. Brigade* were in the support line behind the Russian 5th Division. Behind them, in reserve, were the Russian 2nd Lifeguard Division and the Prussian *Garde Brigade*. Pirch's *10. Brigade* and Jagow's *11. Brigade* were stationed between Leubnitz and Gostritz. Prinz August's *12. Brigade* were behind Gostritz in the second line; the *Schlesisches Ulanen* and mounted *Landwehr* were in the third line; the

---

1   See Map No. 7 Plan of the Battle of Dresden, 15 (27) August.

Prussian reserve artillery were forwards of Nöthnitz. Lederer's cavalry division were stationed behind Zschertnitz; Colloredo's division were behind Räcknitz with Civalart's division and Moritz Liechtenstein's division behind them in the second line; Chasteler's division were to the left of Civalart's force, extending as far as the Plauensche Grund; Nostitz's cavalry division were stationed in the third line of the Austrian contingent; the Russian 1st Grenadier Division were behind Zschertnitz, while Bianchi's and Weissenwolf's Austrian infantry divisions were at Gittersee with Schneller's cavalry division, forming the general reserve. On the left wing, beyond the Plauensche Grund were stationed: Csollich's brigade and Alois Liechtenstein's division, which had arrived during the night, between Dölzschen and Gorbitz; Mesko's division were between Gorbitz and Burgstädtel; Mumb's brigade were behind them in the second line; Mariássy's brigade were in reserve, between Pesterwitz and Altfranken. The three Russian cuirassier divisions and Lifeguard light cavalry remained at Lockwitz.[2]

On Napoleon's part, upon the arrival of *2e Corps* and *6e Corps* during the nights of 14 to 15 (26 to 27) August, the troops were located along the outer edge of the Altstadt and suburbs, as follows: Marshal Mortier was on the left wing between the Elbe and the Großer Garten with Decouz's and Roguet's divisions of the *Jeune Garde*, and General Nansouty with the *cavalerie de la garde* divisions under Ornano [Philippe Antoine d'Ornano] and Lefebvre; Barrois' and Dumoustier's other two divisions of the *Jeune Garde* had assembled at the Falkenschlag under Marshal Ney's command, advanced through the Großer Garten and deployed to the right of Striesen; Marshal Saint-Cyr was stationed facing Strehlen with *14e Corps* and Jacquet's light cavalry brigade [Jean-Pierre Jacquet]; *6e Corps* were either side of the Dippoldiswalde road with Normann's light cavalry brigade [Karl Friedrich Lebrecht von Normann-Ehrenfels], for a total of 42 battalions and eight squadrons, extending their right flank towards Plauen; Marshal Victor's *2e Corps*, were formed up on the left bank of the Weißeritz, forwards of Friedrichstadt, consisting of 38 battalions, together with Teste's division (six battalions) and the cavalry under Latour-Maubourg and Pajol, under the overall command of Murat. The *Vieille Garde* and Walther's division [Frédéric Henri Walther] of the *cavalerie de la garde* were stationed in reserve between lunettes No. III and No. IV. The strength of Napoleon's force overall, as already mentioned, reached 120,000 men.[3]

On the morning of 15 (27) August, the heavy rain continued. The sky was so overcast that any observation, even over short distances, became impossible. Despite this, however, at seven o'clock a powerful cannonade began along the entire line by both sides. At the same time, Emperor Alexander, the King of Prussia and Schwarzenberg arrived on the high ground at Räcknitz, surrounded by their numerous suites. Napoleon also hurried to the battlefield, to lunette No. IV, with the *Vieille Garde*

---

2   Hofmann, *Zur Geschichte des Feldzuges von 1813*, 148; Plotho *Der Krieg in Deutschland und Frankreich in den Jahren 1813 und 1814*, II, 55-66. According to Wagner (*Plane der Schlachten und Treffen, 1813, 14 und 15*, 43) and Richter (*Geschichte des Deutschen Freiheitskrieges*, II, 50), Moritz Liechtenstein's cavalry were stationed by the Plauensche Grund, while Schneller's cavalry division were on the extreme left flank.
3   Aster, *Schilderung der Kriegsereignisse in und vor Dresden, 1813*, 270-271.

stationed nearby. For three hours, the battle was limited to artillery action, because it was almost impossible to fire muskets at all.

Also at dawn, two Prussian battalions located in the Großer Garten Palace (first battalion of *2. Westpreussisches Infanterie* and second battalion of *7. Reserve Infanterie*) evacuated the building and rejoined *10. Brigade*. A battalion from *11. Reserve Infanterie* holding Strehlen, upon being attacked there by Saint-Cyr's force, defended themselves from eight o'clock until ten o'clock and did not retreat until receiving orders to withdraw to Leubnitz. Prinz August's force, lining the right bank of the Kaitzbach and the scrub in the low ground with a dense screen of skirmishers and being supported by the fire of a battery placed on the high ground to the right of Leubnitz, began a heated action with the enemy. At ten o'clock, orders were received to relieve the Prussian force in this village with Russians. The French, believing that the Coalition were intending to retreat, sent a strong column from Strehlen to seize Leubnitz and burst into the village, but were engaged by fire from two guns stationed near the church and were driven off by a bayonet charge from *2. Schlesisches Infanterie*. A little later, the enemy launched another attack on the village, but were repulsed with casualties by the Mogilev Infantry, commanded by General Diebitsch, and retreated beyond the Kaitzbach. Napoleon, who was with Saint-Cyr's force at the time, ordered a battery of *artillerie à cheval* to be driven up to the high ground near Strehlen and intensified the cannonade. Having received a report from Murat in the meantime about the success of the outflanking movement by the force sent to get behind the Austrians, he ordered the storming of Leubnitz once more, but the French column rushing to attack were halted by the fire of Russian batteries and cut down by the Austrian *Chevauxleger von Vincent*. The Coalition managed to keep the village in their hands until nightfall, which put an end to the firefight on the Kaitzbach.[4] At the same time, while the battle in the centre was mostly limited to a cannonade, at about ten o'clock in the morning, the French launched an attack against the right wing of the Coalition army and after that Murat attacked the Austrian left wing.

As has already been mentioned, a force under General Roth was located at the very tip of the Coalition right wing. Their infantry, consisting of nine battalions, were located between the Grünewiese manor and the Tolkewitz forest, holding Gruna and Blasewitz.[5] There were six guns from Colonel Zakharzhevsky's 6th Horse Artillery Company [Yakov Vasilievich Zakharzhevsky] forwards of Grünewiese on the Pirna highway. The Grodno Hussars and Lubny Hussars were deployed behind Grünewiese and Gruna. Rodionov's Cossacks and the Ataman's Cossacks were by the Pillnitz road, with the Sumy Hssars behind them. As early as eight o'clock, elements of Roguet's division moved towards Blasewitz also through the nearby pine woods and, after a short skirmish, forced the Russians back to Tolkewitz. The action was much fiercer at the village of Striesen. Here the French deployed in significant strength with a great deal of artillery, which the Russians could counter with only a few guns. The battalions of *9e voltigeurs* and *10e voltigeurs de la garde* from Decouz's

---

4   Aster, 287-293; Plotho, II, 59; Richter, II, 55; Wagner, 46.
5   The infantry in General Roth's vanguard consisted of: 20th Jägers, 21st Jägers, 25th Jägers, 26th Jägers and 34th Jägers.

division attacked the village of Gruna, while Barrois' and Dumoustier's divisions formed up on both sides of the Pirna highway near the Großer Garten. Roth's men were forced to evacuate Gruna and retreat to Seidnitz, where, having taken up positions, they engaged the enemy with cannon fire, whereupon General Roth (having received orders from Count Wittgenstein, in the event of pressure from superior enemy numbers, not to retreat along the highway, rather, to fall back through Reick and Prohlis towards Torna, and to join the right flank of the army), refusing his right wing in the direction of Tolkewitz, he rested the left on Seidnitz, and moved eight guns to the high ground at Tolkewitz in order to fire on the enemy forces attacking along the Pillnitz road.[6] The French placed a strong battery in front of the woods, and, having silenced the Russian guns, pushed the vanguard beyond the Pirna highway. The stubborn defence of the village of Seidnitz won General Roth enough time to reposition his force between this village and Dobritz, parallel to the highway. After the Russians had evacuated the village of Tolkewitz, Nansouty's French cavalry passed through it and formed up in two lines facing the vanguard's new positions. At the same time, Decouz's division attacked Seidnitz and, after repeated assaults, eventually managed to capture this village. General Roth, outflanked by the enemy on the left, was forced to retreat by ten o'clock. The battery stationed to the right of Dobritz with a cavalry escort, held the French back and enabled the vanguard to retreat to Reick. At the same time, Röder's Prussian reserve cavalry behind the left wing of the Seidnitz position, retreated behind Reick and positioned themselves in two lines forwards of the Dohna road.

At 11 o'clock, as the French were breaking into Seidnitz, Napoleon turned up. Just a few minutes later, while riding through the Großer Garten, he was almost killed by a cannonball that struck by the hooves of his horse. Having evaded a clear threat and having witnessed the success of his forces, Napoleon, in a most cheerful mood, ordered General Pelet to attack Reick with his brigade (*3e Division* of the *Jeune Garde*), supported by the troops of Roguet's *4e Division*. Russian jägers had, in the meantime, already lined the embankment and drainage ditch (Landgraben) that protected this village on its northern and eastern sides. Coalition cavalry were stationed to the right of the infantry with eight guns. On Napoleon's personal orders, the *8e voltigeurs* and *4e voltigeurs* (each of four battalions) proceeded from Grünewiese across the bridge on the Landgraben towards this position. The *9e voltigeurs* were to protect the bridge as the troops crossed the drain. The *10e voltigeurs* closed up to the Landgraben. The *5e voltigeurs* advanced from the eastern side of the village. At the same time, the remaining regiments of the *Jeune Garde* formed up in front of Dobritz, while Nansouty deployed his cavalry to their left. The French advanced to the attack with loud shouts of: *vive l'empereur!* The Russian batteries engaged them with canister. One of the French battalions of *5e voltigeurs*, charged in the flank by the Lubny Hussars, formed square but were scattered by the hussars and lost 11 officers and 300 lower ranks. Unfortunately,

---

6   According to Richter (II, 52), the French *9e voltigeurs* captured three Prussian guns during the attack on the village of Gruna.

during this attack, the hero Melissino died, hit by three bullets.⁷ The French *4e voltigeurs* were also disordered in this attack. Having received word from soldiers fleeing the battlefield that some of the *5e voltigeurs* had rushed into the village of Reick and were holding on there in anticipation of assistance, Mortier sent a company from the *9e voltigeurs* to rescue these troops and led Roguet's division forwards. Nansouty's cavalry advanced, shielding the left wing of the infantry. The defence of Reick by Roth's troops was so stubborn that the French could only eject them by setting fire to the houses on the edges of the village. The Russian jägers continued to defend the southern part of Reick, and in the heat of battle, amid clouds of smoke, in heavy rain, they did not notice that the enemy had managed to get around their right flank and had also cut off their line of retreat to Prohlis. Roth's force, paying no attention, held out in that part of the village they still held. All arms of the army were fighting here as cannon and musket volleys thundered. The entire surrounding area was littered with corpses. Once French forces had captured Reick at noon, the Russian infantry retreated to the high ground near the village of Torna, while the cavalry of the Russian vanguard were stationed behind Prohlis with eight guns from 6th Horse Artillery Company and Röder's Prussian cavalry. The reserve cavalry under Prince Golitsyn [Dmitry Vladimirovich Golitsyn 5th] joined them here after the fighting had ended. The French halted facing Prohlis, limiting themselves to a cannonade, from which several houses in this village burned down, and strongly garrisoned Reick, Seidnitz, Dobritz and Leuben with infantry. Nansouty's cavalry withdrew behind Dobritz and settled for the night, some in bivouacs, some in cramped quarters in Blasewitz and Tolkewitz. Roth's force, with Röder's Prussian cavalry attached, numbering no more than 5,000 men, fighting all day against 20,000 men under Mortier and Nansouty, and prevented them from achieving any breakthrough, capturing many prisoners. According to one of the most truthful foreign historians:

> General Roth, moreover, very successfully accomplished the difficult mission assigned to him, namely, to execute a rearward change of front in the face of superior enemy forces, on completely waterlogged ground, and despite constant, severe enemy pressure on his pivot point. He lost only a few men as prisoners, his troops demonstrated their ability to manoeuvre and gave new evidence of the well-known Russian courage, as the heavy losses of their own and the French testify.⁸

---

7   Several military historians (Aster, 278; Richter, II, 54; Wagner, 45) mistakenly attribute the attack on the *5e voltigeurs* to the Grodno Hussars, while Plotho (II, 60) wrote that the enemy were engaged by Russian jägers and were driven off by the Grodno Hussans, Lubny Hussars and *Schlesisches Husaren*.
8   Richter, II, 54. According to Aster (286): 'General Roth hat übrigens den ihm übertragenen schwierigen Auftrag, eine Schwenkung rückwärts bei überlegenen feindlichen Streitkräften, bei völlig aufgeweichten Boden und bei stetem heftigen Drängen des Gegners auf seinen Drehpunkt, sehr glücklich gelöst. Er verlor dabei nur wenige Mann an gefangenen, seine Truppen bewiesen Manoeuvrirfähigkeit und gaben neue Belege zu der bekannten russischen Tapferkeit, wie diess ihr eigener und der Franzosen grosser Verlust bezeugte.'

But giving due justice to the courage of the small Russian vanguard and the leadership of its commander, one cannot help but notice that the main Coalition commanders, Schwarzenberg and Barclay de Tolly, did not take advantage of the favourable opportunity offered by the rash advance by Mortier and Nansouty between the Elba and the right wing under Count Wittgenstein. The enemy would have suffered an inevitable defeat if the Russo-Prussian reserves had been sent there, or at least the reserve cavalry under Prince Golitsyn, stationed at Lockwitz close to the battlefield and, despite the heavy going, could have operated successfully on the open ground between Prohlis and Leuben.[9]

Generals Moreau and Jomini considered it essential to reopen the Pirna highway, and as Roth's vanguard was retreating from Seidnitz to Reick, they proposed to the Coalition Monarchs that Barclay de Tolly should descend from the high ground with Wittgenstein's and Kleist's corps and with the Russian-Prussian reserves, attack the French forces advancing from Gruna and Seidnitz and push them back towards the Elbe. The proposal was approved by both Sovereigns, and Barclay received orders – directly from Emperor Alexander – to attack the enemy, but, not wanting to leave the advantageous position occupied by him, he replied that, having descended from the high ground onto the swampy plain, he would lose the opportunity to move the artillery again along the mountain slopes. And indeed, the heavy rain has swamped the ground to such an extent that any troop movement became very difficult. At the very moment that the aide de camp sent with this report from Barclay rode up to the Coalition Monarchs, Moreau was seriously wounded a few paces from Emperor Alexander.[10]

General Moreau, one of the most famous military commanders of the era of the revolutionary wars, died in this first battle, without having chance to demonstrate either his abilities or his diligence to Emperor Alexander, to whom he was sincerely devoted. The sole memory of his stay in the Coalition headquarters was a note presented to the Emperor, in Jungfernteinitz [Panenský Týnec, 23 miles southeast of Brüx], a week before the battle of Dresden, which primarily outlined the importance of collecting intelligence on the enemy through informants.[11] Had he not been mortally wounded so unexpectedly in this first battle, then in all likelihood, all subsequent military appreciations by the Russian Monarch would have been influenced by him. On 14 (26) August, Moreau was on horseback almost all day with Emperor Alexander, and at eight o'clock in the evening, wanting to inform the Emperor of his recommendations from his observations, rode through such a thick hail of shell and canister that Colonel Svinin [Pavel Petrovich Svinin], who accompanied him, wondered how both of them remained unharmed. The following day [27 August], Moreau rode across the battlefield from one end to the other, and noticing the weakness of the left wing of the Coalition army, rode to the high ground at Räcknitz to bring this to the attention of Emperor Alexander. Having reached the Emperor at about half past one o'clock in the afternoon, and seeing that the French, who had apparently noticed the large retinue of the headquarters,

---

9   Aster, 272-283; Plotho, II, 59-60; Richter, II, 52-54; Wagner, 44-46.
10 Bernhardi, *Denkwürdigkeiten aus dem Leben Carl Friedrich Grafen von Toll*, III, 172-173.
11 For the text of this note, see Appendix XIV at the end of this chapter.

turned the fire of their battery stationed in the Mosczinski Garten against it, he suggested that the Emperor move to a different vantage point, from where it would be possible to observe the battlefield more clearly and more safely. As it was only possible to move in single file along the narrow path leading there across the lower ground, the Emperor, turning to Moreau, told him: 'go ahead, and we will follow you.' Accompanying Emperor Alexander at that time were: Lord Cathcart [William Schaw Cathcart], the British General Wilson [Robert Thomas Wilson], Colonel Rapatel and several Russian officers. At that very moment, with Moreau two paces ahead of the Emperor, continuing to talk with him about his reconnaissance, saying: 'trust my expertise,' a round shot fired from the French *Garde* battery in the presence of Napoleon himself, hit General Moreau, severed his right leg, and punching through his horse, shattered his left knee. The completely exhausted victim was raised by his friend, Colonel Rapatel. A few minutes later, having come to his senses, he asked about the Emperor, and being reassured about the Tsar, he said to Rapatel: 'I am dying… but do not be sad, my friend! It is good to die for a just cause and within sight of a great Monarch.' Having been carried to Nöthnitz on a stretcher improvised from Cossack lances covered with greatcoats, Moreau endured an operation there – the amputation of both legs above the knee – performed by the Imperial physician Wylie [Yakov Vasilievich Villie or James Wylie]. Then, through rainy weather, during the difficult Coalition retreat to Bohemia, he was carried to Laun [Louny, 15 miles south of Bilin] via Dippoldiswalde and Dux, where he died three days later on 21 August (2 September), retaining his mental faculties until his death, even writing a few lines to his wife and to Emperor Alexander in the last hour of his life.[12] The Emperor, in a rescript to Moreau's wife, expressing his sorrow, wrote: 'The friendship that I have assured your husband extends beyond the grave, and I have no other means of repaying my debt to him, albeit in part, than by doing some good for his family.'[13]

A modest monument has been erected on the hill behind Räcknitz, near the spot where Moreau fell.[14]

The unexpected blow that befell Moreau came at the same time as Barclay was sending a report about the impossibility of going on the offensive with the force entrusted to him. Under such circumstances, it was impossible to expect rapid energetic orders – neither from the Tsar himself, nor from the influential personnel in the headquarters. At the same time, *Flügel-Adjutant* [equerry] Wolzogen [Justus Philipp Adolf Wilhelm Ludwig von Wolzogen] returned, having been sent to the Prinz von Württemberg's detachment to obtain accurate information on the progress of the action in the vicinity of Pirna. His report aroused Emperor Alexander's justifiable

---

12 In the Log of Outgoing Documents there is the following note from Adjutant General Prince Volkonsky to Grand Duke Konstantin Pavlovich: 'If it please Your Imperial Highness to order the immediate assignment of 40 reliable, and strong privates of equal height from the 1st Grenadier Division together with two non-commissioned officers and one officer, who are to be tasked with carrying the wounded General Moreau.'
13 For the text of this letter, see Appendix XV at the end of this chapter.
14 From Prague, where a solemn funeral service was held for General Moreau, his body was transported to St. Petersburg and interred in the Catholic Church, with the same honours as were given to the late Field Marshal Prince Kutuzov.

concerns, as he did not then know of Barclay's detachment of the 1st Lifeguard Division to assist II Corps, and issued orders directly from himself for them to be send as reinforcements to the Prinz von Württemberg. The advance by Barclay's reserves against the left wing of the enemy army was not confirmed, while soon thereafter, the misfortune of the Austrian troops beyond the Plauensche Grund forced the headquarters, and the Commander-in-Chief in particular, to abandon hope of success and undertake the retreat to Bohemia.[15]

The failure suffered by the Austrians on their left wing was a consequence of Schwarzenberg's erroneous orders. The troops stationed on the left side of the ravine (numbering 25 battalions and 12 squadrons, for a total of 20,000 infantry and 2,000 cavalry) were spread out over a large area and did not have sufficient reserves behind them. The main strength of this position lay in the villages across it, but they were very weakly held. Most of the troops stationed there consisted of Hungarian or Galician recruits.

Napoleon, with his customary faith in his military instincts, having assessed the weakness of his adversary's left wing, concentrated significant forces against it in order to deliver the decisive blow, namely: Victor's *2e Corps*, elements of Teste's division, Latour-Maubourg's *1er corps de cavalerie* and Pajols' cavalry, consisting of 46 battalions and 90 squadrons (numbering some 25,000 infantry and some 12,000 cavalry). Victor's force, having assembled at seven o'clock in the morning in front of the Freiberger Schlag, formed up in four columns by ten o'clock, followed by a fifth column consisting of cavalry. There were three batteries forwards of the columns, protected by a screen of skirmishers. Elements of Teste's force were assigned to seize the village of Löbtau, abandoned by the Austrians. Latour-Maubourg's cavalry deployed to the right of Drescherhäuser, while Pajol's cavalry were to the left of Löbtau. Once the French had taken the latter village, Murat opened a strong cannonade against the Austrian front line troops, and meanwhile sent several of Teste's battalions with some of the cavalry down the banks of the Elbe, to Schusterhaus, and on to the Zschonerbach, in order to outflank the enemy position on the left. As soon as these troops had managed to reach their designated locations, the divisions under Dubreton [Jean-Louis Dubreton] and Dufour [François Marie Dufour] (from Victor's corps) attacked the high ground at Naußlitz and Wölfnitz. They were followed by Vial's division [Honoré Vial]. Liechtenstein's skirmishers vainly attempted to defend these villages. The pouring rain made it impossible to shoot and gave Murat's cavalry a decisive superiority over the Austrian infantry. While Victor's force strongly garrisoned both of the villages they had taken and broke into Roßthal, Murat, wanting to split the Austrians into two separate parts, led his cavalry towards Gorbitz. The French generals Bordesoulle [Étienne Tardif de Pommeroux de Bordesoulle], Doumerc and Audenarde [Charles Eugène de Lalaing d'Audenarde] cut into the Austrian squares, competing with each other at the head of their horsemen. The infantry, deprived of the opportunity to shoot back, perished, surrendered, or sought salvation in flight. The Austrians had already been driven into Gorbitz, where the troops under Dufour and Vial broke in after them.

---

15 Bernhardi, III, 173.

Murat, having crashed through the centre of the enemy line, wheeled to the left with Latour-Maubourg's cavalry supported by Dubreton's force towards Dölzschen, against Alois Liechtenstein, in order to push him back into the Plauensche Grund. The Austrians were defending themselves desperately. Liechtenstein himself, roused to higher feats by the hereditary valour of his family, stood at the head of the *Infanterieregiment Wenzel Colloredo* and led them with bayonets fixed. Yet the enemy were getting stronger by the minute, and the brave warriors, betrayed by the mistakes of their commander-in-chief, were forced to retreat. Having reached Altfranken and Pesterwitz, the troops from Liechtenstein's division strongly garrisoned these villages, established communications with Klenau's leading units, stretched out from Tharandt, and avoided destruction by crossing the Weißeritz, at Potschappel [two miles west of Gittersee]. Only the *Infanterieregiment Wenzel Colloredo*, who were covering the retreat of all the others, was surrounded by enemy cavalry and lost many men. Csollich's brigade, under the protection of the *Infanterieregiment Kottulinsky*, who were defending the village of Dölzschen, engulfed in flames, retreated through Potschappel to Gittersee, while Mariássy's brigade retreated to meet the corps under Graf Klenau.

The fate of the forces stationed at Gorbitz was incomparably more disastrous. During the attacks on the villages of Wölfnitz and Naußlitz, some of the infantry from Mesko's division, retreating towards Obergorbitz, rushed into the village, while others joined Mumb's brigade on either side of it, pushing batteries forwards in order to fire at Murat's force. The French, having pushed Liechtenstein's force back from Roßthal towards the Plauensche Grund, wheeled towards the Freiberg road, against the Austrian left wing which they had now isolated. Murat's horse artillery and Victor's and Teste's infantry supported this attack. Mesko's weak cavalry had retreated to Pennrich, Gompitz [two miles north-west of Pennrich], or to Grumbach [4½ miles west of Pennrich] at the very beginning of the battle, while the infantry stationed to the right of Gorbitz formed into four squares, but once the batteries accompanying them were forced to turn their fire against the French artillery, then Murat's cavalry cut into the Austrian squares. Most of the men were cut down or taken prisoner. The remainder fled towards Pesterwitz.

After the French had seized Gorbitz, the Saxon *Kürassier-Regiment Zastrow* were sent past Burgstädtel, into the gap between the villages of Gompitz and Ockerwitz, and after crossing the Freiberg road, they saw an Austrian battery with two squares in front of them. In order to attack these troops, it was necessary to pass alongside a ravine lined with trees and occupied by a dense screen of skirmishers. The cuirassiers were forced to halt, but when a detachment of French infantry came up the road by chance and drove the jägers out of the ravine, the Saxons launched an attack on both squares. The battery left the battlefield, while around 2,000 men of *Infanterieregiment Wacquant*, having repelled two attacks, were overwhelmed and laid down their weapons. Two Colours and one of the departing guns fell into Saxon hands. Following this, Murat's cavalry caught up with Mesko's and Mumb's infantry, who were retreating in square between Gompitz and Pennerich. The Austrians were hurrying towards Pennerich, hoping to take refuge in this village, but it had already fallen to French forces sent on a flanking movement at the beginning of the action. The Austrian infantry, surrounded on all sides by enemy cavalry and struck by fire from French batteries, being unable to return fire, were forced to surrender. The regiments laying down their weapons here were: *Infanterieregiment Beaulieu, Infanterieregiment Saint-Julien, Infanterieregiment Erzherzog Rainer* and *Infanterieregiment Lusignan*. Overall, on this day some 15,000 men were lost to the Austrian army, and *Feldmarschallleutnant* Mesko was among those taken prisoner. At four o'clock, the action on the left wing had already been completely decided, but the French continued to pursue the Austrians along the Freiberg road, hoping to engage Klenau's corps, on whose movement towards Tharandt, in all likelihood, they had no intelligence. They could have known even less that Klenau, having witnessed the defeat of the left wing of the Coalition army, had crossed the Weißeritz and moved onto the Dippoldiswalde road at Rabenau. Throughout the duration of the battle and pursuit, Murat's cavalry captured 16 guns and several Colours.[16]

The defeat of the left wing of the Austrian army had a powerful impact on Schwarzenberg and the main decision-makers on his staff. They all insisted with one voice on the need to retreat to Bohemia immediately. Emperor Alexander did not agree to this, while the King of Prussia proposed to resume the fighting the next day, because most of the army had not yet taken part in the battle. Jomini again gave advice – to retreat to Dippoldiswalde and take up position there on Napoleon's lines of communications. But Schwarzenberg insistently demanded a retreat to Bohemia, pointing out that the Austrian troops had neither provisions nor footwear, and that they had almost no military supplies left with them. This claim was not exaggerated in the least: according to a statement by the *Chef des Stabes* of Klenau's force, Colonel Rothkirch, 'the Austrian soldiers were so exhausted from hunger that many of them were dropping as if lifeless. More than a third of the men were marching barefoot, and so forth.'[17] Yet what conclusions could be drawn regarding the commissariat of the Austrian army, which had allowed this shortage of provisions and footwear right at the beginning of hostilities. This dysfunction had a detrimental effect on the morale of the troops. Contemporaries of the events we describe say that the Russians and Prussians lost confidence in their new ally after the battle of Dresden. In one of Stein's letters [Heinrich Friedrich Karl vom und zum Stein] to Graf Münster [Ernst Friedrich Herbert zu Münster], we find the following assessment:

> Until 1809, the Stadion brothers had sought to raise the spirits of the people and strengthen the army, and achieved their intended aim: the people realised their strength; the troops fought bravely. Currently, at the head of the administration there is a cold, calculating man (Klemens Wenzel Lothar von Metternich) who is averse to any decisive activity, limits himself to insignificant objectives and somehow seeks to darn over the holes (*und mit kümmerlichem Flickwerk sich behilft*), an unnatural marriage, the insane hope of an independent alliance, a puerile congress, a pitiful ultimatum, and such like.[18]

---

16 Richter, II, 60-62; Wagner, 47-48; Aster, 301-317; Lecomte, *Le général Jomini: sa vie et ses écrits*, 177-181.
17 Bernhardi, III, 173-174.
18 Stein's letter dated 23 August, new style, Münster, *Lebensbilder Aus Dem Befreiungskriege*, II, 272.

Under such circumstances, the Coalition monarchs were forced to abandon any further attempts on Dresden. All that remained was to decide along which routes to retreat. The need to move along the highway through Peterswald was obvious, and although Vandamme was astride this route, nevertheless, in the opinion expressed by General Jomini at the time, a 30,000 to 40,000 strong corps could not block the retreat of a 200,000 strong army. In addition to the Pirna highway, two other roads led to Bohemia: from Dohna, via Geiersburg (the old road), or from Dippoldiswalde, but, as King Friedrich Wilhelm noted very pointedly at the time, the former was unsuitable for troop movements.

Based on the general disposition for the retreat drawn up by Radetzky and Toll and approved by the Coalition sovereigns, it was decided to move in three columns:

1. Barclay de Tolly's, with the entire Russo-Prussian contingent, to march via Dohna and Zehista, and then along the highway through Peterswald to Teplitz.
2. The centre, consisting of the majority of the Austrian force (namely the divisions under: Moritz Liechtenstein, Colloredo, Bianchi, Chasteler, Civalart, Crenneville and the cavalry under Lederer and Nostitz), via Dippoldiswalde and Eichwald, towards Teplitz.
3. The left wing (Klenau's corps with Weissenwolf's, Alois Liechtenstein's and Schneller's divisions), via Tharandt towards Freiberg.

The enemy holding both main routes from Dresden, to Pirna and to Freiberg, forced Barclay and Klenau to detour from the routes they had been assigned.

At the end of the two-day battle of Dresden, both the city itself and its surroundings presented a vision of devastation and dismay. Every open space was full of troops. Between the lines of linden trees in the Neustadt camp fires were burning, soldiers were slaughtering cattle and cooking food. The wounded dragged themselves through the streets, or lay on the bare earth side by side with exhausted or dead horses. The population, robbed of everything, wandered around their burned-out homes with their half-naked children, and finding no regret from the men, they cried out to the heavens for aid. Others left in haste, salvaging what remained of their possessions. Outside the city, there were heaps of corpses, naked, mutilated, lying among dead horses, in the mud, in ditches and ravines. Each feat of glory by the powerful nations, vying with each other in the business of mutual destruction, was stained with blood.[19]

The conqueror, averting his gaze from the mournful spectacle of the consequences of his victory, went to the Residenzschloss at six o'clock in the afternoon (at four o'clock, according to other sources), to his ally. Soaked to the skin, he rode through the city streets at a moderate trot. He was accompanied by cheers from the crowd, mindlessly sympathetic to whoever succeeded. Accompanying Napoleon were the captured Austrian generals and an escort from the *Jeune Garde*. Ten

---

19 Richter, II, 63-64.

captured Colours were carried through the city behind him. Following them came the captured guns and thousands of prisoners.

Napoleon was rightly proud of his success. He had been helped by the many errors of his adversaries, but nevertheless the victory won over the Coalition, who had one and a half times his numbers, was amazing. Napoleon had only around 25,000 cavalry, while the Coalition had some 40,000. His troops consisted almost exclusively of conscripts. In contrast, the Coalition had many veteran soldiers in their ranks. Superiority in artillery was also in their favour. But all these advantages could not compensate for the absence of unity of command, for the lack of pace of general decision making and execution of operations. Many of the formation commanders covered themselves in glory, and the troops, for the most part, fought very bravely, but at their head was Schwarzenberg, while at the head of the French was Napoleon. Neither the bright mind of Emperor Alexander, nor the King of Prussia's do-or-die determination to fight, nor the experience of Moreau, nor the profound knowledge of Jomini, could replace the lack of a commander capable of handling the vast army.

Over both days of the Battle of Dresden, the Coalition lost some 30,000 men *hors de combat*,[20] while the French lost between 10,000 to 15,000.[21] But Napoleon had every right to hope for an incomparably better outcome for his victory during the retreat of the Coalition army to Bohemia. The most convenient routes leading there had been cut by French forces during the battle, while Vandamme's corps, numbering some 40,000 men, were astride the Pirna highway, behind the Coalition right wing, threatening to block them on the march, while being pursued by Napoleon.

On 15 (27) August, at dawn on the second day of the Battle of Dresden, General Pyshnitsky set off from the Himmelreich manor with his detachment towards Zehista, to the main body of II Corps. Some time later, the Reval Infantry evacuated Pirna. The enemy, having occupied this location, deployed their forces along the edge of the plateau facing the Gottleuba river. On the Russian side, the force was deployed behind Zehista, under the overall command of Count Osterman, resting their left flank on the Elbe, in three waves: in the first was II Corps, numbering 6,500 men with 40 guns from II Corps and the Lifeguard,[22] and with 4th Jägers

---

20 Coalition losses for the two-day battle of Dresden were given as follows: in Hofmann – 25,000 men; in Plotho – 6,000 taken prisoner and a similar number killed or wounded, 26 guns and 130 ammunition caissons; in Richter – more than 15,000 men; in Aster – 8,000 to 9,000 killed, 10,000 to 11,000 wounded and 14,000 taken prisoner on the second day of fighting; in Thiers – 26,000 to 27,000 men and at least 40 guns; in Vaudoncourt – 6,000 men on the first day and more than 40,000 on the second, 26 guns, 130 ammunition caissons and 18 Colours; in Bernhardi – some 10,000 killed or wounded and some 20,000 taken prisoner.

The dead included: Russian major generals Melissino and Lukov; Austrian *Generalmajor* Andrássy. The wounded included: the Austrians *Feldzeugmeister* Gyulay; *Generalmajor* Mariássy and *Generalmajor* Frierenberger. Prisoners included the Austrian *Feldmarschallleutnant* Mesko.

21 French losses over the two days of the Battle of Dresden were given: in Hofmann – less than half the casualties of the Coalition forces; in Richter – more than 10,000 men; in Aster – from 8,000 to 9,000 killed and 10,000 to 11,000 wounded on the second day of fighting; in Odeleben, from 8,000 to 10,000 men.

22 In Prinz Eugen von Württemberg's diary it states that there were 48 guns in the position at Zehista (Archive of the M.T.D. No. 47,344).

holding the town of Zehista; in the second was Yermolov's 1st Lifeguard Division (12 battalions), numbering 7,000 men; while the third consisted of cavalry, namely: Her Majesty's Leib-Cuirassiers (four squadrons), the Lifeguard Hussars (six squadrons) and Tatar Ulans (six squadrons), with a horse artillery battery, numbering 2,000 men, commanded by Prinz Leopold von Sachsen-Coburg and generals Budberg [Karl Vasilievich Budberg or Carl Ludwig von Budberg-Bönninghausen] and Knorring [Karl Bogdanovich Knorring or Karl von Knorring].

Generals Helffreich and Ilovaisky were still at Cotta and Berggießhübel with their detachments, numbering 2,000 men in all.

Subsequently, the number of troops facing Vandamme would reach no more than 17,500 men.

Under these circumstances, most decisive operations were expected from Vandamme, who commanded twice these numbers. But, instead, for the entire day of 15 (27) August, he remained static on the Pirna plateau, and it was only on the Kohlberg that, from time to time, firefights broke out, interrupted by the heavy rain. The inaction of the French commander was all the more astonishing because, all day long, the cannonade thundering at Dresden could be heard at Pirna and seemed to be calling both sides to battle. The reasons for Vandamme's irresolution, so inconsistent with his character, are unknown to this day. It has been speculated that the following factors may have given rise to this. The commander of the Reval Infantry, Colonel Zhelvinsky [Yakov Sergeevich Zhelvinsky], stationed in Pirna and not anticipating the enemy coming from the direction of the Elbe, did not secure himself with outposts there. Taking advantage of this omission, one of the French columns made its way along the riverbank on the night of 14 to 15 (26 to 27) August and burst into the town at dawn. The regimental commander himself barely had chance to escape. Several sentries and a doctor named May were taken prisoner. *Flügel-Adjutant* Wolzogen, who was on his way from the headquarters to see the Prinz von Württemberg and was looking for him in Pirna, unexpectedly rode into the enemy skirmish line, but was saved by his quick-thinking. 'Cease firing, the town is crawling with Russians!'[23] he yelled at the nearest French officer in the screen. The officer, mistaking him for one of his superiors, ordered a withdrawal, and Wolzogen, taking advantage of his mistake, crossed the Gottleuba river at the mill weir and arrived at II Corps' positions. Thereafter, May was brought to an enemy general, surrounded by a large suite (probably Vandamme himself), who asked him: 'who is the commander of your force?'

'Prinz von Württemberg' replied the doctor.

'What is the strength of your corps?'

'12 regiments, each of 1,500 men, less the casualties they have incurred, and therefore in the corps, together with the cavalry, there should be some 20,000 men, indeed, in addition, the entire Lifeguards of the Russian Emperor and the Prussian King, numbering 50,000 men, are on their way from Dresden to assist.'

May's testimony, which quite skilfully misrepresented the truth, may have misled Vandamme. It has also been claimed that a forester who worked as a double-agent

---

23 'Cessez de tirer, la ville est pleine de Russes!'

for both sides, had deceived the French by informing them of the advance of significant forces from Bohemia to assist the Coalition army.[24]

The Coalition situation at Dresden, despite their superiority in troop numbers, was precarious, while Vandamme's switch to decisive operations on the Army of Bohemia's lines of communications would have made it even more problematic. Yet, in all probability, Napoleon did not have accurate intelligence – neither about the disintegration of the Austrian force, nor about the weakness of the Russian corps stationed facing Vandamme, and therefore believed that the Coalition would once again give battle under the walls of Dresden. Influenced by these convictions, at eight o'clock in the evening on 15 (27) August, Napoleon ordered his *chef d'état-major*, Berthier, that General Dulauloy [Charles François Dulauloy] should assemble his reserve artillery at the headquarters at five o'clock the following morning, together with three batteries of *artillerie à cheval de la garde*, for a total of 58 guns. Orders were issued to occupy the lunettes on the left bank of the Elbe fully, taking the required number of guns and men from the right bank, such that each lunette would have eight guns, 80 gunners, 50 sappers and 50 infantrymen. A dedicated commandant was appointed to each of the lunettes, and it was confirmed that the commandants must defend themselves to the death and under no circumstances to abandon the fortifications entrusted to them.[25] Each of the guns was ordered to have a supply of 250 projectiles and each lunette was to have 10,000 cartridges. At the same time, a commission was appointed to investigate why the commandant of lunette No. III abandoned the post entrusted to him. The *chef d'état-major* was instructed to order the assignment of corps positions and corps quartering on waxed paper. The *Vieille Garde* were ordered to be in the same locations and in the same formation as they had been the day before. The *grenadiers de la garde*, *escadron de service* and Ornano's division were to assemble at lunette No. IV. Nansouty's cavalry were assigned to support the duc de Trévise (Mortier). The Emperor's displeasure was announced to both of them because, throughout the fighting, they had not sent hourly reports on the progress of the battle... Napoleon also ordered that his displeasure be expressed to the *quartier-maître général* for the incompetence of the mobile hospitals. 'It was not until nightfall that wagons were sent to remove the wounded. Every hospital official should have been there...' This was followed by orders for the bakers in Vandamme's corps to stockpile hard-tack, to send 200,000 daily rations upriver to Dresden, and so on.[26]

Napoleon, while celebrating the display of his trophies to the population of Dresden, had no delusions about the state of affairs in general and doubted that the outcome of the war would be favourable to him. On the evening of 15 (27) August, when the Saxon *Militärberater*, General Gersdorff, came to see him and congratulated him on his success, saying that he had witnessed the usual fate of Napoleon's enemies in the defeat of the Austrians, Napoleon replied that the bad weather had saved the Coalition from complete destruction. 'I wanted to take the high ground,

---

24 War Diary of Prinz Eugen von Württemberg's II Corps (Archive of the M.T.D. No. 47,344); Wolzogen, Memoiren, 194-195; Bernhardi, III, 190-191.
25 Up to this point there had been one commandant for every two lunettes.
26 Aster, 331-333.

but I could not do it,' he said, 'because of the rain. I hope to get to Bohemia before my adversaries can retreat there. I shall reach Prague at the same time as them... What do you know of the course of the Eger? Do you have accurate intelligence on Prague?' And when Gersdorff, saying in reply that he was familiar with these areas, expressed the opinion that, after the failure suffered by the Coalition, they would either have to dissolve the coalition or fight again in the open field, Napoleon invited him to follow in the footsteps of the army. 'I want you to return to the King with the news of the former fortunate event,' he said 'I am pleased with the results of this day. However, everything goes badly whenever I am not present.' And as if having glimpsed the mysteries of the future, he continued: 'the force directed against Berlin is defeated. I am also concerned for Macdonald... He is brave, devoted to me, but he lacks good fortune...'[27]

---

27 General Gersdorff's diary; Aster, 333-334.

Appendix XIV

Note submitted to Emperor Alexander by General Moreau a week before the Battle of Dresden

Knowledge of the strength, location and movements of the enemy is essential in order to ensure success and avoid defeat. Based upon this, unerring offensive operations may be conducted and opportunities found to counter enemy offensives.

The skilful management of informants is the most reliable means of acquiring intelligence, without which it is impossible to engage with the enemy in battle. The Austrian and Prussian armies are situated very advantageously in this regard. The population of the country occupied by the belligerent armies is completely devoted to their Sovereigns, embittered against the oppressor, filled with enthusiasm and love for their fatherland, and therefore it is not difficult to find people willing to observe enemy movements and notify the Coalition army commanders of them. All that remains is to redact the observations from the informants and re-word them in such a way that they could not attract enemy suspicion.

We would be able to assess the composition and strength of the French army from intelligence on the movements of generals, and especially of Napoleon himself. It would not be difficult to deduce from where he intends to attack, or where he will concentrate his forces in order to counter his adversaries. And therefore it is very important that Napoleon be surrounded by informants, from whom not a single one of his movements can escape. As soon as he goes anywhere, we must immediately know about it, as well as where and when he has arrived. It is vital also to have similar intelligence on the commanders of large formations in the enemy army. In particular, Marshal Ney and General Latour-Maubourg should be under surveillance, of whom the former commands the largest mass of infantry, and the latter the strongest of the reserve cavalry corps. It is safe to assume that both of them will always be at the most important operational locations. In a similar vein, one should not lose sight of the other marshals and corps commanders, and it seems impossible to doubt that if the flanking corps are moving towards the centre, then the enemy intends to operate from there. Detachments located on the flanks, and used for significant diversions, although they should be under similar surveillance, do not deserve particular attention.

The commanders of forward outposts at which the informants arrive are immediately to provide them with post horses and send them to the headquarters with dispatch riders. However, they may inquire about what is happening facing their force from the informants in order to take necessary precautions, and they are to attempt to capture a few prisoners in order to find out which corps are facing us. Such intelligence would serve to indicate the general direction of the enemy army.

All intelligence that turns out to be accurate must be generously paid for. Napoleon values surveillance of the enemy so much that he takes charge of it himself, but the Coalition army, in this respect, has a greater advantage over him in lands where he is detested.

It is essential to have: one Commander-in-Chief; three large corps, with a battle formation of at least three waves; a strong reserve, formed up behind the centre in two waves and ready to move to any threatened point. A significant corps, currently located on the right wing, manoeuvring with its left wing close to the main army.[1] There should be light troops from each of the Powers in the vanguard of every column, so as not to reveal the overall direction of movement. The Cossacks are to be everywhere.

The corps under the Crown Prince of Sweden must not be defeated, and therefore is to avoid engaging with the main body of the French army, but is to operate determinedly against the enemy rear as soon as Napoleon turns against the Coalition main army.

The troops under General Bennigsen, being concentrated near the Oder, are not vital to the Crown Prince of Sweden as long as he remains on the left bank of this river, because there is no reason to fear that the enemy will cross to its right bank, therefore: Bennigsen should operate on the right bank. If Napoleon heads towards Bohemia, then Bennigsen, having crossed the Oder at Crossen or Breslau, is to operate from Breslau together with Blücher. If Napoleon, having crossed the Elbe in Dresden, turns against the Coalition Main Army, then Blücher is to join it, while Bennigsen is to take his place in Silesia and enter into direct communications with the Crown Prince, who, in all likelihood, will by then be near the Elbe, around Wittenberg.

Having crossed the Oder on his [Bernadotte's] left wing, Bennigsen's force are to establish communications with the prince as well as the main army. They are useless if left behind the Oder. Having crossed on his right wing, either at Crossen or at Frankfurt and closing up to the Crown Prince, they would not strengthen it to such an extent that it could attack the French army, and such a movement would be all the more inappropriate since Bennigsen would be diverted away from the overall Coalition objective,

---

1 Blücher's army.

which consists of pushing forward our left wing in order to cut the enemy army off from Mainz.

Returning to the subject of informants, I ask Your Imperial Majesty to urgently demand from the Coalition monarchs and their generals that every local department be ordered to find the most reliable agents possible who could be infiltrated into every headquarters in the French army and could present themselves at our outposts, from where they should be sent to the headquarters with all possible haste. If they are sound, then the Coalition Army will have the opportunity to be prepared for operations days in advance. Otherwise, the enemy will catch us by surprise, while orders issued in haste are always going to be erroneous and incoherent.

It is vital that the general staff officer, who is to be entrusted with monitoring the situation in the enemy army, notes the changes occurring within it daily, about which intelligence has been obtained through informants, from commanders of the forward units of the force or from other individuals…

Appendix XV

Emperor Alexander's letter to General Moreau's widow

Madam! Since the terrible misfortune which befell General Moreau at my side, depriving me of the knowledge and experience of this great man, I had hoped that through careful treatment we might succeed in preserving him for his family and for my companionship. Providence has ordained otherwise. He died as he lived, with the energy of a strong and constant soul.

There is only one remedy for the great sufferings of life, and that is to watch over those enduring them. In Russia you will find these sentiments everywhere, Madam, and if it were convenient for you to settle there, I would seek by all means to embellish the life of a person to whom I have made it my sacred duty to offer consolation and support. I ask you, Madam, to rely on this as irrevocable, to let me know every situation in which I might be useful to you, and to always write to me directly; It would be my pleasure to anticipate your wishes. The friendship that I have assured your husband extends beyond the grave, and I have no other means of repaying my debt to him, albeit in part, than by doing some good for his family.

In these sad and cruel circumstances, Madam, accept these testimonies of friendship and the assurance of my keen interest.

Madame! Lorsque le malheur affreux, qui atteignit le général Moreau à mes côtés, me priva des lumières et de l'expérience de ce grand homme, je concevais l'espoir qu'on réussirait par un traitement soigneux à le conserver à sa famille et à mon amitié. La Providence en a autrement ordonné. Il mourut comme il a vécu, avec l'énergie d'une âme forte et constante.

Il n'existe pour les grandes souffrances de la vie qu'un seul remède, c'est d'y voir prendre part les autres. En Russie vous trouverez, Madame, partout ces sentimens, et s'il vous convenait de vous y fixer, je chercherais tous les moyens d'embellir la vie d'une personne à la quelle je me fais un devoir sacré d'offrir des consolations et un soutien. Je vous prie, Madame, d'y compter irrévocablement, de me faire connaître toutes les circonstances où je pourrais vous être utile, et de m'écrire toujours directement; ce sera pour moi un bonheur de prevenir vos voeux. L'amitié que j'ai assurée à votre époux s'étend au delà du tombeau, et je n'ai d'autres moyens de m'acquitter, au moins en partie, de ma dette envers lui, qu'en faisant quelque bien à sa famille.

Recevez, Madame, dans ces circonstances tristes et cruelles, ces témoignages d'amitié et l'assurance de mon vif intérêt.

Map of troop movements from Dresden to Kulm.

29

The Coalition retreat from Dresden into Bohemia. Actions at Berggießhübel and Hellendorf

Barclay de Tolly's instructions to Count Osterman. – Amendments to the disposition for the retreat by Barclay de Tolly and Graf Klenau. – The factors preventing the French from persistently pursuing the Coalition army. – The order of the pursuit. – Orders sent to Vandamme from Pirna, at four o'clock on the afternoon of 16 (28) August. – Napoleon's return to Dresden and the cancellation of earlier orders: reasons for this. – Results of the pursuit. – Schwarzenberg's dispositions for the retreat beyond the Eger.

Operations by Count Osterman's force on 16 (28) August. – Barclay de Tolly's instructions. – The Russian formation commanders decide to retreat along the highway to Peterswald. – General Yermolov. – Orders for the retreat. – The actions at Krietzschwitz and on the Kohlberg. – The action at Berggießhübel. – The Prinz von Württemberg's orders. – The action at Hellendorf. – The retreat to Peterswald by the Lifeguard and Helffreich's detachment. – The retreat of II Corps and the Tatar Ulans. – The deployment of Russian forces assembled at Peterswald on the night of 16 to 17 (28 to 29) August. – The deployment of Vandamme's force. – The deployment of the remaining formations of both sides. – The Coalition army's losses. – The excellent condition of the Russian artillery.

Repeated instructions for Vandamme. – Vandamme's report. – Orders by the Russian formation commanders for a further retreat by the forces stationed at Peterswald. – The French strike on Prince Shakhovskoy in Peterswald on 17 (29) August. – The disorder in the Coalition army's rear area. – The retreat of Osterman's force towards Nollendorf and Kulm.

Based on the disposition issued by Prinz Schwarzenberg, the entire Russo-Prussian contingent were ordered to retreat to Bohemia along the Pirna highway, but Barclay de Tolly, having sent orders in this regard to Osterman, added that 'if Count Osterman considers himself cut off from Königstein by the enemy relocating to Berggießhübel, or, more likely, to Hellendorf, then he should move to Maxen, following the main body of the army.'[1] Barclay, considering the vulnerability of the movement of his force along the highway past Vandamme's strong corps, ordered them to go to Maxen and on to Dippoldiswalde. As night fell, the Russo-Prussian reserves were sent there directly. Kleist's corps, on the recommendation of his *Chef des Stabes*, *Oberstleutnant* Grolman [Karl Wilhelm Georg Grolman], moved towards Lockwitz and Maxen. While Count Wittgenstein's corps remained in the rearguard near Dresden with Klüx's Prussian 8. *Brigade* (Roth's detachment at Prohlis, the Russian 5th Division behind Lockwitz, Klüx's brigade at Possendorf [five miles south of Räcknitz]). Thereafter, at eight o'clock in the morning, they followed the main body towards Dippoldiswalde. Having notified Prinz Schwarzenberg of the amendments to the disposition, Barclay asked him to send the Austrian column from Dippoldiswalde towards Saida. The Austrian troops, on the night of 15 to 16 (27 to 28) August, also withdrew from their occupied positions, leaving the *1. leichte Division* under Moritz Liechtenstein in the rearguard at Kaitz until dawn, and retreated to Dippoldiswalde, where on the night of 15 to 16 (27 to 28) August, the headquarters of the Prussian King and Barclay de Tolly was relocated. The headquarters of Emperor Alexander and Prinz Schwarzenberg was in the village of Reichstädt.[2]

Klenau's corps, which was located at Rabenau at the end of the battle of Dresden, having received orders to retreat towards Freiberg on the night of 15 to 16 (27 to 28) August, together with the divisions under Weissenwolf, Alois Liechtenstein and Schneller, could not move there without being exposed to obvious danger, because enemy forces had already cut the Freiberg road and could easily forestall the Austrians in Freiberg, who would have to detour there along a very awkward route through the Tharandt forest. Under these circumstances, at the suggestion of the *Chef des Stabes* of his corps, Colonel Rothkirch, Klenau set off for Pretzschendorf and reported to the Commander-in-Chief about the direction he had taken, also inviting Weissenwolf, Alois Liechtenstein and Schneller to march along the same road.[3]

When the Coalition forces reached Dippoldiswalde, there was an extraordinary congestion of troops, artillery, vehicles and Austrian mobile magazines. The onward march was very slow, due to the awkwardness of the routes leading through Geiersburg and Zinnwald to Teplitz and through Pretzschendorf to Dux.[4] The retreat by the Coalition would have become even more trying if Napoleon had pursued them with his customary aggression. Yet many factors prevented this: even before the battle of Dresden, the French army had been constantly on the march for four days; then they had fought for two days, mostly in inclement weather: however, the labour and hardship that had exhausted the French should not have prevented a rapid pursuit, especially since the Coalition, and the Austrians in particular, were

---

1 See Map No. 8, Map of Troop Movements From Dresden to Kulm.
2 Hofmann, Zur Geschichte des Feldzuges von 1813, 158; Richter, Geschichte des Deutschen Freiheitskrieges, II, 67.
3 Bernhardi, Denkwürdigkeiten aus dem Leben Carl Friedrich Grafen von Toll, III, 175-177.
4 Hofmann, 160.

no less tired and exhausted than the enemy, and if the still continuous rain and bad roads prevented a pursuit at an appropriate pace, then the movement of the Coalition troops was also slowed down by these conditions, being equally unfavourable for both sides. The main cause of the ineffectiveness of the pursuit were erroneous orders from Napoleon himself. He initially expressed his intention to exploit the victory he had won: the very next day after the battle, 16 (28) August, Murat marched towards Freiberg with the troops under Latour-Maubourg and Victor, Marmont to Dippoldiswalde; Saint-Cyr's corps were sent towards Dohna, directed on towards Berggießhübel, but then received orders to move towards Maxen; the entire *Garde* and Napoleon's *quartier général* arrived in Pirna on the same day. Thus, being located at Pirna on the evening of 16 (28) August with the *Garde* and with the force under Vandamme 30 *versts* from Kulm, Napoleon could arrive there the following day and block the passes into Bohemia to the Coalition columns, stretched out along convoluted mountain roads, while Murat, Marmont and Saint-Cyr could press them from behind. At four o'clock in the afternoon, the following orders were issued to Vandamme from the *quartier général*:

> His Majesty desires that you attack the Prinz von Württemberg with your entire force and enter Bohemia via Peterswald. The Emperor believes that your forces can cut the lines of communications leading to Tetschen [Děčín], Aussig and Teplitz before the enemy defeated at Dresden and retreating towards Annaberg (*sic*, Altenberg?) has chance to arrive there.[5]

Following this, further instructions were issued to Vandamme in a similar vein.

But the next day [29 August], the *Vieille Garde* suddenly received orders to return to Dresden, where Napoleon went himself. French historians attribute the countermanding of the earlier orders to Napoleon falling ill, and there is no reason to doubt this, especially after the *Empereur des Français* spent the whole day on horseback in the pouring rain. But it was not this reason alone that forced him to deviate from his usual resolute course of action, and besides, Fain [Agathon Jean François Fain], who was with him, explicitly wrote that he felt unwell on the evening of 16 (28) August (precisely at the point when the cancellation of the persistent pursuit was issued), but was almost completely recovered by the next morning. It is, therefore, very likely that the main reason for Napoleon's return to Dresden with elements of his reserves was news of the failures suffered by his forces in other theatres of the war. Oudinot's defeat was confirmed by new, more definitive information, and then the first news came on the incomparably more disastrous battle for the French on the Katzbach.[6] All these factors diverted Napoleon's attention towards Berlin and Silesia, and the consequences of this were his return march to Dresden with the *Vieille Garde* and

---

5   Vaudoncourt, Histoire de la guerre soutenue par les Français en Allemagne, 157; Beitzke, Geschichte der deutschen Freiheitskriege in den Jahren 1813 und 1814, II, 136-137; Hofmann, 162.
6   Fain, Manuscrit de 1813, II, 298 & 309; Norvins, Portefeuille de 1813, II, 311; Thiers, Histoire du Consulat et de l'Empire, XVI, Edit de Brux, 363-364. Ploto wrote that Napoleon returned to Dresden on the evening of 16 (28) August, Der Krieg in Deutschland und Frankreich, II, 68.

the slow, hesitant advance of other French formations: the *Jeune Garde* received orders to halt in Pirna; the other corps continued to pursue the Coalition, but limited themselves to rounding up stragglers and seizing wagons abandoned on the march by the retreating troops. What was most damaging to the French was that Vandamme's corps, to which Napoleon had assigned the most decisive and, at the same time, the most dangerous mission, did not receive any definitive orders.[7]

Despite the low intensity of the pursuit, its results were significant. Prisoners were constantly being taken, almost exclusively Austrians.[8] In some places, such as near Coschütz and Gostritz, there were long rows of muskets stacked in trestles and many shoes were found stuck in the thick mud. But the prisoners, for the most part, did not come from the rearguard, but consisted of soldiers wandering singly and in groups throughout the surrounding area and looting the villages.[9] On 17 (29) August, the number of prisoners in Dresden reached 20,000. 320 officers had been captured. The next day [30 August], another 1,400 men were brought in, and later 1,700 Russians.[10] Although it is quite difficult to determine the losses from the Coalition army on the return march to Bohemia, it can be said without any doubt that the Coalition, in the battle of Dresden and during the retreat overall lost more than 40,000 men killed, wounded, taken prisoner or deserted. The number of guns and carts lost by the Austrians was very significant, but is not shown precisely.[11]

On 16 (28) August, Prinz Schwarzenberg issued a disposition, on the basis of which all the formations, with the exception of the corps under Count Wittgenstein, Moritz Liechtenstein's Austrian *1. leichte Division* and Crennewitz's reserve division, were to have retreated beyond the river Eger by 21 August (2 September), the Russo-Prussian forces to Budin, and the Austrians to Laun. Wittgenstein's corps, at the same time, was assigned to retreat to Teplitz, leaving Moritz Liechtenstein's division in the rearguard at Altenberg and Crennewitz's division in Neuhausen [four miles north of Böhmisch Einsiedel] on the river Flöha. The reserve artillery and parks were to assemble beyond Laun. *Kolonnen Magasine* (mobile magazines) were to be in Teplitz, Brüx, Komotau (sic, forwards of the deployed main body), Welwarn [Velvary, 11 miles south of Budin] and Jungferteinitz [Panenský Týnec, 7½ miles south-east of Laun], while the sick were ordered to be directed to Prague.[12]

---

7   Hofmann, 162-163.
8   'Man brachte mehrere Gefangene, nur Kaiserliche, die geradehin über Mangel an Schuhen, noch mehr aber über Mangel an Brodt klagten...'(Several prisoners were brought in, all Kaiserliche [Austrians], who complained about the lack of footwear, but even more about the lack of bread). From the Saxon General Gersdorff's diary.
9   Aster, *Schilderung der Kriegsereignisse in und vor Dresden*, 339.
10 Aster, 330.
11 News from the army, published in Le Moniteur on 8 September, claimed that over five days the Coalition lost: 40,000 taken prisoner, 20,000 killed or wounded, and a similar number fallen ill from fatigue and hunger. The following Coalition losses were shown: over 100 guns, 1,500 ammunition caissons blown up or captured by French troops, as well as over 3,000 wagons; 40 Colours or Standards were captured. Among the prisoners taken were 4,000 Russians (sic). It is obvious that the news from the army of 1813 was in no way inferior to the infamous bulletins of 1812.
12 Prinz Schwarzenberg's disposition dated 16 (28) August, extracted from Plotho, II, 68-70.

The retreat of the army beyond the Eger, as proposed by the Commander-in-Chief, did not take place, thanks to the successful action at Kulm.

The news of the Coalition defeat at the Battle of Dresden was delivered to Count Osterman and Prinz Eugen von Württemberg by *Flügel-Adjutant* Wolzogen on the night of 15 to 16 (27 to 28) August, who had been sent to the headquarters the day before, by order of the prinz, in order to report on the situation at Pirna.[13] Subsequently, at dawn on 16 (28) August, Osterman received orders from Barclay de Tolly, which stated 'that if the enemy had already cut the line of retreat to Peterswald, then the troops stationed at Pirna should move through Maxen to rejoin the army.' Compliance with these orders would have gifted the route leading to Teplitz to Vandamme and would have given him the opportunity to occupy the exits from the mountain defiles through which the Coalition army would be moving into Bohemia. Yet in order to forestall the enemy on this route, it was necessary to make a flanking march from Zehista to Berggießhübel, over a distance of two German *Meilen* (about 14 *versts*), past Vandamme's corps, who had twice their numbers. The original idea for such a bold movement belonged to Prinz Eugen von Württemberg.[14] But it was not easy to convince the overall commander, Count Osterman, of its viability, in whose opinion it was necessary to go to Maxen, because the highway had already been cut by the enemy. He made it particularly clear that by making such a move, he would be endangering the Lifeguard. The Prinz von Württemberg vainly tried to convince Count Ostermann that nothing could be more honourable for the Lifeguard than to sacrifice themselves in order to save the army. Eventually, once the prinz had announced that he 'would be going to Peterswald with his force,' Osterman, willing to meet any danger, but still unconvinced by the prinz's arguments, went to Yermolov and, after consulting with him, said: 'Well, I have decided on Peterswald.'[15]

This was the consultation that presaged one of the most illustrious feats of Russian arms. From an impartial study of the events preceding the action at Kulm, it is obvious that Yermolov used his influence over Osterman to induce him to retreat to Peterswald. Yermolov had such an inexplicable, seemingly magical influence over many of his contemporaries, not only in that era when the paths to distinction and glory were wide open to him, but also when he, languishing in inaction, waited for the call to new trials and dangers. The basis of Yermolov's influence on everyone who had the opportunity to know and appreciate this extraordinary man were his personal qualities: his bright mind; blessed with a memory, garnished with a wide and varied knowledge; generosity and selflessness; his very appearance was that of a hero: this was Yermolov! One of the most revered veterans of that Russian army, when asked who should be credited with the honour of the action at Kulm, answered:[16]

---

13 Wolzogen, *Memoiren*, 196.
14 War Diary of II Corps, Archive of the M.T.D. No. 47,344; Lieutenant General Wachten's notes, Archive of the M.T.D. No. 47,353, book No. 36; Wolzogen, 197.
15 War Diary of II Corps, Archive of the M.T.D. No. 47,344; Lieutenant General Wachten's notes; Wolzogen, *Memoiren*, 197-198; Aster, 95-97.
16 Prince Ivan Leontievich Shakhovskoy.

there was a lot of honour, and many should share it. I shall speak only of what I witnessed: that when adjutants and orderlies came to Osterman for orders, he sent them to Yermolov.

The orders for the retreat along the Teplitz highway were as follows: the Prinz von Württemberg was to gather up Helffreich's detachment and swiftly attack the enemy position with the bulk of his corps in the direction of its weakest point at the village of Krietzschwitz; General Yermolov was directed to attack onto the Kohlberg with the 4th Jägers, Reval Infantry, Lifeguard Jägers and Tatar Ulans; Osterman had decided to set out along the highway immediately himself, with the 1st Lifeguard Division, the majority of the artillery and the Lifeguard cavalry, under cover of the attacks by the Prinz von Württemberg and Yermolov, in order to seize Peterswald as quickly as possible; he was to be followed by the troops of II Corps, and at the tail of the column would come the rearguard under General Knorring, consisting of: the Tatar Ulans, 4th Jägers and Reval Infantry.[17] *Flügel-Adjutant* Wolzogen received orders to return to the headquarters and report to Emperor Alexander both about the direction in which Count Osterman's detachment had moved, and about the situation that had prompted this movement. This important information had already been delivered to the Tsar by nightfall on 16 (28) August, in Altenberg during the march of the Coalition army into Bohemia.[18]

On that same day, at about ten o'clock in the morning, Vandamme had sent a report informing Napoleon of the positions of his force on the Pirna plateau, between Pirna and Krietzschwitz, he also wrote that he was 'facing 25,000 enemy troops, being constantly strengthened with reinforcements arriving from Dresden.' It has already been mentioned that the corps under Saint-Cyr and the *Garde* were initially sent to support Vandamme's corps, but subsequently Saint-Cyr received orders to turn towards Maxen, while the *Jeune Garde* were halted at Pirna, and in the meantime, on the basis of the instructions he received, Vandamme was to move with his entire force 'to the high ground at Berggießhübel and Hellendorf immediately after linking up with Saint-Cyr and Mortier, who were heading for Dohna and Pirna.'[19] It is clear that once Mortier had halted at Pirna and Saint-Cyr had turned towards Maxen, Vandamme could be advancing into Bohemia in isolation.

At ten o'clock in the morning, Vandamme began the task of occupying the village of Cotta, abandoned by Helffreich's force. The Prinz von Württemberg immediately supported Helffreich with Wolfe's brigade (Murom Infantry and Chernigov Infantry). The enemy, who had some 3,000 men at this location, were driven out of the aforementioned village and pushed beyond Krietzschwitz, where Wolfe's skirmishers held out until four o'clock in the afternoon. At the same time as the Prinz von Württemberg's attack, Knorring's detachment attacked the Kohlberg, supported by one battalion of Lifeguard Jägers and another from the Lifeguard Semenovsky Regiment under Yermolov's personal command, while the Lifeguard moved along the highway towards Berggießhübel. Knorring's force captured the high ground and

---

17 War Diary of II Corps.
18 Wolzogen, 198.
19 Orders for Vandamme, published in the periodical: *Spectateur militaire*, 1826, 262-266.

pursued the enemy to the Gottleuba river, cheering loudly. The French reoccupied the Kohlberg soon thereafter, but were driven off by the Lifeguard Jägers and Lifeguard Semenovsky, who remained there until II Corps had crossed the Seidewitz ravine [just south of Zehista] entirely and moved along the highway behind the Lifeguard. The enemy, deceived by these determined attacks, began to pull forces from the left wing towards the village of Krietzschwitz, and even sent those elements of the force located between Langenhennersdorf and Berggießhübel there.[20]

A little later, the French launched an attack on the village of Goes [2½ miles north of Cotta], but were checked by the Kremenchug Infantry and Volhynia Infantry, commanded by Major General Pyshnitsky, with 12 guns, which engaged the enemy (*13e léger*) with canister as they attempted to ascend the Kohlberg for a third time, and forced them to retreat. The French, having placed several batteries on the right bank of the Gottleuba, opened fire on the Russian guns, but despite the enemy superiority in the number of guns, or the advantages of their dominant location, the Russians responded with successful counter-battery fire.[21]

During these actions, Prince Shakhovskoy redeployed at the Rothenschenke, near Cotta with the rest of II Corps, while General Yermolov continued to move towards Berggießhübel with the Lifeguard and the artillery. As the units from II Corps left at the Kohlberg and Krietzschwitz were still fighting against a numerous enemy, Count Osterman, concerned that they might be overwhelmed by superior forces, ordered Yermolov to halt the Lifeguard. This order would enable the French to forestall the Russians at the defiles of Berggießhübel and Hellendorf. Prinz Eugen was on the summit of the Cottaer Spitzberg, and having observed that the enemy was already closer to these locations than the leading elements of the Russian column, immediately sent a report on this to Osterman, who was accompanying the Lifeguard, and issued orders to withdraw the units of his corps from combat and to retreat along the highway. Fortunately, not only did Vandamme fail to reinforce the weak detachments sent to Berggießhübel and Hellendorf in sufficient strength, but even ordered those units moving there to turn back to Langenhennersdorf and Bahra [1½ miles south of Langenhennersdorf]. It has been claimed that the reason for this was false intelligence reported by an informant regarding the appearance of a Russian column in Rosenthal [three miles south-east of Langenhennersdorf] that had arrived from Bohemia.[22]

Count Osterman, having received the report on the enemy move towards the defiles on the route to Bohemia, ordered the Lifeguard to break camp and move on. At around two o'clock in the afternoon, the units of 1st Lifeguard Division had already managed to pass through the village of Berggießhübel. The Lifeguard Preobrazhensky Regiment were leading, followed by 24 guns. Having passed the village, as soon as the Russian column began to climb the steep gradient of the Dürrenberg, the leading unit was engaged by artillery fire from a battery stationed on the highway and intense musket fire from the French who had settled astride the road. General Yermolov ordered Ladygin [Nikolai Ivanovich Ladygin] to move four guns up to face

---

20 War Diary of II Corps; Aster, 102-103.
21 Aster, 103.
22 War Diary of II Corps; Aster, 103-104 & 106-107; Hofmann, 166-167.

the enemy, which soon silenced the French battery. Following this, on Yermolov's orders, Major General Rosen [Grigory Vladimirovich Rozen or Georg Andreas von Rosen] sent skirmishers out and, under their cover, moved the first battalion of the Lifeguard Preobrazhensky Regiment to the right of the highway, while leading the second himself directly at the enemy, put them to flight with a bayonet charge and cleared the route for the artillery. Then, General Yermolov ordered two battalions of Lifeguard Jägers, under Major General Bistrom's command [Karl Ivanovich Bistrom 1st or Karl Heinrich Georg von Bistram], to remain to guard the defile just passed until the arrival of II Corps. The third battalion were sent into the forest, towards Langenhennersdorf, to pursue the defeated enemy, while the other guards regiments were ordered to pick up the pace of the march towards Hellendorf.[23]

At the same time, the Prinz von Württemberg, who was further back with his force, having learned that the enemy had checked the Lifeguard at Berggießhübel, issued the following orders: Helffreich's and Prince Shakhovskoy's detachments were immediately sent to assist Osterman with the Tobolsk Infantry, Minsk Infantry, Chernigov Infantry and Murom Infantry; the defence of Krietzschwitz was entrusted to Colonel Wolfe, with the skirmishers from his brigade, supported by the Kremenchug Infantry and Volhynia Infantry commanded by General Pyshnitsky. The chief of staff of II Corps, Colonel Hofmann, received orders to remain with Pyshnitsky's and Wolf's units at Krietzschwitz until the Lifeguard had passed the Berggießhübel defile, and then to proceed as the rearguard. In the event of the enemy cutting the highway again, they were to head onto the old Teplitz road, via Göppersdorf. Colonel Ivanov stationed on the Kohlberg with the 4th Jägers and Reval Infantry, and General Knorring left at Zehista with the Tatar Ulans, were also ordered to retreat along the highway, or, if this march was impossible, to divert through Friedrichswalde [four miles south of Zehista], Borna and Göppersdorf, onto the old Teplitz road. The prinz himself quickly made his way to Berggießhübel, but when he arrived there, the enemy troops had already been pushed back and the Lifeguard continued to move towards Hellendorf.[24]

After pushing the enemy back from the Teplitz highway at the Dürrenberg, the Lifeguard Preobrazhensky Regiment halted, and the Lifeguard Semenovsky Regiment, passing them, moved on as the head of the column followed by the artillery. The enemy, in the meantime, had managed to seize the defile at Hellendorf. The commander of the Lifeguard Semenovsky Regiment, Major General Potemkin [Yakov Alekseevich Potemkin], meaning to help out the artillery, on which the enemy skirmishers had opened a withering fire, sent Colonel Yafimovich [Ivan Lvovich Yafimovich] forward with the second battalion and the third company. The valiant men of the Semenovsky, despite the steepness of the rocky slopes and the density of the forest that covered them, charged with bayonets fixed and put the French to flight. Captain the duc de Broglie [Charles-François-Ladislas de Broglie-Revel] of the Semenovsky Regiment, deployed to pursue them with the third company and the marksmen of the second battalion, seized the village of Hellendorf, but, leaving

---

23 Lieutenant General Yermolov's report No. 1,296 to Count Osterman-Tolstoy dated 22 August [3 September]; War Diary of II Corps.
24 War Diary of II Corps; Bernhardi, III, 195-197.

the highway to his left, was cut off by the enemy and made his way with great difficulty through the mountains to Peterswald.[25]

The Lifeguard regiments passed through the village of Peterswald with the artillery at four o'clock in the afternoon. They were directly followed by Helffreich's detachment. The force under Prince Shakhovskoy, on approaching the Dürrenberg, were attacked by a large enemy column emerging from the forest. The *7e léger*, marching at the head of the French force, attacked the stretched out Russian detachment with fixed bayonets and, cutting the highway at the exit from Berggießhübel, blocked the advance of those regiments from II Corps which had not yet managed to pass the defile. Here a bitter close-quarter fight ensued between the *7e léger* and Murom Infantry. The troops of both sides, intermixed with each other, fought with ferocity. The Prinz von Württemberg, already on the march to Peterswald, turned back towards Berggießhübel with the Chernigov Infantry in order to help the Murom Infantry under attack from incomparably superior numbers, but were unable to rescue them. Both the Murom Infantry and the Minsk Infantry, having been cut off, dispersed and found their way to Peterswald, some along minor roads, with the loss of many men, several ammunition caissons and one gun.[26] The Chernigov Infantry, deployed as skirmishers, were pushed back and retreated to Hellendorf under the protection of the Lifeguard Jägers stationed in column on both sides of the highway. Colonel Wolfe, with his own small detachment, and General Pyshnitsky, with the Volhynia Infantry and Kremenchug Infantry, retreated from Krietzschwitz to Göppersdorf and on to Schönwald, but instead of halting there and re-establishing communications with other elements of II Corps, they retreated to Teplitz and were unable to participate in the action at Kulm on the following day. General Knorring, after the heated combat on the Kohlberg, began to retreat along the highway. Colonel Ivanov, as part of Knorring's detachment, diverted to Göppersdorf, on through Schönwald and arrived at Nollendorf the next morning, where he rejoined the force under Prinz Eugen, while Knorring himself fought his way through the enemy with the Tatar Ulans along the highway and followed the Lifeguard into Peterswald.[27]

The force under Prince Shakhovskoy positioned themselves in front of Peterswald, shielding themselves with forward outposts set up by the Tatar Ulans at the Saxon border. Helffreich's detachment deployed to the right of Peterswald, while the 1st Lifeguard Division deployed behind the village. Of the units from II Corps, only the Tobolsk Infantry, Chernigov Infantry and elements of the Murom Infantry and Minsk Infantry assembled at Peterswald, numbering 2,500 men (according to Prinz Eugen, only 1,500 men). These men had fired off all their cartridges, and the cartridge caissons had been captured by the enemy, or had been diverted along the

---

25 Major General Potemkin's report to Lieutenant General Yermolov. In recognition of this feat, Broglie was awarded the Order of St. George, 4th class.
26 War Diary of II Corps; J.M. von Helldorff, *Zur Geschichte der Schlacht bei Kulm*, 32-34; Aster, III, 112. According to Aster and Helldorff, the disabled Russian cannon was pushed over a stone wall into a ravine and remained there until the Russians launched their counter-offensive into Saxony in early [mid] September and found it in the very place where it had been abandoned.
27 War Diary of II Corps.

old Teplitz road. The losses in II Corps had been significant, but the Russian military commanders had achieved their intended objective: their troops had blocked access to Bohemia with their chests.[28]

Vandamme's leading units, having reached Hellendorf, halted there for the night. Reuß's brigade deployed forwards of the village, Corbineau's division and Gobrecht's brigade were close by, and the main body of the corps were behind them, some along the highway, some between Bahra and Hellendorf.[29]

By nightfall on 16 (28) August, the other formations of both armies were located as follows: on the Coalition side, the Russo-Prussian reserves were at Altenberg, where Emperor Alexander's and Prinz Schwarzenberg's headquarters were also located; Barclay de Tolly's headquarters was at Geising [two miles south-east of Altenberg]; Count Wittgenstein's force, Klüx's Prussian brigade and Moritz Liechtenstein's Austrian division were assigned to the rearguard at Dippoldiswalde, from where Klüx's brigade and Roth's detachment retreated along the road towards Altenberg that same night; Kleist's corps was at Hausdorf ([1½ miles] south of Maxen). On this day, the Austrian army also retreated to Pretzschendorf; Crenneville's reserve division formed its rearguard. The King of Prussia went to Teplitz.[30] On the French side, Mortier was deployed at Pirna with the *Jeune Garde*; Saint-Cyr's *14e Division* had reached Maxen with some of the *artillerie de la garde*; Marmont's *6e Corps* were closing in on Dippoldiswalde; Murat had reached Freiberg with Victor's *2e Corps* and Latour-Maubourg's *1er corps de cavallerie*.[31]

As they were retreating along bad roads, following two days of bad weather, the Coalition, and especially the Austrians, suffered heavy losses in men and vehicles: a number of Austrian guns that had bogged down in the mud were captured by the enemy. The Russians, during the entire retreat from Dresden to the Teplitz valley, did not lose a single gun. They owed this to constant attention from Major General Sukhozanet, who, due to the illness of Prince Iashvili, was entrusted with control of the artillery of the Russian army during the armistice. Subsequently, in conversation with Count Arakcheev [Alexei Andreevich Arakcheev] about the brilliant state of the Russian artillery in the second half of 1813, Emperor Alexander said:

> one only has to compare how things were at Austerlitz and how they are now. During the attack on the French at Dürnstein, Miloradovich could not bring up a single cannon; following our successful fight at Pułtusk, we abandoned 70 guns in the mud; and now, during the disastrous retreat from Dresden, with the French hot on our heels, we have crossed impassable mountains with 500 guns, without losing a single one.[32]

---

28 Aster, 114; Hofmann, 167-168.
29 Aster, 215; Richter, II, 75.
30 Plotho, II, 67.
31 Vaudoncourt, 157.
32 From General-of-Artillery I.O. Sukhozanet's notes [this is at odds with Aster and Helldorff, who claim that a Russian gun was abandoned near Hellendorf – see footnote 26 above. Pototsky's A Century Of Russian Horse Artillery also includes this anecdote: '... before even reaching Berggießhübel, Ensign Pistolkors of Lieutenant Colonel A.A. Bistrom's 3rd Horse Artillery Company were defending a path through the woods with two guns and the support

On the evening of 16 (28) August, Vandamme received via *chef d'état-major* Berthier the following (repeated) instructions from Napoleon:

> The Emperor has ordered that you move towards Peterswald with your entire corps and Corbineau's division, reinforced by 18 battalions from the *42e Division* and Erbprinz Reuß's brigade. Leave the occupation of Pirna to the duc de Trévise (Mortier), who should also relieve your troops from Lilienstein. The Emperor wishes you to enter Bohemia with your entire force and defeat the Prinz von Württemberg should you encounter him. The enemy defeated by us are apparently retreating to Annaberg (*sic*, Altenberg?). His Majesty believes that you will have time to forestall the enemy on their lines of communications leading to Tetschen, Aussig and Teplitz, and shall take possession of all the baggage following their army. The Emperor has ordered the Pirna bridge to be disassembled and a crossing to be set up at Tetschen.[33]

Having in all likelihood not yet received these orders, at half past eight o'clock that evening Vandamme sent the following report to the *quartier général*:

> We have reached Hellendorf. The enemy attempted several times to repulse our brave lads, but were defeated at all points and have retreated in complete disorder. I am facing between 4,000 and 5,000 men. At dawn, I shall attack them and march on Teplitz with the entire *1er Corps*, unless I receive orders to the contrary.[34]

Because the discovery of a French cavalry advance along the road from Raitza [Rájec, two miles north-east of Peterswald] towards Peterswald on the evening of 16 (28) August had revealed the enemy intent – to attack the Russian infantry in the long Peterswald defile, orders were issued for the Lifeguard to withdraw to Nollendorf at five o'clock on the morning of the following day [29 August], shielded by Prince Shakhovskoy's and Helffreich's forces and Her Majesty's Leib-Cuirassiers. At the same time, so as not to subject Shakhovskoy to defeat in detail, at 11 o'clock at night, the Prinz von Württemberg ordered him to withdraw beyond the village of Peterswald and position himself behind it, close to the outermost buildings. The detachment under General Helffreich was ordered to retreat even further back, to the edge of the forest, while General Knorring's Tatar Ulans, having arrived at Peterswald later than the other troops, were ordered to send patrols in all directions, and to withdraw beyond the village at first light and rejoin the troops under

---

of 40 Jägers. A French battalion swooped on the artillery from behind. Pistolkors barely had time to ride away with the limbers and crews. The young ensign reported this woeful event to his commander. He received in response from Anton Antonovich, 'well done riding away with the limbers. Without horses, the French cannot drag the guns off and today we shall take them back,' which is exactly what happened two hours later'].

33 Instructions for General Vandamme, dated 28 August new style, *Geschichte der Kriege in Europa*, X, 196.
34 *Geschichte der Kriege in Europa*, X, 197.

Prince Shakhovskoy.³⁵ As these orders had been issued with the consent of Count Osterman, the Prinz, having spent the night in Peterswald, set off at three o'clock in the morning for the edge of the village where Prince Shakhovskoy's detachment was supposed to be located, and not finding him at the designated place, he believed that he may have moved too far from the road in the thick fog, which made visibility difficult. Then, returning to Helffreich's detachment, stationed facing the mid-point of the village which stretched along the road for a distance of half a *Meile* (3½ *versts*), the Prinz von Württemberg heard several pistol shots: it was enemy cavalry that had made their way into the village along country lanes. At the same time, Prince Shakhovskoy, having found the Prinz, reported that having received orders in the evening, via an officer sent to him from Count Osterman, to light many bivouac fires in order to disguise the weakness of his detachment and to fall back only once the enemy advance had been observed, he had remained forwards of the village until first light, and was now withdrawing with his troops, who were immediately behind him.

Yet a few minutes later, instead of Prince Shakhovskoys force, a number of fleeing infantry soldiers and lancers from Knorring's regiment appeared. Officers galloping back through the village confirmed that all of Shakhovskoy's infantry had been cut down or captured. In fact, what had happened was; the lancers, attacked at dawn by French cavalry, had been driven back and had crashed into the infantry column, which was passing through the village at the time. Emerging through the thick fog at this point, the enemy cavalry smashed into the crowd at several points and scattered the infantry, some of whom fled but managed to rejoin their regiments within a few days. Overall, judging from the course of the action, the Russian losses were fewer than should have been expected, and did not exceed 300 men. Among the prisoners was Colonel Trefurt [Fëdor Fëdorovich Trefurt].³⁶

At the same time, extraordinary chaos reigned on the highway to the rear of the retreating force. The heavy baggage of II Corps, which had remained in the vicinity of Peterswald throughout the duration of the action at Pirna, had set out from there for Kulm before dawn on 16 (28) August, and had spread anxiety and disorder there. That night, just as Ostermann's force had retreated into Peterswald, the convoys departed for Aussig via Karbitz [Chabařovice], and onwards towards Prague, some along the roads, some across country, across mountains and ravines, jettisoning their cargoes from the carts along the way. The following day [29 August], the population discovered barrels of rice, grain and other supplies. The Cossacks escorting the convoy were scattered throughout the surrounding area. As if to crown the chaos, several thousand wagons from Kleist's corps and other formations of the Coalition army were driving down country lanes onto the highway and blocked it all the way from Peterswald to Nollendorf. Since there was no hope of saving these vehicles, some of them were burned, and others were abandoned along the road. The high ground at Nollendorf, over which Osterman's force had to pass, was littered with carts and their wreckage, crates, barrels, and so on. The other routes

---

35 War Diary of II Corps.
36 War Diary of II Corps; Lieutenant General Wachten's notes; Hofmann, 168-169; Helldorff, 34-37.

along which the Coalition army was retreating into Bohemia were choked in a very similar manner. It is easy to imagine what fate would have befallen the long columns stretched out in the mountain defiles if, upon leaving the mountains, they had been met by Vandamme's force and been attacked at the same time from the rear by Napoleon's main body.[37]

The scattering of Prince Shakhovskoy's force obliged Osterman to accelerate his retreat to Nollendorf. No sooner had the Lifeguard regiments set off, than they were caught up by the enemy. Princz Leopold with Her Majesty's Leib-Cuirassiers and Knorring with the Tatar Ulans raced to engage the French, but could not hold them back. The enemy, supporting their cavalry with infantry, pursued persistently. Their skirmishers became mixed up with the Russians and pushed them all the way to the plateau near Nollendorf, where General Yermolov had managed to deploy several guns and pre-position General Khrapovitsky's brigade [Matvei Yevgrafovich Khrapovitsky] in fighting formation together with the following units from II Corps: Murom Infantry, Tobolsk Infantry, Reval Infantry and 4th Jägers (the latter two had only just arrived from Schönwald). This force, having allowed Helffreich's disordered detachment to pass through, halted the French, who, having deployed a strong battery, limited themselves to a cannonade and firefight for more than two hours, despite the thick fog, which prevented them from seeing anything except at very close range. Soon thereafter, the Lifeguard fell back towards Kulm, while Prinz Eugen, who remained with his regiments in the rearguard on the Nollendorf plateau until the fog had completely cleared, also retreated behind the Lifeguard.

At this very moment, Count Osterman received a note from the King of Prussia, in which the King, informing him of the grave situation of the Coalition army, urged him to hold on to the position at Nollendorf to the bitter end. But the enemy were already consolidating on the Nollendorf plateau in significant strength, and there was no way that Osterman could retake it. The loss of this position was completely unintended, and in all likelihood, might not even have happened if Shakhovskoy's detachment had not been scattered in Peterswald, yet it had beneficial consequences for the Coalition. The terrain qualities of the Nollendorf plateau did not allow for a stubborn defence, and Osterman's force, had they remained on it, would have been defeated. The disorder of the Russian force's retreat from Peterswald to Kulm in itself did the Coalition a favour, increasing Vandamme's over-confidence and bewitching him with the promise of reaching Teplitz.[38]

Count Osterman, having received the King's note just as the Lifeguard regiments were passing through Kulm, instructed Yermolov to find the first suitable position and deploy the Lifeguard in it.[39]

The Russian forces halted an incomparably powerful enemy in this position and immortalised the honour of their arms.

---

37 Aster, 118-119.
38 War Diary of II Corps.
39 War Diary of II Corps; Yermolov's report to Count Osterman dated 22 August [3 September].

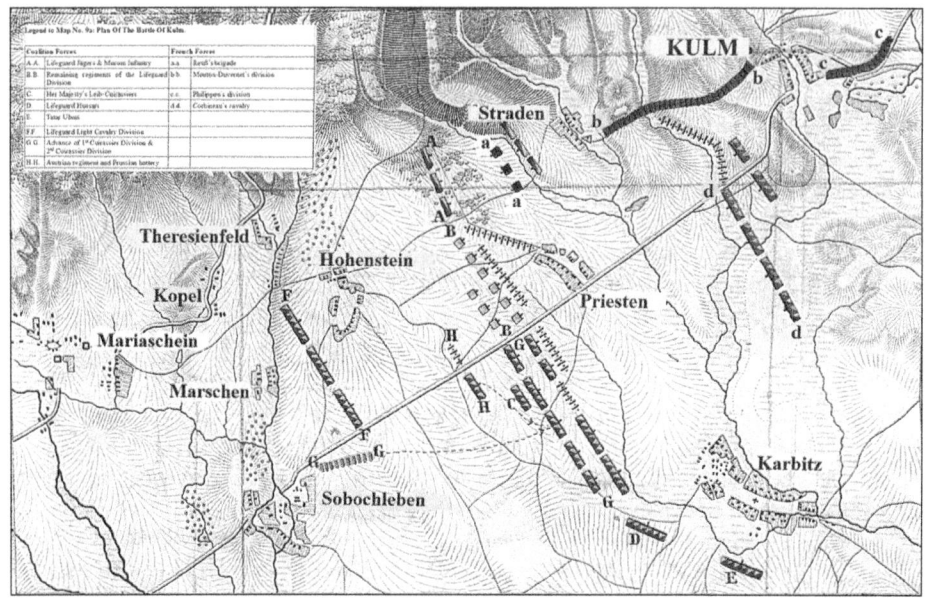

Plan of the Battle of Kulm.

Legend to Map No. 9a
Coalition Forces
A.A. Lifeguard Jägers & Murom Infantry
B.B. Remaining regiments of the Lifeguard Division
C.   Her Majesty's Leib-Cuirassiers
D.   Lifeguard Hussars
E.   Tatar Ulans
F.F. Lifeguard Light Cavalry Division
G.G. Advance of 1st Cuirassier Division & 2nd Cuirassier Division
H.H. Austrian regiment and Prussian battery

French Forces
a.a. Reuß's brigade
b.b. Mouton-Duvernet's division
c.c. Philippon's division
d.d. Corbineau's cavalry

30

The action at Kulm on 17 (29) August

The withdrawal of Osterman-Tolstoy's force into the Priesten position. – Vandamme's advance on Kulm. – Precautions taken by Emperor Alexander I and the King of Prussia. – Description of the positions taken by Osterman's force; their deployment; fighting strength of the Russian corps.

Vandamme's advance. The Erbprinz Reuß's and Mouton-Duvernet's attacks. – The attack by Philippon's division. – The depletion of the Russian reserves. – The arrival or reinforcements for both sides. – Casualties. – The significance of the action at Kulm. – Awards. – The 18 August 1814 Committee. – The movement of Colloredo's and Bianchi's Austrian divisions from Dux in support of Osterman. – Movements by Kleist's corps towards Fürstenwalde. Kleist's intention to advance behind the French corps.

The action at Kulm took place on 17 (29) August, on a day of glory in the annals of Russian military history. At about eight o'clock in the morning, the 1st Lifeguard Division, having passed this village, hurried on towards Priesten [Přestanov], in order to occupy positions assigned there by General Yermolov.[1] The Lifeguard Jägers, who were engaged in a heated firefight with the enemy at Nollendorf, secured the retreat of II Corps and Helffreich's detachment to this location, then also retreated through Kulm to positions at Priesten. After the troops under Helffreich and Knorring withdrew from the Nollendorf plateau, the Prinz von Württemberg (as has already been mentioned) remained on the plateau with Prince Shakhovskoy's detachment until the fog cleared and the enemy, noticing the small size of the Russian rearguard, launched an attack on them. At eight o'clock, shots were fired at Prince Shakhovsky's retreating force from a battery recently placed by the French near the Nollendorf chapel. The following were left in order to delay the enemy: Knorring's Tatar Ulans, 500 paces behind Vorder-Tellnitz [Přední Telnice] with several guns, and Colonel Ivanov's brigade (4th Jägers and the Reval Infantry) with

---

1 See Maps No. 9a and 9b: Plan of the Battle of Kulm.

a half-battery on the Kapellenberg [Horka] by the Dreifaltigkeitskapelle [Kaple Nejsvětější Trojice], forwards of Kulm.²

Following the seizure of Nollendorf, Vandamme sent one battalion of the *57e ligne*, with 300 sappers and two guns, to Postitz [Božtěšice] and on to Aussig, in order to bring this location into a defensible state, while he, having noticed the disorder of the Russian troops in Peterswald, without doubting the success of his advance on Teplitz, moved onwards himself. The Russian detachments left at Tellnitz [Telnice] and Kulm, having delayed the enemy for a short while, retreated in good order to Priesten, while the French, hot on their heels, burst into Kulm just after nine o'clock. At this very moment, the residents of the village, after attended a Divine service in the Dreifaltigkeitskapelle, were returning home. Although the cannonade had thundered from the direction of Nollendorf from the early dawn, the passive inhabitants of the Teplitz valley, unfamiliar with the horrors of war, had not anticipated the storm that broke over their homes. Some of them, completely losing their minds, fled in panic. Others rushed to their homes in order to save their most valuable possessions. They were greeted there by the sobs of frightened women, the screams of children and hand-to-hand combat with bayonets and musket butts. Following this, Vandamme's batteries, unlimbering on the Kapellenberg, opened a strong cannonade on the retreating troops under Prince Shakhovskoy and Knorring. The Russians, in turn, engaged the enemy emerging from Kulm with canister. Shots could be heard from all directions, repeated several times by the echo of the mountains. This was the beginning of the Battle of Kulm.³

At ten o'clock, as the 1st Lifeguard Division was just getting into position, and the other Russian formations were retreating from Kulm to Priesten, the King of Prussia arrived on the battlefield. After a rather lengthy conversation with Count Osterman, he rode back, but remained nearby throughout the battle, sending his aides-de-camp to all the exits from the Ore Mountains, also instructing them to direct the units to assist the Russian corps as they rushed onto the plain.⁴

Equally effective precautions to achieve the same aim were taken by Emperor Alexander. After spending the night in Altenberg, the Tsar set off from there on the morning of 17 (29) August along the road to Dux, to where the headquarters had been assigned. After the long period of bad weather, the sun appeared in all its glory. As soon as Emperor Alexander, surrounded by his large retinue, left the forest covering the ridge at Geiersburg, smoke could be seen to their left. At first it was mistaken for smoke from the bivouac fires, but they soon became convinced that it was from artillery, and a little later they heard gunfire, which gradually became more and more intense. The Tsar diverted from the Dux road towards Graupen [Krupka], and having ascended the commanding high ground, from where he was easily able to view the Teplitz valley, he concluded that the enemy wanted to seize the exits from the mountains in order to block the Coalition's routes into Bohemia. It was vital to reinforce Count Osterman, but the columns of the Coalition army,

---

2   Hofmann, *Zur Geschichte des Feldzuges von 1813*, 170; Aster, *Die Kriegsereignisse zwischen Peterswalde, Pirna, Königstein und Priesten im August 1813 und die Schlacht bei Kulm*, 128-129.
3   Aster, 129-130.
4   Aster, 132.

stretched out in the mountains, were moving very slowly along roads congested with wagons. Emperor Alexander immediately sent General Jomini to meet the Austrian units moving along the Dux road, instructing him to invite whomever was first of the Austrian generals he met at the head of the column, to go to the aid of the troops in combat, to Teplitz. The Emperor went on to Dux himself in order to issue the necessary orders, in collaboration with the Commander-in-Chief, but could not find Schwarzenberg there. Following this, Jomini returned with a reply from Graf Colloredo that, 'having orders to go to Dux and not to Teplitz, without orders from Prinz Schwarzenberg, he would not dare to change the direction of his force.' Having heard this unsatisfactory response, the Emperor sent for Prinz Metternich and explained to him the urgent need to send the approaching Austrian units to Teplitz, instead of the proposed retreat beyond the Eger. During this conversation, General Jomini, having been invited into the Tsar's office, began to explain to Metternich the danger of such a retreat, noting that even if it were decided to continue, it was still necessary to push the enemy corps back, which threatened to sever communications with the formations which had not yet managed to cross the mountains. Prinz Metternich seemed very anxious, but, having been convinced by the soundness of General Jomini's arguments, he decided to fulfil the will of the Tsar and sent a note on this to Graf Colloredo, who, having only received it near Dux, turned towards Teplitz, in order to assist the Russian corps with all the troops under his command, namely with his and Bianchi's infantry divisions and with 'Sorbenberg's' cavalry brigade [alias of Ferdinand Georg August von Sachsen-Coburg-Saalfeld]. The Russian reserve cavalry, emerging from the mountains at that moment, received orders from the Tsar to also hurry to the battlefield.[5]

Emperor Alexander did not limit himself to measures taken to reinforce Count Osterman, he undertook to defeat Vandamme before the other French corps could come to his aid. To that end, the Tsar sent the Prussian *Oberst* Schöler from his retinue to General Kleist, who was marching from Hausdorf to Fürstenwalde with his corps at the time, with instructions to invite him to get behind Vandamme's corps, instead of the proposed move to Teplitz.[6] In expectation of the success of all these orders, the troops under Count Osterman had to repel an enemy twice as strong.

The position chosen by General Yermolov behind the village of Kulm offered many tactical advantages. It is located one German *Meile* (about seven *versts*) forwards of Teplitz, in a place where the picturesque Teplitz valley widens in the direction of Teplitz, having been constrained at Kulm by high ground at Strisowitz [Střížovice] and Böhmisch-Neudörfel [Český Újezd]. On the left flank of the position the slope of the hills rise into dense scrub and forest at the foot of the Ore Mountains. In the centre, near the highway, is the village of Priesten. From there to the right, towards the town of Karbitz, lies a wide meadow, bordered on the Kulm side by a shallow river. The highway running past Priesten was embanked above the surrounding area, and therefore partly protected both this village and the troops occupying it

---

5 Bernhardi, Denkwürdigkeiten aus dem Leben Carl Friedrich Grafen von Toll, III, 219-220; Jomini, Réplique du colonel Jomini à Lord Londonderry, général Stuart, sur les événemens de la campagne de Dresde en 1813, 35; Aster, 134.
6 For details of this mission, see Appendix XVI at the end of this chapter.

from enemy artillery fire. Any enemy breaking into Priesten would be exposed to fire from Russian batteries to its rear, and any crossing of the river on the right wing of the position would be complicated by the positioning of Russian cavalry close to Karbitz: it is obvious that when placing troops in this position, attention had to be paid primarily to the defence of the left wing, which, being closer to the exits from the mountains than other points, presented the greatest advantages for an enemy attack.[7]

Upon retreating into this position, General Knorring's detachment (Reval Infantry, 4th Jägers and Tatar Ulans) were left at Kulm as a rearguard. The other units under Count Osterman, having retreated into the position, deployed themselves as follows: General Bistrom was on the left flank with the Lifeguard Jägers and two battalions of Murom Infantry; Priesten was held by the remaining regiments of II Corps and Helffreich's detachment, under the overall command of the Prinz von Württemberg;[8] the following were stationed 500 paces behind the village in attack columns: the Lifeguard Izmailovsky and Lifeguard Semenovsky in the front line, while the Lifeguard Preobrazhensky were in the support line; forwards of the front line were: on the left wing, Ladygin's 1st Lifeguard Light Artillery Company, with Cheremisinov's 14th Battery Company [Yakov Yakovlevich Cheremisinov] and Baikov's 27th Light Artillery Company [Ivan Ivanovich Baikov] on the right; further to the right was Bistrom's horse artillery battery [Anton Antonovich Bistrom]. The Lifeguard Hussars were stationed behind the infantry, with Her Majesty's Leib-Cuirassiers to their right in the meadow by the river as far as Karbitz (later to be joined by the remaining cavalry). The numerical strength of this force did not exceed 15,000 or 16,000 men, while together with reinforcements that arrived throughout the duration of the fighting on 17 (29) August, or, like the majority, arrived just at the end of the battle, there were some 20,000 men, namely:

Units	Strength according to Prinz Eugen	Strength according to Helffreich
12 Lifeguard battalions	6,500	6,700
Nine weak battalions under Shakhovskoy & Helffreich	2,500	5,500
Cavalry	2,000	2,500
Total:	11,000	14,700
Estimated total including artillerymen:	**12,300**	**16,000**

Adding reinforcements to this total, of which only a few had arrived at the beginning of the battle, it emerges that overall Osterman would have had some 17,000 to 20,000 men, against whom Vandamme had at least 30,000 men. Moreover, according to the

---

7   Richter, *Geschichte des Deutschen Freiheitskrieges*, II, 77-78; Helldorff, *Zur Geschichte der Schlacht bei Kulm*, 40-41; War Diary of II Corps, Archive of the M.T.D. No. 47,344 (handwritten).
8   Prinz Eugen von Württemberg's force in Priesten consisted of: Tenginsk Infantry, Estland Infantry and Her Highness, Grand Duchess Yekaterina Pavlovna's Battalion, from Helffreich's detachment; Tobolsk Infantry, Chernigov Infantry and Minsk Infantry, from II Corps, commanded by Prince Shakhovskoy. Helldorff, 41.

Prinz von Württemberg himself, the regiments of II Corps were already short of ammunition, and Helffreich's detachment had almost none at all.[9]

Throughout the battle, Count Osterman and General Yermolov remained with the guard, while the Prinz von Württemberg, directly commanding the forces under Prince Shakhovskoy and Helffreich, was initially on the highway near Bistrom's battery, and then to the left of Priesten.[10]

Vandamme, hoping to encourage the Russians to continue to retreat through his appearance alone, and in a hurry to reach Teplitz, did not wait for the concentration of his forces and launched an attack on the position at Priesten as soon as Reuß's brigade, marching at the head of his corps, had managed to exit Kulm. At around noon, the units of this brigade (six battalions) were sent against the weakest point of the position – the left wing, towards the village of Straden, but met the most stubborn resistance there. General Bistrom's skirmishers, taking advantage of the wooded area, inflicted significant casualties on the enemy and the brigade commander himself, Erbprinz Reuß, was killed. The arrival, on Yermolov's orders, of the Lifeguard Semenovsky Regiment to assist the Lifeguard Jägers tilted the balance in favour of the Russians. The enemy brigade fell back. But at that very moment General Mouton-Duvernet appeared against the left wing of the position with nine battalions from *42e Division*. The Prinz von Württemberg, seeing this, immediately sent Helffreich's detachment into the gap between the villages of Priesten and Straden and supported him with the Chernigov Infantry and Tobolsk Infantry. Despite this, however, the enemy, taking advantage of their significant numerical superiority, ejected the Russian skirmishers from the forest near Straden, placed strong batteries on the high ground facing the left wing and centre of Osterman's force and smashed them, and, at the same time, wanting to keep the Russian cavalry inactive, deployed Corbineau's division (20 squadrons) and sent Gobrecht's brigade (eight squadrons) out of Kulm along both sides of the highway.

At about two o'clock in the afternoon, the French division under General Philippon approached the battlefield (14 battalions). Vandamme, wanting a decisive resolution of the issue, sent these fresh troops against the Russian position in two columns: *12e ligne* raced towards Straden, while the other three regiments headed for Priesten. General Bistrom, having been forced to cede the village of Straden to the enemy, which was engulfed in flames, fell back and occupied the buildings of the Eggen-Mühle, which served as a stronghold for the left flank of the position. Two French battalions, impetuously chasing after the retreating troops, were surrounded by them in a clearing in the forest and were largely wiped out or captured. An equally fierce battle raged near the Juchtenkapelle [Juchtová kaple, ⅔ mile south-west of Straden]. The enemy quickly attacked this point, wanting to break through the Russian lines. The Lifeguard Semenovsky lost 900 men here. General Yermolov sent two battalions of the Lifeguard Preobrazhensky to reinforce them. Helffreich's detachment, with the Chernigov Infantry and Tobolsk Infantry from II Corps, were also committed to action. The units from both sides fought with varying success and became intermixed with one-another in hand-to-hand combat. At the same time as the attack

---

9   War Diary of II Corps; Helldorff, 41-42.
10 Helldorff, 42.

on the left wing of the position, the enemy attacked the village of Priesten in significant strength, ejected the skirmishers from II Corps and forced Bistrom's horse artillery battery to retreat along the highway, but as soon as the enemy debouched from the village, they were engaged with canister from Russian batteries and were forced to turn back, which allowed Prince Shakhovskoy to reoccupy Priesten with the 4th Jägers, Reval Infantry and Minsk Infantry. The second enemy attempt to establish themselves in this village was equally unsuccessful. Taking advantage of this, the Prinz von Württemberg ordered Colonel Wachten to move Baikov's and Cheremisinov's batteries forward and place them to the left of Priesten in such an alignment that they could fire at the French columns advancing on the left wing of the position, while remaining on a reverse slope in the direction of the enemy artillery stationed forwards of Kulm. The effective fire from these batteries prevented the enemy from enveloping the position from the left flank and forced Vandamme to divert part of his force to the left, against the artillery. The French, despite the canister fire that devastated their ranks, quickly moved forward, with deafening shouts of: '*en avant! Vive l'empereur!*' The Prinz von Württemberg, whose regiments had already been much weakened and had fired almost all their cartridges, sent one of his aides-de-camp (J.M. Helldorff) to Osterman, with a request to support his force with the nearby Lifeguard Izmailovsky regiment.[11]

At this point, one of the battalions from this regiment had already been committed to battle. There were only three battalions left as the reserve of the Russian force, and therefore General Yermolov, as an experienced warrior, wanting to preserve a fresh unit for the final throw, sought to convince Osterman to refuse the reinforcements requested by the Prinz. Foreign historians have attributed the actions of General Yermolov solely to a desire to preserve the Lifeguard.[12] After a heated argument between Yermolov and the Chief of Staff of II Corps, Colonel Hofmann, the Prinz von Württemberg dashed to see Osterman himself and received the battalions who's assistance he wanted. With General Khrapovitsky at their head, they attacked the enemy. According to an eyewitness:

> the advance, the charge and the victory proceeded instantly. The entire battlefield was covered with enemy corpses, the nearest French columns fled, the entire line of Russian troops moved forward, and a strong cannonade was opened from all the batteries in the position. But this truly heroic feat cost the brave Izmailovsky men dearly. General Khrapovitsky himself and Colonel Martynov [Pavel Petrovich Martynov] were seriously wounded…[13]

In order to counter the Russian artillery advanced to the left of Priesten, the French also placed 24 guns on the high ground near Straden, but operations by this battery

---

11 War Diary of II Corps; Wagner, Plane der Schlachten und Treffen, welche von der preussischen Armee in den Feldzügen der Jahre 1813, 14 und 15 geliefert worden. Die Tage von Dresden und Kulm, 101-102; Helldorff, 43-45.
12 For details of this event, see Appendix XVII at the end of this chapter.
13 Helldorff, 46-47. General Khrapovitskiy suffered several bayonet wounds and was wounded in the leg by canister shot. Martynov suffered a gunshot wound to the torso.

could not cause much harm to the Russian force due to the considerable range. Nevertheless, a round shot fired from there severed Count Osterman's left wrist. Retiring from the battlefield, he transferred command of the force to Yermolov.[14]

The Russian troops fought like lions. The regiments vied with each other to dash into the smoke of battle. Musicians, drummers, clerks, begged for muskets. Yermolov wrote in the report on the action at Kulm:

> I could not conceal from the Lifeguard regiments that our army was in the mountains and were unable to arrive soon, that the Sovereign Emperor was with them and had not yet returned. I was not in a position to cheer the soldiers up – the undaunted spirit of their commanders served as an example to them. All of them were impassioned…

Yet every Russian unit was already under fire. Only two companies of the Lifeguard Preobrazhensky Regiment remained in reserve, and the enemy were receiving reinforcements and straining their efforts, trying to break the desperate resistance of this handful of brave men. At about five o'clock in the afternoon, the *7e léger* (the same unit that had fought against the Preobrazhensky at Berggießhübel) marched at an accelerated pace towards Priesten at the head of a huge column. The enemy took this village for the third time and began to cross the ravine that separated it from Baikov's battery. The Russian artillerymen engaged the French with canister shot, but many of them fell under fire from the screen of skirmishers. Lieutenant Colonel Cheremisinov was badly wounded. The enemy were already rushing towards the battery… But at this decisive moment, the Russian cavalry appeared on the battlefield – the Lifeguard Dragoons and Lifeguard Ulans, and behind them the 1st Cuirassier Division. The quartermaster general of Barclay de Tolly's force, Major General Diebitsch, who arrived at the same time, took command of the Lifeguard Dragoons and charged at the French. They were attacked from the other side by the Lifeguard Ulans, commanded by Colonel Prinz Karl von Hessen-Philippsthal [Karl August Philipp Ludwig von Hessen-Philippsthal-Barchfeld], who was badly wounded here. The enemy infantry, driven back by these attacks, lost some 500 men taken prisoner alone and retreated back under the cover of Fezensac's regiments [Raymond Aymeric Philippe Joseph de Montesquiou-Fezensac] proceeding at the tail of the column. At the same time, Gobrecht's cavalry brigade moved forward to check the advancing Russian force: this was the final event of the action at Kulm. Meanwhile, the 1st Cuirassier Division arrived on the right wing of the Russian position, brought up by Lieutenant Diest [Heinrich Ludwig Friedrich Arnold von Diest] of the General Staff, who, acknowledging Count Osterman's desperate situation and using the authority of Barclay de Tolly's name, ordered this division to go straight to the battlefield. The Austrian *Dragonerregiment Erzherzog Johann* arrived almost at the same time as the 1st Cuirassier Division, followed by the 2nd Cuirassier Division. The enemy cavalry stationed behind the river and suffering significant losses from the activity of the Russian artillery (probably Bistrom's horse artillery), moved

---

14 For details of this event, see Appendix XVIII at the end of this chapter.

forward to engage the cuirassiers, but halted and did not charge. On the French side, Dunesme's brigade [Martin François Dunesme] from Dumonceau's division arrived at Kulm, consisting of eight battalions, and were stationed to the left of this village. The action was completely over by seven o'clock in the evening (some sources state six o'clock). The Russian reserves arrived somewhat later: 1st Grenadier Division, commanded by Lieutenant General Raevsky [Nikolai Nikolaevich Raevsky], and 2nd Lifeguard Division under Lieutenant General Udom [Ivan Fëdorovich Udom 1st], and Major General Pyshnitsky and Colonel Wolfe arrived with their detachments from II Corps, which had been rejoined by many soldiers scattered the day before.[15] General Miloradovich, having arrived with the reserves, took command of the entire force assembled to face Vandamme. 1st Grenadier Division were stationed in the front line, relieving 1st Lifeguard Division and the Prinz von Württemberg's force, which were temporarily withdrawn in order to reorganise their disordered battalions. The remainder of the reinforcements took up their assigned positions during the night and the next morning. Prinz Schwarzenberg and Barclay de Tolly arrived just after the fighting had ended. According to Prokesch's biography of Schwarzenberg [Anton Prokesch von Osten], one of the Coalition generals, having gone to meet the Commander-in-Chief, briefed him on the situation as if it were hopeless. He is quoted as saying: '4,000 men of the Lifeguard have fallen on the field of battle; Osterman has been mortally wounded; all is lost.'

'Are the Lifeguard still holding out?' Schwarzenberg asked, and upon receiving a positive response, continued: 'thus nothing is lost as yet, because we have arrived here yet again. Go quickly to Emperor Alexander and tell him that I ordered congratulations for him for tomorrow's victory.' According to Prokesch, Schwarzenberg made arrangements to attack Vandamme the next morning, invited Kleist to assist the rest of the Coalition force, and so forth. In response to all these fabrications, it should be noted that by the time Schwarzenberg arrived on the battlefield, neither he nor any of the other persons present in the headquarters could have known that Napoleon had suspended the advance of his main body, and being unaware of this, it was not realistically possible to hope that Vandamme could be defeated. On the French side, the remaining units of Vandamme's corps arrived at Kulm in the evening and after dark: Doucet's brigade [Pierre Doucet] from Dumonceau's division, consisting of five battalions (as has already been mentioned, one battalion from *57e ligne* had already been detached to Aussig); General Creutzer [Charles Auguste Creutzer] with three battalions from his brigade, from which two remained in Kulm, while Creutzer himself was sent to Aussig with the third battalion as support for the detachment sent there earlier; thereafter the cavalry and artillery from *42e Division* arrived, and finally Quiot's brigade, consisting of six battalions.[16]

The troops from 1st Lifeguard Division, on the day of battle on 17 (29) August, covered themselves with glory, while the line regiments that assisted them were no less selfless or courageous. With the exception of the cavalry charge at the end of the fighting, for six hours the infantry, numbering 12,000 men, fought alone against an

---

15 War Diary of II Corps; Helldorff, 47-49; Alexander Andreevich Shcherbinin's (handwritten) notes.
16 Aster 145.

enemy who eventually built up to 19,000 men (six battalions under Prinz Reuß, nine battalions from Mouton-Duvernet's division and 14 battalions from Philippon's division). But this success was bought at a high price, and the losses to the Russian force in killed and wounded, overall reached some 6,000 men, or almost half of the available number of men taking part in the action, namely: 2,800 men lost to the ranks of 1st Lifeguard Division; 2,400 men from II Corps and Helffreich's detachment; 800 men from the cavalry in Count Osterman's force and those that arrived later.[17]

The number of French *hors de combat* in action on 17 (29) August is not mentioned anywhere. In all likelihood, it was very significant, because some of the enemy battalions were almost completely destroyed.

The action on 17 (29) August at Kulm made it possible for the main Coalition army to retreat back into Bohemia and was the precursor to the defeat of Vandamme's corps, which equalised the outcome of the unsuccessful Coalition attack on Dresden. It displayed the valour of the Russian forces in all their splendour and will remain forever unforgettable in the memory of the Russian people. One of the main enablers of this feat, General Yermolov, testifying to the merits of his worthy colleagues, wrote in the report on the action at Kulm:

> I cannot present particularly outstanding exploits by individual field officers and subalterns. This would necessitate the provision of a list of everyone present. I cannot even present the lower ranks: this would necessitate counting all ranks of the valiant regiments that have the good fortune to bear the title of the Tsar's Lifeguard, whom they idolise.

Emperor Alexander I awarded Count Osterman the Order of St. George, 2nd class. The Preobrazhensky, Semenovsky and Naval Crew received St George's Colours, inscribed: 'For feats performed in combat on 17 August, 1813 at Kulm' (*За оказанные подвиги в сраженіи 17-го августа 1813 года при Кульмѣ*), while the Izmailovsky and Lifeguard Jägers, who already had St George's Colours, were awarded St. George's trumpets inscribed: 'For distinction shown at the Battle of Kulm on 17 August, 1813' (*За отличие, оказанное въ сраженіи при Кульмѣ 17-го августа 1813 года*). The King of Prussia, as a witness to the feats of the Russian troops, awarded the Order of the *Eisernes Kreuz* to every general, officer and lower rank from the Lifeguard who was present on 17 (29) August. When distributing these crosses, the orders issued by Count Miloradovich stated: 'May these new decorations on your chest for the glory of the Russian name and the freedom of Europe be added to the total of those that you acquired through toil and blood in the battles for the salvation of the

---

17 The casualties from 1st Lifeguard Division's regiments in action at Kulm on 17 (29) August were: 700 men from the Preobrazhensky; 900 men from the Semenovsky; 500 men from the Izmailovsky; 600 men from the Lifeguard Jägers, for a total of 2,700 to 2,800 men.
   In addition to those mentioned in the description of the course of the battle, the following were wounded: major generals Ritter and Levashov, and Colonel Mezentsov. Plotho, *Der Krieg in Deutschland und Frankreich in den Jahren 1813 und 1814*, II, 72; Helldorff, 49. In the War Diary of II Corps, it states the Lifeguard casualties, overall, reached some 3,000 men.

fatherland.' Kaiser Franz granted Count Osterman the *Kommandeurkreuz* of the *Maria-Theresien-Orden*. The Bohemian ladies, wishing to express their gratitude to him for blocking enemy access to their country, sent him a goblet decorated with semiprecious stones from each of the districts of the kingdom.[18]

Three monuments stand on the battlefield of Kulm, erected later by the Monarchs of the Coalition Powers, whose forces had taken part in the defeat of Vandamme. Emperor Alexander I has perpetuated the memory of this famous victory with an act of goodness worthy of his benevolence, establishing a Committee exactly a year later to assist all impoverished soldiers who have shed their blood on the field of honour.[19]

The Austrian divisions under Colloredo and Bianchi, who arrived in the vicinity of Dux on the day of the battle of Kulm, 17 (29) August, together with Chasteler's division and the cavalry under Nostitz and Lederer, having received a note from Metternich which changed their original direction (as has already been mentioned), moved towards Kulm and managed take part in the attack on Vandamme the next day, 18 (30) August.[20] The Prussian corps, having set out at two o'clock in the morning on 17 (29) August from Hausdorf (a village two *versts* south of Maxen), headed towards Fürstenwalde. Marshal Saint-Cyr, who was pursuing them with *14e Corps*, having received orders from the *quartier général* to march on Altenberg via Dippoldiswalde, pushed Kleist's corps aside with just his vanguard, which determinedly attacked the Prussian troops proceeding in the tail of the column at Glashütte. But the bold counterattacks by the *1. Schlesisches Husaren*, commanded by *Oberst* Blücher [Franz Ferdinand Joachim von Blücher], made it possible for Kleist to transport all his artillery through the Glashütte defile, and only a few carts were captured by the French.[21] The stage from Hausdorf to Fürstenwalde, along a poor road that was an almost continuous defile, was very difficult, and therefore the Prussian force arrived at Liebenau [2½ miles north of Fürstenwalde] and Fürstenwalde just as dusk was falling. As early as four o'clock in the afternoon, when the battle at Kulm was in full swing, Graf Schweinitz, who was an orderly for King Friedrich Wilhelm, had reached Kleist with orders: 'march as quickly as possible through the mountain passes to the Teplitz valley, to aid Count Osterman-Tolstoy and take part in the battle.' On the way from Teplitz to Kleist's force via Graupen, Graf Schweinitz saw the extent to which this road was congested by Russian units and transport retreating from Dresden. Convinced of the impossibility of moving the corps in the indicated direction in the proper order and arriving in time to help Osterman, Schweinitz reported this to Kleist, who, for his part, emphatically

---

18 This goblet was presented to the Preobrazhensky Regiment by Count Osterman, so that 'every Great Lent at the regimental chapel, after the communion of the Holy Mysteries, it would be passed to the lower ranks, with mulled wine, instead of the vessel used by the Greco-Russian Church for this purpose.' By order of Osterman himself, the names of the commanders of the Lifeguard regiments who took part in the action and those officers killed there were engraved on the goblet.
19 For the details of the establishment of this committee, see Appendix XIX at the end of this chapter.
20 Plotho, II, 74-75.
21 Plotho, II, 73.

assured him that a march through the mountains could not be undertaken before allowing the exhausted troops several hours rest, and that therefore it would be impossible to get to Teplitz before dusk, when, in all likelihood, the outcome of the battle would already have been decided. Based on these considerations, Kleist sent Count Schweinitz back to the King with a report in which he stated that, with exhausted and hungry troops, he had not been able to reach Fürstenwalde before four o'clock in the afternoon, and finding it necessary to pause for a halt, he would be unable to arrive at Teplitz before nightfall and take part in the action, and therefore, moving along bad roads choked with transport, he would needlessly leave his corps vulnerable to the inevitable threats. Kleist responded in a similar vein to the King's repeated command – to detach at least one brigade to help Osterman.

A little later, as the Prussian troops were just entering bivouacs in the vicinity of Fürstenwalde, *Oberst* Schöler arrived there with instructions from Emperor Alexander – prompting Kleist that he should move behind Vandamme's corps. At the same time, Schöler confirmed previous information regarding the complete gridlock on the old Teplitz road. In the meantime, patrols sent from Fürstenwalde towards Nollendorf reported that no enemy troops had been seen in the direction of Peterswald. There was also no threat from Saint-Cyr, because his vanguard had halted at Glashütte. Under these circumstances, a decision was necessary: should they march via Graupen to the Teplitz valley, or to Nollendorf, behind Vandamme? General Kleist, in consultation with his corps *Chef des Stabes*, *Oberstleutnant* Grolman, decided, after giving the troops a much needed rest, to set out for Nollendorf via Streckenwald [Větrov], on the morning of 18 (30) August. The generals and aides-de-camp, who were waiting for orders for the onward march in another room, accepted the decision of their superior with delight, despite the fact that each of them was aware of the danger of such an operation and all were convinced that Napoleon could be following Vandamme into Bohemia with his entire army. On the night of 17 to 18 (29 to 30) August, *Oberst* Schöler returned to Teplitz, having accepted Kleist's orders to convey his intention to the Coalition Sovereigns and Prinz Schwarzenberg.[22]

Thus was Kleist's courageous movement decided, which does him all the more credit since it was left at his discretion whether to undertake it, or to head via Geiersburg: therefore, in the event of failure, a heavy burden of responsibility would have fallen on him for a rash act exposing the troops of the corps entrusted to him to obvious danger.

---

22 Aster, 149-155. For General Yermolov's report on the action at Kulm, see Appendix XX at the end of this chapter.

Appendix XVI

Oberst Schöler's liaison with Kleist at Kulm

From Aster's account (page 152), although it is not explicit that Schöler was sent to Kleist by Emperor Alexander, it is nevertheless impossible to conclude that the King of Prussia sent him. Wolzogen [*Memoiren*, 200] writes definitively that Schöler was sent by the King, but clearly undermines this evidence by stating that Schöler arrived on the battlefield of Kulm together with Emperor Alexander and was sent from there to Kleist. It is known that on this day, 17 (29) August, the Tsar was not on the battlefield, and that Schöler was with him constantly: therefore, it was not the King, but Emperor Alexander who sent Kleist the orders to follow Vandamme. It should, however, be noted that the Tsar was not at all confident in the success of this mission, and evidence of this is another order given to Schöler – to bring the young Prins Frederik van Oranje [Willem Frederik Karel van Oranje-Nassau], with Kleist at the time, to the headquarters. Thus, the decision was left to Kleist whether to follow Vandamme, or go straight to Teplitz.

In Lecomte's more recently published work, *Le Général Jomini, sa vie et ses écrits*, it states:

> Emperor Alexander, for his part, charged Jomini to write to General Kleist to inform him that Vandamme would be attacked at Kulm the next day early in the morning, and to engage this Prussian general into manoeuvring to fall on his right flank via the Geiersburg defile along which he had previously been ordered to proceed. The Prussian ambassador, General Schöler, was good enough to take it upon himself to take this letter to General Kleist, in order to explain the situation to him and to explain to him the importance of this movement.

> (*L'empereur Alexandre, de son côté, chargea Jomini d'écrire au général Kleist àfin de l'informer qu'on attaquerait Vandamme vers Culm le lendemain de grand matin, et d'engager ce général prussien à manoeuvrer pour descendre sur son flanc droit par les défilés de Geyersberg qu'il avait eu précédemment l'ordre de suivre. L'ambassadeur de Prusse, général Schoeler, voulut bien se charger de porter lui même cette lettre au général Kleist, àfin de lui expliquer l'état des choses et de lui démontrer l'importance de ce mouvement*).

Appendix XVII

Yermolov's reluctance to commit the Russian Lifeguard at Kulm

In briefly describing the events at Kulm, Helldorff wrote (pages 45-46) that, having been sent by the Prinz von Württemberg to Count Osterman, with a request to reinforce the units of II Corps with the Lifeguard Izmailovsky Regiment, he found the count together with General Yermolov, and had barely expressed the Prinz's request, when Yermolov said:

> The Prinz places too little value on the blood of the Imperial Lifeguard.' When Count Osterman ordered Yermolov to send the required battalions, Yermolov responded: 'Your Excellency! I consider it my duty to tell you that I shall not accept responsibility before the Tsar for the loss of the entire Lifeguard. The Prinz von Württemberg is to blame for them being destroyed today, but, apparently, he believes that all this has not been enough and demands the remaining battalions. With their loss, the 1st Lifeguard Division will have disappeared.

Whereupon, Helldorff, in response to these words, only managed to say: 'The Prinz…'

Yermolov interrupted his reply, saying:

> The Prinz is German, and it does not matter to him whether we Russians preserve our Lifeguard or not. As for me, I consider it my duty to preserve at least some of them…

Appendix XVIII

Yermolov's succession to command of Osterman's force at Kulm

Some foreign historians (Helldorff, Aster) claim that the Prinz von Württemberg took command after Count Osterman, as the senior of his generals. Indeed, the Prinz was promoted to lieutenant general on 20 October [1 November], 1812, while General Yermolov was promoted later, but with seniority back-dated to 7 [19] August, 1812, that is, from the day of the battle of Lubino [Valutina Gora]. Moreover, Yermolov's report to Count Osterman states: 'Your Excellency, having suffered a wound, was forced to ride away; it was deemed fit to entrust me with command.' From the course of events it is clear that Yermolov was directing operations before the arrival of Count Miloradovich. Alexander Andreevich Shcherbinin's notes, who was serving under General Toll at the time, also mention that Count Osterman handed over command to Yermolov. Finally, in Admiral Shishkov's notes [Alexander Semënovich Shishkov] (second edition, page 155), we find: 'General Yermolov is particularly credited with great honour in this action (Kulm).'

Appendix XIX

Supreme Orders dated August 1814 for the former Committee for the Wounded

The 18 August 1814 Committee was formerly the Committee for the Wounded. The Supreme Orders issued on this day state:

> Warriors! A year ago to this very day, on the fields of Kulm, where your chests halted the enemy striving for Bohemia, I offered solemn thanks to the Almighty, together with you, for His ineffable mercy towards us. Courage, valour, patience and love for Faith and the Fatherland have been your constant companions, have crowned you with new laurels, opened the gates of Paris, granted peace and granted the warrior the complementary pleasure of returning to his State with honour. It is grateful for the service and toil that you have endured. I express gratitude to you in its name. It is on its behalf that I welcome you back to your fatherland. Your heroic deeds have always caught my attention. In order to further commemorate them, and especially the day of 18 [30] August, I am now opening a most convenient path for all those crippled in the last war, unforgettable for their resounding deeds, for generals, field officers and subalterns, both those who have already retired, and those who will henceforth leave the service due to wounds and injuries from this war, and those who have no other income other than a pension determined upon retirement, to revert to me for all their needs. And so that their requests are considered, verified and presented to me immediately, I am establishing a dedicated committee, whose duty will be to accept requests, take care of providing every possible assistance to the poor and injured generals and subalterns, and present their reports on them.

Appendix XX

General Yermolov's report on the action at Kulm

Report to the honourable Lieutenant General and Chevalier, Count Osterman-Tolstoy, from the Commander IV Corps, Lieutenant General Yermolov:

Having had the honour of being under Your Excellency's command of the Lifeguard with the 1st Division, I humbly present the report on their operations.

On the will of Your Excellency, having taken up a position on 15 [27] August, facing Pirna from the direction of the town of Dohna, together with II Corps under Lieutenant General Prinz Eugen von Württemberg, I dispatched Major General Bistrom to the village of Zehista with the Lifeguard Jäger Regiment in order to restore communications with Major General Helffreich, whose detachment, had been cut off by the approaching enemy. Major General Bistrom frustrated the enemy effort and linked up with Major General Helffreich's detachment without hindrance.

On 16 [28] August, Your Excellency deigned to announce the movement of the forces subordinate to you to Peterswald on the road to Teplitz. Once the detachment under Major General Helffreich had gone to occupy the village of Cotta on your orders, and II Corps had moved to block the road there from Zehista, the enemy, seeing the significant separation of the elements of the force, raced to break the link between them. It became essential to push the enemy away. An attack on the Kohlberg heights was unavoidable, whose slopes were extremely steep and, due to the rain-soaked soil, almost inaccessible. No sooner had Major General Bistrom received orders to attack, than the Lifeguard Jäger Regiment appeared on the peak of the mountain – the obstacle had disappeared, the enemy were removed, the Lifeguard Division passed the difficult Zehista defile freely. The Lifeguard Izmailovsky Regiment, sent to reinforce the Jägers, was repulsed by enemy emerging from another direction. The third battalion of the Lifeguard Semenovsky Regiment came to their aid, and the Kohlberg returned to our hands. It was taken for a third time by the second battalion of the Lifeguard Jäger Regiment. The Lifeguard Division passed through Cotta and the troops descended into the frightful defile at Berggießhübel. The Preobrazhensky Regiment were at the head of the column. Behind them were 24 artillery pieces. As soon as they emerged from the defile, they encountered the enemy in twice their strength astride the road. Major General Baron Rosen ordered the skirmishers forward. The first battalion were to go right flanking, while the second battalion were to strike with bayonets fixed. Your Excellency was witness to their success. Nothing compared with the swiftness of the Preobrazhensky's second battalion, and the enemy flight cleared the way for the following units, the artillery was saved. The Lifeguard Jägers relieved the second battalion of the Preobrazhensky Regiment. The Jägers were relieved in turn by troops from II Corps.

The enemy forestalled us once again, occupying the defile and the surrounding high ground near the village of Hellendorf. Once again it was necessary to clear the way by force of arms. Major General Potemkin was directed to attack the enemy blocking the road with the Lifeguard Semenovsky Regiment; none could resist. The first and second battalions prevented the enemy from blocking. Even the steepness of the slopes could not protect them. The artillery passed through safely.

Having ordered Prinz Eugen of Württemberg to hold the enemy, Your Excellency ordered the tired Lifeguard Division to rest. The action was ended by the darkness of the night. We spent the night at Peterswald.

Before dawn on 17 [29] August, Your Excellency ordered me to withdraw with the Lifeguard Division and take up positions nearby. I was stationed on the high ground at Nollendorf, behind which a steep descent immediately begins from the crest of the mountains. Soon II Corps arrived. The enemy coming behind them were engaged with heavy fire from the batteries and skirmishers from the Lifeguard. II Corps deployed. Your Excellency ordered me to descend from the mountains and take up the first position suitable for holding back the enemy. You remained with II Corps yourself in order to discern enemy intentions. Having passed the town of Kulm, I deployed the Lifeguard Division; their left wing extended towards the mountains, the village to our front was held by a battalion of the Jäger Regiment. The cavalry took up positions on the right flank.

We waited in this location for the arrival of the enemy forces, and they appeared in great strength. A powerful bombardment began as the batteries confronted one another. The enemy attacked the village and the entire line in column. I reinforced the fighting line by order of Your Excellency, and within a short time most of the division was in action. The Lifeguard Izmailovsky Regiment struck with fixed bayonets, neither the overwhelming enemy forces nor the fierce fire could stop them. At the head of the regiment, General Khrapovitsky paved the way for those following him. A severe wound took him out of the battle, but the regiment covered the valley with enemy corpses. The artillery commanders, Colonel Baikov and Lieutenant Colonel Bistrom, facilitated the attack through the skilful work of the batteries. Their stronger and heavier-calibre batteries fell silent.

I could not conceal from the Lifeguard regiments that our army was in the mountains and were unable to arrive soon, that the Sovereign Emperor was with them and had not yet returned. I was not in a position to cheer the

Legend to Map No. 9b

Coalition Forces
I.I.   1st Grenadier Division
K.K.   2nd Grenadier Division
L.L.   1st Cuirassier Division & 2nd Cuirassier Division
M.M.   Lifeguard Light Cavalry Division & 3rd Cuirassier Division
N.N.   Prinz Hessen-Homburg's Austrian brigade
O.O.   1st Lifeguard Division
P.P.   Advance of Colloredo's & Bianchi's Austrian divisions
Q.Q.   Kleist's advance behind Vandamme
R.R.   Knorring's cavalry
S.S.   Abele's Austrian brigade
T.T.   Bianchi's division
U.   Colloredo's division
V.V.   Knorring's attack

French Forces
e.   Mouton-Duvernet's division
f.   Philippon's division
g.   Quiot's brigade
h.   Reuß's brigade
i.   Doucet's brigade
k.   Dunesme's brigade
l.   Corbineau's cavalry
m.   Gobrecht's brigade

soldiers up – the undaunted spirit of their commanders served as an example to them. All of them were impassioned, but they found it necessary to tame their ardour. Everyone outdid themselves. After a long resistance, the enemy broke through at one point in strong columns, and after passing through the forest, emerged onto the plain. The Lifeguard Ulans and Lifeguard Dragoons, commanded by Major General Shevich [Ivan Yegorovich Shevich], they struck the columns with incredible intent. One disappeared into the forest, the other had the flames of their audacity extinguished with their own blood. The dead lay in rows, covering the plain in all directions. The second battalion of the Lifeguard Semenovsky Regiment drove the column back and cleared the forest. The Preobrazhensky Regiment marched across the corpses of those who had dared to oppose them. The first battalion of the Izmailovsky Regiment went at the enemy flank through the conflagration of the blazing village. The Lifeguard Jäger Regiment and the third battalion of the Semenovsky Regiment pushed the large numbers of enemy back to the tip of the left wing.

The enemy batteries fell silent in horror. Only two companies remained in my reserve. An advance would be unsafe, the superiority of the enemy numbers was obvious. I gave orders to retreat into the forest. Your Excellency, having suffered a wound, was forced to ride away; it was deemed fit to entrust me with command. Leaving some of the troops in the forest, I directed Major General Potemkin to command the left flank and to form a reserve. Everything was in perfect order, in anticipation of new enemy attacks. Their attacks resumed with ferocity, but not simultaneously and not at multiple locations. The Lifeguard regiments resisted fearlessly, and God blessed them with complete success.

The action had ended by eight o'clock in the evening. The 1st Grenadier Division, which arrived with Lieutenant General Raevsky, relieved the

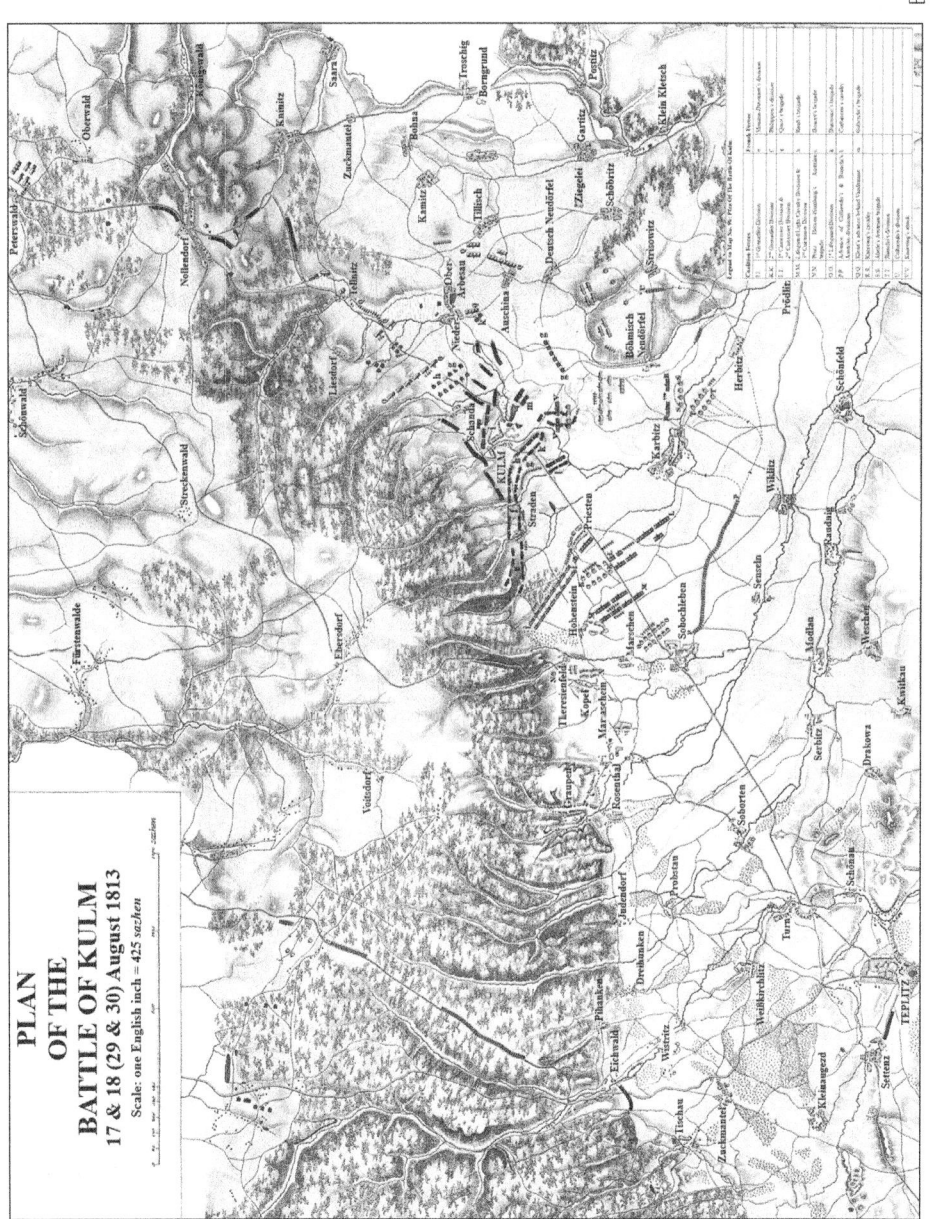

Plan of the Battle of Kulm.

reserves, but the forward outposts and skirmishers from the Lifeguard regiments remained until nightfall.

Having witnessed the diligence, fearlessness and resolve of the honourable generals: I have the honour to present for the favourable attention of the authorities, the commanders from the division, Baron Rosen, Potemkin, Bistrom and Khrapovitsky, with particular respect for services rendered by them this day.

I cannot present particularly outstanding exploits by individual field officers and subalterns. This would necessitate the provision of a list of everyone present. I cannot even present the lower ranks: this would necessitate counting all ranks of the valiant regiments that have the good fortune to bear the title of the Tsar's Lifeguard, whom they idolise.

I have the honour to present the original lists from the honourable unit commanders that I have received. I shall soon present those from other units not from 1st Lifeguard Division, which were under my command, or had been previously, as well as the officers upon whom I was especially reliant.

No. 1296.

22 August [3 September] 1813.

The town of Teplitz in Bohemia.

31

The Battle of Kulm, 18 (30) August

Coalition intentions for 18 (30) August. – Location of Vandamme's force. Deployment of Coalition forces on the morning of 18 (30) August. – Kleist's move to Nollendorf. – Barclay de Tolly's dispositions for battle. – Flanking movement by the right wing of the Coalition army; operations on the left wing and in the centre. – The Coalition advance on the right wing.

The emergence of Kleist behind French lines. – Measures taken by Vandamme. – Operations by the Prussian force. – Attack along the highway by Corbineau's cavalry. – Austrian capture of the village of Nieder Arbesau. – General offensive by the Coalition forces. – Their success. – Capture of Vandamme. – Emperor Alexander and the King of Prussia on the battlefield. – Consequences of the victory. – Trophies. – Casualties. – Awards. – Napoleon's official reporting on the Battle of Kulm. – Comments on operations by the French military commanders.

The deployment of forces by both sides after the Battle of Kulm. Napoleon's attempts to apportion blame for the demise of Vandamme's corps.

At the end of the action on 17 (29) August, the superiority of numbers passed to the Coalition side. Because significant reinforcements were due to arrive from Teplitz the following morning and the troops from Kleist's corps could take part in the fighting, at a conference between Emperor Alexander, the King of Prussia and Prince Schwarzenberg, the following was agreed:

1. That Barclay de Tolly, having taken command of all forces assembled in the position or tasked to reach Teplitz overnight, was to form them up for battle, but was not to go over to an offensive posture until after receiving word of the emergence of Kleist's corps on the highway near Nollendorf.
2. That *Oberst* Schöler should again go to Kleist, and having informed him of the Coalition plans, report to him that he should, if possible, strive to arrive at Vorder-Tellnitz by about ten o'clock in the morning,

because Barclay de Tolly's force could not launch the proposed attack until his appearance had been noted from the high ground of the Teplitzer Schlossberg [Doubravská hora, two miles east of Teplitz].[1]

Vandamme, for his part, having realised that the Russian force fighting against him had received significant reinforcements, did not retreat to Peterswald, but remained at Kulm, confident that the entire French army was hot on the heels of the Coalition. Anticipating the emergence of Napoleon's main body from Geiersburg and having more than 20 battalions that had not yet been in action, Vandamme hoped to resume the battle under the most favourable circumstances and with a greater probability of success. At seven o'clock in the morning of 18 (30) August, his forces were located as follows:

> Mouton-Duvernay's division, consisting of nine battalions, to the right of Straden and between this village and the forest.
> Philippon's division (14 battalions), behind and to the left of Straden.
> Quiot's and Reuß's brigades (20 battalions), either side of the highway, forwards of Kulm.
> Doucet's brigade (five battalions), behind Kulm, to the right of the highway.
> Dunesme's brigade (eight battalions), to the left of the highway. During the night, a horse artillery battery was assigned to this brigade, which was located at the tip of the left wing.
> Two battalions of Creutzer's brigade held the village of Kulm.
> Corbineau's cavalry brigade, consisting of 17 squadrons, were stationed along the left side of the highway, forwards of the left wing of Quiot's brigade.
> Four of Gobrecht's squadrons were to the left of Kulm, behind Dunesme's brigade.[2]

The Coalition forces redeployed during the night of 17 to 18 (29 to 30) August, as follows:

> Stationed on the left wing, facing Straden, in the front line were: Lieutenant General Raevsky's 1st Grenadier Division (12 battalions) and General Pyshnitsky's brigade (Kremenchug Infantry and Volhynia Infantry, consisting of four battalions). The artillery of 1st Grenadier Division were to their front, together with the Prussian *Garde Reitendes Artillerie*. In the second line was Hessen-Homburg's Austrian brigade (four battalions).
> Located in the centre at Priesten in the front line were: the remains of II Corps and Helffreich's detachment, reorganised into six weak

---

1 Aster, Die Kriegsereignisse zwischen Peterswalde, Pirna, Königstein und Priesten im August 1813 und die Schlacht bei Kulm, 156-157.
2 Hofmann, Zur Geschichte des Feldzuges von 1813, 174; Wagner, Plane der Schlachten und Treffen, etcetera, Die Tage von Dresden und Kulm, 104-105.

battalions, with the Lifeguard Hussars (six squadrons), commanded by Prinz Eugen von Württemberg. In the second line were: General Udom's 2nd Lifeguard Division (ten battalions),[3] part of the Lifeguard Light Cavalry Division (Lifeguard Dragoons and Lifeguard Ulans, consisting of 12 squadrons), while General Duka's 3rd Cuirassier Division [Ilya Mikhailovich Duka] (16 squadrons) were behind 2nd Lifeguard Division together with four squadrons from the Austrian *Kürassier-Regiment Kaiser*. 1st Cuirassier Division and 2nd Cuirassier Division (not including Her Majesty's Leib Cuirassiers, 29 squadrons) under generals Depreradovich [Nikolai Ivanovich Depreradovich] and Kretov [Nikolai Vasilievich Kretov] were to the right of the Lifeguard Light Cavalry Division, reaching all the way to Karbitz.

The right wing, assigned to envelope the enemy around their left flank, consisted of the Austrian divisions under Colloredo (12 battalions) and Bianchi (eight battalions). The following cavalry regiments had been assigned to advance ahead of this force, which remained hidden in dead ground, awaiting the emergence of Kleist's corps: Knorring's Tatar Ulans (six squadrons), Her Majesty's Leib Cuirassiers (four squadrons) commanded by Prinz Leopold von Sachsen-Coburg, the Austrian *Dragonerregiment Erzherzog Johann* (six squadrons) and Ilovaisky 12th's Cossacks.

The left wing came under the command of Lieutenant General Prince Golitsyn 5th; the centre under General-of-Infantry Miloradovich; the right wing was commanded by *Feldmarschallleutnant* Graf Colloredo-Mansfeld; the reserves were under His Highness Grand Duke Konstantin Pavlovich.

The 1st Lifeguard Division had been withdrawn towards Sobochleben [Soběchleby].[4]

At the same time as the troops concentrated in the position at Priesten were preparing to attack the enemy, Kleist's Prussian corps was moving towards Nollendorf.

As early as the evening of 17 (29) August, General Kleist ordered the destruction of all transport that might impede the corps' movements, and only those that could not be dispensed with remained with the force: this order, inevitable under the circumstances in which the Prussian force found itself, made a negative impression on the young soldiers. General Kleist made no secret of the dangers of the impending move from the force or brigade and regimental commanders, stating: 'I hope, gentlemen, that you will do everything possible to emerge from these difficult circumstances with honour, and in the event of a success, do not miss the opportunity to deliver a beating to the French.' Zieten's detachment was given the task of protecting the force from the direction of Königstein, consisting of four fusilier

---

3   According to Hofmann (page 175), the Lubny Hussars were with the 2nd Lifeguard Division.
4   Wagner, 106; War Diary of II Corps (Archive of the M.T.D. No. 47,344). For a listing of the Coalition forces assembled against Vandamme on 18 (30) August, see Appendix XXI at the end of this chapter.

battalions and two hussar regiments, with a six-pounder foot battery and four horse artillery pieces.[5] This force received orders to head from Liebenau to Peterswald, to block the enemy if they appeared from the direction of Hellendorf, and notify the corps commander of this. At five o'clock in the morning on 18 (30) August, Kleist's main body set off for Nollendorf, consisting of 30 battalions, 32 squadrons and 9½ batteries. Upon reaching Streckenwald, Kleist received news that the road through Geiersburg was again open and suitable for the movement of troops, however, despite this, he preferred to go to Nollendorf.[6]

No sooner had the leading element of the vanguard managed to pass through the forest between Streckenwald and Nollendorf, than patrols noticed a column on the highway moving from the direction of Peterswald and already approaching Nollendorf. Because this column was apparently stretched out without any security, at first they mistook it for a Russian convoy belonging to Osterman's force, but they soon worked out that they were French from the blue coats. *Oberst* Blücher (the son of the commander-in-chief of the Army of Silesia) charged at the enemy with his *1. Schlesisches Husaren* and captured the convoy. Some of the escort were cut down, the others were taken prisoner, but several fleeing men managed to get to Vandamme's corps with the news of the enemy appearance to their rear. The destruction of the captured convoy delayed the Prussian column for about six hours, such that they could not begin to ascend the Nollendorf plateau before ten o'clock in the morning. The first shots from Kleist's guns from the high ground at Nollendorf should, as already mentioned, have served as the signal for the general attack on Vandamme's corps.[7]

Barclay de Tolly, commanding the entire Coalition force assembled at Priesten, had issued the following disposition:

> Graf Colloredo's division is to move from Sobochleben to the right of the highway and, upon reaching the high ground just to the right of Karbitz, is to deploy covertly behind it.
>
> Baron Bianchi, having left one of his brigades on the high ground behind Sobochleben, is to be located in reserve with the remaining men from his division behind Colloredo's division.
>
> Upon General Bianchi's force reaching the place assigned to them, General Knorring is to attack the high ground upon which the enemy is located between Neudörfel and Karbitz with the detachment entrusted to him. Colloredo's division is to swiftly follow them in two columns, of which one is to move behind the high ground, while the other is to go to the right along the Neudörfel valley. Whereupon Bianchi's division is to occupy the high ground at Karbitz and place its battery there. The artillery from Colloredo's division are also to proceed at the head of the advancing

---

5   Zieten's detachment consisted of: the fusilier battalions of 6. Infanterie, 7. Infanterie, 10. Infanterie and 11. Infanterie; 2. Schlesisches Husaren, Braune's Landwehr Kavallerie; 9. Batterie (six-pounders), 9. Reitende Batterie.
6   Aster, 184.
7   Aster, 184-185.

columns and immediately occupy the high ground between Neudörfel and Deutsch-Neudörfel [Dělouš], in order to cut the line of retreat to Nollendorf.

As soon as the Austrian columns emerge behind the French, all Russian forces located in the centre are to attack the enemy at all points and drive them into the defiles.

General Knorring and his force will be under the command of *Feldmarschallleutnant* Graf Colloredo.[8]

This disposition was issued at eight o'clock in the morning of 18 (30) August, just as a rather heated firefight broke out at Priesten.

The Austrian divisions under Colloredo and Bianchi and 'Sorbenberg's' cavalry brigade, having left the camp at Dux at three o'clock in the morning, arrived at Sobochleben at six o'clock and marched on in the direction assigned to them.[9] Major General Toll accompanied them as Barclay de Tolly's proxy. Graf Colloredo detached one battalion to hold Karbitz, while he headed past Herbitz [Hrbovice] himself with seven battalions to the right of Böhmisch-Neudörfel, onto the high ground at Strisowitz. With Abele's brigade [Franz Abele von und zu Lilienberg] in the first line and eight battalions from Bianchi's division in the second, Knorring proceeded to the left of Böhmisch-Neudörfel. The *Dragonerregiment Erzherzog Johann*, moving towards Herbitz and Böhmisch-Neudörfel, maintained communications between the right wing and the main body of the Austrian force.[10]

While this outflanking movement was taking place, at around seven o'clock in the morning, a heated firefight broke out on the left wing of the Coalition position, at the Eggen-Mühle and Priesten. All the buildings of the Eggen-Mühle, together with the wounded lying in them, fell victim to the flames but despite this, ferocious hand-to-hand combat continued there and at the chapel, (Juchtenkapelle) mostly with musket butts. The French stormed these points several times, defended by elements of 1st Grenadier Division and four battalions from the Kremenchug Infantry and Volhynia Infantry, with the assistance of Hessen-Homburg's Austrian brigade. In the centre, at Priesten, because the enemy remained in place here and Barclay did not want to advance until Kleist had emerged, the action was initially limited to a cannonade and skirmishing.[11]

On the right wing, at half past eight o'clock in the morning, General Knorring advanced to attack with his cavalry and four horse artillery pieces. Behind him came the Austrian infantry. The Tatar Ulans and Her Majesty's Leib Cuirassiers came under heavy canister and musket fire, however, taking advantage of the undulating terrain, they reached the French horse artillery battery stationed on the left wing of Vandamme's force, and charged home, capturing three guns and cutting through one of the battalions of the *13e léger*. The remaining battalions of Dunesme's brigade,

---

8   Disposition signed by Barclay de Tolly on the field of battle, 30 August, new style, at eight o'clock in the morning.
9   For details of the Austrian commitment to this mission, see Appendix XXII at the end of this chapter.
10 Hofmann, 176.
11 Aster, 180-181.

stationed nearby, quickly formed square. At the same time, Heimrod's cavalry brigade (from Corbineau's division) [Friedrich von Heimrod] struck the cuirassiers in the flank and drove them off with casualties, but were checked by Abele's Austrian brigade, which had arrived in the meantime. As Colloredo was moving to the tip of the coalition right wing with his infantry at this time, and began to envelope the French left flank, Vandamme detached Quiot's brigade, forming three two-battalion squares with four guns in their intervals, and positioned themselves at right angles to Dunesme's brigade. Thus, the enemy had 14 battalions and four squadrons here facing Abele's four battalions, supported by Knorring's ten weak squadrons. Colloredo's force, having reached the high ground at Strisowitz, paused, mistaking the Prussian cavalry moving from Arbesau [Varvažov] towards Auschina [Úžín] for the enemy, and Barclay de Tolly, although he had learned of Kleist's appearance behind Vandamme, did not go on the offensive, waiting for the Austrian force to outflank the enemy. General Toll sent *Rotmistr* [cavalry captain] Prince Alexei Fëdorovich Orlov to him, with the notification that the Austrians were about to execute this envelopment immediately, and urged him to bring forward the offensive.[12] At ten o'clock, Knorring attacked the French battery a second time. Gobrecht's brigade, struck him in the flank, and pushed him back to Abele's brigade again. But, shortly thereafter, the Austrian *Infanterieregiment De Ligne* drove the French from the western side of the Strisowitz plateau towards the Ziegelei [brickworks]. As soon as the high ground had been abandoned by the enemy, the Austrians placed a battery to the left of it, between Böhmisch-Neudörfel and Karbitz, pelting the French with canister and causing them heavy casualties. Taking advantage of this, Abele's infantry, with Knorring's support, charged the enemy battery, captured most of the guns and drove Vandamme's infantry back towards Kulm. Colloredo also moved forward, and 'Sorbenberg's' cavalry raced to the right of Deutsch-Neudörfel, onto Vandamme's line of retreat. The French batteries of the left wing, having thundered for three hours, fell almost completely silent: the reason for this being Kleist's appearance behind Vandamme's force.[13]

The French, who were not expecting an attack from this directions at all, mistook the first shots from the high ground at Nollendorf as a signal from Napoleon, that he had arrived with the main body. An extraordinary animation was noticeable along the entire line of the French corps, trumpet and 'column-march' signals were heard, the surrounding area reverberated with the ecstatic cheers of the troops and the Coalition were attacked with greater resolve, the cannonade intensified. But the French misunderstanding was short-lived.[14]

Oberst Blücher, riding at the head of the Prussian corps with his hussars, having descended from the Nollendorf high ground and reaching the last bend of the highway near Vorder-Tellnitz, observed an enemy force with artillery beyond this village, at a distance of about a *verst* from its outermost buildings. Two guns with a weak infantry escort had been stationed facing Tellnitz. The Prussian hussars, still

---

12 Bernhardi, Denkwürdigkeiten aus dem Leben Carl Friedrich Grafen von Toll, III, 247.
13 Hofmann, 177; Aster, 180-184; Richter, *Geschichte des Deutschen Freiheitskrieges* vom Jahre 1813 bis zum Jahre 1815, II, 86-87.
14 Aster, 185; Thiers, Histoire du Consulat et de l'Empire, XVI, Edit de Brux, 385.

in column-of-route, raced into the attack, scattered the escort and captured both guns. But in wanting to drag them off, they became dispersed, and being suddenly attacked by enemy lancers, they were driven off and lost not only the guns they had captured, but also three from the Prussian *7. Reitende Batterie*, which, having only just been unlimbered, fell into the hands of the enemy. Just then, Pirch's *10. Brigade* arrived, putting the enemy under heavy fire, they rescued the Prussian guns and gave the hussars the opportunity to launch another attack, in which the commander of the French lancers was captured. General Pirch, after occupying Tellnitz, placed the six-pounders of *8. Batterie* halfway between this village and Schanda [Žandov], on both sides of the highway. Then, having deployed a screen of skirmishers in order to delay the enemy, under their protection he positioned six battalions from his brigade and attached two further batteries to those sent forward (12-pounders of *3. Batterie* and six-pounders of *11. Batterie*), but strong fire from the French skirmishing screen forced the Prussian artillery to refuse their right flank. At the same time, in order to counter the enemy skirmishers, a battalion from the *7. Reserve Infanterie* was sent to the right of the artillery. The remaining three battalions from *10. Brigade* moved to Arbesau, while the reserve cavalry, after the capture of Ober-Arbesau by the Prussian infantry, deployed between Nieder-Arbesau and Auschina.[15]

When the Prussian force had first appeared behind French lines, Vandamme was on the Kapellenberg by the Dreifaltigkeitskapelle. From there he was able to witness the final intense attacks by his force, but the Coalition, like a solid wall, stood unshakable, and Vandamme soon learned that he would have to deal with a new enemy threatening to cut off the only escape route for the force entrusted to him. The French commander had proved himself to be a resourceful and determined warrior. Assessing the danger of his situation with the usual swiftness of his military intuition, he decided to sacrifice all his artillery and, by concentrating his forces, fight his way along the highway, breaking through the troops of the Prussian corps. From the crest of the Kapellenberg officers galloped in all directions with orders: Reuß's brigade were to pull back to Schanda, and on towards Vorder-Tellnitz, Quiot's brigade were to take Arbesau with the *13e léger* and *25e ligne* (Dunesme's brigade). The remaining battalions under Dunesme were ordered to hold the Austrians and Knorring ('Knorring's many squadrons' – according to Thiers – in reality, there were then no more than 800 men left in both regiments, the Tatar Ulans and Her Majesty's Leib Cuirassiers).[16] Philippon's and Mouton-Duvernet's divisions were initially to hold back the pressure of the Russian force in order to win time for Reuß's and Quiot's brigades to push Kleist aside, and were then to follow them. Finally, all the artillery stationed on the high ground near Kulm was ordered to fight to the last round against the troops advancing from Priesten, while Doucet's brigade were to cover the batteries, and then retreat, abandoning the guns but striving to save the horses and crews.[17] These orders were carried out imme-

---

15 Hofmann, 178; Aster, 185-187; Förster, *Geschichte der Befreiungskriege, 1813, 1814, 1815*, I, 608.
16 'les nombreux escadrons de Knorring.' Thiers, XVI.
17 Wagner, 111; Hofmann, 178-179; Beitzke, *Geschichte der deutschen Freiheitskriege in den Jahren 1813 und 1814*, II, 128; Thiers, XVI, 387-388.

diately: Quiot's brigade moved towards Arbesau; Corbineau's cavalry and Reuß's brigade to Schanda, and on towards Liesdorf [Liboňov]; Dunesme's brigade held the Austrians and assisted Quiot's force in the defence of Arbesau. A little later, first Philippon's division and then Mouton-Duvernet's retreated behind Reuß's brigade, under the covering fire of the reinforced batteries stationed on the high ground in front of Kulm.[18] At this point, Kleist had only Pirch's brigade at hand in order to hold back the French pressure. The rest of the Prussian infantry remained back in the mountain pass, separated from him by the cavalry and artillery that had followed directly behind Pirch's force. General Kleist, considering the seizure of Arbesau to be essential, both to provide a strong point for his left flank and for liaison with the Austrians, ordered the *7. Reserve Infanterie* to take possession of this village. After a bloody battle, in which one of the battalion commanders, Major von Röder [Karl Ferdinand Wilhelm von Röder?], was killed, the Prussian troops established themselves in the upper part of the village (Ober-Arbesau), but all their efforts to dislodge the French from the lower part (Nieder-Arbesau) were unsuccessful. As soon as the Prussian *7. Reserve Infanterie* occupied Ober-Arbesau, the reserve cavalry, the *Schlesische Grenadiere* and two batteries, which could not be deployed near the highway due to lack of space, turned left so that, having passed through the aforementioned village, they could establish communications with the other Coalition forces and operate in accordance with the situation. Once *11. Brigade* had reached *10. Brigade*, *Oberstleutnant* Jagow ordered two battalions from *1. Schlesisches Infanterie* and Dohna's *Schlesisches Landwehr* battalion to head to the tip of the right wing of *10. Brigade* in order to hold the enemy who had pushed the Prussian force back. Two battalions of *10. Reserve Infanterie* and the *Landwehr* battalions under Borke and Geisberg were stationed on either side of the highway. *14. Batterie* relieved *8. Batterie*, which had fired off all their ammunition. But as the enemy skirmishing screen, relieving and strengthening one another, continued to envelope the right flank of Kleist's position, the Prussian troops were forced to retreat in disarray along the highway, abandoning or shoving several damaged guns into the ditch. Many artillery officers and gunners were captured by the enemy, but were soon set free, because the French cared more about their own escape than about trophies. A number of Prussians were captured, robbed and released more than once, and then, in turn, once the Coalition cavalry had caught up with the enemy, they captured their captors. The situation for Kleist's force became even more difficult when, on Vandamme's orders, the *13e léger* and *25e ligne* (Dunesme's brigade), having strongly garrisoned Nieder-Arbesau, were preparing to outflank the Prussian position from there. Right at that moment *12. Brigade* arrived. *Oberstleutnant* Grolman drew the attention of its commander, Prinz August von Preußen, to the danger threatening the corps. Immediately two battalions, Fritsch's and Brixen's [Johann Joseph Franz Maximilian von Brixen] from *10. Landwehr Infanterie*, were sent to capture the village of Nieder-Arbesau. The prinz went to help the troops of *11. Brigade* located on both sides of the highway himself, with *11. Reserve Infanterie* moving at the head of his brigade, and left *2. Schlesisches Infanterie* behind in reserve, with the

---

18 Aster, 188.

12-pounders of *6. Batterie* attached to *12. Brigade*, near the highway. The attack on Nieder-Arbesau was not successful. The battalions from *10. Landwehr* were driven back and swept away the supporting infantry of *2. Schlesisches Infanterie* in their disorder. Most of the Prussian officers were killed or wounded, including the commander of *10. Landwehr*, the Prinz von Anhalt-Pleß [Christian Friedrich von Anhalt-Köthen-Pleß]. All efforts of the commanders to restore order in the force were unsuccessful. Prinz August himself jumped off his horse, grabbed the Colour of *2. Schlesisches Infanterie* and, gathering several hundred men to him, led them against the enemy once more. But at that very moment there was an attack by French cavalry under General Corbineau.

The squadrons of Montmarie's brigade [Aimé Sulpice Victor Pelletier de Montmarie] were racing along the highway at their head, joined by many of the gunners from the artillery that had fallen to the Coalition. They were followed by the rest of Corbineau's cavalry, with whom were also Generals Philippon and Dumonceau. The Prussian artillerymen, stunned by the storm that was breaking over them, only managed to fire canister at the enemy column from a single 12-pounder gun stationed on the highway. Many French horsemen fell to the ground, others galloped at the crew, cut down the gunners and raced further along the highway, cluttered with guns and wagons of all kinds halted in a long convoy. The French cavalry charged at the artillery, cutting down men and horses, and slashing the traces. Four six-pounder and two 12-pounder batteries fell into the hands of the enemy, but having rendered them unserviceable, hastily moved further along the highway. The Prussian infantry had raced off both sides of the highway, leaving the artillery unprotected: *11. Brigade* to their right into the wooded hills, *10. Brigade* and *12. Brigade* into the forest on the left side of the highway, while three battalions from *9. Brigade*, stationed on the high ground forwards of Liesdorf, remained immobile, not daring to shoot into the crowd where the troops of both sides were intermixed. Prinz August was almost captured by the French, but managed to escape by jumping the highway ditch, and reached the battalions located near Liesdorf, who then took refuge in the mountains along with *11. Brigade*. Kleist was himself exposed to the greatest danger and, having been driven away from his corps, made his way via a roundabout route to Zieten's detachment. It has already been mentioned that this detachment had remained at Peterswald for the time being. Subsequently, having received orders to join the corps, Zieten moved along the highway and upon reaching the edge of Jungferndorf [Panenská, one mile north of Nollendorf], he learned of the imminent encounter with enemy cavalry from fleeing Prussian soldiers. General Zieten immediately deployed the leading battalion into the forest along the highway and opened fire on the French, whereupon, once the cavalry had galloped through his force, he deployed his detachment on both sides of the road and moved towards Nollendorf. Many of the enemy were captured by Zieten's troops as they exited Nollendorf along the highway.

Throughout all this chaos on the highway, Dunesme's regiments, *13e léger* and *25e ligne*, were stubbornly defending themselves in Nieder-Arbesau. Graf Colloredo, meanwhile, closing in from the direction of Auschina, attacked the enemy in the aforementioned village with the *Infanterieregiment Czartoryski* and *Infanterieregiment De Ligne*, supported by Chiesa's brigade [Franz von Chiesa] (*Infanterieregiment De*

Vaux and *Infanterieregiment Froon*). The Austrians eventually captured the village, having lost many men, including Major General Chiesa [wounded]. The French, having abandoned their artillery, sought salvation by fleeing up the Tellnitz valley and for the most part fell into the hands of Zieten's detachment. Only those of them who turned to their left from the highway towards Liebenau or [right] towards the Schneeberg managed to escape in time.[19]

At the same time that Corbineau's cavalry were breaking out along the highway, the general attack by the Coalition forces in the position at Priesten was underway. Raevsky's grenadiers, the Austrian Hessen-Homburg brigade, the troops of II Corps, the Lifeguard Light Cavalry Division, supported by 1st Cuirassier Division, under the personal command of Tsarevich Grand Duke Konstantin Pavlovich, attacked the divisions facing them under Mouton-Duvernet and Philippon. The troops of the latter division immediately began to retreat. Mouton-Duvernet's division remained longer and then also retreated along the foothills, where, as with other French forces, some of them made their way through the Prussian corps, and some were cut off. The *17e ligne* (Philippon's division), left to protect a large battery on the high ground between Priesten and Kulm, upon being attacked by the Prinz von Württemberg and disordered by the canister fire from his artillery, raced into the mountains, following the other troops. The commander of the French battery, General Baltus [Basile Guy Marie Victor Baltus de Pouilly], left with no escort, abandoned his guns and left along the highway with most of the crews and horses in the wake of Corbineau's cavalry. The Lifeguard Hussars, having galloped around the left flank of the battery, captured 21 guns here. The Coalition pursued the enemy relentlessly, both along the highway and at the tip of their right flank. The French *1er chevau-légers lanciers*, being isolated and pushed back into a deep ravine by the Tobolsk Infantry, lost many men killed or taken prisoner. The Chevalier Garde Regiment captured six French guns, took more than 300 men prisoner and rescued 16 Prussian guns captured by the enemy.[20] General Knorring dashed towards Kulm with his detachment and the valiant Austrian *Dragonerregiment Erzherzog Johann*, supported by Bianchi's infantry division and Abele's brigade following them up, drove the French reserves back and pursued them towards Schanda. The wagon-laager, stationed behind Kulm, was in complete disarray. The trains-staff were unharnessing their horses and riding off in all directions. The French *16e chasseurs à cheval* attempted to break out along the highway, but were cut off by Prussian infantry, who opened heavy fire and inflicted enormous casualties on them. Knorring's cavalry pursued the enemy into the gap between Schanda and Arbesau and captured nine guns. The Austrian *Infanterieregiment Argenteau* captured 11 guns.[21] About 4,000 men from various French infantry regiments, had been contained in a wide mass between Kulm and Schanda and continued to defend themselves, but being surrounded on all sides and having exhausted their cartridges, laid down their weapons.[22]

---

19 Wagner, 111-114; Aster, 194-201; Bernhardi, III, 248-250.
20 History of the Chevalier Garde Regiment, 112-113.
21 Plotho, Der Krieg in Deutschland und Frankreich in den Jahren 1813 und 1814, II, 80.
22 Aster 202.

Vandamme remained on the Kapellenberg by the Dreifaltigkeitskapelle, for as long as order was maintained in his force, and then he left for the [Baroque] Schloss in Kulm. At about two o'clock in the afternoon, when the Austrians burst in, Vandamme made his way through the park along the highway, and, taking a few steps to one side, reached the village of Schanda. The Russian 4th Jägers took him prisoner here and handed him over to the Cossacks, who took their captive to the Tsar.

At the beginning of the battle Emperor Alexander and the King of Prussia were on the Teplitzer Schlossberg. Once the arrival of Kleist's corps had been noted from there, the Coalition monarchs rode to the battlefield on horseback and on towards Arbesau and Tellnitz. Having observed the many abandoned guns there, Emperor Alexander drew the attention of his ally to these new trophies, but the King, peering closely at said artillery, replied: 'these are actually my guns.'[23] The Emperor immediately ordered the Lifeguard Hussars to take them back. Columns of prisoners passed by the Coalition monarchs continually. Officers were with each platoon, and at the head of the column were the field officers. Whereupon, the Cossacks brought up Vandamme. Emperor Alexander treated him coldly, but ordered that his sword be returned to him and promised to ease his lot. The benevolent monarch, despite the joy of victory, all the more attractive because it had come unexpectedly, ignored the trophies, hastening to express his gratitude to the troops and their commanders, who had laid the foundations for the Coalition success the previous day. The Emperor rode up to each regiment, thanking his heroes, ordering for every possible assistance to be given to the wounded, and, on the way back to Teplitz, having caught up with the convoy carrying the wounded, he stopped repeatedly, asking the sufferers about their condition and paternally ordered that their needs be met.[24]

Vandamme faced a difficult trial. Known throughout Germany as much for his severity as for his avarice, he was hated by the Germans more than almost any of his other fellow countrymen, even Napoleon himself. The news of the disaster that had befallen him caused general delight throughout the surrounding country. On Vandamme's way from Bohemia to Russia, in every German city and town, the residents came running to stare at the prisoner as if he were a fierce beast in captivity. There was no end to the curses and insults.[25] Such was the pitiful fate of the gifted, but cruel, grasping warrior, about whom Napoleon himself once said jokingly: 'If I had two of Vandamme, I would order one of them to be hanged.'

The fighting was over by three o'clock in the afternoon. Following this, Kulm began to burn, where many seriously wounded Frenchmen, hiding in houses, fell victim to the flames. The entire battlefield was covered with the bodies of the wounded, crying out for death as an end to their suffering, and the dead. At every step plundered carts, killed and wounded horses were encountered. Broken weapons and ammunition lay everywhere, jettisoned in order to speed up the escape. Everything presented a frightful vision of destruction and of every possible kind of disaster, the

---

23 'Das sind ja meine Kanonen.'
24 Aster, 122. Verbal testimony from eyewitnesses.
25 Förster, I, 621-622; Shishkov's Notes, second edition, 158-159, for the detailed description of Vandamme's reception, see Appendix XXIII at the end of this chapter.

inseparable companions of war. Where, throughout the duration of the battle, four mighty nations competed with each other in noble feats of self-sacrifice, there also, to the shame of humanity, brutality and lust for personal gain appeared in all their ugliness. The lack of essential supplies – a consequence of the poor management by the Austrian commissariat – gave rise to looting and violence: the last possessions of the unfortunate population were torn away by the rough hands of soldiers who had just come out of combat. The wounded and dying were robbed of every last thing. Foreign historians, having reproached the Russians for devastating the country, state that the Austrians behaved no less harshly with their compatriots, the population of Bohemia.[26] May the sad description of these disasters be used for the benefit of humanity, forcing military commanders to take care of the thousands of people entrusted to them, so as not to lead them into criminality that degrades their noble military status!

The consequences of the Battle of Kulm were very significant. For the Coalition, the spoils consisted of two Eagles, three banners and all the enemy artillery, numbering 81, or, according to other sources, 82 guns; 200 ammunition and cartridge caissons and the entire train fell into the hands of the coalition, or had been destroyed by the French. According to the most conservative estimates, some 10,000 prisoners were taken. Among them were generals: Vandamme, the *chef d'état major* of his corps, général de division Haxo, généraux de brigade Quiot and Heimrod (the latter, a native of Baden [*sic*, Hessen-Hanau], died of wounds). Over 5,000 had been killed in action, including: généraux de brigade Prinz Reuß, Montesquiou-Fezensac and Dunesme.[27] The overall Coalition casualties on this day, *hors de combat*, reached some 3,319 men, including: 1,500 Prussians, 1,002 Russians and 817 Austrians. The dead, as already mentioned, included the Austrian *Generalmajor* Chiesa [*sic*]; the wounded included Major General Tsvilenev [Alexander Ivanovich Tsvilenev] and Lyalin [Dmitry Vasilievich Lyalin].[28] Napoleon shamelessly distorted the truth in the report on the battle of Kulm posted in *Le Moniteur* on 8 September new style, announcing that the French had lost 30 guns and 6,000 men, that the Coalition losses ranged from 4,000 to 5,000 men (therefore – almost equal to the losses of the French force), that Kleist was among those killed, and so on.[29]

The Coalition triumph was multiplied by the news received on the eve of the victory from the Army of Silesia and Army of the North regarding the successes achieved by Blücher on the Katzbach and the Crown Prince of Sweden at Großbeeren.[30] By a strange coincidence, the only man who doubted the victory at Kulm was the one

---

26 Aster, 212-213; Förster, I, 623-62425.
27 Plotho, II, 81; Helldorff, 51; Richter, II, 91-92; Aster, 205. In the War Diary, signed by Adjutant General Prince Volkonsky (Archive of the M.T.D. No. 46,692) the number of prisoners for that day is given as 7,000. Several thousand more prisoners were rounded up on the days following the battle.
28 Plotho, II, 81; Aster, 205; War Diary of II Corps.
29 Vaudoncourt states that the fighting on 18 (30) August cost the French 10,000 men, including 7,000 prisoners, and 30 guns (*Histoire de la guerre soutenue par les Français en Allemagne*, 161). In Thiers the casualties are given as: 5,000 to 6,000 killed or wounded, 7,000 taken prisoner and 48 guns captured (*Histoire du Consulat et de l'Empire*, XVI, Edit de Brux, 390).
30 War Diary signed by Prince Volkonsky.

whose arrival finally decided the outcome of the battle. General Kleist, frustrated at having seen his force pushed aside and thinking all his artillery had been lost, met Zieten's detachment moving from Nollendorf towards Kulm. Stunned by the failure of his force, Kleist wanted to make a last desperate effort: he intended to break through the enemy and link up with the Coalition army by attaching Zieten's detachment to the remnants of the defeated Prussian corps. It is easy to imagine his astonishment at that moment when Major General Diebitsch, who happened to be with Zieten's detachment, informed him of the decisive victory won by the Coalition. General Kleist immediately turned back along the highway through Nollendorf, confirmed the enormous damage suffered by his artillery and infantry for himself, but after inspecting the *Schlesisches Husaren* on the battlefield to the left of Vorder-Tellnitz, he stopped for the night in the village of Arbesau. Meanwhile, the King of Prussia, wanting to award his commander the *Schwarzer Adlerorden*, sent aides-de-camp to find him, but as all their searches were unsuccessful, the King went to Teplitz, ordering Kleist to be told to come to his *Hauptquartier* the following day. Having received this summons during the night, Kleist expected to be put on trial for the rash move behind the enemy, which had resulted in significant losses to the Prussian corps. When the King, having honoured Kleist with a very favourable greeting, wanted to bestow the insignia of the *Schwarzer Adlerorden* on him, he took a pace back and said: 'I do not deserve this; my entire corps has been scattered.' The King, touched by these words, answered: 'I know all of that, it does not matter.'[31] Following this, the King, having invited Kleist to dine with him, proposed a toast to Kleist's health, to which he responded with a request that he be allowed to drink to the health of the brave officers of his corps, and especially to his colleague Jagow. Subsequently, the King elevated Kleist to the dignity of Graf, with the title von Nollendorf, and granted him an estate worth 300,000 *thaler* in Fürstentum Halberstadt.[32]

The Commander-in-Chief of Coalition forces at the battle of Kulm, Barclay de Tolly was awarded the Order of St. George 1st class and the *Kommandeurkreutz* of the *Maria-Theresien-Orden*, while to the worthy colleagues of Count Osterman went: the Order of St Alexander Nevsky to General Yermolov, and the St Vladimir 1st class to Prinz Eugen von Württemberg. A no less flattering reward for the valiant Prinz were the words spoken to him the very next day after the battle by Emperor Alexander: 'I am aware of all that we owe you, but altruism is a most beautiful virtue.'[33] The lower ranks of the Lifeguard Corps were awarded two roubles each.

Napoleon never wanted to admit responsibility for the demise of Vandamme's corps and tried to put the blame for this failure on Vandamme himself. The official report on the battle of Kulm stated:

> On 29 August, General Vandamme crossed the pass through the main ridge with eight or ten battalions and moved towards Kulm. There he encountered the enemy, numbering from 8,000 to 10,000 men and, going into

---

31 '*Ich weiss alles, thut nichts zur Sache.*'
32 Aster, 208-209; Förster, I, 617-618; Johann Heinrich von Minutoli, *Beiträge zu einer künftigen biographie Friedrich Wilhelms III*, 141-142.
33 '*Je sais tout ce que nous vous devons, mais la résignation est la plus belle des vertus.*' Helldorff, 53.

action against them, concentrated his entire corps and immediately drove the enemy force back. But, instead of returning to the ridge, he remained where he was and took up positions near Kulm, occupying the insignificant rise commanding only the highway. Meanwhile, Marshal Saint-Cyr and the duc de Raguse (Marmont) would have arrived at the Teplitz exit no earlier than the evening of 30 August. General Vandamme cared only about blocking the enemy routes and capturing everything that could be cut off. When dealing with an army in flight, *one must arrange a golden bridge for them, or block them with an iron barrier.* But Vandamme's forces were insufficient to form such a barrier.[34]

This report clearly distorts the truth: neither Saint-Cyr nor Marmont could have come to the aid of Vandamme by the evening of 18 (30) August. The former, by that time, had just managed to arrive at Liebenau, while the latter had just reached Altenberg: consequently, both were still separated from Vandamme's corps by the mountain ridge, which they had to cross, as well as overcoming the Coalition army's rearguards left to oppose them. Mortier's force, who could have moved along the highway on 17 (29) August to assist Vandamme, had received orders from the *quartier général* to remain in Pirna. It is not clear, however, why Mortier, about 30 *versts* from Vandamme, and Saint-Cyr, who was even closer, not only failed to maintain proper liaison with him, but also knew nothing of events happening at Peterswald and Kulm: such negligence might be attributed solely to the customary rivalry between French generals of the Napoleonic era, which did not constitute a great disadvantage when he was in personal control of operations, but was very harmful in his absence. Napoleon, not content with accusing Vandamme of complacency, insisted that he had been explicitly ordered to halt on the high ground with his corps and to send only patrols into Bohemia in order to harass the enemy and to collect intelligence on them.[35] But there were no such orders, and if Vandamme can be blamed for anything, then perhaps it is only that he, having insufficient time to break the resistance of Osterman's force on 17 (29) August, and knowing for certain of the arrival of significant reinforcements to assist them, had not retreated that night to Peterswald. But such criticism is hardly justified: Vandamme had received orders to block the routes to Teplitz, and although he did not succeed, by remaining at Kulm, he could have caused great harm to the Coalition had they been persistently pursued by the other French corps. It is much more difficult to justify Saint-Cyr in that, being obliged to pursue Kleist, on 17 (29) August, he marched only six *versts* from Maxen to Reinhardtsgrimma, halted there, awaiting orders from the *quartier général*, and lost contact with the Prussian corps, which, taking advantage of his slowness and inaction gave them the opportunity to move behind Vandamme. Had Saint-Cyr relentlessly pursued the Prussian force, then Kleist would not have dared to go to Nollendorf, and Vandamme's losses would have been much less

---

34 The words in italics were emphasised in the official report. Extracted from *Le Moniteur* dated 8 September new style 1813.
35 Orders for Saint-Cyr, dated 1 September new style.

significant.³⁶ Instead, the Marshal remained in Reinhardstgrimma until 11 o'clock in the morning of the following day, 18 (30) August, and set off from there only once he had received orders: '...to support *6e Corps*, but it would be preferable, if possible, to find a path on the left between the duc de Raguse and the corps under General Vandamme...'³⁷ In executing these orders, Saint-Cyr decided to go to Glashütte and on to Lauenstein, and in order to quicken the pace he left his artillery behind, ordering it to follow the other troops as quickly as they could. Then, having heard the cannonade, the Marshal went forward with a small escort and encountered a disorderly mob leaving Bohemia for Saxony through the mountains. These were the remnants of Vandamme's corps. The daylight was fast failing, and so Saint-Cyr deployed his force at Liebenau.³⁸

The detachment sent to Aussig managed to escape the fate that had befallen Vandamme's corps. As soon as General Creutzer had been informed of the outcome of the battle of Kulm, he ordered his detachment to abandon the town, but before this order was carried out, at four o'clock in the afternoon, the Austrian General Longueville [Johann Baptist von Longueville] emerged from Theresienstadt, with 1,500 infantrymen, a small cavalry detachment and two guns. The French attempted to set fire to the town as they were leaving, in order to delay the Austrians, and moved in perfect order towards the Saxon border, but as they did not know which routes safely led there, in desperation they asked for help from the Bohemian population that they had just robbed. These guides dutifully guided the French into Saxony, but forced them to make their way through the Tyssaer Steine pass [Tiské stěny, three miles east of Peterswald], where they were forced to abandon not only the cattle they had taken from Bohemia, but also their guns, baggage and horses. Whereupon, turning to their right, towards the Schneeberg, Creutzer's detachment reached Königstein.³⁹

By nightfall on 18 (30) August, the day of the battle of Kulm, the troops of both sides were located as follows:

> On the Coalition side, the Russo-Prussian reserves were stationed between Kulm and Teplitz along with Prinz Eugen von Württemberg's force; the Austrian divisions under Colloredo and Bianchi had returned to their camp at Dux, where they joined Chasteler's, Nostitz's, Lederer's and Schneller's divisions that had arrived earlier; Knorring's detachment reached Aussig and sent patrols down the Elbe; Kleist's corps redeployed at Arbesau and Vorder-Tellnitz; his vanguard, commanded by Zieten, was at Peterswald; the Russian 5th Division and most of Klüx's Prussian 9. *Brigade* were at Eichwald under Count Wittgenstein's overall command; his rearguard,

---
36 Mémoires du maréchal Marmont, V, 105.
37 '... L'intention de Sa Majesté est, que dans cet état de choses, vous qppuyiez le 6-me corps, mais il serait préférable que vous pussiez trouver un chemin sur la gauche entre le duc de Raguse et le corps du général Vandamme qui a obtenu de grands succès sur l'ennemi et lui a fait 2,000 prisonniers. Dresde, le 30 août, 1813.'
38 Saint-Cyr, Mémoires, Campagne de 1813 en Saxe, 124-128.
39 Aster, 221-223.

under generals Vlastov and Rüdiger [Fëdor Vasilievich Ridiger or Friedrich Alexander von Rüdiger], having delayed Marmont's force at Altenberg and the Brandstock and Hinter-Zinnwald [Zadní Cínovec] passes, had moved off towards Eichwald; Moritz Liechtenstein's Austrian *1. leichte Division* remained at Klostergrab [Hrob]; Civalart's division was at Nieder Georgenthal [Dolní Jiřetín]; Weissenwolf's and Alois Liechtenstein's divisions were at Saida; Crennewitz's division was at Neuhausen behind the river Flöha; Klenau's corps were at Marienberg: consequently, significant parts of the Austrian force were still on the northern side of the Ore Mountains at this time. Emperor Alexander's, the King of Prussia's, Schwarzenberg's and Barclay de Tolly's headquarters were all located in Teplitz.[40]

On the French side, Murat had reached Zethau [11 miles south of Freiberg] with most of the cavalry and with Victor's corps; Marmont, having reached Altenberg, pushed the vanguard, commanded by Compans [Jean Dominique Compans], to Hinter-Zinnwald; Saint-Cyr's force were deployed at Liebenau and Dittersdorf [2½ miles south-east of Glashütte], where the remnants of Vandamme's corps joined them; Mortier and the *Jeune Garde* remained at Pirna; Napoleon's *quartier général* was in Dresden.[41]

For Napoleon, the defeat of the French corps at Kulm had been completely unexpected. Obsessed with the desire to take revenge on the Crown Prince of Sweden for the defeat suffered by the French at Großbeeren, on 18 (30) August, he had ordered the *Vieille Garde*, two divisions of the *Jeune Garde* (Barrois' and Dumoustier's, commanded by General Curial at the time), and part of Murat's *réserve de cavalerie* to cross to the right bank of the Elbe at Dresden. He had considered it sufficient to send the corps under Marmont and Saint-Cyr for the pursuit of the Army of Bohemia, who were supposed to push the retreating Coalition force back, while Vandamme should only – as Napoleon then thought – exploit any advantages arising from his situation. He had wanted to turn to Berlin with his main body, in the hope that, after the disasters they had suffered in Saxony, the Army of Bohemia would not recover for another three weeks.[42]

At midnight on 18 to 19 (30 to 31) August, the fateful news of the destruction of Vandamme's corps reached Napoleon's *quartier général*. Soon after, General Corbineau arrived, drenched in blood from the enemy and his own wounds. He had a Prussian sabre with him which he had taken to replace his own, broken in battle. Napoleon listened to the details of the casualties suffered rather unemotionally and merely expressed his surprise, saying: 'I do not understand what made Vandamme invade Bohemia.' He repeated several times: 'a golden bridge must be built for a fleeing army, or a steel barrier must be placed in its path. Vandamme should not have considered his corps to be such an obstacle.' Then turning to Berthier, he asked: 'Did we really send him anything that could have inspired such an unfortunate idea? Fetch your file copies. Fain! Let us read mine; Let us check everything we have

---

40 Plotho, II, 81-82.
41 Plotho, II, 82-83; Vaudoncourt, 161.
42 Fain, *Manuscrit de 1813*, II, 312-313.

written.' According to Napoleon's secretary, there was nothing in all these documents that could have prompted Vandamme to advance from Peterswald towards Kulm.[43] But Fain's evidence is clearly contradicted: in the orders sent to Vandamme from the *quartier général* on 16 (28) August and received by this general on the evening of that same day, he was commanded: 'to forestall the enemy on the routes leading to Tetschen, Aussig and Teplitz.'[44]

As has already been mentioned, Napoleon tried to disguise the losses suffered by his forces at Kulm by every possible means, and to that end he ordered the immediate reconstitution of *1er Corps*, but this corps, entrusted to the comte de Lobau (Georges Mouton), numbered fewer than 10,000 of Vandamme's former soldiers in its ranks, and therefore, in all fairness, it should be considered a new formation in the army.[45]

---

43 Fain, II, 319-321.
44 A translation of Vandamme's orders, dated 28 August, new style, regarding the invasion of Bohemia may be found in Chapter 24.
45 Aster, 252; from the diary of Saxon General von Gersdorff: 'the losses were very heavy; between $3/5$ and $4/5$ of Vandamme's strong corps were gone 43.

Appendix XXI

Listing of the Coalition forces assembled against Vandamme on 18 (30) August

Infantry: Russian; 1st Grenadier Division, 12 battalions; General Pyshnitsky's brigade, four battalions; II Corps and Helffreich's detachment, six battalions; 2nd Lifeguard Division, ten battalions; 1st Lifeguard Division, 12 battalions; Colloredo's and Bianchi's Austrian divisions, 24 battalions; for a total of 68 battalions.

> Cavalry: Russian; three regiments from the Lifeguard Light Cavalry Division, 18 squadrons; three cuirassier divisions, 45 squadrons; Her Majesty's Leib Cuirassiers and Tatar Ulans, ten squadrons; Lubny Hussars; Austrian; *Dragonerregiment Erzherzog Johann* and *Kürassier-Regiment Kaiser*, ten squadrons; for a total of 83 squadrons.

> Artillery: seven Russian companies, 83 guns; 1½ Prussian batteries, 12 guns; two Austrian batteries 12 guns; for a total of 107 guns.

In addition, Kleist's Prussian corps arrived from Nollendorf, consisting of 30 battalions, 32 squadrons and 9½ batteries (76 guns). The order of march of Kleist's force was: *Oberst* Blücher's *1. Schlesisches Husaren* with half of *7. Reitende Batterie*; the skirmishers from *7. Reserve Infanterie*; *10. Brigade* with *8. Batterie* (six-pounders) and *3. Batterie* (12-pounders) and half of *7. Reitende Batterie*; the *Reserve Kavallerie Brigade* with *8. Reitende Batterie* and the *Landwehr Kavallerie*; *11. Brigade* with *11. Batterie* and *14. Batterie* (both of six-pounders); *12. Brigade* with *13. Batterie* (six-pounders) and *6. Batterie* (12-pounders); three battalions from *9. Brigade* with *21. Batterie* (six-pounders); half of *9. Reitende Batterie* (the remaining units from *9. Brigade* were with Count Wittgenstein's corps). Aster, 160.

The overall total was:

	Battalions	Squadrons	Batteries	Guns
Russians	44	73	7	83
Austrians	24	10	2	12
Prussians	30	32	11	88
Total:	**98**	**115**	**20**	**183**

But of these troops, the entire 1st Lifeguard Division, as well as most of the cavalry and artillery, did not take part in the fighting on 18 (30) August.

Appendix XXII

Austrian reluctance to fight at Kulm

According to Hofmann (page 173), the divisions under Colloredo and Bianchi set out from Dux the day before, at the insistence of Emperor Alexander, but stopped for the night halfway along the road between Dux and Teplitz.

The notes (*Anmerkungen*) kept in Barclay de Tolly's headquarters (Archive of the M.T.D. No. 47,353, book 27) state:

> at that very moment, as General Barclay de Tolly decided to attack the enemy, there was no appetite for battle in the Austrian Hauptquartier and this is evident not only from the slowness of the advance of Colloredo's and Bianchi's divisions, but also from the following: Barclay de Tolly suggested that these generals send aides-de-camp to obtain the dispositions for the attack. As he was dictating it, Prinz Schwarzenberg arrived with his staff. He did not express an opinion himself, but his entire retinue, Langenau in particular, and even the courageous, forthright Radetzky, considered the enterprise doubtful… Barclay, paying no attention to this, continued to dictate the disposition, and having finished it, ordered it to be presented to the field marshal for signature, but Schwarzenberg, declining responsibility, said that he only wanted to be a witness to the act. However, this did not stop him from writing in a report published in the Austrian newspapers that the attack on Vandamme was executed on his orders…

Appendix XXIII

German reaction to Vandamme as a prisoner of war

Description of Vandamme's reception from Shishkov's Notes, second edition, 158-159.

No sooner had he arrived at the staging post, than this entire street was blocked with people of various classes and titles. For as long as he was sitting at the staging post (which lasted about an hour), the people would not leave. I deliberately walked through the crowds of people and listened to what they were saying. There was not a person who did not come up with some sort of abusive phrase or name for him. Eventually, the *Feldjäger* [Tsar's messenger] who was tasked to lead him to Moscow, a burlier man than Vandamme himself, emerged. The horses were ready, and the carriage drove up to the staging post. The agitation of the people who had come to see him became more animated and noticeable: everyone began to crowd towards the carriage. Someone said to the postmaster: 'Why did you not harness up the dung cart? Even that is too good for him.'

Another said: 'brother, watch that you drive slowly, let the people spit in his face.'

A third: 'tip him out somewhere so that his head will get crushed.'

A fourth: 'he should be driven by swine, not horses.'

Such comments, with additional contemptuous ridicule, were repeated incessantly. The postmaster, joking with them all at his expense, eventually took out his horn and blew it. Everyone laughed and shouted 'well! fine! call him quickly.' Those who were in the upper room with Vandamme said that at that moment a fearful expression crossed his face and he turned pale, but he nevertheless pulled himself together and went out, hurrying to get into the carriage as quickly as possible. Whereupon he was surrounded by a crowd of people. Someone called to him with bitter and reproachful mockery 'what are your orders for Hamburg?' Another: 'what for Lübeck?' A third: 'what for Bremen?' These cities, more than any other location, were witness and victims to his robbery and cruelty. Another shouted at him: '*bon voyage* to Siberia!' Yet another: 'you can catch sables there!' Still more: 'or dig for [silver] ore in Nerchinsk!' Angry voices shouted: '*du Tiger!*' or '*du Krokodill!*' or '*du giftige Schlange!*' (you venomous snake). One, without saying a word, bared his teeth at him in rage and shook his clenched fists.

APPENDIX XXIII 221

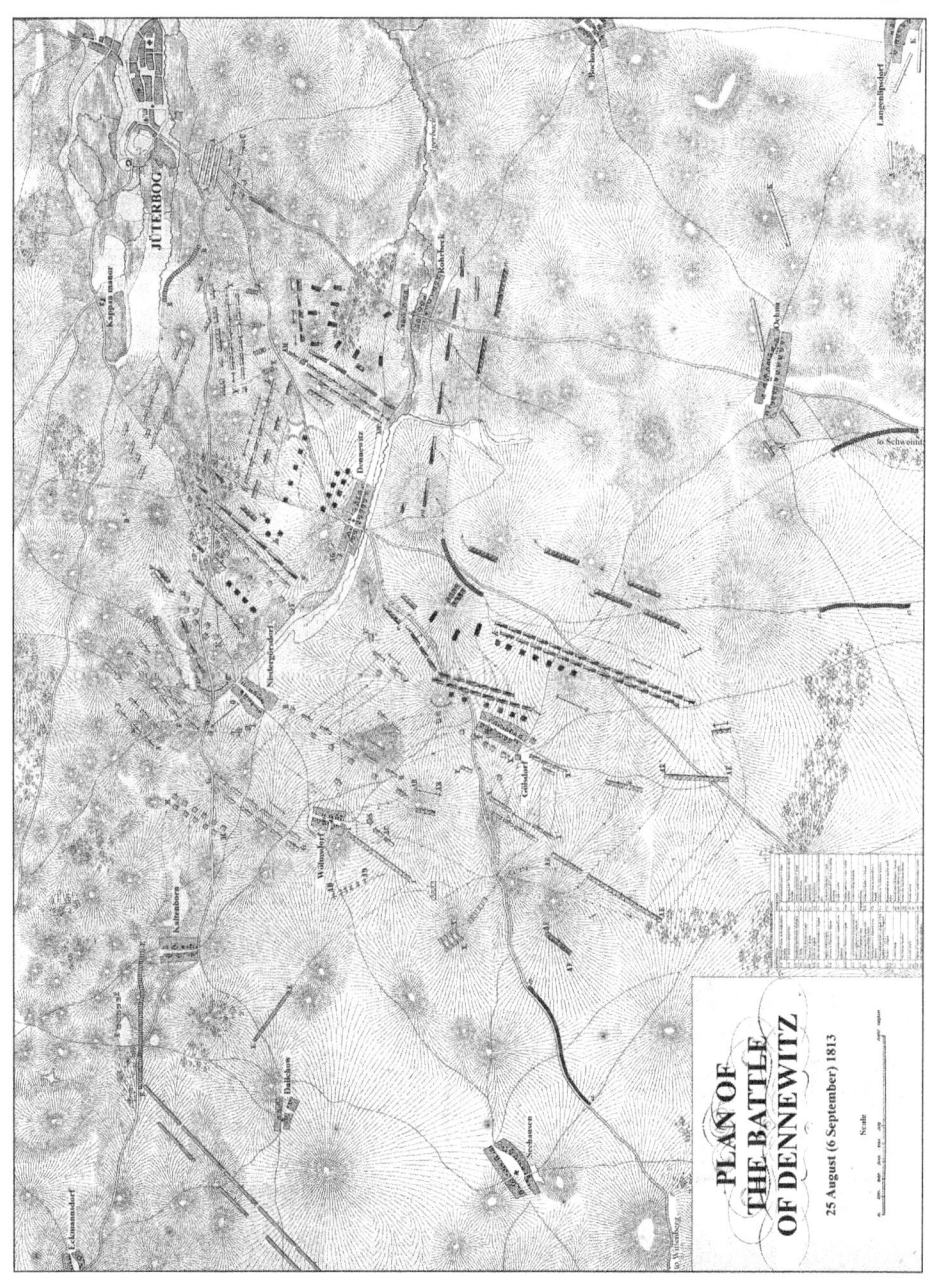

Plan of the Battle of Dennewitz.

Legend to Map No. 10

Coalition Forces

A.A.	Prussian *IV. Korps* on the night before the battle
B.B.	*IV. Korps* move into position
C.C.	Detachment left forwards of Jüterbog
D.D.	*IV. Korps*
E.E.	Advance by Prussian *III. Korps*
F.F.	Thümen's *4. Brigade*
G.G.	Krafft's *6. Brigade*
H.H.	Prinz Hessen-Homburg's *3. Brigade*
I.I.	Oppen's reserve cavalry
K.K.	Advance by Thümen's *4. Brigade*
L.L.	Two battalions from *4. Ostpreußisches Infanterie*
M.M.	Retreat by Thümen's *4. Brigade*
N.N.	*4. Reserve Infanterie* & three battalions from *3. Ostpreußisches Landwehr*
O.O.	Dietrich's Russian artillery
P.P.	Clash between the Prussian *Leib-Husaren* and Polish *Ułanów*
R.R.	Advance by Krafft's *6. Brigade*
S.	Second battalion, *3. Ostpreußisches Infanterie*
T.T.	Attack by four battalions from *3. Brigade*
U.U.	Three battalions from *6. Brigade* & two squadrons *Westpreußisches Dragoner*
V.V.	Advance by 16 Prussian battalions
X.X.	Borstell's *5. Brigade*
Y.Y.	Repeated advance by the Prussian *IV. Korps*
Z.Z.	Cavalry charge
AB.	Swedish battery & Russian ½ battery supporting the *Mörner Husaren*
AC.	Two Russian battalions
AD.	Advance by three Russian batteries
AE.	Prussian cavalry
AF.	Russian cavalry
AG.	Capture of Dennewitz by two battalions of *4. Ostpreußisches Infanterie*
AH.	Thümen's advance towards Rohrbeck

French Forces

a.a.	Advance by Bertrand's *4e Corps*
b.b.	Deployment of *4e Corps* at the start of the battle
c.c.	Advance by Reynier's *7e Corps*
d.d.	Durutte's division
e.e.	French cavalry charge
f.f.	Saxon division
g.g.	Durutte's retreat
h.h.	Move of part of Bertrand's corps to assist him
i.i.	Advance by Oudinot's *12e Corps*
k.k.	Deployment of *12e Corps* into fighting formation
l.l.	Arrighi's cavalry
m.m.	Redeployment of *12e Corps* towards Rohrbeck
n.n.	Cavalry covering the retreat

32

The Battle of Dennewitz

Napoleon's intention – to march on Berlin. – Strength of Ney's force. – Deployment of the Army of the North. – Deployment of the French army on the evening of 24 August (5 September). – Bülow's movement towards the flank of the French army. – Dispositions by the Crown Prince of Sweden. – Description of the terrain around Dennewitz. – Advance by the French army.

Battle of Dennewitz. – Precautions taken by Bülow and Tauentzien. – Tauentzien's operations. – Bülow's advance and the skilful deployment of his forces. – Attack by Tauentzien's cavalry. – Thümen's operations. – Attack on the village of Gölsdorf by Krafft's brigade. – The arrival at Gölsdorf of two Saxon divisions from the enemy side, and Borstell's brigade from the Coalition. – Arrival of Oudinot's *12e Corps* at Gölsdorf. – Guilleminot's attack. – Ney transfers *12e Corps* from the left to the right wing. – Reinforcements reach Bülow. – Flight of the enemy. – The pursuit by Coalition forces. – Losses in the fighting. – Awards. – Russian participation.

Disagreements between the Crown Prince of Sweden and Bülow. – Dissatisfaction of the Saxon forces.

The failure of Marshal Oudinot's offensive did not deflect Napoleon from his intended plan of action. He decided to resume the march on Berlin. The command of Oudinot's army was transferred to Ney; the losses from the battle of Großbeeren were supposed to be made good with an abundance of reinforcements. Napoleon himself had wanted to go to Ney's army with select troops from his *Garde*, and to take command of it. But the blows inflicted by the Coalition on the Katzbach and at Kulm had forced the *Empereur des Français* to turn these reserves initially in the direction of Silesia, and then to the south to Dresden. Only Dąbrowski's Polish division [Jan Henryk Dąbrowski or Jean-Henri Dombrowski] was sent to reinforce Ney, consisting of four battalions and two lancer regiments, numbering 4,000 men, which was not enough even to replenish the losses to the French army since the opening of the campaign: the number of troops assigned to Ney did not exceed

70,000 men.[1] Moreover, the morale of these troops had been crushed by their defeat at Großbeeren. Despite these unfavourable circumstances, however, Ney decided to immediately resume the offensive towards Berlin. On 23 August (4 September), the day after his arrival at the camp at Wittenberg, the Marshal announced at a parade that he would lead the force against the enemy immediately, and indeed on 24 August (5 September) he ordered Bertrand to attack the Prussian detachment under General Dobschütz stationed at Zahna, who retreated to Zallmsdorf after a very stubborn fight with the loss of several hundred men.[2] At this time, the formations of the Army of the North were positioned as follows: Borstell's *5. Brigade* were on the Potsdam road behind the Köpnick and Jahmo defiles; Krafft's *6. Brigade* were behind Kropstädt; Prinz Hessen-Homburg's *3. Brigade* and *Generalmajor* Thümen's *4. Brigade* were at Marzahna; *Generalmajor* Oppen's reserve cavalry were at Wergzahna [2½ miles south of Marzahna]. *Generalmajor* Dobschütz, as already mentioned, had retreated to Zallmsdorf from Zahna with elements of the Prussian *4. Brigade*, consisting of six battalions, four squadrons and a battery, and had been reinforced with six squadrons with four horse artillery pieces.[3] He was joined there by the remainder of the units from *V. Korps*, who had arrived at Gadegast [eight miles south-west of Dennewitz] and Seyda from Luckau, consisting of five battalions and 13 squadrons with 24 guns (first battalion of *2. Neumärkisches Landwehr* remained as the garrison of Luckau, while General Wobeser's force remained in the vicinity of the town). General Dobschütz, temporarily commanding *IV. Korps* in Tauentzien's absence (who had gone to Rabenstein to see the Swedish Crown Prince), deployed his force, numbering 14,000 men with 36 guns, in two echelons, protecting himself on both flanks with Cossacks from Ilovaisky 3rd's regiment [Alexei Vasilievich Ilovaisky] and being attacked again by the French in superior numbers, retreated beyond Mellnitz, and on towards Jüterbog. Overall, the *Korps* losses during the retreat from Zahna reached some 3,000 men.[4] That night, General Tauentzien arrived in Jüterbog, having lost his way on the way back from the Crown Prince's headquarters and narrowly avoided being captured. Having been

---

1 Dąbrowski's division consisted of: II Korpus – 2 Pułk Piechoty and 4 Pułk Piechoty; IV Korpus Jazdy – 2 Pułk Ułanów and 4 Pułk Ułanów (eight squadrons). Wagner, Plane der Schlachten und Treffen, welche von der preussischen Armee in den Feldzügen der Jahre 1813, 14 und 15 geliefert worden, I, 60, according to him, the French army received about 6,000 men as reinforcements; Bernhardi Denkwürdigkeiten aus dem Leben Carl Friedrich Grafen von Toll, III, 496 & 503.
2 Wagner, I, 62-63; Beitzke *Geschichte der deutschen Freiheitskriege* in den Jahren 1813 und 1814, II, 292-294.
3 See Map No. 3, Map to follow operations etcetera [Zahna and Zallmsdorf appear to have been transposed on this map]. Dobschütz's formation consisted of: two battalions each from *1. Kurmärkische Landwehr*, *7. Kurmärkische Landwehr* and *1. Schlesische Landwehr*; two squadrons each from *3. Pommersches Kavallerie* and *7. Kurmärkisches Kavallerie*; *17. Batterie*, all from *IV Korps*; two squadrons of *Brandenburgisches Dragoner*, one squadron each from *Königin Dragoner* and *2. Westpreußisches Dragoner*, and two squadrons of *Berlinsches Landwehr Kavallerie*; *Leutnant* Jenichen's half-battery, all from *III Korps*. Wagner, I, 61.
4 Wagner, I, 63-65; Beitzke, II, 293-295; Vaudoncourt, *Histoire de la guerre soutenue par les Français en Allemagne en 1813*, 170.

unexpectedly halted by the '*qui vive*' of a French sentry, Tauentzien posed as a Saxon officer and escaped the danger that threatened him.[5]

On the evening of 24 August (5 September), the Prussian forces were located in an area stretching about 3½ *Meilen* (25 *versts*) from Jahmo to Jüterbog, while the Russian and Swedish corps were between Lobbese and Marzahna.[6] On the French side, Marshal Oudinot's *12e Corps* had settled down for the night at Seyda, General Reynier's *7e Corps* were between Zallmsdorf and Leetza, while Bertrand's *4e Corps* were at Naundorf [two miles north-west of] Mellnitz.[7]

Ney's offensive against Tauentzien's corps revealed the enemy intent – to envelope the Coalition army's left flank and, by driving them away from Berlin, to capture the capital of Prussia. General Bülow, who was stationed closer to the French army with his corps than any of the Crown Prince's other formations, decided, in the event of a further offensive against Tauentzien, to strike the enemy in the flank and rear. To that end, on the night of 24 to 25 August (5 to 6 September), Bülow moved to Kurzlipsdorf, five *versts* from Bertrand's corps, with the three brigades under the Prinz von Hessen-Homburg, Thümen and Krafft, the reserve cavalry and artillery reserve, and the next morning he moved even closer to the enemy and stationed the infantry at Eckmannsdorf, advancing the cavalry to Dalichow [see Map No. 10, Plan of the Battle of Dennewitz]. Borstell's *5. Brigade*, on the Crown Prince's orders, were left at Kropstädt in order to defend the high ground there and the Köpnick defile, a distance of more than a *Meile* (around nine *versts*) from the main body of the Prussian *III Korps*. General Bülow, wanting to conceal the locations of his force from the enemy, forbade them from lighting camp fires.[8]

On the evening of 24 August (5 September), the Crown Prince issued a disposition for operations on 25 August (6 September), which contained the following orders: Wintzingerode's corps were to concentrate at Lobbese, excluding the vanguard commanded by Count Vorontsov,[9] which was to move towards Zahna and upstream along the Elbe (together with Adjutant General Chernyshev's detachment) and get behind the enemy as soon as they hear a cannonade from Zahna; the Swedish forces were to march to Lobbese and join the Russian corps there; Hirschfeld's detachment were also to go there; Bülow's and Tauentzien's corps were ordered to attack the enemy.[10]

---

5 Richter, *Geschichte des Deutschen Freiheitskrieges vom Jahre 1813 bis zum Jahre 1815*, I, 436.
6 Wagner, I, 65-66; Richter, I, 437.
7 Vaudoncourt, 170; Wagner, I, 66; Beitzke, II, 297-298.
8 Wagner, I, 66-67.
9 On 16 (28) August, Lieutenant General Count O'Rourke's vanguard, commanded by Lieutenant General Count Vorontsov, consisted of: Nezhin Mounted Jägers, Pavlograd Hussars, Poland Ulans, Volhynia Ulans, numbering 2,561 men in 22 squadrons; Grekov 9th's Cossacks, Dyachkin's Cossacks, Melnikov 4th's Cossacks, Melnikov 5th's Cossacks, Andriyanov 2nd's Cossacks, Loshchilin 1st's Cossacks, Tver Coachmen and 1st Bashkirs, numbering 3,376 men in nine regiments; 11th Horse Artillery Company, 13th Horse Artillery Company with 439 crew. Overall, the vanguard numbered 6,376 men with 24 guns. Count Vorontsov's War Diary for 1813 in the Archive of the M.T.D. No. 16,642; Report on force manning for 1813, in the Archive of the M.T.D. No. 46,692.
10 Disposition issued from Rabenstein, signed by Adlercreutz.

The ground where the Coalition were to engage the French is a gently sloping ridge that marks the watershed between the Elbe and Havel basins. In general the surroundings of Dennewitz are undulating and sandy, with small stands of conifers here and there. In some places there are deep swampy ravines, along which rivers flow with no easy fording points. One of them, Aa, or Agerbach [Nuthe], emerging from the marshes near Niedergörsdorf, first heads east through Dennewitz and Rohrbeck, and then meanders north through a large low-lying meadow, past the town of Jüterbog, which lies in a hollow between the hills, one of which dominates the entire surrounding area and is located to the west of the town, near the Kappan manor [*Gutssiedlung*]. The only crossings via bridges over the Agerbach were in Dennewitz, Rohrbeck and slightly downstream of the latter village.

Despite the fact that Ney's force included more than 10,000 cavalrymen, they did not bring any benefit due to their poor quality. The French, surrounded on all sides by Coalition light cavalry and Cossacks, did not dare to send patrols out to any significant distance, and therefore did not know about the deployment of Bülow's corps near their left flank.[11] On 25 August (6 September), the enemy force set off from their overnight camp in accordance with the disposition issued at the time:

> *4e Corps*, having circled to the right of Jüterbog, are to march towards Dahme, *7e Corps* are to go from Zallmsdorf to Gadegast and on to Rohrbeck, *12e Corps* are to stay at Seyda until *7e Corps* have passed, and then are to move towards Oehna. The general direction of the army is to the right to Dahme, and on to Luckau, to link up with the Emperor.[12]

The French army was divided into three columns in order to allow for a quick transition from column-of-route into battle formation, but having emerged from their positions at staggered intervals, they were marching at such a considerable distance from one another that this possibility was lost. In addition, despite the fact that the army was intending to move across open ground, almost all the cavalry was proceeding at the rear of the columns.[13]

General Bülow, having observed the advance of Bertrand's corps, which had set out from their overnight camp together with Lorge's division [Jean Thomas Guillaume Lorge] and the Polish force and was slowly moving through Gölsdorf towards Dennewitz, informed the Crown Prince of his intention to attack the enemy and repeated his request for support for *III Korps* from Borstell's brigade. At the same time, Bülow sent General Borstel orders to march from Kropstädt to rejoin the corps, while General Tauentzien was asked to move from Jüterbog to his right and attach himself to the left flank of *III Korps*. At the same time, Bülow's force had been directed towards Niedergörsdorf and Wölmsdorf, villages located about two *versts* from Dennewitz. It has been claimed that Ney, having observed Bülow's movements,

---

11 Beitzke, II, 299.
12 This disposition was found in the pocket of one of Ney's aides-de-camp captured at the Battle of Dennewitz. Wagner, I, 68.
13 Carl von Weiß (Müffling), Betrachtungen über die grossen Operationen und Schlachten der Feldzüge von 1813 und 1814, 62-63.

mistook his troops for General Reynier's corps and continued to advance towards Jüterbog. Reynier's corps broke camp at eight o'clock in the morning with Defrance's division [Jean-Marie Antoine Defrance], while Oudinot's corps broke camp at nine o'clock with Fournier's division: the former were directed towards Seyda and then wheeled towards Rohrbeck, while the latter were marching on Oehna.

General Tauentzien, having the intention of uniting with Bülow, on the morning of 25 August (6 September), ordered his troops to march to Kaltenborn, while he left Major Kleist on the high ground at Jüterbog with four battalions, two squadrons and 11 guns, with almost no artillery ammunition.[14] But as soon as Tauentzien's corps moved in the indicated direction, they were informed of the enemy advance, which shortly thereafter, actually appeared on the high ground north of Dennewitz. Under these circumstances, Tauentzien decided to occupy the opposite slopes with his force: his infantry stood in two echelons, groups of a few squadrons each were posted behind these lines and on the right wing; 20 guns were deployed in the front line, while the remaining four were in reserve:[15] the strength of Graf Tauentzien's force did not exceed 7,500 men, while together with Kleist's detachment reached some 10,000.[16] Meanwhile, Bertrand's corps, having passed through Dennewitz and encountering the leading Prussian troops, formed up for battle in dead ground and turned towards the high ground facing Tauentzien's corps: in the front line was Fontanelli's Italian division, and then on their right flank, one brigade from Franquemont's Württemberg division [Frédéric de Franquemont] (the other brigade was in the rear guarding the trains); Lorge's cavalry were in the second line; Morand's division [Charles Antoine Louis Alexis Morand] were in reserve: there were no fewer than 18,000 men in these formations in total.[17]

The action began at around nine o'clock in the morning. The weather was clear and began to get quite hot around midday. At the very beginning of the battle, Marshal Ney, riding forward to survey the positions of the Prussian force, was almost captured by skirmishing Cossacks. As soon as the forces of both sides had managed to form up in battle order, they advanced to contact one another. The French, disordered by the cannonade opened up by Tauentzien somewhat earlier than the enemy, brought up some of the troops from the rear into the front line. Tauentzien, wanting

---

14 Major Kleist's force left at Jüterbog consisted of: two battalions of *1. Kurmärkisches Landwehr*, two battalions *1. Schlesisches Infanterie*, two squadrons of *Berlinische Landwehr Kavallerie*, *27. Batterie* (six-pounders, having lost one gun the day before) and *Leutnant* Lent's half-battery of 12-pounders. Wagner, I, 69-70.

15 Tauentzien's battle formation had four squadrons *2. Westpreußisches Dragoner* on the right wing of the front line (one of which was detached to the right to liaise with Bülow), next to them were *6. Reitende Batterie*, then *3. Reserve Infanterie* (three battalions), *17. Batterie* (six-pounders), *5. Kurmärkisches Regiment* (four battalions) and *20. Batterie* (six-pounders). Two squadrons each of *Brandenburgisches Dragoner*, *1. Kurmärkisches Kavallerie* and *7. Kurmärkisches Kavallerie* and three squadrons of *3. Pommersches Landwehr Kavallerie* were behind this line. In the second line were first battalion of *1. Schlesiches Regiment* and three battalions of *2. Neumärkisches Landwehr* with half of *11. Reitende Batterie*. Three squadrons of *3. Ostpreußisches Landwehr Kavallerie* were behind the second line. Wagner, I, 70-71.

16 In Wagner (I, 71) and Beitzke (II, 300), Tauentzien's corps is shown as 10,000 men, clearly including Major Kleist's detachment at Jüterbog.

17 Beitzke, II, 301.

to take advantage of the confusion in Bertrand's corps, advanced across a ravine in battle formation, closed up to the enemy and unleashed a fierce canister and musket barrage. The French unlimbered a large number of guns and forced the Prussians to remain on the defensive, yet despite having twice the number of troops, the French were held for about four hours on the ground occupied by them at the beginning of the battle. Eventually, at around one o'clock in the afternoon, Tauentzien was obliged to withdraw his force behind the ravine. The thick dust and smoke that covered the battlefield prevented him from making this movement in a coordinated manner, but the troops dressed their lines as soon as they had retreated to the high ground. The enemy were preparing to pursue them when a cannonade thundered on their left flank, and they were forced to turn their attention to self-defence. General Bülow had set out from Eckmannsdorf as early as ten o'clock with three infantry brigades and the reserve cavalry. The infantry moved towards Niedergörsdorf in three echelons: in the lead were Thümen's *4. Brigade*, behind them were Krafft's *6. Brigade*, further back came Prinz Hessen-Homburg's *3. Brigade*, the *Leib-Husaren* were on the left flank of the infantry, while Oppen's reserve cavalry, consisting of 20 squadrons, were on the right towards Wölmsdorf.[18] The Crown Prince, who had reached Lobbese that morning from Rabenstein, had already ordered the Russian and Swedish forces to set off for Jüterbog immediately at 11 o'clock, a distance of three *Meilen* (more than 20 *versts*) from the locations where they had halted.[19]

News of the victory on the Katzbach was received just as Bülow's corps were setting off from Eckmannsdorf. The troops, having learned of this, marched to confront the enemy as if on their way to a festival, with joyful cheering.[20]

General Bülow had the option to head along the left bank of the Agerbach and link up with Tauentzien's corps, or along the right bank of this river, in order to isolate the enemy force that had passed Dennewitz from the rest of Ney's army. The former course of action better protected him from defeat by superior enemy forces than the latter, which, conversely, if successful, would deliver a more significant victory. Bearing in mind that Tauentzien had a vital need for reinforcement, but not wanting to lose the opportunity to inflict a decisive blow on the enemy, Bülow took the village of Niedergörsdorf as the focus (pivot) of his operation, from where it was possible, depending on the circumstances, to move along either side of this swampy river. From Niedergörsdorf, Thümen's brigade, numbering 8,000 men, was sent to assist Tauentzien on the left bank of the river, while the other two brigades remained at the aforementioned village in reserve.[21] Just as Thümen was moving towards Dennewitz, Durutte's division from Reynier's *7e Corps*, having crossed

---

18 Oppen's reserve cavalry, advancing on the right wing of Bülow's corps, consisted of: *Königin Dragoner* (four squadrons), *2. Westpreußisches Dragoner* (four squadrons), three squadrons each of *Pommersches National Kavallerie, 2. Pommersches Kavallerie, 2. Kurmärkisches Kavallerie* and *4. Kurmärkisches Kavallerie* (two squadrons of *Brandenburgisches Dragoner* were in Tauentzien's corps. Three squadrons from this regiment had been assigned to *4. Brigade*. One squadron were protecting the trains). Wagner, I, 74.
19 Plotho, *Der Krieg in Deutschland und Frankreich in den Jahren 1813 und 1814*, II, 166-167; Wagner, I, 73-74; Richter, 440-443; Vaudoncourt, 171; Beitzke, II, 301-303 & 305.
20 Beitzke, II, 305.
21 Carl von Weiß (Müffling), 65-66.

the Agerbach, at Dennewitz, made a change of front to the left and formed up in two lines on the high ground between the swampy valley and a stand of conifers, occupying this woods with some of the infantry. Reynier's other two divisions, having reached Rohrbeck were directed, on Ney's orders, along the right bank of the Agerbach, towards Gölsdorf, in order to engage Bülow. Oudinot's *12e Corps* and most of General Arrighi's reserve cavalry were left about five *versts* behind.[22]

General Tauentzien, hearing the cannonade from his right side and observing that the force advancing against him had halted, counter-attacked the enemy with all his cavalry. The valiant Prussian horsemen charged at the French through clouds of dust and smoke. Major Barnekow [Eduard von Barnekow] scattered three battalions with two squadrons of *3. Pommerisches Landwehr Kavallerie* and, with the assistance of the infantry, took most of them prisoner, but was killed himself. The fourth squadron of *Brandenburgisches Dragoner*, followed by *1. Kurmärkische Landwehr* and *7. Kurmärkische Landwehr*, having galloped through the first line of Bertrand's force, scattered two battalions stationed in the second line, drove off a regiment of *chasseurs à cheval* and overran a battery, but only managed to drag away one ammunition caisson. Two Polish *Pułk Ułanów*, rushing to the rescue of the *chasseurs à cheval*, were also scattered by the *4. Kurmärkisches Landwehr* and three squadrons of *2. Westpreußisches Dragoner* and lost many men taken prisoner by the Prussian cavalry. General Tauentzien, meaning to prevent the enemy from turning against Bülow, attacked Bertrand with all his strength and forced him to retreat towards Rohrbeck.[23] At the same time as the above actions by Tauentzien, Bülow's corps was moving towards the enemy. Thümen's brigade, advancing on the left wing,[24] attacked the high ground at Niedergörsdorf, held by Durutte's force, but just as Thümen was crossing a ravine with four battalions from the front line, they were engaged with fierce canister fire and driven back by the numerically superior enemy infantry (overall on the left bank of the Agerbach, Ney had some 26,000 men in Bertrand's corps and Durutte's division against 18,000 with Tauentzien and Thümen). General Thümen lined the ravine with a screen of skirmishers and, under their protection, pushed the second line forward in support of the first, while Bülow reinforced them with units from Prinz von Hessen-Homburg's *3. Brigade*, which had been in reserve, and with Colonel Dietrich's Russian heavy artillery, subsequently reinforced by six more Russian heavy guns.[25] Dietrich's artillery, very advantageously positioned opposite the left flank of the enemy line, weakened their cannonade and musketry through enfilade fire. Taking advantage of this, General Thümen led his infantry with bayonets fixed and drove the French from the high ground they had been

---

22 Wagner, I, 75; Beitzke, II, 307.
23 Wagner, I, 73-74.
24 In Thümen's force, *6. Batterie* (six-pounders) were a little back from the right wing front line; then two battalions of *5. Reserve Infanterie* and two battalions of *Elbe Infanterie*; in the second line: three battalions of *4. Ostpreußisches Infanterie* and two battalions of *5. Reserve Infanterie*. The *Leib-Husaren* were on the left wing; three squadrons of *Brandenburgische Dragoner* behind the centre; two companies of *Ostpreußische Jäger* were following up. Wagner, I, 75.
25 Reinforcements for Thümen were: initially, three battalions of *4. Reserve Infanterie* with Dietrich's heavy artillery company, followed by four battalions of *3. Ostpreußisches Landwehr Infanterie*. Plotho, II, 168.

holding. He had two horses killed under him here. Major Polchinski captured a gun with the third battalion of *4. Reserve Infanterie* and drove two French battalions occupying the pine woods out into the open, where the majority were taken prisoner. Durutte's force fought very bravely, but could not withstand the Prussian onslaught and retreated towards Dennewitz. General Thümen pursued them relentlessly with all 16 battalions from *4. Brigade* and *3. Brigade* and attacked the village, while the skirmishers from the first two battalions of *4. Ostpreußisches Infanterie* captured a 12-pounder cannon.[26]

While Bertrand and Durutte were fighting against Tauentzien and Thümen, both Saxon divisions of *7e Corps* were headed towards Gölsdorf against Krafft's *6. Brigade*, which was formed up in two lines between Niedergörsdorf and Wölmsdorf. Four squadrons of *1. Pommersche Landwehr* guarded the flanks of the infantry of the Prussian brigade. Ahead of the front line were eight six-pounder guns of *16. Batterie* and 12 12-pounder guns of *4. Batterie* and *5. Batterie*.[27] On the enemy side the first Saxon division under Le Coq advanced in the first line, while the second Saxon division were in support (formerly under von Sahr's command). The latter, being surrounded on the march on all sides by Cossacks, were forced to move in long-sided square. Of the two front line brigades, General Mellenthin's had received orders to capture Gölsdorf, while General Brause's brigade was ordered to protect a large battery placed on the Windmühlenberg, north of the village. But in the meantime, because the second Saxon division had already reached this location, General Brause supported the attack by Mellenthin's brigade with his entire force. Defrance's cavalry were stationed behind the right wing of the advancing force. The Saxon cavalry had been left facing Rohrbeck.[28]

As soon as Krafft's force came into contact with the Saxons and got within cannon range, the enemy opened a strong cannonade from the large battery placed on the Windmühlenberg, which soon silenced the Prussian *16. Batterie*. At the same time, several enemy columns, bypassing Gölsdorf, headed towards the flank of *6. Brigade*, which forced Krafft to refuse his right wing. General Bülow immediately sent all remaining battalions of Prinz von Hessen-Homburg's *3. Brigade* to assist them.[29] Major Gleisenberg broke into Gölsdorf with his battalion supported by the fire of *Hauptmann* Neindorff's *5. Reitende Batterie* and *Hauptmann* Glasenapp's six-pounders and sought to hold out there against an incomparably stronger enemy. Having been driven out three times, he attacked the village once more with the assistance of the remaining battalions from *3. Brigade*, which had arrived to help him under the command of Major Sjöholm [Ferdinand Ludwig von Sjöholm]. Just as they

---

26 Plotho, II, 168-169; Wagner, I, 75-78.
27 Krafft's *6. Brigade* were deployed with the *Kolbergische Infanterie* on the right of the front line, *9. Reserve Infanterie* to their left (six battalions) with 12 guns across the front; four battalions of *1. Neumärkischen Landwehr* in the second line, three squadrons of *Pommersche Landwehr* on the right wing and one more on the left. Wagner, I, 75-76.
28 Lecoq's Saxon division and what had been von Sahr's Saxon division, Defrance's French cavalry division and Gablenz's Saxon cavalry brigade, consisting of 19 battalions and about 40 squadrons, had been sent against Krafft's brigade.
29 Three battalions of *3. Ostpreußisches Infanterie*, *2. Ostpreußische Grenadier-Bataillon* and a battalion of *3. Ostpreußisches Landwehr* were sent to assist Krafft. Wagner, I, 79-80.

were about to engage with bayonets fixed, a Swedish battery, escorted by the *Mörner Husaren*, rode up to Gölsdorf and opened fire on the Prussian troops, mistaking them for Saxons. They had already fired five rounds when an aide-de-camp from 6. Brigade, *Leutnant* Kawaczinski, putting himself in obvious danger by galloping up to the battery, disabused the Swedish artillerymen and showed them the position from which they should be supporting the attack on Gölsdorf, together with four Russian guns that had arrived from the reserve.[30] Krafft sent two battalions of *Kolbergische Infanterie* to assist Sjöholm. At the same time, the entire Prussian 6. *Brigade*, reinforced by two squadrons of reserve cavalry (*2. Westpreußisches Dragoner*), moved forward again. Two battalions marched straight at the large battery, which, having fired all its ammunition, was forced to retreat in haste behind the infantry.[31] This attack by six battalions, supported by fire from a large number of guns, overcame the desperate resistance of the Saxons. Bitter fighting broke out with bayonets and musket butts in the village itself and even at the foot of the altar in the church. The enemy were driven out of the buildings of Gölsdorf as they burst into flames. On the left wing of 6. *Brigade*, Major Reckow [Leopold August Eduard von Reckow], with two battalions of *9. Reserve Infanterie*, and Major Kameke [Georg Christian Friedrich von Kameke], with two squadrons of *Westpreußisches Dragoner*, attacked a Saxon battery and captured four howitzers, of which they managed to drag one away. Just at that moment, the thick dust, raised by strong winds, dissipated, and the enemy, noticing the small number of advancing troops, moved forward, but were checked by Reckow's infantry, with the assistance of the newly arrived fourth battalion, *1. Neumärkisches Landwehr*, and Kameke's dragoons.[32]

By four o'clock, matters had taken a favourable turn on the right wing of the Prussian force. The enemy were retreating at all points. Yet every unit had already been committed to battle, and in the meantime three divisions from *12e Corps*, sent to assist the Saxons, arrived with the rest of the reserve cavalry: consequently, about 50 battalions were concentrated against the 15 Prussian battalions located on the right bank of the Agerbach. The enemy opened concentrated fire from several batteries on the troops occupying Gölsdorf and attacked this village with most of Guilleminot's division. Yet the Prussians bravely held out in the ruined houses of Gölsdorf, while Major Bülow, passing through the village with the first battalion *3. Ostpreußisches Infanterie*, and engaging three battalions, scattered the two closest ones, taking many prisoners and forced the third battalion to retreat. This heroic feat was accomplished, however, with great loss life. Bülow himself was wounded and the enemy managed to break back into the village, but Major Gleisenberg, with the third battalion, *3. Ostpreußisches Infanterie*, took cover in a ditch and checked their further progress.[33]

---

30 Wagner, I, 78-80; Beitzke, II, 311-312. According to Beitzke, six Russian guns arrived from the reserve.
31 The second battalion, *Kolbergisches Infanterie* and first battalion, *Neumärkisches Landwehr* were directed against the large battery on the Windmühlenberg. Wagner, I, 81.
32 Beitzke, II, 312-314.
33 Wagner, I, 81-82.

At about four o'clock, at the critical moment when the superior strength of the enemy – it seemed – should have tilted the advantage in their favour, Borstell's *5. Brigade* finally appeared on the battlefield. Having received orders to go to the aid of *III Korps*, General Borstell set off at 11 o'clock for Kurzlipsdorf, and on towards Dalichow. The detachment stationed at Kropstädt were ordered to follow the brigade.[34] The Russian and Swedish corps marched to the left of *5. Brigade*, towards Eckmannsdorf, to where the Crown Prince had also ordered Borstell. But General Borstell did not carry out this order and headed towards Dalichow, and reported to the prince that: 'General Bülow's force are committed to a fierce fight, and therefore, in order to support them, *5. Brigade* are marching towards the enemy left flank.' The Crown Prince, for his part, informed Bülow of the imminent arrival of reinforcements. The prince wrote: 'The battle is won. I am coming with 48 battalions. Your force will form the second line.'[35]

Borstell's brigade marched in two columns, each of which had four battalions. There were 12 guns in platoon column in the interval between the columns, and seven squadrons advanced ahead of the infantry. On the approach to Gölsdorf, the brigade formed two lines to the right of this village: there were four battalions with 12 guns in the front line, and four battalions in the second. The right flank of the brigade was shielded by three squadrons of *Westpreußisches Ulanen*, the *Pommersches Husaren* and two horse artillery pieces.[36]

General Bülow ordered Borstell's brigade to capture the village of Gölsdorf, occupied by enemy troops: the northern end of the village was already being bombarded by a Swedish battery and several Russian guns; while Borstell's artillery opened fire against the southern end. The enemy replied to the cannonade with 16 heavy guns. *2. Reserve Infanterie* burst into the village; the *Pommersche Grenadier-Bataillon* supported them; they were followed by the rest of the infantry from *5. Brigade*. Major von Hövel, passing through the village with second battalion, *2. Reserve Infanterie*, dashed towards the battery, but was forced to retreat. At the same time, taking advantage of the arrival of *12e Corps* on the left wing of the French army, the enemy attacked Borstell's force with six fresh battalions from Guilleminot's division. The other two divisions from Oudinot's corps supported the attack. The Prussian troops were driven out of Gölsdorf; Borstell's artillery, unable to remain under fire from 50 enemy guns, pulled back. Some of the enemy cavalry, hoping to complete the success of the Saxon force, raced in to attack Borstell's brigade, but

---

34 The detachment at Kropstädt consisted of three battalions, two squadrons and two horse artillery pieces. Plotho, II, 171; Wagner, I, 82.
35 Wagner, I, 82-83.
36 The battle formation of Borstell's *5. Brigade* was: two battalions of *2. Kurmärkischen Landwehr*, 12 six-pounder guns from *10. Batterie* and *19. Batterie*, and two battalions of *2. Reserve Infanterie* in the front line; *1. Pommersche Grenadier-Bataillon*, a battalion each of *1. Pommersches Infanterie*, *2. Kurmärkischen Landwehr* and *2. Reserve Infanterie* in the second line. Three squadrons of *Westpreußisches Ulanen*, four squadrons of *Pommersches Husaren* and two horse artillery pieces guarded the right flank. The remaining units: two battalions of *1. Pommersches Infanterie*, one battalion of *2. Kurmärkischen Landwehr* and two squadrons of *Westpreußisches Ulanen* were advancing from Kropstädt and arrived after the fighting had ended. Wagner, I, 83.

were engaged by Oppen's reserve cavalry and were driven back in disorder onto the infantry following up.[37] The Prussian artillery, reinforced by 5. *Reitende Batterie*, rode forward again, while Borstell's infantry, reinforced by 4½ battalions, attacked Gölsdorf once more.[38]

This attack was a last, desperate effort by this valiant Prussian force, and the enemy were already preparing to overwhelm them with superior numbers, but Ney's erroneous orders and the arrival of reinforcements sent by the Crown Prince gave the action an unexpected turn and enabled Bülow's victory.

Marshal Ney, throughout the duration of the battle, was with Bertrand's corps constantly and personally participated in the action instead of monitoring the general course of the fighting. By around five o'clock in the afternoon, the situation of his force operating on the left bank of the Agerbach was becoming very doubtful. Two battalions of *4. Ostpreußisches Infanterie*, having driven the enemy back from the high ground north of Dennewitz, captured this village. The French continued to hold stubbornly forwards of Rohrbeck and even drove forward again to cover the retreat of the force at the tip of their right wing, under pressure from Tauentzien's corps. General Thümen ordered Dietrichs' Russian battery to move forward, and their first rounds set fire to several houses. Whereupon the skirmishers from *5. Kurmärkisches Landwehr*, who had managed to take possession of Rohrbeck woods in the meantime, burst into the village and took two guns. Two squadrons of *3. Ostpreußisches Kavallerie*, galloping through Rohrbeck, bumped into enemy cavalry and scattered eight squadrons. The troops on the French right wing were retreating at all points. But, on the left wing, at Gölsdorf, the enemy were on the verge of a success that would more than compensate for their failures at Dennewitz and Rohrbeck. Fortunately for the Coalition, Ney, concerned only about what was happening in front of his own eyes, and wanting to help Bertrand and Durutte while their forces were still able to defend the high ground forwards of the villages, ordered *12e Corps* to move from Gölsdorf to Rohrbeck. Reynier, seeing the obvious impossibility of holding out with the Saxon contingent alone, vainly sought to persuade Marshal Oudinot to leave at least one of his divisions at Gölsdorf. Oudinot did not want to split his corps up and, sticking to the letter of the orders issued to him, marched towards Rohrbeck. Only a few Bavarian battalions were left to assist the Saxons.[39]

Transferring Oudinot's corps from the left wing to the right took more than an hour, but by the time they had arrived at Rohrbeck, it was no longer possible to rectify the situation. Oudinot's force were dragged back by the right wing of Ney's army, which had fallen into complete disarray, and retreated with them in a similar state of disorder. Thümen's corps, having crossed the Agerbach swamps between Dennewitz and Rohrbeck, pursued the enemy, but they were retreating so hastily

---

37 Plotho, II, 271; Wagner, I, 83-84; Vaudoncourt, 172; Förster, *Geschichte der Befreiungskriege, 1813, 1814, 1815*, I, 801.
38 Borstell's brigade were reinforced by: *2. Ostpreußisches Grenadier-Bataillon* and a battalion of *3. Ostpreußisches Infanterie* from 3. Brigade; *3. Kolbergisches Infanterie* and a battalion of *1. Neumärkischen Landwehr* from 6. Brigade. In addition, two companies from *2. Pommersches Infanterie* were sent by 5. Brigade. Wagner, I, 84.
39 Wagner, I, 86-87; Beitzke, II, 317.

that the infantry could not catch them up, and so the *Brandenburgisches Dragoner* and Major Hiller [Johann Rudolph Christoph Wilhelm Hiller von Gaertringen] with the *2. Neumärkisches Landwehr-Kavallerie* were sent forward.[40]

Meanwhile, on the right wing of the Prussian forces, Bülow ordered Borstell's brigade to resume the attack on Gölsdorf while Oppen's reserve cavalry were sent into action. General Oppen moved to the right of the village and sent forward *Hauptmann* Steinwehr's *6. Reitende Batterie*, escorted by the *Königin Dragoner*. The enemy deployed a howitzer battery to oppose them. The numerous French cavalry tried to check the advance of the Prussian force. But at this very moment, new Coalition forces had arrived: initially, Colonel Pahlen [Matvey Ivanovich Palen 3rd or Carl Magnus von der Pahlen] with the Izyum Hussars, Riga Dragoons and Finland Dragoons. To their right were five Cossack regiments commanded by Ilovaisky 4th [Ivan Dmitrievich Ilovaisky]. Behind them came two battalions of 44th Jägers, who, having joined Borstell's brigade, took part in the final attack and capture of Gölsdorf. Pahlen's regiments, together with Oppen's cavalry, struck the French cavalry in the flank, scattered them and took ten guns. The duty field officer of Ilovaisky's detachment, Colonel Naryshkin [Lev Aleksandrovich Naryshkin], raced into action with the Cossack regiments and captured several guns. Following this, the artillery sent by the Crown Prince turned up: *Överste* Cardell's Swedish battery and Merlin's [Pavel Ivanovich Merlin], Arnoldi's [Ivan Karlovich Arnoldi] and Prince Iashvili's Russian horse artillery companies. This artillery, having driven onto the high ground near the village of Wölmsdorf, at the base of which the battle was raging, unlimbered and opened a powerful cannonade, causing significant damage to the enemy.[41] The Saxon troops fought very bravely, but were driven out of Gölsdorf and were pursued through thick clouds of dust and smoke. By six o'clock in the afternoon, the action was finally decided. The extensive plain south of the Agerbach presented a spectacle of the utter disorder of the enemy army, who, being herded away from the routes leading to Wittenberg, were fleeing towards Torgau. Each of the formation commanders left with the troops entrusted to them, striving to reach the forests near Seyda and Linda [five miles south of Langenlipsdorf] in order to evade the Coalition pursuit there. The enemy attempted a stand at Oehna, but were driven back by the Izyum Hussars, with the assistance of the *Pommersches Husaren*, as a result of which 1,200 men were taken prisoner and 11 guns were captured.[42] *Oberst* Hobe [Karl Friedrich Bernhard Helmuth von Hobe] took three guns with the *Westpreußisches Ulanen*. The cavalry and Cossacks pursued the enemy to Welsickendorf [4½ miles south-east of Langenlipsdorf], Körbitz [three miles south of Langenlipsdorf] and in other directions, until the darkness of the night and the extreme exhaustion of men and horses forced them to stop. The

---

40 Wagner, I, 87.
41 'The Swedish and Russian artillery moved into the fighting line and rendered useful service in the pursuit.' '*Die schwedische und russische Artillerie rückte in die Schlachtlinie ein, und leistete auf der Verfolgung ersprießliche Dienste.*' Wagner, I, 85.
42 Beitzke, II, 318-319; Förster, I, 802-803; Plotho, II, 172, who wrote that those sent to assist Bülow were: Cardell's and Mühlenfels' Swedish batteries, two Russian batteries, some Russian cavalry and a Russian jäger regiment, the Nezhin Mounted Jägers were also mentioned as being part of this force.

infantry of the right wing, namely the brigades under Borstell, Krafft and the Prinz von Hessen-Homburg, reached Oehna, while the formations from the left wing – Tauentzien's corps and Thümen's brigade – reached Langenlipsdorf. The main body of the Russian and Swedish corps settled down for the night between Dennewitz and Jüterbog. Hirschfeld's detachment were at Kaltenborn.[43]

The enemy's further retreat proved disastrous. Ney's force departed along various routes: he headed for Dahme himself with Bertrand's *4e Corps* and Arrighi's cavalry; Reynier's *7e Corps* marched on Herzberg and Annaburg; *12e Corps* made for Annaburg. On the morning of 25 August (6 September), before the outcome of the battle of Dennewitz had been decided, Tauentzien sent orders to General Wobeser to move immediately from Luckau towards Dahma with the troops entrusted to him.[44] Setting out at midnight, Wobeser reached Dahme at dawn [7 September] and attacked the French. *Oberst* Jeanneret [Ferdinand Wilhelm von Jeanneret] was sent to the left onto the Herzberg road with most of the cavalry, while the infantry, supported by the fire of a battery attached to the formation, attacked the town and captured it after a rather bitter struggle. The entire *23e ligne* from Bertrand's corps laid down their weapons. Overall, 18 officers and between 2,500 and 2,800 lower ranks and one gun were captured. Had Wobeser managed to reach Dahme a few hours earlier, he would have found marshals Ney and Oudinot and General Bertrand with their entire staff spending the night in the town. Elements of the enemy force, departing Dahme in the greatest disorder, fled through Schönewalde [10½ miles west of Dahme] towards Annaburg. The Prussian partisans under Major Helwig [Karl Ludwig Friedrich Hellwig] and *Rittmeister* Blankenburg [Friedrich Dionys Ludwig von Blankenburg], having learned of this, set up an ambush near Holtzdorf [5½ miles north-east of Annaburg] and captured ten officers, 300 lower ranks, eight guns and several ammunition caissons. Count O'Rourke's and *Oberstleutnant* Graf Lottum's raiding detachments [Heinrich Christoph Karl Hermann von Wylich und Lottum] caught up with the Saxon force at Herzberg, where the Coalition captured a gun and took some 800 men prisoner. The enemy, wanting to put an end to the persistent pursuit, destroyed the bridges on the Schwarze Elster behind them, at Herzberg and Annaburg, but the Coalition cavalry still crossed the river and reached the bridgehead at the Torgau fortress.[45]

Enemy losses in the battle of Dennewitz and the retreat to Torgau overall ranged from 16,000 to 18,000 men, including some 13,500 taken prisoner. The victor's trophies included 60 guns (80 guns according to some sources), with 400 ammunition and cartridge caissons, and four Colours.[46] The casualties in the Prussian

---

43 Wagner, I, 87-88.
44 Plotho, II, 173.
45 Plotho, II, 173-174; Richter, I, 455-457; Beitzke, II, 325.
46 Plotho, II, 173, states that enemy losses were more than 15,000 men taken prisoner alone, 80 guns, 400 ammunition caissons, four Colours and the entire train; Richter, I, 457, gives 13,500 prisoners, 50 guns and more than 5,000 killed or wounded left on the field of battle; the Crown Prince's dispatches give the overall enemy losses as 16,000 to 18,000 men and 60 guns; Vaudoncourt, 173, gives 10,000 men and 25 guns; Marshal Ney's official report to Napoleon (as published in *Le Moniteur* on 20 September 1813) shows the overall losses as 8,000 men and 12 guns.

force overall were more than 9,000 men, namely: in Bülow's corps there were 204 officers and about 6,000 lower ranks; there were more than 100 officers and 3,000 lower ranks lost in Tauentzien's corps. In Colonel Dietrich's Russian heavy artillery companies, 24 lower ranks were killed or wounded; there is no information on losses from other units that participated at the end of the battle or pursued the enemy.[47]

The victory at Dennewitz, won by 50,000 men under Tauentzien and Bülow over 70,000 men from Ney's army, must primarily be attributed to Bülow's orders. But the Prussian hero's contemporaries treated him unjustly. Public opinion perceived the Swedish Crown Prince as the decisive factor in the victory, and in this capacity he received the highest military honours from every Coalition monarch. Emperor Alexander awarded him the Order of St. George, 1st class. The Austrian Kaiser the *Maria-Theresien-Orden*. The King of Prussia the *Gross Kreuz des eisernen Kreuzes*. General Bülow also received the *Gross Kreuz des eisernen Kreuzes*. Subsequently, but not until 1814, the King elevated him to the dignity of Graf, with the title von Dennewitz.

The Russians took part in this battle, not in significant numbers of fighting men, yet glorious in the manner of their operations. Here is Bülow's own response to Emperor Alexander regarding colonels Dietrichs and Bykhalov [Vasily Andreevich Bykhalov]:

> I am no less fortunate also to have the opportunity to bring more particularly to Your Imperial Majesty's attention the merits of two Russian officers whose valour as well as their unfailing intuition stood out in a very distinguished manner. These were Colonel Dietrichs, commander of the Russian artillery attached to my army corps, whose reasoned calm contributed effectively to the significant enemy losses through directing the fire of his artillery, and Colonel Bykhalov of the Cossacks whose courage deserves the highest praise.[48]

Unfortunately, the victory at Dennewitz gave rise to new disagreements between the Crown Prince of Sweden and Bülow. General Bülow was dissatisfied that, in the official report by the prince, although justice was given to the Prussian troops and their military commanders, Swedish and Russian generals who had not been in combat at all were mentioned along with them. The King, who had heard the rumours of displeasure arising on this occasion, decided to honour General Bülow with the following rescript:

> The Crown Prince of Sweden, fully acknowledging your courage and your military talents, nevertheless has complained that, due to your dislike for him, you do not carry out his orders with such willingness as he has a right to expect based on the relative positions existing between you and him. Because command of the Coalition Army of the North has been entrusted

---

47 The given losses for the Prussian force were extracted from official returns included in Plotho, II, appendix, XXII.
48 For the full text of Bülow's letter to the Tsar, see Appendix XXIV at the end of this chapter.

to the Prince by the Russian Emperor, the British Prince Regent and myself on the basis of the highest political considerations, you can judge for yourself that disobedience towards him may have most disastrous consequences. Therefore, I hope that, guided by your usual feelings of love for the fatherland and devotion to me and to the common cause, you will not give the prince any cause for displeasure, refrain from making unfavourable comments about him and try to maintain the much-needed consensus.[49]

Marshal Ney tried to blame the defeat he had suffered on the Saxon contingent. His report stated:

As the enemy quickly built themselves up with reinforcements, the entire *4e Corps* was committed into action. *7e Corps* kept us waiting. When at last they arrived, I ordered General Reynier to attack the enemy right wing, and at the same time General Morand renewed the assault. These operations were most successful. The enemy retreated a considerable distance. Durutte's division fought bravely. 60 guns fired canister at the enemy, who had been driven into the ravine between Gölsdorf and Wölmsdorf. *12e Corps*, which took an active part in the battle, pushed the right wing of the enemy army back onto their centre isolated from their left wing by *4e Corps*. The battle was as good as won, but at that very moment two Saxon divisions retreated and the entire *7e Corps*, by retreating, carried away part of *12e Corps*, which completely changed the course of events.[50]

General Reynier, upset by this injustice from the marshal, sent a report to Napoleon, in which he recounted all the circumstances of the battle and wrote:

Based on this truthful statement, I hope that Your Majesty will judge that *7e Corps* did everything it could and should have in this action.

In this campaign I have been in two unfortunate actions, where I suffered heavy losses because, driven by the desire to defeat the enemy and win great victories, I may have tempted the fortunes of war too much and relied too much on the support of my superiors and my neighbours.

I ask Your Majesty to be convinced of my devotion, and that I will carry out every operation with which He wishes to entrust me directly, or which might be ordered by other commanders.[51]

---

49 Förster, I, 830.
50 *Le Moniteur*, 20 September 1813.
51 'D'après cet exposé véridique, j'espère que V.M. jugera, que le 7-me corps a fait tout ce qu'il a pu et dû dans cette affaire

J'ai eu dans cette campagne deux affaires facheuses, où j'ai éprouvé de grandes pertes, parcequ' animé du désir de battre les ennemis et d'obtenir de grands succès, j'ai peut-être trop tenté la fortune des armes et trop compté sur l'appui de mes chefs et de mes voisins.

Je prie V.M. d'être persuadé de mon dévouement, et que j'exécuterai bien toutes les opérations, dont Elle voudra me charger directement, ou qui seraient bien commandées par d'autres chefs.'

Ney's report of the cowardice shown by the Saxon troops at the battle of Dennewitz set the French at odds with their allies. Several thousand Saxons captured at the battle of Dennewitz, having been invited to serve in the ranks of the defenders of Germany, for the most part now agreed to this proposal. Following this, the Saxon Major Bünau [Heinrich von Bünau] handed himself over to the Coalition with the battalion from *Infanterieregiment König* entrusted to him and accepted the mission to raise a Saxon legion from the defecting soldiers. But public opinion in Saxony still remained on the French side, and the main reason for this was the devotion of King Friedrich August to Napoleon. Wishing to cement the loyalty of his troops to the French government, on 14 (26) September, the King published an appeal in which he reminded his soldiers of their duties to their sovereign and the fatherland.[52] By remaining unchanged in his attitude towards Napoleon, King Friedrich August violated the incomparably more sacred duty of sacrificing his personal convictions for the good of his country.

---

52 Förster, I, 824-825.

Appendix XXIV

General Bülow's letter to the Tsar after the Battle of Dennewitz

General Bülow's letter to the Tsar (Archive of the M.T.D. No. 29,182, Log of Incoming Documents No. 1,381).

Sire! While I was quite fortunate to have been able to obtain a victory through the bravery of the Prussian forces of which His Majesty the King deigned to entrust me with command, I am no less fortunate also to have the opportunity to bring the merits of two Russian officers more particularly to Your Imperial Majesty's attention, whose valour as well as their unfailing intuition stood out in a very distinguished manner. These were Colonel Dietrichs, commander of the Russian artillery attached to my army corps, whose reasoned calm contributed effectively to the significant enemy losses through directing the fire of his artillery, and Colonel Bykhalov of the Cossacks whose courage deserves the highest praise. I myself was a witness to their glorious efforts at the Battle of Dennewitz and I believe it is my duty as much as it is my pleasure to be able to assure Your Imperial Majesty that they are particularly deserving of Your good grace. I dare most humbly to recommend both to Your supreme benevolence.

Sire! Si j'ai été assez heureux d'avoir pu obtenir une victoire par la bravoure des troupes prussiennes dont Sa Majesté le Roi a daigné me confier le commandement, je ne le suis pas moins d'avoir par-la l'occasion de faire connaître plus particulièrement à Vôtre Majesté Imperiale le mérite de deux officiers russes dont la valeur autant que le juste coup d'oeil se sont signalés d'une manière très distinguée. C'est le colonel de Dietrichs chef de l'artillerie russe attachée à mon corps d'armée, dont le calme raisonné a contribué efficacement aux pertes sensibles de l'ennemi par la bonee direction du feu de son artillerie, et le colonel Bichalof des cosaques dont le courage mérite les plus grands éloges. J'ai été moi-même temoin de leurs efforts glorieux à la bataille de Dennewitz et je crois de mon devoir autant que je ressens de plaisir à pouvoir assurer V.M.I. qu'ils méritent particulièrement Ses bonnes graces. J'ose recommander très-humblement l'un et l'autre à Sa haute bienveillance.

33

Napoleon's Operations against the main army and Army of Silesia from after the Battle of Kulm until the unification of French forces around Dresden

The state of affairs after the battles on the Katzbach, Kulm and Dennewitz. – Dispositions of the Army of Bohemia. – Reorganisation of Austrian formations on 22August (3 September). – Deployment of the Army of the North.

Blucher's advance from the river Queis to Görlitz. – Orders for him to go to the aid of the Army of Bohemia. – Blücher's about-turn and the measures he took for an all-out offensive; the advance towards Bautzen. – Napoleon's arrival. – Blucher's retreat beyond the Löbauer Wasser, beyond the Neisse, beyond the Queis. – Napoleon's return to the Elbe from the Neisse.

The advance of the Army of Bohemia towards Dresden and Schwarzenberg's movements on the right bank of the Elbe. – The French retreat beyond the Müglitz. Napoleon's arrival; the Coalition retreat. – Napoleon's conversation with Marshal Saint-Cyr. – His situation. — Treaties concluded by the Coalition Powers at Teplitz on 22 and 28 August (3 and 9 September).

Locations of French forces in Saxony. – Napoleon's advance towards Geiersburg. – Napoleon calls off the offensive. – The advance towards Nollendorf; Napoleon's return to Dresden. – Dispositions of French forces. – Schwarzenberg's return to the left bank of the Elbe.

Napoleon's intention to march on Blücher. – Blücher's advance from the Queis beyond the Neisse towards Herrnhut. – The reasons for his inaction. – His advance towards Bautzen and Macdonald's retreat to Stolpen.

Invasion of Saxony by the Army of Bohemia. – Coalition opinions. – Napoleon's advance along the Pirna highway. – Coalition Dispositions in order to engage the enemy in the Teplitz valley. – The action at Kulm, 5 (17) September. – Napoleon's return to Pirna. – Condition of the French forces. – Their locations. – Deployment of the Army of Bohemia.

Napoleon, having abandoned his active operations, conducts a reconnaissance in force into Lusatia. – Dispositions of the Army of Silesia and Blücher's preparations for a flanking movement towards the lower Elbe. – The situation of Macdonald's army. – The locations of the French forces on the right bank of the Elbe. – Napoleon's arrival and the advance of Macdonald's army. – Blücher's operational plans. – French forces retreat beyond the Elbe.

The advance of Bennigsen's Army of Poland across Silesia and Lusatia into Bohemia. – The composition and strength of this army. – Dispositions of the Army of the North in anticipation of crossing the Elbe.

In the three weeks that elapsed from the resumption of hostilities to the battle of Dennewitz, the state of affairs had changed completely. Although the coalition had an advantage in troop numbers and quality when the armistice lapsed, Napoleon had compensated for the lack of strength through their skilful use and proved this in practice through the victory at Dresden. But having said that, each of his armies were defeated. His forces, weakened by combat losses and many sick, had lost some 100,000 men overall, namely: the army under his direct command had lost some 40,000, and the others – 30,000 each. More than 250 guns had been lost. With the exception of Davout's corps, garrisons in the fortresses on the Elbe, and so on, there remained some 220,000 men in the active army. Coalition casualties since the resumption of hostilities had reached some 85,000 men, namely: some 45,000 in the Army of Bohemia, while in the others, they were some 20,000 men each, and some 50 guns were lost overall, yet there remained no fewer than 350,000 men, not including Wallmoden's corps or the blockading detachments: the Army of Bohemia, significantly strengthened by newly arrived Austrian troops, had some 200,000 men, while there were 75,000 men in each of the others. Consequently, the Coalition armies were one and a half times stronger than Napoleon's overall, and the arrival of General Bennigsen with 60,000 men would soon give the Coalition a double superiority in troop numbers. Moreover, the victories they had won raised their morale and were the key to future successes.[1]

Justice demands stating, however, that, with the exception of Blücher, the Coalition commanders did not take advantage of the favourable situations in which they found themselves after those battles that they had won. The main army, having

---

1 Beitzke, *Geschichte der deutschen Freiheitskriege in den Jahren 1813 und 1814*, II, 332; Bernhardi, *Denkwürdigkeiten aus dem Leben Carl Friedrich Grafen von Toll*, III, 271.

concentrated in the Teplitz valley, remained there inactive,[2] and only the force under Count Wittgenstein, on 22 August (3 September), marched on Marmont, who was standing in isolation at Altenberg, but Marmont retreated to Dippoldiswalde in good time.[3] All Prinz Schwarzenberg's attention was turned to restoring the Austrian forces to good order and bolstering them with reinforcements. The Austrian army was divided, on 22 August (3 September), as follows: two light divisions under Moritz Liechtenstein and Bubna; four corps under Colloredo, Merveldt [Maximilian von Merveldt], Ignác Gyulay and Klenau, and the reserves under the Erbprinz zu Hessen-Homburg, with an overall composition of 102 battalions, 106 squadrons and 43 batteries.[4] The leading elements of the Army of Bohemia were located on the crest of the Ore Mountains and some were on the northern slopes of the ridge.[5] Some exits from the mountains had been barricaded with palisades. Bridges had been built over the Elbe at Aussig in order to liaise with the Army of Silesia. Because the Army of Bohemia remained in an over-watch stance and only needed to act offensively in the event of Napoleon turning against the Army of Silesia or Army of the North with his main force, it was decided to send several partisan detachments across the enemy lines of communications.[6]

The Crown Prince of Sweden, after the victory at Dennewitz, as well as after the Battle of Großbeeren, remained inactive, despite the fact that Ney's army facing him was in a most pitiful condition. Napoleon had been obliged to disband Marshal Oudinot's corps, to whom he now entrusted the command of the *Jeune Garde*. Ney's other corps (*4e Corps* and *7e Corps*) were incapable of stopping the Army of the North. Nevertheless, the Crown Prince remained in Jüterbog for six days, advancing the Russian and Prussian corps to Schweinitz, Seyda and Luckau, before moving to Seyda, and eventually moved his main headquarters to Zerbst on 3 (15) September, limiting himself to monitoring the fortresses on the Elbe.

In contrast, having reached the river Queis on 19 (31) August following the swift pursuit of the enemy after the battle on the Katzbach, Blücher gave his army just one rest-day. Although the bridges on the Queis had been destroyed by French forces, nevertheless on 20 August (1 September), in anticipation of their repair, the *Brandenburgisches Ulanen* and *2. Leib-Husaren* managed to cross via a ford at Naumburg and move towards Görlitz. They were followed by a fusilier battalion and three jäger companies, which crossed the river over the piers downstream of

---

2 In Schwarzenberg's disposition for 19 (31) August, it states: 'The objective today must be to concentrate the troops as quickly as possible...' '*das Bestreben für den heutigen Tag muss auf die schleunigst mögliche Sammlung der Truppen gerichtet seyn...*'
3 War Diary signed by Barclay de Tolly, Archive of the M.T.D. No. 29,188.
4 For the composition of the Austrian army, see Appendix XXV at the end of this chapter.
5 On 23 August (4 September) the Army of Bohemia were deployed as follows: Zieten's brigade at Peterswald and Count Wittgenstein's I Corps and II Corps at Nollendorf forming the right wing with Wittgenstein's vanguard, commanded by Count P.P. Pahlen at Falkenhain, Moritz Liechtenstein's light division at Altenberg, Kleist's corps and the Russo-Prussian reserves at Teplitz; on the left wing, the Austrian forward elements were at Zinnwald, Klostergrab, Johnsdorf and Sebastiansberg, the main body of the Austrian army were at Brüx and Komotau. Plotho, II, 181-183.
6 Bernhardi, III, 274.

the town. Once the bridge was ready, at two o'clock in the afternoon precisely, the rest of the vanguard force headed towards Görlitz: Katzler's cavalry got as far as this town, while Horn's infantry reached Hohkirch [Przesieczany]. The next day, 21 August (2 September), the Army of Silesia set off from the Queis in three columns: Sacken's corps from Siegersdorf, via Hohkirch, along the main Bunzlau to Görlitz road, Yorck's corps went from Naumburg to Görlitz via Hausdorf and Katholisch Hennersdorf [Henryków Lubański, three miles east of Kieslingswalde], onto the main road from Lauban to Görlitz. Langéron's corps marched from Lauban along the main Görlitz road.[7] No sooner had the troops had chance to move off in the indicated directions, than Schwarzenberg's aide-de-camp, Prinz Wenzel Liechtenstein [Joseph Wenzel Franz Anastasius, von und zu Liechtenstein], reached Blücher in Löwenberg, with 'instructions' on the basis of which Blücher was to go to the aid of the Army of Bohemia with 50,000 men, via Theresienstadt, leaving the remaining 30,000 men, together with Neipperg's Austrian division (subsequently Graf Bubna's division), to shield Bohemia from the direction of Lusatia. Thus, following his victory, Blücher was ordered to stop pursuing a defeated enemy, to divide his army and strengthen Schwarzenberg with the majority of his troops, despite the latter (even without Blücher) still having a significant superiority in numbers over the enemy army operating against him. In Bücher's *Haupquartier* it was quite reasonably thought that he could bring incomparably more benefit to the Army of Bohemia by heading straight towards the Elbe, thus forcing Napoleon to return to Lusatia, rather than by marching to join the Army of Bohemia, through mountains via roundabout routes, which would impede his timely arrival. Moreover, the removal of the Army of Silesia would have made it difficult for the Crown Prince of Sweden to cross the Elbe and would have forced him to remain inactive. Based on these factors, Blücher decided not to comply with the orders received, which fortunately had been issued under Schwarzenberg's name. Although there was no doubt that Schwarzenberg could not issue such important orders without violating the authority of the Coalition monarchs, the matter would have taken a completely different form had Blücher received the orders directly from his Sovereign, or from Emperor Alexander, whose troops made up two-thirds of the Army of Silesia. And therefore, having outlined some of the reasons that prompted him not to execute the orders received, for the sake of decency within the *Haupquartier*, Blücher wrote that he would send elements of the Russian force to assist the Army of Bohemia as soon as Markov's corps [Yevgeny Ivanovich Markov 1st] reached him from Bennigsen's army in Breslau, and that, in any case, the advance of the Army of Silesia directly towards the Elbe would be more likely to protect the Main Army from further attacks by Napoleon than the unification of both armies in Bohemia. At the same time, in a dispatch to General Bennigsen, Blücher requested Markov's corps from him in order to strengthen the Army of Silesia and invited him, in the event of Napoleon invading Bohemia, to march with him towards the Elbe. The Crown Prince of Sweden was also asked to participate in a general offensive.[8]

---

7   Plotho, II, 258.
8   Bernhardi, III, 295-296; Beitzke, II, 229-231.

Blücher's forces continued to pursue the retreating enemy and on 23 August (4 September) forced Macdonald to retreat beyond the Spree, which prompted Poniatowski, who was stationed at Zittau, to retreat to Rumburg and on towards Schluckenau [Šluknov]. The corps under the Army of Silesia reached the Löbauer Wasser on the same day and received orders to move further, but when the vanguard under General Vasilchikov was attacked by superior forces and intelligence was extracted from prisoners regarding the arrival of Napoleon to aid Macdonald with reinforcements, Blücher broke off the offensive. During the pursuit of the enemy from the Queis to Bautzen, a partisan detachment under Colonel Prince Madatov [Valerian Grigorievich Madatov (Madatian)] launched a surprise attack on a battalion stationed in Wurschen and took 700 [sic 500] men prisoner.[9] Thereafter, at Bischofswerda, he dispersed the escort for an enemy park and blew up 100 ammunition caissons. Prussian partisans under Major Falkenhausen and *Rittmeister* Schwanenfeld [Theodor Franz Sartorius von Schwanenfeld?], also surprised an enemy detachment between Görlitz and Bautzen and captured a gun.[10]

The intelligence of Napoleon's arrival with reinforcements turned out to be reliable. Indeed, the *Empereur des Français*, having learned of Macdonald's total defeat, was determined to raise the morale of his force through a decisive offensive and push Blücher back, whose successes threatened the lines of communication between Ney (on his way to Berlin at the time) and Napoleon, who had intended to lead the main body of the French army assembled in Dresden in that direction. Napoleon, upon deciding to march on Silesia, ordered the Dresden fortifications to be strengthened. At the same time, *1er Corps* was reconstituted, which included eight battalions from Teste's division and some of the artillery from other corps. The number of troops in this corps, entrusted to General Mouton, did not exceed 12,000 men. Having left them in the vicinity of Dresden, together with Victor's *2e Corps* and Saint-Cyr's *14e Corps*, facing the Main Coalition Army, on 21 and 22 August (2 and 3 September) Napoleon sent Marmont's corps, Latour-Maubourg's cavalry and the *Garde* along the Bautzen road, numbering some 60,000 men, while he set off following them himself. On his way, he constantly encountered crowds of ragged, exhausted, unarmed soldiers. Napoleon ordered them to be rounded up and reissued with muskets brought from Dresden. Having received weapons instead of bread, they were turned back towards Bautzen. Upon arrival there, on 23 August (4 September), Napoleon went to Hochkirch to meet Macdonald, who was retreating towards the Spree. Irritated by the losses he had suffered, he showered rebukes on the formation commanders, and on General Sébastiani in particular, reminding him of all his failures in Russia, compared with the successes achieved by Latour-Maubourg and concluded his formidable diatribe with the words: 'F... doing as much as them; you command a rabble, not soldiers.'[11]

'Sire! I do not have a rabble,' Sébastiani answered: 'My force has suffered many hardships, and therefore it is impossible to demand more from them than that which they have already achieved.'

---

9 Prince Madatov's detachment consisted of the Alexandria Hussars and one Cossack regiment.
10 Plotho, II, 258-261.
11 'F... faites autant qu'eux; vous commandez de la canaille, et non pas des soldats.'

Macdonald supported him as much as he could, but Napoleon, without paying attention, treated the regimental commanders of Sébastiani's division very badly as they marched past him and continued to praise the exploits of Latour-Maubourg's cavalry.[12]

On that same day, 23 August (4 September), General Vasilchikov, with the leading elements of Sacken's corps and with the vanguard of Yorck's corps commanded by *Oberst* Katzler, left some of the Russian troops on the high ground of the Strohmberg [two miles south of Weißenberg], and six Prussian battalions, commanded by Major Hiller, in an advantageous position on the Pitschenberg [sic, Byčin, Wohlaer Berg, four miles east of Hochkirch?], and moved to Wurschen with the rest of the force, sending Katzler to Hochkirch with the Prussian light cavalry and two battalions. The enemy moved strong batteries to face this town and attacked the forces holding it with ten battalions. The Prussian troops resisted stubbornly, but finally, at about two o'clock in the afternoon, they were forced to retreat to the Pitschenberg. The corps under Sacken and Langéron, having not yet managed to cross the Löbauer Wasser, were ordered to halt, while Yorck' corps, located beyond the river, were moved back to its right bank and retreated to Schöps [1½ miles west of Reichenbach]. The enemy attacked the position on the Pitschenberg with several more battalions and 5,000 or 6,000 cavalry in four large columns at six o'clock, but Major Hiller, yielding every step at a cost in blood, retreated across the Löbauer Wasser at ten o'clock in the evening. The casualties in the Prussian rearguard that day reached some 400 men.[13]

Napoleon, having spent the night in Hochkirch, at nine o'clock in the morning on 24 August (5 September) moved his force along the roads leading to Reichenbach and Löbau along with Macdonald's corps. Poniatowski's corps and Kellermann's cavalry, which was with him at the time, were sent from Gabel towards Löbau. Vasilchikov's rearguard retreated to Reichenbach. His infantry and artillery were located outside the town on the high ground with some of the cavalry, while General Emmanuel, with the Kiev Dragoons, 2nd Ukrainian Cossacks and two squadrons of Alexandria Hussars, stopped the enemy in front of the town and being attacked by Berckheim's light cavalry division [Sigismond-Frédéric de Berckheim] supported by two cuirassier regiments, drove off the incomparably stronger enemy several times. Nevertheless, the rearguard continued the onward retreat behind the army. *Oberst* Katzler, having already passed Markersdorf [four miles west of Görlitz], received orders from General Lanskoy to turn about and attack the enemy, with the objective of making it possible for the other troops to cross the Neisse. But no sooner had *1. Westpreußisches Dragoner* managed to get back through the village, than they came across numerous French cavalry stationed behind the ravine, who engaged them with volleys from their carbines. The Prussian dragoons turned back and disordered the three squadrons of *Brandenburgisches Husaren* that were following them. The enemy cavalry attacked the dragoons and hussars crowded in disarray and completed their disorder. Katzler's other regiments were also driven back, but Major Knobloch [Sigismund Erhard Karl von Knobloch], with the other two squadrons of the *Brandenburgisches Husaren* (third and fourth), raced to engage the enemy,

---

12 Odeleben, *Relation circonstanciée de la campagne de 1813 en Saxe*, I, 170.
13 Plotho, II, 260-261; Beitzke, II, 336-338.

which made it possible for the rearguard to retreat behind the Markersdorf defile and form up in good order in front of Görlitz.[14]

The Army of Silesia crossed the Neisse river during the course of these rearguard actions on three bridges: one on trestles upstream of Görlitz, another in Görlitz, and a pontoon bridge downstream of this town. The crossing of the heavy baggage with the army was carried out in disorder and delayed the retreat of the troops, who rushed in crowds towards the bridges, while the cavalry that had reached there in the meantime increased the general chaos. But old Blücher, at the upper bridge and aware of the danger threatening the army, raced to cross the river on horseback via a ford and, knee-deep in water, with a loud shout of 'follow me!' (*mir nach!*) drew some of the cavalry along with him, and thereby made it easier for the other troops to cross the bridges. Latour-Maubourg's cavalry reached the river and the upper bridge and the town in a huge column formed from regiments in line, commanded by Murat himself. But by this time Blücher's entire army had already retreated, and only one cavalry regiment stood on the right bank of the Neisse. The French cavalry, approaching the left bank, stopped at a distance of about half a *verst* from the Prussian regiment. Murat ordered two horse artillery batteries to open fire on them, but no sooner had they fired a few rounds, than the Prussian cavalry wheeled away to both sides and unmasked the numerous Coalition artillery stationed to the rear. The unexpected cannonade from this battery, composed of heavy guns, had a disastrous effect. Not a single shot aimed at the deep mass of French cavalry was wasted, and by the time they had managed to turn about, some 150 men had already fallen and even more horses, and two guns had been knocked out. Murat hastily withdrew his cavalry, while his infantry moved into Görlitz.[15]

The Army of Silesia, continuing to retreat, withdrew beyond the Queis on the night of 24 to 25 August (5 to 6 September) and the following day. The *Hauptquartier* was in Lauban, Sacken's corps was at Siegersdorf, Yorck was at Naumburg, Langéron was at Lauban. The detachment under the comte de Saint-Priest retreated to Seidenberg [Zawidów] and then towards Lauban. The forward elements halted: Vasilchikov at Hohkirch, while Katzler was at Gruna [Gronów, 1½ miles south of Hohkirch].[16] Yorck and his staff were dissatisfied with the non-stop retreat, and especially with the night marches, which were very exhausting for the troops, who had no essential supplies with them and considered themselves lucky to find a few potatoes somewhere. Yet Napoleon himself assessed his adversary's operations otherwise and, having no chance of inducing Blücher to give general battle, said: 'these animals have learned something.'[17]

The enemy, having reached the river Neisse, halted, from which it might easily be concluded that Napoleon would turn in another direction. In any case, Blücher, who was striving to stay in contact with the French army, would have immediately gone on the offensive, but this turned out to be impossible because Langéron, just as he had

---

14 Droysen, *Das Leben des Feldmarschalls Grafen Yorck von Wartenburg*, III, 80-81; Beitzke, II, 338-340.
15 Droysen, III, 82; Beitzke, II, 341; Bernhardi, III, 299.
16 Plotho, II, 262-263; Beitzke, II, 341-342; Bernhardi, III, 298.
17 '*ces animaux ont appris quelque chose.*' Droysen, III, 82.

before the battle of Katzbach, sent most of the artillery far to the rear. Blücher expressed his displeasure to Langéron and asked him from now on to carry out the dispositions received from the *Hauptquartier* exactly,[18] but was forced to give the army a day's rest on 26 August (7 September) and the very next day he moved towards the Neisse.[19]

Napoleon, having perceived Blücher's intentions somewhat late – to draw him as far from Dresden as possible – and having received a report from Saint-Cyr regarding an offensive by the Army of Bohemia, decided to return to the Elbe with the corps under Marmont, Latour-Maubourg, Kellermann and the *Garde* coming up from Saxony, leaving Macdonald to face the Army of Silesia, as before, with *3e Corps, 5e Corps, 11e Corps* and Sébastiani's cavalry, and reinforcing them with Poniatowski's *8e Corps*, numbering some 70,000 men.[20]

While Napoleon was operating against Blücher, the headquarters of the Army of Bohemia initially believed that he had turned against the Crown Prince of Sweden, and therefore, on the basis of the general plan drawn up at Trachenberg, they decided to make convincing feints (*ernstliche Demonstrationen*) towards Dresden: to that end, on 24 August (5 September), Barclay de Tolly's reserves advanced from Teplitz to Nollendorf; elements of Count Wittgenstein's force (Prince Gorchakov's I Corps) and Zieten's Prussian brigade moved from Nollendorf to Peterswald; Zieten's forward detachment, after a rather heated clash with Mouton's force, captured Hellendorf; Prinz Eugen von Württemberg seized the high ground near the village of Oelsen with II Corps and forced the enemy to retreat to Borna; the detachment under Lieutenant General Count Pahlen [Pëtr Petrovich Palen or Peter Johann Christoph von der Pahlen] was at Falkenhain; Major General Kaisarov's detachment[21] maintained communications between the leading units under Count Palen and Zieten's vanguard.[22] Kleist's Prussian corps remained at Teplitz until 26 August (7 September), and then advanced to Altenberg.[23]

Overall, all intelligence on the enemy received at Schwarzenberg's headquarters was untimely, and therefore Coalition orders were incompatible with the situation. Intelligence on Napoleon's move towards Bautzen with the *Garde* arrived in Teplitz on 24 August (5 September), the day before the French army reserves marched back to Dresden from Reichenbach. The Commander-in-Chief had immediately decided to move up the right bank of the Elbe, into Lusatia, with most of the Austrian army, numbering some 60,000 men. This force was ordered to march in two columns: the left from Aussig to Böhmisch

---

18 Droysen, III, 83; *Militair Wochenblatt, 1844, Beiheft*, 229.
19 Plotho, II, 263.
20 Vaudoncourt, *Histoire de la guerre soutenue par les Français en Allemagne*, 177; Norvins, *Portefeuille de 1813*, II, 345.
21 Kaisarov's detachment consisted of: the Kaluga Infantry, Her Highness Grand Duchess Yekaterin Pavlovna's Battalion, the Austrian *Infanterieregiment Fröhlich*, a squadron each of Sumy Hussars and Tatar Ulans and 30 Cossacks. Plotho, II, 180.
22 War Diary signed by Barclay de Tolly (Archive of the M.T.D. No. 29,188); Plotho, II, 185; Bernhardi, III, 302.
23 'I have the honour to inform You Excellency that the King of Prussia has just written to the Sovereign Emperor to explain that your orders to General Kleist to set off were received very late, and therefore he cannot set off from here before dawn.' Adjutant General Prince Volkonsky's dispatch to General Barclay de Tolly, dated 26 August [7 September]. Log of Outgoing Documents, No. 32 (Archive of the M.T.D. No. 29,190).

Kamnitz [Česká Kamenice] and on towards Rumburg, consisting of the corps under Colloredo, Merveldt and Gyulay; while the right went from Leitmeritz [Litoměřice] to Böhmisch Leipa [Česká Lípa] and on towards Gabel, consisting of Erbprinz zu Hessen-Homburg's Aurstrian reserves, under Prinz Schwarzenberg's personal command. Both columns were supposed to cross the border into Lusatia on 30 August (11 September).[24] Schwarzenberg's orders were fundamentally flawed: having weakened the Army of Bohemia of a whole third of its strength, he directed them along awkward mountain roads, and in the event of Blücher retreating into Silesia, he was in danger of encountering Napoleon's main force holding a central position between the Army of Silesia and his force, which could defeat them in detail in Lusatia.

At the same time as Schwarzenberg's advance on the right bank of the Elbe, Count Wittgenstein's force advanced towards Dresden from Peterswald, and Kleist's force from Altenberg. Kaisarov's detachment were assigned to secure the lines of communication between Kleist's force and the Austrians. Moritz Liechtenstein's *1. leichte Division*, having been relieved by units from Kleist's corps, were located at Seyde. Klenau's corps, at the tip of the left wing of the army, headed from Sebastiansberg [Hora Svatého Šebestiána, four miles south of Reitzenhain] to Marienberg and on towards Freiberg, opposing Victor's *2e Corps* stationed there (the other French corps were stationed as follows: elements of Saint-Cyr's *14e Corps* were forwards of Pirna and around Borna, or on the right bank of the Elbe at Lilienstein, while *1er Corps* were in Dresden). The Coalition forced the enemy to retreat at all points and on 27 August (8 September), pushed them back beyond the river Müglitz. Zieten's vanguard headed to the village of Heidenau [two miles north of Dohna], while Lieutenant General Pahlen, marched to Dohna with the Jäger regiments commanded by Vlastov and the cavalry from Count Wittgenstein's force, supported by 2nd Grenadier Division. But Napoleon, arriving with the reserves himself, counter-attacked the Coalition at Dohna and Heidenau on the same day, at about two o'clock in the afternoon, and forced them to retreat towards Pirna and Zehista, with the loss of some 1,000 men, mostly from Zieten's force. The enemy losses were even more significant. Two squadrons of *14e hussards* were completely wiped out by the Grodno Hussars.

Napoleon returned to Dohna in the evening, where his *quartier général* was located. The French *Garde* were positioned forwards of this location, parts of which had burned down during the fighting. Napoleon, having invited Murat and Saint-Cyr to dine with him, spoke with them for a long time, but did not say a word about future operations. At the same time, the son of General Arrighi [*sic*, Anne-Charles Lebrun] arrived from Ney's force with a detailed report on the battle of Dennewitz. Napoleon, asking him about all the circumstances of this event, with unshakable composure explained the reasons for the failure as clearly as they were correct, but did not express displeasure – neither against Ney, nor against any of his colleagues, attributed the blame solely to the complexities of the art of war, which, according to him, had never been properly explained. He continued: 'If one day I had the time, I would write a book in which I would demonstrate the principles in such a precise manner that they would be within the reach of every soldier, and we would learn war as we might learn

---

24 Bernhardi, III, 302.

any science.' When it came to the art of war acquired through experience, Napoleon admitted that no one had been able to significantly improve their innate abilities through their own experiences with the exception of 'Turenne' [Henri de La Tour d'Auvergne], whose great talents were the fruit of the most profound study, and who had come closest to the goal that he proposed to demonstrate in his work. Upon dismissing Saint-Cyr, Napoleon said that he would arrive at the camp at dawn and, depending on the circumstances, issue orders as necessary.[25]

Such was the capacity of this extraordinary man for self-control, displayed by him during one of the most difficult periods of the campaign, when every benefit of the victory at Dresden had been negated by the mistakes of his subordinates. Napoleon was already aware at that time of the vulnerability of his position and foresaw the need to strengthen the fortresses on the Rhine in case of a defensive war, but concerned about raising doubts about his invincibility, he ordered the duc de Bassano (Maret) to write to the Minister of War, as if from himself, an enciphered dispatch about bringing the fortresses into good condition and about supplying them with artillery as well as both military and essential supplies.[26]

Napoleon's situation was, indeed, precarious. The Austrian government, having earlier been prepared to abandon the coalition after the Battle of Dresden, now sealed the alliance with Russia and Prussia with a treaty signed in Teplitz on 22 August (3 September). Six days later, on 28 August (9 September), other treaties were concluded at Teplitz, on the basis of which the Coalition Powers, Russia, Prussia and Austria, mutually guaranteed the inviolability of their territories, in all their former extent, and pledged to assist each other 60,000 men. The much more important secret terms and conditions of these treaties were as follows:

1. The Austrian monarchy would be restored to the extent to which it existed before the unfortunate campaign of 1805, while the Prussian monarchy would be restored to the same extent as existed before the campaign of 1806.
2. The *Confédération du Rhin* would be dissolved and all territories lying between France and the Coalition Powers would become independent.
3. The House of Braunschweig-Lüneburg would receive the territories taken from them.
4. The Coalition Powers grant themselves the right to decide, by common consent, the future fate of the Duchy of Warsaw.

In addition, the terms of the treaties previously concluded at Trachenberg were confirmed and each of the Coalition Powers was obligated to field at least 150,000 men for operations.[27]

---

25 Saint-Cyr, *Mémoires, Campagne de 1813 en Saxe*, 148-150.
26 Thiers, *Histoire du Consulat et de l'Empire*, XVI, *Edit de Brux*, 491-494.
27 *Mémoires tirés des papiers d'un homme d'état*, XII, 230-231. The treaties were concluded in Teplitz, on 9 September new style between: Austria and Prussia, by Graf Metternich and Baron Hardenberg; Russia and Austria by Count Nesselrode and Metternich; Russia and Prussia, by Count Nesselrode and Baron Hardenberg.

Let us return to the description of military operations.

On the morning of 28 August (9 September), the day after Napoleon had arrived with the reserves to assist Saint-Cyr, The French troops stationed in Saxony were deployed as follows: Mouton's *1er Corps* were on the Teplitz highway opposite Pirna; Saint-Cyr's *14e Corps* were on the old Teplitz road forwards of Dohna; three divisions of the *Jeune Garde*, commanded by Marshal Mortier, and Lefebvre-Desnouettes' *Garde* light cavalry were in reserve at Mügeln. In total, these units possibly numbered from 55,000 to 60,000 men. Victor's *2e Corps* were stationed a short march from the main body, on the road from Altenberg to Dresden. The remaining division of the *Jeune Garde*, the *Vieille Garde* and Latour-Maubourg's cavalry were located in Dresden, while Marmont's *6e Corps*, having been directed towards Hoyerswerda, in order to co-operate with Ney during Napoleon's advance from Lusatia into Saxony with the reserves, had received subsequent orders to move towards Dresden, had left Hoyerswerda in the direction of Ottendorf [near Okrilla].[28]

Upon reaching Saint-Cyr's force and noticing that the Coalition intended to retreat, Napoleon did not want to exhaust his army in a needless pursuit and planned to return to Dresden. But Saint-Cyr suggested that he move quickly along the shortest route through Dohna, Fürstenwalde and Geiersburg, in order to forestall the Coalition in Bohemia, whose main force, according to intelligence just received in the *quartier général* of the French army, were on the Teplitz highway in several echelons. According to Saint-Cyr, the French army, having passed Geiersburg, could turn to the left towards Peterswald and force the Coalition to give battle before the return of Schwarzenberg's force from the right bank of the Elbe and before the arrival of Bennigsen's army in Bohemia. Napoleon, having approved the marshal's proposal, ordered him to march along the old Teplitz road with *14e Corps*, followed by the reserves. The next day, 29 August (10 September), Saint-Cyr's corps deployed somewhat below the mountain ridge, near Ebersdorf [Habartice], while their leading elements had reached Ober-Graupen and descended towards Mariaschein [Bohosudov], no more than five *versts* from Teplitz. Mouton's *1er Corps* had reached Hellendorf; Victor's *2e Corps* were located in the vicinity of Altenberg; the *Jeune Garde* at Liebstadt. Throughout the advance by Saint-Cyr's column, Coalition troops were visible, hastily leaving along the highway parallel to the French line of march. Having guessed Napoleon's intent, Barclay accelerated the retreat by his army. The reserves had arrived in Kulm the day before [9 September]. Wittgenstein's corps also retreated along the highway to Kulm, while Kleist's withdrew from Altenberg to Zinnwald. Klenau's corps were ordered to retreat to Johnsdorf, along the road to Brüx. Only two Prussian lancer regiments and two more of Cossacks remained on the high ground at Nollendorf. The defence of the foothills at Geiersburg was entrusted to General Raevsky with the grenadier corps. The rest of the Coalition troops, under the personal command of Barclay de Tolly, were formed up in two echelons as they arrived at Sobochleben, between Kulm and Teplitz. Having reached the border Bohemian village of Ebersdorf with his entire suite, Napoleon observed the Coalition army before him in the deep valley. Behind

---

28 Marmont, *Mémoires*, V, 155; Thiers, XVI, 494-495.

them, on the edge of the distant horizon, rose the Böhmische Mittelgebirge [České středohoří]. In order to attack the force facing the French, Napoleon had to descend about 2,000 feet along the abruptly steep and densely forested slopes of the ridge. Despite the terrain obstacles, which seemed insurmountable, the deft French *voltigeurs* descended into the valley and began a firefight with the Russian grenadiers. But since the enemy had failed to drag a single gun over the crest, their infantry, lashed by canister and attacked by superior numbers, were driven back into the defile. Napoleon, wanting to ensure that it was possible to debouch at this point, ordered General Drouot [Antoine Drouot] to survey the ground right to the bottom of the descent. It turned out that it was impossible for a significant force to invade Bohemia from here. The French troops were ordered to bivouac on the crest of the ridge, which had the appearance of a wilderness. The failure of the planned invasion was an embarrassment to Napoleon. In addition, he had received at this point detailed information regarding Ney's defeat at Dennewitz. Perhaps this factor interfered with Napoleon's usual determination to act, despite the fact that (according to Saint-Cyr) French sappers, with the help of infantry soldiers, could soon have improved the road. Calling the marshal to him, he said:

> I do not want to attack the enemy in this position; I am going to withdraw, but let everyone believe that my intention is still to give battle; do not change anything in your disposition; continue to have the mountain path repaired today and tomorrow in order to further maintain the enemy and my troops in this deception. I shall support you, if you are attacked.[29]

Whereupon Napoleon left for Breitenau, spent the night there and the next day, 30 August (11 September), having reached Hellendorf along a very bad country lane, he ordered *1er Corps* located near this village to march on Nollendorf. The Coalition cavalry stationed there were driven off. Mouton's force, supported by the *Jeune Garde*, occupied Nollendorf almost without resistance and began a rather heated firefight with the infantry under Count Shakhovskoy, who were defending the abatis at Tellnitz. At dusk, Napoleon, seeing the danger of a further advance into Bohemia, ordered Mouton, like Saint-Cyr before, to remain in a threatening stance, while he returned to Dresden himself the next day, 31 August (12 September).[30] The *Jeune Garde* deployed at Cotta. Mouton's corps were in echelons on the highway, at Nollendorf, Peterswald and Berggießhübel. Saint-Cyr's corps were at Fürstenwalde and Borna. Victor's corps were at Rechenberg and Seyde, while Marmont's corps moved to Großenhain on 1 (13) September and came under Murat's command, together with the strong cavalry corps located there. This force was escorting 20,000

---

29 *'Je ne veux point attaquer l'ennemi dans cette position; je vais me retirer, mais laissez croire à tout le monde que mon intention est toujours de livrer bataille; ne changez rien à vos dispositions; continuez, aujourd'huis et demain, à faire réparer le chemin de la montagne, pour entretenir davantage l'ennemi et mes troupes dans cette persuation. Je vous soutiendrai, si vous êtes attaqué.'*
30 War Diary signed by Barclay de Tolly; Saint-Cyr, *Mémoires*, 151-158; Bernhardi, III, 313-318; Thiers, XVI, 495-500.

hundredweight (around 7,000 *Chetvert* [one *Chetvert* equals 5.772 Imperial Bushels)] of flour being rafted up the Elbe from Torgau to Dresden.[31]

On 31 August (12 September), the Austrian corps sent to the right bank of the Elbe returned to the Kulm area. A thanksgiving service was performed in the camp of the Coalition army on the occasion of the news of the Dennewitz victory received at this time, after which a triple gunfire salute by all the infantry and artillery was sounded in the nearby towns within sight of the enemy forward outposts still on the ridge at Geiersburg.[32]

Thus, Napoleon's offensive, launched with insufficient forces, was unsuccessful. There is no doubt that had he managed to get at least some of the army through the mountain range on 29 August (10 September), or at least on the morning of 30 August (11 September), before the Austrian force, sent to the right bank of the Elbe could rejoin the Russo-Prussian army, then the cautious Barclay de Tolly would have retreated into Bohemia.[33] But this would not have improved Napoleon's position in the least, indeed, on the contrary, the deeper he went into this country, the greater would be the vulnerability of his lines of communication with Saxony, which served as his base of operations.

Napoleon fully appreciated the difficulty of invading Bohemia, in view of the Coalition army being twice as strong and, in the event of failure, he would have had to retreat by scrambling up the steep slopes at Geiersburg. He preferred to wait for the Army of Bohemia to cross the mountains again and, in the meantime, would turn to Lusatia, where his arrival with reinforcements was needed.

As has already been mentioned, as soon as the enemy force pursuing the Army of Silesia halted upon reaching the river Neisse, Blücher decided to go on the offensive once more. Reliable intelligence of Napoleon's departure was extracted from one of the officers from his *quartier général*, captured by Figner between Reichenbach and Bautzen. General Blücher, intending to fix Macdonald frontally, envelope him on his left flank using Langéron's and Yorck's corps and sever his line of retreat with the assistance of Bubna's division, sent Langéron's corps from Lauban towards Ostritz on 27 August (8 September), ordering him to close up to the Neisse as covertly as possible. The detachment under the comte de Saint-Priest was intended to move to the left via a roundabout route, get to Bernstadt behind enemy lines, and form the vanguard of Langéron's force. Yorck's corps, preceded by Katzler's vanguard, was also ordered to close up to Radmeritz [Radomierzyce] covertly, while Sacken's corps was directed towards Görlitz. But Blücher's plan failed and the Prussian commander blamed Langéron for prematurely revealing his force to the enemy, and Saint-Priest for not arriving at Bernstadt. Irritated by comte Langéron's disobedience, Blücher complained to King Friedrich Wilhelm, but the matter remained without further consequences.[34]

---

31 Plotho, II, 198; Marmont, V, 161.
32 Plotho, II, 198.
33 Barclay de Tolly's report to Emperor Alexander, dated 10 September, new style; Bernhardi, III, 317.
34 Droysen, III, 83-88; Richter, *Geschichte des Deutschen Freiheitskrieges vom Jahre 1813 bis zum Jahre 1815*, II, 130; Beitzke, 344-345.

On the following day, 28 August (9 September), the Commander-in-Chief, based on the operational plan he had drawn up, ordered the following: Saint-Priest was to march towards Löbau, Langéron towards Reichenbach and Yorck towards the Landeskrone; Sacken's corps was to remain in Görlitz. But Macdonald avoided the danger threatening him by quickly retreating to the river Spree. Poniatowski's corps, which had been left as a rearguard at Löbau, upon being attacked by the comte de Saint-Priest, fought stubbornly and, having received some of Lauriston's force as reinforcements, took up an offensive stance, which gave him the opportunity to delay Saint-Priest's vanguard supported by Kaptsevich's corps from noon until four o'clock, and shield the retreat by Macdonald's main body. The casualties on each side reached 500 men. On 29 August (10 September), Macdonald retreated to the high ground in front of Bautzen. Blücher, having no chance of isolating the enemy, pursued them with his forward detachments alone, and gave the remainder of the force a rest day. Blücher's *Hauptquartier* was in Herrnhut. His partisans raced off behind French lines and reached the Elbe.[35] Meanwhile, after the headquarters of the Coalition Sovereigns, had decided to move the Army of Silesia to Bohemia, Blücher would remain inactive in anticipation of the cancellation of this order. Nevertheless, Macdonald, concerned that he might be cut off from the Elbe, on 31 August (12 September) retreated to Stolpen, where he deployed one stage from Dresden. Three days later, on 3 (15) September, Blücher moved Sacken's corps towards Kamenz, and Yorck's and Langéron's corps to Bautzen, where the army *Hauptquartier* was also moved. Katzler's vanguard was located near Stolpen, while Graf Bubna's division was located facing Lilienstein, beyond the river Sebnitz.[36]

During the course of these operations, the Amy of Bohemia invaded Saxony once more.

The Coalition, having learned from their surveillance that Napoleon had abandoned his operations in Bohemia, launched an offensive once more with the aim of taking advantage of the dislocation of the enemy corps at the northern foot of the Ore Mountains from the Pirna highway to the Freiberg to Dresden road. On 1 (13) September, Lieutenant General Count Pahlen moved to the high ground at Nollendorf with the majority of Count Wittgenstein's force in three columns: the right hand column, under Count Pahlen's direct command, was directed towards Königswald [Libouchec] and consisted of nine [sic, 12] battalions and 12 squadrons; the centre column, under Prinz Eugen von Württemberg, headed towards Zuckmantel [Žďárek] and consisted of seven battalions, two squadrons and 12 guns; the left hand column, under Major General Rüdiger, headed for Hinter-Tellnitz and consisted of two battalions, four squadrons and one Cossack regiment.[37] Count Wittgenstein

---

35 Beitzke, II, 346-348.
36 Vaudoncourt, 177-178; Beitzke, II, 358.
37 Lieutenant General Count Pahlen's detachment consisted of: right column – four battalions from 4th Division, eight battalions from 14th Division and 12 squadrons from Pahlen's vanguard; centre column – seven battalions from 3rd Division and 4th Division, two squadrons of Lubny Hussars and 12 guns; left column – two battalions from 5th Division, the Grodno Hussars and one Cossack regiment; for a total of 21 weak battalions and 18 squadrons with 12 guns. Prinz Eugen von Württemberg's diary (Archive of the M.T.D. No. 47,344); Bernhardi, III, 330.

located forwards of Kulm with the remaining battalions from 5th Division of Prince Gorchakov's I Corps with Graf Colloredo's Austrian division, were to support Pahlen, while Prinz August's Prussian brigade were assigned to assist them from Ebersdorf, from the direction of Geiersburg.[38] On the following day, 2 (14) September, Prinz Eugen von Württemberg, moving towards Kninitz [Knínice], attacked Dumonceau's division from Mouton's corps, stationed at Nollendorf, with all the skirmishers from his column, commanded by Colonel Reibnitz [Karl Pavlovich Reibnitz], supported by the Tobolsk Infantry, followed by General Pyshnitsky with the Kremenchug Infantry and Volhynia Infantry and with a battalion from the Minsk Infantry. The enemy force, having not yet had chance to recover from the defeat they had suffered at Kulm, fled, but were caught beyond Peterswald by the Sumy Hussars and Lubny Hussars and were scattered in total disarray. One of the battalions of the *33e ligne*, cut off by the hussars and under attack from Reibnitz's marksmen, laid down their arms. The Prinz von Württemberg intended to outflank the enemy who had taken up positions at Berggießhübel, but having learned about a significant French force at Breitenau, he was forced to halt at Oelsen, where the forces under Prince Shakhovskoy and Rüdiger joined him. Count Pahlen's column, having passed through Hellendorf, positioned themselves facing the enemy [Berggießhübel] position frontally. The force under Prince Gorchakov was at Hellendorf, while Prinz August's Prussian brigade faced the enemy holding Breitenau. General Kaisarov's small detachment was sent to monitor Königstein. On this day [14 September], more than 700 men were taken prisoner by Russian troops.[39]

Count Pahlen's advance was the beginning of the Coalition's large scale offensive. At a conference on 1 (13) September, it was decided that Prinz Schwarzenberg would move through Marienberg and into Saxony with the entire Austrian force. Barclay received orders to support the Austrian offensive by moving to Brüx with the Russo-Prussian reserves. Wittgenstein was instructed to position himself at Dux and guard the roads leading to Johnsdorf and Zinnwald, while Kleist was tasked with occupying the high ground at Nollendorf, monitoring access along the highway and through Geiersburg towards Zinnwald. The Army of Bohemia was supposed to remain in these positions until relieved by troops expected from Silesia, and was then to launch a general offensive into Saxony.[40] In the event of Napoleon's entry into Bohemia before the arrival of Coalition reinforcements from Silesia, it was planned to direct Kleist's force towards Aussig, while Wittgenstein's and Barclay's went towards Bilin [Bílina], across the river Biela [Bílina], and were also to hold in the defiles leading through the Böhmische Mittelgebirge while Schwarzenberg's force would retreat along the road from Marienberg back to Bohemia. But before the proposed moves could be carried out, intelligence was received that Napoleon was advancing with reserves to assist the corps facing the Coalition army.[41]

---

38 Bernhardi, III, 330.
39 Prinz Eugen von Württemberg's diary; War Diary signed by Barclay de Tolly.
40 It was to that end that Blücher's Army of Silesia had initially been ordered to go to Teplitz in Bohemia and then, after the cancellation of these orders, Bennigsen's army, which had arrived in Breslau from the Duchy of Warsaw on 27 August (8 September).
41 Bernhardi, III, 330-332.

Indeed, having learned of the Coalition crossing of the Bohemian border, Napoleon arrived at Langenhennersdorf on 3 (15) September, with two divisions of the *Jeune Garde*, and headed towards Markersbach, directly against Kaisarov's detachment and outflanking Pahlen, stationed forwards of Hellendorf. His other formations were: the remaining two divisions of the *Jeune Garde*, the *Vieille Garde* and Latour-Maubourg's cavalry, gradually moving along the highway in several echelons in support of Mouton; Saint-Cyr's corps moving towards Geiersburg; while Victor's corps were even further to their right. The Russian forces, attacked along the highway by superior numbers, had retreated to Hellendorf by three o'clock in the afternoon. Count Pahlen's vanguard checked the enemy here with support from Mezentsov's 5th Division and Prinz August's Prussian *12. Brigade*, which had arrived from Ebersdorf via Schönwald. The French, disordered by the fire of a Prussian battery defending a defile on the highway and attacked by Russian cavalry, turned back, while the enemy light infantry which had attempted to envelope the Hellendorf position on its left flank, were attacked by the Sumy Hussars and Chuguev Uhlans and were driven off with the loss of 400 men taken prisoner. The Prinz von Württemberg contributed to halting the enemy with a show of force by 3rd Division along the Oelsen road.[42]

On 4 (16) September, based on the general dispositions, it was necessary for Kleist's corps, with the exception of Klüx's brigade which was blocking the passes via Geiersburg, to concentrate on the right flank and relieve Wittgenstein's force defending the Teplitz highway. While waiting for the Prussian brigades to assemble, Count Pahlen's vanguard and Mezentsov's division remained on the highway. As the enemy had revealed significant strength at Hellendorf, the Coalition forces retreated to Peterswald. Pahlen's cavalry were placed forwards of this village. Behind them, resting their right flank on the village, was Prinz August's brigade. To the right of Peterswald were *1. Schlesisches Husaren* under *Oberstleutnant* Blücher (son of the Commander-in-Chief of the Army of Silesia). Mezentsov's division was behind the village.

Napoleon, having managed to assemble his reserves and concentrate some 50,000 men near the highway, deployed significant forces against the Coalition position. General Kleist retreated along the highway under the protection of Pahlen's cavalry and, having reached the forest between Peterswald and Nollendorf, he relieved the Russian force: thus, pending the concentration of his corps, he had only one brigade with a few squadrons. At this precise moment as the Prussian and Russian formations were moving towards each other, the Nollendorf defile to Kleist's rear was congested with artillery and carts. Taking advantage of this, Polish lancers rushed the *Schlesisches Husaren* and scattered them, where the valiant regimental commander, Blücher, the son of the Commander-in-Chief of the Army of Silesia, was seriously wounded and captured. Upon being introduced to Napoleon, Blücher was asked: 'Does your King have many troops?'

He answered: 'My Sovereign has as many soldiers as there are loyal subjects.'[43]

---

42 War Diary signed by Barclay de Tolly; Plotho, II, 205-206; In the work by General Helldorff (*Aus dem Leben des Prinzen Eugen von Württemberg,* 62) it states that Prinz Eugen's show of force took place on 4 (16) September.
43 Plotho, II, 206; Richter, II, 107.

The arrival of the Prussian brigades under Zieten and Pirch enabled Kleist to retreat to Kulm without further loss. General Zieten, positioning himself at Nollendorf as the rearguard with his brigade and with the Sumy Hussars and Chuguev Uhlans, covered the retreat of the corps on the morning of 5 (17) September, and then followed him to Kulm, leaving one fusilier battalion for the defence of the Tellnitz abatis and another battalion with two companies of skirmishers in the village of Tellnitz. The defence of Kulm was entrusted to II Corps under Prinz Eugen von Württemberg with Zieten's brigade. Behind them were the rest of Count Wittgenstein's and Kleist's forces. Barclay's reserves were stationed at Sobochleben. The Austrian forces were positioned as follows: Graf Merveldt's *II. Korpus* were to the north of Aussig, having garrisoned this town with Longueville's mixed brigade. Graf Colloredo's *I. Korpus* were on the high ground at Strisowitz. Prinz Hessen-Homberg's reserves were to the right of Karbitz on the Bihana Höhe [Na Běhání, one mile south of Herbitz]. Graf Gyulay's *III. Korpus* formed the general reserve at Dux. Overall, the entire Army of Bohemia was concentrated in the vicinity of Kulm, except for Klenau's corps stationed at Marienberg, and Count Bubna's division on the right bank of the Elbe. The strength of the Coalition force overall reached some 160,000 men.[44]

On the morning of 5 (17) September, Napoleon surveyed the ground and the Coalition positions from a rise near the Nollendorf chapel, but thick fog, as on the previous day, prevented him from seeing anything, even at close range. Despite all this, however, at around noon, the enemy launched an attack with troops from Mouton's corps, supported by the *Garde*. Zieten's leading units defended the Tellnitz abatis for more than three hours, then conducted a fighting retreat to Kulm where they were supported by the corps under Wittgenstein and Kleist. II Corps manned the Kulm perimeter, while Zieten's brigade was located to the left of the village in the forest with the Volhynia Infantry and Kremenchug Infantry. The enemy, on their part, were steadily growing stronger. The cannonade sounded louder and louder. The French, having widened the frontage of their attack, seized Arbesau, Tillisch [Dělouš] and Johnsdorf [Habrovice, one mile west of Troschig], but were held frontally by Russo-Prussian troops, while Colloredo's corps descended from the high ground at Strisowitz towards Arbesau, on the enemy's flank. The Austrian horse artillery, having silenced the nearest French batteries, opened fire on the troops advancing towards Kulm. General Nansouty boldly charged at the Austrian battery with the *cavalerie de la Garde* and captured several guns, but at that very moment they were counterattacked by Röder's Prussian cavalry and several squadrons of *Hessen-Homburg Husaren*, which forced them to abandon the captured guns and retreat behind the infantry stationed nearby. Graf Colloredo, exploiting the success of the Coalition cavalry, moved towards Arbesau and captured this village, where the Austrians took an Eagle and three guns. Pahlen's cavalry assisted the Austrian force. Zieten's brigade and II Corps also attacked the enemy. The marksmen from the fusilier battalion of *1. Schlesisches Infanterie* captured General Creutzer, several officers and around 200 lower ranks. The disordered enemy were pursued beyond the Tellnitz abatis,

---

44 Prinz Eugen von Württemberg's diary; Plotho, II, 208-209; Beitzke, II, 382-383; Helldorff, 63.

but heavy rain forced the Coalition to halt and facilitated the French retreat. The loss to Napoleon's force taken prisoner reached some 1,000 men.[45]

General Creutzer and all the other prisoners unanimously claimed that their force constituted only the vanguard of the French army, and that Napoleon intended to give battle again. Based on this intelligence, the Coalition spent the entire next day [18 September] awaiting the advance of Napoleon's forces. Emperor Alexander, the King of Prussia and Schwarzenberg were constantly on horseback, but the entire action was limited to a few skirmishes between the forward outposts, on the highway at Tellnitz, and on the Geiersburg at Graupen. Napoleon knew that his forces were insufficient for a decisive invasion of Bohemia, and was unwilling to move away from Dresden, because Blücher was just two marches away from this city with the main body of his army, while the Crown Prince of Sweden could not be held by the completely demoralised force under Marshal Ney. Having surveyed the Coalition positions with the help of a telescope from the high ground at Kninitz, Napoleon said to his closest associate Berthier: 'all I can see consists of two corps, with a strength of about 60,000 men. They will need more than a day to concentrate and attack us.' These words were spoken with such indifference, as if the Coalition army was not worth the effort of continuing the offensive. Later, at four o'clock in the afternoon, he went to Pirna, ordering the reserves and *2e Corps* to go there. The other French corps, Mouton's and Saint-Cyr's, retreated to Nollendorf and Fürstenwalde that night.[46]

Forced marches, a lack of essential supplies, inclement weather and – most of all – the constant failures had a very unfavourable effect on the morale and discipline of the French army.[47] But the Coalition troops, especially the corps under Wittgenstein and Kleist, exhausted from ceaseless marches along awkward mountain roads in rainy weather and also suffering from a lack of food, since the battle of Kulm had lost many more men to the influence of these unfavourable circumstances rather than in combat with the enemy, and had a vital need for a rest. The cavalry were forced to send out daily foraging parties four *Meilen* or more (some 30 *versts*). All this forced the Commander-in-Chief, with the consent of the Coalition monarchs,

---

45 Prinz Eugen von Württemberg's diary; Plotho, II, 209-210; Beitzke, II, 383-385; Helldorff, 62-63; Vaudoncourt, 179; Norvins, II, 350-351.
46 Plotho, II, 212-214; Beitzke, II, 386.
47 Odeleben, *Relation circonstanciée de la campagne de 1813 en Saxe*, II, 198. 'An order from Napoleon had been published as early as 5 September to have all stragglers arrested and one in ten of them shot, but the entire force no longer resembled anything but bands of stragglers and pillagers. A cavalry division [probably meaning a pair of squadrons] encamped on the high ground near Meißen, according to eyewitness reports, amused themselves by shooting at peaceful travellers passing across the plain, threw the bread that had been distributed to them into the Elbe, and procured other supplies at the expense of the peasants. One of them dared to shoot an officer who wanted to prevent these excesses...'
'Dès le 5 setpembre, on avait publié un ordre de Napoléon, pour faire arrêter tous le traîneurs et en faire fusiller un sur dix, mais toutes les troupes ne formaient plus que des bandes de traîneurs et de pillards. Une division de cavalerie campée près de Meissen, d'après le rapport des temoins oculaires, s'amusait à tirer des hauteurs sur les paisibles voyageurs passant dans la plaine, jetaient dans l'Elbe le pain qu'on leur distribuait, et se procuraient d'autres vivres aux dépens des paysans. L'un d'eux osa tirer un officier qui voulait empêcher ces excès...'

to rest all the troops entrusted to him until the arrival of Bennigsen's army, sending the cavalry and some of the artillery into Bohemia, where obtaining forage was less difficult than in the northern part of the region. The move into Saxony was postponed and Napoleon was able to continue to stay in the vicinity of Dresden. But this would not bring him any advantage, and he was aware of the Coalition superiority in numbers himself, stating: 'the enemy position does not allow for an attack. So I have decided to stick to the back and forth and wait for the opportunity.'[48]

Meanwhile, Macdonald had been pushed back to Stolpen by Blücher, Napoleon, deciding to go to Lusatia with the reserves to face the Army of Silesia, positioned his other formations to cover Dresden on the main roads leading there from Bohemia: Mouton's corps at Berggießhübel, Saint-Cyr's corps at Borna, Victor's corps on the road from Marienberg to Freiberg.[49]

After Napoleon's departure, the Army of Bohemia repositioned itself as follows:[50] the leading elements occupied the crest of the Ore Mountains; the main body was stationed at Teplitz, Dux and Brüx; the headquarters were at Turn [Trnovany] near Teplitz. Klenau's Austrian corps was at Marienberg; the cavalry and reserve artillery were behind the crest of the Böhmische Mittelgebirge, in the Eger river valley. General-of-Cavalry Count Platov [Matvey Ivanovich Platov] was directed towards Frauenstein with four Cossack regiments, ten Don artillery pieces and Prince Kudashev's detachment (consisting of two Cossack regiments and two Don artillery pieces), to cut the enemy lines of communications and to support the partisan detachments under General Thielmann [Johann Adolf von Thielmann] and Graf Mensdorff sent there earlier.[51] The raiding detachments under Major Colomb [Friedrich August Peter von Colomb] and *Rittmeister* Graf Pückler [Wilhelm Erdmann Karl August von Pückler-Groditz] were also sent behind enemy lines at this time.[52]

Let us turn to Napoleon's operations against Blücher.

The situation for the *Empereur des Français* became even more problematic after his second attempt to invade Bohemia. His units, hastily formed from conscripts and foreigners, were apparently melting away from losses in combat, from forced marches, deprivation and desertion. According to Odeleben, Napoleon had been forced to fill the ranks of his army with Polish prisoners and often to form battalions entirely from them. It has even been claimed that Austrians, Bohemians, Hungarians and even Prussians and Russians were forced by the purgatory of imprisonment, hunger and coercion to join the French forces and were sent to serve in Spain.[53] The Coalition armies, like menacing storm clouds accumulating from various directions, were gradually constraining Napoleon: the main army was preparing to march into

---

48 'la position de l'ennemi ne permet pas de l'attaquer. Je me suis donc arrêté au parti de m'en tenir au va et vient et d'attendre l'occasion.' Plotho, II, 214-216; Beitzke, II, 387; Bernhardi, III, 335-336.
49 Saint-Cyr, 170 & 172.
50 War Diary signed by Barclay de Tolly.
51 Ataman Platov's detachment consisted of: the Ataman's Cossacks, Grekov 5th's Cossacks, Chernozubov 5th's Cossacks, 2nd Teptyar Cossacks and ten Don artillery pieces; Prince Kudashev's detachment: one Don Cossack regiment and one Black Sea Cossack regiment, with two Don artillery pieces. War Diary signed by Barclay de Tolly.
52 Plotho, II, 218.
53 *Österreichische Militärische Zeitschrift*, 1838, III, 128.

Saxony again; Blücher stood two short stages from Dresden; the Crown Prince could cross the Elbe and, having driven back Ney's weak army, could move towards the French lines of communication. Under these circumstances, Napoleon, of necessity, having decided on a most daring undertaking, wanted to cross at Pirna, attack the left flank of the Army of Silesia and, having defeated them, link up with Murat and Marmont, who were stationed at Großenhain and Königsbrück. Then, in conjunction with Ney's force located at Torgau, he intended to march against the Crown Prince of Sweden. Napoleon considered the corps under Mouton, Saint-Cyr and Victor sufficient to delay the Army of Bohemia for some time, which, in the worst case, could retreat to the significantly strengthened Dresden fortifications. But in the meantime, while he was in Pirna preparing to execute the operational plan he had conceived, he received news, first from Ney, on the crossing of the Elbe by the Crown Prince with 80,000 men, and then, from Macdonald and Murat, on the move towards the lower Elbe by the Army of Silesia. This report, which later turned out to be false, and the inclement weather, delayed Napoleon's bold manoeuvre and forced him to limit himself to a reconnaissance in force towards Bautzen.

At the time that he was preparing to march against Blücher, the Army of Silesia was still at Bautzen and Kamenz. Having finally received word on 6 September regarding permission for him to move to the right and unite with the Crown Prince of Sweden, via the returning Major Rühle von Lilienstern [Johann Jakob Otto August Rühle von Lilienstern], Blücher remained awaiting the transfer of Bennigsen's army into Bohemia, which he was supposed to shield from interference from the enemy facing him, indeed, Blücher's own flanking movement required that he first push Murat's strong detachment located at Großenhain back as far as possible. Not content with this, Blücher undertook to envelope the enemy from several directions with superior forces, and to that end, began liaising with General Tauentzien, who, being on the left wing of the Army of the North, could conveniently assist him with part of his corps. Tauentzien expressed complete readiness to cooperate with Blücher's proposal for the impending attack on the French, promising to arrive from Elsterwerda and Ortrand with 10,000 or 11,000 men. For his part, Blücher gave his word that he would send a whole corps to meet him, which was intended to cut the enemy off from Dresden, while he intended to remain facing Macdonald himself, with the corps under Langéron and Yorck, of which the former was at Bautzen, while the latter was south of this town, on the left wing of the army. Bubna's division was located even further to the left, near Neustadt and Hohnstein. Saint-Priest's corps were stationed at Bischofswerda. Macdonald's army, constrained within the radius of one stage from Dresden and surrounded by Coalition light troops, did not dare to send foragers out of the encampment and suffered an extreme shortage of provisions and fodder. If half of the infantry in the Army of Silesia were barefoot, looting was extremely widespread, the troops were taking not only essential supplies, but also livestock, horses and committed highway robbery, often remaining without bread, and even more often without fodder, then one can imagine the state of the enemy army in a devastated country, being completely deprived of the opportunity to forage.[54]

---

54 Beitzke, II, 400-406.

The French forces stationed on the right bank of the Elbe were positioned as follows: the corps under Lauriston, Macdonald and Souham were at Harthau; Poniatowski's corps was at Stolpen; Macdonald's *quartier général* was in Fischbach, 2½ *Meilen* (18 versts) from Dresden; Murat was at Großenhain and Radeberg, with the corps under Marmont and with Sébastiani's, Kellermann's and Latour-Maubourg's cavalry.[55]

Napoleon reached Macdonald's *quartier général* on 10 (22) September, with just his personal escort, consisting of one battalion of *Vieille Garde*, a squadron of *chasseurs à cheval* and 60 hand-picked *gendarmes*.[56] Having reviewed several battalions, he distributed crosses of the *Légion d'Honneur* and presented an Eagle to the 49e ligne [sic, there was no such regiment at the time] with the usual ceremony, which foreshadowed a heated engagement. And indeed – at two o'clock in the afternoon Macdonald's corps was ordered to attack the Coalition forward outposts at Goldbach, Großdrebnitz and Pulsnitz. Preparations for the battle took about two hours. Then, upon a signal, the French went on the attack. General Emmanuel and *Oberst* Katzler, who commanded Saint-Priest's and Yorck's vanguards, decided to retreat beyond Bischofswerda without committing to an unequal battle. The enemy, persistently pursuing the Coalition, rushed into the town after them, but being engaged with canister from horse artillery covertly placed behind the ruins of houses and by skirmishers, they suffered heavy casualties. Paying no heed to this, Napoleon ordered his troops to take possession of the town, which was done. Then the French, advancing further, attempted to seize the forest, but were checked by the Coalition until nightfall. On the following day, 11 (23) September, Napoleon remained undecided for a long time – whether to continue the offensive towards Bautzen, or return to Dresden. The number of troops that he could commit against Blücher barely reached 60,000 men who were in a pitiful condition. The devastated surroundings did not provide any resources to resupply the army with vital provisions. Autumn was coming. Under such circumstances it was impossible to move away from Dresden and, in order to concentrate his forces, it was even necessary to evacuate the right bank of the Elbe. Eventually, after a lengthy hesitation, Napoleon ordered the troops to march towards Bautzen, with the objective of pushing Blücher further back and gaining the time necessary to cross the Elbe. The French moved forward, at about 11 o'clock, some along the high road, some to the left towards Geißmannsdorf, and forced the Coalition to evacuate the forest behind Bischofswerda, but as soon as the enemy, having deployed entire battalions as skirmishers, came out into the open, they were attacked by 15 squadrons under Katzler, Emmanuel and de Witt,[57] who, having scattered the French skirmisher screen, drove off several cavalry regiments and captured ten officers and 300 lower ranks from the Westphalian *Garde*. Despite even these heavy casualties to the French army in killed and wounded, however, Napoleon persistently continued the pursuit, participating in the action himself and exposing himself to the greatest danger, and by the evening had reached Göda, from

---

55 Vaudoncourt, 181; Marmont, V, 161; Beitzke, II, 406.
56 Beitzke, II, 402.
57 Nine squadrons from Katzler's vanguard; two squadrons of Kiev Dragoons and four squadrons of Ukrainian Cossacks. Blücher's report to Emperor Alexander from Bautzen, dated 13 (25) September (Log of Incoming Documents, No. 1,475); Beitzke, II, 410.

where he went back to Harthau for the night. On this day, the Coalition lost six officers and more than 200 lower ranks killed or wounded, including 33 Russians.[58]

The Commander-in-Chief of the Army of Silesia, having realised the weakness of the enemy force, not only did not want to retreat from the position he had taken up at Bautzen, but had the intention of counterattacking Napoleon. Taking advantage of the forward position of Sacken's corps, he ordered them to move to Kloster St. Marienstern behind enemy lines during the night of 11 to 12 (23 to 24) September and, in order to divert the attention of the French, Saint-Priest's detachment was to make a feint attack on their right wing. General Sacken, having received these orders too late, did not have chance to get across the line of retreat of the enemy army. All this notwithstanding, however, Napoleon, having received news, on the one side from Macdonald, regarding Blücher's readiness to give battle and about Sacken's move to get behind the French, and on the other side from Ney – regarding the Coalition construction of a bridge on the Elbe, at Wartenburg, he ordered Macdonald's force to retreat to Dresden, while Murat was to retreat to Meißen, and on the evening of 12 (24) September, he returned to the Saxon capital himself.[59]

On the morning of 13 (25) September, in the headquarters of the Army of Silesia, word was received from the forward outposts regarding the retreat of the enemy army. At the same time, because the last units of Bennigsen's army had crossed the mountain passes at Zittau, the Army of Silesia could immediately undertake a flanking move to the right, in order to get closer to the Army of the North and to cross the Elbe.[60]

The army entrusted to General-of-Cavalry Baron Bennigsen consisted of troops previously located in the Duchy of Warsaw, with the addition of some units from the Reserve Army under Prince Lobanov-Rostovsky [Dmitry Ivanovich Lobanov-Rostovsky] and *opolchenie*. This army, referred to as the Amry of Poland because it was formed in Poland, had crossed the Oder at Breslau and upstream of Steinau [Ścinawa] at the end of August (early September, new style), and arrived in the vicinity of Liegnitz on 1 (13) September.[61] On 5 (17) September, Bennigsen's force reached the Bober,[62] and then, having crossed this river and the Neisse shielded by the Army of Silesia located at Bautzen, they moved towards the passes through the Lusatian mountains in two columns: the right hand column consisting of regular troops under the personal command of Bennigsen himself, crossed the mountains at Rumburg on 10 (22) September, reaching Leitmeritz on 14 (26) September; while the left hand column, consisting of *opolchenie* commanded by Count Tolstoy [Pëtr Alexandrovich Tolstoy], arrived in Aussig via Zittau on 20 and 21 September (2 and 3 October).[63] On 15 (27) September, Bennigsen's vanguard relieved units from the

---

58 Beitzke, II, 409-412; Bernhardi, III, 342-343.
59 Plotho, II, 274; Bernhardi, III, 343-344.
60 Plotho, II, 274.
61 General Bennigsen's reports to Emperor Alexander dated 31 August (12 September) and 1 (13) September from Breslau (Log of Incoming Documents, No. 1,337 and No. 1,346).
62 General Bennigsen's report dated 5 (17) September, from Löwenberg (Log of Incoming Documents, No. 1,389).
63 March routes attached to Adjutant General Prince Volkonsky's dispatch to General Bennigsen, dated 7 (19) September (Log of Outgoing Documents, No. 64).

Main Army in the forward outposts, which, after moving to their left to Komotau, set off for Saxony.[64]

Upon their arrival at Teplitz, the Army of Poland consisted of: 43 battalions, 40 squadrons, nine regiments (27 battalions) of foot *opolchenie* and five regiments (27 squadrons) of mounted *opolchenie*; ten Cossack regiments; 17 artillery companies with 198 guns and four companies from the Department of Engineers, numbering: 28,924 infantry lower ranks, 12,595 *opolchenie* lower ranks, 5,530 regular cavalry lower ranks, 2,705 mounted *opolchenie* lower ranks, 3,565 irregular cavalry lower ranks, 3,950 artillery and engineer lower ranks, for a total of 57,269 lower ranks.

Included in this force were some 15,000 *opolchenie* who had received inadequate tactical training and were armed, in part, with very poor muskets and even pikes: in Major General Muromtsov's corps there were only 3,677 serviceable muskets for 6,140 infantry men, while in Major General Titov's corps of 6,455 infantry men there were 4,403 muskets.[65]

The Crown Prince of Sweden, in anticipation of the approach of the Army of Silesia, was preparing to cross to the left bank of the Elbe. To that end, Tauentzien's corps was ordered to monitor the Torgau fortress; General Dobschütz, stationed on their left wing with two battalions, four squadrons and two guns, at Mühlberg on 7 (19) September, stumbled upon the *8e Chasseurs à cheval* and *19e Chasseurs à cheval* from Latour-Maubourg's corps, based around Großenhain, and attacked them with the assistance of Ilovaisky 4th's Cossack detachment. The French valiantly engaged the Coalition, but upon being caught in the left flank by the Cossacks, they were completely scattered. Among the more than 500 prisoners were Colonel Talleyrand-Périgord [Alexandre Edmond de Talleyrand-Périgord] and 16 officers. No more than 30 men escaped.[66] Bülow's corps, reinforced by Hirschfeld's detachment, approached Wittenberg and, in anticipation of the siege artillery that was to arrive from Berlin and Spandau, collected materials for the construction of a bridge near the town of Elster. A bridge of boats was completed there by 12 (24) September. Whereupon a siege park including a British rocket battery arrived near Wittenberg and a proper siege of the fortress began. The Swedish corps moved up to Roßlau, and the Russians to Aken. The Coalition built bridges at both of these points and protected them with fortifications. The partisan detachment under Adjutant General Chernyshev had crossed to the left bank of the Elbe at Aken on 2 (14) September, occupied Bernburg and sent patrols out along the river Saale. The Crown Prince's headquarters were located in Zerbst in anticipation of the proposed crossing.[67]

---

64 War Diary signed by Barclay de Tolly; Plotho, II, 229-234; Beitzke, II, 388-389.
65 For details of the composition of Bennigsen's army, see Appendix XXVI at the end of this chapter.
66 Plotho, II, 305-306.
67 Plotho, II, 302-306.

Appendix XXV

Composition of the Austrian army from 22 August (3 September)

1. leichte Division: *Feldmarschallleutnant* Prinz Moritz von Liechtenstein.

Brigade	Unit	Battalions	Squadrons
Generalmajor Haugwitz	*1. Jäger-Bataillon*	1	
	2. Jäger-Bataillon	1	
	Chevaulegers Kaiser		6
Generalmajor Schreither	Grenzregiment Broder	1	
	7. Jäger-Bataillon	1	
	Chevaulegers Vincent		6

One brigade battery (three-pounders); one horse artillery battery (six-pounders), for a total of: four battalions, 12 squadrons and two batteries.

2. leichte Division: *Feldmarschallleutnant* Graf Bubna.

Brigade	Unit	Battalions	Squadrons
Generalmajor Zechmeister von Rheinau	Grenzregiment Peterwardein	1	
	6. Jäger-Bataillon	1	
	Husaren Liechtenstein		6
Generalmajor Neipperg	*5. Jäger-Bataillon*	1	
	Husaren Kaiser		6
	Husaren Blankenstein		6

One brigade battery (three-pounders); one horse artillery battery (six-pounders), for a total of: three battalions, 18 squadrons and two batteries.

I. Korpus: *Feldzeugmeister* Hieronymus von Colloredo-Mansfeld

Division	Brigade	Unit	Battalions	Squadrons
Feldmarschallleutnant Schneller	*Generalmajor* Prinz Gustav zu Hessen-Homburg	Grenzregiment Deutsch-Banater	2	
		Husaren Hessen-Homburg		4
		Dragoner Riesch		5
		Horse artillery battery		

Division	Brigade	Unit	Battalions	Squadrons
Feldmarschallleutnant Graf Wimpffen	*Generalmajor* Torry	*Infanterie Froon*	3	
		Infanterie de Vaux	3	
		Six-pounder battery		
	Generalmajor Czerwenka	*Infanterie Argentau*	2	
		Infanterie Erbach	2	
		Six-pounder battery		
Feldmarschallleutnant Greth	*Generalmajor* Mumb	*Infanterie de Ligne*	2	
		Infanterie Czartorski	2	
		Six-pounder battery		
	Generalmajor Quosdanovich	*Infanterie Albert Gyulay*	2	
		Infanterie Reuß-Plauen	2	
		Six-pounder battery		

Reserve artillery: one six-pounder battery and two 12-pounder batteries.
Total: 20 battalions, nine squadrons and eight batteries.

II. Korpus: *General der Kavallerie* Graf von Merveldt.

Division	Brigade	Unit	Battalions	Squadrons
Feldmarschallleutnant Lederer	*Generalmajor* 'Sorbenberg'	*Grenzregiment Gradisker*	1	
		Husaren Kienmayer		4
		Dragoner Erzherzog Johann		4
		Three-pounder battery		
	Generalmajor Giffing	*Infanterie Strauch*	2	
		Infanterie Bellegarde	2	
		Six-pounder battery		
Feldmarschallleutnant Prinz Alois von Liechtenstein	*Generalmajor* Klopstein von Ennsbruck	*Infanterie Kaunitz*	2	
		Infanterie Wenzel Colloredo	2	
		Six-pounder battery		
	Generalmajor Mécsery de Tsoor	*Infanterie Vogelsang*	2	
		Infanterie Reuss-Greiz	2	
		Six-pounder battery		

Reserve artillery: one six-pounder battery and two 12-pounder batteries.
Total: 13 battalions, eight squadrons and seven batteries.

III. Korpus: Feldzeugmeister Graf Ignác Gyulay.

Division	Brigade	Unit	Battalions	Squadrons
Feldmarschallleutnant Crenneville	Generalmajor Hecht	Grenzregiment Warasdin-Kreuzer	1	
		Grenzregiment Warasdin-St Georg	1	
		Chevaulegers Klenau		5
		Chevaulegers Rosenberg		5
		Six-pounder horse artillery battery		
Feldmarschallleutnant Murray de Melgum	Generalmajor Herzogenberg	InfanterieErzherzog Ludwig	2	
		Infanterie Würzburg	2	
		Six-pounder battery		
	Generalmajor Reichlin	Infanterie Mariássy	2	
		Infanterie Ignác Gyulay	2	
		Six-pounder battery		
	Generalmajor Csollich	Infanterie Kottulinsky	2	
		Infanterie Kaiser	2	
		Six-pounder battery		
	Generalmajor Grimmer von Riesenberg	Infanterie Kolowrat	2	
		Infanterie Fröhlich	2	
		Six-pounder battery		

Reserve artillery: one six-pounder battery and two 12-pounder batteries.
Total: 18 battalions, ten squadrons and eight batteries.

IV. Korpus: General der Kavallerie Graf Klenau.

Division	Brigade	Unit	Battalions	Squadrons
Feldmarschallleutnant von Mohr	Generalmajor Paumgartten	Grenzregiment Walachisch	1	
		Grenzregiment Walachisch-Illyrisch	2	
		Chevaulegers Hohenzollern		4
		Husaren Palatinal		5
		Husaren Erzherzog Ferdinand		5
		Six-pounder horse artillery battery		

Division	Brigade	Unit	Battalions	Squadrons
Feldmarschallleutnant Hohenlohe-Bartenstein	*Generalmajor* Schäfer	*Infanterie* Joseph Colloredo	2	
		Infanterie Zach	3	
		Six-pounder battery		
	Generalmajor Splény	*Infanterie* Württemberg	3	
		Infanterie Lindenau	3	
		Six-pounder battery		
Feldmarschallleutnant Mayer von Heldensfeld	*Generalmajor* Abele	*Infanterie* Alois Liechtenstein	3	
		Infanterie Coburg	3	
		Six-pounder battery		
	Generalmajor De Best	*Infanterie* Erzherzog Karl	2	
		Infanterie Kerpen	2	
		Six-pounder battery		

Reserve artillery: one six-pounder battery and two 12-pounder batteries.
Total: 24 battalions, 14 squadrons and eight batteries.

Reserves: *General der Kavallerie* Prinz von Hessen-Homburg.

Division	Brigade	Unit	Battalions	Squadrons
Feldmarschallleutnant Graf Weissenwolf	*Generalmajor* Fürstenwerther	*Grenadiere* Czarnotzky	1	
		Grenadiere Obermayer	1	
		Grenadiere Berger	1	
		Grenadiere Oklopsia	1	
	Generalmajor Gabelkoven	*Grenadiere* Habinay	1	
		Grenadiere Portner	1	
		Grenadiere Fischer	1	
		Grenadiere Rüber	1	
		Two six-pounder batteries		
Feldmarschallleutnant Bianchi	*Generalmajor* Prinz Philipp zu Hessen-Homburg	*Infanterie* Hiller	2	
		Infanterie Hieronymus Colloredo	2	
		Infanterie Hessen-Homburg	2	
	Generalmajor Quallenberg	*Infanterie* Simbschen	2	
		Infanterie Esterhazy	2	
		Infanterie Davidovich	2	
		Three six-pounder batteries		
Reserve cavalry: *Feldmarschallleutnant* Graf Nostitz.				

Division	Brigade	Unit	Battalions	Squadrons
Feldmarschallleutnant Graf Ignaz Hardegg	*Generalmajor* Rothkirch	Kürassier Kronprinz Ferdinand		4
		Kürassier Erzherzog Franz		4
Feldmarschallleutnant Graf Klebelsberg	*Generalmajor* Rogécourt	Kürassier Hohenzollern		4
		Kürassier Sommariva		4
Feldmarschallleutnant Civalart	*Generalmajor* Des Fours	Kürassier Kaiser		6
		Kürassier O'Reilly		5
	Generalmajor Kuttalek	Kürassier Herzog Albert		4
		Kürassier Lothringen		4
		Three six-pounder horse artillery batteries		

Total reserves: 20 battalions, 35 squadrons and eight batteries.

Overall, the Austrian army assembled in Bohemia consisted of: 102 battalions, 106 squadrons and 43 batteries (Fighting Composition of the Austrian Army, 3 September new style 1813, Archive of the M.T.D. No. 29,184).

Appendix XXVI

The composition of General Bennigsen's Army of Poland

Vanguard: commanded by Lieutenant General Markov; cavalry commanders, major generals Dyadkov and Dekhterev; Cossack commander, Major General Prince Bagration [Roman Ivanovich Bagration]; *opolchenie* commander, Major General Prince Tenishev.

Formation	Unit	Battalions	Squadrons	Officers	Lower Ranks
16th Division: Major General Bulatov	Neyshlot Infantry	3		45	1,805
	27th Jägers	3		59	2,199
	43rd Jägers	3		47	1,597
13th Division (one brigade): Major General Ivanov	Saratov Infantry	3		56	2,026
	Penza Infantry	2		39	1,373
	Infantry Total:	14		246	9,000
Regular Cavalry	Orenburg Ulans		2	18	202
	Vladimir Ulans		3	19	385
	1st Hussar Regiment		5	33	824
	1st Ulan Regiment		5	21	695
	Regular Cavalry Total:		15	91	2,106
Artillery	16th Battery Artillery Company			7	249
	56th Light Artillery Company			6	183
	30th Horse Artillery Company			4	133
	10th Horse Artillery Company (half)			2	105
	Artillery Total:			19	670
Engineers	Captain Stender's sapper company			3	105

Formation	Unit	Battalions	Squadrons	Officers	Lower Ranks
Irregular Cavalry	Vlasov 2nd's Cossacks			12	358
	Platov 5th's Cossacks			10	325
	Andriyanov 3rd's Cossacks			13	502
	Shamshev 2nd's Cossacks			13	419
	4th Ural Cossacks			8	233
	9th Bashkirs			15	314
	11th Bashkirs			15	340
	14th Bashkirs			25	340
	15th Bashkirs			14	302
	Irregular Cavalry Total:			125	3,130
Opolchenie	Siberia Opolchenie Cossacks			19	494
	Penza Opolchenie Cossacks			13	446
	Opolchenie Cossack Total:			32	940
	Vanguard Total Manning:			516	15,951

Vanguard total units: 14 battalions, 15 squadrons, nine irregular cavalry regiments, two opolchenie regiments, one sapper company, 3½ artillery companies with 12 heavy guns, 12 light guns and 14 horse artillery pieces.

Right Flank Corps: General-of-Infantry Dokhturov [Dmitry Sergeevich Dokhturov]; cavalry commander, Lieutenant General Musin-Pushkin; reserve artillery commander, Colonel Kolatinsky.

Formation	Unit	Battalions	Squadrons	Officers	Lower Ranks
12th Division: Major General Prince Khovansky	Smolensk Infantry	2		53	1,388
	Narva Infantry	2		44	1,439
	Alexopol Infantry	2		39	1,399
	Novoingermanland Infantry	2		32	1,398
	6th Jägers	2		53	1,671
	41st Jägers	2		41	1,172
26th Division: Major General Paskevich	Nizhegorod Infantry	2		39	1,473
	Ladoga Infantry	2		61	1,341
	Poltava Infantry	2		46	1,546
	Orël Infantry	2		45	1,277
	5th Jägers	2		39	1,467
	42nd Jägers	2		31	1,230

Formation	Unit	Battalions	Squadrons	Officers	Lower Ranks
13th Division (reserve brigade): Major General Lindfors	Velikiye Luki Infantry	3		58	2,146
	Galits Infantry	2		36	977
	Infantry Total:	29		617	19,924
Regular Cavalry	Combined Dragoons		5	13	760
	1st Mounted Jägers		4	14	524
	2nd Mounted Jägers		4	9	616
	2nd Ulans		4	15	552
	Taganrog Ulans		4	24	622
	Siberia Ulans		2	20	174
	Zhitomir Ulans		2	13	176
	Cavalry Total:		25	108	3,424
Artillery	45th Battery Artillery Company			9	254
	1st Light Artillery Company			5	150
	26th Battery Artillery Company			5	258
	47th Light Artillery Company			4	157
	2nd Horse Artillery Company			7	302
	Artillery Total:			30	1,121
Lieutenant Colonel Afanasiev 3rd	Mining Company			3	71
Reserve Artillery	22nd Battery Artillery Company			7	274
	18th Light Artillery Company			8	159
	48th Light Artillery Company			5	171
	53rd Light Artillery Company			5	175
	9th Horse Artillery Company			5	287
	Reserve Artillery Total:			30	1,066
Engineers	1st Pontoon Company[1]				
	5th Pontoon Company			5	171
	Right Flank Corps Manning:			794	25,777

---

1   En route from Warsaw.

Right Flank Corps total: 29 battalions, 25 squadrons, two engineer companies and ten artillery companies with 48 heavy guns, 48 light guns and 24 horse artillery pieces.

Left Flank Corps: Lieutenant General Count Tolstoy.

Major General Muromtsev's corps.

Formation	Unit	Battalions	Squadrons	Officers	Lower Ranks
Nizhegorod Opolchenie	Mounted Regiment			17	563
	1st Foot Regiment			34	1,276
	2nd Foot Regiment			34	1,374
	3rd Foot Regiment			35	1,400
	4th Foot Regiment			34	1,090
Kostroma Opolchenie	Mounted Regiment			25	471
Cossacks	5th Ural Cossacks			18	435
Artillery	52nd Battery Artillery Company			6	237
	22nd Horse Artillery Company			8	222
Engineers	Captain Shevich's pioneer company			3	104
	Muromtsev's corps Total:			214	8,172

Muromtsev's corps total: four *opolchenie* foot regiments, one irregular cavalry regiment, two opolchenie mounted regiments, one pioneer company, two artillery companies with 24 guns.

Major General Titov's corps.

Formation	Unit	Battalions	Squadrons	Officers	Lower Ranks
Penza Opolchenie	1st Foot Regiment			43	1,182
	2nd Foot Regiment			44	1,556
	3rd Foot Regiment			31	1,162
	Artillery detachment (two guns)			2	52
Artillery	64th Light Artillery Company			5	131
Ryazan Opolchenie	Mounted Regiment			23	515
	3rd Foot Regiment			46	1,182
	1st Jäger Regiment			41	1,373
Kazan Opolchenie	two mounted sotnia			6	216
	Titov's corps manning:			240	7,369

Titov's corps total: five opolchenie foot regiments, 1½ opolchenie mounted regiments, 1½ artillery companies with 14 guns.

Left Flank Corps total: nine opolchenie foot regiments, 3½ opolchenie mounted regiments, one engineer company and 3½ artillery companies with 40 guns.

Bennigsen's Army of Poland total: 43 regular battalions, 27 opolchenie battalions, 40 regular squadrons, 10 irregular cavalry regiments, 5½ opolchenie mounted regiments, four engineer companies and 17 artillery companies with 198 guns.

Manning total: 19 generals, 1,764 officers and 57,269 lower ranks.

Extracted from Army of Poland strength reports dated 11 and 15 [23 and 27] September, signed by General Bennigsen.

34

Measures taken by the Coalition in order to concentrate their forces

> Blücher is ordered to attach most of his force to the Army of Bohemia. – A memo from General Jomini regarding future operations. – The proposal for operations drawn up by Schwarzenberg's headquarters staff. – Blücher receives orders to attach his entire force to the Army of Bohemia. – Blücher's letter to Emperor Alexander. – General Knesebeck's memo. – Barclay de Tolly's opinion on future operations. – Blücher's second letter and the arrival of Rühle von Lilienstern at the headquarters of the Coalition sovereigns. – Instructions issued to Blücher and Bennigsen. – Letter from Emperor Alexander to the Crown Prince of Sweden regarding future operations.

When describing the operations that were taking place simultaneously at various points in the theatre of war, it has been necessary to limit ourselves to only briefly indicating the most important decisions taken at the commanders' conferences at the headquarters of the Army of Bohemia. Although the vast extent of the theatre of war did not allow centralised control of operations by all the Coalition armies, and therefore the general orders from headquarters, for the most part, turned out to be untimely, nevertheless, for an accurate and complete understanding of the struggle between the Sovereigns, the nations of Europe and Napoleon, it is necessary to know exactly what was decided in the councils of war by the monarchs unitedly mobilised for collective defence.

The failure suffered by the Coalition at the Battle of Dresden led many to doubt the merits of the general plan of action drawn up at Trachenberg. It was obvious that if Napoleon could manage to defeat an army that outnumbered him by almost one and a half times, then he could also achieve success over the weakest armies, those of Silesia and the North. Although the action at Kulm, on 17 (29) August, showed what a handful of brave men led by decisive and skilful commanders were able to achieve, it did not dispel the doubts that darkened the horizon in Schwarzenberg's headquarters. On the morning of 18 (30) August, neither he himself nor his advisers were sure that an attack on Vandamme would be successful. In their opinion, the objective of the imminent battle should be limited to being able to retreat beyond the river Eger without further loss and await the arrival of reinforcements there, without whose assistance any enterprise against Napleon seemed to them to be pointless. Influenced by these opinions, Schwarzenberg then sent one of his aides-de-camp, Prinz Wenzel von und zu Liechtenstein, to Blücher with news of the losses suffered by the Coalition and with a request for his speedy assistance to the Army of Bohemia. The instructions given to Liechtenstein and officially presented to Blücher stated that: 'as a consequence of the events from 15 to 18 (27 to 30) August, it is necessary of at least half of Blücher's army not only to close up to, but to link up with the Army of Bohemia. If the former consists of 80,000 men, then 50,000 of them may join the Main Army, and the other 30,000, together with the Austrian division under Graf Bubna, will be enough to cover not only Silesia but also Bohemia by taking a flank position, either at Sankt Georgenthal [Jiřetín pod Jedlovou] or Zittau. A movement by 50,000 men to join the main army towards Theresienstadt could be carried out from Zittau, Bömisch Leipa, Graber [Kravaře v Čechách] and Leitmeritz. It is desirable that this corps should have from 5,000 to 6,000 Cossacks in order to rush them from the left wing of the Main Army, across the Eger, into the enemy lines of communications.[1] Since, in all likelihood, Napoleon will direct the bulk of his forces along the left bank of the Elbe into Bohemia facing the Main Army, which will take up a position on the right bank of the Eger in the vicinity of Budin or Laun, it is imperative that His Royal Highness, the Crown Prince of Sweden crosses the Elbe as quickly as possible, wherever possible, and moves into the rear of the enemy army.'[2]

The unexpected success of the attack on Vandamme on 18 (30) August and the victory on the Katzbach forced the Coalition to abandon the retreat beyond the Eger proposed by Prinz Schwarzenberg. According to General Jomini, 'it was necessary to take advantage of Napoleon's weakening and operate on the offensive. The Coalition could:

1. Send the main army to Rumburg and on towards Bautzen, to divide the enemy forces and to operate in the rear of the forces stationed against Blücher. Should the roads leading there prove suitable and the ground be open, then this modus operandi should be preferred, as most consistent with the principles in the current state of Napoleon's army.[3]

2. March on Freiberg, but for this it is necessary to send at least 150,000 men in that direction, and to have sufficient strength at Peterswald to protect the Teplitz highway. In this case it is vital to:
    a) reinforce the corps at Peterswald with part of the Theresienstadt garrison and fortify the position there and the routes leading from Saxony to Bohemia.

---
1 The retreat across the river Eger was considered inevitable by the Austrian army headquarters staff.
2 Extracted from instructions given to Prinz Wenzel Liechtenstein, under the signature block: 'General Duka, as ordered by *Feldmarschall* Prinz Schwartzenberg.' *Militair Wochenblatt (Beihefte zum)*, 1844, 205-206.
3 *le plus conforme aux principes dans l'état actuel de l'armée de Napoleon.*

b) garrison the bridgehead at Melnik with a dedicated unit from the force.
c) invade Saxony with 170,000 men, of whom 150,000 will march on Freiberg, while of the rest, some will go towards Dresden, some in the role of partisan detachments towards Leipzig and Zwickau in order to collect provisions and to sever enemy communications. In the event of a battle, these units may rejoin the army.
d) set up magazines in Eger and Karlsbad [Karlovy Vary] and transfer some of the supplies from Prague thence.
e) stock the parks; have a pontoon park accompany the army, which was omitted during the first offensive.
f) take urgent measures to attach 12 Cossack regiments to the army, which can bring greater benefit nowhere than in Bohemia, being located close to the enemy lines of communications.
g) order Blücher to move into Bohemia, and Bennigsen to replace him on the Katzbach and the Bober. Leaving Saint-Priest's detachment at Gabel and some of the force at Böhmisch Kamnitz, Blücher could replace the corps located at Peterswald, or, depending on the circumstances, could move in the wake of the Main Army.
h) pay attention, in the event of a general battle, primarily to protecting the army from the right flank.
i) not march blindly without espionage (*ne pas marcher en aveugles sans espionnage*).
j) give the appointed Commander-in-Chief complete freedom of action having properly established his staff.

3. The army may be sent from Peterswald towards Dresden, to take up positions half a march from this city (*à trois lieues*) and a vanguard sent to monitor the enemy. Having taken up this observation position, we could move closer to the enemy lines of communications, but, in my opinion, the axis leading towards Freiberg should be preferred if Blücher is able assist the Main Army.[4]

Three days later [5 September, new style], in Schwarzenberg's headquarters, the following planning assumptions were drafted for operations by the Main Coalition Army.

'Emperor Napoleon, after his armies have suffered several partial defeats, has concentrated forces in Dresden in order to attack the Coalition in superior strength, wherever he is most likely to succeed. He may:

1. advance to engage Blücher's victorious army.
2. defend himself with part of the force while attacking the army of the Crown Prince of Sweden with the main body.

---

4   General Jomini's memo, dated 21 August (2 September), Archive of the M.T.D. No. 29,184.

3. having achieved some successes, turn back towards Bohemia, against our Main Army.
4. abandon the Elbe and concentrate his forces at Leipzig in order to decide the fate of Saxony with a pitched battle.

In the first case (Napoleon advancing against Blücher), it will be possible to use bridges that are to be built at Aussig to cross the 50,000 or 60,000 strong corps assigned to debouch from Bohemia across the enemy lines of communications via Zittau or Rumburg, while the army under General Blücher, by falling back and uniting with the army under General Bennigsen, may resume a decisive offensive with the assistance of the Main Army.

In the second case (Napoleon advancing on the Crown Prince of Sweden. In Schwarzenberg's headquarters it was considered all the more likely that, according to the latest intelligence, the enemy would advance against the Army of the North from several directions), General Blücher should march on the flank of the French force moving from Dresden to Berlin, moreover, his lines of communications, in any case, would be secured by Bennigsen's army, which would advance to Görlitz. The main army will operate towards Dresden at the same time and will try to capture the Pirna camp in order to distract the attention of the enemy.[5]

In the third case (Napoleon advancing on the main army), it will be enough to check the heads of the enemy columns on the Teplitz position. Once we are convinced that Napoleon really intends to invade Bohemia, then our army will retreat beyond the Eger, and Blücher will be asked to move to Aussig or Leitmeritz into the enemy flank by forced marches.

Finally, in the fourth case (which Schwartzenberg's staff considered the least likely to happen), if Napoleon, having abandoned the defence of the line along the Elbe, concentrates his forces at Leipzig, the Main Army would move towards Plauen and Zwickau, General Blücher would hastily head towards the Elbe, and Bennigsen towards Dresden, to invest the bridgehead there, should it still be occupied by the enemy. The Crown Prince, depending on the circumstances, is to take steps to facilitate a general offensive.

From all this it follows that it is necessary: to build two bridges at Aussig and, as quickly as possible, to improve the roads from there towards Rumburg and Zittau. To concentrate the troops assigned to reinforce Blücher between Karbitz and Türmitz [Trmice] and give definitive orders to Bennigsen to move forwards in order to support Blücher in the various operations that may be undertaken by him.

It appears that Emperor Napoleon wants to hold persistently on the Elbe. Therefore, light detachments must be sent across his lines of communications in order to interrupt the food supply to his troops from distant regions, who are already beginning to suffer from a lack of essential supplies. In order to achieve this objective, the 3,000 men commanded by General Thielmann and *Oberst* Mensdorff are not enough. It is vital to reinforce them with all the Cossacks attached to Blücher's army, which, due to his position, cannot operate to advantage as partisan detachments.

---

5 *La grande armée opérera sur Dresde en même tems et tàchera d s'emparer du camp de Pirna pour attirer l'attention de l'ennemi.*

The regular troops from this army should be sufficient for service in the forward outposts and for the pursuit of a defeated enemy. General Klenau's corps are to advance for two days in order to support the detachments sent across the enemy lines of communications...'[6]

Because it was believed in the headquarters of the Army of Bohemia that, after the battle of Kulm, Napoleon had turned with all his might against the Crown Prince of Sweden, it was decided: that the main Coalition army would launch a significant show of force towards Dresden. This plan was immediately executed: on 24 August (5 September) and on the following day (as shown in Chapter 33), the Coalition force crossed the Saxon border, and at the same time a dispatch was sent to Blücher, in which Schwarzenberg wrote that he completely agreed with him regarding the cancellation of the move into Bohemia by the Army of Silesia, and that he hoped to draw Napoleon from the right bank of the Elbe to the left through a strong show of force. At the same time, it was proposed that Blücher advance towards the Elbe with the assistance of Graf Bubna's *2. leichte Division*.

When, soon thereafter, intelligence was receive that Napoleon was not heading against the Crown Prince, rather towards Bautzen against Blücher, Schwarzenberg immediately decided to march from Rumburg and Gabel into Lusatia with 60,000 Austrian troops in two columns. Having started the move on 25 August (6 September), it was planned to cross the Bohemian border on 30 August (11 September). The Russo-Prussian forces were intended to remain on the left bank of the Elbe, with Klenau's corps and Moritz Liechtenstein's division, under the overall command of Barclay de Tolly. Barclay, recognising the move by the Commander-in-Chief to the right bank of the Elbe as sound, I found it inappropriate that only Austrian troops had been assigned for this and not Russians who, being located on the right wing of the army, could have moved into Lusatia faster than the Austrians stationed on the left wing. In particular, he was concerned that the *Feldmarschall* might stretch the entire army out over a significant area, in the form of a cordon. Taking advantage of Schwarzenberg's withdrawal, Barclay made a feint of a decisive invasion of Saxony. The offensive by this force began on 25 August (6 September), the same day that Schwarzenberg advanced to the crossings on the Elbe, and Napoleon moved back from the Neissa towards Dresden. We have already seen that Napoleon's operations against the Army of Bohemia forced the Coalition to retreat behind the Ore Mountains and to cancel Schwarzenberg's proposed campaign in Lusatia. Following this, orders were sent to Blücher to join the Main Army with his entire force and to cover their lines of communications prior to an attack on Chemnitz. To that end, Blücher had to march towards Pirna, or, having advanced his vanguard as close as possible to Dresden, to make a flanking move under the cover of this vanguard and Bubna's division, through Rumburg and Bömisch Kamnitz, or through Zittau and Bömisch Leipa, towards Leitmeritz.[7] Meanwhile, the main army, having evaded the encounter with Napoleon, managed to concentrate behind the crest of the Ore

---

6 Proposal for operations, dated 5 September, new style, signed by Prince Schwarzenberg. Archive of the M.T.D. No. 29,184.
7 Emperor Alexander's letter to General Blücher, dated 28 August (9 September), with an annex containing the operational plan for the Coalition armies. Archive of the M.T.D. No. 29,190;

Mountains when news of the victory at Dennewitz arrived, and on 1 (13) September a letter from Blücher was received, in which he, comparing the advantages of moving his army to Pirna in Saxony, or to Leitmeritz in Bohemia, wrote that the likely consequences that the victory at Dennewitz might bring, prompted him to prefer an offensive into Saxony. That this victory, having changed the situation, would provide the opportunity to shift the theatre of operations onto the left bank of the Elbe, and that he had already made a proposal to the Crown Prince of Sweden to that effect. If the Army of the North were to cross between Wittenberg and Magdeburg and move towards Leipzig, then, in all likelihood, Napoleon would be forced to abandon his position near Dresden and fall back. The Army of Silesia could also immediately cross the Elbe between Dresden and Torgau in order to establish communications with the Main Army, which, for its part, could undoubtedly advance towards Altenberg and Leipzig. Otherwise, if the Army of Silesia army moved six marches away from the Crown Prince, he would obviously remain inactive, and even then, during the move into Bohemia, the Army of Silesia could not participate in operations against the enemy for ten whole days. At the conclusion of his assessment, Blücher wrote that he would take up a central position between Bautzen and Schluckenau, and that Bennigsen's arrival on the Neisse would enable the Army of Silesia to operate on the offensive again, moving to their right to link up with the Crown Prince, or, in the event of Napoleon invading Bohemia, crossing the Elbe and moving up behind him. Should Napoleon turn against the Army of Silesia, they would retreat beyond the Neisse, or to a flanking position towards Zittau or Rumburg. If General Bennigsen had reached them by that time, it would be preferable for him to move towards Zittau, because this would force the enemy to divide their forces and would enable one of our armies to operate against his flank. Similar advantages could be expected should the Crown Prince cross the Elbe, and the Army of Silesia move to link up with him at Elsterwerda.[8]

At the same time that Blücher wrote his assessment, on 30 August (11 September), Emperor Alexander wrote to him:

> based on reliable intelligence, it is known that Napoleon has crossed the Elbe with the majority of his forces and is moving against the Army of Bohemia... It is highly likely that the corps under Ney, Lauriston, Poniatowski and Sébastiani, having fallen back, will join him via Königstein. From this it follows that you will not be able to head towards Pirna, but must move towards Rumburg and Leitmeritz...[9]

Once the headquarters of the Army of Bohemia had received Blücher's dispatch dated 30 August (11 September), then, at a meeting attended by Emperor Alexander,

---

Log of Outgoing Documents, No. 44. From the Tsar's letter it is clearly His wish for Blücher to move to Rumburg.
8 Blücher's letter to Emperor Alexander dated 11 September, new style. Archive of the M.T.D. No. 29,182, Log of Incoming Documents, No. 1,330.
9 Extract from Emperor Alexander's letter to Blücher. Log of Outgoing Documents, No. 48.

the King of Prussia and Schwarzenberg, it was decided to confirm the orders issued to Blücher, setting out the reasons for this in a memo drafted by General Knesebeck [Karl Friedrich von dem Knesebeck] and sent to the headquarters of the Army of Silesia on 1 (13) September. Considering the question: following the victory at Dennewitz, should the Army of Silesia move to their right to join the Crown Prince, or to the left to join the Army of Bohemia via Leitmeritz, Knesebeck gave preference to the latter course of action, because:

1. A concentration of Coalition troops on the middle Elbe, in the vicinity of Torgau, would force the enemy to move closer to their sources of resupply and thereby strengthen them; conversely, it is more advantageous to strengthen the Coalition in Bohemia, as this would facilitate cutting them off from these resources.
2. 'If Blücher's army does not come to Bohemia, then the Main Army, being forced to leave 50,000 men to protect its key-point (*point d'appui*) on the Elbe, would not dare to march on Chemnitz across the enemy lines of communications. Just as Napoleon, being in Dresden, could reach Teplitz in three marches, the Main Army, without properly protecting their lines of communications, would not dare to move more than three marches away from Teplitz, and therefore, having reached Sebastiansberg, would halt in order to be able to return to their base of operations, if necessary: therefore, they would lose the opportunity to operate on the lines of communications of the enemy army in significant strength.
3. The Army of Silesia, having encountered great difficulties in crossing the Elbe in the vicinity of Torgau, might fail in its enterprise and remain inactive on the right bank of the river, and since the Army of the North is in the same situation, the enemy could turn against the Army of Bohemia with their main force.
4. Even if the Army of Silesia did manage to cross the Elbe, they would be forced to give battle, because, having a river to their rear, they could not, as before, evade the fight. The success of such a battle without the assistance of the Army of the North is highly doubtful.
5. By uniting with the force under the Crown Prince, the Army of Silesia would lose its independence, which is completely contrary to its primary mission.'

The move into Bohemia was not intended to be carried out until after Bennigsen's arrival and the relief-in-place of the Army of Silesia by his formations, and since the drafter could not help but admit that it was necessary to operate in accordance with a situation that could not be foreseen ahead of time, the final decision on this matter rested with Blücher.

This memo overlooked the fact that the Crown Prince of Sweden considered it too dangerous to cross the Elbe without the assistance of the Army of Silesia and that, conversely, a crossing by the Army of the North and the Army of Silesia and their advance towards the enemy lines of communication, by prompting Napoleon to abandon his defensive line along the Elbe, would serve to protect Silesia more reliably than protecting this region with a dedicated army.[10]

In Barclay de Tolly's opinion, it was more advantageous to bring Blücher closer to the Main Army by the shortest route to Pirna, rather than along a roundabout route via Rumburg and Leitmeritz, because the Main Army, having carried out an offensive along the left bank of the Elbe, which would not present any particular difficulties, and having built bridges, could establish liaison with Blücher and could sever the communications of the enemy army. But, as Barclay pointed out, since the Army of Silesia may have already moved in the direction assigned to it, it would be better to stick to the plan, even if it might be less advantageous, than to amend it. It would simply be desirable that, having attached one of the best formations of the Coalition army to the main force, it should not be doomed to the same inaction in which the situation had hitherto kept the largest of our armies, while others, incomparably less powerful, decided the fate of the campaign… By moving towards the enemy lines of communications with the main mass of troops from our left wing, we could induce them to divide their forces or retreat, but, judging from the beginning of the campaign, we would not dare to undertake such a bold undertaking, which, if successful, could lead to the destruction of the enemy, yet would bring associated heavy losses if unsuccessful. Therefore, it follows, that by limiting ourselves to dispatching a fairly substantial corps across Napoleon's lines of communications, while directing the main force against him frontally and giving a defensive battle in a good position, the loss of which would put the enemy, enveloped from behind, in a very dangerous situation, and even if they managed to defeat us, it would not lead to anything other than an opportunity to turn against the corps deployed across their communications. Barclay de Tolly believed that no time should be wasted waiting for Blücher's army, which needed at least seven days to join the main army, rather, upon reaching Leitmeritz it should immediately go into reserve, and therefore the main force could immediately be advanced to the exits from the mountains leading to Pirna, and part of the army could be assigned to operate towards Chemnitz across enemy communications or, depending on the situation, towards Hof. In the conclusions to his opinion, Barclay repeated that the advance of the main force towards the communications of the enemy army would have a more decisive outcome than a detachment outflanking a smaller element of the force, but that as a result of earlier events there clearly appeared a determination not to be exposed to any kind of risk…[11] From this it is clear that Barclay de Tolly did not approve of the slow, indecisive modus operandi adopted by Schwarzenberg's headquarters staff at all, but both the Russian military commanders and Emperor Alexander himself, guided by political considerations, were forced to coordinate their actions with the Austrian military plans.

While the headquarters of the Army of Bohemia believed that the Army of Silesia was executing its mission and had already set out for Bohemia, Blücher, taking

---

10 Bernhardi, Denkwürdigkeiten aus dem Leben Carl Friedrich Grafen von Toll, III, 327-329.
11 Assessment, signed by Barclay de Tolly, in his letter to the Emperor, dated 31 August [12 September], submitted on 3 (15) September. Archive of the M.T.D. No. 29,182, Log of Incoming Documents, No. 1,338.

advantage of the right granted to him to choose between Leitmeritz or Pirna, and not in the least wanting to join the Main Army, immediately upon receipt of Emperor Alexander's orders dated 30 August (11 September), replied that:

> in all probability, Your Majesty is not yet fully aware of the consequences of the victory at Dennewitz, which would force the mission issued to the Army of Silesia to be changed. The enemy forces opposed to me are very significant (some 50,000); the army defeated at Dennewitz numbered from 60,000 to 70,000, and therefore Napoleon cannot send more than 100,000 men against the Army of Bohemia.
>
> Because the supply trains and parks of the Army of Silesia have not yet managed to cross the Neisse, and the troops are stretched out across a front from Kamenz to Schandau, only the vanguard could reach Leitmeritz by 19 September (new style); therefore, the arrival of the Army of Silesia in Bohemia will not deliver the expected advantage.
>
> Ney's army has retreated towards Leipzig for the most part, and the Crown Prince of Sweden is able to cross the Elbe without further difficulty, as I have strongly urged him so to do. Therefore, until I receive a response to this report, I shall not inform the prince of any move to Bohemia by the Army of Silesia, so as not to give him grounds for the postponement of the proposed crossing.
>
> If it is considered necessary to strengthen the Main Army, then may I dare to propose that Your Imperial Majesty send Bennigsen's army to Bohemia, in two columns, via Zittau and Rumburg. This movement would be shielded by the Army of Silesia, which would, otherwise, have to withdraw from its current position in view of the enemy, and would be pursued by them becoming entrapped in rearguard actions. In addition, the enemy would take possession of important posts at Zittau and Gabel, so as to prevent us from resuming offensive operations from there.[12]

Not content with this assessment alone, Blücher considered it necessary to send Major Rühle von Lilienstern, of the general staff, to Teplitz to the Coalition monarchs, being instructed to verbally brief on the observations that had guided Blücher. General Gneisenau's doubts regarding the Crown Prince of Sweden's lack of activity were not hidden from the sovereigns. Schwarzenberg merely commented that the Army of Silesia was already very close to the enemy and that they should not lose contact with them. This gifted officer sent by Blücher executed his assignment perfectly. It was proposed to send Bennigsen's army to Bohemia, rather than the Army of Silesia. Blücher was ordered to move to his right, to cross the Elbe between Torgau and Wittenberg, thus prompting the Crown Prince to cross this river as well, and to operate in conjunction with the Army of the North. Emperor Alexander, delighted with the clarity of Major Rühle's arguments, embraced him in the presence of Friedrich Wilhelm and congratulated the King on having such an exemplary

---

12 General Blücher's letter to Emperor Alexander I, dated 13 September, new style, from Herrnhut. Archive of the M.T.D. No. 29,182, Log of Incoming Documents, No. 1,331.

officer in his army. But Blücher's evasion of the instructions he had received from the headquarters, although justified in practice, nevertheless aroused displeasure against him but even more against his faithful colleague Gneisenau, whom many tried to present before the eyes of the Coalition monarchs as an ambitious man who would sacrifice the common good in order to achieve his personal objectives.[13] Upset by the machinations of his ill-wishers, Gneisenau wrote to Graf Münster:

> Would that Emperor Alexander himself might take supreme command, to put an end to the innumerable differences, losses of time, and jealousies. As little as I intend to abandon my lord and king and the good cause, I must fear that ingratitude and hatred might almost induce me to withdraw as soon as the main work is done. In this case, I claim Your Excellency's goodwill to prepare me an asylum, where I can escape so many people who are ill-disposed towards me, and not be compelled to endure many faces marked by laziness or wickedness.[14]

On 6 (18) September, Major Rühle returned from Teplitz with approval from the Coalition sovereigns of everything proposed by Blücher. The Commander-in-Chief of the Army of Silesia received permission to advance to link up with the Army of the North in order to induce the Crown Prince to take decisive action. Blücher destroyed the dispatch written on this subject upon receipt, and a whole week later, on 13 (25) September, instructions were sent from the headquarters of the Coalition sovereigns to Blücher and Bennigsen.[15]

The orders for General Blücher contained the following instructions:

> The united army (of Bohemia) should soon enter Saxony, towards Chemnitz, or closer to the Elbe, depending on intelligence on the enemy.
> General Bennigsen's army is to hold the high ground at Nollendorf and secure our main communications with Prague along the Teplitz highway.
> Napoleon might hasten towards Bennigsen with his entire force, or against us via Freiberg in order to preserve his lines of communication. In the first case, that is, if he moves towards Teplitz, which judging by his previous attempts is most likely, such a course of action would be disastrous for him: General Bennigsen is to withdraw slowly and in good order with 60,000 or 70,000 men to a position at Laun, beyond the river Eger, holding the enemy frontally, while the main army, turning back, is to move on his flank (*flanquerait constamment l'ennemi*), while the army entrusted to you, having crossed the Elbe at Pirna, or at another point, at your discretion, is to move up behind and is to pursue him relentlessly.

---

13 Bernhardi, III, 331-332; Beitzke, Geschichte der deutschen Freiheitskriege in den Jahren 1813 und 1814, II, 355-356.
14 From General Gneisenau's letter to Graf Münster, from Bautzen, dated 18 September, new style. *Lebensbilder Aus Dem Befreiungskriege*, II, 325.
15 Bernhardi, III, 339; Beitzke, II, 359.

General Bubna may monitor the movements of the enemy army from the flank with his division, heading along the right bank of the Elbe towards Leitmeritz, or towards the bridgehead at Melnik, in order to delay any enemy crossing at this point.

These are the measures to be taken with the consent of *Feldmarschall* Prinz Schwarzenberg.

All that remains is to determine how your army should operate in the event of the enemy moving towards Freiberg. Indeed, in this case, you are to cross the Elbe, wherever you find it most appropriate, and decisively attack the enemy army from the rear together with General Bennigsen, or move to your right, towards Leipzig, along the Wurzen highway and establish communications with the Crown Prince. The latter course of action should be preferred by you only once you have confirmed that the Army of the North has crossed to the left bank of the Elbe, and even in that case it would be more advantageous to quickly pursue the enemy from behind, maintaining liaison with General Bennigsen, and if the enemy has left significant forces in Dresden, to besiege the city together with him, or to seize this place if it is occupied by a small number of troops.

In summary, continue to operate as you have before – do not lose contact with Napoleon and constantly try to coordinate your movements with those that are to be undertaken by the units of the Main Army.

Since crossing the Elbe in the vicinity of Dresden is very difficult, it should be decided upon only in the event that there are no enemy there, indeed, in general it would be better to cross at Pirna, under the protection of Bennigsen's army, by agreement with him regarding the time of his arrival at this location. Because such a move should only be made once Napoleon is on his way to Freiberg with his main force, the simultaneous arrival of both your armies at Pirna may be easily coordinated by having the ability to enter into communications with each other via Tetschen.

I propose that you inform Me about yourself every day, also informing Me of everything you know regarding the Crown Prince of Sweden and regarding the enemy army.[16]

General Bennigsen was sent the Tsar's Supreme Orders, dated 3 (15) September, regarding the cancellation of the mission previously assigned to him – to relieve the Army of Silesia, which had been intended to move into Bohemia. Instead, Bennigsen received orders to move there with the force entrusted to him, in two columns: the first, consisting of regular troops, directed via Rumburg and Böhmisch Leipa, was to arrive at Leitmeritz by 14 (26) September, while the second, consisting of *opolchenie*,

---

16 A copy of Emperor Alexander's instructions to Blücher, signed by Adjutant General Prince Volkonsky, dated 13 (25) September, is in the Archive of the M.T.D. No. 15,314.

was also to proceed to Leitmeritz, via Zittau and Gabel, to arrive by 19 September (1 October).[17]

The instructions to General Bennigsen, sent to him at the same time as those sent to Blücher, were as follows:

> The army entrusted to you is assigned to protect the lines of communication of the Main Army. In order to achieve this objective, you are to take up positions at Kulm, forwards of Teplitz, sending a vanguard up to Nollendorf or Peterswald, and flank detachments to guard Vorder Zinnwald and the road to Altenberg. Therefore, send partisans in this direction and along the Peterswald highway as far as possible, but avoiding a decisive engagement, so as not to attract the attention of the enemy. All defiles leading to your position must be fortified as thoroughly and as quickly as possible.
>
> Throughout the offensive by the Main Army, the enemy might turn towards Teplitz via Peterswald with significant forces in order to get out of difficulty by abandoning his line of operations and seizing: his previous attempts provide grounds for this assumption. Having fully realised the importance of the mission assigned to you, you must exploit every terrain advantage in order to delay the enemy through stubborn rearguard actions and retreat to Laun, to the fortified position behind the Eger, striving to protect Budin. Stay in this position as long as possible and remain in constant communication with Blücher, informing him of every enemy move such that he may support you, as necessary. You are also to come to an agreement with the commandants of Theresienstadt and the bridgehead at Melnik and with *Felmarschall* Kolowrat [Johann Nepomuk Karl Joseph von Kolowrat-Krakowsky] in Prague on everything related to the protection of these points from enemy attacks.
>
> Finally, I instruct you, general, in particular to send reports to Me twice daily, such that the Main Army can hurry to your aid if the enemy begins to pressure you strongly. But you must have reliable intelligence on the number of enemy troops advancing against you in order not to force us to abandon the movement we have undertaken due to some hollow rumours. In order to achieve this objective, you are to stay on high ground for as long as possible, because once the enemy has driven you into the valleys, they can conceal all their movements.
>
> If Napoleon moves towards Freiberg against the Main Army, or towards Frauenstein, about which it should be easy for you to obtain intelligence from partisans or informants, in this case, you may leave part of your army in the position assigned to you, and move towards the enemy left flank and

---

17 Supreme Orders for General Bennigsen, dated 13 [25] September and Prince Volkonsky's dispatch to him dated 7 [19] September. Archive of the M.T.D. No. 29,190, Log of Outgoing Documents, No. 51 and No. 64.

rear with the rest of the force, in order to force them to divide their forces and make it easier for Blücher to cross the Elbe…[18]

At the same time, a letter was sent to the Crown Prince of Sweden from Emperor Alexander, in which the Tsar, informing him of the imminent arrival of Bennigsen's army in Bohemia, which was intended to trigger the invasion of Saxony via Marienberg by the Main Coalition Army, set out His views on the Crown Prince's operations, as follows:

> In all probability, our offensive will draw Napoleon's main force towards the Army of Bohemia, or towards Bennigsen, who will remain guarding the Teplitz highway. It is desirable that Your Highness, taking advantage of favourable circumstances with the usual faithfulness of your military intuition, cross the Elbe and seize Leipzig with your vanguard. The occupation of this city will deprive the enemy of immense resources, because all their communications pass through there and it is from there that they receive their essential resupply. As soon as Napoleon, having left just a garrison in Dresden, turns with all his strength against our Main Army, then if you decide to commit to cross, General Blücher will move to his right to assist the Army of the North. Instructions have accordingly been sent to Blücher, but you definitely need to notify him of your intentions and everything that is to happen subsequently. You alone may judge, based on intelligence on the enemy, whether it would be possible to launch the proposed operations. It is vital to increase our efforts to induce the enemy to abandon the Elbe line, which provides them with so many advantages, and to overcome the obstacles separating our armies. Having achieved this objective, we have a right to hope for the most brilliant outcome, because in this case we may give our operations the completeness and strength necessary for success.[19]

Thus, the storm-clouds of the battle of the nations of Europe at Leipzig were approaching to surround Napoleon from all sides. But before following him there, we consider it necessary to take a quick look at the bold raids by the Coalition partisans in the lands still under the yoke of the conqueror.

---

18 A copy of Emperor Alexander's instructions to General Bennigsen, dated 13 (25) September is in the Archive of the M.T.D. No. 15,314.
19 Letter to the Crown Prince of Sweden, dated 13 (25) September, Log of Outgoing Documents, No. 80.

35

Partisan operations since the ending of the armistice

Partisans from the Army of Bohemia. Detachments on the enemy lines of communications: *Oberst* Graf Mensdorff; *Generalleutnant* Thielmann. – Counter moves by General Lefebvre-Desnouettes. – The assignment of Count Platov to assist the partisans. – The actions at Altenburg and Zeitz.

Partisans from the Army of the North. *Oberst* Marwitz's expedition to Braunschweig. Adjutant General Chernyshev's expedition to Kassel. King Jérôme and the Kingdom of Westphalia. – The Westphalian army. – Dispositions of Westphalian forces. – Chernyshev's detachment; crossing the Elbe and deployment to Bernburg. – The move towards Roßla. – The diversion to Sondershausen and on towards Kassel. – Deployment of the force. – The attack on the city. – Extraction to Melsungen. – Dispersion of Bastineller's detachment. – The arrival of Zandt's detachment in Kassel from Göttingen. – The composition of the Kassel garrison. – The recruitment of Westphalian infantry and artillery by the Coalition. – Chernyshev's second advance on Kassel. – Unrest in the city. – Negotiations. – The surrender of Kassel. – Trophies. – Casualties in the Russian detachment. – Dissolution of the Kingdom of Westphalia. – Chernyshev's return march to the Elbe. – The consequences of the Kassel expedition. – The Crown Prince of Sweden's dispatch regarding this expedition.

Partisans from the Army of Silesia.

Following the battle of Kulm, General Toll submitted a memo highlighting the successes achieved by the Russian partisans in the War of 1812. He proposed sending several light detachments into Saxony along the roads from Dresden to Leipzig, Altenburg and Chemnitz in order to operate against the communications of the enemy army and for waging guerilla warfare. To that end, it was necessary, in his opinion, to reassign 12 Cossack regiments from Blücher's army to the Army of Bohemia. Though such operations, it would be possible not only to deprive the enemy of the resources supplied by the regions of Saxony, but also to establish magazines in Zwickau and Hof for the Main Army, which was soon to move towards Leipzig, to link up with the army under the Crown Prince of Sweden.[1] Toll's proposal was approved and at the same time, on 20 August (1 September), the Austrian *Oberst* Graf Mensdorff was sent from Komotau towards Chemnitz with four Austrian squadrons and two Cossack regiments, numbering some 1,000 men, while the next day, 21 August (2 September), *Generalleutnant* Baron Thielmann, in Russian service, followed him with eight squadrons, three Cossack regiments and two Don guns,[2] numbering about 1,500 men.[3] General Thielmann, knowing the terrain of this country completely from his service fighting against the Herzog von Braunschweig [Friedrich Wilhelm von Braunschweig] in 1809, hoped to take advantage of good relations with the population in order to cause harm in the enemy army rear areas, where confusion and disorder reigned. Wounded and unwounded soldiers who had fled from the battlefields of Großbeeren and Kulm were drawn, singly and in whole crowds, along every route leading to the Rhine.[4] Moving from Komotau through Altenburg, Thielmann reached Weißenfels on 30 August (11 September), where the enemy detachment assigned to escort convoys with provisions and other supplies heading to Leipzig was located at the time, numbering 4,000 infantry and 500 cavalry,. General Thielmann, catching the enemy with a surprise attack at dawn, took around 1,300 men prisoner; the next day [12 September, new style], the town of Naumburg [8½ miles west of Weißenfels] surrendered to a Prussian squadron under *Rittmeister* Graf Wartensleben, where 400 French were captured, together with 600 sick. On 6 (18) September, Thielmann overran Merseburg, where he took 700 armed and 1,500 unarmed enemy prisoner and released 2,000 Coalition army sick and wounded from captivity. After that, General Thielmann, together with Mensdorff, took several hundred more men prisoner, intercepted couriers with important dispatches and freed some 600 Austrian and Russian prisoners of war.[5]

The successes of the Coalition partisans forced Napoleon to take measures to secure his army's communications: to that end, général de division Lefebvre-Desnouettes received orders to clear the country to the rear of the army of Coalition partisans, with the *chasseurs à cheval de la Garde* division and three batteries, having assimilated to his force the march battalions and cavalry depots located in Leipzig commanded by General Margaron [Pierre Margaron].[6] As soon as this

---

1 Major General Toll's memo submitted to *Feldmarschall* Prinz Schwarzenberg on 20 August (1 September).
2 General Thielmann's detachment consisted of: a Russian contingent commanded by Colonel Orlov: three Cossack regiments and two Don Cossack guns; an Austrian contingent: two squadrons each from the *Husaren Hessen-Homburg* and *Chevaulegers Klenau*; a Prussian contingent commanded by *Generalmajor* Prinz Biron von Curland: two squadrons each from the *2. Schlesisches Husaren* and *Schlesisches National Kavallerie*.
3 Plotho, Der Krieg in Deutschland und Frankreich in den Jahren 1813 und 1814, II, 180-181.
4 Förster, Geschichte der Befreiungskriege, 1813, 1814, 1815, II, 28-29.
5 Beitzke, Geschichte der deutschen Freiheitskriege in den Jahren 1813 und 1814, II, 398-399.
6 The sources for the composition and strength of Lefebvre-Desnouette's force are very contradictory: in Vaudoncourt's *Histoire de la guerre soutenue par les Français en Allemagne*, 182, 4,000 men are shown; in Richter's *Geschichte des Deutschen Freiheitskrieges vom Jahre 1813 bis zum Jahre 1815*, II, 113 and Beitzke, II, 399, 7,000 are shown, and so on.

intelligence was received at the headquarters of the Army of Bohemia, a Cossack detachment under Count Platov (to which Prince Kudashev's detachment was also subordinated), numbering some 2,000 men with ten guns,[7] and the small Prussian detachments under *Rittmeister* Colomb and *Rittmeister* Graf Pückler were sent to assist Thielmann and Mensdorff on 10 (22) September.[8] Upon reaching Penig [13 miles north-west of Chemnitz] on 15 (27) September, Platov met with Thielmann and Mensdorff, who were based nearby, and agreed on an attack on Lefebvre-Desnouettes, located near Altenburg, for the following day. Early on the morning of 16 (28) September, even before Thielman had chance to arrive from the direction of Zeitz, Prince Kudashev attacked the enemy on the river Pleiße with Platov's vanguard, captured the village of Windischleuba [2½ miles north-east of Altenburg] and blocked the road to Leipzig. Lefebvre-Desnouettes, intending to shield the line of retreat to Zeitz, took up positions on the high ground behind Altenburg, but once two Cossack regiments and one Austrian squadron enveloped them on their right flank, at nine o'clock in the morning, the enemy force began to retreat in haste towards Zeitz. Upon reaching Meuselwitz, the French halted and checked Kudashev's detachment, but upon being attacked from the right flank by Thielmann's force, they continued their onward retreat towards Zeitz, while Thielmann, moving parallel to them, harassed them with attacks and almost destroyed the entire enemy rearguard. Lefebvre-Desnouettes, upon reaching Zeitz, held the high ground to the front with two batteries in order to give his force time to retreat through the town. The *Husaren Hessen-Homburg* and *Schlesisches Husaren* formed up facing this artillery and suffered heavy losses, but after that Prince Kudashev, having placed several Don guns on the enemy flank, put their position under enfilade fire and forced the French batteries to withdraw. At this very moment, the cavalry under Platov, Thielmann and Mensdorff raced into the attack: in the lead, the Black Sea Cossack regiment were first to break into the town. Some of the enemy infantry, ensconced in factory buildings in front of the town (Albrechtsche Fabrik Gebäude), fired at the Coalition cavalry, forcing them to dismount and storm the factory. The Cossacks and hussars, under the command of Prinz Biron von Curland [Gustav Kalixt von Biron], drove the enemy out of the buildings they held, wiped out some of the force, capturing 36 officers and 1,380 lower ranks, and took three banners and five guns in combat (three were taken by Platov's men and two by Thielmann's). The Coalition lost some 300 men in this action; Prinz Biron was among those lightly wounded.[9] Emperor Alexander, having received the report on this successful feat, ordered the

---

7   Count Platov's and Prince Kudashev's detachments consisted of: the Ataman's Cossacks, Grekov 5th's Cossacks, Chernovuzov 5th's Cossacks, 1st Teptyar Cossacks, Chikilev 1st's Cossacks and Black Sea Cossacks, with ten Don artillery pieces. Plotho, II, 218. In the force strength returns, dated 1 [13] September, signed by Barclay de Tolly, Prince Kudashev had two guns, while no artillery are shown with Platov.
8   *Rittmeister* Colomb's detachment consisted of: nine officers and 160 lower ranks from various Prussian cavalry regiments (*Aus dem Tagebuche des Rittmeisters von Colomb*, 87). *Rittmeister* Graf Pückler's detachment consisted of: 50 *Brandenbugisches Husaren* and 30 Cossacks from the 4th Ukrainian Regiment (Plotho, II, 218).
9   Plotho, II, 232-234; War Diary signed by Adjutant General Prince Volkonsky; Vaudoncourt, 182-183.

detachment under Count Platov to be reinforced with two more regiments; 3rd Orenburg Cossacks and 11th Bashkirs.[10]

Throughout the Army of the North's inactive period after the battle of Dennewitz, its detachments operated successfully on the left bank of the Elbe, commanded by brave and skilful leaders.

On 10 (22) September, *Oberstleutnant* Marwitz, in Prussian service, with the 3. *Neumärkischen Landwehr Kavallerie*, numbering 400 men, having crossed the Elbe at Ferchland, two *Meilen* (around 15 *versts*) upstream of Tangermünde, reaching Braunschweig, one of the most significant cities in the Kingdom of Westphalia, at dawn on 13 (25) September, garrisoned by 980 men from various units, commanded by the decrepit and indecisive *Brigadegeneral* Klösterlein. On that same day, as Marwitz was preparing to attack the city, Klösterlein sent his entire trains to Salzgitter, on the road to Kassel, while he set out for Wolfenbüttel himself with his troops, leaving *Oberst* Bork with a single company of carabiniers in Braunschweig. After Klösterlein had departed, Marwitz attacked the city from several sides, overran it almost without a shot and sent *Leutnant* Graf Finckenstein [Carl Ludwig Wilhelm Bonaventura Finck von Finckenstein] with 50 horsemen in pursuit of Klösterlein, who, having learned in Wolfenbüttel of the seizure of Braunschweig by Russian troops, set off to continue down the Goslar road, but had barely passed the village of Halchter [1½ miles south of Wolfenbüttel], when he was caught by the Prussians. Finckenstein himself, galloping up to the Westphalians, shouted: 'You would not shoot at your German brothers, would you?'[11] The Westphalian soldiers immediately handed themselves over to the Prussian detachment, while Klösterlein and other commanders were forced to seek salvation in flight. The overall number of Westphalian prisoners reached 25 officers and 350 lower ranks. Most of them expressed a desire to enter Prussian service. Since so many students from the *braunschweigischen Militärschule* also volunteered to serve in the Coalition army, a *freiwillige Jägerschwadron* [volunteer jäger squadron] was formed within 3. *Neumärkischen Landwehr Kavallerie* from all these volunteers. The population of Braunschweig greeted and saw off their liberators with delight and hope for a better future. Having accomplished the expedition with brilliant success, Marwitz's detachment returned to Ferchland along country lanes, via Burgstall and Grieben [12½ miles east of Burgstall].[12]

The expedition to the Kingdom of Westphalia by Adjutant General Chernyshev would have incomparably more important consequences.

In the work by the Hessian *Hauptmann* Specht (*Das Königreich Westphalen und seine Armee im Jahr 1813*), we find a gloomy depiction of the situation in this country. Upon the conclusion of the Treaty of Tilsit, having merged the *Kurfürstentum* [Electorates] of Hessen, Braunschweig and Hannover together with Prussian territory lying on the left bank of the Elbe, under the designation of the Kingdom of Westphalia [*Königreich*

---

10 Adjutant General Prince Volkonsky's dispatch to Count Platov, dated 20 September [2 October], Log of Outgoing Documents, No. 88.
11 'Ihr werdet doch nicht auf euere deutschen Brüder feuern?'
12 Plotho, II, 307-308; Richter, II, 115-116; Beitzke, II, 453-454; F.A.K. von Specht, *Das Königreich Westphalen und seine Armee im Jahr 1813*, 97-105.

Westphalen or *Royaume de Westphalie*], as one of the members of the *Confédération du Rhin*, Napoleon gave it to his younger brother Jérôme. Not only did the new king know neither the language, nor the culture and customs of the country under his control, but he also never bothered to learn them. Distracted by festivities and amusements, he gave no consideration at all to reinforcing his dubious rights to the throne through wise governance, and therefore, despite his natural intelligence and kindness, he alienated himself from all those on whom he should have been reliant in dangerous moments. The constant associates for him and the French who were with him were solely the corrupt who held public opinion from their countrymen in contempt. State revenue was consumed by the pomp of the Court, which was onerous for his subjects, yet did not inspire respect for their ruler – the puppet of his powerful brother. The king was obliged to send his troops everywhere at Napoleon's behest: the war in Spain cost the Westphalians at least 7,000 men; the war of 1809 against Austria required new sacrifices; of the 25,000 men sent to Russia, no more than 2,000 returned; in the War of 1813, losses reached a third of the available troops (some 8,000 men): consequently, in the space of five years, some 40,000 Westphalians had died fighting for Napoleon. At the same time, the people, impoverished by the introduction of the Continental System [*le blocus continental*] and the decline of trade, were oppressed by exorbitant taxes and extorted loans. In addition to the enormous costs of maintaining the Court and the army, which consisted of 26,000 Westphalians and 18,600 French, the King was forced to pay Napoleon more than 30,000,000 [*sic*, 13,000,000] francs annually (around 3,500,000 roubles). The national debt had reached 94,000,000 francs (more than 25,000,000 roubles), and the war indemnity imposed on the country by Napoleon in 1812 had reached 16,000,000 francs (4,500,000 roubles), when two-thirds of it had already been paid. In 1813, the Westphalians contributed more than 18 francs (five roubles) per head to the treasury, and yet the deficit had reached 9,500,000 francs (more than 2,500,000 roubles). The Ministry of Finance was concerned only with raising revenue, without any concern for the future.[13]

Of the 30,000 Westphalian troops, two-thirds were distributed among various French corps, while the remaining 10,000 (6,850 infantry, 3,046 cavalry and 416 artillerymen) were stationed in the vicinity of Kassel and Braunschweig. The borders of the state were completely open. With the exception of a small corps of *gendarmes*, which constituted an excellent cavalry force completely loyal to the French, every other regiment was formed from recruits who were serving under duress. Deserters caught by the *gendarmes* were being shot almost daily around Kassel.[14] The King of Westphalia and those close to him distrusted the loyalty of the troops but at least tried to draw the officers to themselves by generously distributing honours and awards. For greater security, the King surrounded himself with conscripted French troops, equipped in Kassel and enlisted into the *Garde*, and they were granted important privileges. The *Garde-Chevauxlegers* were forced to give the *Hieronymus-Napoleon-Husaren* their best horses, but both the officers and the lower ranks of this French-manned unit had few military veterans, and were not even skilled horsemen.[15]

---

13 Specht, 4-36.
14 Specht, 69-83.
15 Specht, 86-88.

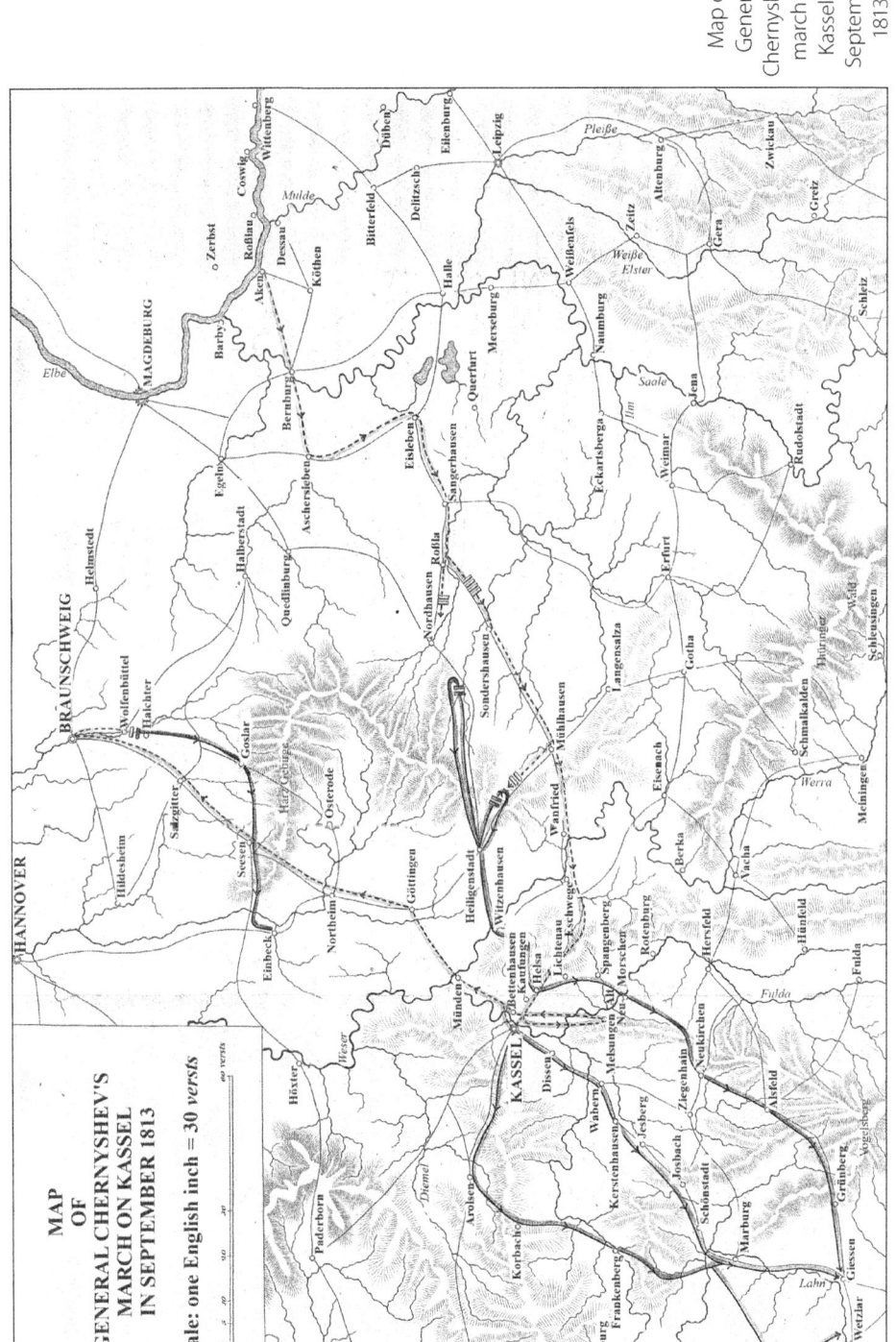

Map of General Chernyshev's march on Kassel in September 1813.

The suspicions of the French regarding the loyalty of the Westphalian troops were not slow to justify themselves in practice. On the night of 10 to 11 (22 to 23) August, two of the best regiments in the Westphalian army, the *1. Husaren* and *2. Husaren*, stationed at Reichenberg in Silesia, defected to the Austrians in Bohemia. Two of their detached squadrons were later taken prisoner (probably willingly), on 6 (18) September, by the Austrian partisan, *Oberst* Schniter, at Freiberg in Saxony.[16]

The defeats suffered by Napoleon's military commanders and the raids by Coalition partisans forced the Westphalian government to take measures to protect the kingdom's capital, Kassel, from the direction of the river Saale. To that end, detachments were positioned on the main approach routes from there as follows: two squadrons at Göttingen, numbering some 300 men commanded by General Zandt, and one battalion from *7. Infanterie* supporting them from Münden, numbering 840 men; a cuirassier brigade, *3. Leichteinfanterie Batallion* and two guns at Heiligenstadt, numbering 1,200 cavalry, 1,000 infantry and 70 artillerymen, commanded by *Brigadegeneral* von Bastineller.[17] The Kassel garrison consisted of 3,060 infantry, 906 cavalry and 336 artillery, for a total of 4,200 men with six guns. In addition, there were 28 guns in the city.[18]

The displeasure that prevailed against King Jérôme and the French in Westphalia was known in the headquarters of the Army of the North. Adjutant General Chernyshev, one of the most outstanding Russian partisans, quite reasonably believed that the occupation of Kassel by the Coalition, by ending the existence of the Kingdom of Westphalia, could incite an uprising against Napoleon in other German territories. Due to the location and terrain around Kassel providing the means for a stubborn defence and due to the rather significant number of troops holding it, the capture of this city without the aid of infantry presented extreme difficulties for a light detachment, consisting mostly of Cossacks. Nevertheless, General Chernyshev decided on this undertaking, hoping for the assistance of the population and national troops, and realising that the success of the proposed attack depended not so much on the strength of the detachment entrusted to him, but on the suddenness of its appearance.

Having requested permission from the Crown Prince of Sweden to march on Kassel, General Chernyshev set off for the Elbe with a detachment consisting of eight squadrons and five Cossack regiments, with four horse artillery pieces (other sources show six), numbering some 2,300 men.[19] The Cossack regiments were commanded by Colonel Benckendorff (Konstantin Khristoforovich Benkendorf [or Konstantin Friedrich von Benckendorff]); the artillery by Captain Lishin; the quartermaster of

---

16 Specht, 88-89.
17 Specht, 95-96.
18 Specht, 137-139.
19 See Map No. 11, General Chernyshev's march on Kassel. Specht (146) shows Chernyshev's deatchment as: three squadrons of combined hussars, three squadrons of Izyum Hussars, two squadrons of Finland Dragoons, Sysoev 3rd's Cossacks, Zhirov's Cossacks, Grekov 18th's Cossacks, Vlasov 3rd's Cossacks, Balabin 2nd's Cossacks, and six horse artillery pieces, numbering 2,300 men. In Lieutenant Colonel Balmain's manuscript, the regular cavalry are shown as two squadrons each of Izyum Hussars, Riga Dragoons and Finland Dragoons, with the same Cossack regiments, but only four horse artillery pieces, numbering 1,200 to 1,300 men.

the detachment was Colonel Bogdanovich; Among the volunteers were: Lieutenant Colonel Count Balmain [Alexander Antonovich de Balmain] (subsequently, as a Russian commissar, he was on the island of St. Helena during Napoleon's incarceration there.), Major Dörnberg and Prussian officers: *Oberst* Barnekow, *Rittmeister* Arnim and *Rittmeister* Fabeck, among others.[20] Having crossed the Elbe near Aken by boat on the night of 2 to 3 (14 to 15) September, General Chernyshev deployed at Bernburg and sent patrols out in various directions in order to distract the enemy and to collect intelligence, as necessary.[21] One of these patrols, consisting of 80 Cossacks, commanded by *Rittmeister* Fabeck, managed to attack Querfurt, catching the garrison by surprise and took 40 officers and 500 lower ranks prisoner there.[22]

On 12 (24) September, General Chernyshev's detachment set off from Bernburg and arrived at Roßla the next day [25 September, new style]. Movement once inside enemy occupied territory was carried out in compliance with full precautions: the troops stopped for the night for the shortest time, in places remote from any habitation; when they happened to make short halts in towns or villages, the detachment was cordoned off by Cossack outposts that prevented any of the residents from leaving the villages; when setting off on the onward march, the *Bürgermeister* [mayor] and other local officials were invited to accompany the troops and were not released until the detachment had moved a fairly considerable distance; the guides did not know the true end-point of each stage, and they were also questioned about routes along which there was not intention to travel at all; the troops often turned away from the intended direction and returned to it once there were no outsiders with the detachment, except for informants of proven loyalty, upon whom one could fully rely.[23]

Upon reaching Roßla, Adjutant General Chernyshev received intelligence that General Bastineller was still stationed at Heiligenstadt, having pushed forward outposts towards Nordhausen. Chernyshev had no choice but to take a roundabout route, evading Bastineller's detachment in order to mask the movements of the Russian force towards Kassel for as long as possible. A large patrol was sent to Nordhausen in order to engage the enemy frontally. Chernyshev moved to the left himself, along a poor road to Sondershausen, presenting the detachment as the vanguard of a significant corps and ordering provisions to be prepared for 30,000 men; everyone travelling towards Kassel was detained. The reigning Fürst von Schwarzburg-Sondershausen [Günther Friedrich Carl I], submitting to the force of circumstances, went to meet the unexpected guests with his entire retinue, received the officers in his palace and bade the detachment farewell as they set out on their next march.[24] The force arrived at Mühlhausen on the morning of 15 (27) September and moving on from there that same day, they made a forced march of 11 *Meilen*

---

20 Lieutenant Colonel Balmain's manuscript notes.
21 According to a statement by Captain Lishin, who participated in the expedition, the men crossed by boat with the saddles and other harness, the horses swam, while guns, limbers and ammunition caissons, were carried across individually, on boats rafted up in pairs and decked with planks.
22 Plotho, II, 305.
23 Captain Lishin's manuscript notes.
24 Balmain's notes; Specht, 148.

(around 80 *versts*), through Wanfried, Eschwege and Waldkappel [8½ miles southeast of Lichtenau], and reached Kassel at half past six o'clock in the morning of 16 (28) September completely undetected, which was facilitated by the thick fog that blanketed the outskirts of the city. Despite the measures taken by Chernyshev to hide the objective of his mission, Bastineller had learned about the movements of the Russian detachment from the patrols sent out; and a courier had been sent to Kassel from Mühlhausen, with a report from the local administration there about the presence of Russian troops. General Chernyshev, having learned about this, sent a Cossack patrol after the courier, and although the Cossacks managed to intercept him, an undercover *gendarme* who was travelling with him, taking advantage of the darkness of the night, managed to escape and reached Kassel.[25]

Thus, the Westphalian government was forewarned of the threat, but the measures taken to repel the Russian force were most insubstantial: a small detachment sent from the city to engage them was defeated with losses in the suburb of Bettenhausen; six guns placed in a battery near the Forstfeld meadow [one mile south of Bettenhausen] without an escort, were captured by the Cossacks. Continuous thick persistent fog delayed the advance of the Russian detachment until half past ten o'clock in the morning.[26] General Chernyshev, hoping that the failure suffered by the enemy forward detachment would force King Jérôme to leave Kassel, issued orders to sever the routes leading to the Rhine and Paderborn: Colonel Benckendorff was sent to Neue Mühle [three miles south of Kassel] with Zhirov's Cossacks and with one squadron of Riga Dragoons in order to cross the Fulda upstream of the city and to block the Frankfurt road, while a half-*Sotnia* of Cossacks were sent to Wolfsanger [3½ miles north-east of Kassel] in order to cross downstream of the city and to block the roads to Paderborn and Arolsen. The attack on the city was entrusted to Colonel Bedryaga [Yegor Ivanovich Bedryaga], with two squadrons of Izyum Hussars, Vlasov's Cossacks, Grekov's Cossacks and two guns under Captain Lishin. In order protect the detachment from behind, from Bastineller on the march from Heiligenstadt to Witzenhausen, a Cossack *Sotnia* and a squadron of dragoons were ordered to occupy the defile at Kaufungen and to set up an outpost at Helsa. All other units remained in reserve.[27]

Colonel Bedryaga overran a company of *Garde Jägers* sent forwards, and as soon as two rounds of canister had been fired at the remaining companies, he launched an attack upon them; the battalion managed to form square, but became disordered and were, for the most part, taken prisoner. The enemy force retreated behind the Wahlebach stream [less than a mile east of the Fulda river]. But this success was bought at a high price: Colonel Bedryaga was among the wounded, mortally hit by two bullets.[28]

During the course of these actions, Colonel Benckendorff had crossed the Fulda at Neue Mühle with most of his detachment and drove off the *Garde Husaren* sent to

---

25 Balmain's notes; Specht, 149.
26 Specht, 151-154.
27 Specht, 183-185.
28 Lishin's notes; Chernyshev's report to General Wintzingerode, dated 19 September (1 October), from Kassel (Log of Incoming Documents, No. 1,580); Specht, 157 & 185.

engage him, but having learned from prisoners taken that King Jérôme had already managed to escape along the Frankfurt road, and having been engaged by an enemy superior in numbers, crossed back to the right bank of the Fulda; he had captured ten officers and 250 cavalrymen from the force accompanying the King. General Chernyshev, having received the information on the flight of the King with his most loyal troops and about General Allix's assumption of command in the city [Jacques Alexandre François Allix de Vaux], decided to attack the enemy who had retreated behind the Wahlebach; the units in reserve were ordered to close up in order to guarantee the success of the assault.[29]

No sooner had the tireless men of the Don enveloped the enemy on both flanks, having forded the [Wahlebach] stream, than Chernyshev launched an attack in two columns: the Izyum Hussars advanced frontally, the Cossacks went right-flanking. One of the enemy guns was knocked out. After several rounds of canister from Lishin at the troops stationed behind the bridge, both Russian columns rushed at the infantry standing opposite them, dispersed them, captured a damaged gun and reached the Leipziger Tor [gatehouse]. Several shells lobbed into the city were effective in causing its defenders to flee. The Cossacks rode up to the gate, opened it with the help of several townspeople, and galloped through the Unterneustadt to the bridge on the Fulda. Since the enemy had not bothered to occupy the Schloß [Rathaus], a strong building dominating the bridge and a large square, the Russians, having occupied it, consolidated themselves in the Unterneustadt, but upon being engaged at the bridge by withering musketry from every nearby building, they were forced to halt. *Garde Husaren*, supported by infantry, turned against Benckendorff, and two cuirassier regiments with two guns from Bastineller's detachment, appeared behind Chernyshev's force. Although having subsequently changed his original intention – to march to Kassel, General Bastineller was now moving towards Lichtenau in order to make his way to the Rhine, this fact was unknown to Chernyshev at the time, who, considering himself surrounded by superior forces and not having the infantry needed to capture the city with him, decided to retreat to Melsungen, a short march from Kassel. At about 11 o'clock, the troops received orders to break off the attack and leave the city, which was achieved without interference from the enemy. Benckendorff's detachment were left near Kassel as the rearguard, while Sysoev's Cossacks, positioned to monitor Bastineller in the vicinity of Kaufungen, retreated at dusk, following the other units towards Melsungen.[30] Bastineller's men, exhausted from the forced pace of the retreat and with collapsing morale, mostly scattered; the rest fell into such disorder that their commander, having reached Alt-Morschen, ordered that the two guns that were with the detachment, due to the exhaustion of the horses and being unable to take them any further, be pushed into the Fulda river.[31] General Chernyshev, who had meanwhile stationed himself at Melsungen with his main force, having learned about the pitiful state of the enemy detachment, sent *Khorunzhy* [Cossack cornet] Sevastyanov with a *Sotnia* of Cossacks to pursue them, caught up with Bastineller's rearguard and stragglers at Alt-Morschen, put

---

29 Specht, 186.
30 Lishin's notes; General Chernyshev's report from Kassel; Specht, 186-190.
31 Specht, 196.

them to flight, and took 20 cuirassiers prisoner, retrieved both guns from the Fulda and returned to Melsungen.[32]

Zandt's detachment, which was in Göttingen on 16 (28) September, 40 *versts* from Kassel, having received orders issued to them the day before, were to march to the capital, and should be able to reach there by making one forced march. But General Zandt, an inexperienced and timid man, owing his position to the whim of King Jérôme, instead of immediately setting out for Kassel, initially postponed the march until four o'clock in the morning on 17 (29) September, and then, having sent the first battalion of *7. Infanterie* to Kassel, which had arrived from Münden two days before, remained static for several hours with his cavalry. Thereafter, moving towards Münden, General Zandt overtook the infantry there, gave the entire detachment a long rest and for a long time could not decide whether to go to Kassel via the shortest route through Lutterberg [4½ miles south of Münden] and Landwehrhagen [six miles north-east of Kassel], or to cross the Fulda and move towards Wilhelmshausen [9½ miles north of Kassel]. Meanwhile, the halt in Münden had very serious consequences. The soldiers who had previously been placed in quarters there heard exaggerated stories from the residents, that the Russians had already captured Kassel and all the Westphalian units had fled. At the same time, the townsfolk in Münden challenged the soldiers to refuse to soldier on, telling them: 'Are you going to Kassel and will you fight for the French against the Russians and your German brothers who have come to liberate you?' and such like. The indecisiveness and lateness of Zandt's orders instilled doubt in the ranks of his force, who, having moved his infantry from one bank to the other several times, did not advance. Eventually, once it was already seven o'clock in the evening, the detachment moved up the left bank of the Fulda. The soldiers, stretched out in the darkness of the night, along bad roads through the forests, mixed into a discordant crowd and began to scatter in various directions. The men from Hannover and Braunschweig were the first to go; then the Hessians dispersed as they approached their homeland. At ten o'clock in the morning on 17 (29) September, Zandt's detachment reached Kassel, having lost a significant number of men. Only 200 men remained in the battalion from *7. Infanterie* out of 816. Indeed, the Kassel garrison had been significantly weakened overall by desertion and the consequences of the unsuccessful action on 16 (28) September. There remained just 500 infantry, and 350 cavalry. General Allix, wanting to reassure the inhabitants of the city and arouse loyalty to the French among the troops, ordered the following news to be published in *le Moniteur* on 17 (29) September:

> Yesterday several hundred Cossacks appeared in front of the city, but they were engaged in such a way that they lost the desire to advance again and fled into the forests with heavy losses.
>
> The peace in the city was not disturbed for a single minute, and both residents and troops behaved in the best possible manner.

---

32 General Chernyshev's report from Kassel; Specht, 199.

Despite these assurances, however, Allix himself recognised the impossibility of a prolonged defence, given the small numbers in the garrison, the unreliability of the troops and the hostile disposition of the population, and therefore limited himself to placing two guns in front of the Friedrichsplatz and two on the Weinberg, a hill [⅓ mile] south of the city, and lining the Fulda embankment with 6. *Jäger Kompagnie*.[33]

Throughout 17 (29) September, General Chernyshev remained at Melsungen with his detachment, receiving intelligence from informants, defectors and people devoted to the German cause, regarding everything that was happening in Kassel, and especially about the morale of the troops. *Oberst* Barnekow, *Rittmeister* Fabeck and *Rittmeister* Arnim were instructed to form a battalion of 300 men from prisoners of war, defectors and volunteers. All the captured guns were supplied with crews from the dragoons and Westphalian artillerymen who volunteered to operate alongside the Russians. Allix, having received word of the advance by the Russian detachment, ordered the checkpoints to be closed and occupied by troops; the Fulda bridge was also barricaded with wagons and a gun was placed behind it with an escort; the two guns stationed on the Weinberg were driven to the Friedrichsplatz, where a battery of four guns was formed, with protection from the remnants of 7. *Infanterie* and the *Garde Jäger Bataillon*; the cavalry were located on the Linden Allee, near the Friedrichsplatz.[34]

General Chernyshev, having reached the city, ordered the artillery to open fire both on the city buildings and on the troops stationed on the Friedrichsplatz. The city residents begged Allix to spare them by concluding a capitulation, he replied: 'I have been ordered to defend the city to the bitter end, and I shall fulfil the orders issued to me.' This response agitated the citizens; young men walked the streets in crowds, announcing that since the French were no longer able to defend the city, and any further resistance could only lead to its ruin, they would force open the city gates to the Russians. Matters got to the point that the Kassel residents began to obstruct the troops in the performance of their duties. The *Garde Husaren* were obliged to fire into the crowds of people, who threw stones at the soldiers and at Allix himself, and left the city to engage the Russian force. As soon as Colonel Benckendorff advanced towards the Leipziger Tor with the Westphalian battalion and two squadrons of dismounted dragoons, the carabinier company stationed there, without waiting for the attack, handed the checkpoint over to the Russians, who, having manned the outpost, entered the city. Nevertheless, General Chernyshev, wanting to save the inhabitants from the destruction that threatened them, sent Count Balmain to Allix, as a *parlementaire*, with a letter in which Chernyshev informed the French general of the destruction of Bastineller's detachment and proposed that he surrender the city, inviting the Westphalian *Garde* to fight alongside the Russian forces. Allix wanted to detain both Balmain and Colonel Benckendorff, who had been sent after him, but having encountered resistance from his closest colleagues and being threatened with a general uprising by the residents of Kassel, he sent *Oberstleutnant* Bolte to General Chernyshev, expressing his consent to surrender the city on the following conditions:

---

33 Specht, 200-210.
34 Lishin's notes; General Chernyshev's report from Kassel; Specht, 210-213.

1. To hand over the city in 48 hours.
2. To take his artillery with him.
3. To respect and maintain the integrity of royal property.

In anticipation of the conclusion of the capitulation, Allix left the city and bivouacked outside the Kölnische Tor with the remaining cavalry. Negotiations were conducted on the Russian side by Colonel Benckendorff, with the assistance of Count Balmain and Major Dörnberg. Eventually, at dusk, General Allix signed the surrender, which contained conditions demanded by Chernyshev, namely:

1. The Westphalian and French troops were to leave the city that evening, with personal weapons and purely military baggage, but without artillery.
2. The city would be occupied by Imperial Russian troops that evening.
3. In order to protect the Westphalian and French troops from attacks by Cossack detachments roaming in every direction, the units under General Allix were to be accompanied by a Cossack regiment for a distance of two *Meilen* from Kassel.
4. Members of the diplomatic corps and citizens could obtain safe passage documents for wherever they wished to go during the next two days.
5. Anything that had not been removed from the city that day, under the protection of Russian forces, as well as any royal possessions, would be considered booty.
6. The terms of this surrender would come into effect in two hours time.

General Allix departed from Kirchditmold [2½ miles west of Kassel] towards Arolsen at seven o'clock in the evening. He was accompanied by the French generals and officials, yet very few of the Westphalian officers and soldiers, indeed, even these returned to Kassel upon reaching the borders of the kingdom.[35]

The entry of Russian troops into Kassel was postponed until the morning of 19 September (1 October). Following a thanksgiving service, General Chernyshev ceremonially entered the city. The people greeted him as their liberator with joyful cheers. He assigned the Berlepsh residence in Bellevue [Schöne Aussicht] to house the detachment headquarters; the royal palace was left unoccupied, and everything in it was preserved intact.[36] Found in the city were: 30 guns (other sources report 20), many different types of weapons, cartridges, munitions and a war chest with 79,000 Thalers.[37] Some 1,000 French were taken prisoner (including those sick in hospital). Of the guns that were taken as trophies, 22 with their ammunition caissons were sent under reliable escort to Berlin. Of the cash recovered, 15,000 Thalers were distributed to the troops of the detachment, 4,000 were allocated to Major

---

35 Balmain's notes; General Chernyshev's report from Kassel; Specht, 213-223.
36 General Chernyshev's report from Kassel; Specht, 226.
37 In Adjutant General Chernyshev's report to Baron Wintzingerode, dated 19 September (1 October) it seems that ten guns were taken in combat and 17 guns were found in the city.

Dörnberg to equip the newly formed battalion, while the remaining 60,000 Thalers were sent to the military treasury of General Wintzingerode's corps.[38]

The detachment's losses, killed and wounded during the entire expedition, did not exceed 70 men. Among those officers were: Colonel Bedryaga killed; Lieutenant Colonel Raisky and majors Chelobitchikov and Dörnberg wounded.[39]

On the evening of 19 September (1 October), the following appeal was printed and the next morning was posted at every street corner.

> To the inhabitants of the Kingdom of Westphalia.
>
> At the very moment of victory of my forces conquering your capital, I announce to you, in the name of His Majesty the Emperor of All Russia, and on the basis of the orders of His Royal Highness the Crown Prince of Sweden, Commander-in-Chief of the Army of Northern German, that the Kingdom of Westphalia (composed of regions taken from your legitimate sovereigns by force) is to be dissolved, not to be dealt with as with a conquered country, but to liberate you from French domination. The magnanimous mindset of our great Monarch is known to all. Having mobilised his people in order to liberate Germany from the foreign yoke and to grant the light of peace, He has given his word – not to lay down his arms until this noble objective has been achieved.
>
> The right hand of God himself is the obvious patron of this sacred cause. Over the course of several weeks, the enemy have lost more than 300 guns and 100,000 prisoners. Bavaria and Württemberg have broken away from them; most of Germany is preparing to rebel against them.
>
> Each of you who joins this noble coalition, and thereby shows himself to be a worthy son of Germany, will be willingly accepted by us, will be our brother, a comrade in our military exploits and will earn the patronage of our Monarch.
>
> I do not think that any of you will remain loyal to the cowardly government which abandoned you in the moment of danger. But if this should happen, then anyone who attempts any act causing general harm shall be subject to the harshest penalties.[40]

This proclamation ended the existence of the Kingdom of Westphalia. Although, after the departure of the Russians, Allix reoccupied Kassel and remained there for 19 days, from 25 September to 14 October (7 to 26 October), although King Jérôme returned to his capital and attempts were made to restore his reign, nevertheless, it had collapsed irrevocably.

On 20 September (2 October), the flankers (*Jäger-Schwadron*) of the *Neumärkisches Dragoner* arrived in Kassel, numbering 150 cavalrymen, commanded by *Rittmeister*

---

38 Specht, 223, 238-239 & 241.
39 General Chernyshev's report to Baron Wintzingerode, dated 19 September (1 October); Specht, 223.
40 Appeal dated 19 September (1 October), signed by Adjutant General Chernyshev.

Rohr, who, having been sent to Halle to seize the local magazines by General Thielemann, following the occupation of Merseburg, on 6 (18) September, had become separated from the main body of the detachment by General Lefebvre-Desnouettes' offensive and therefore turned, initially towards Eisleben, and then towards Kassel, in order to join forces with Chernyshev.[41]

Just as there was no doubt that the French reserves assembled on the Rhine were heading towards Kassel, they would also be able to eject the Russian partisans from there, so General Chernyshev undertook a reverse movement towards the Elbe. On 21 September (3 October), the spoils of their victory were sent along the road to Hannover. The troops would march to Göttingen, Northeim, Braunschweig and on to Salzwedel [48 miles north of Helmstedt], to Dömitz, cross the Elbe there and rejoin the Army of the North.[42]

The success of General Chernyshev's expedition aroused sympathy for the Coalition cause in every Rhineland territory in Germany. Napoleon supporters and the French could not consider themselves safe anywhere. Cossacks were seen everywhere, whose speed and tirelessness were exaggerated beyond the limits of the possible by rumours. One of Napoleon's vassals, the *Fürstprimas* [prince primate], the *Großherzog* [Grand Duke] of Frankfurt (Dalberg [Karl Theodor Anton Maria von und zu Dalberg]) fled from his residence in Aschaffenburg to Konstanz.[43]

Chernyshev attached Jérôme's report to Napoleon on the loss of his capital, which had been intercepted by Cossacks, to his report to General Wintzingerode on the capture of Kassel. Both of these dispatches were forwarded to the Crown Prince of Sweden and were presented to Emperor Alexander I by him, along with the keys to Kassel, with the following appraisal of General Chernyshev.

> Sire! I have already informed Your Imperial Majesty of the departure of General Chernyshev on a secret expedition. I would undoubtedly diminish the virtues of this intrepid and intelligent officer if I described to Your Majesty his march, his battles and his successes. I therefore believe that I can do no better than to place before Your Majesty the original reports which he addressed to General Wintzingerode. This general has just sent me the keys to Kassel, which I hasten to forward to Your Imperial Majesty via Captain Davidov who accompanied General Chernyshev, and I find myself all the more happy to be able to announce to Your Majesty the capture of the capital of the Kingdom of Westphalia as I was not without concern about the outcome of this enterprise, given the distance that General Chernyshev found himself from any assistance. Independently of the arrangements made to support him from the direction of Halle and Bernburg, I also had a bridge thrown across the Elbe at Ferchland and I sent four squadrons to meet him in the vicinity of Gifhorn and Braunschweig…[44]

---

41 Specht, 237-238.
42 Plotho, II, 312.
43 Richter, Geschichte des Deutschen Freiheitskrieges vom Jahre 1813 bis zum Jahre 1815, II, 123.
44 'Sire! J'ai déja instruit Votre Majesté Imperiale du départ du général Czernitscheff pour une expedition secrete. J'attenuerais sans doute le mérite de cet intrépide et intelligent officier si je

In recognition of the conquest of Kassel, Emperor Alexander awarded Adjutant General Chernyshev the Order of St. Vladimir, 2nd class.

The partisans of the Army of Silesia, the Russians Prince Madatov and Colonel Figner and the Prussians Major Falkenhausen and *Rittmeister* Schwanenfeld, being at a considerable distance from the Elbe, were forced to limit the extent of their operations to raids on the communications of Macdonald's army, in whose rear areas they intercepted couriers, destroyed parks and convoys, and even attacked quite significant enemy detachments. According to accounts from the few surviving contemporaries of this era, Figner's detachment included soldiers of all nations, including several Spaniards who had been serving under duress in Napoleon's forces and defected to the Coalition at the first convenient opportunity. This volunteer group were not distinguished by their discipline and had the appearance of a band of robbers. There was no mercy for any of the French who fell into the hands of Figner's partisans. Figner himself fell victim to the disorder and negligence that prevailed in his detachment. Caught by surprise near Wörlitz [8½ miles east of Dessau] by incomparably superior enemy numbers – according to rumour – he dashed towards the Elbe with several Cossacks in order to swim to the near bank and was reported missing, believed dead.

---

fesais à Votre Majesté la description de sa marche, de ses combats et de ses succès; je crois donc ne pouvoir mieux faire qu'en mettant sous les yeux de Votre Majesté les rapports originaux qu'il a adressés au général Wintzingerode. Ce général vient de m'envoyer les clefs de Cassel, que je m'empresse de transmettre à Votre Majesté Imperiale par le capitaine Davidoff qui a accompagné le général Czernitscheff, et je me trouve d'autant plus heureux de pouvoir annoncer à Votre Majesté la prise de la capitale du Royaume de Westphalie que je n'ai pas été sans inquietude sur l'issue de cette entreprise, vu l'eloignement où le général Czernitscheff se trouvait de tout secours. Indépendamment des dispositions prises pour le soutenir du coté de Halle et de Bernbourg, j'ai fait jetter un pont sur l'Elbe à Ferckland et j'ai fait passer quatre escadrons pour aller à sa rencontre aux environs de Giffhorn et de Brunswic...'

36

Operations by Graf Wallmoden's Corps. The action at Göhrde and capture of Bremen

> Davout's retreat behind the Stecknitz River. – Movements by Graf Wallmoden with elements of the Coalition Combined Corps on the left bank of the Elbe. – Location of General Pécheux's detachment near Göhrde. – The action at Göhrde. Losses on both sides. – Eleonore Prochaska. – Wallmoden's return to the right bank of the Elbe.
>
> General Tettenborn is detached to the left bank of the Elbe. The expedition to Bremen and the surrender of this city. Final liberation of Bremen.

The failure of Marshal Oudinot's offensive towards Berlin and the defeat of General Girard at Hagelberg (see Chapter 25) resulted in the retreat of Davout's corps to Ratzeburg and of Napoleon's Danish allies to Lübeck. Soon thereafter, on 21 August (2 September), Davout withdrew behind the Stecknitz to a position protected by natural and man-made obstacles. Graf Wallmoden followed him, but being inferior to the enemy in numbers, he was forced to restrict himself to observation and skirmishes at the forward outposts. Tettenborn and other enterprising partisans often crossed to the left bank of the Elbe upstream of Boizenburg and operated on the lines of communications of Davout's corps. One of the Coalition detachments managed to capture a French artillery officer with dispatches, from which it emerged that Marshal Davout had sent Pécheux's division [Marc Nicolas Louis Pécheux] to the left bank of the Elbe, and that there were orders for rations to be prepared for 10,000 men along the route assigned to them. Thus, the opportunity arose to attack an element of the enemy corps with superior forces, but in order to do this it would be necessary to weaken the force facing the French positions. Graf Wallmoden, counting on Davout continuing to remain inactive, decided to take advantage of this promising opportunity and to attack General Pécheux with the main body of his corps.[1]

In order to shield the flanking movement up the Elbe, Vegesack's Swedish division was left on the Stecknitz, while several of Lützow's battalions, the *Hanseatische*

---

1 Beitzke, Geschichte der deutschen Freiheitskriege in den Jahren 1813 und 1814, II, 459-460.

infantry and *2. Husarenregiment* of the Russo-German Legion, held the sector from Roggendorf ([four miles] west of Gadebusch) to Boizenburg: overall, some 11,000 men were left facing Davout.[2] On 1 (13) September Graf Wallmoden moved to his left with the remaining units of the Combined Corps, numbering some 10,000 men, through Vellahn, the Langenheide and Lübtheen, to Dömitz, crossed the Elbe the next day [14 September, new style] via a bridge of boats and reached Dannenberg on 3 (15) September.[3] On the same day, Major General Tettenborn, having been sent to the Göhrde Wald [seven miles north-west of Dannenberg], discovered the enemy.[4]

On 2 (14) September, General Pécheux crossed [the Elbe] at Zollenspieker [five miles north of Winsen] with a detachment of six battalions, one squadron of *chasseurs à cheval* and eight guns, numbering 4,500 men, advanced through Lüneburg and arrived at Dahlenburg on 3 (15) September.[5] Their *chasseurs à cheval*, having engaged a Cossack patrol, took prisoners from whom they learned of the advance of a Coalition formation towards Göhrde in significant strength. Pécheux, an experienced and brave general, having received this intelligence, halted the advance of his detachment and reported the threat to Marshal Davout, who, meanwhile, concluding from a show of force by the Coalition units facing him that Graf Wallmoden's main body was stationed to his front, either paid no attention to the received report, or did not have chance to issue appropriate orders. On the night of 3 to 4 (15 to 16) September, General Pécheux deployed his detachment on the high ground on both sides of the Lüneburg road, between the villages of Oldendorf [3½ miles south-east

---

2   In the periodical Oestereichische Militärische Zeitschrift, 1827, IV, 40, the following units are shown as being left facing Davout: Vegesack's division (Mecklenburg-Schwerin and Swedish-Pomeranian brigades), 7,500 men; Hanseatische Brigade, 2,450 men; Russo-German Legion 2. Husarenregiment with two guns from Lützow's detachment, 450 men; three battalions from Lützow's detachment, four Hanseatische squadrons and one Cossack regiment, 1,900 men: total, not including Vegesack's division: 4,000 infantry and 800 cavalry; thus, the total left facing Davout was 12,300 men. Yet the number of troops shown here are for the opening of the campaign after the armistice, a whole month later there could not have been more than 11,000 men in these units from Wallmoden's corps.
3   In the periodical *Oestereichische Militärische Zeitschrift, 1827*, IV, 41, the following units are shown as having been assembled for operations against General Pécheux: six battalions of the Russo-German Legion, six Hanoverian battalions, one battalion of the British 73rd Foot arrived from Stralsund, Reiche's battalion, 400 infantry from Lützow's detachment, three Cossack regiments, two hussar regiments (including *1. Husaren* of the Russo-German Legion), two squadrons of Hanoverian hussars, 300 cavalry from Lützow's detachment, for a total of 16 (*sic*, 15) battalions, three Cossack regiments and 20 (*sic*) squadrons, numbering 7,800 infantry and 2,800 cavalry, with 28 guns (in addition, the detachment had a British rocket battery). There may have been some 11,000 men in all these units at the opening of the campaign and some 10,000 a month later. Beitzke (II, 460) shows 12,000 men, while Plotho (II, 323) shows 16,000, which is clearly an exaggeration.
4   Plotho, Der Krieg in Deutschland und Frankreich in den Jahren 1813 und 1814, II, 322-323.
5   General Pécheux's detachment consisted of: four battalions of *3e ligne*; two battalions of *105e ligne*; one squadron of *28e chasseurs à cheval*; eight guns (extracted from Bernhardi Denkwürdigkeiten aus dem Leben Carl Friedrich Grafen von Toll, III, *Beilagen*, 501). Vaudoncourt (*Histoire de la guerre soutenue par les Français en Allemagne*, 187-188), shows similar, but just one battalion from *105e ligne* and six guns. The troop strength is shown as 7,000 to 8,000 men in Oestereichische Militärische Zeitschrift, 1827, IV, 41, which is clearly an exaggeration.

of Dahlenburg] and Eichdorf, and stationed skirmishers in the Göhrde *Jagdschloß* (hunting lodge) to his front.[6]

General Wallmoden, moving through undulating and wooded terrain, was hoping to conceal the advance of his force and lure the enemy out of their position. But the French detachment held their ground, and therefore Graf Wallmoden, concerned that they might retreat back to Hamburg, decided to attack them: General Tettenborn was ordered to fix them frontally with the Cossack regiments, two battalions, four squadrons and four horse artillery pieces from Lützow's detachment; *Oberstleutnant* Pfuel [Ernst Heinrich Adolf von Pfuel] was to head through the forest to go left- flanking with six battalions, four squadrons and 12 guns from the Russo-German legion; the remaining units, under Wallmoden's direct command, were to follow Tettenborn's cavalry in reserve.[7] Pfuel's force, who had been assigned to make the outflanking movement, set off from their location at noon, while Tettenborn, moving off at one o'clock in the afternoon (two o'clock according to other sources), attacked both flanks of the enemy position with the Cossacks. At the same time, Lützow's jägers, having occupied the right side of the forest, began a fierce battle with the French skirmishers in the *Jagdschloß*. At the same time, a cannonade was heard from the direction of Boizenburg, on the right bank of the Elbe. There was no doubt that the Coalition forces facing Davout frontally, if attacked by superior numbers, would be placed in a dangerous situation, but Graf Wallmoden, being unable to go to their aid, decided to continue the operations already in progress against Pécheux. The enemy, entrenched in a ditch at the exit of the forest, held out stubbornly, but were eventually forced to retreat to their main position. A swamp stretched forwards of the high ground they held; their flanks were protected by the villages. There were two guns on the right wing, five guns on the left, and one howitzer in the centre on the Lüneburg road. As soon as Tettenborn's men emerged from the forest onto the open ground, they were engaged by a cannonade.

Meanwhile, Pfuel's detachment, moving around the right wing of the enemy position, had not yet arrived at the place assigned to them. While waiting for them, Tettenborn opened fire with his guns, which were gradually joined by other batteries. The Coalition infantry formed up for battle; the Cossacks and cavalry, positioned in dead ground, waited for an opportune moment to attack. But, based on intelligence received, because they considered the enemy to be much stronger than they actually were, Graf Wallmoden halted the main column advancing frontally, intending to attack as soon as Coalition troops appeared to the rear of the French position. The daylight was already fading when Dörnberg's cavalry outflanked the enemy left wing. Following this, a cannonade was heard to the left beyond the forest; this was artillery fire from the Russo-German Legion to the rear of the enemy position; the

---

6 Plotho, II, 323; Vaudoncourt, 187-188; Beitzke, II, 460-461.
7 Plotho, II, 323. According to other sources, Tettenborn had: two battalions, four squadrons, three Cossack regiments and four guns; Pfuel had: six battalions, one hussar regiment and 12 to 16 guns; Dörnberg had his cavalry and a rocket troop. Beitzke, II, 461. In the *Oestereichische Militärische Zeitschrift, 1827*, IV, 42-43, Tettenborn is shown with: two battalions, four squadrons, three Cossack regiments and four guns; Pfuel (Arentschildt) had: six battalions, one hussar regiment and two batteries; Dörnberg had: ten squadrons, 14 guns and the rocket troop; General Lyon, in reserve, had: six battalions and 12 guns.

infantry under *Oberstleutnant* Pfuel, having captured the villages on this flank, had cut the French line of retreat; *Oberstleutnant* Lützow attacked them frontally with his cavalry and forced the enemy squadron to fall back behind their infantry, which, forming several squares, repelled the attacks by the Coalition cavalry with musketry; the French artillery, firing canister at very short range, also inflicted significant casualties on the Coalition. Lützow suffered two wounds himself; his *schwarzen Reiter* were forced to fall back. But Lützow's *Jäger zu Fuß* quickly dashed forwards, drove the enemy from the high ground near the Lüneburg road and captured the howitzer stationed there. At the same time, the Hanoverian battalions under General Lyon [James Frederick Lyon] and nine squadrons under General Dörnberg were brought into action; Lützow's cavalry went on the attack again. Every French gun had been captured by the Coalition. The enemy, surrounded on all sides, lashed by canister shot, defended themselves with musketry, and were eventually utterly disordered. General Pécheux attempted to make his way to his left with the remnants of his detachment, towards the Elbe. Yet no sooner had he managed to rally any of his scattered soldiers, than the Coalition artillery, having caught up with them, pelted the French with canister shot. It has been claimed that the Congreve rockets especially struck fear and confusion in the ranks of the enemy: this was one of the very rare examples of the successful use of combat rockets, which, in all likelihood, would never be destined to play an important role in military actions. *Oberstleutnant* Goltz [Alexander Wilhelm von der Goltz], with the *1. Husarenregiment* of the Russo-German Legion, broke one of the enemy squares and, alongside the rest of the cavalry, completed the defeat of the enemy detachment.[8]

The darkness of the night interrupted the pursuit by the Coalition cavalry and gave the French the opportunity to take refuge in the forest and make their way through Lüneburg to Zollenspieker. Pécheux himself, under whom two horses were killed, left on foot and rallied barely half of the detachment entrusted to him on the Elbe. All his artillery had been captured by the Coalition. General Melchinsky [*sic*, Miączyński?], 100 officers and 1,900 lower ranks were taken prisoner (including 800 wounded); some 500 Frenchmen were killed in action.[9] Overall, the Coalition lost some 1,000 men killed or wounded.[10] Among those killed was Major Deveaux. History should not leave in oblivion the name of the Prussian heroine Eleonora Prochaska [Marie Christiane Eleonore Prochaska], who fell on the field of honour serving in Lützow's jägers under the name Renz. 21 years old, tall, gifted with a strong physique and extraordinary dexterity, this Jeanne d'Arc of the modern era concealed her gender from her military comrades in Lützow's jägers, earned their respect and was distinguished by her aptitude for military skills, to which she devoted herself out of love for the fatherland. A canister shot shattered her leg in the

---

8   Plotho, II, 323-324; *Oestereichische Militärische Zeitschrift, 1827*, IV, 43-46; Sporschill, *Die große Chronik*, I, 609-613; Beitzke, II, 461-463.
9   *Oestereichische Militärische Zeitschrift, 1827*, IV, 46; Karl Ferdinand von Rau & Emil Heinrich Hänel von Cronenthal, *Der Krieg der Verbündeten gegen Frankreich in den Jahren 1813, 1814 und 1815*, I, 131.
10 Plotho, II, 324. Other sources show Coalition losses as not more than 500 men *Oestereichische Militärische Zeitschrift, 1827*, IV, 46.

action at Göhrde. Languishing in the most severe agony, she endured it resolutely and smiled in the face of death.[11]

Davout's attack on the Coalition force left facing him frontally forced Count Wallmoden to return to the right bank of the Elbe via Dömitz the very next day after the action at Göhrde, 5 (17) September. Major General Tettenborn remained on the left bank of this river with three Cossack regiments, detachments of Lützow's cavalry and jägers, Reiche's battalion and four horse artillery pieces, numbering 2,100 men.[12] Tettenborn was directed to go to Lüneburg and to send patrols from there towards Harburg and across enemy lines of communications with Bremen. Later, he received orders to return to Dömitz via Dannenberg.[13] Because Chernyshev had launched an expedition to Kassel, anxious to compete with this brilliant success, Tettenborn asked Graf Wallmoden for permission to make an attempt on Bremen. Setting out from Boizenburg on 27 September (9 October), General Tettenborn crossed the Elbe at Bleckede, advanced by forced marches to Bienenbüttel, Soltau and Visselhövede [11 miles west of Soltau], to Verden arriving there on 30 September (12 October). The winding country lanes along which the detachment intended to travel had become almost impassable due to heavy rains; the carts on which the infantry were mounted became bogged down at every step; the guns followed the force with extreme difficulty. Despite all this, however, the detachment covered 20 *Meilen* (140 *versts*) over the course of 72 hours. All that remained was to complete the stage from Verden to Bremen, four *Meilen* (about 30 *versts*), through deep sand. It was known that Bremen was surrounded by an earthen rampart with a wide water-filled ditch and palisades, and that the garrison, numbering 1,500 men, was commanded by Colonel Thuillier, a veteran, experienced officer, famous for his determination. Under such circumstances, success would depend more on the surprise of the attack than on the strength of the assigned force. General Tettenborn's detachment immediately advanced towards Bremen. Replacement horses were sent ahead in order to bring up the artillery without pause. The force reached the outskirts of the city before dawn on 1 (13) October. Two Swiss companies stationed in the village of Hastedt [three miles south-east of Bremen], one of the city's suburbs, were taken by surprise and scattered. Only a few of the Swiss managed to escape over the drawbridge into the city. The Cossacks pursued the enemy persistently, and several of them even managed to break into the city just as the the French were trying to raise the bridge. General Tettenborn, being forced to halt on the outskirts, positioned his guns facing the city ramparts, from which quite frequent shots was fired, and ordered numerous shells to be lobbed into the city; a fire broke out from their detonations, but in spite of all this the the garrison enforced the loyalty of Bremen's large population. Attempts to persuade the commandant to surrender were also unsuccessful; Thuillier gave orders to shoot at officers sent to him as *parlementaire*.

---

11 Eleonore Prochaska died in Dannenberg on 5 October, new style. Förster, *Geschichte der Befreiungskriege, 1813, 1814, 1815*, I, 859-860.
12 General Tettenborn's detachment consisted of: three Cossack regiments, 800 men; Lützow's cavalry, 450 men; Lützow's and Reiche's jägers, 800 men four *Hanseatische* guns. *Oestereichische Militärische Zeitschrift, 1827*, IV, 43-48; Förster, I, 615-617.
13 *Oestereichische Militärische Zeitschrift, 1827*, V, 120; Sporschill, I, 615-617.

Under these circumstances, an assault had to be planned in order to capture the city. A reconnaissance conducted by the Coalition convinced them of the possibility of scaling the ramparts in two places where it would be easy to fill the ditches with fascines due to their insignificant depth. Tettenborn's small groups were already preparing for the assault when Thuillier, who had been observing the Coalition locations through a telescope from the city ramparts on the morning of 2 (14) October, was fatally struck by a bullet. Tettenborn received intelligence on this from a resident of Bremen who had climbed down the rampart and crossed the ditch, and at the same time he was informed that the new garrison commandant, Lieutenant Colonel Devallant, a native of Switzerland, was ready to surrender the city but only if relatively mild terms were offered to him. The consequence of this was the conclusion of capitulation, according to which Tettenborn's detachment would occupy Bremen on 3 (15) October, and the French force, numbering 1,200 men, would march to the Rhine, with weapons and baggage, pledging not to serve against the Coalition for a year.

The entry of the valiant partisans into the liberated city was festive: the residents of Bremen embraced their deliverers, greeted them with loud cheers, and showered them with wreaths. Everything that had belonged to the French government, money, stores of munitions, huge warehouses full of cloth and other supplies, all of this was given to the Coalition soldiers. A significant part of the produce was sold for a song at public auction; several hundred carts loaded with tobacco, cloth, complete uniforms, cochineal, and colonial goods were sent under escort to Mecklenburg territory; 110,000 francs were distributed to the troops in the detachment; 150,000 francs were delivered to Emperor Alexander's headquarters. The spoils of victory were 16 guns. Most of the Swiss expressed a desire to enter Coalition service; in addition, several Bremen students and young merchants joined Lützow's detachment.[14]

Enemy troops sent from Nienburg to assist the Bremen garrison were engaged and driven off by one of Tettenborn's patrols. Whereupon, the commandant of Nienburg, concerned at the surrender of Bremen, fell back towards the Rhine, having demolished the bridges on the Weser.[15]

General Tettenborn, having sent the captured trophies across the Elbe, set off on 6 (18) October for Verden. A Cossack detachment, commanded by *Rottmeister* Schultz, remained in Bremen until 10 (22) October, when an advance by General Lauberdière [Louis-François-Bertrand du Pont d'Aubevoye de Lauberdière] from Osnabrück with 1,500 men forced the Cossacks to evacuate the city; but the days of Napoleonic rule in Germany were already numbered, and soon news of the outcome of the battle of Leipzig forced the French to march back to Osnabrück on 14 (26) October.[16]

---

14 Plotho, II, 506-507; *Oestereichische Militärische Zeitschrift, 1827*, V, 127-129; Sporschill, I, 618-621; Beitzke, II, 465-466; Förster, I, 863-869.
15 *Oestereichische Militärische Zeitschrift, 1827*, V, 129.
16 Förster, I, 869.

37

Blücher's flank-march from Bautzen to the Elbe. The Battle of Wartenburg. The Crown Prince of Sweden crosses the Elbe

Blücher's proposal to cross the Elbe. – Detachment of the corps under Prince Shcherbatov and the division under Graf Bubna in Lusatia. – Flanking movement by the Army of Silesia. – Factors that influenced the choice of crossing point. – Construction of bridges near the village of Elster.

Composition, numbers and quality of Ney's force. – Deployment of Ney's corps for the defence of the Elbe crossings. – The position at Wartenburg and the deployment there of Bertrand's force.

The battle of Wartenburg. Blücher's battle speech. – Advance by the Prussian force. – General Yorck's dispositions. – Troop numbers assigned to attack the enemy position. – Attack on Bleddin by the Prinz von Mecklenburg. – Horn's attack on Sauanger. – The capture of Wartenburg. – Steinmetz's attack. – Flanking movement by the Prinz von Mecklenburg. – Deployment of Blücher's force after the battle. – The pursuit. – Losses on both sides.

Construction of a fortified camp at Wartenburg. – The Crown Prince of Sweden crosses the Elbe and Ney's retreat to Eilenburg. – Movements by the Coalition armies on both banks of the Mulde. – Plan of operations drafted in the headquarters of the Army of Silesia. – The Crown Prince's meeting with Blücher. – The intentions of the Coalition commanders to march on Leipzig. – News of Napoleon's offensive. – The Coalition decision to cross to the left bank of the Saale.

Following the retreat from the outskirts of Bautzen to the Elbe on 12 (24) September by Napoleon's forces operating against the Army of Silesia, Blücher, having secured Bennigsen's transfer from Silesia to Bohemia, began to execute a movement aimed at crossing the force entrusted to him over the Elbe and advancing alongside the

Army of the North under the Crown Prince of Sweden. Up until this point, the Coalition armies were separated from each other by considerable distances: the Bohemian and Silesian Lusatian mountains were crossed by difficult indirect roads such that although the distance from Bautzen to the Teplitz valley, as the crow flies, does not exceed ten *Meilen* (70 *versts*), nevertheless, in order to move troops from Bautzen, via Zittau, Gabel, Böhmisch-Leipa and Leitmeritz required a journey of 20 *Meilen* (140 *versts*). The distance between the main bodies of the Army of Silesia and Army of the North reached some 25 *Meilen* (more than 170 *versts*). Napoleon occupied a central position on the Elbe with crossings at the fortresses; in contrast, the Army of Silesia and Army of the North could only establish communications with the Army of Bohemia by building bridges within the radius of operations of the main body of Napoleon's forces and in the vicinity of French occupied fortified points. An offensive on enemy lines of communications by all the Coalition armies would deprive him of the benefits provided by occupying a line along the Elbe and could prompt Napoleon to fight under circumstances very unfavourable to him. It has already been stated that Blücher's intentions, although they did not align with the views in Schwarzenberg's *Hauptquartier*, had nevertheless been approved by the Coalition Sovereigns. Yet only a few of Blücher's colleagues were aware of the Monarchs' consent to the execution of his plans. The Prussian General Rauch [Johann Justus Georg Gustav von Rauch], who was at his *Hauptquartier* in order to take measures to protect the Silesian fortresses, knowing their poor condition, considered a flank-march by the army to the Elbe to be extremely dangerous, which, in his opinion, would gift these fortresses into enemy hands. General Tuyll [Fëdor Vasilievich Teil van Seraskerken or Diederik Jacob van Tuyll van Serooskerken], the Russian resident to Blücher, a physically courageous man, but cautious to the point of timidity in his strategic assessments, strongly urged the veteran commander not to allow himself to be drawn into such a dangerous enterprise. Blücher loved Tuyll, who had served under him for a long time, and treated him as an old friend, but did not feel himself obliged to follow his advice. He said: 'Rest assured, my friend, everything has been thoroughly thought through.' When Tuyll ventured to protest formally against the flanking move, Blücher reminded him that he was at the headquarters of the Army of Silesia as a Russian attaché, but had no right to give advice on military operations. Rauch's opinions provoked an even sharper response from the old commander. Because Blücher did not keep the consequences of his meetings with generals Tuyll and Rauch in confidence, both of them soon left the army.[1]

By making a move towards the Elbe, Blücher intended, in the event of Napoleon retreating towards Leipzig, to cross at Mühlberg in order to maintain communications with the Main Army; if Napoleon were to remain on the Elbe, Blücher intended to cross the river at its confluence with the Schwarze Elster and liaise with the army under the Crown Prince of Sweden.[2] The Austrian light division under Graf Bubna was left at Neustadt (eight *versts* south-east of Stolpen) in order to shield

---

1   Müffling, *Aus meinem Leben*, 71-72; Beitzke, *Geschichte der deutschen Freiheitskriege in den Jahren 1813 und 1814*, II, 417-418.
2   General Baron Tuyll's letter to Adjutant General Volkonsky, dated 17 (29) September, from Elsterwerda (Log of Incoming Documents, No. 1,491).

the route from Lusatia to Bohemia via Rumburg,[3] while VI Corps under Lieutenant General Prince Shcherbatov was on the route leading from Dresden to Silesia via Bautzen, consisting of two divisions, with two cavalry regiments, one of Ukrainian Cossacks, 150 Cossacks from Isaev 2nd's Don Cossacks and five Cossack artillery pieces, numbering some 8,000 men.[4] On 14 (26) September, the flanking move by the main body of the Army of Silesia began, which consisted at this point of 70,000 men, excluding the corps under Prince Shcherbatov.[5] Sacken's corps, shielding the other formations from the direction of the Elbe, headed for Großenhain and halted there, pushing a vanguard forwards towards Meißen, where the Russians got into a rather heated action with the enemy;[6] the remaining corps reached Elsterwerda on 17 (29) September. Blücher intended to cross the Elbe close to the confluence with the Schwarze Elster, opposite Wartenburg, where the river forms a tight loop, and where, by order of the Crown Prince of Sweden, a bridge was being built across the Elbe. But on 15 (27) September, upon arrival in Königsbrück, Blücher had received a letter from General Tauentzien, from Liebenwerda, with the news that the Crown Prince had ordered the dismantling of the bridge at Elster because several enemy battalions had appeared at Wartenburg.[7] Based on this information, Blücher decided to build a bridge and cross at Mühlberg, where there were also great tactical advantages. But since this point is located between Torgau and Meißen, where the enemy held bridges, Sacken was ordered to destroy the bridge at Meißen in order to deprive them of the opportunity to debouch onto the right bank of the Elbe from there,

---

3 Graf Bubna's light division consisted of: *Generalmajor* Baron Zechmeister's brigade: *Grenzregiment Peterwardein, 6. Jäger-Bataillon, Husaren Liechtenstein* (six squadrons), one three-pounder battery; *Generalmajor* Graf Neipperg: *5. Jäger-Bataillon, Husaren Kaiser, Husaren Blankenstein* (six squadrons), one six-pounder horse artillery battery, for a total of three battalions, 12 squadrons and two batteries.
4 Price Shcherbatov's detachment consisted of: nine battalions from Major General Talyzin's 7th Division; six battalions from Major General Benardos' 18th Division; cavalry under Major General Panchulidzev of: three squadrons of Chernigov Mounted Jägers, two squadrons of Tver Dragoons, 1½ *Sotnia* of Isaev 2nd's Don Cossacks, five guns from 2nd Don Cossack Artillery Company, 28th Light Artillery Company and 34th Light Artillery Company (War Diary of VI Corps, 1812, 1813 & 1814, Archive of the M.T.D. No. 44,585).
5 Beitzke, II, 418.
6 Extract from the War Diary of Sacken's corps for 2 [14] January 1813 to 19 [31] March 1814.
7 'The great general of the right wing is operating in such a manner that it is only through God's will that things are still going well... I have just received a letter from General Borstell, in which he informs me that he has received orders to demolish the bridge of boats that has been built with so much effort at Elster, because several enemy battalions have positioned themselves and resisted the establishment of a bridgehead... I shall hold the position here behind the Elster until I can contribute something to the larger objectives in cooperation with Your Excellency's Army.'
   'Der grosse Feldherr auf dem rechten Flügel operirt auf eine Weise, das es Gottes Wille sein muss, dass die Sachen noch so gut stehen... Ich erhielt so eben ein Schreiben vom Gen. Borstell, laut welchem er mir anzeigt, dass er Befehl erhalten, die bei Elster mit so vieler Mühe geschlagene Schiffbrücke wiederum abzubrechen, weil einige feindliche Bataillone gegen Anlegung eines Brückenkopfs sich aufgestellt und widersetzt haben... Ich werde hier die Position hinter der Elster so lange halten, bis ich in Übereinkunft mit Ew. Exc. Armee zu grösseren Zwecken etwas beitragen kann.' Extract from General Tauentzien's letter to Blücher, from Elsterwerda.

which was done by his vanguard, supported by some of the infantry, on 17 (29) September. The French, having been attacked by Russian troops, believed that the Coalition really intended to cross there and dismantled the bridge themselves.[8]

Despite this success, which would have facilitated a crossing for the Coalition at Mühlberg, Blücher decided to move downstream along the Schwarze Elster, to build a bridge opposite Wartenburg and cross the Elbe there. The reason for this was the Prussian generals' distrust of the Crown Prince of Sweden. He had given cause for their displeasure himself, sparing the Swedish troops in the main and showing favour towards the Russians. He often admired the youthfulness and helpfulness of the Pavlograd Hussars in his suite; it has also been claimed that, watching Russian jägers passing by him near Dresden, he turned to his retinue and said: 'There, gentlemen, look at how one should go into action.'[9] He was subjected to even greater criticism for remaining passive during the battles of Großbeeren and Dennewitz and allowing Ney's defeated army to evade complete destruction. Throughout his stay in the vicinity of Zerbst with the bulk of the army, the Crown Prince paid attention exclusively to operations against Danish forces. Wanting to induce the Danes to part from Napoleon, he ordered Graf Wallmoden to attack Davout's larger force, located in an advantageous position behind the Stecknitz, and wanted to send the Prussian contingent under his direct command there. It was in all probability to that end that he ordered Tauentzien, who had already established communications with the Army of Silesia at Mühlberg, to cross the Elster at Jessen and Schweinitz. Suspicions of the Crown Prince's coolness towards the common cause reached the extent that Graf Tauentzien expressed his readiness to cross the Elbe to Blücher in cooperation with the Army of Silesia, even without the consent of his Commander-in-Chief. General Bülow, located closer to the prince's headquarters with his corps, not yet committed to such a bold step, promised to assist Blücher as much as possible.[10] However, King Friedrich Wilhelm would not consent to the unauthorised detachment of the Prussian corps from the Army of the North, and therefore Blücher decided, by crossing the Elbe closer to the Crown Prince, to induce him to attack, and meanwhile, the very next day after the army had departed from the Bautzen area, 15 (27) September, he sent Major Rühle von Lilienstern to him with notice of his intentions. When asked by the prince – with what number of troops did Blücher intend to cross the Elbe? Major Rühle replied that he would cross with the entire army, the Crown Prince promised to assist the Army of Silesia. In his opinion, the most advantageous place for Blücher's crossing was the village of Elster, of which Major Rühle was also convinced, having observed the ground around this location himself. Having received a letter from the prince, in which he promised to cross to the left bank of the Elbe in three or four days, as soon as his bridgeheads were ready, Blücher abandoned the crossing at Mühlberg and moved down

---

8 The attack on the Meißen bridge was led by the 49th Jägers, supported by the 8th Jägers, Kamchatka Infantry and Okhotsk Infantry. General Sacken's report to Barclay de Tolly, dated 1 [13] October (Archive of the M.T.D. No. 16,644); Blücher's report to Emperor Alexander I, dated 18 (30) September (Log of Incoming Documents, No. 1,503).
9 Lieutenant Colonel Balmain's (manuscript) notes.
10 'so weit es seine untergeordnete Stellung nur irgend verstatten würde.'

the course of the Schwarze Elster to Herzberg on 19 September (1 October) and to Jessen on the following day [2 October, new style]. Sacken's corps proceeded in the same direction followed by what had been their vanguard force.[11] On the night of 20 to 21 September (2 to 3 October), two bridges were built by Russian pontoniers, commanded by lieutenant colonels Ivanov and Shishkin: one pontoon bridge, and the other on trestles, and according to a statement by Blücher himself, 'the army is indebted to their activity for the opportunity to cross at five o'clock the following morning.'[12] The construction of the bridges was carried out under the protection of several battalions from Bülow's corps, reinforced by three of Yorck's battalions, with one horse artillery battery and one foot battery, commanded by *Oberstleutnant* Siegholm.[13]

At this time, as the Army of Silesia and Army of the North were preparing to cross the Elbe with some 150,000 men, Marshal Ney could concentrate no more than 34,000 men to oppose them, namely: the corps under generals Bertrand and Reynier, each of which had three infantry divisions and one cavalry brigade, numbering 15,000 men each, and the cavalry corps under General Arrighi, numbering 4,000 men following the detachment of the division under General Lefebvre-Desnouettes, conducting counter-partisan operations against the Coalition. In these formations, barely half were Frenchmen: in Bertrand's corps there were: one French infantry division, another Italian and a third Württemberg; the cavalry brigade consisted of Westphalians and Württembergers, while in Reinier's corps there were: two French infantry divisions, one Saxon and a Saxon cavalry brigade. The French could not rely on the loyalty of the German soldiers, who very often defected to the Coalition. On 15 (27) September, one of the Saxon battalions stationed near Berlin in contact with Swedish forces, came over to them in its entirety.[14]

Because the forces under the Crown Prince of Sweden had begun to build bridges on the Elbe simultaneously at Aken, Roßlau and Elster, and his light detachments appeared on the left bank of the river in order to protect these works, Marshal Ney, having managed to assemble his forces in the vicinity of Eilenburg somewhat, sent the corps under Bertrand and Reynier towards Dessau. For four days, from 14 to 17 (26 to 29) September, quite fierce fighting took place between Reynier's force and elements of the Swedish corps protecting the bridge at Aken; yet the Coalition managed to repulse the enemy; in contrast, at Elster, as soon as Bertrand's corps appeared at Wartenburg in the vicinity of this point, orders had been issued to dismantle the bridge being built there, ditching some of the materials in the river

---

11 The Crown Prince's letter to Blücher, dated 29 September, new style, from Zerbst (Log of Incoming Documents, No. 1,503).
12 Blücher's report, dated 21 September (3 October), from Wartenburg (Log of Incoming Documents, No. 1,547).
13 The contingent from the Army of Silesia assigned to protect the Elbe bridges at Elster consisted of: two battalions from *2. Ostpreußisches Infanterie* of *1. Brigade*; Fischer's *Landwehr* battalion of *2. Brigade*. Plotho, *Der Krieg in Deutschland und Frankreich in den Jahren 1813 und 1814*, II, 279; Beitzke, II, 426.
14 Vaudoncourt, *Histoire de la guerre soutenue par les Français en Allemagne en 1813*, 180. According to Plotho, II, 306, [and Cerrini] the Saxon battalion [König] defected to the Coalition on 11 (23) September.

and removing others. Following this, Bertrand's troops settled down between Wartenburg and Pretzsch [7½ miles upstream], while Reynier's corps remained at Dessau: thus monitoring the sector where the Coalition intended to cross, Ney hoped to block their access to the left bank of the Elbe, especially since only a few battalions had hitherto appeared against him, at Aken and Elster, and operations by the Army of the North in general had been slow and hesitant. The French were completely unaware of Blücher's arrival at the mouth of the Schwarze Elster. The location of the detachments under Prince Shcherbatov and Graf Bubna, at Bautzen and Stolpen, in the same places where the forward elements of the Army of Silesia had previously been stationed; the movement to the army's left by Vasilchikov's, Katzler's and Rudzevich's light detachments, which formed an impenetrable screen against the enemy; Sacken's attack on Meißen and the Coalition attempt to build a bridge at Mühlberg: all this diverted the attention of the French from the point chosen for the crossing of the Army of Silesia. General Bertrand, one of the best engineers of the Napoleonic era, having examined the area around Elster, chosen by the Crown Prince of Sweden for the construction of the bridge, found it most advantageous for crossing to the left bank of the river, but at the same time it presented extreme difficulties for the debouching of significant forces. Having deployed his force in positions at Wartenburg and Bleddin, Bertrand wrote to Napoleon that he 'hoped to deter the enemy from crossing at this point.'[15]

Indeed, the ground at Wartenburg was very advantageous for defence.[16] The river Elbe forms a tight loop there, with a dyke across its base. Bertrand's corps was located behind this dyke. Their flanks were shielded by the villages of Wartenburg and Bleddin; in front of the left wing stretched a deep arm of the Elbe; in front of the centre there was a swamp; the right wing was somewhat more accessible than other points. Much of the low-lying ground was very swampy in the spring and contributed to defensive operations, making it difficult for forces to advance or to deploy them into battle formation. In addition, scrub partially covering the ground between the river and the dyke obstructed observation of the position. The French had set up abatis in some places and prepared the village of Wartenburg for defence.

General Bertrand's formations were positioned as follows: Morand's division at Wartenburg; Franquemont's Württemberg division at Bleddin, consisting of four battalions, numbering no more than 1,500 to 2,000 men; Fontanelli's Italian division was to the right of Wartenburg; the Westphalian-Württemberg cavalry brigade was forwards of the village of Globig, consisting of 12 squadrons.[17]

General Blücher, intending to conceal the arrival of the Army of Silesia at Wartenburg until the engagement with the enemy facing elements of Bülow's

---

15 Beitzke, II, 426-428. At the end of September new style Napoleon's other corps were located as follows: the *Garde, 1er Corps, 3e Corps, 5e Corps, 11e Corps, 14e Corps, 2e corps de cavalerie* and *4e corps de cavalerie* were at Dresden, Weißig and Pirna; *2e Corps* were at Freiberg; Prince Poniatowski was at Penig and Altenburg with *8e Corps* and Lefebvre-Desnouettes' cavalry; Marmont was at Leipzig with *6e Corps, 1er corps de cavalerie* and *5e corps de cavalerie*; Augereau was moving up from the Main.
16 See Map No. 12, Plan of the Battle of Wartenburg.
17 Wagner, *Plane der Schlachten und Treffen, welche von der preussischen Armee in den Feldzügen der Jahre 1813, 14 und 15 geliefert worden*, II, 58-59.

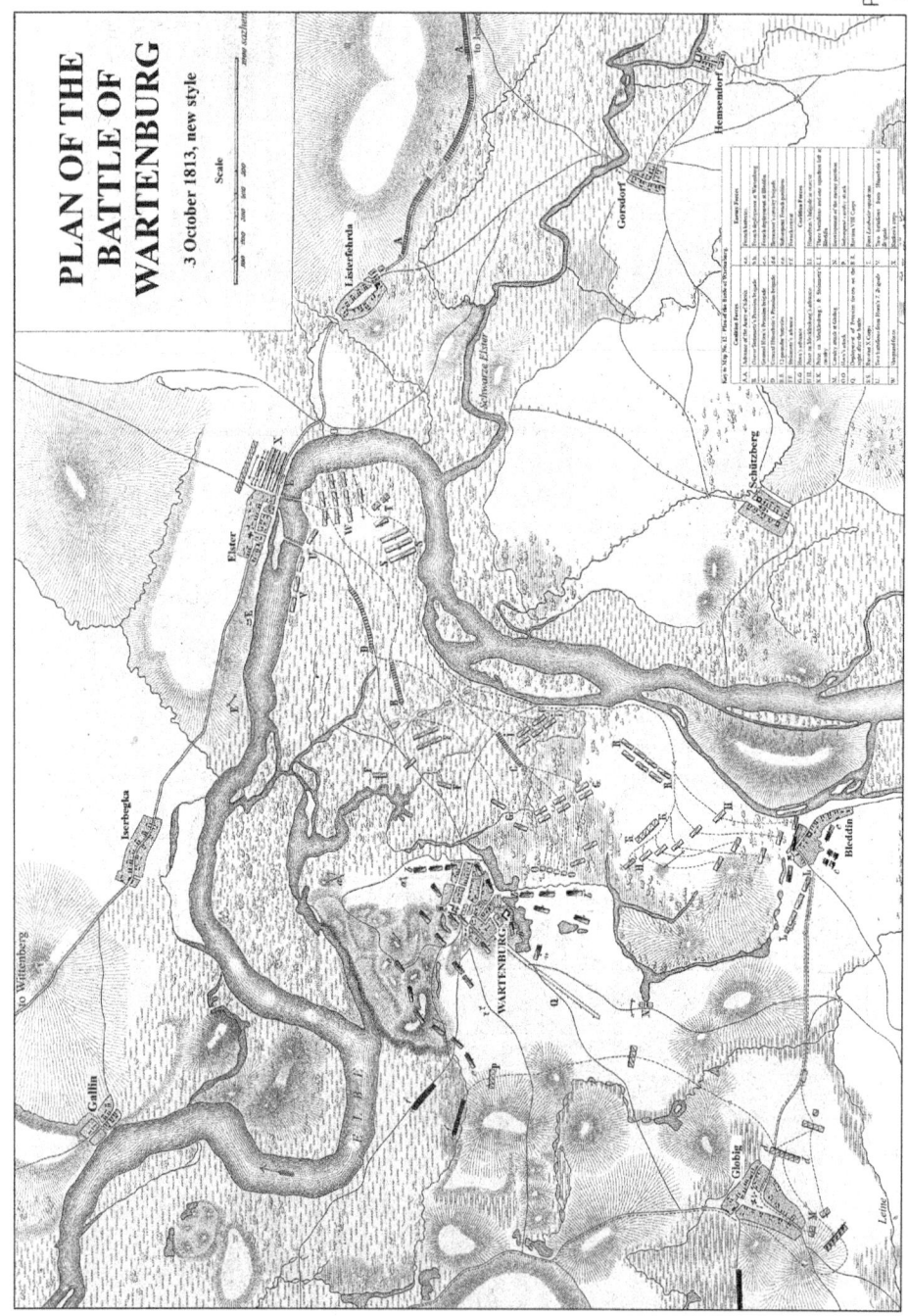

Plan of the Battle of Wartenburg.

Legend to Map No. 12

Coalition Forces

A.A.	Advance of the Army of Silesia
B.	*Oberst* Steinmetz's Prussian brigade
C.	General Horn's Prussian brigade
D.	General Hünerbein's Prussian brigade
E.E.	12-pounder batteries
F.F.	Steinmetz's advance
G.G.	Horn's advance
H.H.	Prinz zu Mecklenburg's advance
I.I.	Hünerbein's brigade in reserve
K.K.	Prinz zu Mecklenburg's & Steinmetz's cavalry
L.L.	Three battalions and one squadron left at Bleddin
M.	Cavalry attack at Globig
N.	Envelopment of the enemy position
O.O.	Horn's attack
P.	Subsequent cavalry attack
Q.	Deployment of Prussian forces on the night after the battle
R.R.	Russian VIII Corps
S.S.	Russian X Corps
T.	Four *Landwehr* squadrons
U.	Two battalions from Horn's *7. Brigade*
V.	Two battalions from Hünerbein's *8. Brigade*
W.	Vanguard force
X.	Sacken's corps

Enemy Forces

a.a.	French batteries.
b.b.	French deployment at Wartenburg
c.c.	French deployment at Bleddin
d.d.	Beaumont's cavalry brigade
e.e.	Subsequent French positions
f.f.	French retreat

Prussian corps, appointed Yorck's corps to attack the position. To that end, on 21 September (3 October), at seven o'clock in the morning, Prinz Karl zu Mecklenburg crossed the Elbe with three of *Oberstleutnant* Siegholm's battalions and moved towards Wartenburg.[18]

The Commander-in-Chief accompanied these troops himself and reached the left bank of the river in front of them. 'Forwards, boys! Hold fast! Wartenburg must be stormed. I shall let the bridge burn down behind us.'[19] This short speech did not please some of the veteran soldiers.

'He has no reason to doubt us,' they grumbled. 'It is all the same to us if the bridges are behind us or if they are burned.'

'Don't be sly, boys! I did not mean it like that; yes, we know each other!'[20] The response to this was the joyful cheering of enthusiastic Prussian soldiers. When,

---

18 Blücher's report to Emperor Alexander I, dated 21 September (3 October), from Wartenburg.
19 '*Vorwärts, Kinder! Gut ausgehalten! Wartenburg muss erstürmt werden. Die Brücke lass ich hinter uns abbrennen.*'
20 '*Seid doch gescheidt, Kinder! So habe ich das nicht gemeint; wir kennen uns ja!*'

after that, Fischer's *Schlesisches Landwehr* battalion passed by, Blucher, seeing that the warriors were in rags, barefoot, of the most unkempt appearance, cried out: 'Lads! You look like swine! Yet you beat the French well on the Katzbach. That was not the end; you must beat them again today, or we shall all be gone…'[21]

A few hundred paces from the pontoon bridge, Prinz Karl encountered a screen of enemy skirmishers, who, conducting a fighting retreat, fell back towards Wartenburg. Because there was no doubt that the French were holding the position in significant strength, the remaining six battalions of *Oberst* Steinmetz's *1. Brigade*, with a six-pounder battery, and then another five battalions from *2. Brigade* were sent up in support of the prinz. *7. Brigade*, *8. Brigade*, the *Mecklenburgisches Husaren* and *2. Leib-Husaren*, also crossed to the left bank of the Elbe. General Yorck, having surveyed the enemy position under a hail of canister shot, as much as could be seen in this enclosed and intersected terrain, issued the following orders at nine o'clock:

> *Oberst* Steinmetz is ordered to hold in the position he has taken with *1. Brigade* facing Wartenburg to the last man, positioning his *2. Batterie* in such a way as to counter the enemy artillery.[22] *Oberstleutnant* Schmidt has been ordered to place the 12-pounder guns which remain behind the Elbe, on the high ground of the right bank in order to enfilade the left flank of the French positions. The brigade under Prinz Karl zu Mecklenburg is to make a determined attack on the village of Bleddin, to drive the enemy from there and is to strive to envelope the right flank of their position. Horn's brigade is to take up concealed positions behind Prinz Karl's force, while Hünerbein's brigade remains in reserve on the approaches to the bridges. As soon as Prinz Karl has taken possession of Bleddin and is enveloping the enemy right wing, the brigades under Steinmetz and Horn are to attack frontally, storm the village of Wartenburg with several battalions and envelope it on both sides with the rest of their forces.[23]

Overall, the following were assigned to attack the enemy position from the units in Yorck's corps: 27 battalions and seven squadrons with three batteries, numbering from 15,000 to 16,000 men.

General Bertrand had entrusted the defence of Bleddin to General Franquemont, with the Württemberg division, which had suffered extraordinary losses in the battle of Dennewitz and consisted of four weak battalions with six guns. To Franquemont's concerns that the forces allocated to the defence of this rather extensive and most accessible sector of the position were insufficient, Bertrand replied that he 'would not

---

21 '*Kerls! Ihr seht ja aus wie die Schweine! Aber an der Katzbach habt ihr die Franzosen gut geschlagen. Damit ist's noch nicht genug; ihr müsst sie heute wieder schlagen, sonst sind wor alle…*' Richter, *Geschichte des Deutschen Freiheitskrieges vom Jahre 1813 bis zum Jahre 1815*, II, 142-143; Varnhagen von Ense, *Leben des Fürsten Blücher von Wahlstadt*, 209.
22 The disposition ordered the four guns form Prinz Karl's brigade battery to be left behind to attach to this battery, but they joined their brigade and operated on the left wing.
23 Droysen, *Das Leben des Feldmarschalls Grafen Yorck von Wartenburg*, III, 109-110. According to Plotho, *7. Brigade* and *8. Brigade* crossed the Elbe as early as 11 o'clock, whereupon the general disposition for the attack was issued by General Yorck.

permit the enemy to turn past Wartenburg towards Bleddin in significant strength.' At the same time, he lost sight of the fact that the swamps that made it difficult for the Coalition to approach Wartenburg were an equally important obstacle to the debouching of his own force. Franquemont's division was positioned as follows: two battalions with four guns were stationed on the fairly extensive Schützberg meadow, 1,200 paces forwards of Bleddin, having sent a skirmishing screen onto the marshy lowland (kleine Streng); the other two battalions with two guns remained in reserve behind the village.[24]

The Prinz zu Mecklenburg, having received orders to attack the enemy located at Bleddin, could not fulfil the orders issued to him for some time, due to extreme difficulties encountered on the way to this village. Eventually, with the help of guides from the population of the surrounding country, having managed to find a way through with the troops and drag his artillery (*1. Batterie*, reinforced with five guns detached from Horn's *3. Batterie*) onto the meadow (Schützberg), Prinz Karl brought forward all his guns and opened fire on the enemy skirmishing screen, which occupied the edge of the swampy scrub; then, having withdrawn the infantry, he formed them into three echelons on the left, each of two battalions, and deployed both hussar regiments (seven squadrons) behind the infantry.[25] The remaining three guns from *3. Batterie* and six battalions from *7. Brigade* were stationed in the forest in front of the swampy stream (kleine Streng), while two battalions from this same brigade (the fusiliers from the *Leib-Infanterie* and *Thüringisches Infanterie*) were detached to the right, in order to protect the force attacking Bleddin from being outflanked from the direction of Wartenburg.[26] The appearance of Prinz Karls' artillery came as a complete surprise to the enemy, who had considered it impossible to move artillery across the swamps and onto the meadow. As soon as the cannonade from the Prussian battery was heard, *Oberstleutnant* Lobenthal closed on Bleddin with two battalions of *1. Ostpreußisches Infanterie*, which formed the left echelon, along the river bank shielded by an embankment. The second battalion of *2. Ostpreußisches Infanterie* was sent to support them. General Franquemont, having withdrawn his forward battalions to the village, defended himself stubbornly; but his troops, being struck by Prussian artillery fire and attacked by superior numbers, were forced to retreat towards Globig, under the protection of Beaumont's Westphalian-Württemberg [Marc-Antoine Bonnin de la Bonninière de Beaumont] cavalry, which had arrived to assist them. At two o'clock in the afternoon, Prinz Karl, having occupied Bleddin, led the hussars through this village and sent them in pursuit of the enemy. Beaumont's cavalry halted, but did not wait to be attacked and turned back to form up to the right of Globig. *Oberstleutnant* Warburg [Ernst Wilhelm Christoph Friedrich von Warburg] struck the enemy cavalry on both flanks with the *Mecklenburgisches Husaren*, scattered them and took more than 200

---

24 Beitzke, II, 431-432.
25 According to Wagner, four guns from *1. Batterie* were left behind, and there were only the other four guns from this battery with Prinz Karl's brigade. But the plan attached to his description of the battle shows all eight guns of *1. Batterie*, along with five guns from *3. Batterie*.
26 Wagner, II, 61-62; Droysen, III, 111.

men prisoner, while Major von Stössel [Johann Otto Sigismund von Stössel] caught up with Franquemont's retreating infantry behind Globig, capturing five guns and six ammunition caissons and forced the enemy to retreat in haste along the road to Düben.[27]

At the same time as these actions on the left wing of the Prussian corps, a heated struggle was taking place in the centre, on the Sauanger [common], and on the right wing, at Wartenburg.

At one o'clock in the afternoon, two battalions from Horn's *7. Brigade*, the fusiliers of the *Leib Infanterie* and the *Thüringisches Infanterie*, were advancing on the Sauanger. Here, south of Wartenburg, an enemy force consisting of five battalions were protected by two embankments, which greatly facilitated the defence. As soon as Horn's infantry approached the nearest dyke, they were engaged by fire from a very dense screen of skirmishers and canister from several guns. Following this, the enemy crossed the embankment and counter-attacked the advancing force, disordered by the casualties they had suffered. General Yorck, wanting to help them out, ordered *Oberst* Weltzien [Heinrich Wilhelm von Weltzien] to attack the village of Wartenburg from the right flank with two battalions from the *15. Landwehr Infanterie*, while General Horn was to move to the left with the remaining four battalions from his brigade and three guns from *3. Batterie*, and having outflanked the village, take possession of the embankments. Hünerbein's brigade were ordered to move forward in support of the attack. In the meantime, Langéron's entire corps had managed to cross the Elbe. Should the attack by Yorck's force fail, Blücher planned to bring the Russians into action, and galloped up to Langéron's corps himself, which was stationed in column near the bridges, and turning to General Kern [Yermolai Fëdorovich Kern], asked him to interpret his speech to the troops in Russian, saying: 'You old Muscovites, you have never shown your backs to your enemies; I shall lead you myself. You must attack those lads, the French; I know you will not show your backs to them today either. Forwards!' This speech was greeted with a loud Hurrah! The Russians quickly went to help their comrades in arms, but at this very moment, word was received that General Horn had captured the embankment and Langéron's troops were ordered to halt.[28]

This truly heroic feat by Horn was accomplished as follows: as soon as the Weltzien's *Landwehr* approached the Sauanger, at Rötkolk [the lake immediately south of Wartenburg], the enemy entrenched behind the embankment engaged them with canister and musketry. This firefight was disadvantageous for the Prussian force and could not lead to success, therefore Horn decided to cross the swamp that protected the enemy positions at a place where they were linked by a ditch, and storm the embankment. General Yorck, with *7. Brigade* at the time said: 'Yes, Horn, now is the time.' Hünerbein's brigade had not yet arrived, and, as it turned out later, having strayed from the direction assigned to them, found themselves behind the right wing. Yet Horn, undaunted despite this, stood at the head of the second battalion of

---

27 Wagner, II, 62.
28 *'Ihr alten Moskowiter, ihr habt euren Feinden noch nie den Rücken gekehrt; ich werde mich an eure Spitze setzen. Ihr sollt die Kerls, die Franzosen da angreifen; ich weiss, Ihr werdet ihnen auch heute nicht den Rücken zeigen. Paschol!'* Droysen, III, 115; Wagner, II, 63; Beitzke, II, 441.

the *Leib Infanterie* and lead the assault, with a loud shout of: 'Anyone still shooting is a son of a bitch [*Hundsfott*]! On attack, muskets by the right!'²⁹ The battalion, roused by the example of their beloved commander, rushed forwards with drums beating, crossed the ditch waist-deep in mud, and quickly climbed the embankment. Other battalions from the brigade came rushing after them. The enemy, astonished by the appearance of Prussian troops, retreated behind the second embankment, but did not dare to try to hold there either. General Horn, exploiting this success, seized both embankments and pursued the defeated force for several hundred paces. *Hauptmann* Holleben [Heinrich Ludwig Friedrich Karl von Holleben], captured a gun with the skirmishers from the *Leib Infanterie*. *Oberst* Weltzien also crossed the ditch with his two *Landwehr* battalions and, having scaled the dyke, broke into the village of Wartenburg. Morand's force dislodged them, but not for long. Of the three guns that were with Horn's brigade, the Prussian artillerymen managed to transport one to the dyke with a broken carriage, but the others were intact, from which *Leutnant* Neander opened fire with canister at the exits to the village. The enemy skirmishers attempted to capture the damaged gun, but were repulsed by Major Kotulinski's *Landwehr* battalion who, together with Sommerfeld's battalion [Karl August Wilhelm von Sommerfeld], broke into the village of Wartenburg and captured it.³⁰

Oberst Steinmetz contributed to the success of this attack by crossing the swampy lowland and outflanking Wartenburg from the north, despite the fact that the very muddy terrain and enemy abatis made this advance extremely difficult. But eventually, the Prussian forces overcame each of the terrain obstacles here, crossed the embankment and pursued the French who had evacuated the village.

On the left wing of Yorck's corps, the Prinz zu Mecklenburg, in compliance with orders issued to him, having occupying Bleddin, advanced towards Wartenburg and engaged units from Fontanelli's Italian division on the way to this village after they had been driven out by Horn. The enemy turned towards Wittenberg in complete disorder and most of the retreating battalions would have been cut off if the prinz had any cavalry, but the reserve cavalry were still crossing the Elbe and the hussar regiments attached to *1. Brigade* were already committed to the pursuit towards Globig. All this notwithstanding, *Oberst* Warburg quickly managed to round up two squadrons from both regiments, and riding up to the prinz with them, received orders to attack the enemy. The Italians tried to form square, but were scattered and lost four guns. Major von Stössel racing up the left with a squadron of Prussian *Leib-Husaren*, captured another gun and many carts. General Horn, having occupied Wartenburg, linked up with the prinz. Aware that the enemy still remained on the high ground behind the village, he attacked Morand's division located there, and finally forced the French to retreat down the Elbe. Some battalions from *7. Brigade* pursued them almost as far as Wittenberg.³¹

---

29 '*ein Hundsfott wer noch schiesst! Zur Attaque Gewehr rechts!*'
30 Droysen, III, 116-117; Richter, II, 149-150; Wagner, II, 63-64. According to whom, four guns were captured during the seizure of Wartenburg.
31 Droysen, III, 117-118; Wagner, II, 64; Beitzke, II, 444-446.

During the night after the battle, Yorck's force settled down near Wartenburg, anchoring their right wing to this village. Langéron's corps, having crossed the Elbe, were stationed in front of the bridges, along with those elements of Yorck's corps which had not had chance to take part in the action.[32] Sacken's corps reached the crossing point after dark and crossed the Elbe the next day [4 October, new style]. The following were detached in order to pursue the enemy: *Oberst* Katzler's cavalry were sent towards Wittenberg; Major General Emmanuel was sent towards Kemberg with 1st Ukraine Cossacks, 3rd Ukraine Cossacks, two Don Cossack regiments and six guns from Lieutenant Colonel Shusherin's [8th] horse artillery company [Zakhar Sergeevich Shusherin]; while Major General Yuzefovich went upstream along the Elbe towards Pretzsch and Schmiedeberg [four miles south-west of Pretzsch] with the Kiev Dragoons, Kharkov Dragoons, Kalmyks and two Don artillery pieces.[33]

The enemy losses in killed and wounded in the action at Wartenburg did not exceed 500 men, because their troops were fighting from behind embankments, walls and other terrain obstacles; but, having said that, they lost some 1,000 men taken prisoner, 11 guns and 70 wagons or ammunition caissons captured.[34] Losses in the Prussian corps reached 67 officers and 2,012 lower ranks.[35] The second battalion of the *Leib-Infanterie* had distinguished themselves most of all. On the day after the battle [4 October, new style], as they marched past Yorck, this general, generally stern and ungenerous with praise, took off his hat and held it in his hand until the last platoon of the battalion had passed. 'This valiant battalion has earned the respect of the world,' Yorck told his retinue, who, following his example, paid the same complements to these brave warriors. With regard to one of the heroes of the Wartenburg action, General Horn, he said: 'Compared to him, Bayard was just an oaf.'[36] Subsequently, King Friedrich Wilhelm elevated Yorck to the dignity of Graf, adding the title von Wartenburg to his surname.[37]

One of the officers from the Crown Prince of Sweden's headquarters, who was a witness to the victory, was sent to him to report on the outcome of the battle. Blücher hoped that the Crown Prince would cross the Elbe, but was not yet sure whether he would agree to commit to a pitched battle. Under such circumstances, it was a necessary precaution to secure a return crossing by the Army of Silesia to the right bank of the Elbe by fortifying the position at Wartenburg. To that end, orders were issued to provide 4,000 labourers from every corps each day, being divided into three shifts

---

32 The units from Yorck's corps that were not sent into action at Wartenburg were: two Landwehr battalions each from *7. Brigade* and *8. Brigade*; the entire vanguard, consisting of 8¾ battalions and 20 squadrons, and all the reserve cavalry, consisting of 17 squadrons, four horse artillery batteries, two six-pounder batteries and one three-pounder battery.
33 Log of the movements of Adjutant General Baron Korff's corps; Plotho, II, 283; Wagner, II, 64-65; Beitzke, II, 447.
34 Droysen, III, 119; Wagner, II, 64; Beitzke, II, 447; Vaudoncourt, 192. According to the latter, the French lost no more than 100 men taken prisoner.
35 Plotho, II, *Beilagen*, 104. According to him, Yorck's corps lost: 11 officers and 291 lower ranks killed; 56 officers and 1,539 lower ranks wounded and 182 lower ranks missing. In Beitzke (II, 447) and Förster (*Geschichte der Befreiungskriege*, I, 747) the overall losses to Yorck's corps are given as: 67 officers and 1,550 lower ranks.
36 'Gegen ihn selbst Bayard nur ein Lump gewesen.' Droysen, III, 120.
37 Charter, signed by King Friedrich Wilhelm III, dated 3 June, 1814.

and working day and night, with the assistance of sappers, under the direction of the Prussian engineer *Generalmajor* Rauch, were to complete the proposed fortifications by 29 September (10 October). It was planned to put the entire area from Wartenburg to Bleddin in a defensible state, building three redoubts on the right wing and constructing two large batteries: one for 50 guns forwards of Wartenburg, while the second would have 100 guns between Wartenburg and Bleddin.[38] But the lack of entrenching tools made the work extremely slow.[39]

The Crown Prince of Sweden kept this promise, also moving his forces to the left bank of the Elbe. On 22 September (4 October), Wintzingerode's Russian corps crossed at Aken, while the Swedish corps crossed at Roßlau, which forced Ney to retreat to Bitterfeld with Reynier's force; on that same day, the Crown Prince moved his headquarters to Dessau. On 23 September (5 October), the corps under Bülow and Tauentzien crossed the Elbe, at Roßlau, with the exception of the following formations left by the Elbe: Hirschfeld's detachment securing the bridges at Roßlau; Thümen's brigade blockading the fortress of Wittenberg from the right bank of the river, and Wobeser's brigade monitoring the bridgehead fortifications at Torgau. Whereupon Ney retreated to Delitzsch, where both French corps linked up, numbering some 30,000 men.[40] The troop strength of the Army of Silesia, following the detachment of several thousand men as labourers and prisoner escorts, reached more than 60,000 men, while the Army of the North had some 80,000 men. Napoleon could bring no more than 100,000 to help Ney: therefore, the combined strength of both Coalition armies was sufficiently strong to counter the French. In addition, Ney's force, consisting of officers and soldiers of various nationalities and influenced by the failures they had suffered, completely lost heart. The raiding detachments sent after the enemy brought back several hundred prisoners every day. The Coalition had the chance to exploit these favourable circumstances and complete the destruction of Ney's corps, or at least to inflict even greater losses on them. Yet the Crown Prince, although he had moved his army across the Elbe, did not advance from the vicinity of Dessau. Blücher, hoping to inspire him through his example and to encourage the Army of the North to take action, moved the corps forward: Yorck towards Gräfenhainichen, Langéron towards Düben, Sacken in the direction of Mockrehna near Eilenburg. These moves which threatened Ney's communications with the main body of the French army located in the vicinity of Dresden, forced him to destroy all the bridges on the Mulde and, on 25 September (7 October) to move towards Eilenburg, where Marmont joined him, with *6e Corps*, the cavalry under Latour-Maubourg and Arrighi (*1er corps de cavalerie* and *5e corps de cavalerie*) and Dąbrowski's Polish division which, together with Ney's force, numbered some 50,000 men.[41]

---

38 Plotho, II, 284; Weiß (Müffling), *Zur Kriegsgeschichte der Jahre 1813 und 1814*, 62.
39 Beitzke, II, 449.
40 Plotho, II, 314-315; Vaudoncourt, 193.
41 Blücher's report to Emperor Alexander I, dated 5 October, new style, from Kemberg (Log of Incoming Documents, No. 1,570); Plotho, II, 286 & 288; Weiß, 62-63; Beitzke, II, 450-452. Marmont, who remained in Leipzig for several days with his force until 21 September (3 October), moved to Düben on 22 September (4 October) and to Eilenburg on 24 September (6 October), *Mémoires du maréchal Marmont*, V, 166-167.

After crossing the Elbe, a proposal was drawn up in Blücher's *Hauptquartier* for operations by both Coalition armies, which had the following in mind:

1. In the event of an enemy attack in superior strength against one of these armies, it was intended to retreat to a fortified position, while the other army was to operated against the flank of the advancing enemy.
2. In the event of enemy forces concentrating near Leipzig, to attack them with all forces simultaneously with the Army of Bohemia.
3. In the event of an enemy attack on the Army of Bohemia, to send the vanguards of the other armies into their rear, each numbering 20,000 men, composed predominantly of cavalry and horse artillery.[42]

The Crown Prince, having received this draft operational plan, invited Blücher to a meeting in Mühlbeck, where both commanders-in-chief arrived on 25 September (7 October).[43] Accompanying Blücher were the brother of the King of Prussia, Prinz Wilhelm [Friedrich Wilhelm Karl von Preußen], Graf von der Goltz and Müffling, while with the Crown Prince were generals Adlercreutz and Bülow. It had been intended to send both armies towards Leipzig simultaneously.[44] The following day [8 October, new style], every corps of the Army of Silesia reached the Mulde: Yorck deployed at Mühlbeck; Langéron at Düben, where Blücher had his *Hauptquartier*; Sacken was at Mockrehna; his vanguard was at Eilenburg. Because the enemy did not have chance to destroy the bridge at Mühlbeck, Yorck's vanguard crossed the Mulde and moved towards Sausedlitz, [6½ miles north-east of Delitzsch]. At the same time, work began on constructing pontoon bridges upstream and downstream of Düben, and on repairing the bridge at Eilenburg. The Army of the North also moved forwards and on 25 September (7 October), positioned itself between Radegast, Zörbig and Jeßnitz, except for Tauentzien's corps, which was left at Dessau. The engineer General Sparre [Bengt Erland Franc-Sparre] was tasked with laying bridges over the Mulde and protecting them with bridgeheads. But the next day, 26 September (8 October), intelligence was received of an enemy advance in significant strength towards Oschatz [7½ miles west of Riesa] and Wurzen and of Napoleon's march through Meißen. The situation had changed completely. It was obvious that the Army of Silesia and Army of the North, moving towards Leipzig, would be engaged by the main body of Napoleon's force before they could establish communications with the Army of Bohemia. Not knowing what the Crown Prince intended to do under these circumstances, Blücher sent Major Rühle to investigate, who arrived in Zörbig at night and although the prince was already in bed, was immediately received by him. As soon as Rühle expressed Blücher's wish to know the Crown Prince's intentions, he announced that he had no intention of waiting for

---

42 A copy of the projected operational plan, signed by Blücher, is held in the Log of Incoming Documents, No. 1,570.
43 For the text of the Crown Prince's letter to Blücher, see Appendix XXVII at the end of this chapter.
44 Baron Tuyll's letter to Prince Volkonsky, dated 26 September (8 October) from Düben (Log of Incoming Documents, No. 1,612); Beitzke, II, 479.

Napoleon's attack, he would recross the Elbe at Roßlau and Aken, and dismantle the bridges, and that the Army of Silesia should also recross at Wartenburg in order to avoid an engagement with Napoleon and to shield Berlin. Major Rühle replied to the prince that Blücher would not agree to retreat behind the Elbe, especially since there were no resources to feed the troops there. When the prince asked: 'what does he intend to do?' Rühle responded very smartly: 'he will move across the Saale.'

'Very well,' answered the prince, 'I shall also cross over the Saale; should Napoleon follows us, we can recross the Elbe at Ferchland, where a bridge has already been laid, and will protect Berlin once more.'

But Major Rühle emphatically announced that Blücher would not fall back, and that if it pleased the prince, the Army of Silesia would move to link up with the Army of Bohemia alone.

'What will happen to Berlin?' asked the prince.

'If Moscow burned down, then why not sacrifice Berlin,' Rühle answered.

The Crown Prince, astonished by this speech, abandoned his previous intention, expressed consent to cross the Saale and promised to build a bridge at Wettin.

Upon the return of Major Rühle to the headquarters of the Army of Silesia on 27 September (9 October), Blücher, who had arrived in order to respond to the prince's aide-de-camp, expressed his consent to withdraw behind the Saale after consulting with Gneisenau. The Commander-in-Chief of the Army of Silesia, by undertaking such a movement, had to leave not only the fortified position at Wartenburg and the bridges on the Elbe, but also completely abandon communications with Silesia, which had hitherto been the only source of food for his army, and with Mark Brandenburg. Nevertheless, he decided to take this bold step, not wanting to give the Crown Prince a reason to retreat behind the Elbe and hoping that the deployment of 140,000 Coalition troops on the left bank of the Saale, between Merseburg and Bernburg, would lead to the establishment of communications with the Army of Bohemia and put Napoleon in a very dangerous position.[45]

Such was the course of events at the point when Napoleon turned against the Army of the North and Army of Silesia with the bulk of his forces.

---

45 Baron Tuyll's letters to Prince Volkonsky, dated 8 & 9 [20 & 21] October (Log of Incoming Documents, No. 1,612 & No. 1,613); Plotho, 287-292 & 316-317. For a breakdown of Yorck's force on 3 October, new style, see Appendix XXVIII at the end of this chapter.

Appendix XXVII

Bernadotte's letter to Blücher, dated 6 October, 1813, new style

The Crown Prince's letter to Blücher, dated 6 October, 1813, new style (Log of Incoming Documents, No. 1,607).

My dear General Blücher!
I have received the letter you sent to me yesterday from Kemberg. The enclosed Memorandum is perfectly in alignment with my ideas, on the whole, as I had informed Graf von der Goltz of a similar project even before having read it. Nevertheless, in situations which may become so decisive, we cannot shield ourselves too much against fate. This consideration and the desire to renew my old acquaintance with you makes me strongly hope that it would be possible for you to meet in Mühlbeck, where we could consult together and shorten the slow process that correspondence entails, through a conference. I am moving my headquarters to Radegast tomorrow and tomorrow evening we can see each other. I repeat to you the assurance of my sincere attachment being
    Yours affectionately etcetera,
    brother in arms
    Charles Jean.

Mon cher Général de Blucher!
J'ai reçu la lettre que Vous m'avez adressée hier de Kemberg. Le Mémoire qu'elle contient est parfaitement d'accord avec mes idées, quant à l'ensemble, car avant de l'avoir lu j'avais fait part d'un projet semblable au comte de Goltz. Cependant dans des circonstances qui peuvent devenir aussi décisives, nous ne saurions trop nous prémunir contre les évènemens. Cette considération et le désir de renouveler avec Vous une ancienne connaissance me font vivement désirer qu'il Vous soit possible de nous réunir à Mühlbeck, où nous pouvions nous concerter ensemble et abréger par une conférence tout ce qu'une correspondance entraine de lenteur. Je porte demain mon quartier-général à Radegast et demain au soir nous pouvons nous voir. Je Vous renouvelle l'assurance de mon sincère attachement étant
    Votre affectionné etc.
    frère d'armes
    Charles Jean.

Appendix XXVIII

Composition of Yorck's force, dated 21 September (3 October)

Vanguard commanded by *Oberst* Katzler:
Cavalry: five squadrons of *Brandenburgisches Husaren*; two squadrons of *2. Leib-Husaren*; four squadrons of *Brandenburgisches Ulanen*; five squadrons of *Ostpreußisches National Kavallerie*; four squadrons of *5. Landwehr Kavallerie*; for a total of 20 squadrons.

    1. *Reitende Batterie*.
    2.

Infantry, commanded by Major Hiller: one battalion of *Leib-Grenadiere*; one battalion of *Westpreußisches Grenadiere*; second battalion of *12. Reserve Infanterie*; first battalion of *Brandenburgisches Infanterie*; fusilier battalion of *2. Ostpreußisches Infanterie*; Reckowski's *Landwehr* battalion; Thile's *Landwehr* battalion; Wedel's *Landwehr* battalion; three jäger companies; for a total of 8¾ battalions.

Prinz zu Mecklenburg's brigade:
One battalion of *Schlesisches Grenadiere*; three battalions of *1. Ostpreußisches Infanterie*; second battalion of *2. Ostpreußisches Infanterie*; Kosetski's *Landwehr* battalion; four squadrons of *Mecklenburgisches Husaren*; three squadrons of *2. Leib-Husaren*; *1. Batterie* (eight six-pounders); *3. Batterie* (five six-pounders); for a total of six battalions, seven squadrons and 13 guns.

Steinmetz's brigade:
One battalion of *1. Ostpreußisches Grenadiere*; first battalion of *2. Ostpreußisches Infanterie*; Fischer's *Landwehr* battalion; Mumm's *Landwehr* battalion; Seidlitz's *Landwehr* battalion; Walter's & Kronegg's *Landwehr* battalion; Larisch's *Landwehr* battalion; Martitz's *Landwehr* battalion; for a total of eight battalions (Borwitz's battalion had been left at Görlitz).

Generalmajor Horn's brigade:
Three battalions of *Leib-Infanterie*; one battalion of *Thüringisches Infanterie*; Sommerfeld's *Landwehr* battalion; Pöttinghofer's *Landwehr* battalion; Reichenbach's *Landwehr* battalion; Kotulinski's & Knorr's *Landwehr* battalion; *3. Batterie* (three

six-pounders); for a total of eight battalions and three guns (Reibnitz's and Körber's battalions had been left guarding bridges).

Oberst Hünerbein's brigade:
Two battalions of *Brandenburgisches Infanterie*; two battalions of *12. Reserve Infanterie*; Kempski's *Landwehr* battalion; for a total of five battalions (Brixen's and Gfug's battalions had been left on the banks of the Elbe).

Reserve cavalry commanded by Oberstleutnant Jürgaß:
Five squadrons of *Litauisches Dragoner*; four squadrons of *1. Westpreußisches Dragoner*; four squadrons of *10. Schlesisches Landwehr Kavallerie*; four squadrons of *1. Neumärkisches Landwehr Kavallerie*; *1. Reitende Batterie*; *3. Reitende Batterie*; for a total of 17 squadrons and 16 guns.

38

The concentration of forces by both sides at Leipzig. Cavalry action at Liebertwolkwitz

The factors that prompted Napoleon to move against the Army of the North and Army of Silesia. – His intention to abandon Dresden completely. – Situation of Saint-Cyr's force. – Current locations of the French army. – Napoleon's advance towards Düben. – Napoleon and the Saxon forces. – Blücher's crossing to the left bank of the Mulde; Sacken's precarious situation during the withdrawal behind the Mulde. – Indecisive operations by the Crown Prince of Sweden. – Retreat by both Coalition armies across the river Saale. – Locations of the units left on the Elbe.

Reynier's and Ney's advance towards the Elbe. – Divergent points of view between the Coalition commanders. – Napoleon's intention to move up the right bank of the Elbe and sever the Army of Bohemia's lines of communications. – Napoleon in Düben. – His administrative instructions. – Conferences on impending operations. – Napoleon decides to march to Leipzig. – The final orders issued by him in Düben.

The advance of the Main Army from Bohemia into Saxony. – Slow and indecisive orders from Prinz Schwarzenberg during the advance towards Leipzig. His intention to make a flanking march beyond the Elster and establish communications with the other Coalition armies. – Orders to Bennigsen and Graf Colloredo to move towards Leipzig.

Schwarzenberg's dispositions for a reconnaissance of the positions occupied by Murat forwards of Leipzig. – Murat's intention to retreat behind the Parthe. – His deployment at Wachau and Liebertwolkwitz. – The cavalry action at Liebertwolkwitz, 2 (14) October. – The Army of Bohemia on the march directly towards Leipzig. – Deployment of the formations of this army, 3 (15) October.

The advance of the Army of Silesia and Army of the North towards Leipzig. Operations by General Bennigsen's Army of Poland. – The advance to Dresden. – Locations of Saint-Cyr's forces. – Action at Dresden. – Detachment of Count Tolstoy to Dresden with elements of the army and the movement towards Leipzig by Bennigsen, Colloredo and Bubna. – The composition of the Army of Poland.

Napoleon arrives Leipzig. – Deployment of his forces. – Composition of the French forces. – Napoleon postpones the battle until 4 (16) October. – The factors that prompted the Coalition to also postpone the battle. – Napoleon reviews his army. – Appeal from Prinz Schwarzenberg.

By this point the Coalition, having assembled their armed forces into two significant masses, were advancing towards Leipzig from opposite sides and were preparing to link up in the rear of the enemy army, Napoleon, confined to a small area in the vicinity of Dresden, intended to prevent the execution of this plan by moving against one of the masses that threatened him, and having broken it, turn against another. All that remained was to decide: where should he go first? Napoleon realised that the Army of Silesia and Army of the North were just one or two marches from Leipzig, while the Army of Bohemia had barely crossed the mountains separating them from Saxony and was moving very slowly; moreover, in the event of failure, they could evade defeat by retreating behind the mountain range and onwards beyond the Eger, while the Army of the North and Army of Silesia, having been defeated, would be forced to cross the Elbe between fortresses held by French garrisons. All these circumstances caused Napoleon to charge against the Crown Prince of Sweden and Blücher initially, leaving only minor forces facing the Army of Bohemia. Napoleon even intended to evacuate Dresden and absorb the forces there into the main body, but changed his mind, wanting, if successful, to retain this important point under his control and continue to defend the line of the Elbe.[1]

Saint-Cyr himself wanted to keep Dresden under his protection. The situation of the French forces in Dresden and the area surrounding this city was very problematic. Providing the troops with essential supplies became ever more difficult, because the country had been exhausted. Deliveries along the Elbe had been interrupted; the magazines were empty; constantly repeated requisitions had given rise to unlimited abuse by the petty officials of the commissariat, whose numbers had risen to 5,000 or 6,000. According to one eyewitness to the events described: 'in addition to the French army, armed with muskets and sabres, who were just as onerous to allied countries as to those of the enemy, there was also a corps in Saxony at that time armed with quills, commanded by Daru [Pierre Daru], which consumed everything the army had conquered.' Hunger forced the soldiers to forage, which gave rise to pillage. The horses, due to a lack of fodder, were in a most pitiful condition. The troops stationed in the vicinity of Dresden, not content with plundering everything that could be carried away, devastated the country, needlessly cut down chestnut and fruit trees and turned the meadows, fields and gardens of beautiful Saxony into a barren steppe.[2]

---

1 Saint-Cyr, Mémoires, Campagne de 1813, en Saxe, 185-189.
2 Odeleben, *Relation circonstanciée de la campagne de 1813 en Saxe*, II, 202-204; *Napoleon in Dresden*, II, 54.

On 26 September (8 October), on the very day that the Crown Prince of Sweden and Blücher were in Zörbig and Düben, Napoleon's forces occupied the following positions: *1er Corps* and *14e Corps*, commanded by Saint-Cyr, remained defending Dresden and the routes leading to Bohemia; Murat was stationed between Penig and Freiberg with *2e Corps*, *5e Corps* and *8e Corps*, in order to delay the main Coalition army marching from Bohemia towards Leipzig; Napoleon had departed Dresden himself on 25 September (7 October), arriving in Wurzen with the *Garde* on the following day. The remaining formations were assembling in the vicinity of this point and, on the evening of 26 September (8 October), were located as follows: Souham's *3e Corps* near Wurzen; Macdonald's *11e Corps* and Sébastiani's *2e corps de cavalerie* were at Dahlen; Bertrand's *4e Corps* was at Schildau; Reynier's *7e Corps*, Dąbrowski's Polish division, Latour-Maubourg's *1er corps de cavalerie*, Sébastiani's *2e corps de cavalerie* [sic], and elements of *3e corps de cavalerie* (Fournier's division and one of Defrance's brigades) were in the Eilenburg area; Marmont's *6e Corps* with Lorge's division from *3e corps de cavalerie* were at Taucha, a half-stage from Leipzig. The total number of fighting men concentrated under Napoleon's direct command ranged from 125,000 to 130,000 men. In addition, some 15,000 men had been left in Leipzig.[3]

Following Napoleon, the King of Saxony left Dresden for Wurzen, under escort by *2e division de la Vieille Garde*; for the onward journey to Eilenburg, and then on to Leipzig, he was accompanied by 30 men of the *Vieille Garde* and the Saxon *Leibgrenadiergarde*.[4]

Napoleon had no accurate intelligence on the strength or disposition of the Coalition armies: he believed that the Crown Prince had no more than 40,000 men and that he had not yet managed to establish communications with Blücher. Hoping to defeat the Army of Silesia in isolation, Napoleon directed his forces towards Düben on 27 September (9 October) in three columns: the right hand column was directed towards Mockrehna, consisting of Bertrand's and Macdonald's corps, Sébastiani's cavalry and Chastel's division (from *1er corps de cavalerie*); the centre column, commanded by Ney, was directed along the right bank of Mulde towards Düben, consisting of Dąbrowski's division, Fournier's cavalry and one of Defrance's brigades (*3e corps de cavalerie*), *3e Corps* and *7e Corps*, followed by the reserves (the *Garde* and the cavalry corps under Latour-Maubourg and Kellermann); the left hand column, commanded by Marmont, was also directed towards Düben, but along the left bank of the Mulde, consisting of *6e Corps* and Lorge's division (from *3e corps de cavalerie*).[5]

Napoleon, upon arrival at Kültzschau [two miles east of Eilenburg], on the morning of 27 September (9 October), reviewed *7e Corps*, at the end of which he called all the officers and non-commissioned officers from the Saxon division to the front and delivered the following speech, instructing Caulaincourt [Armand Augustin Louis de Caulaincourt] to translate it into German:

---

3   Vaudoncourt, Histoire de la guerre soutenue par les Français en Allemagne, 193-194; Bernhardi, Denkwürdigkeiten aus dem Leben Carl Friedrich Grafen von Toll, III, 366-367.
4   Förster, *Geschichte der Befreiungskriege, 1813, 1814, 1815*, II, 7.
5   Bernhardi, III, 369.

brave Saxons! You have been unlucky in your recent actions against the enemy. The Emperor has arrived; he will stand at your head to give you the opportunity for victory in your turn. You will be in action against the Prussians who want to annex Saxony. This is not the first time that Saxon banners have flown alongside those of France. We have been fighting side by side since the Seven Years' War; we have fought together at Friedland and Wagram. Can the Emperor rely on the brave Saxons, on their loyalty to their King? One of you, who owed his rise to French service, has betrayed you and his fatherland. Those who have gone over to the enemy's side have become enemies of their country. If any of you does not share this conviction, let him leave the ranks of our army. Go and tell this to your soldiers.

Napoleon's speech was not distinguished by his usual energy and was conveyed incorrectly and haltingly by Caulaincourt, producing no reaction. The sullen silence of the Saxon warriors was a harbinger of their defection from the French.[6]

On 27 September (9 October), on the same day as the French forces were moving towards Düben, Blücher, arriving in the village of Pouch [1½ miles south of Mühlbeck], learned of the offensive by the enemy main force against him. This obliged him to speed up the crossing of the Mulde. Yorck's corps, which had arrived at Jeßnitz in the evening and bivouacked there, was ordered to move overnight to the left bank of the river, near this village and at Raguhn, and reposition themselves on the left bank. In the meantime, the pontoon park had just arrived and another bridge was built at Jeßnitz. Langéron's corps, which had been marching all night, crossed in the morning, but General Sacken did not receive timely orders cancelling the previous ones, and was heading towards Düben, and would encounter Napoleon's main force. But the experienced warrior evaded the danger that threatened him. Having learned of the offensive by strong columns towards him from the front and from the left flank, he initially had the intention of retreating to Wartenburg, but such a movement would have isolated him from the other corps of the Army of Silesia, and therefore he preferred to head through the forest towards Jeßnitz, and upon reaching Schköna, to the south-east of Gräfenhainichen, he received orders from Blücher to go to Raguhn and cross the Mulde there. Having crossed the river on the morning of 28 September (10 October), Sacken's corps deployed at Jeßnitz, where on that same day all his units that had remained far behind rejoined him, and after that the pontoon bridge was dismantled. The remaining two corps of the Army of Silesia were stationed at Zörbig, to where Blücher relocated his *Hauptquartier*. The forward elements were redeployed: Katzler towards Brehna, Rudzevich towards Roitzsch, Yuzefovich towards Bitterfeld.[7]

The Crown Prince of Sweden was very reluctant to begin crossing to the right bank of the Saale, pointing out to Blucher that the Army of the North could not

---

6   Odeleben, II, 5-6; Förster, II, 11-12.
7   Tuyll's letter to Prince Volkonsky, dated 28 September (10 October) from Jeßnitz (Log of Incoming Documents, No. 1,623); Plotho, *Der Krieg in Deutschland und Frankreich in den Jahren 1813 und 1814*, II, 293-295; Beitzke, *Geschichte der deutschen Freiheitskriege in den Jahren 1813 und 1814*, II, 485-486.

move away from the Elbe, exposing their communications to the enemy and isolating the blockade formations detached from them; and therefore the prince wanted the Army of Silesia to move to form the right wing of a general deployment. This proposal aroused such suspicion among the Coalition generals subordinate to the prince that Bülow and Wintzingerode were prepared to abandon him and join Blücher. Tauentzien's corps had been directed to monitor the fortresses on the Elbe and protect Berlin. Consequently, had the other corps commanders dared to depart from the Army of the North, then the Crown Prince would have only the Swedish corps alone remaining. But General Gneissenau managed to persuade the prince to keep his promise to move to the left bank of the Saale, which was also facilitated by the British military commissioner who was with him at the time, Sir Charles Stewart, who announced that, in the event of the prince's refusal, the agreed British subsidies would not be paid to him.[8]

At five o'clock in the morning of 29 September (11 October), the Army of Silesia set off towards Wettin on the Saale, where the Crown Prince had promised to build a bridge. Blücher, for his part, had ordered the pontoons from Jeßnitz to be sent there in order to build another bridge. Yorck's corps marched to Ostrau and on towards Krosigk, Langéron's corps to Rieda and on towards Trebitz [one mile north-east of Sylbitz], while Sacken went to Radegast and on towards Löbejün; the vanguards of the first two corps remained in place to shield the movement of the army; Sacken's vanguard followed his corps. Upon the arrival of the columns under Yorck and Langéron in the vicinity of Petersberg, news was received that the pontoons on their way from Jeßnitz would not arrive at Wettin before nightfall, and that there was not so much as a rumour of the construction of the bridge ordered by the Crown Prince of Sweden. Blücher immediately decided to turn left, along the Magdeburg to Halle road, and to cross to the left bank of the Saale at Halle. In order to do this, it was necessary to conduct a march of about 30 *versts* in one day, and since the crossing at Halle was carried out over a single bridge, Yorck's force, proceeding behind Langéron's corps, only managed to cross to the far side of the river at two o'clock in the morning and deployed partly to the west of Halle in the villages of Nietleben and Zscherben [four miles and five miles west of Halle, respectively], partly in the town itself and on its outskirts. The reserve cavalry from Yorck's corps remained on the right bank of the river at Diemitz, two *versts* from the town. The cavalry from Langéron's corps, having not received timely orders to go to Halle, marched to Wettin and were sent towards Halle upon arrival there. Having reached the outskirts of this town at midnight, they settled down for the night, and the following day (12 October, new style), having crossed the Saale, they bivouacked between Schlettau and Beuchlitz [five miles and 5½ miles south-west of Halle, respectively]. The troops under the comte de Saint-Priest occupied Merseburg. Sacken's corps, having spent the night at Löbejün, crossed the next day, 30 September (12 October), at Wettin, and took post on the right wing of the army between Langenbogen [nine miles west of Halle] and Teutschenthal [nine miles south-west of Halle]. The Army of the North also crossed the Saale on 29 September (11 October) at Rothenburg and Alsleben,

---

8   Beitzke, II, 486-487.

and deployed at Rothenburg. Hirschfeld's detachment remained at Aken; Thümen's brigade was monitoring Wittenberg, while Wobeser's brigade was observing Torgau. General Graf Tauentzien, stationed at Dessau with the rest of his corps, received orders to protect the bridge at Roßlau, and in the event of the enemy crossing the Elbe, to concentrate all the detachments remaining on the right bank of this river and protect the approaches to Berlin. As early as 28 September (10 October), General Prince Shcherbatov had been sent orders by Blücher to go to the village of Elster by forced marches and await further orders there, leaving only a small cavalry detachment facing Dresden for surveillance.[9]

Following the retreat of the Army of Silesia and Army of the North across the river Saale, only scattered Prussian detachments remained facing Napoleon across a considerable front. On 28 September (10 October), having reached Düben, he learned that his hopes of defeating Blücher in isolation had been dashed. On 29 September (11 October), Reynier's *7e Corps* and *3e Corps* commanded by Ney were sent towards the Elbe: the former towards Wittenberg, and the latter towards Dessau. As far as can be judged from the orders issued by Napoleon and from his correspondence, he intended to force the Army of Silesia and Army of the North to return to the right bank of the Elbe by threatening Berlin. Napoleon hoped to defeat the Coalition, should they be willing to give battle, and then to turn on Bennigsen and relieve Dresden, which, in all probability, would prompt Schwarzenberg to retreat into Bohemia.[10] All the other French corps proceeded behind Reynier and Ney, except the *Vieille Garde*, which remained with the *quartier-général* in Düben. General Reynier, crossing at Wittenberg, forced Thümen to retreat to Roßlau, where this Prussian detachment joined the force under Tauentzien on 30 September (12 October) and, having destroyed the bridge at Roßlau, retreated together to Zerbst in the early hours of 1 (13) October. The Prussian casualties in combat against enemy forces three times as strong did not exceed 800 men (Tauentzien lost 500 while Thümen lost 300), but the forced marches cost them many more. Count Tauentzien, concerned that the enemy might forestall him in Berlin, retreated there in haste and arrived in Potsdam with his force, exhausted from fatigue, on the night of 2 to 3 (14 to 15) October.[11]

---

9 Adjutant General Korff's corps diary; General Sacken's report No. 274 to Barclay de Tolly, dated 1 [13] October, from Teutschenthal (Archive of the M.T.D. No. 16,644); War Diary of Prince Shcherbatov's VI Corps; Plotho, II, 331, 334-335 & 340; Beitzke, II, 487-489.

10 '… The Emperor is in Wittenberg (sic), which His Majesty has relieved. The Army of Silesia is in retreat in all directions on the left bank. Tomorrow His Majesty will force the enemy to accept battle, or to dismantle their bridges at Dessau and Wartenburg. Perhaps he will then decide to move to the right bank with his entire army; it is via the right bank that the Emperor will move towards Dresden.' *Extrait de la lettre du major-général au maréchal Saint-Cyr, Duben, le 10 octobre.*

'… L'empereur est à Wittenberg, que S.M. a debloqué. L'armée de Silésie est en retraite de tous côtés sur la rive gauche. Demain S.M. obligera l'ennemi à recevoir bataille, ou à se laisser enlever ses ponts de Dessau et de Wartenbourg. Peut-être se décidera-t-elle alors à passer sur la rive droite avec toute son armée; c'est par la rive droite que l'Empereur se portera sur Dresde.'

11 Vaudoncourt, 197, according to whom, the Prussian forces on the retreat to Roßlau lost 3,000 men and six guns; Plotho, II, 332-333, 338-340, 348 & 356; Hofmann, *Zur Geschichte des Feldzuges von 1813, Zweite Auflage*, 234.

The French advance towards the Elbe was regarded in Blücher's *Hauptquartier* as a feint. In contrast, the Crown Prince took it to be the beginning of a decisive offensive by Napoleon's army towards Berlin. As soon as he received news of the lifting of the blockade of Wittenberg, the concentration of significant enemy forces between the Mulde and the Elbe and Napoleon's arrival in Düben, he transferred his army to Köthen in order to be closer to the Elbe, and wrote to Blücher, on 1 (13) October, that Napoleon was heading towards Wittenberg with four corps, and that therefore the Army of the North found it necessary to move to the right bank of the Elbe at Aken, where the bridge built by the Coalition still remained intact. At the same time, the Crown Prince reported that, in accordance with Emperor Alexander's comment to him, that, in some cases, Blücher was to obey the prince, and therefore, on this basis, the Army of Silesia should follow the Army of the North onto the right bank of the Elbe. The officer who arrived with the prince's letter repeated the most exaggerated rumours regarding Napoleon's intentions. Some claimed that he would march down the Elbe to join Marshal Davout; others thought that the objective of his operations could be the occupation of Berlin; others believed that he would move on Stralsund. Finally, some expressed their fears to the point that they foresaw the appearance of Napoleon on the Oder and an uprising in Poland. The Crown Prince, sharing some of these opinions himself, ordered General Rauch to float the pontoons down the Elbe from the village of Elster and, once he had constructed another bridge at Aken, to protect it with a bridgehead on the right bank of the river. But by this time the French were closing on Aken from Roßlau, and General Rauch, by order of Blücher, had already moved the pontoons from Elster to the Saale: thus, the Crown Prince, having lost the chance to cross the Elbe at Aken, was forced to halt at Köthen. In response to his recall, Blücher wrote that the Army of Silesia had moved to the left bank of the Saale at the suggestion of the prince himself. Blücher continued:

> Currently, Your Royal Highness would like to cross the Elbe via the Aken bridge. In this event, upon being separated from the Army of the North, necessity would dictate that I march to join the Army of Bohemia. I do not know how Your Royal Highness would be able to complete the proposed crossing, or how you could operate in the confined area between the enemy, the Elbe, Magdeburg and the Havel...

Blücher did not write a word about his subordination to the prince, but wanting to show that the situation was not at all as desperate as was perceived in the headquarters of the Army of the North, he informed the prince of the conclusion of a treaty of alliance between the Austrian and Bavarian governments in Ried [Ried im Innkreis] on 26 September (8 October), as a result of which a strong Austro-Bavarian corps would be moving towards Würzburg. The Crown Prince of Sweden, still not abandoning his intention to cross to the right bank of the Elbe, ordered General Rauch, who had arrived in Köthen with the pontoons, to go back to Aken and construct a bridge there. These orders gave rise to disagreements between the Coalition commanders; but at the same time, Napoleon turned towards Leipzig, and the Crown Prince, having received news of this from Blücher, decided to go with him after the enemy once more, in order to get closer to the Army of Bohemia.[12]

Napoleon had indeed changed his intentions – planning to cross to the right bank of the Elbe with all the formations he had assembled. By undertaking this movement, he hoped to divert both Coalition armies advancing against him from the north and defeat them there, isolated from the Army of Bohemia, or at least to drive them a considerable distance away from each other; thereafter, having destroyed every crossing on the Elbe except for those located in the fortresses held by his troops, he planned to move up the right bank of this river to Torgau or Dresden, cross at one of these points onto the left bank of the Elbe once more, and if he main Coalition army was continuing the offensive they had begun and reached Leipzig, to strike them from behind and push them back into the Mulde and the Elbe, away from their lines of communications with Bohemia. Based on the above assumptions, Napoleon sent out the necessary enciphered instructions, revealing his deepest secret to all who received them, in his own words, that 'the salvation of the Empire depends' on their execution over the next three days. In a letter from the duc de Bassano (Maret) to Marshal Saint-Cyr we find:

> the King of Naples (Murat) is retreating to Leipzig; if he is forced to evacuate this city, then, having driven the Army of Silesia and Army of the North onto the right bank of the Elbe, the Emperor intends to cross after them and destroy them; and if the enemy remains on the left bank of the river, to use Magdeburg and Dresden as the focus of operations. His Majesty would best like you to maintain communications with Torgau. Having concluded matters with the Army of Silesia and Army of the North, His Majesty will immediately establish communications with you...[13]

The *chef d'état-major*, Berthier, on Napoleon's instructions, on 28 September (10 October), ordered Murat to delay the enemy advance and hold Leipzig behind him in order to give the Emperor time to defeat the Army of Silesia; in the event that the King were forced to cede Leipzig, he was to retreat towards Torgau and Wittenberg behind the Mulde or even behind the Elbe, in anticipation of Napoleon moving his main force onto the left bank at Torgau or Dresden and his advance into the rear of the Army of Bohemia.[14] General Arrighi received orders to send essential supplies, munitions, clothing and footwear from Leipzig to Torgau; he was also instructed to write to Erfurt and Mainz such that they would not be alarmed in the event of an enemy seizure of Leipzig, which might occur in the course of operations destined to end with a lightning blow.[15]

Thus, Napoleon intended to abandon communications with the Rhine temporarily, which were less important to him now than before, because his final expected

---

12 Beitzke, II, 503-509; Müffling, *Zur Kriegsgeschichte der Jahre 1813 und 1814 – Die Feldzüge der Schlesischen Armee*, 72-73.
13 Saint-Cyr, 448-449.
14 Letter from the *chef d'état-major* to Murat, dated 10 October, new style, from Düben.
15 'par un coup de foudre.' Thiers, *Histoire du Consulat et de l'Empire*, XVI, Edit de Brux, 566-567.

reinforcements, two divisions from Augereau's corps [Charles Pierre François Augereau] and cavalry sent from Spain, had already reached the Leipzig area. But the following were vital for this bold concept from a brilliant commander to succeed:

1. That the Army of Silesia and Army of the North must be driven a great distance away from the Army of Bohemia.
2. That the Army of Bohemia must operate slowly and hesitantly and could not be given time to achieve significant success before the appearance of Napoleon's main force to their rear.

The first intelligence Napoleon received in Düben was quite favourable: among all the uncertainties of the collected intelligence, it seemed certain that the rapid advance by the French army had forced Blücher to retreat behind the Mulde and the Saale, while the Crown Prince of Sweden had to cross back over the Elbe.[16] From the opposite direction, news came in from the comte de Lauriston regarding the successes the French had won over the forward elements of the Army of Bohemia.[17] But it soon emerged that the evasion of an engagement with Napoleon's main force by the Army of Silesia and Army of the North was intended to concentrate the entire Coalition force, or at least the main army and Army of Silesia, across his communications.[18] On the other hand, Murat reported that he, by avoiding a clash with the superior numbers of the army advancing against him, had retreated to take up positions forwards of Leipzig and would hold there to the last man.[19]

Napoleon, while waiting for confirmation of all these circumstances and remaining in Düben for several days, could not find subsistence for any energetic activity, and was involuntarily limited to instructions regarding food supply and the tactical restructuring of the army. The huge parks and mobile magazines which had hitherto moved along with the *quartier général*, were distributed down to the corps. Commissariat reserves of clothing and footwear were distributed to the troops; He then wrote several times regarding demands agreed with the local government of Saxony for the supply of 30,000 pairs of shoes for the French army. Anticipating an imminent clash with the Coalition, who were superior in strength, Napoleon ordered the infantry to form up in two ranks rather than three which, in his opinion, without weakening either firepower when deployed in line or shock

---

16 Thiers, XVI, 573.
17 'On 8 October, Prince Poniatowski defeated 3,000 cavalry at Frohburg. He killed many men and took prisoners. General Sokolniki was attacked in Penig. He repelled the enemy and pursued them for a league. The King of Naples marched to Fröhburg with *2e Corps*. He sent Prince Poniatowski to Altenburg with *5e corps de cavalerie...*' Extract from comte de Lauriston's letter to the duc de Bassano, dated 9 October, new style, from Rochlitz.

'Le 8, le prince Poniatowsky a battu à Fröhburg 3,000 hommes de cavalerie. Il a tué beaucoup de monde et fait des prisonniers. Le général Sokolnicki a été attaqué à Penig. Il a repoussé l'ennemi et l'a poursuivi une lieue. Le roi de Naples s'est porté à Fröhburg avec le 2me corps. Il a fait marcher le prince Poniatowsky sur Altenburg avec le 5me corps de cavalerie...'
18 For the contents of Berthier's letter to Murat in this regard, see Appendix XXIX at the end of this chapter.
19 Thiers, XVI, 575-576.

action when in column, encouraged the perception of greater numbers to an enemy force than was actually the case. In conversations with Marshal Marmont and his other associates, he discussed measures to mitigate the risks that threatened him. They all suggested that he continue the offensive down the Elbe, assimilating the force under Saint-Cyr and some of Davout's corps, and abandoning the previous lines of communications with France via Mainz, establish new ones via Wesel. According to Saint-Cyr, having temporarily adopted Magdeburg as the focus of his operations (*pivot de ses opérations*), a large and strong fortress, abundantly stocked with military and essential supplies, Napoleon could have drawn the Coalition from Bohemia, which offered the opportunity of threatening their lines of communications while preserving his own; but with this course of action the outcome of the matter would be delayed, and Napoleon wanted to decide the fate of the war as soon as possible.[20] The German population were hostile to him; their rulers, influenced by the turbulent flow of public opinion, wavered in their loyalty to the conqueror. The Italians who fought under his flag in northern Germany yearned for *farniente* [relaxation]. The French themselves were looking forward to victory or peace. In this state of affairs, there was nothing left to do but muster as much strength as possible in order to resolve the issue with one blow.

On 30 September (12 October), having received word from Murat on the advance of the Army of Bohemia towards Leipzig, while strong patrols sent out from Marmont's corps reliably confirmed that not only the Army of Silesia, but also the Army of the North had retreated behind the river Saale, Napoleon amended his original operational plan. It was vital to prevent a Coalition concentration at Leipzig. To that end, Napoleon decided to go to Murat's aid and fight the Army of Bohemia. Notifying him of his intent, he ordered Murat to inform him whether he could hold his position at Leipzig until the morning of 2 (14) October, and in this case he intended to support him with his main body; if Murat found it necessary to abandon Leipzig, then Napoleon intended to assemble the army on the Mulde, holding the sector from Wurzen to Grimma with Murat's force and repositioning the remaining corps from Wurzen to Eilenburg.[21] Marmont, having marched to Delitzsch on that same day [12 October, new style] with his force, numbering 20,000 men, was placed at Murat's disposal and could link up with him on 1 (13) October; Augereau's corps, numbering some 15,000 men, had arrived the day before: therefore, on 1 (13) October, Murat could assemble some 90,000 men. The *Garde* and Latour-Maubourg's cavalry corps, some 45,000 men in all, were ordered to march from Düben at dawn on 1 (13) October and move quickly towards Leipzig. These formations would arrive there on 2 (14) October and, together with Murat's corps, would form an army of more than 130,000 men. At the same time as the departure of the *Garde*, orders were sent to Bertrand, who was still in Wartenburg destroying the fortifications built there by Blücher's troops, and to Macdonald, directed to Wittenberg in support of Reynier's corps, to get themselves to Düben by forced marches; the latter, in addition to his own forces, was to bring Sébastiani's cavalry

---

20 Saint-Cyr, 229-231; Marmont, *Mémoires*, V, 169.
21 Instructions to Murat and the duc de Bassano (who was in Eilenburg), dated 12 October, new style.

corps, detached to the Elbe, so long as General Reynier could manage without their assistance: thus, Napoleon hoped to concentrate some 170,000 men at Leipzig by 3 (15) October.[22] The addition of Reynier's corps and Dąbrowski's division, numbering 15,000 to 20,000 men sent across the Elbe to destroy the bridges at Barby [12 miles downstream of Aken], and Ney, with 15,000 men moving down the Mulde to seize the crossing at Dessau, could have brought the French army to over 200,000 men, but Napoleon did not want these corps to report to Leipzig before completing their missions, and believed that Ney could still arrive on 3 (15) October.[23]

The final orders dictated by Napoleon to *chef d'état-major* Berthier, before departing Düben for Leipzig, contained the following instructions: 'Generals Bertrand and Latour-Maubourg are to report their estimated time of arrival at Göbschelwitz ([four miles] north-east of Wiederitzsch) in advance, such that I have time to send them definitive instructions; if these have not been received by them before arriving at the aforementioned village, then Bertrand's corps are to take up positions on both sides of the Dessau road, the units under Latour-Maubourg are to be positioned in a similar manner, while the parks and trains are to be further back. General Latour-Maubourg is to direct send reconnaissance forces along the roads to Delitzsch and Landsberg. The duc de Reggio (Oudinot), if he has not received other orders, is to deploy at Seehausen [two miles east of Wiederitzsch], resting his right flank on the Parthe [south of Seehausen], while the duc de Treviso (Mortier) is to deploy at the village of Wiederitzsch, with his right flank on the Delitzsch road, and his left on the Elster. In the event of Bertrand or Latour-Maubourg hearing a strong cannonade from Leipzig, they should accelerate their march. I shall be on the road from Düben to Leipzig and will leave a picket of selected *gendarmes* at the Pfaffendorfer bridge [one mile north of Leipzig] to indicate the location at which I may be found after crossing the Parthe. Write to General Durrieu [Antoine Simon Durrieu] such that the pontoons, the trains of the quartier général, the artillery and engineering parks are to be transported to the left bank of the Mulde, and that he entrusts the Bavarian general with guarding Eilenburg, deploying his own infantry and artillery with them.[24] He should also be required to provide information about the size and condition of the trains, their estimated times of departure and arrival in Leipzig. He must be ready to move with the entire train within an hour of receiving orders.'[25]

Let us turn to the advance towards Leipzig by the Army of Bohemia and towards Dresden by Bennigsen.

Having been relieved by units of the Army of Poland the Russo-Prussian units stationed on the right wing of the Army of Bohemia began to move; on 16 (28) September, the corps under Count Wittgenstein and Kleist moved to their left towards Komotau and arrived there the following day. They were followed by the Grenadier Corps and the Russo-Prussian guard, and finally the Austrian *II. Korpus* under Graf Merveldt, stationed at Aussig. The flank march by the troops was carried

---

22 Instructions issued at five o'clock and six o'clock in the morning of 13 October, new style.
23 Instructions issued at three o'clock in the morning of 14 October, new style.
24 From this it is clear that Napoleon did not yet know about Bavaria's defection from him.
25 Instructions issued on 14 October, new style.

out extremely slowly. The headquarters did not move to Brüx (15 *versts* from Teplitz) until 18 (30) September and remained there for four days until 23 September (5 October); thereafter, having moved another 15 *versts* to Komotau, they halted for two more days, then, having completed a similar stage, reached Sebastiansberg on 26 September (8 October). The reserve cavalry remained, as before, between the Böhmische Mittelgebirge and the river Eger during the flank march. The Austrian corps under Klenau, constantly stationed on the left flank of the army at Marienberg, at a fairly considerable distance from Victor's corps, which was monitoring them, according to the general disposition, was to form the lead element of the right hand column once the army advanced into Saxony; Gyulay's corps, which was to follow them, did not arrive at Marienberg until 19 September (1 October), as did Moritz Liechtenstein's light division at Annaberg; the rest of the Austrian formations were still trailing behind at intervals of several stages. Count Wittgenstein's corps, assigned to move as the lead formation of the left hand column, departed from Komotau no earlier than 20 September (2 October), and advanced across the main ridge, arriving at Annaberg together with Kleist's corps on 3 October new style. The remaining Russian and Prussian formations crossed the mountains over the following days; the last echelon, consisting of the Russo-Prussian reserve artillery, moved into Saxony from Sebastiansberg on 24 September (6 October): consequently, the army's march through the mountains took eight days, during which the headquarters moved six *Meilen* (a little over 40 *versts*).[26]

The French corps defending the approaches to Saxony were located at a considerable distance from the main mountain crest: the reason for this was the weakness of their forces and the inability to feed the troops in a country devastated by the constant presence of huge armies. Mouton's *1er Corps* and Saint-Cyr's *14e Corps*, under the command of the latter, were protecting Dresden, holding the sector between Dippoldiswalde and Königstein; Murat's force, assigned to defend Leipzig, numbering more than 40,000 men, were located as follows: Victor's *2e Corps* at Freiberg; Lauriston's *5e Corps* at Mittweida [eight miles south of Waldheim], Poniatowski's *8e Corps* at Frohburg.[27] Despite the triple superiority in the strength of the Army of Bohemia over the force under Murat, *Feldmarschall* Schwarzenberg, calculating the full strength of enemy forces concentrated in Saxony, moved forward step by step, as if in the dark, and the further he moved away from the mountains that served him as a refuge, the stronger became his concerns. Nevertheless, the news he received on 23 September (5 October) of Blücher's crossing and victory had to prompt him to greater activity.[28] If the Prussian commander had dared to cross the Elbe in full view of the enemy, then there was nothing preventing him from

---

26 Log of military movements and operations of the Russo-Prussian army, signed by Barclay de Tolly (Archive of the M.T.D. No. 29,188); War Diary signed by Prince Volkonsky; Plotho, II, 224-227, according to whom, the last column of the Army of Bohemia did not enter Saxony until 26 September (8 October).
27 For a comparison of estimates of Murat's troop strength, see Appendix XXX at the end of this chapter.
28 Poltho, II, 236; The War Diary signed by Barclay de Tolly states that the news of Blücher's victory at Wartenburg was received at the headquarters of the Army of Bohemia on 25 September (7 October).

advancing towards Leipzig together with the Crown Prince, and in this case, on the basis of the action plan drawn up in Trachenberg, Schwarzenberg was obliged to race to link up with the Army of the North and the Army of Silesia. In addition, as if to dispel the doubts that worried him, he received premature, but seemingly reliable, intelligence of Napoleon abandoning the line of the Elbe.[29] All this forced Schwarzenberg to speed up the advance by the leading corps: on 24 September (6 October), the forces under Count Wittgenstein and Kleist deployed at Zwickau, the Austrian corps under Klenau and Gyulay were at Chemnitz and Waldkirchen [2½ miles north-east of Zschopau]. Wittgenstein's vanguard, commanded by Lieutenant General Count Pahlen, had been pushed up the Altenburg road; the vanguard of Klenau's corps were moving towards Penig, while *Feldmarschallleutnant* Graf Murray was heading for the river Flöha with the vanguard of Gyulay's corps.[30] Murat, who was stationed at Oederan [9½ miles west of Freiberg] at the time with Victor's corps and Sułkowski's *chasseurs à cheval* brigade [Antoni Paweł Sułkowski], calculating that the best way to delay the army advancing against him was to defeat any one of its forward detachments, attacked Murray at the village of Flöha [eight miles east of Chemnitz], drove them back over the river and pursued the defeated force for several *versts*.[31]

Schwarzenberg, having reached the Chemnitz area on 26 September (8 October), learned of the unexpected defeat of his vanguard and decided to attack Murat, located between Zschopau and Flöha with Victor's corps, *4e corps de cavalerie* and *5e corps de cavalerie*. To that end, the Austrian *III. Korpus* and *IV. Korpus* were directed against them; but the enemy retreated to Mittweida without waiting for the attack. The Austrians occupied Oederan. Unfortunately, the *Feldmarschall* then received intelligence that Napoleon was marching from Wurzen towards Leipzig with the bulk of his forces; it was also known that Augereau's reserve corps was moving through Weimar towards Leipzig as well: all this made Schwarzenberg concerned for an attack on the left flank; the advance by Wittgenstein and Kleist towards Altenburg was suspended. Poniatowski, taking advantage of the Coalition hesitancy, attacked the forward detachment from *Feldmarschallleutnant* Mohr's division [Johann Friedrich von Mohr], which was holding Penig, and ejected them from there. The next day [9 October, new style], having received reliable news of Napoleon's moves down the Elbe and Mulde, Schwarzenberg ordered the advance towards Leipzig to resume as quickly as possible.[32] The Austrian formations deployed at Chemnitz, except for Klenau's corps advanced to Penig. The corps under Count

---

29 Plotho, II, 236.
30 Count Pahlen's vanguard consisted of: Ilovaisky 11th's (*sic*, 12th?) Cossacks; Grodno Hussars, Sumy Hussars; Prussian *Neumärkisches Dragoner*; four regiments from 14th Division; 7th Horse Artillery Company and four heavy guns; Plotho, II, 238. General Nikitin's notes state that Pahlen's vanguard consisted of: Sumy Hussars, Grodno Hussars, Lubny Hussars; Chuguev Ulans; Major General Nikitin's 7th Horse Artillery Company, numbering 1,700 men with 12 guns.
31 Plotho, II, 239; Beitzke, II, 391-392.
32 'According to consistent reports, because the enemy march downstream between the Elbe and Mulde has proved successful, the main Army of Bohemia is to continue its march in the direction of Leipzig as quickly as possible.'

Wittgenstein and Kleist occupied Altenburg; Count Pahlen's vanguard was directed up the road towards Borna; on 28 September (10 October), the reserves arrived in Chemnitz.[33] The Coalition army could easily have arrived at Leipzig on 1 (13) October, but, instead, it did not arrive there until 3 (15) October. The leading corps advanced no more than 40 *versts* in five days. What would Suvorov [Alexander Vasilievich Suvorov] have said about the speed of Schwarzenberg's movements?

Because only part of the Coalition army advanced to confront Murat, and the other corps were slowly proceeding behind their forward detachments, the enemy dared to give battle several times on the march from Penig and Altenburg towards Leipzig. On 27 September (9 October), the leading Coalition corps were in the following locations: Count Wittgenstein's vanguard, commanded by Lieutenant General Pahlen, was at Borna; 3rd Division and 5th Division were on the road between Altenburg and Borna; General Rüdiger's small cavalry detachment had been pushed forwards towards the village of Eschefeld [2½ miles west of Frohburg], and for their support, General Zieten with the Prussian *11. Brigade* and Prinz Eugen von Württemberg with 4th Division were headed there from Windischleuba; the Prussian *10. Brigade* were stationed at Windischleuba, while Kleist himself was at Altenburg with *9. Brigade* and *12. Brigade*. Count Platov's Cossack detachment held Pegau, from where patrols had been sent out towards Naumburg, Weißenfels, Lützen, Merseburg and Halle. Thielmann's detachment and the Austrian light division under Moritz Liechtenstein were moving towards Naumburg, held by Augereau's corps on the march towards Leipzig, and the following day [10 October, new style], following a fierce battle at Wethau [two miles south-east of Naumburg], retreated towards Zeitz, protected by Colonel Orlov's rearguard. *Oberst* Graf Mensdorff was sent towards Weißenfels during this action. The advance by Wittgenstein's force towards Borna had been carried out without orders from Schwarzenberg, who, remaining unaware that it had been taken, ordered Count Wittgenstein to occupy Borna on 29 September (11 October). Poniatowski's corps had been enveloped on the right flank by the corps under Wittgenstein and Kleist, but remained facing Graf Klenau's Austrian corps, which had reached Penig at the same time as the seizure of Borna by Russian forces. On 28 September (10 October), concerned about losing communications with Leipzig, Murat concentrated his forces between Frohburg and Rochlitz, retreated through Priessnitz and Flössberg [3½ miles and three miles south-west of Lausick] to the right bank of the Jordanbach and took up positions on the high ground at Gestewitz, [three miles] north of Borna. Prince Poniatowski, who was shielding this move, upon being pursued by the troops under Zieten, was engaged by the vanguard under Pahlen from the direction of Borna and lost several hundred men taken prisoner. The losses in the Russian force, killed and wounded reached some 300 men. Zieten's force took Frohburg and pursued the enemy as far as the

---

'*Da nach den übereinstimmenden Nachrichten, der Marsch des Feindes zwischen der Elbe und Mulde abwärts sich bewährt, so soll das böhmische Hauptheer seinen Marsch, in der Richtung gegen Leipzig, auf das schleunigste fortsetzen.*'

33 Prinz Schwartzenberg's dispositions for 9 October, new style; War Diary signed by Barclay de Tolly; Beitzke, II 393.

Jordanbach, but despite these successes, Murat concentrated his forces across the shortest route to Leipzig.[34]

On that same day [10 October, new style], intelligence was received at Schwarzenberg's headquarters that Bennigsen, who was advancing towards Dresden at the time, was facing no more than 15,000 to 20,000 enemy troops, and that Blücher's army was at Düben, while the Crown Prince was at Radegast. The conclusion drawn from all this, was that since no significant forces were concentrated against any one of the aforementioned Coalition armies, Napoleon was preparing to assemble his forces around Leipzig. In order to counter him, the Austrian Commander-in-Chief also undertook to concentrate the Coalition army, but instead of bringing in the corps stretched over a considerable distance by the shortest route, to face the enemy frontally, and attacking Murat without giving him time to bring up reinforcements, it was decided to go left flanking and envelope the French army's right flank. To that end, orders were issued for: Wittgenstein and Kleist to unite at Borna; Klenau to move from Penig to Rochlitz; the corps under Gyulay, Merveldt, the Prinz von Homburg and the Russian grenadiers with 3rd Cuirassier Division to move from Chemnitz and Zschopau to Altenburg, while the Russo-Prussian guard and the first two cuirassier divisions were to go from Marienberg to half way between Penig and Altenburg.[35]

It emerges from all the orders by Schwarzenberg that he was constantly unaware of the locations of the corps entrusted to him and was therefore worried by irrelevant concerns; he was particularly concerned about delays to the Austrian *I. Korpus* under Graf Colloredo, temporarily attached to the Army of Poland, which had been sent orders from the headquarters on 26 (8 October) to march on Leipzig. Because it had become apparent in the meantime that Dresden was defended by insignificant forces, Emperor Alexander I ordered Colloredo's corps to move to Dippoldiswalde and on towards Freiberg, and then, depending on the situation, towards Waldheim or some another direction in order to establish communications with the Army of Bohemia; Bennigsen's army was also ordered to march on Leipzig, leaving some of the force to monitor Dresden and Königstein, under the command of Count Tolstoy, also to facilitate the crossing of the Elbe by the detachments under Prince Shcherbatov and Graf Bubna.[36]

On 29 September (11 October), the formations of the Army of Bohemia carried out the movements in accordance with the disposition issued the day before by the Commander-in-Chief, except for the Russian grenadiers, who only managed to reach Langenleuba, five *versts* north-west of Penig, and the guards who arrived at Penig at dusk.[37] The lateness of Schwarzenberg's orders allowed Murat to remain in the position he had taken up at Gestewitz near Borna until 30 September (12

---

34 War Diary signed by Barclay de Tolly; Prinz Eugen von Württemberg's diary (Archive of the M.T.D. No. 47,344); Bernhardi, III, 401-403.
35 Prinz Schwarzenberg's dispositions for 10 and 11 October, new style; Sporschill, *Die große Chronik*, I, 667, is of the opinion that the flanking march by the Army of Bohemia on the way to Leipzig had the objective of linking up with the Army of Silesia and besieging Leipzig.
36 Adjutant General Volkonsky's dispatches to General Bennigsen dated 26 and 27 September [8 and 9 October], Log of Outgoing Documents, No. 108 and No. 114.
37 War Diary signed by Barclay de Tolly; Alexander Andreevich Shcherbinin's (manuscript) notes.

October).³⁸ On this day, instead of a persistent pursuit, the Coalition directed only the forward detachments under Count Pahlen and Zieten after the enemy, who, having pushed Murat's rearguard, consisting of 14 squadrons, back to Magdeborn, and took up positions at Mucken [two miles south-east of Magdeborn]. Count Wittgenstein's force was stationed at Espenhain and Borna; Kleist's corps were at Borna and Rohrbach [5½ miles south of Naunhof]; Mohr's division were at Lausick; their leading elements being [4½ miles further north] at Otterwisch; Klenau's corps were in Frohburg. Kaisarov's detachment was at Rötha adjoining Count Pahlen's outposts; Platov was pushed back from Lützen to Pegau by Augereau's corps, which had arrived to reinforce the French army. Gyulay's Austrian *III. Korpus* moved to Zeitz and linked up with Moritz Liechtenstein's division and Thielmann's detachment there. General 'Sorbenberg's' cavalry brigade (Austrian *II. Korpus*) was stationed at Lucka [four miles north of Meuselwitz] in order to liaise between the forces at Zeitz and Wittgenstein's corps at Borna. The Austrian corps under Merveldt and Prinz Homburg, and the Russo-Prussian reserves were at Altenburg together with the headquarters of Emperor Alexander and Prinz Schwarzenberg.³⁹

On the following day, 1 (13) October, a reconnaissance-in-force of the enemy position was ordered to be carried out, for which, just as before the Battle of Dresden, quite significant numbers were assigned, namely: the Russian I Corps and II Corps, Pahlen's cavalry, Platov's Cossack detachment, Kleist's Prussian corps and Klenau's Austrians, for a total of 60,000 men under the overall command of Count Wittgenstein. This force, supported by the corps following behind them, could have defeated Murat and captured Leipzig even before Napoleon's arrival, which would have made the concentration of the enemy army problematic. But in the disposition by the Commander-in-Chief, Wittgenstein was constrained to: '… carry out a reconnaissance today in conjunction with *General-der-Cavalerie* Graf Klenau, in order to entice the enemy to commit his forces without engaging in a full-scale attack.'⁴⁰ It was proposed that:

> Klenau's corps are to head from Otterwisch, in two columns, towards Rohrbach and Pomßen [3½ miles south of Naunhof], seize the Universitäts Waldungung [Oberholz, three miles east of Gossa] and attack the enemy left wing from the front and flank. As soon as Graf Klenau opens a cannonade, four battalions from Pahlen's vanguard are to seize the villages on the Göselbach [flowing from Otterwisch to Rötha], while 16 squadrons with a horse artillery battery are to deploy between the Göselbach and the

---

38 Plotho, II, 336; Shcherbinin's notes state that the enemy withdrew towards Leipzig as early as 29 September [11 October]; Vaudoncourt, *Histoire de la guerre soutenue par les Français en Allemagne*, 198, also states that Murat withdrew to Wachau and Liebertwolkwitz on 11 October, new style.
39 [On Map No. 3, Magdeborn and Rötha have been transposed]. Prinz Eugen von Württemberg's (manuscript) diary; Plotho, II, 336-337; Sporschill, I, 667-668.
40 '… *in Vereinigung mit den General der Cavalerie Graf Klenau eine Recognoscirung heute vorzunehmen, um den Feind zur Deployrung seiner Kräfte zu verleiten ohne hierbey sich in einen vollkommen Angrief sich einzulassen.*' Prinz Schwarzenberg's dispositions for 13 October, new style (Log of Incoming Documents, No. 1,608).

Pleiße; the remaining units from the Russian vanguard and the Prinz von Württemberg's II Corps, with two cavalry regiments and a horse artillery battery from Kleist's corps, are to remain at Großpötzschau [three miles north of Espenhain] until they hear the cannonade from Graf Klenau's corps, and are then to cross the river, attack the Störmthaler Wald and strive to take the village of Störmthal [two miles south-east of Gossa]; the Prussian *10. Brigade* and *11. Brigade* are to support this attack. Prince Gorchakov, with I Corps, having crossed at Oelzschau [four miles north-east of Espenhain], must assist Count Pahlen's attack on Störmthal and maintain liaison with Klenau's corps; the other units are to remain in reserve between Espenhain and Mölbis [one mile north-east of Espenhain].[41]

This reconnaissance was postponed until the following day, because Klenau, whose cannonade was supposed to signal the advance of the other troops, was late and only reached Pomßen as darkness was falling.[42] His vanguard, commanded by General Mohr, occupied Großpösna [two miles south-west of Fuchshain]. On the left flank, having encountered enemy forward troops near Markkleeberg [five miles west of Liebertwolkwitz], Count Platov drove them back behind the Pleiße, but having discovered a significant French camp behind this village, he retreated in the direction of Zwenkau. The losses on both sides were insignificant, but among the seriously wounded was the brave partisan, General Prince Kudashev.[43]

Meanwhile, having retreated to the outskirts of Leipzig and concerned at be overwhelmed by the superior numbers of the Army of Bohemia, Murat intended to retreat behind the Parthe,[44] but Napoleon sent Gourgaud to him with news of his impending arrival in Leipzig on 2 (14) October, and Murat, reassured by this promise, decided to give battle forwards of Leipzig.[45]

On the morning of 2 (14) October, Murat's formations were positioned as follows: Prince Poniatowski's *8e Corps* of around 8,000 men were between Connewitz [2½ miles south of Leipzig] and Markkleeberg; Victor's *2e Corps* of some 20,000 men were on the high ground from Markkleeberg to Wachau [two miles west of

---

41 Disposition issued by Count Wittgenstein on 1 (13) October.
42 General Toll, sent to Espenhain by Count Wittgenstein, wrote from there at a quarter to four o'clock in the afternoon on 1 (13) October: 'I very much doubt that we will be able to conduct a reconnaissance today, because we still have heard nothing from Klenau. General Mohr only reached Otterwisch at one o'clock in the afternoon, having sent patrols to Pomßen. While Klenau stopped for lunch in Lausick, because he was on his way from Frohburg today, which Radetzky, of course, did not know about, because according to his disposition, he had been assigned to go to Köhra [2½ miles south-west of Naunhof], which would have been a stage of some five *Meilen*. I shall stay on here; maybe Klenau will arrive to be a spectator of the action.' Log of Incoming Documents, No. 1,602; The War Diary signed by Barclay de Tolly states: 'When the Austrian corps did not arrive at their designated point, this attack was not launched.'
43 War Diary signed by Barclay de Tolly.
44 Berthier's letter to Murat (see Appendix XXIX at the end of this chapter); Murats letter to Marmont, dated nine o'clock in the evening of 13 October, new style; Aster, *Die Schlachten bei Leipzig im October 1813*, I, 243; Marmont, *Mémoires*, V, 174, however, he does not mention this letter, saying that he returned to the right bank of the Parthe from Stötteritz at Napoleon's behest.
45 Aster, I, 244.

Liebertwolkwitz]; Lauriston's *5e Corps* numbering 17,000 men were on the high ground from Wachau to Liebertwolkwitz, put into a defensible state and heavily occupied by troops from Maison's division; Augereau's reserve corps of some 10,000 men were forwards of Leipzig at Straßenhäuser; *4e corps de cavalerie* and *5e corps de cavalerie* of some 7,000 men were behind the left wing at Liebertwolkwitz (the latter were composed mostly of the excellent cavalry that had arrived from Spain along with the infantry that Augereau had assembled on the Main). Overall, there were over 60,000 men in the position forwards of Leipzig, not including the 25,000 men from Marmont's *6e Corps* and various depots, some in Leipzig, some to the north and west of this city.[46]

Feldmarschall Schwarzenberg, having established communications with the Army of Silesia via Weißenfels and Merseburg to Halle, decided to move closer to Blücher. To that end, on 1 and 2 (13 and 14) October, the Army of Bohemia continued to move to their left, towards the enemy lines of communications, at the same time that Count Wittgenstein was instructed to carry out a reconnaissance-in-force fixing the enemy position frontally. The division under Moritz Liechtenstein moved from Zeitz towards Lützen with Thielmann's and Mensdorff's detachments, while Gyulay's Austrian *III. Korpus* went from Zeitz, via Hohenmölsen [ten miles north of Zeitz], towards Muschwitz (midway between Pegau and Weißenfels); the Austrian *II. Korpus* and their reserves advanced towards Groitzsch in the sector between the Elster and Pleiße; the Russian grenadiers and 3rd Cuirassier Division proceeded from Borna in support of Count Wittgenstein; the Russo-Prussian guard and two cuirassier divisions were directed from Altenburg along the road to Zeitz.[47] According to a statement from one of the officers serving under General Toll, the Austrian general staff had decided to avoid a general battle, but Toll, having learned of this, persuaded the Austrians to amend their plans and send their main force to Pegau rather than to Zeitz.[48]

Count Wittgenstein issued the following orders for the attack on Murat's position: Lieutenant General Count Pahlen was to proceed at the head of the left hand column towards Magdeborn with the Sumy Hussars, Grodno Hussars, Lubny Hussars, Chuguev Ulans and Major General Nikitin's 7th Horse Artillery Company [Alexey Petrovich Nikitin], numbering 1,700 men with 12 guns, supported by ten squadrons from the Prussian *Neumärkisches Dragoner*, *Ostpreußisches Kürassiere* and *Schlesisches Ulanen* with *10. Reitende Batterie*; because the 3rd Cuirassier Division, assigned to assist Pahlen, had not yet come up, Kleist reinforced Pahlen with all the remaining regiments from Röder's cavalry reserve, comprising 16 squadrons with one horse artillery battery. The Prussian cavalry total, together with the *freiwillige Jäger* attached to the regiments, reached some 4,000 men: thus there were probably 6,000 men under Pahlen's command.[49] The following Cossack regiments advanced on the flanks of the Russian cavalry: Ilovaisky 12th's towards Cröbern [4½ miles

---

46 Aster, I, 252; Hofmann, *Zur Geschichte de Feldzuges von 1813*, 248, which states that Murat had 70,000 men.
47 Hofmann, 243.
48 Shcherbinin's (manuscript) notes.
49 Count Nikitin's (manuscript) notes; Hofmann, 243; Aster, I, 254; Beitzke, II, 524.

north of Rötha] and Grekov's towards Störmthal. Count Wittgenstein's infantry were to advance behind Pahlen's force: Helffreich in the direction of Cröbern with 14th Division; Prinz Eugen von Württemberg towards Gossa [Güldengossa] with II Corps; Prince Gorchakov towards Störmthal with 5th Division; Kleist's corps towards Magdeborn. *Feldmarschallleutnant* Mohr, at the head of the right hand column, having occupied the Universitäts Waldung was to seize Liebertwolkwitz, while Graf Klenau was to support him with units of the Austrian *IV. Korpus*.[50]

The Coalition were confident that the enemy would defend the defiles on the Göselbach at Göhren [one mile south-west of Gossa] and Cröbern, but Murat, concerned at being enveloped on his left flank via the Universitäts Waldung, fell back and repositioned himself (as already stated) on the high ground either side of Wachau. Count Wittgenstein, believing that this position had been taken in order to protect an onward French retreat, decided to attack the enemy immediately. As soon as Pahlen's Russian cavalry reached the Auenhain manor farm (Vorwerk Auenhain), a message was received from Ilovaisky regarding the location of enemy infantry at Markkleeberg in great strength; Count Pahlen stopped short of Auenhain, sent Major General Rüdiger up to support Ilovaisky with the Grodno Hussars and directed the Lubny Hussars to reconnoitre the enemy to the right towards Liebertwolkwitz. It emerged that there was a significant line of cavalry there, adjoining their left flank to the aforementioned village. Thus, convinced of the superior enemy strength and their intention to hold the positions they occupied, Pahlen considered it necessary to await the arrival of the Prussian cavalry. At this very moment Diebitsch, the quartermaster general of Barclay's force, rode up to him. It was the opinion of the passionate Diebitsch that the French should be attacked immediately; but Pahlen waited for the leading Prussian regiment, namely the *Neumärkisches Dragoner*, to reach them, and as soon as they crossed the dyke near the village of Gossa, he moved forwards with the Sumy Hussars and Nikitin's battery to the right of an alder grove near the village of Wachau. Because General Rüdiger had informed them at this time that enemy strength was increasing between Markkleeberg and Wachau, nine Landwehr squadrons were sent to assist him, which were covertly positioned near Auenhain and helped the Grodno Hussars in repelling the Polish cavalry until 3rd Cuirassier Division arrived on the battlefield. On the right wing, General Nikitin dashed a considerable distance forwards with his battery and opened fire on the enemy cavalry stationed at Liebertwolkwitz. Murat, noting the distance of the Russian battery from their escort, attacked them with the hand-picked regiments that had arrived from Spain. The battery, engaging them at very close range with canister, were in great danger but were rescued by the Sumy Hussars. When Murat's cavalry drove them back, the *Neumärkisches Dragoner* went on the counterattack, followed by the *Ostpreußisches Kürassiere* and *Schlesisches Ulanen*, who, striking the enemy in both flanks, put them to flight; soon thereafter, the Chuguev Ulans and Grekov's Cossacks also arrived on the scene. The *Schlesisches Kürassiere* and *Brandenburgisches Kürassiere* deployed to the left of the *Ostpreußisches Kürassiere*. The *Neumärkisches Dragoner* and Sumy Hussars reformed behind them while the

---

50 Hofmann, 244; Aster, I, 255.

cuirassiers went on the attack: the cavalry action continued intermittently in this manner for several hours. The charges were executed, for the most part, by single regiments; and sometimes two at a time. Murat, having assembled a significant mass of cavalry under his command, including the excellent dragoon regiments recently arrived from Spain, boldly led them into battle, exposed to obvious danger. During one of the pauses, as the regiments on both sides, equally disordered by the fierce fighting, were reforming, gathering their strength for renewed combat, *Leutnant* Guido von der Lippe of the *Neumärkisches Dragoner*, having spotted Murat showing off in his theatrical costume with his large retinue in front of the French cavalry, decided to capture or kill him. Hastily gathering several flankers who were wheeling between the front lines of both sides, the brave warrior rushed at full speed with them towards the royal retinue and scattered them; only one horseman remained with Murat. Guido loudly yelled '*Halt, halt! König!*' several times while pursuing the astonished foe. He was just about to catch up with his prey, when at that very moment Murat's only companion inflicted a mortal blow on him and saved the King from death or captivity. During the battle of Liebertwolkwitz, the most significant cavalry battle of the entire war of 1813, Murat did not demonstrate his ability to command and control large masses of cavalry: charges followed one after another, without any overall objective. The desire to test his strength against the enemy was the only evident motive of this famous cavalryman. The superiority of French numbers gave them the opportunity to maintain equilibrium in the battle for several hours, but by the end of the action the advantage had passed to the Coalition side: the reasons for this, in addition to the greater control of their commanders, were:

1. Maintenance of the horses in better condition in the Coalition cavalry, as became apparent during the final attacks.
2. Arming a significant proportion of the Coalition horsemen with lances (Cossacks and the front ranks of lancers and hussars).

According to General Nikitin:

> in this action the enemy suffered many killed and wounded, such that the entire field was covered with the bodies of their men and horses, both from the successful action of our battery and from attacks by lance-armed cavalry. This weapon is the only (best) one for cavalry, especially at this time when it was of a greater length than now.

Count Pahlen, wanting to prolong the action until Klenau's arrival, refused the left wing of his force and supported it through the action of two Prussian horse artillery batteries; the right wing, in contrast, was moved forward. On the French side, significant forces were deployed on their right wing, while large batteries were located on the high ground between Wachau and Liebertwolkwitz operating against the left flank of the Coalition cavalry. Murat, believing them already to be completely weakened from previous attacks, sent the dragoon regiments of *5e corps de cavalerie* against them towards the end of the action. These elite horsemen, suddenly appeared from the clouds of smoke in front of the Coalition cavalry in a deep column; but Nikitin's

7th Horse Artillery Company and the Prussian *7. Reitende Batterie*, stationed on the left flank of Pahlen's cavalry, engaged the enemy with canister and completely disordered the head of the French column. Exploiting this advantage, the Russian hussars, Prussian lancers and the *Brandenburgisches Kürassiere* that joined them raced to engage the enemy. At this time (two o'clock in the afternoon), Graf Klenau, having arrived at Liebertwolkwitz from Threna [two miles south of Fuchshain] with the main body of his corps, opened a strong cannonade on the French infantry occupying Liebertwolkwitz and directed the *Kürassier-Regiment Kaiser* and part of the *Chevauxlegers-Regiment O'Reilly* towards the flank of Murat's cavalry; while the cavalry brigade, screened by two squadrons from *Husaren-Regiment Erzherzog Ferdinand* and *Chevauxlegers-Regiment Hohenzollern*, were positioned so that the guns, in conjunction with the other Coalition artillery, could catch the enemy in a crossfire. Murat's cavalry, disordered by the fire from the batteries and driven back by the coordinated attacks of Pahlen's and Klenau's cavalry, were pursued almost as far as Probstheida [three miles north-west of Liebertwolkwitz] and no longer returned to the battlefield, but the enemy artillery intensified their fire and caused great harm to the Coalition cavalry. On the left wing of Count Pahlen's force, the Grodno Hussars, with the assistance of the *Schlesisches Landwehr Kavallerie* and Ilovaisky's Cossacks, prevented the Polish cavalry from achieving the slightest success; with the arrival of 3rd Cuirassier Division, the enemy, having halted their cavalry attacks, pushed forward significant masses of infantry, which, having come under crossfire from the Prussian batteries, retreated to the high ground occupied by them at the beginning of the action. The Prinz von Württemberg, having witnessed the advance of the enemy infantry, asked Count Pahlen for permission to go into action, but Pahlen refused, believing it was pointless to expand the scope of a battle that had no crucial objective. Following the retreat of the enemy infantry, operations were restricted to a cannonade. Count Wittgenstein intended to attack the enemy with his full strength, but at six o'clock in the afternoon he received orders from Prinz Schwarzenberg to wind the action down. The Russian light cavalry, upon falling back, positioned themselves to the right of Gossa; the Prussian cuirassiers were stationed to their left near this village; the *Landwehr Kavallerie* were forwards of Cröbern; General Helffreich was in reserve behind Cröbern with 14th Division and the Prussian *10. Brigade* and *11. Brigade*; the Prinz von Württemberg was behind Gossa with his corps; Prince Gorchakov was at Störmthal with 5th Division, Kleist was at Magdeborn with the Prussian 9. Brigade and 12. Brigade, the Grenadier Corps was at Espenhain; Count Wittgenstein's headquarters was in Mölbis. Graf Klenau, who had been holding Liebertwolkwitz, was pushed back to Pomßen.

In the action at Liebertwolkwitz, the losses on both sides were significant: the casualties in the French army reached 600 men killed or wounded; generals Pajol and Montmarie were among the seriously wounded. The Austrian *IV. Korpus* lost some 1,000 men overall; casualties among the other Coalition forces are not known, but they were heavy, judging by the fact that in the *Schlesisches Kürassiere* 13 officers and 69 lower ranks were killed or wounded.[51]

---

51 Count Nikitin's (manuscript) notes; Plotho, II, 353-354; Hofmann, 243-247; Aster, I, 255-267; Bernhardi, III, 410-412; Beitzke, II, 524-528.

Thus, the reconnaissance-in-force undertaken by the Coalition, beyond their expectations, turned into a bloody battle. Up to this point, the Commander-in-Chief had still not abandoned his intention to close up to the Army of Silesia by way of a flank march to the left, who, for their part, were supposed to cross the Merseburg road and advance towards Lindenau [two miles west of Leipzig] in conjunction with Gyulay's corps; but Blücher rejected this proposal, preferring to head for Leipzig by the shortest route via Schkeuditz. Major Rühle, sent to Schwarzenberg's headquarters in order to deliver a verbal briefing on this subject, suggested that the Crown Prince, being in coordination with Blücher, could operate more decisively than would be the case if he were to be separated from the Army of Silesia.[52] The cavalry success at Wachau finally prompted the Coalition monarchs to demand that the troops entrusted to Prince Schwarzenberg be sent directly towards Leipzig, whence the other Coalition armies were also advancing at this same time. Nevertheless, the existing orders from the Austrian headquarters had an unfavorable impact on operations on the first day of the Battle of Leipzig: a significant number of troops, assembled to no purpose in the narrow swampy sector between the Elster and the Pleiße, weakened that part of the army located on the right bank of the Pleiße and (as will be described later) almost led to a Coalition defeat.[53]

The following day, 3 (15) October, Count Wittgenstein's force remained in almost the same locations they occupied at the end of the Liebertwolkwitz action. The other formations of the Army of Bohemia were positioned as follows: the Austrian *III. Korpus* was at Lützen together with Thielmann's detachment and Moritz Liechtenstein's *1. leichte Division*; Mensdorff's detachment was at Markranstädt; the Austrian *II. Korpus* was at Zwenkau; Barclay de Tolly's headquarters was at Audigast, with the Austrian reserves and Russo-Prussian guard nearby; Platov's Cossack detachment, having driven the enemy out of Gautzsch [six miles north of Zwenkau], moved to Seifertshain [one mile north-west of Fuchshain] on the night of 3 to 4 (15 to 16) October in support of Klenau's corps. Emperor Alexander's headquarters as well as that of Prinz Schwarzenberg relocated to Pegau, while the *Hauptquartier* of the King of Prussia and the Austrian Kaiser's *Hoflager* were in Altenburg.[54]

During 3 (15) October, while the elements of the Army of Bohemia were converging on Leipzig, Prince Schwarzenberg personally reconnoitred the course of the river Pleiße in the vicinity of Gautzsch, from where he intended to send most of the force entrusted to him around the enemy right flank and into their rear. But this reconnaissance apparently was not used by the Commander-in-Chief to properly survey the terrain, which was most inappropriate for the deployment of significant forces. At around noon, the outposts reported an advance by enemy cavalry proceeding from our left flank towards Liebertwolkwitz. The Coalition generals who rode up to the forward screen believed that the enemy intended to attack the units facing them but it soon turned out that the French were on parade awaiting inspection. From the high ground near the village of Gossa, using a telescope one could see a

---

52 Bernhardi, III, 414.
53 Beitzke, II, 529.
54 Plotho, II, 359; Aster, I, 317-319.

horseman and behind him many others quickly dashing along the ranks of troops. It was Napoleon, who had arrived in Leipzig the day before.[55]

The Army of Silesia was also moving towards Leipzig.

It has already been mentioned that on 2 (14) October, the Crown Prince of Sweden received word of the retreat by French forces towards Leipzig from the Elbe and Düben, from Blücher. At the same time, the Prussian commander informed the Crown Prince of Prinz Schwarzenberg's intention to attack the enemy in conjunction with the other Coalition armies, and invited him to head for Leipzig immediately. The Crown Prince, now utterly convinced that Napoleon had abandoned his attempts on Berlin, remained on the left bank of the Elbe but, on 2 (14) October, instead of moving from Köthen towards Landsberg along the shortest route to Leipzig and arriving in the vicinity of this city on 3 (15) October, he headed along the road to Halle that day, halted the advance of his army after Petersberg having traveled only 18 versts, and settled down for the night in the village of Sylbitz. He also remained there on the morning of 4 (16) October, throughout the duration of the fighting, despite the continuous cannonade audible from Leipzig, deaf to the representations of the Coalition commissioners, generals Stewart, Pozzo di Borgo [Karl Osipovich Potstso di Borgo or Charles André Pozzo di Borgo] and Saint Vincent [(Nikolaus) Karl von Vincent], who were at his headquarters,[56] and only managed to reach Landsberg, still about 20 *versts* from the battlefield, in the evening, having covered three *Meilen* (20 *versts*).[57]

In contrast, Blücher sent word to the headquarters of the Army of Bohemia on the movement of Napoleon's army towards Leipzig, repeating his previous promise to take part in a general battle. On the morning of 3 (15) October, he received a dispatch from the headquarters of the Army of Bohemia regarding Prinz Schwarzenberg's intention to attack Napoleon on 4 (16) October with his full strength south of Leipzig, near Wachau, and regarding the simultaneous advance by Gyulay's corps towards Lindenau, along the Erfurt road. Having informed Blücher of all this, Schwarzenberg expressed the hope that the simultaneous advances by the Army of Silesia and Army of the North towards Leipzig would prevent the enemy from concentrating their dispersed forces. On that same day [15 October, new style], Blücher advanced from Halle to Schkeuditz, sending Saint-Priest's corps from Merseburg towards Lindenau and ordering him to spread rumours that the entire Army of Silesia was following him along the same route. Informing the Crown Prince of Sweden of his advance, Blücher wrote to him that he anticipated his arrival in Delitzsch on 3 (15) October, and hoped for his participation in the impending battle. Nevertheless, the experienced commander took precautions to be able to attack the enemy without the assistance of the Army of the North, just in case.[58]

---

55 Aster, 308-309 & 312-313.
56 Weiß (Müffling), *Die Feldzüge der schlesischen Armee*, 77; Hofmann, *Zur Geschichte des Feldzuges von 1813*, 249-250; Beitzke, II, 508-512.
57 Plotho, II, 394; for the text of a letter from the Crown Prince justifying his slow advance, see Appendix XXXI at the end of this chapter.
58 Varnhagen von Ense, *Leben des Fürsten Blücher von Wahlstadt*, 222-223.

The army under General Bennigsen and Graf Colloredo's Austrian *I. Korpus* were on the march from Dresden to Leipzig, but would not reach the battle on 4 (16) October.

Upon the completion of the flanking march by the Army of Bohemia towards Komotau, General Bennigsen had been entrusted with guarding the passes through the Ore Mountains with the units of the so-called Army of Poland and the Austrian *I. Korpus*, in the sector from the Elbe to Johnsdorf. All these passes were occupied by Russian troops, except for the post at Nollendorf, where a vanguard, comprising a multi-national force, was stationed commanded by *Feldmarschallleutnant* Graf Hardegg. Bennigsen's force remained in place until 26 September (8 October). The day before, intelligence had been received regarding Napoleon's departure from Dresden with the main body of the French army. As it could be assumed from this that the force left to protect Dresden had been weakened, General Bennigsen decided to carry out a reconnaissance-in-force. To that end, Paskevich's 26th Division [Ivan Fëdorovich Paskevich] was sent to Hellendorf with four additional squadrons, Hardegg's detachment was directed on Breitenau, supported by three battalions of Poltava Infantry, Ladoga Infantry and the Cossack detachment under Prince Bagration, while Kreutz's detachment [Kiprian Antonovich Kreutz] was to head towards Liebstadt. Thick fog made visibility extremely difficult, but despite this, the Coalition were convinced that the enemy had abandoned the positions they had previously occupied, at the exits from the mountains. Taking advantage of this, General Bennigsen ordered all his remaining units to advance: General Markov's and Count Tolstoy's corps from Peterswald towards Berggießhübel, while Dokhturov's and Klenau's corps were to advance from Schönwald and Breitenau towards Göppersdorf. In the evening, General Paskevich reached the enemy fortifications at Berggießhübel with three battalions from 5th Jägers and 42nd Jägers, four squadrons from the Taganrog Ulans and Siberia Ulans and several guns, captured them without much opposition, in the presence of King Friedrich Wilhelm who was accompanying Bennigsen's force at the time. Hardegg and Kreutz reached Breitenau and Liebstadt. The remaining units of the Army of Poland reached Hellendorf and Peterswald except for the *opolchenie* under Count Tolstoy who remained at Aussig; Colloredo's corps reached Altenburg. The King of Prussia returned to Teplitz at the end of the action.[59]

Since 14 (26) September, the forces protecting Dresden under Marshal Saint-Cyr had been located as follows: *43e Division* (*14e Corps*) were at Pirna; *42e Division* (*14e Corps*) were at Königstein, along both banks of the Elbe; *1er Corps* were in the Berggießhübel area; *44e Division* and *45e Division*, commanded by General Bonet [Jean Pierre François Bonet], were at Borna and Dippoldiswalde. The advance by Bennigsen's force obliged General Mouton to withdraw across the river Müglitz with *1er Corps*. The units from *14e Corps* stationed at Borna, Pyrna and Königstein followed the movements by *1er Corps*, destroying the bridge of boats that served as their link to Lilienstein.[60] Bennigsen pursued them relentlessly: General Markov,

---

59 War Diary of the Army of Poland, signed by the Chief-of-Staff, Lieutenant General Opperman (Log of Incoming Documents, No. 1,822); Plotho, II, 245-247.
60 Saint-Cyr, 176-177 & 179.

having supplemented his vanguard with Paskevich's 26th Division at Zehista, moved towards Dohna, while Hardegg advanced from Borna, enveloping the right flank of the enemy position held by forces under Saint-Cyr, numbering 20,000 men. The French, coming under attack at Dohna on 27 September (9 October), frontally by Paskevich's 26th Division and from the left flank by Bulatov's 16th Division [Mikhail Leontievich Bulatov], defended stubbornly, but upon being threatened with envelopment on both flanks, they retreated towards Dresden at dusk. Enemy losses in the action at Dohna reached some 250 men taken prisoner alone.[61]

On 28 September (10 October), the French force, having retreated towards Dresden, deployed between Gruna and Räcknitz, and the following day [11 October], upon being attacked on the high ground at Räcknitz, retreated behind the Dresden fortifications, leaving small detachments in the nearby villages. At the same time, in accordance with Napoleon's repeated orders, the departure of trains, parks and 3,000 sick and wounded began by boat from Dresden to Torgau. But by this time the right bank of the Elbe had already been occupied by units sent up by Prince Shcherbatov and Graf Bubna, and therefore only a few of the ferryboats managed to reach their destination.[62]

At the same time as the arrival of Bennigsen's army at Dresden, Graf Colloredo received orders from the headquarters of the Coalition sovereigns to move up swiftly to join the main army via Dippoldiswalde and Freiberg; while Graf Bubna's Austrian 2. *leichte Division*, located on the right bank of the Elbe, was assigned to support the Army of Poland, which crossed the river on rafts at Pratzschwitz [2½ miles downstream of Pirna], opposite Heidenau on 1 (13) October; a detachment was left on the right bank near Dresden consisting of three Austrian battalions and three Russian squadrons.[63] Lieutenant General Prince Shcherbatov, also stationed on the right bank of the Elbe opposite Dresden, having received orders from Blücher on 27 September (9 October) to move to the left bank of the river, moved to the village of Elster, but upon arriving there, found the bridge there had been destroyed, as had the bridge at Roßlau. Because significant enemy forces had appeared there by this same time, and the Prussian corps under Tauentzien, having lifted their siege of Wittenberg, had retreated to Berlin, then in order to move closer to them, Prince Shcherbatov moved to Jüterbog, from where, after the battle of Leipzig, he proceeded behind the Coalition armies towards the Rhine.[64]

On 1 (13) October, the *opolchenie* arrived at Dresden from Aussig, under the command of Lieutenant General Count Tolstoy. In the meantime, having received orders from the Tsar to leave a suitable number of troops to monitor the enemy at Dresden and Königstein, and to march towards Leipzig with the remaining formations, Bennigsen ordered General Paskevich to attack the French on 30 September (12 October), in order to conceal this movement. The enemy abandoned their

---

61 War Diary of the Army of Poland; Plotho, II, 253, gives the enemy losses as 300 taken prisoner and one banner. On the Russian side, 26th Division alone suffered some 800 killed or wounded.
62 Saint-Cyr, 198-201.
63 War Diary of the Army of Poland.
64 War Diary of VI Corps.

occupation of the villages of Gostritz, Kaitz and Plauen in front of the fortifications almost without resistance; but the next day [13 October], Saint-Cyr, having only enough provisions left for a week upon Napoleon's departure, and forage for three days, concerned most of all at being bottled up in the city, attacked the Russians with all his strength. At seven o'clock in the morning, the French launched an attack, directing their main effort towards the village of Plauen and captured it, driving the 5th Jägers and 42nd Jägers from the place; but the 41st Jägers, Orël Infantry and Nizhegorod Infantry held back further enemy attacks, having been sent forwards by order of the Commander-in-Chief, with four light guns located on the high ground at the exits from the village. Bennigsen, wanting to force the French to reveal all the units occupying Dresden, deployed the troops under Dokhturov and Markov on the high ground at Räcknitz and deployed strong batteries. The fighting descended into a cannonade and firefight, which continued until nightfall. The French *voltigeurs*, skilfully using terrain cover, inflicted significant losses on the Russian jägers, who lost some 600 men killed or wounded, while on the enemy side, by their own admission, 28 officers and 500 lower ranks were *hors de combat* from *42e Division* and *45e Division* that actually took part in the fighting.[65] King Friedrich Wilhelm and the Crown Prince of Prussia, who had arrived from Teplitz the day before, remained on the battlefield at Plauen throughout the entire morning under heavy cannonade.[66]

At two o'clock in the afternoon the vanguard of Bennigsen's force,[67] commanded by Lieutenant General Count Stroganov [Pavel Alexandrovich Stroganov], set out for Wilsdruff, and the remaining formations of the army followed him after dark, except for the Combined Corps under Lieutenant General Count Tolstoy, left at Dresden.[68] Bennigsen's main body marched to Nossen, linking up there with Graf Bubna's *2. leichte Division* and reached the outskirts of Waldheim (60 *versts* from Leipzig) late at night between 3 to 4 (15 to 16) October.[69] Colloredo's corps was located at Penig, at almost the same distance from Leipzig, therefore, neither Bennigsen nor Colloredo could reach the battlefield before 5 (17) October. In addition, the Army of Poland was utterly exhausted from forced marches. The chief of staff of this army,

---

65 War Diary of the Army of Poland; General Bennigsen's letter to the Tsar, dated 1 (13) October, gives Russian losses as some 500 men; Plotho, II, 345-346; Saint-Cyr, *Campagne de 1813 en Saxe*, 204, 'They (the Russians) lost a lot of men here, because we fought stubbornly and with valour on both sides, but with more skill on our part…' '*Ils (les Russes) y perdirent beaucoup de monde, parceque l'on y combattit des deux côtés avec vaillance et opiniatreté, mais avec plus d'adresse du nôtre…*'
66 Plotho, II, 346; General Bennigsen's letter to the Tsar, dated 1 (13) October, from Wilsdruff (Log of Incoming Documents, No. 1,628).
67 Lieutenant General Stroganov's vanguard consisted of four battalions of jägers, one hussar regiment and two more of Cossacks, with six guns.
68 Count Tolstoy's corps consisted of: the *opolchenie* (see Appendix XXVI at the end of Chapter 33), reinforced with 16th Division, two ulan regiments, one Don Cossack regiment and another of Bashkirs, with two batteries, commanded by General Markov (General Bennigsen's letter to the Tsar, dated 1 (13) October, from Wilsdruff). This force numbered some 24,000 men with 64 guns.
69 General Bennigsen's letter to Adjutant General Volkonsky, dated 3 (15) October, from Waldheim (Log of Incoming Documents, No. 1,635).

Lieutenant General Opperman [Karl Ivanovich Opperman], outlined the condition of the troops in a letter to Prince Volkonsky, as follows:

> From Liegnitz itself we have constantly been following in the footsteps of other armies, our own and the enemy's. Throughout these movements, we have been unable to find sufficient essential supplies anywhere, which is why the men are suffering in need, and the horses even more so. The soldiers, in crossing the steep mountains, have worn out their footwear, while the disastrous slowness of the administration in the Duchy of Warsaw has led to the fact that the boots completed on the banks of the Vistula in August have not yet reached the army. From this one can see that we are not in a brilliant condition, and that if we must always follow other armies, then complete destruction awaits us. In addition to all this, I consider it my duty to note that the mission entrusted to our force to monitor Dresden, Sonnenstein [one mile south-east of Pirna] and Meißen has greatly weakened the army, which now comprises only 12th Division, 13th Division, 26th Division and one cavalry division, formed mostly from recruits.[70]

Napoleon's forces were moving just as quickly towards Leipzig.

Napoleon, having left Düben himself at seven o'clock in the morning on 2 (14) October, arrived in Leipzig at around noon. Uproar and confusion reigned in the city, arriving units passed, orderlies and couriers galloped, the wounded were escorted or carried from the direction of Wachau, from where a strong cannonade could be heard from time to time; gunfire was audible to the north being exchanged between the leading units under Blücher and Marmont. The weather was cloudy, cold, with strong gusts of wind. Napoleon, upon reaching the Hallisches Tor at the same time as elements of the *Vieille Garde* and the *cavalerie de la Garde*, rode around the city and along the avenues to the Grimmaisches Tor and stopped outside the city limits, north of the road to Wurzen. A huge bonfire was lit here, around which he, together with Berthier and Caulaincourt, walked for a long time at a fast pace, first in one direction then in the other, glancing from time to time at a map laid out on his camp table. Aides-de-camp and other officers were constantly riding up to him with news from Murat about the progress of the battle. Some of them, having been lightly wounded, appeared spattered with blood, having had no time to dress their wounds. Napoleon issued orders to them himself, or instructed his *chef d'état-major* to issue the necessary orders. As they were laying out the groundsheet preparatory to serving his lunch, several carriages appeared protected by troops. It was the King of Saxony, with his wife and daughter, having arrived from Eilenburg under the protection of his ally. He was escorted by Polish lancers, Saxon dragoons and *Leib-grenadiere*. Behind them came the *2e Division* of Napoleon's *Vieille Garde* and several regiments from the *cavalerie de la Garde*. Napoleon, after talking for a few minutes with the King and Queen, returned to his camp fire, while the King rode off to the city on horseback. As the formations approached Leipzig, they were

---

70 General Opperman's letter dated 2 [14] October, from Nossen (Log of Incoming Documents, No. 1,637).

sent to various points in the city area. The *2e Division* of the *Vieille Garde*, having reached the village of Taucha, received orders to go to Holzhausen and halted there for the night. *6e Corps* deployed at Breitenfeld [2½ miles north of Möckern], the *Jeune Garde* moved to their left towards Eutritzsch [1½ miles south of Wiederitzsch]. At about four o'clock in the afternoon, an aide-de-camp rode up with news of the arrival of *1er Division* of the *Vieille Garde* at the Grimmaisches Tor across the city. Napoleon ordered to beat the muster and, joining *1er Division* with the units he brought with him, positioned them on both sides of the road to Wurzen, while he went to Reudnitz [1½ miles south-east of Leipzig] himself and moved his *quartier général* to the estate of the banker, Vetter. Meanwhile, the number of wounded and refugees leaving the battlefield was constantly increasing; crowds of them together with the units within the city completely blocked the streets, such that it was impossible to make way through them except by exposing oneself to danger.

4e Corps reached Hohenossig [4½ miles north-east of Wiederitzsch] at seven o'clock in the evening; from there they received orders to go to Eutritzsch, which was only achieved after dark. *1er corps de cavalerie* and *2e corps de cavalerie* positioned themselves between Göbschelwitz and Podelwitz [three miles north-east of Wiederitzsch] facing Blücher, having sent light cavalry to observe towards Delitzsch. *11e Corps* arrived at their night-halt at Wölkau, 2½ *Meilen* (18 *versts*) north-east of Leipzig; *3e Corps* crossed the Mulde bridge at Düben in the evening, while *7e Corps*, passing through Wittenberg, reached Kemberg during the night of 2 to 3 (14 to 15) October. At dusk, the *Jeune Garde* and *1er corps de cavalerie* moved through the city towards Strassenhäusern and Stötteritz [three miles north-west of Holzhausen].[71]

On the morning of 3 (15) October, Murat visited Napoleon to deliver a verbal report on the action at Liebertwolkwitz. Napoleon had intended to attack the main Coalition army on that same day, but cancelled his plans because not all of his corps had managed to reach Leipzig during the morning. Of the elements of *3e Corps*, which had received orders to assemble at Mokau on the Parthe [three miles north of Leipzig] on 3 (15) October, only two divisions had arrived, while the third, under General Delmas [Antoine Guillaume Muralhac Delmas], had been left behind to destroy the Roßlau bridge and stretched along the road to Düben escorting the parks and convoys of the entire corps, for a distance of a whole stage from Leipzig. Fournier's cavalry division remained at the Düben bridge together with a battalion until *7e Corps* arrived there. Although *11e Corps* had set off from Wölkau at two o'clock in the morning, they did not reach Panitzsch, 2½ miles south-east of Taucha, until four o'clock in the afternoon.[72] In general, the French troops had been extremely fatigued by the forced marches and night moves along bad roads in the cold and rainy season. The soldiers, not having been issued rations or receiving them in insufficient quantities, were forced to fend for themselves. For the hungry men, soaked to the skin and freezing, no compassion was forthcoming from the population of this country, even though they were regarded as the most faithful of France's allies. The soldiers plundered anything edible, stole livestock, pulled down entire villages for firewood, burned doors, window frames, stairs, agricultural tools,

---

71 Aster, I, 281-287; Hofmann, 251.
72 Aster, I, 293-294.

books, paintings, musical instruments: there was no mercy for anyone or anything. The avenues and orchards that beautified the outskirts of the city were cut down. The French lit fires near buildings and fences in order to get some shelter from the blustery wind, which often burned out of control. The town of Liebertwolkwitz, in which fires broke out during the action on 2 (14) October, fell victim to the flames. The Saxon warriors, upset by the rampages of their fellow French soldiers, did not hide their displeasure and were constantly brawling with them; sometimes these brawls ended in murder. It was easy to foresee the outcome of the mood of the Saxon troops, devoted to their King and fatherland, but embittered against the brilliant warrior, who, having subjected their country to every kind of catastrophe, could no longer dazzle his victims with the splendours of victory.[73]

Napoleon decided to attack the Army of Bohemia the next day, 4 (16) October, hoping that the other Coalition forces would be unable to take part in the battle. In any case, he could have better protected himself from an attack by Blücher had he transferred the entire army to the left bank of the Parthe, holding the line with one of his corps: by operating in this way, he could have opposed the Army of Bohemia with the overwhelming majority of his strength. Moreover, Leipzig should have been put in a defensible state, fortifying this city, both on the southern, northern and western sides, and building several bridges over the Pleiße and Elster in order to secure the line of retreat towards Naumburg.[74]

In the Coalition headquarters it was also decided to attack the enemy army on 4 (16) October, despite the fact that the Army of the North and Army of Poland, numbering about 100,000 men, could not arrive before 5 (17) October. The factors that prompted the Coalition commanders to attack Napoleon urgently were the desire to prevent a concentration of his forces and the concern that he, taking advantage of his central position, might defeat the Army of Silesia in isolation.

Throughout 3 (15) October, those forces from both sides that had managed to assemble in the vicinity of Leipzig rested while awaiting reinforcements. As has been mentioned, Napoleon reviewed his troops. At two o'clock in the afternoon, they formed up in a long line from Markkleeberg to Liebertwolkwitz. Napoleon had visited Poniatowski in Dölitz [four miles west of Liebertwolkwitz] initially, enquired about the nature of the Pleiße in detail and ordered the destruction of some bridges on branches of this river, which, however, was not carried out. Then he galloped to Liebertwolkwitz along the entire front, greeted by loud exclamations of *Vive l'empereur*! Only the Saxon *Leib-Grenadiere* remained silent. Three regiments from Augereau's reserve corps received their Eagles with the usual ceremonial. Napoleon returned to Reudnitz at the conclusion of the review at dusk.[75]

In preparation for the decisive battle, Prinz Schwarzenberg issued the following order to the army entrusted to him:

> The most important hour of this sacred struggle has come, valiant warriors! Prepare yourselves for battle. This coalition concluded for the common good

---

73 Aster, I, 288-289.
74 Hofmann, 252.
75 Aster, I, 299-300; Karl Gustav von Berneck, *Die Schlachten bei Leipzig*, 101.

by these powerful nations shall be cemented on the battlefield. Russians, Prussians, Austrians! You are striving for one thing: for your independence, for the immortality of your repute. All for one, and one for all; go into battle with this noble motto; victory shall accompany you.[76]

At eight o'clock in the evening, three white rockets were launched from Pegau; a few minutes later, four red ones soared skywards from the direction of Halle: these were the mutually agreed signals for the main army and the Army of Silesia to show their readiness for the imminent battle.[77]

---

76 Plotho, II, 366.
77 Beitzke, II, 540.

Appendix XXIX

Berthier's letter to Murat, dated 12 October, new style

Chef d'état-major Berthier's letter to Murat, dated 12 October, new style (Saint-Cyr, 450-451)

The Emperor has instructed me with the honour of informing Your Majesty that we have seized the enemy bridges; that it appears that the Prince of Sweden has returned to the right bank of the Elbe with the army of Berlin. With this state of affairs, the Emperor is ready to move on Leipzig with his army, which, combined with yours, will make up more than 200,000 combatants. The Marshal duc de Raguse [Marmont] will spend the night between Düben and Leipzig; he should therefore be in this city early tomorrow. The Emperor will be within reach of Leipzig at some point tomorrow with his entire *Garde*, and the day after tomorrow, 14 October, the entire army will be there, but, Sire, all these arrangements now depend on what you are able to do. If it is possible for you to hold your position throughout the day on 13 October, as well as the city of Leipzig, the Emperor will immediately order the movements which I have just mentioned to you. If, on the contrary, Your Majesty were forced to evacuate your position and the city of Leipzig tomorrow, 13 October, the Emperor will no longer be able to execute his manoeuvre, and from this moment you should move, as you proposed, towards the Mulde, taking Wurzen as your point of direction. The question therefore consists of knowing, yes or no, whether you are able to hold your position and Leipzig with your own forces until the morning of 14 October…

L'empereur me charge d'avoir l'honneur de prévenir Votre Majesté que nous nous sommes emparés des ponts de l'ennemi; qu'il parait que le prince de Suède, avec l'armée de Berlin, a repassé sur la rive droite de l'Elbe. Dans cette situation des choses, l'empereur est prêt à se porter sur Leipzig avec son armée, ce qui, réunie à la vôtre, fera plus de 200,000 combattants. Le maréchal duc de Raguse couché ce soir entre Duben et Leipzig; il pourra donc être demain de bonne heure sur cette ville. Dans la journée de demain, l'empereur, avec toute sa garde, sera à portée de Leipzig, et après-demain 14, toute l'armée y sera rendue, mais, Sire, toutes ces dispositions dépendent désormais de ce que Vous pouvez faire. S'il vous est possible de conserver votre position toute la journée du 13, ainsi que la ville de Leipzig, l'empereur ordonnera sur-le-champ le mouvement dont je viens de Vous parler. Si au contraire V.M. était forcée d'évacuer demain 13 sa position et la ville de Leipzig, l'empereur ne sera plus à temps d'exécuter son mouvement, et dès ce moment vous vous porteriez, comme vous le proposiez sur la Mulde, prenant pour point de direction Wurtzen. La question consiste donc à savoir, oui ou non, si Vous pouvez, avec vos propres troupes, conserver votre position et Leipzig jusau'au 14 au matin...

Appendix XXX

Comparison of estimates of Murat's troop strength before Leipzig

The strength of Murat's force, is given by Beitzke (II, 390) as 37,000, including General Sébastiani's cavalry (which was at Wittenberg at the time). This figure, in all likelihood, was derived from Vaudoncourt, who, in every case, tries to show the strength of the French to be less than their actual number. Including the Leipzig depots, Murat's army consisted of:

Plotho, *Der Krieg in Deutschland und Frankreich in den Jahren 1813 und 1814*, II, 369		Schütz/Schulz, *Geschichte der Kriege in Europa seit dem Jahre 1792*, XI, 1 Band, 182-185	
Victor's *2e Corps*	15,000	Victor's *2e Corps*	16,000
Lauriston's *5e Corps*	10,000	Lauriston's *5e Corps*	13,400
Poniatowski's *8e Corps*	10,000	Poniatowski's *8e Corps*	5,400
4e corps de cavalerie	4,000	*4e corps de cavalerie*	2,150
5e corps de cavalerie	4,000	*5e corps de cavalerie*	4,600
Total:	**43,000**	**Total:**	**42,350**

Appendix XXXI

Bernadotte's letter to Emperor Alexander, dated 15 October 1813, new style

The Crown Prince of Sweden explained the reasons that delayed his arrival at Leipzig in a letter to Emperor Alexander I, as follows:

> As all the secret agents and intelligence received from my outposts appeared to confirm the march of an enemy army towards the Elbe in considerable strength, with the intention of crossing this river, I initially halted the advance that I had made jointly with General Blücher behind the Saale. Soon thereafter, Graf Tauentzien informed me that he had been forced to evacuate Dessau, to retreat to the right bank of the Elbe and to dismantle the Roßlau bridge. A strong French column had emerged from Wittenberg and forced General Thümen to retreat. The *Jeune Garde* and several army corps were located between the Elbe and the Mulde. The town of Aken was attacked from this direction, but having been repulsed, the enemy bombarded it from the right bank of the Elbe, also without success; the bridge was destroyed on my orders.[1] Being in this situation, and as everything indicated that Emperor Napoleon was advancing on Berlin with significant forces, I resolved to move from Rothenburg to Köthen, in order to cross the Elbe at Aken and pursue the enemy line of march, in the hope that the main Army of Bohemia would meanwhile destroy everything before it and would then proceed in the footsteps of the *Empereur des Français*. Deceived by this movement, the enemy is moving, in all probability, from the Elbe through Taucha and on to Leipzig. We have even observed from Petersberg this evening columns filing from Delitsch towards the latter town. So today I have decided to move from Köthen to Halle. On the road, I received the dispositions for a battle which is presumed to take place tomorrow. I halted all the units under my command here, near Petersberg and at Zörbig, the troops being exhausted from a difficult march on terrible roads. If there is no threat on my left flank from the direction of the Mulde, I shall move forward towards Leipzig tomorrow, and I will in any case be able to arrive on the battlefield towards evening with at least part of my cavalry, in order

---

1 The Aken bridge was not destroyed; War Diary of Prince Shcherbatov's VI Corps.

to support the efforts of the combined army as necessary, should the great battle begin.

From my headquarters in the village of Sylbitz, a good *Meile* from Halle, on 15 October, 1813.

Archive of the M.T.D. No. 1,645.

Tous les agens secrets et les nouvelles reçues de mes avantpostes paraissant confirmer la marche des forces considérables de l'armée ennemie vers l'Elbe, dans l'intention de passer ce fleuve, j'arretai d'abord le mouvement que j'avais fait, conjointement avec le général Blücher, derrière la Saale. Bientôt après le comte de Tauentzien m'apprit, qu'il avait été forcé d'évacuer Dessau, de se rétirer sur la rive droite de l'Elbe et de couper le pont de Rosslau. Une forte colonne française déboucha de Wittenberg et força le général Thümen à se réplier. La jeune garde et plusieurs corps d'armée se trouvaient entre l'Elbe et la Mulda. La ville d'Acken fut attaquée de ce côté, mais l'ennemi ayant été repoussé, on la canonna de la rive droite de l'Elbe, également sans succès; le pont fut rompu par mon ordre. Dans cet état de choses, et lorsque tout annonçait que l'Empereur Napoléon s'avançait avec des grandes forces sur Berlin, je resolus de me porter de Rothenbourg sur Cöthen, afin de passer l'Elbe à Acken et suivre la marche de l'ennemi, dans l'espérance que la grande armée de Bohème détruirait en attendant tout ce qui se trouverait devant elle et se porterait ensuite sur les traces de l'Empereur des Français. L'ennemi, trompé par ce mouvement, se reporte, d'après toutes les probabilités de l'Elbe sur Taucha et Leipzig. On observa même ce soir de Petersberg des colonnes qui filent de Delitch vers cette dernière ville. J'ai donc pris la parti de me reporter aujourd'hui de Cöthen vers Halle. En chemin j'ai reçu la disposition pour la bataille, qu'on présume avoir lieu demain. J'ai arreté ici, à côté de Petersberg et à Zörbig, toutes les troupes sous mes ordres, étant très fatiguées par une marche difficile dans des chemins horribles. Si rien ne menace mon flanc gauche du côté de la Mulda, je me porterai en avant demain vers Leipzig, et je pourrai toujours, avec une partie de ma cavallerie au moins, arriver vers le soir sur le champ de bataille, à fin d'appuyer en cas de besoin les efforts de l'armée combinée, si la grande bataille s'engage.

A mon quartier-général du village de Sylbitz, à une bonne mille de Halle, le 15 Octobre 1813.

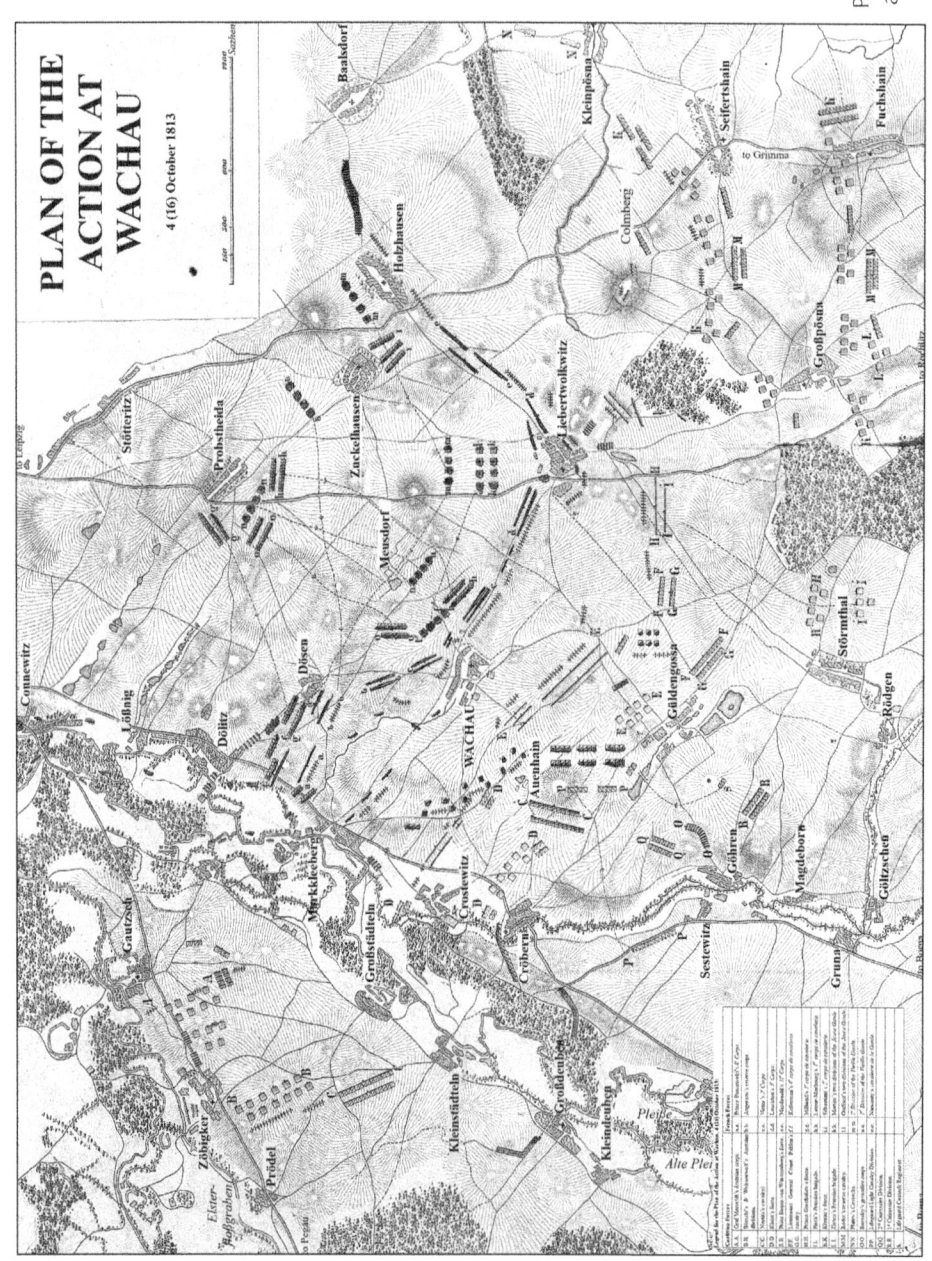

Plan of the action at Wachau, 4 (16) October 1813.

39

The Battle of Leipzig. The actions at Wachau and Lindenau on 4 (16) October

The nature of the terrain around Leipzig. – Disposition of Napoleon's forces on the morning of 4 (16) October. – Enemy troop numbers. – Prinz Schwarzenberg's operational plan. – Emperor Alexander's opinion. – Prinz Schwarzenberg's dispositions. – The composition and strength of Coalition forces assigned to attack the enemy position. – The number of troops advancing towards Leipzig overall: Russian, Prussian, Austrian, Swedish.

The actions at Wachau and Connewitz. – Advances by Kleist's and Prinz Eugen von Württemberg's forces. – Capture of Wachau by the Russians. – The powerful enemy cannonade. – Capture of Markkleeberg by Prussian forces and their subsequent retreat. – The advance by Prince Gorchakov towards Liebertwolkwitz. – Graf Klenau's attack on this village. – Attack and capture of the Colmberg by the Austrians. – Macdonald's advance. – The units under Graf Klenau, Prince Gorchakov and Count Pahlen are forced to retreat. – Reasons for the failure of the Coalition offensive. – Merveldt's attempt to cross the Pleiße.

Napoleon's arrival on the battlefield. – The arrival of the Coalition monarchs. – Orders by Emperor Alexander for the concentration of forces at both Güldengossa and Auenhain. – Napoleon's orders for the defence of the positions held by his forces. – His operational plan to eject the Coalition from Wachau, Markkleeberg and Liebertwolkwitz. – Murat's cavalry attack. – Counter-attack by Count Orlov-Denisov. – Retreat by the Prinz von Württemberg and Klüx to Güldengossa and Auenhain. – Arrival of the Russian reserves. – Operations by the Russian reserve artillery. – Failure of Murat's attack. – The offensive against Kleist by Kellermann and Poniatowski. – The arrival of the Austrian reserves. – Their capture of Markkleeberg and Auenhain. – Napoleon plans to resume the attack. – Merveldt's crossing at Dölitz.

The action at Lindenau. – Gyulay's inaction. – The advance of his forces and their return move to Markranstädt.

The locations of the formations of both sides during the night of 4 to 5 (16 to 17) October.

The fates of nations have repeatedly been decided by bloody battles on the fields of Leipzig. The reasons for this were:

1. The wealth of this city and the fertility of Saxony facilitated the concentration of significant forces around Leipzig, because it provided plentiful resources for the subsistence of the troops.
2. This location formed the hub of the main routes across Northern Germany.
3. Advantages of the terrain for forces occupying Leipzig and the surrounding country.

Leipzig lies on an extensive fertile plain, intersected by many rivers and streams flowing through shallow valleys. In general, this entire area, although undulating, does not have dominant high ground. The terrain around Leipzig is open for a considerable distance, and the rather large Universitäts Waldung is only found 12 *versts* south-east of the city. Many villages, with masonry buildings, strong walls and isolated churches outside built up areas, facilitate defensive operations; the main obstacles to troop movement are the flowing waterways crossing the terrain in many directions. The most important of them are the courses of the Elster and Pleiße, intertwined with many channels and branches, forming a vast lowland of meadows and swamps, in places covered with scrub, intersected by ditches and crossed by causeways and footbridges. Thus, communications from Leipzig to Lindenau (on the road to Lützen), over a distance of half a *Meile* (about 3½ *versts*), are via a causeway with six bridges.[1] The river Parthe forms another important obstacle as it flows north of Leipzig, almost at right angles, into the Pleiße. Although fordable almost everywhere, nevertheless, on the lower reaches of its course it presents an obstacle to the movement of cavalry and guns, and therefore, together with the villages located on it, may serve to shield troops from the front or flank. The defensive lines formed by the course of the Elster, in conjunction with the Pleiße and course of the Parthe, divide the Leipzig area into three sectors, namely:

1. West of the Pleiße and Elster, around Lindenau.
2. East of the Pleiße and south of the Parthe, around Wachau.
3. East of the Pleiße and north of the Parthe, around Möckern

Fighting took place in all these sectors, from the cavalry action at Liebertwolkwitz described above until the Coalition capture of Leipzig on 7 (19) October.

---

1 The first at the exit from the city into the Ranstädt suburb over the Pleiße; the second at the exit from this suburb, over a branch of the Elster; the third and fourth over other branches of the Elster; the fifth over the Kuhburger Wasser, and the sixth over the river Luppe near the village of Lindenau.

Throughout this entire period the weather was cloudy. On the night of 2 to 3 (14 to 15) October, a powerful storm tore away roofs, felled large trees and unleashed a downpour that extinguished every campfire. The first day of the Battle of Leipzig, 4 (16) October, was showery and overcast; while on 5 (17) October it rained almost incessantly from early morning until evening.[2]

Napoleon had intended to thrust against the Army of Bohemia with his full strength early on the morning of 4 (16) October, but not having had chance to concentrate his troops by that time, he was forced to postpone the proposed attack, and, instead of attacking the Coalition, was attacked by them in the positions at Wachau. Meanwhile, the arrival of the Army of Silesia at Möckern forced him to detach part of the French force there, and thereby weaken himself at the decisive point of the battlefield.

On the morning of 4 (16) October, Napoleon's forces assembled in the vicinity of Leipzig were positioned as follows:

Prince Poniatowski's *8e Corps* were *en echelon* between Markkleeberg, Dösen and Connewitz;[3] Marshal Victor's *2e Corps* were either side of Wachau; General Lauriston's *5e Corps* were between Wachau and Liebertwolkwitz. General Kellerman's *4e corps de cavalerie* were to the right of Dösen behind the infantry of *8e Corps*; the four divisions of the *Jeune Garde*, commanded by Mortier and Oudinot, were behind the infantry of *5e Corps*, while the *2e Division* of *Vieille Garde* were behind them under General Curial; *1er corps de cavalerie* and *5e corps de cavalerie* under Latour-Maubourg and Milhaud, together with General Friant's *1er Division* of *Vieille Garde* and Nansouty's *cavalerie de la Garde*, were forwards and to the right of Probstheida, from where, at nine o'clock in the morning, *1er corps de cavalerie* with 18 horse artillery pieces moved to Meusdorf. Macdonald's *11e Corps* were still on the march towards Holzhausen; General Sébastiani's *2e corps de cavalerie* had been ordered to hold behind this village, while Augereau's reserve corps were behind Zuckelhausen. The total strength of these formations assembled by Napoleon south of Leipzig, ranged from 100,000 to 120,000 men. To the north of Leipzig were stationed: Marshal Marmont's *6e Corps* between Breitenfeld and Radefeld [five miles east of Schkeuditz]; General Bertrand was at Eutritzsch with *4e Corps*, along with Ney's *quartier général*; two divisions (under Brayer [Michel Silvestre Brayer] and Ricard [Étienne Pierre Sylvestre Ricard]) from General Souham's *3e Corps* and Defrance's cavalry division were at Mockau [three miles north-east of Leipzig]; Dąbrowski's and Fournier's divisions were just upstream on the Parthe; Lorge's division was forwards of the other formations. The total strength of Napoleon's forces north of Leipzig reached some 50,000 men.[4] Having added the Leipzig garrison and depots, numbering some 60,000 men,[5] to the listed corps it emerges that Napoleon had from 160,000 to 173,000 in the Leipzig area, and if we

---

2   Beitzke,*Geschichte der deutschen Freiheitskriege in den Jahren 1813 und 1814*, II, 535-536.
3   See Map No. 13, Plan of the Actions at Wachau and Connewitz, 4 (16) October 1813.
4   For a comparison of numbers reported in Plotho, Vaudoncourt and Schulz, see Appendix XXXII at the end of this chapter.
5   The Leipzig garrison was 3,500 strong while General Lefol's depots [Étienne Nicolas Lefol] had 2,250 men. Schulz, XI, *1 Band*, 185.

include General Reynier's *7e Corps* and Delmas's division from *3e Corps* who had not yet arrived,[6] from 170,000 to 190,000 men with 700 guns; among these troops there were from 23,000 to 24,000 cavalry.[7]

From an examination of the positions occupied by the enemy south of Leipzig, it is obvious that the course of the Pleiße and the swamps lying between this river and the Elster completely protected their right flank from being enveloped; in contrast, their left wing at Liebertwolkwitz was being outflanked (which forced Napoleon to refuse it, almost at a right angle back to Holzhausen). However, based on an idea by General Langenau, Prince Schwarzenberg chose to conduct the main attack on the village of Connewitz, and having captured it, to get around behind the enemy.[8] No matter how hard biased historians have tried to obscure the truth by keeping silent about the disposition issued by the *Feldmarschall* on the eve of the battle, nevertheless, the second disposition they cite, which was issued on 4 (16) October, the first day of the battle of Leipzig, is sufficient to explain how the commander-in-chief and the *Generalquartiermeister* from his staff had misread the terrain on which they were to operate. Always preferring the indirect approach everywhere rather than a committed action from the front, Prinz Schwarzenberg wanted to send two Austrian corps to Lindenau along the Lützen road; to send the Austrian reserves, the Russo-Prussian Guard and Russian cuirassiers from Audigast into the impassable ground between the Elster and Pleiße, and to move the rest of the formations from the Army of Bohemia along the right bank of the Pleiße: Thus, the Coalition, upon advancing towards Leipzig, would be dividing their army into three isolated elements. General Jomini, having become aware of the planning in the Austrian *Hauptquartier*, reported to Emperor Alexander that although the idea of directing the efforts of the Coalition to the left across the enemy lines of communications made sound strategic sense, nevertheless, they were unnecessarily obsessing over this, and were operating contrary to basic tactical principles and would expose the army to obvious danger. In his opinion, the Coalition, in deciding to head between Leipzig and Lützen, would have to move the main body of the Army of Bohemia there, as well as that of Blücher and the Crown Prince of Sweden, and not split their force into five elements deprived of mutual support.[9]

General Toll, for his part, considered the disposition drawn up by the staff of the *Feldmarschall* to be highly inappropriate to the situation and tried to convince both Prinz Schwarzenberg in person as well as his advisers. In his opinion, it would be impossible to cross at Connewitz under canister and musket fire, and even if it were possible to cross the swamps and rivers there, it would be on a narrow frontage,

---

6 General Reynier's *7e Corps* had 13,800 men while Delmas' division had 4,000. Schulz, XI, *1 Band*, 182 & 185.
7 Schulz, XI, *1 Band*, 182-185. According to whom, there were a total of 190,775 men, including some 30,000 cavalry (363 battalions and 400 squadrons) in the corps assembled at Leipzig by Napoleon on 4 to 5 (16 to 17) October 4-5; Hofmann, *Zur Geschichte des Feldzuges von 1813, Zweite Auflage*, 260, shows Napoleon as having 170,000 men, of whom 24,000 were cavalry, with 260 guns; Vaudoncourt, 201-202, shows the cavalry, not including those attached to the infantry corps, to have been 22,800 men.
8 Prinz Schwarzenberg's disposition, issued on 3 (15) October.
9 Ferdinand Lecomte, *Le général Jomini:sa vie et ses écrits*, 206-207.

requiring considerable time to redeploy into battle formation and this would facilitate an enemy counterattack in superior strength and result in the destruction of the leading units before the others could debouch from the defile and arrive in time to assist them. Based on these arguments, General Toll believed that it was necessary to send the main body of the army along the right bank of the Pleiße and envelope the position on the enemy's left flank. Because all his efforts to deflect the Austrian strategists from their intent were unsuccessful, he asked Prinz Schwarzenberg not to issue the disposition to the corps commanders until Emperor Alexander had expressed his consent, and he immediately went to the Emperor and reported to him regarding the Commander-in-Chief's plans. It was not difficult for Toll to defend his convictions as they were shared by generals Barclay de Tolly and Diebitsch. The Emperor gave orders for Prinz Schwarzenberg to be summoned, who, having arrived together with Radetzky and Langenau, stubbornly defended his operational planning. Emperor Alexander, usually accommodating and compliant in meetings, was finally driven to impatience by the stubbornness of the *Feldmarschall* and told him with obvious irritation:

> Well, *monsieur* Marshal, since you persist, you may do as you wish with the Austrian army, but as for the Russian forces under Grand Duke Konstantin and Barclay, they will advance to the right of the Pleiße, where they should be, and not otherwise.[10]

Subsequent events have fully vindicated the Tsar's insistence.

Despite warnings from the talented military men at Emperor Alexander's headquarters, Prinz Schwarzenberg made only slight amendments to the orders issued on the eve of the battle. The disposition issued on 4 (16) October ordered:

> At six o'clock in the morning, *Feldzeugmeister* Gyulay's *III. Korpus* is to assemble at Markranstädt together with *1. leichte Division* under Prinz Moritz von Liechtenstein and General Thielemann's detachment, where, in all likelihood, they will also be joined by the corps under Lieutenant General the comte de Saint-Priest. At seven o'clock in the morning, Graf Gyulay is to depart Markranstädt and advance towards Leipzig. The main objectives of this column are to maintain communications between the main army and the Army of Silesia, and to facilitate the attacks by other formations by diverting enemy attention from them. Should Gyulay's corps be attacked by superior forces and find it necessary to retreat, they must withdraw towards Hohenmölsen and then towards Zeitz, whence the battalions left at Weißenfels and Naumburg are also to retreat.
>
> *II. Korpus* under General Graf Merveldt are to form up in column at six o'clock in the morning; behind them are to proceed: Nostitz's

---

10 '*Eh bien, monsieur le maréchal, puisque vous persistez, vous ferez avec l'armée autrichienne ce que vous voudrez, mais quant aux troupes russes du grand duc Constantin et de Barclay, elles iront à la droite de la Pleisse, òu elles doivent être, et pas ailleurs.*' Bernhardi, *Denkwürdigkeiten aus dem Leben Carl Friedrich Grafen von Toll*, III, 422.

cavalry, Bianchi's division, the reserve artillery of *II. Korpus* and finally Weissenwolf's division. This force, under the overall command of the Erbprinz zu Hessen-Homburg, are to depart Zwenkau at seven o'clock in the morning for Connewitz, and are to seize the bridges and town, deployed in battalion column, in three waves: Merveldt's corps in the first, Bianchi's division in the second, and Weissenwolf's in the third. Nostitz's cavalry, upon the capture of Connewitz, are to form up in regimental column to the right of Merveldt's corps. A pioneer half-company with pontoons is to be assigned to Graf Merveldt's corps in order to repair the Connewitz bridges.

All Russian cavalry and infantry reserves, as well as the Russo-Prussian Guard, having set off from their overnight halt locations at four o'clock in the morning, are to advance through Pulgar [between Audigast and Zwenkau] to Rötha, cross the Parthe [*sic*, Pleiße] there and are to position themselves on the right bank of this river in such a way that they can serve as a reserve for both the force under Count Wittgenstein and the Prinz zu Hessen-Homburg (*sic*). The cavalry are to be stationed on the right wing of the infantry in column, in chessboard formation. General Barclay will command all forces on the right bank of the Pleiße.

General Count Wittgenstein, at seven o'clock, with his own corps, Graf Klenau's and Kleist's is to attack the forces facing them and drive them towards Leipzig. The Russian grenadiers and cuirassiers are primarily to serve as the reserve for this right wing, but are to be committed to battle only in the event of a crisis.

In general, during the advance, units are to be formed in battalion or regimental column, in a chessboard formation; the batteries are to move forwards and back in a similar formation.

In the event of a retreat, the formations are directed as follows: the Prinz zu Hessen-Homburg's column via Pegau towards Zeitz; Count Wittgenstein's column towards Altenburg; Graf Klenau's column towards Penig; the Russian reserves, depending on the circumstances, towards Zeitz or Altenburg.

I. Korpus under *Feldzeugmeister* Graf Colloredo is to advance as far forwards as possible from Borna towards Leipzig, and is to serve as a reserve for the force under Graf Klenau, and in the event of a retreat is to march towards Chemnitz. The army under General Baron Bennigsen will reach Colditz tomorrow and is to move towards Grimma and Wurzen.

All trains, without exception, are to go to Zeitz and are to be positioned outside this town on the road to Gera.

At the beginning of the action, I myself shall be with the force under the Prinz zu Hessen-Homburg, and thereafter with the Russian reserves.

The dressing station shall be on the left wing, at Zwenkau.

Throughout the duration of the action, corps commanders are to send me reports hourly.[11]

---

11 *Angriffs Disposition auf der 16ste October 1813* (Log of Incoming Documents, No. 1,642). Although Plotho and Hofmann have written that this disposition was drafted in Pegau on

THE ACTIONS AT WACHAU AND LINDENAU 369

The Coalition forces were distributed for the advance on Leipzig as follows:[12]

The Austrian *III. Korpus*, with Moritz von Liechtenstein's *1. leichte Division*, Thielmann's and Mensdorf's detachments, numbering around 20,000 men with 60 guns, were to approach from Kleinzschocher [five miles east of Markranstädt] to Lindenau along the left bank of the Elster.

Merveldt's Austrian *II. Korpus*, supported by the reserves of the Erbprinz zu Hessen-Homburg, numbering 29,000 men with 114 guns, in the sector between the Elster and Pleiße, were to head from Zwenkau towards Connewitz.

On the right bank of the Pleiße, under the overall command of Barclay de Tolly, the formations, numbering 84,000 men with 404 guns, were positioned in two lines with a reserve as follows: first line – commanded by Count Wittgenstein, stationed on the left wing at Cröbern were *Generalleutnant* Kleist with the Prussian *12. Brigade*, Russian 14th Division, second brigade of 3rd Cuirassier Division and Lubny Hussars; in the centre at Güldengossa were the Prinz von Württemberg with II Corps and the Prussian *9. Brigade*; between Güldengossa and Störmthal were Prince Gorchakov with the Russian 5th Division and Prussian *10. Brigade*; on the right wing at Großpösna, commanded by Graf Klenau, were the Austrian *IV. Korpus*, Prussian *11. Brigade* and reserve cavalry; Platov's Cossack detachment was at Seifertshain; second line – commanded by Lieutenant General Raevsky, behind the centre of the first line were the grenadier corps and first brigade of 3rd Cuirassier Division; in reserve, behind Magdeborn and Cröbern, commanded by the Tsarevich Konstantin Pavlovich, were Count Miloradovich's infantry consisting of Yermolov's Lifeguard infantry corps and the Prussian guard infantry brigade; Lieutenant General Prince Golitsin 5th's cavalry from 1st Cuirassier Division and 2nd Cuirassier Division, Prussian guard cavalry brigade, Russian Lifeguard light cavalry division and the Russian reserve artillery.

Blücher was advancing from the direction of Schkeuditz, with Langéron's and Sacken's Russian corps and Yorck's Prussian corps, numbering 60,000 men with 315 guns.[13] Consequently – in the fighting on 4 (16) October, the Coalition had some 193,000 men (not including Cossacks), with 893 guns, which increased over the next two days with the arrival of the Army of the North, numbering 58,000, with 256 guns, and Bennigsen's Army of Poland, with Colloredo's and Bubna's Austrian

---

14 October new style, it is clear from the Log of Incoming Documents that it was received in Emperor Alexander's headquarters on 4 (16) October.
12 For details of the Coalition forces, see Appendix XXXIII at the end of this chapter.
13 According to returns signed by comte Langéron on 21 September (3 October), his effective troop strength reached 36,000 non-commissioned officers and privates, but some 9,000 men from the corps under Prince Shcherbatov should be subtracted, remaining on the left bank of the Elbe, and losses over the 13 days, up to 4 (16) October, were some 1,000 men. Therefore, 26,000 men with 151 guns remained in Langéron's corps, along with seven guns of the Don Cossack artillery. According to returns signed by Baron Sacken on 25 September (7 October), his effective troop strength reached 13,540 men. Losses for the nine days until 4 (16) October, did not exceed 500 men. Therefore Sacken had 13,000 men with 60 guns. Returns shown in Droysen, *Das Leben des Feldmarschalls Grafen Yorck*, III, 481-483, Yorck's corps numbered 21,000 men on 3 (15) October. According to returns signed by York himself, the corps lists 13 batteries with 104 guns.

forces, numbering some 54,000 men with 186 guns.¹⁴ Thus, more than 300,000 men were concentrated around Leipzig, of which there were some 56,000 cavalry, with 1,335 guns. These included:

	Russian	Prussian	Austrian	Swedish
Army of Bohemia	38,870	29,751	89,457	-
Army of Silesia	39,000	21,500	-	-
Army of the North	20,000	20,000	-	18,000
Army of Poland	30,000	24,000	-	-
Total:¹⁵	126,870	95,251	89,457	18,000

The Coalition offensive towards Leipzig on 4 (16) October resulted in the following battles:

1. To the south of the city at Wachau and Connewitz.
2. To the west at Lindenau.
3. To the north at Möckern.

The fighting at Wachau and Connewitz

The Coalition forces, having formed up for battle at seven o'clock in the morning, moved in to the attack. General Kleist and Prinz Eugen von Württemberg reached Markkleeberg and Wachau at about eight o'clock, while Klenau, advancing to the right towards Liebertwolkwitz, was somewhat late. The forward enemy units, which seemed very weak, retreated back, leaving seven guns on the high ground between Wachau and Liebertwolkwitz, which opened fire as soon as the Prinz von Württemberg approached to within cannon range. The force under the Prinz von Württemberg launched their attack in three columns: Colonel Reibnitz over the causeway below Güldengossa towards Wachau with three battalions from the

---

14 According to returns signed by General Wintzingerode, it is evident that there were more than 20,000 Russian troops in the Army of the North not only before the battle, but also after the battle of Leipzig; in the Swedish corps, which had suffered minor losses, there were some 18,000 men, while in Bülow's Prussian corps there were 20,000 (Schulz, XI, *1 Band*, 180). Artillery totals were: 92 guns in Wintzingerode's and Vorontsov's corps; 80 Prussian and 22 Russian guns in Bülow's corps; 62 guns in Stedingk's Swedish corps (returns signed by General Wintzingerode; Bernhardi, III, 517-518). The number of troops in Bennigsen's army reached some 30,000 men with 132 guns, according to returns dated 15 (27) September, excluding the Consolidated Corps under Count Tolstoy, left near Dresden, and losses from the time the army arrived in Bohemia until the battle of Leipzig; there were 20,000 men with 48 guns in Graf Colloredo's corps (Hardegg's, Wimpffen's and Greth's divisions); Plotho and Hofmann show Graf Bubna as having from 7,500 to 8,000 men in his division, but this is an obvious exaggeration.
15 Plotho, II, 368-369, shows the four Austrian corps, Austrian reserves and *1. leichte Division* as having 70,000 men, indeed, *2. leichte Division* is shown with 8,000 men, for a total of 78,000 in the Austrian forces. Yet at the same time, reinforcements arriving from the depots in Bohemia were not taken into account.

Tobolsk Infantry and Minsk Infantry;[16] while Prince Shakhovskoy and Pyshnitsky went to his right through the village of Güldengossa; a battery of 24 guns from 24th Battery Company and 6th Light Company, commanded by Colonel Dietrichs, moving ahead of the latter two columns, opened fire on the enemy, blew up an ammunition caisson and forced the French battery to pull back. At the same time, Reibnitz had seized the village of Wachau. Count Wittgenstein admired these successes, but matters soon took a different turn. Over the course of a quarter of an hour, the enemy moved some 100 guns onto the high ground between Wachau and Liebertwolkwitz. The bombardment from this huge battery had a terrible effect. According to one of those who took part in the battle, it seemed as if the thunder of the guns was shaking the entire area, nothing was visible through the smoke and flames; within a few minutes, 17 (according to other sources 19) Russian and five Prussian guns had been knocked out. Many men were killed or wounded; Reibnitz, seriously wounded, was carried from the battlefield; the enemy reoccupied Wachau. General Klüx sent the fusilier battalion from *1. Westpreußisches Infanterie* and the first battalion of *6. Reserve Infanterie* to the Russians, supporting them with three and a half battalions from his brigade. The brave fusiliers burst into the village at half past ten o'clock, and although they were ejected from there, nevertheless, with the assistance of Klüx's other units, they held out in the scrub near the village until three o'clock in the afternoon. During the course of these actions, the Prinz von Württemberg transferred the Chernigov Infantry and 4th Jägers from the right flank of his corps to the left wing, towards Wachau. Having received orders to take possession of the village, the Russians not only drove the enemy out of Wachau, but pursued them right up to the muzzles of the guns stationed on the high ground. The enemy, having cut down many brave men with canister shot, attacked the survivors with bayonets fixed, and having pushed them back, reoccupied the village. A Prussian battery, sited near the scrub occupied by Klüx's skirmishers, was knocked out to the last gun, but every attempt by the French to debouch from the village into the open was thwarted. For several hours, operations by both sides were limited to a cannonade, from which the Coalition troops, having incomparably less artillery with them, suffered heavy losses. Despite all this, however, the Prinz von Württemberg, convinced of the importance of the ground he was holding in the line of advancing formations, ordered the troops to remain in place, and even forbade the removal of batteries that had fired the last of their projectiles. He even exposed himself to the greatest dangers: a shell exploded a few paces away killing or wounding 25 men; after that, at a similar close range, an ammunition caisson detonated, and then a horse was killed under him by round shot.[17]

General Kleist attacked the enemy at about eight o'clock in the morning. *Oberstleutnant* Loebell [Ernst Friedrich Christian von Loebell], with two battalions from the Prussian *12. Brigade*, marched from Crostewitz towards Markkleeberg, Helffreich's division, with two Russian and eight Prussian guns, headed for the high ground between Markkleeberg and Wachau, while the Lubny Hussars

---

16 The road from Leipzig to Borna was later built over this causeway.
17 Prinz Eugen von Württemberg's diary (manuscript in the Archive of the M.T.D. No. 47,344); Hofmann, 261-263; Aster, *Die Schlachten bei Leipzig in October 1813*, I, 376-383.

monitored the fairly significant gap between the forces under Kleist and the Prinz von Württemberg. After a stubborn fight between the skirmishers, supported by cannonade from both sides, the Prussian force captured Markkleeberg, but in their haste to pursue the enemy, they were ambushed and lost some 100 men taken prisoner by Polish lancers. Encouraged by this success, the enemy launched an attack on Markkleeberg with infantry in battalion columns and captured the village, which changed hands several times. Augereau's corps, arriving to help Poniatowski at about ten o'clock, from Zuckelhausen, on Napoleon's orders, tilted the advantage to the enemy side. Helffreich's force, in attempting to cross the low ground and reach the heights, were completely disordered by canister fire from the French batteries. The enemy, taking advantage of the large gap between the columns under Kleist and the Prinz von Württemberg, charged at the flank of the Prussian batteries, almost all of whose horses had been killed, but Count Pahlen, on Kleist's request, sent the *Neumärkisches Dragoner* and a division [pair of squadrons] of *Schlesisches Ulanen*, to assist them and, although they suffered heavy casualties from the cannonade, nevertheless, they managed to protect the artillery while spare draught horses were brought up to them. At the same time, several battalions were sent from the left wing into the gap on the right flank of Kleist's force, which, together with the 4th Jägers that had arrived from the Prinz von Württemberg, resumed the attack on the high ground between Markkleeberg and Wachau; the enemy skirmishers were driven back on their supports; nevertheless, the French repulsed the Prussian force twice with fixed bayonets and forced them to retreat to Cröbern. Polish cavalry from *4e corps de cavalerie* hastened to pursue Kleist's force, but were engaged and driven back by Levashov's cuirassiers [Vasily Vasilievich Levashov], who valiantly supported the Kleist's infantry throughout the duration of the battle.[18]

The columns under the Prinz von Württemberg and Kleist, as stated above, were the first to enter combat. In contrast, Prince Gorchakov, having received orders to attack Liebertwolkwitz together with General Klenau, waited for him to arrive. But once the strong cannonade from the French batteries against II Corps could be heard, Gorchakov considered it necessary to assist him, and advanced at nine o'clock from Störmthal through the Universitäts Waldung with 5th Division and started a rather heated action against the enemy at Liebertwolkwitz. Pirch's Prussian *10. Brigade*, which had arrived in the meantime, took up post in the second line. Noticing that the French, pressing forwards, threatened to envelope the troops of 5th Division, Prince Gorchakov shifted them to the right, and moved Pirch's brigade into the front line in place of 5th Division. But his over-extended force was unable to launch a decisive attack on Liebertwolkwitz, and the action was reduced to a powerful cannonade, in which, in addition to Prince Gorchakov's batteries, the 6th Horse Artillery Company and 7th Horse Artillery Company attached to Pahlen's cavalry took part. The Russian artillery suffered very significant losses in crew and horses. The commander of 6th Horse Artillery Company, Colonel Zakharzhevsky, had his leg severed by round shot.

---

18 Hofmann, 260-261; Aster, I, 383-387; Berneck, *Die Schlachten bei Leipzig*, 108-109.

The Russian batteries were relieved by two Prussian ones, which were soon also forced to pull back.[19]

Emperor Alexander, not entirely convinced of the reliability of the Austrian generals, instructed General Toll to accompany Graf Klenau's force and assist him; but Toll's presence was resented both by Klenau himself and his chief of staff, *Oberst* Rothkirch, and therefore did not have a noticeable impact on the outcome of the battle.

Graf Klenau, intending to take Liebertwolkwitz from the flank, directed Mohr's vanguard in this direction from Großpösna, at nine o'clock, with three battalions, 14 squadrons and six guns, supported by four battalions from the *Erzherzog Karl Infanterie* and *Kerpen Infanterie* (from Mayer's division), with another six guns. Two battalions of *Erzherzog Karl Infanterie* attacked the village, while two battalions of *Kerpen Infanterie* raced to the right with both batteries, towards the Colmberg. A bitter struggle ensued in the ruins of the village, burned down on 2 (14) October; but in the end the Austrians, threatened with envelopment on their right flank, were forced to retreat. Graf Klenau, having noted the advance of strong cavalry columns from Holzhausen to Hirschfeld [two miles east of Baalsdorf], demanded the assistance of some of the cavalry. The Prussian brigades under Wrangel [August Friedrich Ludwig von Wrangel] and Mutius [Johann Karl Jakob von Mutius], consisting of 16 squadrons with a horse artillery battery, were sent to reinforce him. Because the French had not occupied the dominant high ground of the Colmberg, the Austrians drove 12 guns up onto it, placed several squadrons on either side and set up a skirmishing screen in the ravine at the northern foot of the slopes. The main body of the column, namely the Austrian division under the Prinz zu Hohenlohe-Bartenstein and Zieten's Prussian *11. Brigade*, still remained back between Seifertshain and Großpösna, at a distance of more than 2,000 paces from the Colmberg. General Toll, on the high ground, having examined the dense masses of Macdonald's corps, approaching from the direction of Holzhausen, commented to Graf Klenau that his second line was stationed at a significant distance from the front. 'It is still a long time until nightfall' answered Klenau. 'We will have time to bring the reserves into action.' Following this, however, having noticed the advance by Sébastiani's cavalry on the left wing of the French infantry, Graf Klenau and Rothkirch sent orders to the Prinz zu Hohenlohe to bring several battalions up to the Colmberg. But these orders would not improve the situation. The Austrian skirmishers had already been driven out of the ravine, and Charpentier's entire division, numbering 4,000 men, formed up in regimental columns, were headed for the Colmberg, while Marchand's [Jean Gabriel Marchand] and Ledru's divisions were advancing on Seifertshain with Sébastiani's cavalry. Napoleon, having witnessed the destructive effect of the Austrian battery stationed on the Colmberg himself, rode up to Charpentier's division. Noticing that these troops had halted, not daring to close with bayonets fixed, he turned to the head of the column and asked: 'Is the *22e ligne* really standing idle under canister fire?' Hearing these words, the soldiers of the *22e ligne* dashed forward in double-time; behind them the entire division advanced with bayonets

---

19 General Nikitin's notes (handwritten, in the Archive of the M.T.D. No. 47,353); Aster, I, 387-388; Berneck, 109.

fixed, with drums beating, with colours unfurled. The battalions of the *Kerpen Infanterie* fell back; the batteries, having fired their last rounds of canister, withdrew from their positions; but only eight guns managed to escape, while four were captured by the enemy. Klenau at the head of the second battalion of the lead regiment of Hohenlohe's division, raced to engage the French and was almost captured himself. At the same time as the action on the Colmberg, Sébastiani was engaging the cavalry of Klenau's corps and Zieten's brigade.[20] The Coalition attacks were initially successful and they even managed to recapture three of the guns taken by the enemy; but subsequently they were driven back in complete disorder. Fortunately, however, at this very moment 16 Prussian squadrons sent by Pahlen appeared (two cuirassier regiments and two Landwehr regiments).[21] The cuirassiers, forming line, let the crowd of disordered horsemen pass through and then attacked the enemy cavalry frontally. Whereupon Count Platov suddenly arrived from the direction of Kleinpösna. The Cossacks struck the French in their left flank. Sébastiani, baffled by these attacks, retreated behind the Colmberg, which made it possible for Graf Klenau to rally his units between Großpösna and Fuchshain.[22]

The column under Prince Gorchakov, also unable to hold off the advance of the numerically superior enemy, retreated into the Universitäts Waldung, while Count Pahlen, having sent 16 squadrons to help Klenau and six to escort Kleist's batteries, withdrew to the high ground forwards of the Grünen Teiche (Green Ponds) with the remaining 26 squadrons.[23]

Thus, the attack by Count Wittgenstein had been repulsed, despite the bravery of his troops, and the leadership and selflessness of unit commanders. Napoleon's units stationed somewhat behind the front lines before the start of the battle, safe from the fire of the Coalition batteries, had retained the ability to engage the advancing troops at each of the locations attacked, in superior numbers and with fresh forces. In contrast, the Coalition launched their attacks across the entire sector from the Pleiße to Liebertwolkwitz, in an arc more than eight *versts* long, over-extending their forces in order to maintain communications between the isolated elements of the army and suffered untold losses from their artillery fire before reaching the enemy.

The operations by Austrian forces between the Elster and Pleiße were even less successful. General Merveldt, having received orders from the Commander-in-Chief to seize the crossing at Connewitz, advanced towards this village through dense forest and undergrowth. The French had destroyed almost every bridge that could serve as a link between the branches of the Pleiße, and the swampy terrain prevented any off-road movement. Eventually, once the *Bellegarde Infanterie*, marching at the head of the column, managed to reach the bridge at Connewitz, it emerged that the enemy had placed strong batteries on the high ground on the right bank of the river and

---

20 The offensive on the right wing of the Coalition army involved the *Hohenzollern Chevaulegers*, *Palatinal Husaren* and *Erzherzog Ferdinand Husaren* (14 squadrons in total); the Prussian *1. Schlesisches* (four squadrons and *Schlesisches Landwehr Kavallerie* (two squadrons).
21 *Oberst* Wrangel's brigade consisted of the *Ostpreußisches Kürassiere* and *Brandenburgisches Kürassiere*. while *Oberst* Mutius' brigade consisted of *7. Landwehr Kavallerie* and *8. Landwehr Kavallerie*.
22 Hofmann, 263-264; Aster, I, 388-390 & 413-417; Bernhardi, III, 429-433.
23 Hofmann, 264-265; Berneck, 109.

occupied the village and scrub with a dense screen of skirmishers, protecting them and the columns stationed behind them completely. The Austrians wanted to place several guns to counter the enemy artillery, but could not find suitable firing points anywhere. The marksmen, sent to the water's edge, were forced to fire by instinct, unable to see the enemy who were hitting them at will. During the first two hours, five officers and 200 lower ranks were lost to the *Bellegarde Infanterie*. In addition, the recruits who formed the majority of the *Wenzel Colloredo Infanterie*, stationed behind the *Bellegarde Infanterie*, perched on the boughs of the trees, were hitting their own troops. The Austrians, finally acknowledging that it would be impossible to cross at Connewitz, attempted to repair the bridge between this village and Lößnig, and then to cross even further upstream, but these attempts were not successful.[24]

Napoleon had arrived at the Galgenberg (gallows hill) between Wachau and Liebertwolkwitz as early as nine o'clock, where Murat was waiting for him. Having surveyed the advancing columns of the Army of Bohemia through a large telescope, he made no changes to the orders he had issued.[25]

The Coalition monarchs reached the Wachberg, between Güldengossa and Göhren, just after nine o'clock. Emperor Alexander arrived from Pegau, the Austrian Kaiser from Borna, and the King of Prussia from Gruna near Magdeborn. The Tsar's escort, the Lifeguard Cossack Regiment commanded by Adjutant General Count Orlov-Denisov [Vasily Vasilievich Orlov-Denisov], were stationed on the reverse slope.[26] Shortly before this, having passed Magdeborn and ascended the high ground from where the enormous enemy forces were visible, ready to engage the Coalition, Emperor Alexander ordered his *Flügel-Adjutant*, Colonel Wolzogen, to go to Prinz Schwarzenberg, who was still back at Connewitz, and in the name of the Emperor, to demand that the Austrian reserves be transferred to the right bank of the Pleiße. At the same time, having assigned several Lifeguard Cossacks to Wolzogen, Emperor Alexander ordered him to send them back with a report on the progress of operations between the Elster and the Pleiße, as well as beyond the Elster and from Blücher's army. Colonel Wolzogen, having struggled to get across Pleiße at Gaschwitz [west of Cröbern], found the *Feldmarschall* near Gautzsch together with his Chief of Staff, Radetzky, and announced Emperor Alexander's will to him. Prinz Schwarzenberg excused the losses suffered at Connewitz. 'Merveldt has lost 4,000 men' he said, 'and there is little hope of matters improving.' Radetzky added that he had never expected anything better from this undertaking, and urged the *Feldmarschall* to accelerate the crossing by the reserves without losing a moment, because the move to Gaschwitz, the crossing of the Pleiße there and the advance to Markkleeberg required at least four hours.[27] General Jomini, who was with Prinz Schwarzenberg at the time and had already tried several times to dissuade him from attacking Connewitz, seeing the futility of his arguments, asked the *Feldmarschall* to send one of his aides-de-camp up the Gautzsch bell tower, from where it was possible to survey the surrounding area for a considerable distance. Because the

---

24   Aster, I, 396-400; Beitzke, II, 560-562.
25   Aster, I, 391.
26   Aster, I, 391.
27   Wolzogen, *Memoiren*, 212-213.

direction of the cannonade indicated that the French were moving forwards, the Commander-in-Chief ordered two Austrian officers, Graf Clam [Karl Johann Nepomuk Gabriel Clam-Martinic] and Wrbna [Dominik von Wrbna-Freudenthal?], to observe the enemy from the bell tower together with General Jomini. Their observations utterly convinced them of the danger threatening the Coalition on the right bank of the Pleiße. The *Feldmarschall*, having heard their report, sent the reserves under the Prinz zu Homburg to Gaschwitz and Großdeuben, but still left Merveldt's corps between the Elster and the Pleiße in order to renew the attack on Dölitz. Thus, having finally managed to persuade Prinz Schwarzenberg to move the reserves to the right bank of the Pleiße, General Jomini then sent his aide-de-camp Baron Friedrichs to Emperor Alexander, with a hastily scribbled note in pencil, in which he reported on the imminent French offensive and the need for the Russian reserves to be brought up.[28]

But even before receiving this note, having ascertained the vulnerability of the Coalition situation, Emperor Alexander had ordered the Lifeguard light cavalry to go to Cröbern, while Duka's cuirassiers and Raevsky's grenadiers were to move to Auenhain; the 1st Cuirassier Division and 2nd Cuirassier Division were directed up onto the high ground between Magdeborn and Güldengossa, while the remaining Russian-Prussian reserves were to go to Magdeborn.[29]

Napoleon, for his part, was also taking steps to strengthen the force assembled in the positions at Wachau.

Augereau's reserve corps had been sent to reinforce Prince Poniatowski as soon as Kleist and the Prinz von Württemberg had attacked the right wing of the French army and, setting out from Zuckelhausen, Augereau had arrived in the gap between Wachau and Dösen at about ten o'clock in the morning. Latour-Maubourg was stationed at Wachau with the *1st corps de cavalerie* in the second line behind Victor's corps, where they had suffered significant casualties from the cannonade by the Prinz von Württemberg and Prince Gorchakov: 11 of his 32 guns had been destroyed in the course of one hour. Latour-Maubourg himself lost a leg. The *1er Division* of the *Vieille Garde* and the *cavalerie de la Garde* were stationed at Meusdorf behind *1er corps de cavalerie*. Four divisions of the *Jeune Garde* were stationed on the left wing, behind Lauriston's corps, in the second line, while the *2e Division* of the *Vieille Garde* were behind them in reserve, having had arrived from Holtzhausen, via Zuckelhausen. When the French were driven out of Wachau by Russo-Prussian forces, Napoleon sent the *3e Division* and *4e Division* of the *Jeune Garde* to assist Victor; the other two divisions, *1e Division* and *2e Division*, were left at Liebertwolkwitz.

After all these movements, by 11 o'clock in the morning, the French army was deployed as follows:

Prince Poniatowski's *8e Corps* was between Connewitz and Markkleeberg; Augereau's reserve corps was between Dösen and Wachau; Kellerman's *4e corps de*

---

28 Aster, I, 394; Lecomte, 209-210.
29 Aster, I, 394; War Diary signed by Barclay de Tolly, which states that 1st Grenadier Division was directed towards the Universitäts Waldung, while 2nd Grenadier Division was directed towards Auenhain.

cavalerie and Milhaud's *5e corps de cavalerie* were to the right of Augereau's corps. Victor's *2e Corps* was behind Wachau; behind them, in the second line were Latour-Maubourg's *1er corps de cavalerie*, while the reserves were forwards of Meusdorf, consisting of Nansouty's *cavalerie de la Garde* and Friant's *1er Division* of the *Vieille Garde*; Oudinot was on the march from Liebertwolkwitz to Wachau with *3e Division* and *4e Division* of the *Jeune Garde*. Lauriston's 5th Corps was stationed between Wachau and Lieberwolkwitz; behind them in the second line were Marshal Mortier's *1er Division* and *2e Division* of the *Jeune Garde*, while Curial's *2e Division* of the *Vieille Garde* was in reserve; Sébastiani's *2e corps de cavalerie* had advanced between Liebertwolkwitz and Seifertshain; Macdonald's 11th Corps, having arrived from Holzhausen, was deployed at a shallow angle to the left wing of Lauriston's corps.

Napoleon had hoped to reinforce these formations with two more, *3e Corps* and *6e Corps*, although Marshal Marmont had reported to him the day before about the advance of the Army of Silesia and Army of the North towards Leipzig. Paying scant attention to these reports, Napoleon considered it sufficient to leave Bertrand's *4e Corps* to shield the city on its northern side.[30] But when Gyulay's Austrian corps advanced from Markranstädt towards Lindenau, General Arrighi, who was there with four battalions, asked Marshal Ney to reinforce him with some of the units stationed north of Leipzig. Because there seemed to be no danger from the direction of Halle, Ney sent *4e Corps* to occupy Lindenau, a very important point through which passed the sole French army line of communications with the Rhine. Defrance's division was sent to Leipzig from *3e corps de cavalerie* in order to maintain communications with the main body of the army. The remaining formations, *3e Corps* and *6e Corps* and elements of *3e corps de cavalerie*, were supposed to be sent to Liebertwolkwitz.[31] At the same time (at 11 o'clock in the morning) Marshal Marmont reported to Napoleon on the appearance of the enemy on the roads from Halle and Landsberg and about his intention, in spite of this to go to Liebertwolkwitz.[32] Ney had actually intended to relieve *6e Corps* at Lindenthal [two miles north of Möckern] with *3e Corps*, but since this would have cost too much time, Marmont was left there with *6e Corps*, while Ney moved over to Schönefeld [five miles east of Möckern] himself, with two divisions from *3e Corps* located at Mockau [two miles south-east of Wiederitzsch], receiving several contradictory sets of orders from Napoleon's *quartier général* and spent the rest of the day in pointless counter-marching, without taking part in the actions taking place at Wachau and Möckern.[33]

Napoleon, having shored up all the most threatened points of his position and repelled the Coalition attacks, decided to counterattack in the centre, at Güldengossa, with a significant mass of cavalry from *1er corps de cavalerie* and *5e*

---

30 Marmont, *Mémoires*, V, 174-175.
31 Marshal Ney's report dated half past ten o'clock in the morning on 16 October, new style, from Eutritzsch.
32 Marshal Marmont's report dated half past ten o'clock in the morning on 16 October, new style, from Radefeld.
33 Marmont, V, 180.

corps de cavalerie, and then, in the event of this attack succeeding, to move forwards with the main body of the army assembled south of Leipzig: Marshal Victor was to seize Auenhain with *2e Corps* supported by *3e Division* and *4e Division* of the *Jeune Garde*, General Lauriston was to occupy Güldengossa with *5e Corps*, Marshal Mortier was to clear the Universitäts Waldung with *1er Division* and *2e Division* of the *Jeune Garde*, while Marshal Macdonald was to envelope the Coalition right flank at Seifertshain with *11e Corps* and *2e corps de cavalerie*. Napoleon hoped to smash through the units of the Coalition line in the centre, or to push them back to the Pleiße and the Elster, cutting them off from direct communications with Bohemia.[34]

Fortunately, the high ground between Güldengossa, Störmthal, Magdeborn and Göhren prevented the enemy from observing that strong reserves were being concentrated at the very point where they wanted to make their breakthrough with a huge mass of cavalry, reserves that would make it possible to repel the blow that threatened the destruction of the Coalition army.

While the cavalry of Latour-Maubourg's *1er corps de cavalerie* and part of Milhaud's *5e corps de cavalerie*, comprising around 100 squadrons and numbering 8,000 horsemen, were forming up for the attack, Kleist's force, supported by the Malorussia Cuirassiers, Novgorod Cuirassiers and Lubny Hussars attached to them, were still fighting with more or less success against an incomparably stronger enemy (the corps under Poniatowski, Augereau and Kellerman's cavalry), but were finally forced to retreat back to Cröbern. The Prinz von Württemberg, wishing to maintain the links to Kleist's force, sent the Kremenchug Infantry, 20th Jägers and 21st Jägers to the left, which weakened II Corps, which had already been disordered by the losses they had suffered.[35] It has already been mentioned that Klenau had been forced to retreat from Liebertwolkwitz and the Colmberg to the positions he had held at the beginning of the battle, and that Prince Gorchakov and Count Pahlen had also retreated to the Universitäts Waldung and to the high ground by the Grünen Teiche. The Prinz von Württemberg, wishing to increase the fire from his batteries, many of whose guns had been destroyed, sent his aide-de-camp Wachten to bring up the artillery. He was sent Count Arakcheev's Lifeguard Battery Company as reinforcements, which, having taken up position on the left flank of II Corps, opened up a cannonade that had a remarkably successful effect.[36]

At about two o'clock in the afternoon, the French cavalry assigned to the main attack had formed up in two waves to the east of Wachau; the *cavalerie de la Garde* were stationed in reserve. The attack was entrusted to Murat; under his command were *1er corps de cavalerie* with *général de division* Bordesoulle having replaced Latour-Maubourg, and Milhaud's *5e corps de cavalerie*. Shortly before the attack, General Drouot rode forward with 60 guns from the reserve artillery, and supported the operations of several disordered French batteries. At three o'clock in the afternoon, trumpets sounded the signal for the attack. The closest enemy batteries ceased

---

34 Aster, I, 408.
35 Aster, I, 411; Hofmann, 268, states that the gap that had opened up between the Russian 3rd Division and the Prussian 9. *Brigade* was further increased by the need to reinforce the troops on the flanks. Only the Kremenchug Infantry remained in this gap.
36 Hofmann, 268-269.

firing. The command was given: *marche*! *marche*! The cavalry set off at a trot and gradually quickening their pace, swooped first on Güldengossa, and then to the right towards the ponds lying to the west of this village. As to their formation during the attack, eyewitness accounts disagree: some say that they were in line; others claim that they moved and attacked in column.[37]

As soon as the Prinz von Württemberg saw this mass of cavalry forming up against him, he sent for reinforcements from General Duka, who was stationed behind Auenhain with his 3rd Cuirassier Division at the time, to the right of Cröbern. But the enemy cavalry were already charging at full gallop; Murat at their head attacked a battery of 30 guns and the Kremenchug Infantry stationed nearby himself with the cuirassiers from Berckheim's brigade [Sigismond-Frédéric de Berckheim]. The second battalion of this regiment was partly wiped out, partly captured together with their commander, Lieutenant Colonel Kiselevsky, but their Colours were saved by a wounded Junker and carried by a Prussian Landwehr cavalryman to the first battalion of the same regiment, commanded by Lieutenant Colonel Cheodaev [Mikhail Ivanovich Cheodaev]. Having dispersed the battery's escort, the French rushed the guns, cutting down the crews and horses, slashing the traces, rendering almost all the Prinz von Württemberg's artillery immobile in its place, and headed towards the causeway at Güldengossa, breaking through II Corps' lines at their weakest point, exactly on their boundary with the remainder of 4th Division. The Russian 3rd Division and Klüx's Prussian brigade quickly formed battalion squares with the Russian regiments attached to them and stood firm. At the same time as the attack on the large battery, the Saxon *Garde du Corps* regiment was sent to the right against Count Arakcheev's battery. These elite warriors raced towards the guns located half a *verst* forwards of the ponds to the west of Güldengossa, cut down their crews and drivers and attempted to drag away the artillery.[38]

At this very moment, Lieutenant Yaroshevitsky of His Highness' Lifeguard Battery Company, finding himself near the attacked battery by chance and witnessing the disaster befalling his fellow soldiers, noticed Russian cavalry passing about a *verst* away from Göhren towards Cröbern, galloped towards them and informed the commander of the nearest regiment of the loss of the battery. Colonel Khilkov [Stepan Alexandrovich Khilkov] immediately turned about with the Lifeguard Dragoons and hurried to the rescue of the artillery; the Lifeguard Ulans and Lifeguard Hussars also galloped after him. General Shevich, riding at the head of the Lifeguard Light Cavalry Division, believing that his cavalry had received orders to attack, followed them; but he had barely managed to turn his horse when he was fatally struck by round shot; the commander of the Lifeguard Hussars, Colonel Davydov [Yevgraf Vladimirovich Davydov], had both legs severed by round shot.[39] Despite the loss of

---

37 Hofmann, 269; Aster, I, 430-431; According to Bordesoulle, commander of 1er *corps de cavalerie*, only two divisions took part in the attack: his own division, formed in three waves, and Doumerc's division moving behind them in reserve, numbering some 4,000 men.
38 Prinz Eugen von Württemberg's diary; Hofmann, 269; Aster, I, 433-435.
39 [The Russian Biographical Dictionary states that Davydov was wounded in the right leg by a shell fragment and suffered a head contusion from round shot but remained on duty (later that day, round shot severed his right hand and left leg at the knee)].

their commanders, however, the Lifeguard cavalry boldly charged at the enemy, and did not withdraw until they were engaged by the brigade under General Bessières [Bertrand Bessières], which had been committed from Bordesoulle's reserve and had begun to move beyond the swamps and ditches connecting the series of ponds to the west of Güldengossa.[40] The enemy, tenaciously pursuing the Russian regiments, appeared at the ponds and near the village, at a distance of no more than 800 paces from the high ground on which the Coalition monarchs had been located since early morning as well as Prinz Schwarzenberg, who had arrived from Connewitz. Some of the generals who were in Emperor Alexander's suite asked him to leave, but the Emperor, paying no heed to the threat, was concerned only with reinforcing the troops fighting at Güldengossa and Auenhain: part of 1st Grenadier Division and Pirch's Prussian brigade were ordered to go to Güldengossa; the 2nd Grenadier Division was sent to Auenhain. Emperor Alexander summoned the commander of the Russian artillery, General Sukhozanet,[41] who had just arrived from Liebertwolkwitz, and pointing to the battlefield spread out at their feet, said: 'do you see, the one who gets here first right now has the advantage; how far away is your reserve artillery?'

'They will be here in two minutes' answered Sukhozanet, who had earlier sent his aides-de-camp off with orders to bring all the reserve artillery to Güldengossa at the trot. They were indeed already approaching at the head of the Lifeguard corps, which the Tsar himself had sent for. Seeing the horse artillery companies forming up in dead ground, with his usual thoughtful smile, the Emperor said: 'Excellent!' and having ridden back a little together with the King of Prussia, he ordered his escort to protect the 10th Horse Artillery Company as they advanced forward. Meanwhile, Adjutant General Count Orlov-Denisov, returning from Magdeborn, where he had been sent by the Tsar with orders for Barclay de Tolly to send the cuirassiers up immediately, noticed the movement of the Lifeguard Cossacks through the clouds of smoke and, headed with them towards the nearby causeway. Having assessed that it would be impossible for one artillery company to beat off the overwhelming enemy numbers, Count Orlov-Denisov left them on the south side of the defile and moved the Cossacks by files across the very narrow embankment, whereupon, having redeployed the first squadron, he led them up the reverse slope into the attack, while the other squadrons were deploying. At the same time, the 10th Horse Artillery Company, together with Colonel Markov's 23rd Horse Artillery Company [Alexander Ivanovich Markov], which General Sukhozanet had positioned right next to the pond, caught the French cavalry in a crossfire of canister shot. The unexpected attack by the Lifeguard Cossacks on the French left flank, surprising the enemy and checking their advance, won time for the disordered regiments of the Lifeguard light cavalry to rally. General Chicherin [Pëtr Alexandrovich Chicherin], having hastily reformed them, joined the Lifeguard Cossacks and cooperated in their brilliant feat. Emperor Alexander personally expressed his satisfaction to Count Orlov-Denisov in the most flattering terms; the

---

40 Hofmann, 269-270; Yaroshevitsky's manuscript notes on the battle of Leipzig on 4 [16] October.
41 Major General Sukhozanet was the commander of the Russian artillery at this time, due to Prince Iashvili being ill.

Austrian Kaiser, on the recommendation of Prinz Schwarzenberg, who had witnessed the attack by the Lifeguard Cossacks, granted the *Maria-Theresien-Orden* to the Count that same day.[42] His feat was immortalised by the Sovereign Emperor Nicholas Pavlovich of blessed memory, who ordered the establishment of a sacred holiday for the Lifeguard Cossack Regiment on 4 [16] October.

Although he had been attacked by the enemy in considerable strength himself, Count Pahlen, nevertheless, having assessed the danger threatening the centre of Wittgenstein's force, sent the *Neumärkisches Dragoner* and *Schlesisches Kürassiere* to Güldengossa, who cut into the enemy cavalry and, having mixed with the French in hand-to-hand combat, pursued them right up to their batteries. General Bordesoulle, fearing that they would capture the entire *artillerie de la Garde*, asked their commander, Drouot, to engage the crowd galloping towards them at full speed with canister shot, which was done. This bombardment and the arrival of fresh French regiments halted the brave Prussian cavalry.[43]

Murat's cavalry attack, having split Prinz Eugen von Württemberg's force into two separate parts, forced them to retreat in different directions: the Murom Infantry, Reval Infantry, 20th Jägers, 21st Jägers and a battalion of Kremenchug Infantry with several guns fell back towards Güldengossa, while the other units of II Corps and Klüx's brigade withdrew towards Auenhain. The Russian regiments had been weakened to the point that some of them had no more than 100 men left. The grenadiers sent to reinforce II Corps were: Choglokov's 2nd Grenadier Division formed up in square to the right of the units retreating to Auenhain, and a brigade from 1st Grenadier Division, of St. Petersburg Grenadiers and Taurida Grenadiers, holding Güldengossa, together with Pirch's Prussian brigade.[44]

While the bitter fighting was raging at Güldengossa and Auenhain, the entire reserve artillery, numbering about 100 guns, managed to line up on the high ground behind the village of Güldengossa and the ponds, and opened fire, to which the French responded with equally intensive action from their batteries. The cannonade continued for an hour and a half at a range of no more than 1,000 paces, which Miloradovich said was louder than that at Borodino. This bought time to reinforce the units fighting in Güldengossa with the Leib Grenadiers, Pavlovsk Grenadiers, Lifeguard Jägers and Lifeguard Finland Regiment, and to bring all other reserves up closer to the centre. The batteries of both sides initially worked with equal success, but eventually the Russian artillery gained the upper hand and forced the French batteries to abandon their positions one by one and retreat out of cannon range. Their cannonade carried on, but diminished to the point that General Sukhozanet managed to drag away the damaged guns abandoned on the far side of the ponds by II Corps during the melee.[45] Napoleon, having received news of Macdonald's

---

42 General Sukhozanet's manuscript notes on the battle of Leipzig; Count Orlov-Denisov's manuscript notes on the battle of Leipzig on 4 [16] October.
43 Aster, I, 440-441.
44 Prinz Eugen von Württemberg's diary; Plan of the battle of Leipzig on 4, 6 and 7 [16, 18 and 19] October, signed by General Diebitsch (Archive of the M.T.D. No. 20,012); Plan of the battle of Leipzig on 4 (16) October (Archive of the M.T.D. No. 20,015).
45 General Sukhozanet's notes. The 23rd Horse Artillery Company under Colonel Markov particularly distinguished themselves here, engaging the enemy cavalry with fire as soon as

capture of the Colmberg and the breakthrough at Güldengossa by Murat's cavalry, ordered congratulations for the King of Saxony for the victory and to ring all the bells, both in Leipzig and in the surrounding villages held by French forces.[46] But the stubborn resistance by the Prinz von Württemberg and Kleist, the valiant charge by the Lifeguard Cossacks, the successful work by the Russian artillery and the timely arrival of reserves at the decisive point of the battlefield snatched victory from the hands of the brilliant commander and was a precursor of the triumph of Europe, which had risen up in defence of its independence.

It has already been mentioned that Kleist's force, having fought for several hours with varying success against Poniatowski and Augereau, supported by Kellermann's cavalry, had finally been forced to retreat from Markkleeberg in the direction of Cröbern. Napoleon, wishing to complete the success at this point, had reinforced Kellerman's corps with a brigade of *Dragons de la Garde* under Letort [Louis-Michel Letort de Lorville] and sent them against Kleist's force; this attack was supported by Poniatowski's infantry, formed in several squares, and strong batteries. But the commander of the Austrian reserve cavalry, Graf Nostitz, having gone ahead of his force as they moved from Gautzsch to Cröbern, in order to get early news of the developing situation, and having seen that Kleist and Helffreich had been pushed back almost to the Göselbach, sent orders to the cavalry to pick up the pace. At two o'clock in the afternoon, having passed Cröbern, his vanguard attacked and drove back the Polish cavalry under Kellerman and Letort's *Dragons de la Garde*; and thereafter, charging at the infantry, they broke through between the squares; while these attacks were going on, the Austrian infantry division under Bianchi crossed to the right bank of the Pleiße. Formed of select Hungarian regiments, at three o'clock they advanced from Cröbern towards Markkleeberg and relieved Kleist's units there, weakened from eight hours of combat, who withdrew to the second line. The Austrian batteries, putting the enemy line extending forwards from Wachau under enfilade fire, forced the French to retreat. Exploiting this success, General Graf von Haugwitz [Eugen Wilhelm von Haugwitz], with the right column from Bianchi's division, consisting of two battalions of *Prinz von Hessen-Homburg Infanterie*, pushed the enemy back even further and took six guns, including five Prussian ones, abandoned during the retreat by Kleist's force.[47] Bianchi himself, with the left hand column, consisting of the *Hiller Infanterie, Colloredo Infanterie* and one battalion of *Esterhazy Infanterie*, having passed through Markkleeberg, drove the enemy out of the scrub, pursuing them almost to the village of Dölitz and captured three more guns.[48]

Murat raced towards Güldengossa, and losing most of their crews. When Markov visited his wounded after the end of the fighting, the dying asked him: 'Papa Alexander Ivanovich! Have we pleased our Tsar? Have we pleased you?' When Markov expressed his gratitude to them, they replied: 'Well, bless us, dear father, we shall not enter the damp earth in dishonour.' (Markov's notes).

46 Odeleben, *Relation circonstanciée de la campagne de 1813 en Saxe*, II, 21; Beitzke, II, 566; Aster, I, 423.
47 Plotho, II, 377.
48 Austrian communique on the battle of Leipzig, published by the *Hofkriegsrat*.

Following the mass cavalry attack, part of the Prinz von Württemberg's force, which had retreated towards Auenhain, were ejected from there by Victor's corps, supported by two divisions of the *Jeune Garde*. But any further advance by the French was checked by the 2nd Grenadier Division, under Raevsky's personal command. The courageous grenadiers, having formed battalion squares, repelled the enemy almost without firing a shot, using only the bayonet. Raevsky, wounded by a bullet in the shoulder, pulled the bloody lead out of the wound himself and, upon showing it to the poet Batyushkov [Konstantin Nikolaevich Batyushkov] his aide-de-camp, recited a famous French rhyme:

Of my life-giving blood, nothing remains;
For my homeland it was spilt from my veins.[49]

Emperor Alexander passed the command of the grenadier corps to Adjutant General Prince Trubetskoy [Vasily Sergeevich Trubetskoy].[50] By about five o'clock in the afternoon, all the French attacks had been repulsed, but the enemy still held Auenhain, the most important location in the Coalition centre, whose loss meant they could not remain in the positions they currently occupied. Prince Schwarzenberg, considering it vital to conclude the fighting by retaking this location in order to raise the morale of the troops, assigned the *Simbschen Infanterie* for the assault (left in Cröbern by General Bianchi) supported by all the regiments from Weissenwolf's division. Victor, having strongly garrisoned Auenhain and placed strong batteries to the sides of this location, defended himself stubbornly, but the Austrians, paying no attention to the canister shot that was thinning their ranks, drove the enemy out. The loss of Auenhain forced the French *2e Corps* to retreat to their former positions at Wachau.[51]

Napoleon had intended to deliver a decisive attack at five o'clock, but he suspended it, noticing an alarm to the rear of his right wing. The reason for this was Merveldt's appearance there.[52]

The advance of Bianchi's division from Markkleeberg in the direction of Dölitz had enabled Merveldt's force to occupy the left bank of the Pleiße. At five o'clock, *Feldmarschallleutnant* Liechtenstein, having positioned two howitzers by Schloß Dölitz with two companies of *Kaunitz Infanterie*, opened fire on the flank of the French retreating along the far bank of the river, which forced them to flee. Merveldt wanted to take advantage of the favourable situation and cross the river via a footbridge. The enemy, however, having noticed the preparations for this crossing, placed a battery facing it and placed General Rottembourg's brigade [Henri Rottembourg] of the *Vieille Garde* on either side of it in several columns. General Merveldt, having approached the footbridge, mistook these troops for Hungarian infantry, and despite warnings from Alois Liechtenstein and Colonel Wolzogen, who were accompanying

---

49 'Je n'ai plus rien du sang, qui m'a donné la vie; Ce sang est épuisé pour la patrie.'
50 Mikhailovsky-Danilevsky, Campaign Memoirs of 1813; Mikhailovsky-Danilesky, Description of the War of 1813, II, 131-132.
51 Austrian communique; Plotho, II, 379.
52 Hofmann, 273.

him, crossed over the footbridge with a battalion of *Strauch Infanterie* onto the far bank of the river and approached to within 20 paces of the enemy. The French fired a volley, wounding Merveldt and killing his horse, and, having captured him, ran onto the left bank of the river together with the *Strauch Infanterie* battalion; but upon being engaged by the nearby Austrian *Wenzel Infanterie, Colloredo Infanterie* and *Strauch Infanterie*, they withdrew to the right bank of the Pleiße.[53] The action at Dölitz was insignificant, but it had diverted Napoleon's attention from the location at which he had intended to operate decisively, and in the meantime the light was failing and the battle ceased without bringing any significant advantage to either side. As has already been mentioned, Napoleon's forces had lost Markkleeberg and were forced to retreat from Auenhain and Güldengossa to Wachau and Liebertwolkwitz; Mortier had attempted to seize the Universitäts Waldung with two divisions of the *Jeune Garde*, but had been held in check by the troops under Prince Gorchakov; Macdonald, although he managed to take Seifertshain, was unable to hold on to it and retreated to the Colmberg and Kleinpösna.[54]

There is no reliable data on the casualties suffered by each side in the fighting on 4 (16) October at Wachau. What is known, however, is that on the Coalition side the greatest losses were suffered by the Prinz von Württemberg's II Corps and Kleist's Prussian *II Korps*. In the former, almost two thirds of the available number of men were *hors de combat*, namely: 15 field officers, 125 subalterns and 3,400 lower ranks; in the latter: 160 officers and 6,425 lower ranks (not including losses to Zieten's *11. Brigade* or Röder's reserve cavalry, which are not recorded). It is believed that the losses in Wittgenstein's force overall ranged from 15,000 to 20,000 men and that the French forces operating south of Leipzig lost no fewer.[55]

The action at Lindenau

On the western side of Leipzig, where only four French battalions had been stationed early in the morning, Graf Gyulay, instead of taking advantage of the enemy's weakness, remained inactive, awaiting the advance of the Army of Silesia. But because there was still no news from Blücher by eight o'clock, and from the Markranstädt bell tower they had, in the meantime, observed the advance of the Coalition columns down the Pleiße, the Austrian forces eventually set off from their positions and approached Leipzig, at the same time that Bertrand, having arrived at Lindenau with *4e Corps*, numbering 10,000 men, had fitted out the fortifications

---

53 Vaudoncourt, 208; Aster, I, 463-464.
54 Aster, I, 473-474.
55 Prinz Eugen von Württemberg's diary; Aster, I, 487-488. Every regimental commander in II Corps was rendered *hors de combat*. When one of the battalion commanders of the 21st Jägers, Lieutenant Colonel Bushen, reported to the commander of 3rd Division, Prince Shakhovsky, about the fatal loss of the commander of the aforementioned regiment, Colonel Stepanov, Shakhovsky replied: 'Well, what now? They will kill you and then they will kill me; take the regiment under your command.' The icy composure of Prince Shakhovsky, who had been a good friend of Stepanov's, amazed everyone around him; but when the action was all over, this courageous warrior broke down in tears like a child.

being built there with ten or 12 guns each. At around nine o'clock, when the fighting at Wachau was already in full swing, Gyulay's force, numbering some 20,000 men, advanced in three columns: General Csollich's right hand column consisting of his own brigade and Moritz von Liechtenstein's *leichte Division* towards Kleinzschocher and Plagwitz [2½ miles west of Leipzig]; the centre column under Gyulay's personal command, of three battalions and the cavalry under Crenneville, Thielmann and Mensdorff with four batteries, along the highway past Schönau [four miles east of Markranstädt]; the left hand column under Prinz Philipp zu Hessen-Homburg, of Weigl's brigade [Joseph Weigl von Löwenwarth], *2. Jäger Bataillon* and *Saint-Georg Bataillon* with a Cossack regiment, directed towards Leutzsch [three miles north-west of Leipzig]. Two battalions of the *Kolowrat Infanterie* remained in reserve, behind the village of Schönau, half a *Meile* (3½ *versts*) from Lindenau. Graf Gyulay intended to approach Lindenau with the centre column, open a cannonade on the enemy from the front, and conduct a decisive attack from the flanks with the side columns. The Austrian cavalry drove the enemy back twice. Whereupon Gyulay, having deployed the infantry of the centre column against Lindenau, advanced 24 guns and opened a heavy bombardment. General Csollich, after a very bitter fight at Kleinzschocher, captured this village, but, moving on, was driven back from Plagwitz. The enemy, having disordered his force with canister shot and musketry, attacked them with cavalry, but Colonel Orlov charged at the flank and rear of the enemy with a Cossack regiment, rescued the Austrians and gave them the chance to rally. The Prinz zu Hessen-Homburg drove the French out of Leutzsch and twice broke into Lindenau, but each time, being subjected to the strongest cannonade from the French batteries stationed behind the village, he was forced to retreat to Leutzsch. The small detachments sent to establish communications with Blücher returned having failed to complete the mission given to them, except for a half-company from the *2. Jäger Bataillon* under *Leutnant* Gelber, which managed to link up with the Army of Silesia at Stahmeln, [2½ miles] north-west of Möckern, having crossed the Luppe and several branches of the Elster. By evening Gyulay had withdrawn to Markranstädt, leaving four battalions in Kleinzschocher and Leutzsch and holding the line between these villages with outposts. The losses to his force amounted to 2,000 men.[56]

The other formations of the Army of Bohemia, on the night of 4 to 5 (16 to 17) October, were deployed as follows: the Austrian *II. Korpus*, commanded by Prinz Alois zu Liechtenstein, was on the left bank of the Pleiße, between Connewitz and Oetzsch [a half-mile north-east of Markkleeberg]; the Austrian reserves were between Markkleeberg and Auenhain; Kleist's force was close to Cröbern; the 3rd Cuirassier Division were to the right of this village, facing towards Güldengossa; the 2nd Grenader Division were at Auenhain; the Lifeguard Light Cavalry were between Auenhain and the Güldengossa ponds; Klüx's brigade and elements of II Corps were behind the Lifeguard Light Cavalry, while the other regiments from II Corps and Pirch's brigade were behind the village of Güldengossa, which was garrisoned by a brigade from 1st Grenadier Division, the Lifeguard Jägers,

---

56 Hofmann, 274-275; Aster, I, 401-404, 450-452 & 468.

Lifeguard Finland Regiment and Pavlovsk Grenadiers; Count Pahlen's cavalry were between Güldengossa and the Universitäts Waldung with 2nd Cuirassier Division behind them, the forest being held by the Russian 5th Division; a brigade of 1st Grenadier Division was behind the forest; the Prussian foot Guards were behind the Güldengossa ponds; five Russian Lifeguard regiments, 1st Cuirassier Division and the cavalry of the Prussian Guard were to the right of Magdeborn; the Russian reserve artillery were behind Güldengossa and the ponds; Klenau's corps, Zieten's brigade and the Prussian reserve cavalry were between Großpösna and Fuchshain, with a detachment in Seifertshain; Platov's Cossack detachment were to the right of Seifertshain.[57] In summary, the front line of the Coalition forces' combat deployment, on the right bank of the Pleiße, extended from Markkleeberg through Auenhain to Güldengossa, and onwards, forming a shallow angle, along the outer edge of the Universitäts Waldung, and through the villages of Großpösna and Fuchshain. Emperor Alexander's and Prinz Schwarzenberg's headquarters were located in Rötha; the King of Prussia was in Borna, and the Austrian Kaiser's *Hoflager* was in Pegau.[58]

No definitive news was forthcoming from Blücher, until the early hours of the morning, but, from the thunder of the cannonade, it could be concluded that the Coalition were closing in on Leipzig. Colloredo's Austrian corps had reached Borna. The vanguard of the Army of Poland and Bennigsen's headquarters reached Grimma at midnight, while Dokhturov's corps would arrive at six o'clock in the morning on 5 (17) October.[59]

The French army, on the night after the battle at Wachau, occupied the following positions on the right bank of the Pleiße:

Prince Poniatowski's *8e Corps* stretched from Dölitz to Connewitz; General Curial's *2e Division* of the *Vieille Garde* were behind the right wing of *8e Corps*; Kellerman's *4e corps de cavalerie* were to the right of Dösen, Augereau's reserve corps were between Dösen and Wachau; Victor's *2e Corps* were partly in Wachau, partly between Wachau and Auenhain; *3e Division* and *4e Division* of the *Jeune Garde* were to the left of Wachau and on the high ground facing Guldengossa, under Oudinot; Lauriston's *5e Corps* were between Wachau and Liebertwolkwitz; *1er Division* and *2e Division* of the *Jeune Garde* were in the Niederholz forest, facing Großpösna, under Mortier; from Macdonald's *11e Corps*, Charpentier's division was opposite Großpösna; Ledru's division was facing Seifertshain; Marchand's division was on the Colmberg, while Gérard was at Kleinpösna, *1er corps de cavalerie* and *5e corps de cavalerie* were to the left of Gérard's division, on the march towards Stötteritz. Friant's *1er Division* of the *Vieille Garde* were in bivouacs at the brickyards behind Meusdorf. Bertrand's *4e Corps* were deployed behind Lindenau and in Leipzig.[60]

The forward outposts of both sides were very close to each other, and from time to time isolated shots were heard from the screen. The troops, after ten hours of bitter

---

57 Plan of the Battle of Leipzig, 4 (16) October (Archive of the M.T.D. No. 20,015); Hofmann, 275-276.
58 Hofmann, 276.
59 Plotho, II, 386; Hofmann, 276.
60 Aster, I, 473-474.

struggle, had a vital need for rest, but, having no straw, were forced to lie on the wet ground. The soldiers were hungry and exhausted, yet could hardly close their eyes amidst incessant shouts of: *qui vive? wer da?* and *kto idët?* It is not hard to imagine the situation of the wounded, who remained mostly on the scene of the slaughter.[61]

Napoleon was still on the battlefield when the captured General Merveldt was brought to him. Having first met him in 1797, on the occasion of the armistice negotiations in Leoben, Napoleon treated him favourably, gave orders for his wound to be bandaged and to take care of him, while he went to spend the night behind the Meusdorf brickyards himself, where the usual five tents had been pitched for the *Empereur des Français* and his *quartier général* on ground formed on the site of a drained pond, where a huge bonfire was also blazing. The *1er Division* of the *Vieille Garde* bivouacked around Napoleon. The news received during the night from various points on the battlefield, and especially the reports from Marmont and Poniatowski, convinced Napoleon that he could not consider the bloody battle of 4 (16) October to be a victory. There was no word from General Reynier's *7e Corps*.[62]

---

61 Aster, I, 476-477.
62 Aster, I, 477-485.

Appendix XXXII

Comparison of estimates of Napoleon's troop strengths at Leipzig

The strength of Napoleon's forces south of Leipzig are shown as follows:

	Plotho	Vaudoncourt	Schulz
Marshal Victor's *2e Corps*	15,000	16,000	16,800
General Lauriston's *5e Corps*	10,000	9,000	13,400
Prince Poniatowski's *8e Corps*	10,000	8,000	5,400
Marshal Augereau's reserve corps	10,000	10,000	10,000
Marshal Macdonald's *11e Corps*	14,000	15,000	19,000
General Latour-Maubourg's *1er corps de cavalerie*	6,000	4,500	7,100
General Sébastiani's *2e corps de cavalerie*	5,000	4,500	4,420
General Kellerman's *4e corps de cavalerie*	4,000	3,000	2,150
General Milhaud's *5e corps de cavalerie*	4,000	3,000	4,600
Jeune Garde	15,000	16,000	22,500
Vieille Garde	4,000	4,000	8,500
Cavalerie de la Garde	5,000	4,800	5,600
Total:	102,000	97,300	119,470

The strength of Napoleon's forces north of Leipzig are shown as follows:

	Plotho	Vaudoncourt	Schulz
General Bertrand's *4e Corps*	14,000	15,000	9,695
Marshal Marmont's *6e Corps*	20,000	18,000	17,700
Two divisions from Souham's *3e Corps*	12,000	15,000	12,000
Dąbrowski's division	-	-	3,000
General Arrighi's *3e corps de cavalerie*	3,000	3,000	5,340
Total:	49,000	51,000	47,735

Plotho, *Der Krieg in Deutschland und Frankreich in den Jahren 1813 und 1814*, II, 369; Vaudoncourt, *Histoire de la guerre soutenue par les Français en Allemagne en 1813*, 201-202; Schulz, *Geschichte der Kriege in Europa seit dem Jahre 1792*, XI, 1 Band, 181-185.

Appendix XXXIII

Coalition forces at the actions at Wachau and Connewitz on 4 (16) October 1813

	Battalions	Squadrons	Men
Gyulay's Column			
Austrian *III. Korpus* (Crenneville's, Murray's & Prinz Philipp zu Hessen-Homburg's divisions)	15	9	13,678
Prinz Moritz von Liechtenstein's *1. leichte Division*	4	16	4,537
General Thielmann's detachment (400 Prussians, remainder Austrians)	-	8	842
Oberst Mensdorf's detachment	-	6	680
Total (with 60 guns):	19	39	19,737
Erbprinz zu Hessen-Homburg's Column			
Austrian *II. Korpus* (Lederer's & Alois von Liechtenstein's divisions)	17	10	13,050
Graf Nostitz's cuirassier corps	-	40	3,840
Reserves (Bianchi's & Weissenwolf's divisions)	20	-	12,060
Total (with 114 guns):	37	50	28,950
Kleist's Force			
Prinz August's Prussian *12. Brigade*	8	-	5,400
General Helffreich's Russian 14th Division	8	-	1,600
Russian cuirassier brigade and Lubny Hussars	-	14	1,400
Total (with 20 guns):	16	14	8,400
Prinz Eugen von Württemberg's, Count Pahlen's & Prince Gorchakov's Force			
II Corps (Prince Shakhovsky's & Pyshnitsky's divisions)	15	-	5,200
General Klüx's Prussian *9. Brigade*	8½	-	5,820
Pahlen's cavalry	-	20	2,000
General Mezentsov's Russian 5th Division	11	-	4,100
General Pirch's Prussian *10. Brigade*	7	-	4,770
Total (with 62 guns):	41½	20	21,890
Graf Klenau's Force			
Austrian *IV. Korpus* (Mohr's, Hohenlohe's & Mayer's divisions)	24	14	17,170
General Zieten's Prussian *11. Brigade*	7½	6	5,661
General Röder's Prussian reserve cavalry	-	26	2,600

389

	Battalions	Squadrons	Men
Total (with 72 guns):	31½	46	25,431
Barclay de Tolly's Second Line Force			
General Raevsky's Russian grenadier corps (Sulima's & Choglokov's divisions)	24	-	9,100
First brigade of General Duka's 3rd Cuirassier Division	-	8	800
Total (with 34 guns):	24	8	9,900
Tsarevich Grand Duke Konstantin Pavlovich's Reserves			
Lieutenant General Yermolov's Lifeguard infantry corps (Rosen's & Udom's divisions)	21½	-	8,070
Oberstleutnant Alvensleben's Prussian guard infantry brigade (with *Freiwillige*)	8	-	4,300
General Depreradovich's 1st Cuirassier Division & General Duka's 2nd Cuirassier Division	-	34	3,400
Oberst Werder's Prussian guard cavalry brigade	-	11	800
General Shevich's Lifeguard light cavalry division	-	22	2,200
Total (with 60 guns):	29½	67	18,770

Russian reserve artillery consisted of 92 guns, while the Prussian reserve had 64 guns.

Data for the composition and troop numbers was extracted from returns on the state of the forces, signed by Barclay de Tolly, and from the tables published in Plotho, II, *Beilagen*, 38-44, Hofmann, 312-315 and Schulz, XI, *1 Band*, 175-179.

Legend to Map No. 14

Coalition Forces
A.A. Infantry of Hiller's Prussian vanguard
B.B. Kleist's Prussian corps
C.C. Comte Langéron's corps
D.D. General Korff's cavalry
E.E. General Vasilchikov's cavalry
F.F. Comte Saint-Priest's corps
G.G. Kaptsevich's advance
H.H. Advance by Rudzevich's vanguard
I.I. Advance by Emmanuel's cavalry
K.K. Cossacks
L.L. General Olsufiev's force
M.M. General Udom's advance
N.N. Katzler's Prussian vanguard cavalry
O.O. Prinz Karl zu Mecklenburg's *2. Brigade*
P.P. Steinmetz's *1. Brigade*
Q.Q. Horn's *7. Brigade*
R.R. Hünerbein's *8. Brigade*
S.S. Jürgaß's Prussian reserve cavalry
T. Bistrom 2nd's advance
U. Major General Vasilchikov's advance

French Forces
a.a. First position of Marmont's *6e Corps*
b.b. Second position of Marmont's *6e Corps*
c.c. Third position of Marmont's *6e Corps*
d.d. Fourth position of Marmont's *6e Corps*
e.e. Dąbrowski's division
f.f. Normann's cavalry
g.g. Lorge's cavalry
h.h. Delmas' division
i.i. Parks & trains escorted by *3e Corps*
k.k. Dąbrowski's retreat
l.l. Dąbrowski's advance with Delmas
m.m. Retreat by French forces
o.o. Lagrange's division
p.p. Compans' division
r.r. Friederichs' division

APPENDIX XXXIII 391

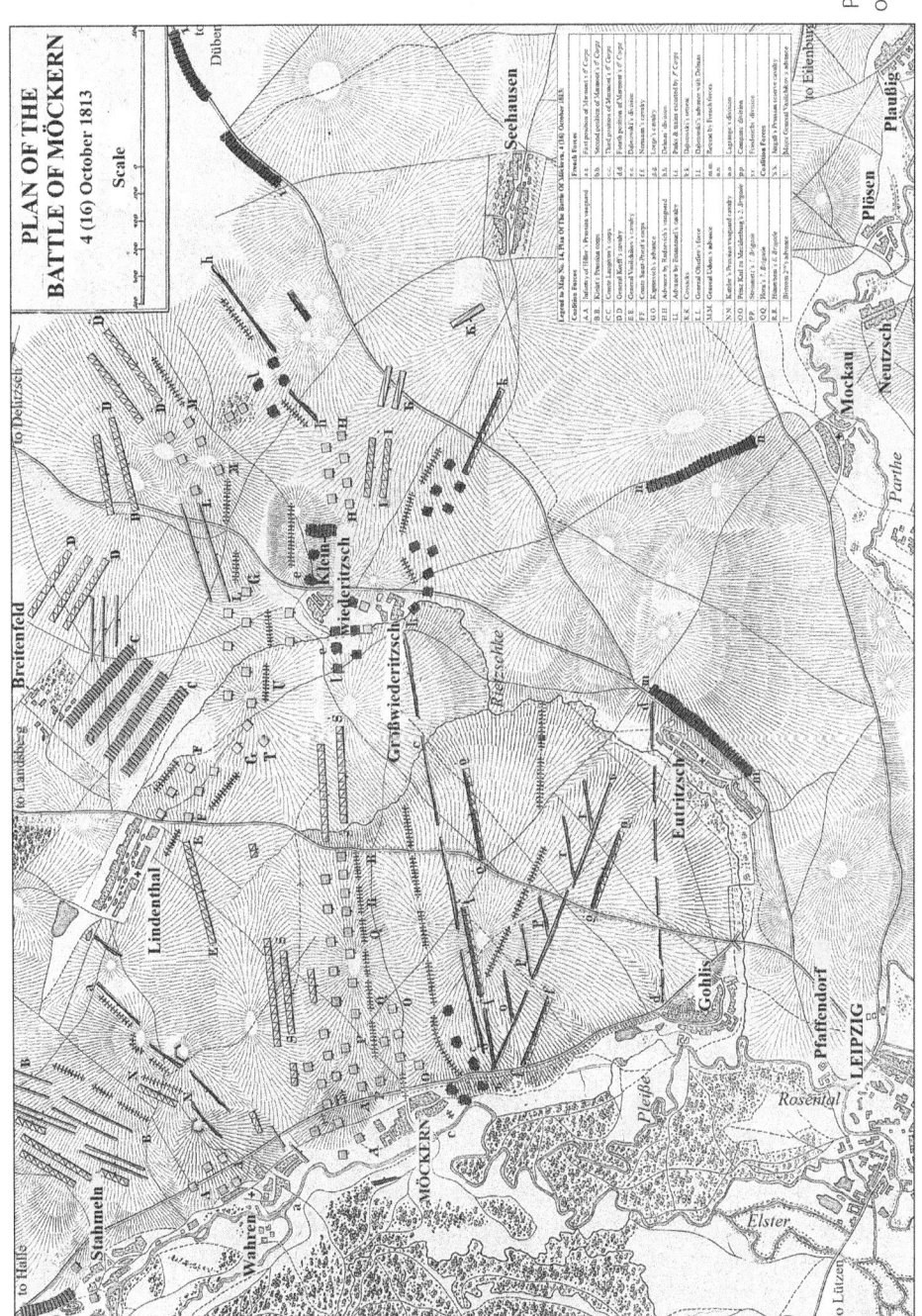

Plan of the Battle of Möckern, 4 (16) October 1813.

40

The Battle of Leipzig (continued)

The Battle of Möckern. Marshal Marmont's position at Lindenthal and his withdrawal to the position at Möckern. – Blücher's offensive; his pre-battle motivational speech. – The deployment of Marmont's force. – Blücher's orders. – Hiller's attack on the village of Möckern.

The capture of Wiederitzsch by Langéron's troops. – Emmanuel's attack. Prinz Karl zu Mecklenburg's attack on Möckern. – Marmont's advance to engage him. – The fighting in the village. – Steinmetz's attack. – Attack by the Brandenburg Hussars and Yorck's other cavalry.

Operations on the left wing of the Army of Silesia. – Langéron's force is driven out of Wiederitzsch. – The second offensive by the Russian forces. The final defeat of the enemy and their retreat to Euteritzsch and Gohlis. – The spoils of victory. – Losses. – Remarks.

The deployment of the Army of Silesia on the evening of 4 (16) October, after the battle.

The reorganisation of Yorck's corps. – Wintzingerode's cavalry arrive in Lindenthal on the morning of 5 (17) October. – Vasilchikov 1st's attack. – The enemy retreat to the Halle Gate.

The Coalition postpone the attack on Napoleon until 6 (18) October. – The arrival of reinforcements. – Napoleon decides to retreat. – His conversation with General Merveldt. – Orders for the retreat. – Blücher's conference with the Crown Prince of Sweden.

The Battle of Möckern

Having received Napoleon's orders to deploy north of Leipzig, in order to protect the city from the direction of Halle and Landsberg, as early as the night of 2 to 3 (14 to 15) October, Marshal Marmont was reporting to him that he had found a position at Lindenthal, near Breitenfeld, which, although too extensive for *6e Corps* to hold alone, nevertheless, if reinforced with field fortifications and occupied by 30,000 men, should be able to delay the Army of the North and Army of Silesia for a full 24 hours. Napoleon responded to the marshal that he should begin work immediately, and that his force would be supplemented in due course by *3e Corps*. Having received these orders, Marmont began to set up abatis in the forest between Radefeld and Lindenthal, and stationed the vanguard in Radefeld. Throughout the day and night of 3 to 4 (15 to 16) October, he kept Napoleon informed of the progress of the Army of Silesia and the Army of the North and asked for reinforcements from *3e Corps*, but at eight o'clock in the morning on 4 (16) October, received instead a dispatch in which Napoleon expressed doubts about the reliability of the intelligence delivered by the marshal, and wrote to him that he must cross through Leipzig and should become the army reserve. The reason for Napoleon's misperception, in all likelihood, was rumours spread by Saint-Priest about an advance by the entire Army of Silesia from the direction of Merseburg. Units from *6e Corps*, having withdrawn from the position forwards of Lindenthal, began to retreat towards Leipzig, but being harassed by Blücher, were forced to halt and take up new positions between Möckern and Eutritzsch, which, being less advantageous than the previous position, could nevertheless be defended by a smaller force, and in addition Marmont received news from Ney about his willingness to support *6e Corps* with the entire strength of *3e Corps*. The French force, having retreated under the protection of Coehorn's brigade [Louis Jacques de Coehorn] and Normann's Württemberg cavalry left as the rearguard at Radefeld, took up positions with their right flank adjoining the village of Eutritzsch and the Rietzschke stream, and their left flank adjoining Möckern;[1] Dąbrowski's division, having occupied the village of Wiederitsch behind the stream but ahead of the right flank, threatened to envelope the advancing Coalition force and shielded the Düben road, along which Delmas was moving with one of the divisions from *3e Corps*.[2] The strength of Marmont's force overall reached 22,000 men with 84 guns.[3]

At 11 o'clock in the morning on 3 (15) October, units of the Army of Silesia arrived at Schkeuditz, having set out from the vicinity of Halle, and were stationed as follows: Yorck's corps, just short of this village, on both sides of the highway; Langéron's corps, two *versts* to the left; Sacken's corps in reserve at Gröbers about 5½ miles north-west of Schkeuditz. The vanguard of Yorck's corps was pushed about half a *Meile* (about four *versts*) forwards of Schkeuditz, to Hänichen. On the morning of 4 (16) October, Blucher carried out a reconnaissance-in-force himself, with all the cavalry from the three Coalition corps, from which it emerged that Radefeld,

---

1 See Map No. 14, Plan of the Battle of Möckern, 4 (16) October 1813.
2 Marmont, *Mémoires*, V, 174-177.
3 Schulz, *Geschichte der Kriege in Europa seit dem Jahre 1792*, XI, *1 Band*, 183 & 185, shows Marmont's force as having: from *6e Corps*: Compans' division, Legrange's division and Friederich's division each with 14 battalions and 5,600 men; Normann's cavalry brigade with eight squadrons and 900 men, for a total of 42 battalions, eight squadrons and 17,700 men; Dąbrowski's division of four battalions, ten squadrons and 3,000 men; Lorge's division from *3e corps de cavalerie* with 30 squadrons and 1,500 men, for a grand total of 46 battalions, 48 squadrons and 22,200 men. Marmont, *Mémoires*, V, 177, shows 84 guns, which is very close to the number shown by General Pelet, *Spectateur militaire*, IV, *Tableau de la grande armée en Septembre et Octobre 1813*.

Lindenthal and the pine forest between these villages were heavily occupied by the enemy, and that their troops were also at Podelwitz. Just after nine o'clock, a disposition for the army's advance was issued: Langéron's corps were ordered to advance towards Radefeld, Yorck's towards Lützschena [Stahmeln] and then, to wheel left off the highway towards Lindenthal; Sacken was to proceed as the reserve; Saint-Priest's detachment were to cross to the right bank of the Elster at Schkeuditz and thereafter to move up behind Langéron's force. Preparing for battle, Blücher and his staff rode along the line of his beloved combat arm – the cavalry, addressing the regiments with a short speech: 'Lads, today we are going to strike them in the old Prussian manner' he said to the *Ostpreußisches National Regiment*. To others he said: 'Whoever is not either dead or in intoxicated bliss this evening has fought like a disreputable son of a bitch.'[4]

At half past one o'clock in the afternoon, Langéron, having encountered Marmont's vanguard at Radefeld, forced them to retreat, ejected the enemy from the pine forest and, leaving Lindenthal to his right, headed for Breitenfeld. Earlier Yorck's force had moved along the highway, and in the meantime the vanguard cavalry commanded by *Oberst* Katzler, had deployed to the left in order to shield the advance by the rest of the force. Having observed several enemy squadrons stationed forwards of Lindenthal, Katzler ordered the *National Regiment* to attack them, but, being engaged by fire from infantry occupying the pine forest and attacked by Normann's Württemberg cavalry, were driven back. The Prussian *2. Reitende Batterie*, having fired all their projectiles, retreated; but immediately afterwards the enemy leading units, under attack by superior numbers, were forced to retreat to the main position. At the same time, the vanguard infantry commanded by Hiller, captured the villages of Stahmeln and Wahren and closed in on Möckern.[5]

Marmont, believing that the main Coalition attack would be directed along the highway towards Möckern, had changed front, wheeling by brigade, advancing the right flank; thus, six echelons were formed, of which the left hand, foremost one, held Möckern and the area closest to this village, and the others formed a staggered line resting their right flank on the Rietzschke. Dąbrowski's division, holding Klein- and Großwiederitzsch, was forwards of the right wing, and had been assigned to operate against the flank of the force advancing against this position. The defense of Möckern was entrusted to the *2e régiment de marine*; all the artillery was placed on the high ground in front of the infantry; 12 heavy guns fired from the right at the village of Möckern and the main road; the cavalry were in the second line behind the left wing and the centre.[6]

As soon as the Coalition noticed that the enemy had rested their left wing on the river Elster, General Yorck, instead of wheeling left towards Lindenthal, advanced

---

4   General Sacken's report No. 284 to Barclay de Tolly dated 18 October [new style?] from Rothkirchen; Droysen, Yorck's Leben, III, 143-145, '*Kinder, heut haut einmal auf altpreußische Art ein... wer heut Abend nicht entweder todt oder wonnetrunken ist, der hat sich geschlagen wie ein infamer Hundsfott.*'
5   Wagner, *Plane der Schlachten und Treffen, welche von der preussischen Armee in den Feldzügen der Jahre 1813, 14 und 15 geliefert worden*, II, 81-82; Droysen, III, 145; Aster, *Die Schlachten bei Leipzig*, I, 517-522.
6   Wagner, II, 84; Marmont, V, 177-178.

in such a way that the right wing of the main body of his corps attached itself to the vanguard directed toward Möckern. In the meantime, because Langéron's corps had been directed to their left past the pine forest, towards Breitenfeld, a large gap opened up in the centre of the Coalition army. The Commander-in-Chief ordered Sacken's cavalry and the units under the comte de Saint-Priest to fill this gap, while the cavalry from Langéron's corps were detached to Podelwitz to shield the army's left flank from the enemy moving in from the direction of Düben. But the cavalry from Sacken's corps, due to a misunderstanding, also headed for the left wing, and subsequently deployed to the south of Lindenthal.[7] Because at this time both the strength and the location of the enemy north of Leipzig were as yet unknown, Blücher was taking precautions to protect himself from being enveloped from the left flank and was constantly with Langéron's corps himself, leaving Yorck to operate on the right wing.[8]

At about two o'clock in the afternoon, the Coalition closed up to the villages occupied by the enemy on the flanks of their position. At three o'clock, Major Hiller received orders to take Möckern with eight battalions and three companies of jägers from Yorck's vanguard;[9] his infantry advanced up a ravine; the six-pounders of *12. Batterie* were to assist the attack by advancing alongside the infantry; while the batteries from *7. Brigade* and *8. Brigade* (*3. Batterie* and *15. Batterie*) supported by the 12-pounders of *1. Reserve Batterie* and *2. Reserve Batterie*, and *1. Reitende Batterie* and *3. Reitende Batterie* were advanced against the centre of the enemy position; they were followed by: Horn's *7. Brigade* and Hünerbein's *8. Brigade* in the front line, Prinz Karl zu Mecklenburg's *2. Brigade* and *Oberst* Steinmetz's *1. Brigade* in the second, with Jürgaß's reserve cavalry, who had been joined by Katzler's cavalry, further back.[10]

Major Hiller attacked the village of Möckern as soon as the mutual cannonade began. The Prussian force broke in several times, but on each occasion, being greeted with highly effective fire from the French batteries on the high ground, they were forced to retreat; a small detachment of Austrian jägers from Prinz Moritz von Liechtenstein's division took part in operations by the Prussian vanguard, having crossed the swamps and branches of the Elster and Pleiße to Stahmeln with extreme difficulty. Marshal Marmont sent the *4e marine* and *37e légère* up in support of the *2e marine*, who fought stubbornly, but despite this, the Prussian force eventually managed to gain a foothold in a few houses in the burning village. This success was bought at a high price: many brave men had fallen; among the wounded were Hiller and Major Klüx, who had taken his place. General Yorck, believing that the success of the battle depended primarily on the capture of Möckern, supported the vanguard infantry with the Prinz zu Mecklenburg's *2. Brigade* and placed

---

7   Hofmann, *Zur Geschichte des Feldzuges von 1813*, 277; Aster, I, 517-520.
8   Aster, I, 522-523.
9   Wagner, II, 96, the infantry of Hiller's vanguard consisted of: the fusilier battalion of *2. Ostpreußisches Infanterie*, *Leib Grenadiere*, *Westpreußisches Grenadiere*, first battalion of *Brandenburgisches Infanterie* and second of *12. Reserve Infanterie*, three *Landwehr* battalions, two companies of *Ostpreußisches Jäger* and one of *Garde Jäger*, with *12. Batterie*, for a total of eight battalions, three companies and eight guns, numbering 4,000 men.
10 For details of these formations, see Appendix XXXIV at the end of this chapter.

Steinmetz's *1. Brigade* in reserve behind them. Marmont, for his part, reinforced Lagrange's division [Joseph Lagrange] defending Möckern with nearby regiments from Compans' division, which enabled the French to hold out in this village for more than three hours and inflict significant damage on the Prussian force with their artillery, which was very advantageously located on the high ground to the right of the village.[11]

Throughout the duration of these actions at Möckern on the left wing of Marmont's corps, Dąbrowski was also fighting on their right wing.

Count Langeron's force, having passed Breitenfeld, advanced in two directions: Kaptsevich's X Corps towards Kleinwiederitzsch, followed by 9th Division from Olsufiev's IX Corps, while General Rudzevich moved to the left with the vanguard, supported by Korff's cavalry, into the gap between Wiederitzsch and Seehausen. On Dąbrowski's side, four or five battalions held Kleinwiederitzsch, while some ten squadrons of cavalry were stationed to the right. Comte Langéron attacked Kleinwiederitzsch with the regiments from X Corps and directed Major General Emmanuel against the enemy cavalry with the Kharkov Dragoons, Kiev Dragoons, Novorossia Dragoons and Major General Pahlen 2nd's brigade (Dorpat Mounted Jägers and Livland Mounted Jägers). The Poles holding the villages of Kein- and Großwiederitzsch, resisted very stubbornly, but having been driven out of there, began to retreat towards Eutritzsch, while General Emmanuel attacked the cavalry at the same time with the 1st Ukrainian and 3rd Ukrainian Cossacks, who struck them in the flank, under the command of generals Count de Witt and Prince Obolensky [Vasily Petrovich Obolensky]. The attack was a complete success: the Polish cavalry were routed, with the loss of seven guns and 500 prisoners.[12]

Meanwhile, as the desperate struggle continued on the Coalition right wing in the village of Möckern, the Prinz zu Mecklenburg, sent to assist the vanguard with *2. Brigade*, quickly moved to the left of the village straight in front of the batteries and approached to within 300 paces of them. Marmont hurried with the nearest battalions himself in order to secure the artillery. The regiments under the Prinz zu Mecklenburg, engaged with canister shot, lost many men. Taking advantage of this, several French battalions closed in on the advancing force. The *mariniers de la Garde* [*sic*, probably *4e marine*], having allowed the fusilier battalion of *1. Ostpreußisches Infanterie* to come within 50 paces, fired a volley at them. The fusiliers were completely disordered and were forced to take cover in the village. *Oberstleutnant* Lobenthal dashed forward with two battalions from the same regiment, and, having driven off the sailors, advanced with drums beating towards the nearest battery. But he was engaged here by enemy battalions under Marmont's personal command. Prinz Karl swiftly rode forward and was badly wounded. He handed over command of the brigade to the brave Lobenthal. *Oberst* Sjöholm [Friedrich Wilhelm von Sjöholm] deployed the combined battalion from *2. Ostpreußisches Infanterie* along a ravine, from there they shot down the French battery's crews and the infantry protecting them with accurate fire. At the same time, the commander of artillery of Yorck's corps, *Oberstleutnant* Schmidt, blew up four enemy ammunition

---

11 Wagner, II, 85-86; Beitzke, II, 576-577; Marmont, V, 178; Aster, I, 523-527.
12 War Diary of comte Langéron's corps; Aster, I, 527-528.

caissons; one of Marmont's 12-pounder batteries was forced to cease firing; their escort fell back. The *Ostpreußisches Infanterie* battalions raced at the two nearest guns and bayoneted their crews. Marmont, forced to commit Compans' entire division into action, charged with fixed bayonets with the *20e régiment provisoire* and *25e régiment provisoire*. He said, 'never before had I come so close to the enemy.' Outnumbered, the Prussian troops were forced to retreat. The French pursued them, but were engaged by fire from the six-pounders of *1. Batterie* and the 12-pounders of *2. Reserve Batterie*, and were charged by the *Mecklenburgisches Husaren*, and halted. *2. Brigade* lost almost half of its available men; every battalion commander was killed or wounded, including Lobenthal.[13]

A desperate struggle was still going on inside the village of Möckern. The Prussian units, broken down into groups of 30 to 40 men, systematically stormed the houses and other buildings held by the French. The losses suffered in the fighting brought the ferocity of both sides to the point that after the capture of a building, all its defenders would be mercilessly executed with bayonets or musket butts. Finally, at around five o'clock in the afternoon, the French abandoned the village completely.[14]

By this time the Prussian *1. Brigade* had also been committed into action.[15] The advance of these units was supported by the fire of both 12-pounder batteries (*1. Reserve Batterie* and *2. Reserve Batterie*) and the six-pounder *2. Batterie*, while to their left the 14 guns of *1. Reitende Batterie* and *3. Reitende Batterie* and five six-pounders from *15. Batterie* continued to fire. The brigade commander, *Oberst* Steinmetz, led his infantry forwards at such an angle that the right-flank battalions from both lines would pass through the village of Möckern, while all the others faced the enemy held high ground. Two battalions of *13. Landwehr Infanterie* approached to within 150 paces of the French batteries, but having lost many men and all their field officers, they halted and fired ragged volleys from their column, despite the efforts of the officers to restore order in the ranks of their units. Major Maltzahn, with the grenadier battalion of the *1. Ostpreußisches Infanterie* and two battalions of the *5. Landwehr Infanterie*, stationed in the second line, advanced ahead of the first line and charged with lowered bayonets. *Oberst* Steinmetz and *Oberst* Losthin [Michael Heinrich von Losthin], majors Mumm and Leslie were wounded here; majors Maltzahn and Kosetzki were killed; many officers and soldiers were *hors de combat*, but the *Landwehr*, stepping over the bodies of their comrades, continued to advance; behind them the first line had rallied and rejoined them. The battalions moving on the right flank, through the blazing village of Möckern, drove out the French, who continued to defend themselves in the gardens and behind fences, and pursued them with the assistance of the *Brandenburgisches Husaren*.[16] But every last battalion of Yorck's infantry had already been committed to action; *1. Brigade* and *2. Brigade* had lost many men and were in complete disarray; the Prussian artillery was

---

13 Droysen, III, 154-155; Marmont, V, 178-179; Aster, I, 537-538, states that the detonation of the ammunition caissons occurred somewhat later, namely, during the advance by the Prussian *1. Brigade*.
14 Aster, I, 535.
15 Aster, I, 535.
16 Wagner, II, 87-89; Aster, I, 536-537.

gradually falling silent; while the enemy intensified their devastating cannonade. The outcome of the battle was in the balance. Under such circumstances, the resolute Yorck decided to commit his entire force to the battle. Noticing some wavering in the ranks of the advancing French units, he ordered Major von Sohr [Friedrich Georg Ludwig von Sohr], who was stationed behind Möckern with three squadrons of *Brandenburgisches Husaren*, to hurry into the attack, also sending for the reserve cavalry. Horn's and Hünerbein's brigades, which had not yet closed to close-quarter combat, were ordered to fix bayonets. At the same time, the Commander-in-Chief sent orders for General Sacken's corps to move towards Möckern.

Major von Sohr, closing with the enemy infantry pursuing the Prussian troops through the thick gunpowder smoke, ordered the attack signal to be sounded and charged at the nearest two columns with loud cheers of 'Hurrah!' scattering them and capturing six guns. General Normann quickly moved to engage them with the Württemberg cavalry but was hit in the flank by the *Brandenburgisches Ulanen* and *5. Schlesisches Landwehr Kavallerie*, brought up by the aide-de-camp Reyher [Karl Friedrich Wilhelm Reyher]. The Württemberg cavalry were driven back onto the infantry, several squares were broken and the second line of enemy cavalry (possibly one of the brigades from Lorge's division) were forced to retreat.[17] The hussars captured ten more guns, five ammunition caissons and many prisoners. During a second attack, von Sohr was wounded himself in the right arm by a bullet but remained with his cavalry. Major von Stössel, with two squadrons of *2. Leib Husaren* attached to *1. Brigade*, cut into one of the squares, and then, having encountered enemy cavalry, was forced to retreat, but having quickly rallied his hussars, he attacked the enemy once more, routing their cavalry and captured five guns (other sources state two) and two banners. To his left, *Oberst* Warburg broke a square with the *Mecklenburgisches Husaren*, took their Eagle (*einen Vogel*, as the Prussian hussars reported it) and captured 700 prisoners. The entire vanguard and reserve cavalry, having caught up with the enemy, attacked them under the personal command of Yorck himself. The *1. Westpreußisches* and *National Kavallerie* captured four guns each.[18]

At the same time as Yorck's general cavalry attack on the enemy left wing, the brigades under Horn and Hünerbein charged at the centre and right wing with bayonets fixed; two Russian artillery companies advanced on the end of the left flank, Colonel Bellingshausen's 32nd Battery Company and 33rd Light Company

---

17 Marmont, V, 178, 'I ordered the Württemberg cavalry brigade, commanded by General Normann, to charge this infantry, which presented a vision of the utmost confusion. They initially refused to carry out my orders, and once the moment had passed, there was nothing useful left for me to do. Upon receipt of a second order, however, they moved, but threw themselves at a battalion of the *1er régiment de marine*, routing them instead of charging towards the enemy who had rallied and resumed their advance...' '*Je donnai l'ordre à la brigade de cavalerie wurtembergeoise, commandée par le général Normann de charger cette infanterie présentant à la vue la plus grande confusion. Elle refusa d'abord d'exécuter mes ordres, et le moment passé, il m'y avait plus rien à entreprendre de bien lutile. A l'arrivée du second ordre, elle s'ébranla cependant, mais se jetant sur un bataillon du 1er régiment de marine, le culbuta au lieu de se précipiter sur l'ennemi qui se retablit et recommença son offensive...*'
18 Wagner, II, 90-91; Droysen, III, 160-163 & 165-167; Aster, I, 538-540.

under Colonel Bashmakov [Flegont Mironovich Bashmakov], escorted by the Wilmanstrand Infantry, and two squadrons of *Brandenburgisches Husaren*. Graf Schwerin [Johann Christoph Herrmann von Schwerin], on Horn's orders, having led the *Leib Infanterie* from the second line into the first, charged without firing a shot towards a French battery, with loud cheers of 'Hurrah! Long live the King!' Enemy cavalry raced to engage the Prussian regiment, but Schwerin, paying no attention to them, continued to move forward, forced the cavalry threatening him to fall back behind their infantry, assisted the *Mecklenburgisches Husaren* in their brilliant attack on a square and captured a howitzer. Graf Reichenbach [Christoph Joachim Heinrich von Reichenbach-Goschütz], with a battalion of *Schlesisches Landwehr*, repelled an attack by French cavalry. *8. Brigade*, although it had lost almost all of its commanders, nevertheless, having quickly formed into a single line, attacked the enemy; three French squares were driven back and pursued into the defile at the bridge over the Rietzschke.[19]

On the left wing of the army, comte Langéron had captured the villages of Kleinwiederitzsch and Großwiederitzsch (as has already been mentioned). But then, at about three o'clock in the afternoon, Dąbrowski attacked the Russian force using units from Delmas' division, which was escorting the trains and parks moving from Düben to Leipzig, drove the Russians out of both villages and forced them to retreat back across the river, causing them great harm with their artillery; Lieutenant Colonel Voevodsky of the Staroskol Infantry was killed; the commander of the Arkhangelogorod Infantry, Colonel Shenshin [Vasily Nikanorovich Shenshin] and commander of the 4th Jägers, Lieutenant Colonel Prigara [Pavel Anufrievich Prigara?] were wounded. At the same time, General Olsufiev received orders to position himself on the left wing with 9th Division, at a salient angle to the rest of the force, because a strong column had appeared at Hohenossig from the direction of Düben. The reserve cavalry deployed further to the left, in the direction of the village of Podelwitz. The enemy column spotted on the Düben road was actually the parks and trains of the French *3e Corps*, with a weak escort, moving to join the army; but comte Langéron, unaware of this, considered it necessary to reinforce his left wing, which cost him the opportunity to assist Yorck's corps and separated the forces under Kaptsevich and the comte de Saint-Priest. In order to hold off the enemy advancing behind the left flank, Olsufiev ordered General Udom to occupy a small forest with the 10th Jägers 38th Jägers and the marksmen from the Nasheburg Infantry, Apsheron Infantry and Yakutsk Infantry.[20] Delmas' force attacked them, which forced Olsufiev to bring forwards the 29th Light Artillery Company under Colonel Zasyadko [Alexander Dmitrievich Zasyadko] from the reserve and to reinforce Udom with the Ryazhsk Infantry and Kolyvan Infantry. Very bitter fighting broke out at this location, in which the Ryazhsk Infantry particularly distinguished themselves by capturing a banner from the *125e ligne*.[21] The French were forced to

---

19 Aster, I, 541-542.
20 The Apsheron Infantry had recently joined comte Langéron's corps.
21 [Bogdanovich is mistaken, the Ryazhsk Infantry may have captured a banner, but not from this regiment because the (Dutch) *125e ligne* did not exist in 1813; it was not reformed after its destruction at the Berezina crossing in 1812].

retreat through Seehausen to Plösen and Neutzsch, and crossed there via a footbridge to the left bank of the Parthe. Elements of the French parks and trains were caught by the Cossacks, six guns, about 100 wagons and some 500 prisoners were taken. Generals Langéron and Rudzevich attacked the enemy with the valiant Schlüsselburg Infantry supported by jägers in the villages of Kleinwiederitzsch and Großwiederitzsch, without firing a shot and drove them out into the open, while Emmanuel's cavalry chased them over the Rietzschke. Meanwhile, Dąbrowski attempted to cross this river downstream of the villages and to push Langéron's force away from the corps under the comte de Saint-Priest, but was engaged from Langéron's side by Major General Vasilchikov 3rd, with the Vyatka Infantry, Arkhangelogorod Infantry and 34th Battery Company under Colonel Magdenko [Mikhail Semënovich Magdenko], and from Saint-Priest's side by Major General Bistrom 2nd [Adam Ivanovich Bistrom or Adam Otto Wilhelm von Bistram], with the 1st Jägers and 33rd Jägers, which forced Dąbrowski's division to retreat beyond the Parthe towards Schönefeld; while the units of the French *6e Corps* retreated to Eutritzsch and Gohlis with Lorge's attached cavalry.[22]

At eight o'clock in the evening, Blücher sent one of his orderly officers from the battlefield to the headquarters of the Coalition monarchs via Schkeuditz with the news of the victory. But this officer, riding at night through the marshy Elster floodplains, lost his way, and so the first news of the victory at Möckern was received at the headquarters at three o'clock the following afternoon, from the Commander-in-Chief's aide-de-camp, Colonel Graf Goltz, who was sent together with the Eagle captured from the French.[23]

The Coalition trophies were: an Eagle, three banners (one taken by the Russians), 53 guns (40 taken by the Prussians and 13 by the Russians). 2,000 men were taken prisoner; in addition, the enemy lost no fewer than 67,000 men killed or wounded. Marmont was one of those wounded as were *généraux de division* Compans and Friederichs [Jean-Parfait Friederichs].[24] The Coalition losses were very high, most especially among the Prussian force: Yorck lost 172 officers and 5,508 lower ranks killed or wounded; the field officers killed included Maltzahn, Krosigk [Heinrich Ferdinand von Krosigk], Retkowski [Johannes Franz von Wrycz-Retkowski], Kosetzky, Gädeke [August Hans Friedrich Gädeke], Schleuse [Daniel Gottlob Schleuse] and Wedel. In comte Langéron's corps, there were 1,500 men *hors de combat* overall.[25]

In the opinion of some military commentators, the Coalition could have achieved their objective – the defeat of Marmont's force – more conveniently and with fewer losses if, instead of stubbornly trying to take Möckern, they had launched an attack on the centre or the left wing of the enemy position. If Yorck's corps had succeeded in bypassing Möckern, the French would have been forced to abandon this location,

---

22 War Diary of comte Langéron's corps; Wagner, II, 92-94; Aster, I, 528-531; Marmont, V, 180.
23 Carl von Weiß (Müffling), *Die Feldzüge der Schlesischen Armee*, 84-86.
24 Plotho, II, 392-393; Droysen, III, 169; Aster states that the Coalition took 43 guns, more than 200 wagons, one Eagle and one banner; Marmont, V, 179, admits losing 27 Guns; Vaudoncourt, 210, states that ten guns were lost.
25 Plotho, II, 393; Aster, I, 547.

the further defence of which exposed them to the risk of being pushed back into the Elster. Moreover, by advancing in this direction, Yorck's corps would be in communications with Langéron's corps, and in the event of a reverse, the Army of Silesia could retreat along the Magdeburg road towards the Army of the North, moving towards Landsberg at the time.[26] In all probability, Yorck would have had to change Blücher's dispositions and direction of the main attack along the Halle road, having neither reliable intelligence of the enemy locations nor of the properties of the ground they were holding. During the reconnaissance-in-force carried out in the morning immediately before the battle, the location of elements of the French force at Hohenossig and Podelwitz had been observed. It remained to be decided whether the Army of Silesia should attack the enemy in the positions they occupied, or to head straight towards Leipzig. Hoping for the assistance of the Crown Prince of Sweden and upon the cannonade from Wachau having become audible, Blücher decided to head for Leipzig, yet at the same time, having received news of the advance of the Army of the North towards Halle from Sir Charles Stewart, who had arrived from the prince's headquarters, he amended his intent and attacked the enemy, who, instead of taking up positions at Hohenossig and Podelwitz, had withdrawn to positions between Lindenthal and the Elster. The weakest point of this position, without any doubt, was its right wing, which Blücher himself had directed to be attacked, but General Yorck, instead of assisting Langéron's corps by attacking the enemy centre, having observed the French force on the high ground near Möckern, directed the main attack on this village, and upon being forced to commit half of his corps there, thereby lost the opportunity to attack the centre of the enemy position decisively.[27]

On the evening after the battle, the Army of Silesia army was deployed as follows: Blücher's Hauptquartier was in the village of Großwiederitzsch; Yorck's corps was on the battlefield, forwards of Möckern; Sacken's corps was behind them in reserve, behind Möckern; Langéron's corps was at Wiederitzsch.[28]

At dawn on 5 (17) October, Sacken's corps moved into the front line at Möckern, relieving Yorck's corps, which was withdrawn to Wahren to rest and reorganise after the losses they had suffered. Every two battalions were consolidated into one, and the four brigades were reformed into two divisions: *1. Brigade* and *8. Brigade* became General Hünerbein's *1. Division*, while *2. Brigade* and *7. Brigade* became General Horn's *2. Division*.[29]

The Crown Prince of Sweden, at the insistence of Sir Charles Stewart, sent General Wintzingerode to reinforce Blücher, with all the cavalry from his corps numbering some 5,000 men, who, arriving in Lindenthal on the morning of 5 (17) October, moved on to Taucha in order to seize the bridge on the Parthe there and to establish communications with the Main Army.[30]

Early on the morning of 5 (17) October, Blücher, having arrived at the forward outposts, found that the enemy still held the villages of Eutritzsch and Gohlis,

---

26 Aster, I, 554-555.
27 Carl von Weiß (Müffling), 78-79.
28 War Diary of Sacken's corps; War Diary of Langéron's corps; Plotho, II, 393.
29 Plotho, II, 396.
30 Carl von Weiß (Müffling), 87.

and that their skirmishers were scattered along the upper Rietzschke and were exchanging shots with the Russian jägers. Comte Langéron received orders to place 24 heavy guns forwards of Wiederitzsch, which was carried out immediately under the protection of General Kaptsevich's force. General Vasilchikov moved towards Eutritzsch and enveloped this village with 2nd Hussar Division, several Cossack regiments, and the comte de Saint-Priest's corps, while Sacken's corps moved towards Gohlis. The enemy held out in Eutritzsch but becoming aware of flanking movements by the Russian infantry, retreated to Gohlis, under the protection of Arrighi's *3e corps de cavalerie*, which was positioned on the right wing resting their right flank on the Parthe level with Dąbrowski's infantry at Gohlis. General Sacken attacked the enemy holding this village frontally with the 8th Jägers, Okhotsk Infantry and Kamchatka Infantry under the command of Colonel Rakhmanov [Pëtr Alexandrovich Rakhmanov], and from the [enemy] left flank along the river Elster with the 50th Jägers under Colonel Kologrivov [Alexey Semënovich Kologrivov]; but the enemy fought so stubbornly that at this point Sacken's entire force was committed to action and units from Yorck's corps were sent up to him as reinforcements. The Commander-in-Chief, approaching the right wing of the enemy position, ordered Vasilchikov's hussars to attack the French cavalry. Vasilchikov 2nd's Mariupol Hussars and Akhtyrka Hussars, advancing in column-of-march, without wasting time on forming line, dashed towards the enemy; they were swiftly followed by the Alexandria Hussars and Belorussia Hussars. The enemy engaged them with the most powerful canister fire, yet nothing was able to hold them back. The French cavalry, shaken, retreated behind their infantry towards the [outer] Hallisches Tor. The hussars pursued the French past their infantry and artillery to the bridge itself, taking five guns, and cutting down and capturing cavalry and infantry. Dąbrowski's troops quickly formed square and lashed the bold horsemen with musketry and canister shot. But the Russian hussars completed their brilliant feat and, having surrounded their booty, five guns and some 500 prisoners, they used their weapons to cut their way back to Sacken's force fighting at Gohlis.[31]

This cavalry attack, having played on enemy concerns for their only line of retreat, passing over the bridge on the Parthe at the [outer] Hallisches Tor, hastened the capture of Gohlis by General Sacken. The forces under Marmont and Ney (which had come to his aid), were forced to restrict themselves to holding and defending the Pfaffendorf manor, the Hallische Vorstadt and the fortifications built forwards of it. At the same time, once Blücher had received word from the headquarters of the Coalition sovereigns that the attack on the enemy army had been postponed until 6 (18) October, the corps under Sacken and Yorck, numbering 25,000 men, were positioned facing the aforementioned suburb, while Langéron's corps remained behind them in an over-watch position.[32]

The enemy suffered considerable losses in the cavalry action on 5 (17) October. In particular, they had an unfavourable effect on the morale of the French *7e Corps*, which, having arrived at Taucha at four o'clock in the morning, had set out from there at dawn and, upon reaching the Heiterblick manor [two miles west of Taucha],

---

31 War Diary of Sacken's corps; War Diary of Langéron's corps; Müffling, 88-89; Aster, II, 43-44.
32 Müffling, 90; Aster, II, 44-45.

encountered a mob of troops and transport fleeing from the battlefield.[33] Blücher was delighted with this action. Enthused by memories of his own exploits, he preferred cavalry attacks to every other action, and considered any battle in which cavalry had not taken part as imperfect.[34]

After the fighting at Wachau ended, Prinz Schwarzenberg had intended to renew the battle the following day, but since the expected reinforcements, namely the Austrian corps under Graf Colloredo and Bennigsen's army, had only arrived in the early morning and had a vital need to rest, therefore at a meeting called by the *Feldmarschall* in the village of Sestewitz, it was decided to wait for the arrival of Bennigsen's army and to attack the enemy on 6 (18) October together. Emperor Alexander, upon informing General Bennigsen of this, ordered that he be told that

> the battle scheduled for the following day would be fought on the anniversary of the victory he [Bennigsen] had won at Tarutino, which marked the beginning of the successes of Russian arms, and that the Tsar expected the same tomorrow from his talents and combat experience.[35]

Graf Colloredo's corps arrived at Magdeborn at about 11 o'clock in the morning; the vanguard of Bennigsen's army reached Fuchshain at four o'clock in the afternoon, while the main body was stationed between Naunhof and Fuchshain by late evening; Graf Bubna's division had reached Brandis [two miles south of Machern]; while Count Platov's Cossack detachment, spent the night of 5 to 6 (17 to 18) October at Beucha [four miles north of Naunhof]. The Crown Prince of Sweden, having set out from Landsberg at two o'clock in the morning on 5 (17) October with the main body of his army, arrived at Breitenfeld at eight o'clock in the morning; his vanguard, commanded by General Wintzingerode (as has already been mentioned), had pushed on to Taucha.[36]

On the morning of 5 (17) October, Napoleon was convinced from the reports he had received that significant reinforcements were reaching the Coalition army. In contrast, the only reinforcements available to the French army were Ney's corps, which had not yet managed to take part in the battle, and Reynier's corps, which had not yet arrived, numbering some 30,000 men, of whom several thousand Saxons and Württembergers were already preparing to defect to the Coalition side. Nevertheless, despite both the superiority in numbers of the Coalition armies, and the defeat suffered by French forces at Möckern, Napoleon, wishing to show his readiness to resume the battle, ordered his army to stand to arms at dawn on 5 (17) October. French forces were deployed across the area from the Pleiße to Liebertwolkwitz; sappers had spent the previous night fortifying the Colmberg, and in the morning a 12-pounder battery was brought up there with an escort of Baden troops. As the

---

33 Aster, II, 46-47.
34 Richter, *Geschichte des Deutschen Freiheitskrieges vom Jahre 1813 bis zum Jahre 1815*, II, 261; Varnhagen von Ense, *Leben des Fürsten Blücher von Wahlstadt*, 232.
35 Bernhardi, *Denkwürdigkeiten aus dem Leben Carl Friedrich Grafen von Toll*, III, 445-446; Aster, II, 15 & 20-21.
36 Plotho, II, 397; Aster, II, 19-20 & 23; Bernhardi, III, 446-447.

Coalition also continued to move up without pause throughout 5 (17) October, both sides remained in anticipation of combat. But evening came, and, apart from the cavalry attack on the outer Hallisches Tor, everything remained calm on the fields of Leipzig.[37] Napoleon, with his characteristic insight, had fully assessed the entire situation. It was not difficult for him to be convinced of the need to retreat; but his troops were tired and disordered; it was necessary to somehow rally and put the army in order and await the arrival of Reynier's corps, which was lagging behind. Moreover, having ceded Leipzig, Napoleon could not hold anywhere until the Rhine itself. He would not only have to give up his long-standing dominance over Germany, but to make an even greater sacrifice by leaving a quality force of more than 100,000 men in Danzig and in the fortresses on the Oder and Elbe. And so it was quite natural that, finding himself in such a hopeless situation, Napoleon hesitated and was undecided. Wanting to buy some time, hoping to induce the Coalition into opening negotiations and being prepared to make significant concessions, he thought of sharing his opinions by sending Graf Merveldt, captured the day before, to the headquarters of the Coalition army. At two o'clock in the afternoon of 5 (17) October, Napoleon, having summoned Merveldt to him, spoke flatteringly about the attempt by the Austrians to attack the French army from behind, and then announced to him that, as a sign of his respect, he intended to release him on his word of honour. Then, after asking a few questions about the strength of the Coalition armies, Napoleon admitted that he had not considered them to be so significant.

'Were you aware that I was here with the army?' he asked.

'Without a doubt,' replied Merveldt.

'So you really wanted to give battle with me.'

'Yes, Your Majesty.'

'You were mistaken about my strength; how many men did you calculate that I had?'

'Some 120,000 men.'

'I have 200,000. I have also, in all probability, underestimated your actual strength; how many troops do you have?'

'More than 350,000.'

When Napoleon asked whether the Coalition intended to attack him the following day, Merveldt answered in the affirmative.

'Will this be the end of this war?' Napoleon asked. 'It is time to end it.'

'Sire! Everyone desires it; it was incumbent upon your Majesty to conclude peace at the Prague Congress.'

'They dealt with me unjustly; they were disingenuous (*on a finassé*), they set me an immutable deadline; such an important matter cannot be completed in ten days. Austria has missed the opportunity to be pre-eminent in European affairs; I would have done everything according to the wishes of the Austrian government, and we could have obliged everyone to obey our will.'

---

37 Aster, II, 27-28.

'I do not dare to conceal from Your Majesty that in Austria, French dominance is feared most of all.'

'But someone needs to open negotiations; let them leave it to Austria! Russia is under the influence of England, which does not want peace at all.'

General Merveldt replied that he did not know the views of the Austrian government, but that it would undoubtedly negotiate only in concert with the Coalition. With regard to Napoleon's criticism of Britain, Merveldt noted that they needed peace themselves, but wanted the terms of the peace treaty to guarantee their status.

'What do you think these guarantees might comprise?' asked Napoleon.

'A balance of power between the European states, which would put limits on the dominance of France.'

'Let England return the islands to me; I would return Hanover to her, I would renounce the departments annexed to France, I would give up the Hanseatic cities.'

'I believe, Sire, that the Coalition would wish for the restoration of Holland.'

'Oh! Holland cannot exist independently; it would become dependent upon England.'

'It seems to me that the policies adopted by the British government were a consequence of the war and would end with it. In that case, your Majesty would have no reason to seek the retention of Holland.'

Napoleon expressed great readiness for peace. 'I would make concessions, and still greater ones,' he said, 'but there are things which are dear to my honour, and which, especially in my position, I cannot give up: for example, the Protectorate of Germany.'[38]

'Your Majesty is well aware that such French influence over Germany is contrary to the restoration of the balance of power in Europe, and therefore it cannot be assumed that it would be supported in a treaty of peace. Our relations with Bavaria and other members of the *Confédération du Rhin*, the necessary occupation of Saxony by our forces: these have all deprived your Majesty of some of your allies, and we are confident that our decisive superiority will oblige others to follow their example.'

'Oh! Those who do not want my patronage may do whatever they want. They will have cause to repent, but honour does not allow me to give up the title of Protector for the remainder.'

'Your Majesty once considered it essential for the peace of Europe that France be separated from the other major European Powers by a number of small independent states. Observance of this basic principle would ensure the prosperity of Europe.'

Napoleon, after a moment's silence, said: 'Very well, we shall see, but all this would not lead to peace; how is it possible to negotiate with the English, who want me to have no more than 30 ships of the line?'

General Merveldt replied that 'such demands from England could have arisen from concerns at the French occupation of a vast coastline from the North Sea to the Adriatic, and that concessions in Italy would have reassured Europe and, being considered a generous sacrifice by the French government, would have led to the

---

38 '... mais il y a des choses aux quelles mon honneur tient, et dont surtout dans ma position je ne saurais me départir: par exemple le Protectorat de l'Allemagne.'

rejection of demands for any restrictions on the fleet incompatible with the dignity of France.'

Napoleon agreed that such a concession would be less onerous. 'But, in any case,' he said, 'I will never allow the old order to be restored in Italy. This country must be united into a single state.'

'Your Majesty would probably have to renounce the Duchy of Warsaw.'

'Indeed, I offered that, but my concession was not accepted.'

'Spain might also provide grounds for dispute.'

'No! Spanish affairs are a dynastic matter.'

'That is quite true, but I believe that the belligerent parties cannot agree on which dynasty.'

'I have been forced to abandon Spain, therefore the matter has already been decided.'

'And so, evidently, we can make peace.'

'Well then, send me one of your trusted people and we shall settle the matter. I stand accused of always proposing armistices, therefore I shall not propose one, although it would serve the common good. Perhaps I should retreat behind the Saale, the Russians and Prussians behind the Elbe; you to Bohemia, and unfortunate Saxony, having suffered such destruction, should remain neutral.'

'Saxony supplies our army with provisions, and besides, we have the advantage in numbers, and we are hopeful that Your Majesty will retreat even behind the Rhine this autumn.'

'For that to occur, I must lose this battle; that may come to pass, but it has not happened yet…'

Napoleon, upon releasing Merveldt, gave him a letter addressed to the Austrian Kaiser.[39] There was no response, indeed, there could not be one. The Coalition Sovereigns had resolutely decided to reject any request from the *Empereur des Français* for a separate peace. The Russian and Prussian monarchs did not want to stop fighting until such time as the Coalition had undoubted guarantees of victory. The successful operations by their forces after the armistice had completely changed the situation. The German princes, and even Kaiser Franz himself, despite the ancestral pride of the House of Habsburg, tacitly recognised Emperor Alexander as the Agamemnon of the European Coalition. Prussia, recently weakened and humiliated by the proud conqueror, had acquired a decisive voice in all matters of the German community through the prudence of its Sovereign and the courage of its population. The ruling princes sought the patronage of the Prussian heroes, who often made them aware of the pre-eminence of their fatherland. A few days before the battle of Leipzig, at a conference for Yorck's entire General Staff attended by the Erbprinz von Hessen, who was a volunteer with the Prussian corps, the prince, turning to General Hünerbein, asked: 'is it too much to hope that, in the event of a successful end to the war, the territories would be returned to my father, who has donated such significant sums for the liberation of Germany?' Hünerbein replied: '… if it were up to me, Your Highness would receive less land than I have dirt under my fingernails.'

---

39 Bernhardi, III, 445 & 521-524.

When the prince wanted to know Yorck's own opinion, he was told in response that 'Hünerbein should have expressed himself more diplomatically.'[40]

Napoleon, having received no reply to his message, at seven o'clock in the evening, finally decided to retreat, but instead of leaving his position that evening and withdrawing beyond the Elster defiles at night, he postponed the retreat until the following morning. Marshal Ney received orders to send Bertrand's corps, reinforced by Guilleminot's division (7e Corps) with a 12-pounder battery, to Lützen; orders were issued to send all the parks past the choke-points at night, along the same route; the units stationed at Wachau withdrew a short distance and took up a less extensive position between the Pleisse and the Parthe. Napoleon intended to make a further withdrawal beyond the Elster the following day within sight of the Coalition, in the hope that they, content with that, would 'build him a golden bridge:'[41] this withdrawal would thus have the appearance of an unforced movement, which counted for a lot in the eyes of Napoleon and would serve to maintain, at least for a short time, his power over the Members of the *Confédération du Rhin*. The executor of this concept, Berthier, concerned about giving the regiments a pretext to retreat from the army, did not take all the precautions that were necessary for the situation at that time. Thus, the construction of bridges and the advance deployment of reserve artillery, parks and supply trains were overlooked. Some of the parks assigned to Weißenfels and Freyburg were turned back towards Leipzig, because, as Berthier assured them, the Emperor was absolutely anxious to resume offensive operations.[42]

Napoleon and his *chef d'état major* were equally mistaken about the Coalition. Having held out at Güldengossa, having won at Möckern, being reinforced the next day with more than 100,000 men, they wanted to fight, being certain of success. The Crown Prince of Sweden himself, who had hitherto avoided active participation in the struggle between Europe and France, was enthused by the general belligerence of his fellow combatants. Both the Russian and Prussian generals had not concealed their doubts about the prince's devotion to the common cause; the Swedes themselves, having reached the open ground at Breitenfeld, where the memories of the valour of their ancestors called them on to new feats with every step, expressed to the prince through the Chief-of-Staff of their corps, General Adlercreutz, a desire to test themselves against the French. Yielding to general opinion, but still not intending to operate independently, the Crown Prince proposed to Blücher that he should cross to the left bank of the Parthe with the troops of the Army of Silesia, while he wanted to remain north of Leipzig himself with his entire army. But Blücher would not agree to this, and at a conference in Breitenfeld, on the night of 5 to 6 (17 to 18) October, both commanders, in the presence of Prinz Wilhelm, the brother of the King of Prussia, agreed that the Army of the North should cross the Parthe and be reinforced by 30,000 men from the Army of Silesia. Blücher agreed to this, at the request of the Crown Prince of Sweden, not wanting to give him any reason to

---

40 Droysen, III, 130, '... *geht es nach meinen Willen, so bekommen Ew. Hoheit nicht so viel zurück, als Schmutz unter meinem Nagel ist.*'
41 '*Il faut faire un pont d'or à un ennemi qui se retire.*' was one of the old principles of war.
42 Aster, II, 33; Thiers, XVI, 655.

avoid participating in a general battle, and having assigned Langéron's corps, which constituted half of the Army of Silesia, to assist the prince, he intended to cross over to the left bank of the Parthe himself together with these troops, where, in all likelihood, the fate of the battle was to be decided. He had only just returned to Eutritzsch on the morning of 6 (18) October when the cannonade rang out along the entire length of the arc around Leipzig held by the French. This was the beginning of the Battle of Nations for the independence of Germany and Europe.[43]

---

43 Müffling, 92-94; Varnhagen von Ense, 234-238.

Appendix XXXIV

Composition and deployment of Coalition forces at Möckern

In support of the assault on Möckern, *7. Brigade* and *8. Brigade* were deployed in battalion column in two waves:

The first wave of *7. Brigade* consisted of: first battalion of *15. Landwehr*, two battalions of *4. Landwehr* and the *Thüringisches Bataillon*; in the second: the *Leib Infanterie*, second battalion of *15. Landwehr*; four squadrons of *Landwehr Kavallerie*; *3. Batterie*.

The first wave of *8. Brigade*: second and third battalions of *Brandenburgisches Infanterie* and third battalion of *12. Reserve Infanterie*; in the second: first battalion of *12. Reserve Infanterie* and a battalion of *Landwehr*; two squadrons of *Brandenburgisches Husaren*; *15. Batterie*.

For a total for both brigades of: 13 battalions, six squadrons and 16 guns, numbering 7,000 men (Wagner, II, 83 & 97).

2. Brigade were also deployed in two waves:

The first wave consisted of: the fusilier battalion of *1.* were also deployed in two waves: *Infanterie* and a mixed battalion from *2. Ostpreußisches Infanterie*; in the second were: two musketeer battalions of *1. Ostpreußisches Infanterie* and a *Landwehr* battalion deployed as skirmishers. The brigade included four squadrons of *Mecklenburgisches Husaren* and *1. Batterie*.

1. Brigade were also deployed in two waves:

In the first wave were: three battalions of *13. Landwehr* and the *Schlesisches Grenadiere*; in the second were: three battalions of *5. Landwehr* and the *Ostpreußisches Grenadiere*. The brigade included two squadrons of *2. Leib Husaren* and *2. Batterie*.

For a total for both brigades of: 13 battalions, six squadrons and 16 guns, numbering 7,000 men.

The reserve cavalry commanded by *Oberst* Jürgaß consisted of: the *Litthauisches Dragoner*, *Westpreußisches Dragoner* and *Neumärkisches Landwehr*, for a total of 13 squadrons, with *1. Reitende Batterie* and *3. Reitende Batterie*, numbering 1,500 men (Wagner, II, 86, 88 & 96-97).

The cavalry vanguard commanded by *Oberst* Katzler consisted of: two squadrons of *2. Leib Husaren*, three squadrons of *Brandenburgisches Husaren*, the *Brandenburgisches Ulanen*, *Ostpreußisches National Kavallerie* and *5. Landwehr*, for a total of 18 squadrons with *2. Reitende Batterie*, numbering 1,800 men (Wagner, II, 96).

Plan of the Battle of Leipzig, 6 (18) October 1813.

APPENDIX XXXIV

Legend to Map No. 15

Coalition Forces
1. Platov's Cossacks
2. Graf Bubna's Austrian *leichte Division*
3. Kreutz's detachment
4. Prince Khovansky's 12th Division
5. Paskevich's 26th Division
6. Hohenlohe's Austrian division
7. Mayer's & Baumgarten's Austrian divisions
8. Austrian *Prinz Coburg Infanterie* & 12-pounder battery
9. Abele's Austrian brigade (Mayer's division)
10. Zieten's Prussian *11. Brigade*
11. Prussian battery
12. Lieutenant General Pahlen's cavalry
13. Prince Gorchakov's I Corps
14. Prinz Eugen von Württemberg's II Corps
15. Kleist's corps
16. 2nd Grenadier Division
17. 3rd Cuirassier Division & Lifeguard Light Cavalry Division
18. 2nd Cuirassier Division & two squadrons of Lubny Hussars
19. Prussian reserve cavalry
20. Russo-Prussian Guard Infantry, 1st Cuirassier Division & Prussian Guard cavalry
21. Wimpffen's Austrian division
22. Hardegg's Austrian *leichte Division*
23. Greth's Austrian division

25. Bianchi's Austrian division
27. Austrian cavalry
29. Giffing's Austrian brigade
31. Beck's Austrian brigade
33. Advance by the Swedes to Plaußig
35. Langéron's corps
37. Rudzevich's vanguard & Emmanuel's cavalry
39. Langéron's battery
41. Bülow's corps
43. Sacken's corps
45. Prussian battery
47. Prinz Hessen-Homburg's Prussian brigade
49. Colonel Dietrich's two Russian heavy batteries & British Rocket Battery
51. Borstell's Prussian brigade
53. Wintzingerode's force
55. Manteuffel's & O'Rourke's cavalry

French Forces
a.a. Prince Poniatowski's *8e Corps*
b.b. General Semellé's force
c.c. *4e corps de cavalerie*
d.d. *2e Divsion* of the *Jeune Garde*
e.e. Augereau's reserve corps
f.f. Victor's *2e Corps*
g.g. *5e corps de cavalerie*
h.h. *1er corps de cavalerie*
i.i. Macdonald's *11e Corps*
k.k. Lauriston's *5e Corps*
l.l. *2e corps de cavalerie*
m.m. Nansouty's *cavalerie de la Garde*
n.n. *Vieille Garde*
o.o. Saxon division (Reynier's *7e Corps*)
p.p. Durutte's division (Reynier's *7e Corps*)
q.q. Ney's *3e Corps*
r.r. Marmont's *6e Corps*
s.s. Defrance's cavalry division
t.t. Fournier's cavalry division
u.u. Lefebvre-Desnouettes' cavalry

v.v. Ricard's division (*3e Corps*)

Coalition Forces
24. Alois Liechtenstein's Austrian division
26. Weissenwolf's Austrian division
28. Austrian cavalry
30. Two Austrian batteries
32. Advance by the Swedes to Plaußig
34. Advance by the Swedes to Plaußig
36. Russian 36-gun heavy battery
38. Artillery from Rudzevich's vanguard
40. Part of Kaptsevich's X Corps
42. Graf Stedingk's Swedish corps
44. Yorck's corps
46. Russo-Prussian battery
48. Oppen's Prussian reserve cavalry
50. Coalition attack on Paunsdorf
52. Krafft's Prussian brigade
54. Count Vorontsov's force
56. Russo-Swedish battery

41

The Battle of Leipzig, 6 (18) October 1813 (continued)

Withdrawal of the French army to the position at Probstheida. – Deployment of Napoleon's forces. – Their strength. – Coalition orders for the attack on the enemy positions; composition of the columns and strength of the Coalition forces.

The course of the battle from dawn until two o'clock in the afternoon. Platov's move to the Eilenburg road, Garf Bubna's move towards Mölkau, Bennigsen's move towards the Colmberg and onwards towards Holzhausen and Zuckelhausen; the enemy retreat to Probstheida and Stötteritz. – The advance of Barclay de Tolly's force to Liebertwolkwitz and Wachau; the enemy retreat to Probstheida. – The advance by the Erbprinz zu Hessen-Homburg along the Pleiße; the enemy switch to a counter-attack; the move by Gyulay's corps and elements of the Russian reserves to assist Prinz Homburg. – Napoleon's initial orders. – Deployment of the Saxon contingent. – Crossing to the left bank of the Parthe by Langéron's corps. – The first attack on Schönefeld. – Part of the Saxon contingent and Normann's Württemberg brigade defect to the Coalition. – Crossing of the Parthe by the Army of the North. – Sacken's attack on Pfaffendorf.

The course of the battle from two o'clock in the afternoon until the end of the fighting. Bülow's offensive. – The Saxon division defects to the Coalition side; strength of the Saxon force. – Movement of French reserves to assist Ney. – The enemy retreat to Stötteritz. – Barclay's attempt to seize Probstheida. – Napoleon's arrangements for the defence of that location. – Operations by the Austrians on the left wing of the Army of Bohemia. – Operations by Sacken north of Leipzig. – Departure of Yorck's corps to Merseburg. – Langéron's attempt to seize Schönefeld. – The advance by the Army of the North; operations by the Russian cavalry. – The capture of Schönefeld by the Russians. – The conference of the Coalition commanders. – Proposals for operations on the following day.

Napoleon decides to retreat. – Dispositions of forces on both sides during the night of 6 to 7 (18 to 19) October. – Leipzig during the battle. Napoleon's intention to fight the following day; the real reasons for his retreat. – The number of projectiles expended during the battle of Leipzig.

Napoleon, having decided to retreat to Probstheida and to take up positions in the vicinity of this village, withdrew his army on the night of 5 to 6 (17 to 18) October. The units withdrew from their previous positions in pouring rain, leaving forward outposts to maintain the camp fires and to delay the Coalition. Napoleon set off in a carriage himself from his overnight halt in the village of Stötteritz at two o'clock in the morning, through the bivouacs of the *Vieille Garde*, in the direction of Probstheida; in the vicinity of this village, the French artillery were burning ammunition caissons at the time, which, due to a shortage of horses, they could not take with them, and since some of the caissons still contained projectiles, detonations were happening constantly. Napoleon turned back towards Reudnitz, wanting to find Ney, found him and his entire staff still sleeping, went on to Lindenau via Leipzig, ordering Bertrand to go to Weißenfels with *4e Corps* and returned to Stötteritz at about eight o'clock in the morning. At this time the French forces were deployed as follows:[1] the right wing of the army, having changed front with its left flank refused, was located between Connewitz and Probstheida, namely: Prince Poniatowski, promoted to Marshal the day before, remained on the extreme right wing with *8e Corps*, resting on the Pleiße at Connewitz and Lößnig; elements of Augereau's reserve corps were stationed to the left of Poniatowski's force, while the remainder held the scrub between Dölitz and Lößnig; Kellerman's *4e corps de cavalrie* were the reserves for this force, supported by the cavalry from Dąbrowski's division, commanded by General Krukowiecki [Jan Krukowiecki], and Oudinot with *2e Division* of the *Jeune Garde*. To Oudinot's left were the units of Victor's *2e Corps*, stationed as far as Probstheida, with *5e corps de cavalerie* behind them. Mortier had also been assigned to support Victor with two divisions of the *Jeune Garde*, but he was subsequently ordered to relieve Bertrand in Lindenau. *1er corps de cavalerie* were deployed behind the village of Stötteritz. All the corps listed on the right wing of the army were under Murat's overall command. In the centre were: Macdonald's *11e Corps* at Holzhausen, with Lauriston's *5e Corps* behind them, forwards of Stötteritz; *2e corps de cavalerie* were between Holzhausen and Baalsdorf. On the left wing, under Ney's overall command, were: the Saxon division of Reynier's *7e Corps* at Paunsdorf and Heiterblick; Durutte's French division from this same corps, was between Paunsdorf and Schönefeld; elements of Souham's *3e Corps* and Marmont's *6e Corps* initially occupied the left bank of the Parthe from Schönefeld to Cleuden; and later, once units of the Army of the North had outflanked this position on the right, they changed front with the right flank refused; *6e Corps* were stationed at the end of the left wing, at Schönefeld, *3e Corps* to their right, and *3e corps de cavalerie* behind them, in reserve. Nansouty's

---

1 See Map No. 15, Plan of the Battle of Leipzig, 6 (18) October 1813.

cavalerie de la Garde were to the left of Stötteritz while the *Vieille Garde* were to the right of this village as the general reserve. Finally, Dąbrowski's division held the Pfaffendorf and Rosental manors to the north of the city. The strength of Napoleon's forces assembled on the left bank of the Parthe, between this river and the Pleiße, amounted to 108,000 men, while together with Dąbrowski's division and the Leipzig garrison, to 150,000 men.[2]

Coalition orders for the attack on the enemy on 6 (18) October were as follows:

The Army of Bohemia assembled on the right bank of the Pleiße (excluding Gyulay's corps, who were to remain on the left bank of the Elster, and Lederer's division, between the Elster and the Pleiße), and supported by formations under Bennigsen and Graf Colloredo to the sum of 150,000 men, were to advance in three main columns: the left, commanded by the Erbrinz zu Hessen-Homburg, from Dölitz and Dösen; the centre under Barclay de Tolly, from Wachau and Liebertwolkwitz towards Probstheida; the right under General Bennigsen, from Holzhausen and Baalsdorf towards Zweinaundorf.[3] The Coalition sovereigns at the beginning of the battle were on the Galgenberg, east of Wachau, and later on the high ground north of Liebertwolkwitz, near the old brick factory, which has since been renamed the Monarchenhügel.[4]

The formations of the Army of the North, numbering 58,000 men, set out from Breitenfeld at nine o'clock in the morning and moved towards Plaußig, Seegeritz, Grassdorf and Taucha, where they were to cross the Parthe. Langéron's corps with Saint-Priest's force, 25,000 in total, headed towards Mokau with the same objective, where a bridge had been hastily laid, and towards Plösen, but later elements of Langéron's force crossed the river by fording. Meanwhile, the Crown Prince of Sweden sent orders for Langéron to head for Taucha and cross at this point, which would have caused him to lose at least four hours, but Blücher, who was accompanying units of the Russian corps at the time, replied to the prince that General Langéron would come under his command on the left bank of the Parthe, at Abtnaundorf, and ordered the corps to continue its move towards Mokau without halting.[5] The remaining corps of the Army of Silesia, Sacken's and Yorck's, numbering 25,000 men, were to advance on Leipzig from the direction of Gohlis and Eutritzsch;

---

2   Schulz, *Geschichte der Kriege in Europa seit dem Jahre 1792*, XI, 1 Band, 117-118; Aster, *Die Schlachten bei Leipzig im October 1813*, II, 73-77.
3   Schulz, XI, Band I, 119-120, the composition of the columns in the Army of Bohemia was:
      Left – 19,800 men in Colloredo's corps; 15,400 in the Erbprinz's corps; 8,400 in Alois von Liechtenstein's division; numbering 43,600 Austrians;
      Centre – 8,400 men in Prince Gorchakov's and Prinz Eugen von Württemberg's corps, Lieutenant General Count Pahlen's cavalry and those commanded by Count Wittgenstein; 9,800 men from Kleist's Prussian corps of Klüx's, Pirch's and Prinz August's brigades, with Röder's reserve cavalry; 28,900 men in the Russo-Prussian reserves, for a total of 47,100 men, of whom 32,600 were Russian and 14,500 were Prussian;
      Right – 28,000 men from the Army of Poland; 23,500 men from Klenau's corps and Bubna's division; 5,000 men from Zieten's brigade; 3,000 men from Platov's detachment, for a total of 59,500 men, of whom 31,000 were Russian, 23,500 were Austrians and 5,000 were Prussians.
4   Aster, II, 78.
5   Varnhagen von Ense, *Leben des Fürsten Blücher von Wahlstadt*, 238-239; Aster, II, 82.

Gyulay's corps, numbering 18,000, from the direction of Lindenau. Therefore, the Coalition had 280,000 men on the battlefield that day.⁶

The fighting on 6 (18) October, for the sake of convenience, may be divided into two parts:

1. From dawn until two o'clock in the afternoon.
2. From two o'clock in the afternoon until nightfall.

In the course of the first part of the battle, the main army and Army of Poland, having occupied the area where the enemy advanced outposts had been, approached Probstheida and Zweinaundorf, while the Army of the North crossed the Parthe with Langéron's corps and moved towards Schönefeld and Paunsdorf. The second part of the battle includes: the attacks by the main army and Army of Poland on Probstheida and Zweinaundorf, the defection of the Saxon forces to the Coalition side, the attack by the Army of Silesia on Pfaffendorf, the arrival of the Army of the North on the battlefield, the attacks by this army and Langéron's corps on the left wing of the French position, the attempts by the Coalition to seize the villages of Probstheida and Stötteritz and the measures taken by the enemy at the end of the battle to defend the positions they still occupied.⁷

The course of the battle from dawn until two o'clock in the afternoon

Operations by Platov's Cossack detachment and Bennigsen's army

At three o'clock in the morning, Platov, who was on the extreme right wing of the Army of Poland, set off from Zweenfurth [one mile east of Althen], crossed the Wurzen road and, having reached the Eilenburg road, linked up with General Emmanuel's patrols. The unexpected appearance of Cossacks caused great alarm in the enemy trains stationed between Sommerfeld and Mölkau. Graf Bubna, at three o'clock in the morning, advanced from Machern through Brandis to Beucha [four miles south-west of Machern], in order to cross the Parthe there and close the gap to the right flank of the Army of Poland, but because floodwaters that had arisen from the rain had washed away the bridge, the troops were forced to cross the river via a ford more than two feet deep; the guns were also moved across by fording, while the ammunition caissons crossed via the bridge at Borsdorf [two miles east of Sommerfeld]. At eight o'clock in the morning, Graf Bubna's division, having completed the crossing, advanced towards Mölkau. The formations of the Army of Poland were directed as follows: General Kreutz's detachment from Kleinpösna towards Baalsdorf, followed by Count Stroganov's vanguard and Chaplits' cavalry

---

6 Coalition forces taking part in the fighting on 6 (18) October were: 43,600 men with the Erbprinz zu Hessen-Homburg; 47,100 with General Barclay de Tolly; 59,500 with General Bennigsen; 83,000 with the Crown Prince of Sweden and General the comte de Langéron; 25,000 with generals Sacken and Yorck; 18,000 with Graf Gyulay; 4,000 in General Lederer's division, for a total of 280,200 men.
7 Aster, II, 87-88.

[Yefim Ignatievich Chaplits]; General Dokhturov was to envelope Holzhausen from Kleinpösna with 26th Division and 12th Division; Klenau's corps was to envelope both flanks of the Culmberg and take this high ground together with Ivanov's 13th Division and Zieten's brigade.[8] Overall, Bennigsen, wanting to establish communications with the Crown Prince as quickly as possible, extended his army over a considerable front.

Bennigsen's force, having set off from their overnight halt before dawn, had reached Seifertshain at seven o'clock in the morning; by this time the enemy had already abandoned the Colmberg. The units under Kreutz and Count Stroganov captured Baalsdorf almost without resistance. At the same time, Klenau was moving towards Holzhausen, while Zieten was on the way to Zuckelhausen; the capture of these villages was vital for securing further operations by Bennigsen's column. Holzhausen was occupied by Marchand's division, made up of contingents from Hessen-Darmstadt and Baden, while Zuckelhausen was held by Charpentier's French division. In front of the villages and on the high ground of the Steinberg there were strong batteries; Gérard's division were stationed behind the Steinberg; in the space between the villages there was a dense screen of skirmishers lying in wait in a ravine. Graf Klenau, approaching the enemy position, advanced several batteries under the protection of the *Liechtenstein Infanterie*, *Hohenzollern Chevaulegers* and *Kaiser Kürassiere*. After a fairly strong cannonade, General De Best [Adalbert Johann De Best] and his *Württemberg Infanterie* and *Kerpen Infanterie* attacked Holzhausen, while General Abele advanced to storm Zuckelhausen with the *Liechtenstein Infanterie* and Zieten's brigade. The enemy stubbornly defended Holzhausen, and although the Austrians broke into this village, they were nevertheless ejected from there; the French also reoccupied Baalsdorf. Bennigsen supported the Austrians with the Narva Infantry and 45th Battery Company under Colonel Begunov; this force, subsequently reinforced by the remaining regiments from 12th Division, with the 47th Light Artillery Company and 55th Light Artillery Company, and both regiments from Major General Ivanov's 13th Division, with half of 10th Horse Artillery Company, forced the French to completely evacuate the village by two o'clock in the afternoon. Because the enemy continued to stubbornly defend the positions they held, General Paskevich was sent to their flank towards the Steinberg with 26th Division. The French opened a heavy cannonade which caused considerable damage to the advancing columns; among the wounded was General Lindfors [Fëdor Andreevich Lindfors or Axel Friedrich Lindfors], whose leg was severed by round shot. Sébastiani's cavalry then raced up to attack 12th Division, but were repelled by the Smolensk Infantry and Narva Infantry, which particularly distinguished themselves and captured two guns. The Austrian cavalry, led by Graf Klenau in person, pursued the enemy retreating from Holzhausen to Steinberg and captured three guns. The French retreat also forced the Baden and Hessen-Darmstadt troops to withdraw towards the Steinberg. Kreutz's detachment, supported by some of Chaplits' cavalry, commanded by General Dekhtyarev, and three squadrons of Penza *Opolchenia* Cossacks under Colonel Bezobrazov [Lavrenty

---

8   General Bennigsen's War Diary (Log of Incoming Documents, No. 1,822); Hofmann, *Zur Geschichte des Feldzuges von 1813, Zweite Auflage*, 291-292; Aster, II, 90-97.

Afanasievich Bezobrazov], having passed through the village of Zweinaundorf, occupied by Stroganov's force, engaged in a ferocious melee with enemy cuirassiers. The French batteries inflicted great damage on our cavalry, but were disrupted by the fire of 56th Light Artillery Company under Lieutenant Colonel Taube [Maxim Maximovich Taube or Magnus von Taube]. Here, the Combined Dragoon Regiment, under the command of Colonel Klebeck, particularly distinguished themselves by saving the 1st Light Artillery Company under Lieutenant Colonel Shishkin, which was under attack from Walther's *cavalerie de la Garde*. The enemy force holding the Steinberg, worried that they might be cut off, retreated towards Probstheida. Taking advantage of this, Bennigsen ordered several Austrian batteries and two Russian heavy artillery companies to be deployed onto this high ground, who immediately opened fire on the enemy units and batteries retreating to Stötteritz. On the extreme right wing, Graf Bubna's division captured Paunsdorf, but was ejected from there by troops from Durutte's division of *7e Corps*.[9]

Operations by Barclay de Tolly's force

At seven o'clock in the morning, Count Wittgenstein's corps formed up for battle between Güldengossa and the Universitäts Waldung; to their left stood Kleist's force; while the grenadiers, Guard, and Russian cuirassiers remained in reserve. The Coalition monarchs and the Commander-in-Chief, proceeding step-by-step behind the advancing troops, positioned themselves on high ground to the right of the Monarchenhügel, from where they could conveniently observe the progress of the battle. At eight o'clock, Prince Gorchakov moved towards Liebertwolkwitz with I Corps, Prinz Eugen von Württemberg moved into the space between Liebertwolkwitz and Wachau with II Corps; Kleist advanced directly towards Wachau with three brigades from his corps; Lieutenant General Count Pahlen maintained communications between the columns under Bennigsen and Barclay with his light cavalry and 2nd Cuirassier Division. The weather had turned clear after several rainy days; the units advanced quickly, with drums beating and bands playing. The enemy forward detachments, having delayed Kleist's advance at Meusdorf, fell back to the main position. At about ten o'clock, Wittgenstein's force, having engaged the French beyond Liebertwolkwitz, opened a strong cannonade on them, but were ordered to halt in anticipation of the ongoing advance of the columns under Bennigsen and the Prinz zu Hessen-Homburg. The attack on the village of Probstheida, with its many solidly-built masonry buildings and enclosures, presented extreme difficulties. The enemy, convinced of the paramount importance of this location, the loss of which would oblige them to abandon the defence of the occupied positions and retreat to Leipzig, strongly garrisoned the buildings, gardens and enclosures in the village with infantry, placed abundant reserves behind them and set up large batteries on either side of Probstheida, covering every approach to the village under crossfire. In the meantime, because the force under the Prinz zu Homburg, advancing on the left wing along the Pleiße river, had been repelled with losses, while Bennigsen's army had not yet managed to come level with the force under Barclay de Tolly, which

---

9 General Bennigsen's War Diary; Plotho, *Der Krieg in Deutschland und Frankreich in den Jahren 1813 und 1814*, II, 407-409; Hofmann, 291-292; Aster, II, 90-97.

had pushed forward, the Coalition monarchs ordered his columns to halt. At this location the battle was limited to a cannonade and skirmishing until two o'clock in the afternoon. General Count Pahlen was ordered to attack the enemy, who were retreating in disorder from Holzhausen towards Stötteritz. His cavalry raced forwards, ignoring the intense fire from the enemy batteries stationed at Probstheida, but did not manage to cut off their infantry, and only some of its accompanying artillery was captured by the Grodno Hussars.[10]

Operations by the Prinz zu Hessen-Homburg's force

The Austrian force under the Prinz zu Hessen-Homburg, having formed up for battle at Markkleeberg at the same time as the force under Barclay de Tolly, had orders to remain on the defensive, yet as soon as the enemy withdrawal from Wachau was observed, the Austrians immediately moved into the area between Dösen and Lößnig, resting their left flank on the Pleiße and maintaining communications with Kleist's froce advancing towards Probstheida on their right flank: Bianchi's division were in the front line, Weissenwolf's division in the support line, the cavalry behind them, and finally the reserves of Alois Liechtenstein's division and Graf Colloredo's *I. Korpus*. The force under Prince Poniatowski holding Dölitz, Dösen and Lößnig were driven back, but Napoleon, who was at the Quandtsche Tabaksmühle [now marked by the Napoleonstein] south of Thonberg at the time, having observed the Coalition successes, immediately sent two divisions of the *Jeune Garde* commanded by Marshal Oudinot to shore up his right wing. The battle resumed with extraordinary ferocity; the casualties on both sides were very high, and the Prinz zu Hessen-Homburg was himself among the wounded. Graf Nostitz, who had taken over command of the force, was obliged to cede the aforementioned villages to the enemy; the entire Austrian reserve had already been committed to action. The Commander-in-Chief, concerned about the dubious course of the action at this point, sent *Hauptmann* Adelstein of the General Staff to General Gyulay, with verbal orders to go to Cröbern in order to assist the force fighting on the right bank of the Pleiße. Gyulay's move towards Cröbern was carried out at the same time that the French corps under Bertrand, having been relieved by two divisions of the *Jeune Garde* commanded by Mortier, were advancing from Lindenau towards Markranstädt. Thus the only line of retreat to the Rhine was exposed to the enemy. In 1820, Schwarzenberg subsequently justified the arrangements he had made, saying that it was not necessary to push an enemy who had retained significant forces to extremes; but having accepted such a conclusion, it would have been necessary to willingly renounce any opportunity to inflict significant damage on the enemy. Many have attempted to excuse the errors of the Coalition Commander-in-Chief as the policy of the Viennese Cabinet, which wanted to weaken rather than destroy Napoleon's regime. In any case, the movement prescribed to Gyulay was useless, because he could not arrive on the right bank of the Pleiße in time and spent the whole day in pointless marches, having squandered the opportunity to operate

---

10 Barclay de Tolly's diary (Archive of the M.T.D. No. 29,188); Prinz Eugen von Württemberg's diary (Archive of the M.T.D. No. 47,344); Plotho, II, 402-405; Beitzke, *Geschichte der deutschen Freiheitskriege in den Jahren 1813 und 1814*, II, 602-605; Aster, II, 98-102.

decisively on the lines of communications of the enemy army. Only Csollich's brigade managed to reach Gautzsch, and even then the danger had already passed. Elements of the Russian reserves were also sent to assist the Austrians (namely, 2nd Grenadier Division and 3rd Cuirassier Division), but by then a general offensive by the Coalition had forced the enemy to pay exclusive attention to defending the positions they held.[11]

Napoleon's initial orders

During the general advance by the Army of Bohemia and Army of Poland, Napoleon was on the high ground at the Quandtsche Tabaksmühle windmill south of Thonberg. The *Vieille Garde* also moved across to there. After resting for a few minutes on the bare ground, he mounted his horse again and rode forward to the *artillerie de la Garde* pushed up to the high ground near the village of Probstheida. The cannonade was continually gaining in intensity; several round shot flew over Napoleon's head and over Berthier and Murat, who were accompanying him. Having observed the Coalition preparations for an attack, he ordered the *2e Division* of the *Vieille Garde* to form up in column and placed them behind the batteries. The Saxon and Westphalian Guard battalions were sent to assist Poniatowski.[12]

The Saxon contingent, who had not inspired much confidence in their loyalty to the French, had been ordered to go to Torgau early in the morning. But after General Reynier had personally conducted a reconnaissance, it emerged that the road to Eilenburg and Torgau was blocked by the Coalition, whereupon the Saxon infantry division which had already set out from Paunsdorf towards Heiterblick, turned back and at about nine o'clock in the morning took up positions at Paunsdorf together with their artillery and a squadron of hussars on both sides of the Wurzen road; the rest of the Saxon force (a light cavalry brigade, *Schützen bataillon von Sahr* and Birnbaum's horse artillery battery) remained between Heiterblick and Taucha, having advanced outposts as far as the Parthe river; one of the battalions held Taucha. Thus this weak force, and especially the light cavalry and the two battalions pushed far forwards, had been placed in a very dangerous situation. General Reynier, commanding *7e Corps* which included the Saxon division, enjoyed the deep respect of his subordinates, but otherwise the Saxons generally detested the French. Indeed, it could not be otherwise: their beautiful country was being devastated by Napoleon's forces; fighting against their fellow German speakers for a cause not in the interests of their homeland, they constantly suffered great shortages of provisions, and in addition, the French had deeply insulted them by attributing the loss of the Battle of Dennewitz to them. This was the situation in which they found themselves on 6 (18) Octobe just before Coalition forces emerged facing them.[13]

The crossing onto the left bank of the Parthe by Langéron's corps

The Crown Prince of Sweden, having set off for Taucha with his army, in order to cross the Parthe there, had ordered Langéron 'to be stationed on the right bank of

---

11 Plotho, II, 402; Aster, II, 103-110 & 115-116; Berneck, *Die Schlachten bei Leipzig*, 135-136.
12 Aster, II, 116-118.
13 Aster, II, 119-120; Beitzke, II, 611.

the Parthe with units from his corps at Mockau and Plösen' and, with the agreement of Blücher, was to come under the prince's command, whereupon he was 'to protect the crossing by the Army of the North, and was to proceed onto the left bank of this river.' The units under Langéron and Saint-Priest reached Mokau at nine o'clock in the morning; 36 heavy guns immediately opened fire on the units from General Souham's *3e Corps* located at Neutzsch. Operations by this artillery, reinforced by another 36 heavy guns placed on the Keulenberg, had silenced the French batteries by ten o'clock; taking advantage of this, General Rudzevich crossed the Parthe waist-deep in water, near Mokau with Langéron's vanguard, captured the Kirche Hohen Thekla despite enemy resistance, who had strongly garrisoned the churchyard with skirmishers and artillery, and pushed the enemy back towards Schönefeld, to their main positions.[14] General Korff's cavalry, having crossed the ford at Plösen, reached the Leipzig to Taucha road. During these operations, the Crown Prince of Sweden, having lost much time in the indirect move towards Taucha, ordered Langéron's force to go there, upstream along the Parthe; but Blücher, who was accompanying the Russian corps, rejected these orders, and reported to the Prince that 'comte Langéron, in anticipation of orders, has already crossed to the left bank of the Parthe.' Whereupon, Langéron, having asked the prince for permission to attack Schönefeld, advanced towards this village at one o'clock in the afternoon. VIII Corps and X Corps advanced in the lead, followed by IX Corps and Korff's cavalry, with the exception of Emmanuel's regiments, which had been directed towards Heiterblick. The 29th Jägers, 37th Jägers, 45th Jägers and Staroskol Infantry boldly assaulted and broke into the village, despite stubborn resistance from the French under the personal command of Marshal Marmont. But the enemy, reinforced by fresh units, drove the Russians out of Schönefeld, where the Staroskol Infantry suffered in particular. Major Filipov was killed; General Kaptsevich and artillery Colonel Magdenko were wounded. Kaptsevich, having rallied the defeated force at Abtnaundorf, reinforced them with the Vyatka Infantry and Olonets Infantry, under the command of Major General Turchaninov [Pavel Petrovich Turchaninov], and ordered the attack to be resumed; General Olsufiev proceeded in reserve with IX Corps. At the head of the assault column, Colonel Vasilchikov 3rd charged into the village with the Vyatka Infantry; the troops from both sides became intermixed, fighting with bayonets and musket butts; eventually, the Russians were forced to evacuate the buildings they had cleared. General Langéron ordered Olsufiev to go into action. Colonel Poltoratsky [Konstantin Markovich Poltoratsky] attacked the village for a third time with the Nasheburg Infantry and Yakutsk Infantry, supported by the Staro-Ingermanland Infantry; thereafter Colonel Kern went into the assault with the Ryazan Infantry and Belozersk Infantry, as well as General Pillar [Yegor Maximovich Pillar or Georg Ludwig Pilar von Pilchau], with the Brest Infantry and Wilmanstrand Infantry; the rest of Saint-Priest's force followed them in. A

---

14 General Rudzevich's vanguard consisted of: 7th Jägers, 12th Jägers, 22nd Jägers, 30th Jägers, 48th Jägers, Schlüsselburg Infantry, Olonets Infantry; Emmanuel's brigade of: Kharkov Dragoons and Kiev Dragoons. War Diary of Langéron's corps; Adjutant-General Korff's War Diary; Aster, II, 133.

terrible fire that engulfed the village and the desperate French defence forced the Russians to retreat. Many wounded from both sides fell victim to the flames.[15]

Almost at the same time as Olsufiev's attack on Schöndfeld, the Saxon light cavalry brigade and *bataillon von Sahr* defected to General Emmanuel.

This force, as had already been stated, were located between Heiterblick and Taucha, in front of the main position. As early as nine o'clock in the morning, the commander of one of the regiments, Major Fabrice [Friedrich Joseph Anton von Fabrice?], convinced of the willingness of his subordinates to surrender to the Coalition, sent an officer to General Zeschau [Heinrich Wilhelm von Zeschau], who was stationed at Paunsdorf with the infantry, informing him of the dangerous situation in his brigade and of the intention of the officers and soldiers to defect from the French. General Zeschau, after consultation with the commanders of the infantry brigades, *Generalmajor* Ryssel and *Oberst* Brause, announced to the officer sent by Fabrice that, 'without specific orders from the King, I could not do anything contrary to the duties entrusted to me.' This emphatic response did not change the intentions of the Saxons, however. Meanwhile, at 11 o'clock, Emmanuel's dragoons and Platov's Cossacks appeared at Heiterblick; a little later, Wintzingerode's cavalry approached from the direction of Taucha. The Saxons, numbering about 700 horsemen, raced into the attack, but were driven off; then, having rallied once more, they went to engage the Cossacks a second time, but this time without drawing their sabres from their scabbards, they halted a short distance away and greeted the Russians with a loud shout of 'Hurrah!' General Emmanuel rode out to meet the Saxon officers who had advanced ahead of their units, and, having become convinced of their desire to fight in the ranks of the Coalition, reported this to comte Langéron. The *bataillon von Sahr* followed the cavalry; Birnbaum's horse artillery and several cavalry officers and soldiers went back to the infantry division stationed at Paunsdorf.[16]

At the same time, the Württemberg cavalry brigade, numbering about 600 horsemen, surrendered to Platov. But their commander, General Normann, declared that his troops would not fight against the French without orders from their King.[17]

The crossing of the Parthe by the Army of the North

The army under the Crown Prince of Sweden, directed by an indirect route from Breitenfeld to Taucha, crossed the Parthe later than the corps under comte Langéron: Wintzingerode's force, having left their overnight camp at nine o'clock in the morning, moved towards Grassdorf, repaired the bridge there under fire from enemy skirmishers and crossed to the left bank of the river, detaching some of the cavalry under Major General Count Pahlen, along the right bank, towards Taucha. The Saxon battalion holding this village with several guns, upon being surrounded by Russian troops, laid down their arms after a rather sharp struggle in which the commander of the 13th Horse Artillery Company, Colonel Arnoldi, lost a leg. Following this, Pahlen's cavalry crossed the Parthe. After them, formations from Bülow's corps crossed at noon: the Prinz zu Hessen-Homburg's brigade at

---

15 Aster, II, 137-138.
16 Aster, II, 121 & 123-125.
17 Aster, II, 126.

Grassdorf, Borstell's and Krafft's brigades and Oppen's cavalry at Taucha; while the Swedish corps crossed at one o'clock in the afternoon: the infantry at Plaußig, over the repaired bridge, while the cavalry forded across. Whereupon, the reserve artillery, parks and trains of the Army of the North crossed over, and by three o'clock, had taken their designated place between Langéron's corps and Bennigsen's force, located facing Paunsdorf and Stötteritz.[18]

Operations by the Army of Silesia to the north of Leipzig

At about nine o'clock in the morning, as soon as Blücher, who was with Langéron's corps on the high ground of the Windmühlenberg at the village of Mokau, had seen the Army of Bohemia advancing, he ordered Sacken to attack the Pfaffendorf manor and seize the Hallisches Tor, while General Yorck, who had managed to reorganise the rest of his force into two divisions, at nine o'clock was ordered to deploy between Gohlis and Eutritzsch and to support Sacken's attack. The Russian units moved forward. The cavalry of the duc de Padoue (Arrighi) were pushed back into the suburbs, but Dąbrowski's infantry, supported by units from the French depots, defended themselves with extraordinary tenacity. Lieutenant General Neverovsky, with the regiments of the 27th Division, attacked Pfaffendorf, while Colonel Rakhmanov moved from Gohlis towards Rosental with the Okhotsk Infantry and Kamchatka Infantry.[19] General Huene [Yakov Yegorovich Gine or Jakob von Hoyningen-Huene], having positioned 24 guns of Captain Ericks' 13th Battery Company and Lieutenant Colonel Novosiltsov's 35th Light Artillery Company to the left of the manor, within pistol range of the city walls, paved the way for the troops through the Hallisches Tor and was mortally wounded. Colonel Rakhmanov and the commander of the Kamchatka regiment, Major Salmanov [Zakhar Ivanovich Salmanov], were killed. The enemy, having received reinforcements from *Garde* units, repelled the Russian force. In order to support Sacken, Horn detached the fusilier battalions from the *Leib Infanterie* and *Ostpreußisches Infanterie*, with whose assistance the Russian force defeated the enemy who were attempting to seize Gohlis.[20]

Thus, by two o'clock in the afternoon, every attack by the Army of Bohemia and Army of Silesia had been repelled by the French, Bennigsen's force, having pushed the enemy back to the villages of Stötteritz and Paunsdorf, which were heavily garrisoned by French troops, had halted, awaiting assistance from the other armies, the troops of the Crown Prince of Sweden had only just reached the battlefield, and the force under Gyulay was wasting time in a pointless move. But the Coalition armies, were now forming a continuous arc of fire and iron in the sector between the Pleiße and Parthe, and were preparing to resume the battle that would decide the fate of Europe.

---

18 Plotho, II, 410-411; Aster, II, 139-141; Beitzke, II, 618-619.
19 Known for publishing the excellent, given the state of Russian military literature at that time, Military Journal.
20 War Diary of General Sacken's corps (Archive of the M.T.D. No. 16,343; Aster, II, 141-142.

Course of the battle from two o'clock in the afternoon until the fighting ended

The continuation of the advance by Bennigsen's forces and the defection of the remaining Saxon troops to the Coalition side.

At around two o'clock in the afternoon, at the same time as Graf Bubna, having been driven out of Paunsdorf, opened a cannonade on Durutte's division, the advance by the Army of the North from Taucha was observed, which forced General Reynier to withdraw the Saxon division towards Sellerhausen.

At three o'clock in the afternoon, the leading units from Bülow's corps, having joined their left wing to the right wing of Graf Bubna's division, moved towards Paunsdorf, captured this village (as will be described later, under operations by the Army of the North), and pushed Durutte back towards Sellerhausen. At this very moment, the Saxon troops decided to defect to the Coalition.[21]

They had been waiting for a convenient opportunity for this for a long time. Their commander, General Zeschau, having received news of the defection of the light cavalry, wrote to King Friedrich August regarding this, asking for instructions, and reporting to him that the entire Saxon force was willing to defect to the coalition unilaterally, which would be incomparably more harmful to the country than a declared breach with the French. Captain Nostitz, sent with this report, returned at three o'clock with the following handwritten note from King Friedrich August.

> To the honourable *Generalleutnant* Zeschau! I have always had confidence in my troops, even now more than ever. They can show their loyalty to me only through the execution of their duties, and I am convinced that they will strive to vindicate my confidence. Thereafter, I pray to God to receive them under his holy protection.[22]

General Zeschau read the King's response to the brigade commanders and urged them to carry out the will of their Sovereign precisely, but his subordinates found this answer ambiguous and believed that the King could not write otherwise, being in thrall to Napoleon, and that for the good of Saxony it was necessary to defect to the Coalition immediately.[23]

General Reynier, who was with the Saxon force during the retreat by Durutte's division, wishing to secure the 12-pounder battery that was with them, ordered it to withdraw behind the second brigade located at Sellerhausen. But instead, the battery moved to meet Bennigsen's force in platoon column. The cavalry under Sébastiani and Walther, sent out to attack Bennigsen's overextended army, having observed the advance of the battery and not understanding their true intent, greeted the Saxons with cheers of: *'vive l'empereur!'* The infantry of the first Saxon brigade moved in the wake of the battery; the second brigade rushed at an increased pace in the same direction. General Zeschau and Reynier himself tried to stop these formations, but all their efforts were in vain; the remaining Saxon guns followed their infantry, and

---

21 War Diary of the Army of Poland; Aster, II, 148-149.
22 Aster, II, 144.
23 Aster, II, 128-129 & 144-145.

in the meantime the Russian artillery and the British rocket battery were pelting Durutte's division with round shot, shell and rockets. The Saxon troops who had defected to the Coalition were received very favourably, but of their number only four horse artillery pieces were allowed to take part in the battle; the rest of their artillery and all the infantry were bivouacked at Engelsdorf, and the light cavalry brigade with Yorck's corps. General Reynier withdrew to Leipzig with the 24 officers and 600 lower ranks from the Saxon force that had stayed with him. French military historians and Napoleon himself, exaggerating the importance of the Saxon defection, have attributed the loss of the battle of Leipzig to it. But such an opinion is very mistaken. The number of Saxon troops was so small that their defection to the Coalition could not have had any effect on the outcome of the battle, in which more than 400,000 men participated on both sides. On 6 (18) October, the Saxon infantry had 96 officers and 3,246 lower ranks with the Colours; the artillery consisted of 15 officers and 506 lower ranks with 22 guns (of which only 19 were battle-worthy).[24] Consequently, the division had a total of 111 officers and 3,752 lower ranks, while excluding those who were *hors de combat* that day, or on various missions or had returned to Leipzig, the number of troops who defected to the Coalition at Stünz did not exceed 3,000 men with 12 guns.[25]

The Coalition monarchs, having learned of this event from Bennigsen's report, wished to see the brigade commanders, *Generalmajor* Ryssel and *Oberst* Brause, and expressed their good will to them for the devotion they had shown for the common cause of Germany. The King of Prussia, however, remarked that 'the Saxons have kept us waiting for a long time.'[26]

As soon as Reynier reported on the withdrawal of the Saxon force to Ney, measures were taken to defend the territory they had abandoned. The force that Napoleon had recently dispatched in order to split the Army of Poland from the Army of Silesia, namely the light *cavalerie de la Garde* under Nansouty with 20 guns from the *artillerie de la Garde* and the *chasseur* brigade of the *Vieille Garde* under General Christiani [Charles-Joseph Christiani], at three o'clock in the afternoon, hurried from Crottendorf to face 26th Division and Graf Bubna's Austrian *leichte Division*, who were advancing on the right wing of Bennigsen's force; *2e corps de cavalerie* and *5e corps de cavalerie* supported this attack; Bennigsen was located there and was almost captured by the sudden surge of French horsemen; but, on Dokhturov's orders, the enemy were engaged with fire from the heavy artillery companies under Begunov and Shulman, and upon being forced to halt, limited themselves to a relatively fierce cannonade, in which the four Saxon horse artillery pieces took part.[27] Their commander, *Hauptmann* Birnbaum [Heinrich Moritz Birnbaum], was wounded. One Russian horse artillery company and one Austrian *reitende Batterie* were deployed on either side in support of the Saxon battery, whose successful fire silenced Nansouty's artillery. Taking advantage of this success, General Chaplits attacked the French *cavalerie de la Garde* and drove them off with considerable losses.

---

24 Aster, II, 152-153.
25 Details of the defection of the Saxon division to the Coalition can be found in Aster, II, 150-155.
26 Aster, II, 156.
27 War Diary of General Bennigsen's Army of Poland.

At this point (at around four o'clock in the afternoon) Grand Duke Konstantin Pavlovich reached the Army of Poland with a message from Emperor Alexander to express the Tsar's favour to Bennigsen for the successes he had achieved and to congratulate the Crown Prince of Sweden on his arrival on the battlefield. Meanwhile, Stroganov had managed to seize control of Zweinaundorf; Macdonald's force drove him from there, but General Paskevich reoccupied the village once more with 26th Division. At the same time, General Glebov had captured the scrub to the right of Zweinaundorf with the 6th Jägers and 41st Jägers. The French attempted to block the Coalition advances with cavalry attacks, but were repulsed each time by the cavalry under Chaplits and Kreutz, with the assistance of the Penza *Opolchenie* Cossacks and Lieutenant Colonel Taube's 56th Light Artillery Company. At dusk the cannonade died down and eventually stopped completely, but near the villages of Probstheida and Stötteritz the cannonade and shooting continued into the night. Paskevich's force, having passed through Zweinaundorf, occupied the high ground of the Windmühlenberg forwards of this village; while Graf Klenau, having taken Ober Zweinaundorf in combat, led the *Zach Infanterie* and *Joseph Colloredo Infanterie* from there in order to assault Stötteritz, but upon being engaged with a hail of canister shot, retreated to Zweinaundorf with losses.[28]

The assault on Probstheida by Barclay's force

The Coalition had not intended to attack Probstheida until they had advanced the columns under Bennigsen and the Erbprinz zu Hessen-Homburg farther forward; thus hoping to compromise the defence of this village by outflanking it. But instead, at two o'clock in the afternoon, the Prussian *10. Brigade* and *12. Brigade* from Kleist's corps received orders to attack Probstheida immediately; *9. Brigade* was to support the attacking force, while *11. Brigade*, temporarily re-subordinated to Bennigsen, upon reaching Zuckelhausen, was to establish communications with Kleist's other brigades.

The village of Probstheida, which formed the salient point of the position of the French forces, consists of sturdy masonry buildings; it is surrounded by solid walls made of masonry and clay. Victor's entire *2e Corps* and elements of Lauriston's *5e Corps* had been assigned to defend it, supported by General Sébastiani's *2e corps de cavalerie* located close by. There were strong batteries on either side of the village. The attack was carried out almost simultaneously from two directions: Prich's *10. Brigade*, *9. Landwehr Infanterie* crossed the pair of walls of the gardens on the southwestern side of the village, while Prinz August's *12. Brigade*, *2. Schlesisches Infanterie* and *11. Reserve Infanterie*, went into the assault from the eastern side, facing Zuckelhausen. The Prussian troops broke into the village, but, upon being disordered by canister fire, were forced to fall back a distance of 600 to 800 paces. Zieten's *11. Brigade*, after occupying Zuckelhausen, took part in the attack on Probstheida: two battalions of *10. Reserve Infanterie* and the fusilier battalion of the *Schlesisches Infanterie* quickly pushed into the village with a company of jägers, but were also unable to hold on and retreated back to Zuckelhausen. Prinz Eugen von Württemberg, who was stationed behind the Prussian force with the remainder of

---

28 War Diary of General Bennigsen's Army of Poland; Aster, II, 158-162.

his II Corps, numbering just 1,800 men, wishing to buy them time to reorganise, also attacked the village. Prince Shakhovskoy scaled the wall from the direction of Liebertwolkwitz at the head of 3rd Division but the enemy pushed them out into the open and forced the Russian units to retreat under fire from the screen force lining the wall. The casualties to II Corps in this action reached some 600 men. The French, having seen the Coalition retreat, chased after them, but, being engaged with canister shot, returned to their positions, and the action was reduced to a cannonade. Napoleon, concerned at attacks on the most important location within his positions, hastened to Probstheida himself, strengthened the defences of the village with the fusiliers [sic, *chasseurs à pied*?] of the *Vieille Garde* and several hundred dragoons and, wishing to motivate his warriors, rode out into their front ranks and was exposed to the greatest danger. Having been informed that the artillery were already running low on ammunition, Napoleon ordered the rate of fire to be reduced. The French, who were no longer fighting for a victory but for their own survival, showed courage worthy of their reputation. The *2e ligne, 4e ligne* and *18e ligne* distinguished themselves in particular under the command of *général de division* Vial, who was killed instantly by round shot. General Rochambeau was also among those who fell in the defence of Probstheida.[29] The Saxon and Württemberg troops coming over to the Coalition not only failed to weaken the French soldiers' morale, but, on the contrary, aroused self-sacrifice and a thirst for vengeance in them. For this reason, the German troops still in Napoleon's army found the idea of fighting against their fellow countrymen repugnant. The commander of the Saxon cuirassier brigade protecting a French battery near Stötteritz, General Lessing, having received orders from General Bordesoulle to engage the Russian cavalry threatening to attack the battery, remained in place, claiming their horses were utterly exhausted. Napoleon tried to conceal the Saxon defection from the troops of the *Confédération du Rhin* by every means and even ordered a rumour to be spread among the Saxon cuirassiers that General Thielmann and 6,000 men had been captured, and so on. But all these ruses were in vain, and the Saxon cuirassiers, as well as the *Leibgrenadier Bataillon*, which was part of the *2e division* of the *Vieille Garde*, learned of the defection of their comrades to the side of the defenders of Germany that same day or the following night.[30]

Operations by Graf Nostitz's Austrian force
After the French had repulsed the Austrian attacks on the villages of Dösen, Dölitz and Lößnig, Wimpffen's division [Maximilian Alexander von Wimpffen], which was positioned to the right of the scrub at Dösen, limited themselves to a cannonade on the village of Probstheida; at two o'clock in the afternoon, Alois Liechtenstein's division engaged the enemy in a heated skirmish in the Dösen scrub, while the troops from Bianchi's division fought against Poniatowski at Dölitz. Beck's brigade [August von Beck] of the same division attacked Lößnig, but encountered very stubborn resistance there; Augereau's force held Connewitz in strength, and Decouz's division

---

29 Prinz Eugen von Württemberg's diary; Vaudoncourt, *Histoire de la guerre soutenue par les Français en Allemagne*, 214-215; Aster, II, 163-169.
30 Aster, II, 169-170.

of the *Jeune Garde*, under Oudinot's command, located behind the Lößnig ponds, held back the Austrian advance. Colloredo led Greth's division to assualt Lößnig himself, which forced Napoleon to reinforce the right wing of his position with General Rottembourg's *Vieille Garde* brigade. After taking Lößnig, Graf Colloredo, having garrisoned this village with two battalions of *Czartoryski Infanterie*, deployed his front line in column forwards of Dölitz and Dösen and attacked the Connewitz churchyard, but was repelled by Poniatowski. Fighting continued at this location, with varying success, until nightfall. Graf Nostitz suffered a severe contusion to the leg, but remained with his troops both that day and the next. At dusk, on Napoleon's orders, the Saxon and Westphalian *Garde* battalions and Rottembourg's brigade returned to the Tabaksmühle to the south of Thonberg. Christiani's brigade also arrived there from the left wing, from Stötteritz and Reudnitz. Napoleon, wishing to mark the location for his overnight halt more clearly, ordered a large fire to be lit near the mill, but as soon as the fire began to flare up, an incoming shell struck it and scattered the wood in all directions; The *Empereur des Français* remained imperturbable within lethal range of the exploding shell, but when the newly rebuilt fire was scattered once more, this time by round shot, it was ordered not to be lit.[31]

Operations by the Army of Silesia and Army of the North from two o'clock in the afternoon until the end of the fighting

After the village of Gohlis was occupied by elements of Yorck's force, General Sacken and his corps moved towards the Pfaffendorf manor and seized the buildings there, but when the enemy opened fire on the advancing troops, both from Rosental and from a battery placed forwards of the Hallisches Tor, the Russians were forced to evacuate the manor after it caught fire. The flames spread so quickly that many of the wounded did not have chance to escape. By evening, Sacken's force had crossed the Pleiße into Rosental, but were unable to hold out there and withdrew to Gohlis. However, Sacken's attacks had an impact on the overall course of the battle, delaying the movement of enemy forces sent from Leipzig towards Schönefeld. Yorck's corps remained between Gohlis and Eutritzsch until evening; and once the Coalition successes on the southern side of Leipzig made retreat by the enemy army inevitable, Blücher, who had constantly remained at Mockau and Eutritzsch, at seven o'clock in the afternoon, sent General Rauch to Yorck with orders to hold the crossings at Halle and Merseburg and to pursue the French. Yorck immediately recalled to his corps the two battalions sent to Gohlis; two Cossack regiments, a detachment from *2. Jäger Bataillon*, which had joined the Prussian force on 4 (16) October, and the Saxon light cavalry were also attached to him.[32]

At three o'clock in the afternoon, Langéron's corps received orders from both Blücher and the Crown Prince of Sweden to storm Schönefeld once more, as soon as the Army of the North had managed to take up their assigned places on the battlefield. The bombardment of the village was intensified by fire from several batteries placed on the right bank of the Parthe on Blücher's orders.

---

31 Aster, II, 171-173.
32 Carl von Weiß (Müffling), *Zur Kriegsgeschichte der Jahre 1813 und 1814*, second edition, 96-97; Aster, II, 180-183.

Saint-Priest's force, under heavy canister fire, attacked this village defended by *2e Division* and *3e Division* of *6e Corps* under the command of Lagrange. According to Marmont himself, 'never before had troops fought so heroically.' Neither side was willing to be outshone by the other in selflessness; attacks followed one another in quick succession. Amid the yells and shouts of the soldiers, the thunder of the cannonade, the rattle of musketry, the detonation of shells, the blazing bell tower suddenly collapsed, the light was dimmed by clouds of smoke and dust, and the darkness of the evening interrupted the efforts of the struggling troops for several minutes. General Olsufiev reinforced Saint-Priest with the divisions under Rudzevich and Udom. Marshal Ney, having been forced to yield Paunsdorf to the Coalition, had decided to hold out to the bitter end in Schönefeld, which served as the buttress for his left flank. He angled the right flank of his force in the direction of Stünz. Ney's infantry were deployed in this position in battalion column, in a chessboard pattern; all the batteries were placed forwards: such were his dispositions for engaging the Army of the North as it came into the general line of the Coalition forces at the same time as Durutte's French division, having reoccupied Paunsdorf, separated Bennigsen's force from the Army of Silesia. General Bülow immediately attacked the enemy with the Prinz zu Hessen-Homburg's brigade at the head of his corps and Oppen's reserve cavalry, with one Prussian horse artillery battery and two Russian battery companies under Colonel Dietrichs and with Holtzendorff's reserve artillery; the remaining brigades under Borstell and Krafft, received orders to leave two battalions with three guns to defend the bridges at Taucha and hurry to the battlefield. One Russian and one Prussian horse artillery battery were quickly moved forward along the Taucha road, in order to support Major General Pahlen's cavalry brigade; Bülow raced to the left of the main road himself, with the Prinz zu Homburg's brigade, straight towards Paunsdorf, and sent the cavalry even further to the left to link up with Graf Bubna's division. The Russian battery companies under Dietrichs, the Prussian six-pounder battery under *Hauptamnn* Glasenapp and the British rocket battery under Captain Bogue opened fire on the village of Paunsdorf, while the Prussian brigade, having formed two lines, moved to the assault. Two battalions of *4. Reserve Infanterie* and one of *3. Ostpreußisches Infanterie*, with the assistance of the Austrian *6. Jäger Bataillon*, broke into the village, drove the French out and put them to flight towards Sellerhausen, with the loss of four guns and 60 men taken prisoner. At the same time, the Russian and Prussian batteries advancing along the road from Taucha, closed up towards the enemy and began to fire at them; but the rocket battery moved forward carelessly and obstructed the Prussian horse artillery battery, which forced them to stop firing. The enemy skirmishers, taking advantage of this, rushed towards the rocket launchers, and without giving them chance to launch a single rocket, killed the battery commander and wounded many horses. However, after that, several rockets launched at the enemy forced them to retreat. French cuirassiers charging at two Prussian battalions sent towards Sellerhausen were repelled by canister shot by Colonel Dietrichs and *Hauptmann* Glasenapp.

By five o'clock the remaining formations of the Army of the North had reached the battlefield. Borstell's brigade formed up between Paunsdorf and the Taucha road; the first wave were deployed in line, while the second were in column; Krafft's brigade stood in reserve. Wintzingerode's corps occupied the sector between the Taucha road and Langéron's force, while the Swedish corps formed the general reserve. The left wing of the enemy army, between Schönefeld and Stünz, was lined with strong batteries. 24 Russian guns, sent with a cavalry escort from Count Vorontsov's force in order to counter this artillery, threw the enemy into disarray, taking advantage of which Colonel Yakhontov [Alexander Andreevich Yakhontov] raced to attack the infantry with his Volunteer Regiment, taking four guns and 800 prisoners, and was himself seriously wounded. Because the enemy were still attempting to counterattack the Prinz zu Hessen-Homburg and Bubna, Bülow reinforced his battle lines with four battalions from Krafft's brigade and engaged the French with fire from 76 guns. At the same time, Nansouty's cavalry were struck from the other side by fire from Bennigsen's and Bubna's batteries, and was forced to retreat. At the same time, Grand Duke Konstantin Pavlovich, having met with the Crown Prince Sweden on the left flank of the Army of the North, greeted him on behalf of his August brother. The Crown Prince, upon his appearance on the battlefield, no longer influenced by political considerations, rather, by his innate propensity for the military art, he calmly directed the operations of his forces under the most brutal fire, paying no heed to the thousands that threatened him with death. At six o'clock Bülow received orders to seize the villages of Stünz and Sellerhausen. Several more batteries were brought up to fire on them, including the Russian under Lieutenant Colonel Taube, and a total of 150 guns were deployed from the Army of the North. Dietrichs' battery company, approaching Stünz, opened a strong cannonade and assisted majors Müllenheim [Carl Heinrich August von Müllenheim von Rechberg] and Frisius in taking control of the village with two battalions from *3. Ostpreußisches Infanterie*. Whereupon, the jägers from the second battalion of *3. Ostpreußisches Infanterie* stormed Sellerhausen and captured two guns (other sources show third battalion of *1. Neumärkisches Landwehr* and skirmishers from *1. Kolbergisches*). At the same time, units under Stroganov and Bubna captured the village of Mölkau, from where the French retreated towards Crottendorf. After the Coalition forces had occupied the aforementioned villages, Bülow reinforced them with elements of the reserves and deployed his entire corps in battle formation for the night.

At the time of Bülow's operations just described, the cavalry from Wintzingerode's corps, commanded by generals O'Rourke and Manteuffel [Ivan Vasilievich Manteifel or Gotthard Johann von Manteuffel], attacked Delmas' division and Beurmann's brigade (*3e Corps*) [Frédéric Auguste de Beurmann] as they were advancing from Volkmarsdorf, drove them back and captured four guns, but lost one of the most outstanding cavalry commanders, Count Manteuffel. The French were still holding out on the crest of a gentle rise between Schönefeld and Volkmarsdorf. The Russian artillery, deployed to counter the enemy batteries, had fired off almost all of its projectiles, and so the Crown Prince sent General Cardell from the reserve with 20 Swedish guns, which, together with the batteries under Saint-Priest, forced the enemy to withdraw from their position. Taking advantage of this, the formations under Rudzevich and Count Vorontsov moved forward. The French, reinforced by Ricard's division (*3e Corps*) from Reudnitz, attempted to stop the Russians, but were driven back with great losses; among those killed [mortally wounded] was Delmas, among the wounded were Ney and Souham. Meanwhile, Langéron's forces assaulted

Schönefeld several times, and finally, having driven back Ricard's division, which had arrived to assist Marmont, at about six o'clock in the evening they captured this important location on the eighth attempt and held on to the ruined village despite subsequent French counterattacks. The losses suffered by Russian forces during the attacks on Schönefeld amounted to 4,000 men, but the enemy also lost no fewer. The *chef d'état-major* of *6e Corps*, General Richemont [Christophe François Camus de Richemont], was killed; generals Friederichs, Coehorn, Compans, Pelleport [Pierre de Pelleport] and Choisy [Jacques Robert Souslier de Choisy] were wounded. Many of Marmont's aides-de-camp and officers fell victim to the desperate fighting; of the marshal's aides-de-camp, only Damrémont [Charles-Marie Denys de Damrémont] and Fabvier [Charles-Nicolas Fabvier] survived unscathed.[33] Following the occupation of Schönefeld, the formations under Rudzevich, Vorontsov, Wintzingerode and Bülow occupied the ridge of high ground extending from this village through Sellerhausen to Stünz. The capture of Schönefeld by the Russians, exposing the French to the risk of losing communications with Leipzig, should have forced the immediate abandonment of their positions in front of the city, had the onset of darkness not put an end to the successes of the Coalition forces.[34]

At dusk the Commander-in-Chief summoned all the corps commanders who were nearby to the Monarchenhügel in order to make arrangements for operations for the following morning with the agreement of Emperor Alexander and the King of Prussia.[35] The troops were ordered to prepare for renewed combat at dawn; should the enemy abandon the positions they were holding, the Coalition armies were to move towards Leipzig and storm the city. Emperor Alexander proposed to send the Russo-Prussian reserves immediately onto the left bank of the Elster via Pegau in order to operate on the flank of the retreating enemy. According to the honest Plotho, the Emperor aroused general astonishment with the clarity, determination and merits of his strategic assessments, but in response he was informed of the fatigue of the troops and the lack of vital supplies, which forced the postponement of the departure of the reserves until the following morning: thus the opportunity to strike a decisive blow at Napoleon's army was missed![36] Yorck's and Gyulay's corps were assigned to operate on the enemy lines of communications. Yet the former, although he had already advanced upstream on the Elster on the evening of 6 (18) October, was unable to reach the enemy army's line of retreat in time due to the marshy nature of the terrain between the Elster and the Luppe, which forced Yorck to take the indirect route via Merseburg towards Freyburg. The corps under Graf Gyulay, already on the left bank of the Elster, could operate on the flank of the enemy more easily than any other formation, received orders to go to Pegau together with Moritz Liechtenstein's *1. leichte Division* and the detachments under Thielmann and Graf Mensdorff, who having driven their adversaries away, in addition were told, in any event, 'to be careful not to suffer a defeat, and as soon as the French had an open line of retreat, to pursue them with cavalry

---

33 Marmont, *Mémoires*, V, 183-185; Varnhagen von Ense, 241; Aster, II, 183-195.
34 Aster, II, 195.
35 The Austrian Kaiser had left for Rötha at six o'clock in the afternoon.
36 Plotho, II, 414.

alone.'³⁷ Obviously, with such instructions, one could not expect a decisive operation. Graf Bubna's *2. leichte Division* and Platov's Cossack detachment were also assigned to pursue the retreating enemy; yet these two formations were on the right wing of the Coalition army, at a distance of about one and a half *Meilen* (ten *versts*) from the Elster; however, the haste of the pursuit was of little general concern at Schwarzenberg's headquarters: Bubna's detachment only received orders to advance towards Pegau at eight o'clock in the morning the next day.³⁸

The retreat of the enemy army had begun before midday on 6 (18) October. First, Bertrand's *4e Corps* moved toward Lützen; the supply trains followed; at about five o'clock in the afternoon, the *1er corps de cavalerie* was ordered to move through Leipzig and Lindenau; then followed *3e corps de cavalerie* and *5e corps de cavalerie*; during the night, the artillery parks set off, having replenished the batteries' ammunition and destroying some of the empty caissons. Napoleon left the bivouac at the Tabaksmühle himself for the Hôtel de Prusse [Preußischer Hof] at seven o'clock in the evening. He spent most of the night issuing various dispositions to the formatins; but neither he nor his chief comrade-in-arms, Berthier, ensured that bridges were built for the retreat.³⁹

On the night of 6 to 7 (18 to 19) October, the right wing of the French army remained between Connewitz and Probstheida; further on, at right angles, stood the formations of the centre, from Probstheida, through Stötteritz to Crottendorf; the left wing extended from Crottendorf, through Volkmannsdorf, to Reudnitz, and onwards through the Hallische Vorstadt to Rosental. The reserves were behind Stötteritz. The French surrounded the entire outer line of their bivouacs with a dense screen of vedettes, maintained fires and occupied the villages lying within the perimeter of their army's deployment with strong detachments in order to conceal their retreat for as long as possible.

The Coalition forces were positioned as follows during the night: the Army of Silesia from Gohlis to the river Parthe and onwards from Schönefeld to Sellerhausen; the Army of Poland, together with the attached formations under Bubna and Zieten, were at Mölkau, Zweinaundorf, Holzhausen and Zuckelhausen; Lieutenant General Pahlen's cavalry and 2nd Cuirassier Division were stationed with their right flank forwards of Zuckelhausen, resting their left flank against Wittgenstein's force deployed facing Probstheida; Colloredo's force was at Dösen, Dölitz and Lößnig; the Russian 2nd Grenadier Division was behind Wittgenstein's corps; the Lifeguard Light Cavalry Division and 3rd Cuirassier Division were behind Kleist; the Prussian reserve cavalry were to their left; the Russian 1st Grenadier Division was south of the old brickworks astride the Colditz road; thr Russo-Prussian Guards were between Liebertwolkwitz and Wachau; Lederer's division were on the left bank of the Pleiße, facing Dölitz and Connewitz; Gyulay's corps was on the right bank of the Elster at Knauthain [2½ miles west

---

37 Aster, II, 178-179.
38 Bernhardi, *Denkwürdigkeiten aus dem Leben Carl Friedrich Grafen von Toll*, III, 460.
39 Aster, II, 198; Pelet, *Spectateur militaire*, 1830; Fain, *Manuscrit de 1813*, II, 442, both of the latter state that Napoleon ordered temporary bridges to be built along the army's line of retreat, but these orders were not carried out.

of Markkleeberg]. The outposts of both sides were so close to each other that the challenges of the enemy sentries were audible.[40]

Throughout the Battle of Nations on 6 (18) October, in which some 400,000 men took part with 1,500 guns, the inhabitants of Leipzig were in agonising anticipation of every possible catastrophe. From early morning the cannonade rang out, constantly getting louder as the fighting approached the city; the injured were endlessly being carried in and out, along with long lines of walking wounded. The surrounding villages were bursting out in ominous flames. By evening round shot and shells began to crash into the city, killing residents and setting city buildings on fire. Some of the population left the city, carrying away their most precious possessions; others climbed into attics and roofs and watched the progress of the battle from there. Confusion and disorder reigned in each of the suburbs, and especially in the Hallische Vorstadt, which increased with the onset of darkness, when the troops and the remaining trains crowded at the exit for the Lützen road; the infantry and cavalry intermixed and pushed past each other, soldiers threw down their weapons; guns and pouches were strewn about in every street. The shortage of rations, and especially bread, had reached the point that it was with great difficulty that any could be obtained for Napoleon himself and those closest to him, and even then it cost more than 17½ groschen (60 kopecks).[41]

The King of Saxony, having become a victim of Napoleon's rule, witnessed the suffering of his subjects with sorrow and could do nothing to comfort them. The conqueror's narcissism prevented him from admitting the failure he had suffered: at eight o'clock in the evening, when the Coalition were already standing at the gates of Leipzig, the duc de Bassano (Mare) sent an officer to Friedrich August with the news that 'the battle has been won and the Coalition would certainly be retreating during the night.'[42] According to Pelet, the duc went to the King and persuaded him, in the name of Napoleon, to break off the alliance with France. Nevertheless, Friedrich August did not dare to accompany the French army and preferred to remain in Leipzig.

French historians have asserted that Napoleon, having repelled all the attacks by Coalition forces on the positions he had occupied in front of Leipzig, intended to hold on to them the following day, and that he was prompted to retreat by a shortage of ammunition.[43] But this assertion is as inconsistent with the evidence as the claim by the French that the defection of the Saxon troops was the cause of the loss of the battle. Napoleon's failure, without resorting to fabrication, can be easily explained by the enormous numerical superiority of the Coalition forces: at the end of the fighting on 6 (18) October, all of Napoleon's formations, except for some elements of the *Vieille Garde*, had already been committed to battle; in contrast, the Coalition had conserved their reserves. Under such circumstances, by persisting in continuing the unequal struggle, Napoleon would have suffered the same fate that befell him on the fields of Waterloo, and would have lost the opportunity to form a new army over the next four months.

---

40 Hofmann, 298; Aster, II, 200-203.
41 Aster, II, 225-226 & 230-232.
42 Aster, II, 228.
43 Vaudoncourt, 218-219; Fain, *Manuscrit de 1813*, II, 430-432; Norvins, *Portefeuille de 1813*, II, 414.

Since the widespread introduction of firearms there had never yet been, and in all probability there will not be for a long time, such a battle as took place on 6 (18) October on the fields of Leipzig. It is believed that the number of artillery projectiles fired by the French amounted to: some 84,000 on 4 (16) October; 95,000 on 6 (18) October; while overall, from 2 (14) October until 6 (18) October, some 220,00 rounds. On the Coalition side, judging by the strength of their artillery, even more rounds were expended, and therefore, without any exaggeration, it may be assumed that on 6 (18) October both sides fired some 250,000, and in the preceding five days some 500,000 artillery projectiles and several million musket cartridges.[44]

---

44 Beitzke, II, 634; Hofmann, 305, states that over the preceding four days, the French artillery fired 175,000 rounds; Vaudoncourt, 218, states that 250,000 rounds were expended from 3 (15) October, while around 100,000 were fired on 6 (18) October.

42

The Battle of Leipzig (conclusion)

The capture of Leipzig by Coalition forces. Leipzig in 1813. – Disposition of Napoleon's forces for the defence of the city. – Napoleon's departure. – The advance by the Coalition armies. – The deputation from Leipzig. – The mission assigned to Toll and Natzmer.

The advance by the Army of Bohemia and Army of Poland. The advance by the Army of the North. The advance by the Army of Silesia. – The arrival of the Coalition sovereigns at the Marktplatz and occupation of the city by their forces. – Demolition of the bridge on the Elster. – Desperate situation of the enemy units left in the city. – Death of Prince Poniatowski.

Emperor Alexander in Leipzig. – The Saxon King acknowledged as a prisoner of war. – Casualties to both sides in the battle of Leipzig. – Awards.

The deployment of forces on both sides on the night of 7 to 8 (19 to 20) October.

Throughout the night following the bloody battle of 6 (18) October, the leading Coalition units heard a great commotion and noticed constant movement in the enemy positions. Some attributed this to the French retreating; others thought that they, in preparing to defend the city, were barricading the gates, breaching loopholes, and so on. On the morning of 7 (19) October, once the fog cleared, the sun rose and it was a clear day, it turned out that the enemy, having completely abandoned the positions at Probstheida, were hastily retreating towards the city.[1]

In the half century that has passed since the gigantic battle of Leipzig, some gates and streets have been renamed, and almost every gate has been moved to a different location. In 1813, the inner city was surrounded by an ancient, rather weak stone wall, with four gates: the Peterstor, through which the Pegau road passed; the Grimmaisches Tor, where the roads from Rochlitz, Grimma and Wurzen met; the Hallisches Tor, on the northern side, and the Ranstädter Tor, on the western side of

---

1 Beitzke, *Geschichte der deutschen Freiheitskriege in den Jahren 1813 und 1814*, II, 636.

the city. The inner city was separated from the surrounding extensive suburbs by a fairly wide space, partly lined by boulevards, partly turned into esplanades. From the suburbs there were exits into the open through ten outer gates, namely:

1. Floßtor [or Münztor].
2. Outer Peterstor [or Zeitzer Tor].
3. Windmühlentor on the road to Thonberg.
4. Sandtor.
5. Hospitaltor.
6. Outer Grimmaischer Tor [or Kohlgärtnertor].
7. Hintertor on the Schönefeld road [also known as Schönefelder Tor or Tauchaer Tor].
8. Gerbertor with a masonry bridge over the Parthe on the Halle road [also known as the Äußere Hallische Tor].
9. Rosentaltor on the road to Gohlis.
10. Outer Ranstädter Tor [also known as Äußeres Rannisches Tor, Frankfurter Tor or Wassertor].

The perimeter wall around the suburbs was of brick or wooden planking construction with loopholes, while the gates were blocked with barricades, palisades, and so on. The French had intended to set fire to the Ranstädter Vorstadt after passing through it, and to that end they had demanded 36 *Centner* (90 *Pud*) of pitch from the city, but this plan was never carried out.[2]

The formations assigned to the defence of Leipzig were stationed in the suburbs as follows: Poniatowski's *8e Corps* and Macdonald's *11e Corps* were supposed to form the rearguard after the withdrawal of all other elements of the army from the city, and were placed between the Pleiße and the road to Grimma; Souham's *3e Corps* were between the Grimmaisches Tor and Hallisches Tor; Marmont's *6e Corps*, were in the Hallische Vorstadt and Pfaffendorf along with Durutte's and Dąbrowski's divisions; one division from *11e Corps* was stationed in reserve on the esplanade forwards of the outer Peterstor (later renamed Königsplatz). Macdonald was ordered to hold the town with *8e Corps* and the *11e Corps* until at least noon and was then to withdraw, blowing up the bridge on the Elster.[3] The army's retreat along a single route through Lindenau to Markranstädt presented extreme difficulties. A few broken carts would be enough to stop the movements of every unit and convoy behind them. Some of Napoleon's companions suggested that he burn the suburbs of Leipzig and defend himself behind the city walls; but he would not dare to destroy one of the finest German cities, which belonged to his most faithful ally: that which was necessary for him as a commander could not be fulfilled by him as a Sovereign without violating international law. At nine o'clock in the morning, having completed all the arrangements for the defence of the suburbs, Napoleon went to the city, visited King Friedrich August and left the Saxon Guard with him; then, having said his farewells, he went to the Ranstädter Tor; but the crowds of men

---

2   Sporschill, *Die große Chronik*, I, 768-769; Aster, *Schlachten bei Leipzig*, II, 266 & 270.
3   Vaudoncourt, *Histoire de la guerre soutenue par les Français en Allemagne*, 220.

and vehicles prevented him from going there directly, and therefore he was forced to make his way through side streets and only got out of the city with great difficulty.[4]

The Coalition forces started to move towards Leipzig before dawn. The Army of Bohemia, from the south of the city towards the Peterstor; the Army of Poland towards the Sandtor and Hospitaltor; the Army of the North from the east towards the Grimmaisches Tor and Hintertor; while the Army of Silesia came from the north towards the Gerbertor, and on towards the Hallisches Tor. Platov's Cossack detachment and Graf Bubna's Austrian *leichte Division* received orders to cross the Pleiße and Elster upstream of Leipzig and move towards Pegau, while the cavalry of the Army of Silesia, after crossing the Elster at Schkeuditz, was ordered to head towards Lützen.[5]

As soon as Emperor Alexander and the King of Prussia, together with the Commander-in-Chief, reached Thonberg, a deputation of Leipzig citizens and *Oberst* Ryssel [Anton Friedrich Karl von Ryssel], sent by King Friedrich August, came out to meet them, proposing the surrender of the city, on condition of unhindered withdrawal of the forces located in it, and entrusting the fate of the population to the magnanimity of the victors. Emperor Alexander expressed his willingness to spare the city to the deputation; at the same time General Toll and the Prussian King's *Flügeladjutant*, *Oberstleutnant* von Natzmer [Oldwig Anton Leopold von Natzmer], were sent to Leipzig with the following letter for King Friedrich August:

> Negotiations with the King of Saxony, after every previous proposal from the Coalition has been rejected, are out of the question. The city will be spared if the enemy evacuate it immediately; Saxon troops will not be considered hostile forces as soon as they abandon all participation in the fighting and pile their muskets.[6]

General Toll was ordered to announce to the King that he was granted half an hour to comply with the aforementioned conditions. Further delay would have given the enemy the opportunity to save the troops and supply trains that were at risk from the rapid advance of the Coalition armies. But the mission entrusted to Toll and Natzmer could not be completed in such a short time. The chaos and confusion in the city were extreme. It was necessary to make their way with great difficulty along side streets, in crowded condition and under fire. The envoys were initially taken to Prince Poniatowski, then to Augereau, to Victor, and finally to the King of Saxony. Here they were told that the King 'was busy' but when Toll announced to Minister Einsiedel [Detlev von Einsiedel] that the Russian Monarch wished to receive an immediate answer, and that any delay might give rise to catastrophe, the King received him and Natzmer, in the same costume in which he had, half an hour before, bade Napoleon farewell, in a white uniform with a star, silk stockings and shoes. General Toll delivered the letter to him and the words of the Tsar. The

---

4   Vaudoncourt, *Histoire de la guerre soutenue par les Français en Allemagne*, 220.
5   Plotho, Der Krieg in Deutschland und Frankreich in den Jahren 1813 und 1814, II, 416;
    Bernhardi, Denkwürdigkeiten aus dem Leben Carl Friedrich Grafen von Toll, III, 461-462.
6   Bernhardi, III, 464.

King, without mentioning the mission he had assigned to Ryssel, suggested that the envoys should refer to the duc de Padoue (Arrighi) with regard to measures for the preservation of the city, as he had been appointed governor of Leipzig by the will of Emperor Napoleon, *'sein hoher Alliirter'* (his high ally). In the King's opinion, Saxon troops could not be withdrawn from the fighting, because they, being at the disposal of Emperor Napoleon, his high ally, received orders from him and from his marshals. When Toll reminded the King that this answer was not in accord with the statement from the city deputation, which had presented itself to the Coalition monarchs in the name of the King himself, Friedrich August replied that he had previously believed that Emperor Napoleon had yielded to the Coalition (*habe die Sache aufgegeben*), but that just half an hour ago, Emperor Napoleon, having visited him, had assured him that he was leaving Leipzig with the sole intention of manoeuvring in the field, and that in two or three days he would liberate the city. Since nothing could be expected from the King after this response, Natzmer set out, together with Einsiedel and General Zeschau, to look for the duc de Padoue, but could not find him, and in the meantime the Coalition had already broken into the city and the negotiations were over. *Oberstleutnant* Natzmer hurried to meet the Prussian fusiliers and, taking one of the companies, placed it, together with the Saxon Guard, by the house occupied by King Friedrich August, in order to protect his person, while General Toll, hearing the sound of jägers' bugles and single shots, rushed to the window and shouted to the Prussian soldiers hurrying into the square that they should not shoot at the Saxon grenadiers standing by the royal apartments; whereupon, running down the stairs, he turned to the Baden troops passing close by, and pointing to the Prussian skirmishers, said: 'these are your friends; they are fighting for the freedom of Germany; join them against our common enemy, the French. Long live Emperor Alexander! Long live the Coalition monarchs!' At the same time, *Oberstleutnant* Natzmer urged the Saxons to show themselves worthy sons of Germany and to turn their weapons against the French. The residents of all the nearby houses welcomed the envoys as harbingers of peace and salvation for the city; in every window, ladies, making signs with their handkerchiefs, urged their fellow compatriots, the Saxon warriors, 'to fight for the just cause.' The *Grenadier Bataillon von Anger* and some of the Saxon Guard, carried away by the general enthusiasm, immediately came over to the Coalition side.[7]

The attack on Leipzig was carried out by all four Coalition armies

The advance by the Army of Bohemia and Army of Poland

At about eight o'clock in the morning, the leading formations of the Army of Bohemia moved towards Probstheida and Dölitz (Count Wittgenstein's corps on the right wing, Kleist's corps in the centre, Graf Colloredo's corps on the left wing), but by this time the French had already retreated to the Leipzig suburbs, having destroyed some 50 ammunition caissons and buried 12 guns. Barclay de Tolly's force, having

---

7   Plotho, II, 416-417; Bernhardi, III, 464-469.

received orders to advance further, at about ten o'clock set off towards the Sandtor and the Windmühlentor). The enemy, having placed batteries at the entrances to the suburbs, opened fire, which was countered by the Coalition artillery. The Russians, having crossed themselves, were preparing to storm the city, but were ordered to halt, because other columns were already breaking into the suburbs at other points and it was easy to foresee that the enemy would soon be forced to retreat. The Austrian force under Graf Colloredo, sent to Kleist's left, towards the Peterstor, engaged the retreating troops, but having reached the suburbs, they also halted and at three o'clock in the afternoon received orders to advance towards Gautzsch and on towards Pegau. General Bennigsen, having marched through Stötteritz at seven o'clock in the morning, moved towards the Sandtor and the Hospitaltor with the infantry of the Army of Poland and brought up 60 guns from his artillery reserve, under the command of General Rezvy [Dmitry Petrovich Rezvy], to a range of 300 paces from the perimeter wall.[8] The actions of the Russian batteries soon silenced the enemy, but then ceased firing for the duration of the visit of the Leipzig deputation to the Coalition sovereigns. Once the negotiations had failed and General Bennigsen received orders to resume operations against the city, the bombardment restarted and orders were given to storm the place, but at the same time the troops were informed that 'the Tsar has ordered Leipzig to be spared and it is forbidden to plunder in the city and its suburbs under penalty of death.' The attack was crowned with complete success: Bennigsen broke through the Grimmaisches Tor (sic, Hospitaltor?) himself with Paskevich's 26th Division; 12th Division burst into the Petersvorstadt, while 13th Division pushed through a breach made in the wall by the courageous sappers from Lieutenant Colonel Afanasiev's company. Despite stubborn resistance from the French skirmishers entrenched in the gardens, the Russians reached the boulevard separating the suburbs from the city, captured some of their artillery and took many prisoners. Major General Savoini [Yeremey Yakovlevich Savoini] captured 18 guns with the Ladoga Infantry and Poltava Infantry; the Orël Infantry took three, 5th Jägers took eight; Major Semenovich of the second battalion of the Narva Infantry took General Małachowski [Kazimierz Małachowski], 15 officers, 300 lower ranks prisoner, and captured 17 guns and 27 ammunition caissons.[9]

The advance of the Army of the North

Bülow's corps set off from their overnight camp at Paunsdorf at seven o'clock in the morning, took the villages abandoned by the French, and reached Leipzig at eight o'clock, at the same time that Bennigsen's force were just breaking camp. The brigade under Prinz Ludwig von Hessen-Homburg marched at the head of the Prussian corps towards the outer Grimmaisches Tor; Borstell's brigade proceeded to their right, somewhat further back, in the direction of the Milchinsel park and the Hintertor, while Krafft's brigade were in reserve. At nine o'clock, the Prussian force began a cannonade and firefight, in which Bennigsen's force also joined in an hour later; and at 11 o'clock the brigade under the Prinz von Hessen-Homburg went on the attack. Major Friccius' *Königsberger Landwehr Bataillon* [Karl Friedrich Friccius] were the

---

8   Bennigsen's diary states that the Army of Poland attacked the Grimmaisches Tor.
9   War Diary of General Bennigsen's Army of Poland; Aster, II, 275.

first to break through the rubble barricading the gate and suffered heavy losses; they were followed by two battalions of 3. *Ostpreußisches Infanterie*.[10] The enemy fought very stubbornly; among the wounded was Prinz Ludwig von Hessen-Homburg himself. 'Lads! Keep standing firm' he said to Friccius' warriors as they carried him away from the scene of slaughter.[11] General Borstell, having taken command of Bülow's vanguard, directed his brigade at the Hintertor; the brave Pomeranian battalions burst into the suburb and captured 25 guns. At the same time, the Crown Prince of Sweden reinforced Borstell with two Swedish battalions and sent General Count Vorontsov to the Hospitaltor with five battalions, who drove the enemy out of the suburb, pushed them back to the city even reaching the Roßplatz. Colonel Krasovsky [Afanasy Ivanovich Krasovsky] particularly distinguished himself with the 14th Jägers here, taking several guns.[12]

The advance of the Army of Silesia
The attack on the city from the north presented the greatest difficulties, because the enemy paid particular attention to the defence of Pfaffendorf and the Hallische Vorstadt, which lay close to their line of retreat towards Lützen. While awaiting the arrival of Langéron's force on the right bank of the Parthe, Blücher ordered Sacken to take Pfaffendorf, which was successfully achieved. At the same time, an heavy artillery company, positioned on the right bank of the river by Blücher himself, fired at the area between the city and the village of Reudnitz and greatly assisted Bülow's advance. At around 11 o'clock, comte Langéron's force reached the scene of the fighting. General Kaptsevich was ordered to storm the flèche at the outer Hallische Tor [Gerbertor], which protected the bridge on the Parthe; this fortification was armed with three guns, while the gardens and houses on the far bank of the river were heavily garrisoned with artillery and marksmen. The operations by the Russian batteries on the Hallische Vorstadt, however, forced the enemy and the *magistratus* of Leipzig to plead for mercy for the city; but Blücher replied that he would cease firing only when the city surrendered, and ordered Sacken and Langéron to seize the Hallisches Tor immediately. At one o'clock in the afternoon, just as Bülow's force were breaking into the city and had compromised the defence of the flèche by threatening to envelop the enemy holding it from the rear, General Kaptsevich assaulted the fortification with the Arkhangelogorod Infantry and Staroingermanland Infantry; Blücher personally supervised the assault himself, rousing the advancing columns with shouts of: '*Vorwärts! Vorwärts!*' The Arkhangelogorod Infantry under Lieutenant Colonel Shenshin particularly distinguished themselves, suffering such losses here that after the capture of Leipzig, only 30 officers and 180 lower ranks remained. At the same time as this assault, comte Saint-Priest received orders to bypass the flèche by moving to the left, along the bank of the Parthe, but all his efforts to get into the suburbs were unsuccessful, due to the marshy terrain intersected by branches of the river, which forced Saint-Priest

---

10 The author of a very good work on the war of 1813: *Geschichte des Krieges in den Jahren 1813 und 1814, mit besonderer Rücksicht auf Ostpreußen und das Königsbergsche Landwehrbataillon.*
11 '*Kinder! Haltet eich verner brav.*'
12 Plotho, II, 419-420; Aster, II, 283-292; Beitzke, II, 644-646.

to attack the flèche frontally, together with Kaptsevich's men. General Bistrom 2nd (Adam Ivanovich), with the Yekaterinburg Infantry and Rylsk Infantry, went into the assault; the French, under the command of Durutte, defended themselves desperately; the Russian troops lost some 1,000 men, but eventually Major Bogdanovich [Vasily Ivanovich Bogdanovich] broke into the fortification with the Yekaterinburg Infantry, captured the three guns stationed there, crossed the bridge and drove the defeated enemy along the Gerberstraße, where he was seriously wounded. The rest of Kaptsevich's and Sacken's forces raced up behind them, and during the assault on the flèche, managed to seize Rosental. The enemy were pursued by the victors through the Hallische Vorstadt right up to the boulevard itself with loud shouts of 'Hurrah!' from where some of their troops turned towards the Ranstädter Tor in complete disorder; still others surrendered to Langéron and Sacken with all the artillery that was with them (numbering more than 50 guns). From these latter forces, 8th Jägers and 39th Jägers under Colonel Akhlëstyshev [Mikhail Fëdorovich Akhlëstyshev], who was wounded, particularly distinguished themselves.[13]

At around midday, just after Bülow's and Bennigsen's troops had broken into the suburbs, Wittgenstein's and Kleist's corps were ordered to continue the offensive. Shortly before, General Stockhorn [Karl Ludwig Wilhelm Stockhorner von Starein], who was stationed at the Grimmaisches Tor with the Baden brigade from Marchand's division, received orders to go to the assistance of the force defending the Peterstor and to come under Marshal Augereau's command. But before the Baden men had chance to arrive at their assigned place, one of the regiments, on Marchand's orders, had turned back to the Grimmaisches Tor, whereupon *Markgraf* Wilhelm von Baden [Wilhelm Ludwig August von Baden] moved them on to the Marktplatz; the other regiment, located at the Peterstor, were enveloped from the rear by Bennigsen's force and obliged to lay down their arms. The Polish units stationed alongside them surrendered willingly.[14]

The Coalition sovereigns, having issued orders to the troops under Wittgenstein and Kleist to enter the city, accompanied them. Emperor Alexander, expressing his goodwill to the regiments going into the assault for the courage they had shown the day before, reminded them not to abuse the civilian population. 'Lads' he said 'you have shown yourselves to be brave warriors once more; be merciful to the vanquished and to the unfortunate inhabitants of this city. Your Tsar asks this of you, and if you are devoted to me, as I am sure you are, then you will carry out my orders without exception.'[15] Even amidst the thunder of war, and in the joy of a decisive victory, bought at the cost of many years of care, exertion, and sacrifice, the Blessed Monarch encouraged his warriors not simply to crush the foe, but rather to spare those showing submission. Occasional shots were still being fired in the city

---

13 War Diary of Baron Sacken's corps; War Diary of comte Langéron's corps; Plotho, II, 420; Richter, *Geschichte des Deutschen Freiheitskrieges vom Jahre 1813 bis zum Jahre 1815*, II, 315-316.
14 Vaudoncourt, 221; Norvin, *Portefeuille de 1813*, II, 420, these and other French historians claim that the Baden troops voluntarily let the Coalition in through the Peterstor; but this is inconsistent with the evidence presented in *Militär-Wochenblatt*, 1830, No. 714 & No. 715.
15 Förster, *Geschichte der Befreiungskriege, 1813, 1814, 1815*, II, 322-323.

when Emperor Alexander, the King of Prussia and Prinz Schwarzenberg, with their numerous retinue, passed through the Grimmaisches Tor at one o'clock in the afternoon, rode through the suburbs and continued their festive procession, through the ranks of victorious warriors, to the great Marktplatz. The sounds of military music, the roar of the cannonade at the Ranstädter Tor, the deafening 'Hurrahs!' from the Coalition soldiers and the joyful cheers of the population, who merged their welcome for the salvation of the city and the freedom of Germany with each other. Upon reaching the large square, the monarchs were met by the Crown Prince of Sweden and General Bennigsen; the other commanders of the Coalition formations gradually gathered there. The King of Saxony, leaving the house where he was residing, stopped on the portico, hoping that Emperor Alexander and King Friedrich Wilhelm would pay him a visit, but, after talking for a few minutes with the Crown Prince of Sweden, they set off for the Ranstädter Tor. They met Blücher on the way there as he was riding up from the Hallische Vorstadt, and having expressed their gratitude to him, they wanted to make their way to the Ranstädter Steinweg, but were forced to abandon this plan, due to the crowds of troops and vehicles jammed along the avenues littered with the bodies of the dead, the wounded, wreckage of guns, carts, weapons, as so on. Moreover, several shells fired from the direction of Lindenau by the French burst near Emperor Alexander, and all those surrounding the Tsar begged him to leave. The Coalition monarchs, having entrusted command of the formations that had entered the city to the Crown Prince of Sweden, rode to the Grimmaisches Tor and, having met up with Kaiser Franz, dismounted their horses and congratulated him on his victory. Thereafter, the Austrian Kaiser departed via the Marktplatz and Peterstor to Rötha, while Emperor Alexander, at the invitation of the Crown Prince, having reviewed the Swedish corps bivouacked at Reudnitz, returned to Leipzig together with the King of Prussia.[16]

At the same time as the Coalition sovereigns were making their festive entrance to the conquered city, Napoleon managed to escape with great difficulty, being obstructed at every step by units and vehicles leaving along the only line of retreat – via Lindenau. He had barely crossed the masonry bridge over the Elster when a terrible explosion was heard: the bridge had been destroyed and the French forces remaining in the city were now deprived of the opportunity to evade death or capture. Napoleon's detractors claimed that, obsessed solely with his own salvation, he had ordered the bridge to be destroyed as soon as he had crossed it with his retinue. But this accusation has not been proven in any way, indeed, there was no need to ensure Napoleon's escape by such a desperate measure: as soon as they managed to get out onto the Lützen road, the many defiles behind them gave his formations the means to check the Coalition pursuit. If Napoleon and the chief executor of his concepts, Berthier, deserve criticism, it is not for selfishly sacrificing the troops in pursuit of self-preservation at all, but rather for their negligence regarding precautions taken to secure the army. Since it was a matter of withdrawing 100,000 or 120,000 men with huge parks and baggage trains through the long defiles formed by the branches of the Pleiße and Elster, it was necessary to take care of the construction

---

16 Aster, II, 324-327.

of additional bridges, which would speed up the crossings and give the army mitigation against unanticipated incidents. But this was not done, and the troops were dragged down a single road, through a long series of defiles, where a few broken carts were enough to delay the entire army. In order to prevent coalition forces from crossing the Elster behind the French rearguard, orders were issued to lay demolition charges under the masonry bridge and to blow it up after the army had crossed to the left bank of the river.[17] The *État-major général du Génie*, Dulauloy, entrusted the execution of this order to his *chef d'état-major*, Colonel Montfort, who, leaving a corporal with three sappers at the bridge, went to Lindenau, to Berthier, to clarify exactly under which circumstances the bridge should be blown up. But Berthier, ignorant of the situation inside the city, could not resolve his doubts, and Montfort, instead of remaining at the bridge himself, again distinguished himself by ordering the sappers left there to light the fuse as soon as the enemy reached it. Meanwhile, at one o'clock in the afternoon, Sacken's skirmishers, having taken Rosental, made their way to the Jakobshospital over one of the branches of the Elster, across the still intact hospital footbridge and then through the gardens towards the masonry bridge and began shooting at the troops and vehicles passing over it. As was stated in the French report, the corporal was 'a man without intelligence and a poor understanding of his mission,' believing that delay was no longer possible, lit the fuse, blew up the bridge and severed the only line of retreat for the French army.[18] The news quickly spread among the troops who had not yet managed to leave the city, leaving them stricken with horror. Those enemy under pressure from all sides by Coalition forces threw down their weapons and surrendered; others, scattered along the floodplains of the Pleiße and Elster, threw themselves into the water and swam across the branches of these rivers, or drowned. Major General Emmanuel, as one of the first to enter Leipzig with an escort of 14 men, captured first 12 cuirassiers of the Guard [sic], then General Vissaut [sic, Louis Vasserot?], and galloped to the recently demolished bridge. Seeing the French attempting to cross the river on planks, Emmanuel forced them to turn back; Lauriston was among them.[19] An enemy column was approaching the river at that very moment. The French, astonished at the sight of their corps commander and a Russian general standing together, halted. General Emmanuel, taking advantage of their bewilderment, rode up to them determinedly, and, having demanded that the column lay down their arms, allowed the officers to keep their swords on their word of honour, since it was impossible to disarm them: thus, he had captured two generals, 17 officers and some 400 lower ranks with his small escort. Another corps commander, Reynier, and generals Kamieński and Grabowski [Stefan Grabowski] were captured by Bülow's men.[20]

---

17 To that end, on the night of 6 to 7 (18 to 19) October, a small boat was moored under the bridge with three barrels of gunpowder secured to it.
18 '*homme sans intelligence et comprenant mal sa mission.*'
19 Emperor Alexander, who knew General Lauriston personally, since he had been the French ambassador in St. Petersburg, received him very graciously and ordered that his needs be met and all possible favours be done for him.
20 *Moniteur de 30 d'octobre 1813*; Richter, II, 323; Aster, II, 300-304 & 320; Beitzke, II, 649-650. Colonel Montfort and the corporal who lit the fuse faced a *cour martiale*.

Marshal Prince Poniatowski was among the enemy fallen. The small remnant of the Polish force, having been pushed back into the parks laid out along the left bank of the Pleiße, tried to cross from there to the Lützen road. Prince Poniatowski, wounded on 2 and 4 (14 and 16) October, and receiving a third wound during the defence of Leizig on 7 (19) October, also galloped there. Having reached Richters Garten, he addressed the Polish officers surrounding him with a short speech: 'we must die here with honour!' he said, jumping his horse into one of the wide ditches (the Diebesgraben) linking the Pleiße with the Elster. But the muddy bed of this ditch prevented him from crossing; his horse got stuck and, having abandoned it, he barely managed to scramble up the other side of the ditch himself, with the help of his suite. His strength was completely gone, but despite this, he mounted another horse and, having seen that Prussian skirmishers were catching up to him, galloped towards the Elster, threw himself into the water on horseback and died, having been hit by a bullet. Many officers who also attempted to swim across the Elster drowned along with him. The same fate befell the French *Général* Dumoutier [sic], *Chef d'état-major* of *11e Corps*. Marshal Macdonald, on the other hand, managed to cross the Elster safely and reported to Napoleon in person, who remained in the Lindenauer Mühle with his *Chef d'état-major* until three o'clock in the afternoon, and then went to spend the night in Markranstädt.[21]

Emperor Alexander spent the entire night of 7 to 8 (19 to 20) October dealing with diplomatic and military business. According to contemporaries and eyewitnesses, Kröller's house [the Griechenhaus] on the Katharinenstraße, where the Tsar's headquarters were located, became the epicentre of all European politics at this time. The King of Saxony sent General Zeschau to the Austrian Kaiser and the King of Prussia, expressing a desire to visit them. When the coalition monarchs, instead of responding, ordered the general to present himself before Emperor Alexander, the Tsar promised to send an answer later. At eight o'clock in the evening, the Russian Privy Councillor Anstett [Ivan Osipovich Anshtet or Johann Protasius von Anstett] went to Friedrich August and, in the name of His Majesty, announced to the King that his 'personal security and safety required his departure from Leipzig to Berlin, where all preparations would be made for his residence, and that Privy Councillor Anstett had been instructed to accompany the King there with his family and the retinue that was accompanying him.' Thus, Friedrich August was acknowledged as a prisoner of war. In response to this decision, the King of Saxony, having set out the factors which had prompted him to take Napoleon's side after the battle of Lützen in a letter to the Tsar, concluded his explanation with the following words:

> Victory has decided it. I am in the hands of Your Imperial Majesty. The conditions that You propose to offer me can only be just and in accordance with my interests and those of my people. In which case, I am ready to accede to them and maintain them with the same rigour that has been the principle of my actions thus far. May Your Imperial Majesty grant me

---

21 Aster, II, 317-318 [Aster only mentions a *Général* Dumoutier, not the appointment of *Chef d'état-major* of *11e Corps*, which is given in other sources as *Général* Grundler, who died in 1833].

a new sign of Your benevolence, by not delaying in letting me know Your intentions and those of Your powerful allies in this regard.[22]

The Tsar replied:

> The respect I owe to the unfortunate position in which Your Majesty finds yourself imposes on me the duty of not entering into a discussion on the motives which guided your political course. Military interests alone must, in the current circumstances, direct the views that I may follow with regard to Your Majesty.[23]

The losses on both sides in the four-day battle of Leipzig were enormous, although, considering the number of troops involved, it was less bloody than the battles of Preußisch Eylau or Borodino. The troop losses have been given as:

	Plotho	Hofmann	Schulz	Aster
French Army	15,000 killed. 30,000 wounded.[24] 15,000 prisoners. Total: 60,000 men, 300 guns, 900 ammunition caissons & vehicles.	30,000 killed & wounded. 30,000 prisoners.[25] Total: 68,000 men, 300 guns.	At least 60,000 casualties. More than 300 guns.	13,000 killed & wounded. 30,000 prisoners. 23,000 sick. Total: 66,000 men.
Russian Army	19,535 killed & wounded.[26]	20,800 killed & wounded.	**Beitzke** 22,604 killed & wounded.	12,653 casualties (not including 4 (16) October). 1,844 killed. 12,697 wounded & prisoners. Total: 14,541 men.
Prussian Army	15,470 killed & wounded.	14,170 killed & wounded.	16,430 killed & wounded.	
Austrian Army	2,058 killed. 5,308 wounded. 1,040 prisoners. Total: 8,406 men.	7,360 killed & wounded.	8,399 killed & wounded.	
Swedish Army	310 casualties.	310 casualties.	103 casualties	

---

22 'La victoire en a décidé. Je suis entre les mains de Votre Majesté Impériale. Les conditions qu'Elle daignera m'offrir ne peuvent être qu justes et conformes à mes intérêts et à ceux de mes peuples. Je suis prêt dans ce cas à y accéder et à les maintenir avec la même rigueur qui a été jusqu'ici la règle de mes démarches. Que Votre Majesté Impériale veuille m'accorder une marque nouvelle de Sa bienveillance, en ne tardant pas à me faire savoir à cet égard Ses intentions et celles de Ses puissans alliés.'
23 'Les égards que je dois à la position malheureuse, où Votre Majesté se trouve, m'imposent le devoir de ne pas entrer en discussion sur les motifs qui out guidé sa marche politique. L'intérêt militaire doit dans les circonstances actuelles diriger seul les vues que Je puis suivre à l'égard de Votre Majesté.'
24 Of these, 23,000 were sick and were in Leipzig hospitals.
25 Including many of those that were sick.
26 The Russian casualties were broken down as: killed: 15 field officers, 95 subalterns, 199 non-commissioned officers, 2,761 privates. Wounded: 102 field officers, 568 subalterns, 952 non-

From all these statements it may be assessed that the French army in the fighting around Leipzig, from 4 to 7 (16 to 19) October, lost a total of over 60,000 men and 300 guns. Even Vaudoncourt admits that the French lost 20,000 killed, 30,000 prisoners and 150 guns. According to Thiers, the French army lost from 60,000 to 70,000 men; and there remained between 100,000 and 110,000 men with the Colours, in a most miserable condition. In the Coalition armies, some 50,000 men were *hors de combat*, of whom 22,000 were Russians, 16,000 were Prussians, 12,000 were Austrians, and between 100 and 300 were Swedes.[27]

The French generals killed were: Marshal Prince Józef Poniatowski, *généraux de division*: Vial, Rochambeau, Delmas, Friederichs, Richemont and Dumoutier (the latter drowned in the Elster); those wounded were: marshals Ney, Marmont and Macdonald, Prinz Emil von Hessen-Darmstadt [or Aemilianus Maximilian Leopold von Hessen und bei Rhein], corps commanders: Lauriston, Reynier, Latour-Maubourg (the latter died a few days later [*sic*, he died in 1850]), Sébastiani, Souham and Pajol; *généraux de division*: Maison, Compans, Charpentier, Rożniecki [Aleksander Antoni Jan Rożniecki] and *général de brigade* Krasiński [Izydor Zenon Tomasz Krasiński?]; those taken prisoner included: Prinz Emil von Hessen-Darmstadt, *Markgraf* Wilhelm von Baden, Lauriston, Reynier, Charpentier, Rożniecki, *généraux de brigade*: Bertrand ([Antoine Joseph Bertrand] Commandant of Leipzig), Pino [Domenico Pino?], Denen [*sic*], Dorsenne [*sic*], Dubois [*sic*], Couloumy [Annet-Antoine Couloumy], Aubry [Claude Charles Aubry de La Boucharderie], Montmarie, d'Haugéranville [François Charles d'Avrange d'Haugéranville?], Brenoville [*sic*], Krasiński, Umiński [Jan Nepomucen Umiński], Slivarich [Marc Slivarich de Heldenbourg, or Marko Šljivarić] and Rautenstrauch [Józef Rautenstrauch]; the Bavarian *Generalleutnant* Raglovich [Clemens von Raglovich], Baden generals: Stockhorn, Hochberg and Schäffer [Konrad Rudolf Schäffer], Württemberg *Generalleutnant* Beurnonville [*sic*]; Saxon lieutenant generals Zeschau and Gersdorff; *Generalmajor* Bose.[28]

The Russian dead included: lieutenant generals Shevich and Neverovsky, major generals: Manteuffel, Huene, Reven, Prince Kudashev and Lindfors; wounded included: lieutenant generals Raevsky, Duka and Kretov; major generals: Levashov, Kreutz, Pisarev [Alexander Alexandrovich Pisarev], Lieven, Stavitsky [Maxim Fëdorovich Stavitsky], Pahlen, Benckendorff and Kryzhanovsky [Maxim Konstantinovich Kryzhanovsky]; colonels: Arnoldi and Dietrichs. The Prussian dead included: *Obersten* Maltzahn and Krosigk; the wounded included: Prinz Ludwig von Hessen-Homburg, Prinz Karl zu Mecklenburg-Strelitz; *Obersten*: Steinmetz, Katzler, and others. The Austrian dead included: generals Fenner [*sic*] and Giffing [Samuel von Giffing]; the wounded included: *General der Kavallerie* the

---

commissioned officers, 21,065 privates. Missing: 15 subalterns, 78 non-commissioned officers, 2,685 privates. For a total of: 117 field officers, 678 subalterns, 1,229 non-commissioned officers, 17,511 privates.
27 Plotho, II, 422-424; Hofmann, *Zur Geschichte des Feldzuges von 1813*, 305; Vaudoncourt, 222; Schulz, *Geschichte der Kriege in Europa seit dem Jahre 1792*, XI, *1 Band*, 152-153; Aster, II, 221-224; Beitzke, II, 654; Thiers, *Histoire du Consulat et de l'Empire*, XVI, 699-700.
28 Sporschill, I, 934-935; Aster, II, 356-357.

Erbprinz zu Hessen-Homburg, *Feldmarschallleutnanten*: Nostitz, Hardegg, Mohr and Graf Radetzky, *Generalmajor* Splény [Franz Splény de Miháldy].[29]

Emperor Alexander, on the night following the battle that decided the fate of Leipzig, bestowed many awards on his companions: the Order of St. George 1st class for Prinz Schwarzenberg and Blücher;[30] the Order of St. George 2nd class was awarded to Tsarevich Konstantin Pavlovich, Prinz Eugen von Württemberg and Kleist; Bennigsen and Barclay de Tolly were raised to the dignity of counts; Count Miloradovich and Count Platov were awarded the Order of St. Andrew the First-Called; Count Wittgenstein received a Golden Sabre with laurels; Konovnitsyn [Pëtr Petrovich Konovnitsyn], Prince Gorchakov and Sabaneev [Ivan Vasilievich Sabaneev] received the Order of St. Vladimir 1st class; comte Langéron received the Order of St. Alexander Nevsky with diamonds; Prince Volkonsky, Lieutenant General Count Pahlen, Vasilchikov, Count Vorontsov, Count Shuvalov [Pavel Andreevich Shuvalov], Count Stroganov and the Prussian General Gneisenau received the Order of St. Alexander Nevsky. The following were promoted to full general: Raevsky, Uvarov and Wintzingerode; those promoted to lieutenant general included Diebitsch and Paskevich. Blücher, having been promoted to the rank of *Feldmarschall* by King Friedrich Wilhelm, also received the *Großkreuz* of the *Maria-Theresien-Orden* from Kaiser Franz, which was also awarded to Prinz Schwarzenberg. Both also received the Prussian *Schwarzer Adlerorden*.

After the capture of Leipzig, the city garrison was formed from 2,000 Russian and Prussian troops; General Shuvalov was appointed the interim governor of Leipzig. The following were located around the city, in bivouacs, on the evening of 7 (19) October: the corps under Wittgenstein and Kleist, the entire Austrian force, except for Gyulay's *III. Korpus* and both *leichte Divisionen*, Count Bennigsen's entire Army of Poland, except for 26th Division under Paskevich and Kreutz's cavalry detachment, and the entire Army of the North, except for the detachment under Adjutant General Chernyshev. The following measures were taken for the pursuit of the enemy: from the formations of the Army of the North, Yorck's Corps, numbering 13,400 men, having occupied the crossings at Merseburg and Halle, sent the reserve cavalry under *Oberst* Jürgaß along the Lützen road, where the cavalry from Sacken's Corps, commanded by Vasilchikov, were also headed; the corps under Langéron and Sacken crossed over at Schkeuditz. As early as the evening of 6 (18) October, General Gyulay, who was with the Austrian *III. Korpus* on the left bank of the Elster, having received orders to forestall the enemy in Naumburg, was to occupy the Kösen defile [4½ miles west of Naumburg] and to defend the crossing over the

---

29 Sporschill, I, 936-937; Aster, II, 357.
30 At the time of the assault of Leipzig, Emperor Alexander and King Friedrich Wilhelm awarded Prince Schwarzenberg the Order of St. George, 1st class, and the *Schwarzer Adlerorden*, congratulating the Commander-in-Chief on a victory that would perpetuate his renown. The *Feldmarschall* replied that he was 'merely an executor of the orders of the Coalition monarchs and that all the glory of the victory belongs to them, as well as to the commanders and troops who were fighting for the independence of Germany'. Plotho, II, 417-418; Varnhagen von Ense, *Leben des Fürsten Blücher von Wahlstadt*, 250-251, claims that Emperor Alexander presented Blücher with a jewelled sabre for distinction in the battle of Leipzig.

river Saale to the last man, immediately sent the detachments under Thielmann and Mensdorff towards Naumburg, the Austrian *1. leichte Division* to Pegau, while he set off there himself with the rest of the force at two o'clock in the morning on 7 (19) October. Lederer's division and Nostitz's reserve cavalry were assigned to support him, but both of these formations were unable to cross the Elster that day, and Gyulay, upon reaching Pegau, having received emphatic orders to hold the Kösen defile, set off towards Naumburg. On the way there, at Dobergast [8½ miles north of Zeitz], the Austrian force, due to a mistake by headquarters, stumbled across a large Cossack detachment in a ravine cluttered with artillery and trains, which forced the Austrians to halt for the night at this defile and continue moving towards the Saale river the next day [20 October, new style]. Fortunately for the Coalition, the enemy did not have chance to exploit their mistake and seize the crossing at Kösen, which was so vital to them. At eight o'clock in the morning, the detachments under Thielmann and Mensdorff reached Naumburg, and together with five companies under Major Graf Gatterburg [Karl Josef von Gatterburg] that had also arrived there, they took up positions at the Kösen bridge. The leading units of Bertrand's French corps appeared at the bridge in the evening, but Graf Gatterburg delayed them and made his small detachment appear stronger than it really was, which forced the enemy to abandon the crossing at this point and turn towards Weißenfels and take the Freyburg road, and the next day, 8 (20) October, in the evening, Gyulay and Nostitz reached Naumburg, but instead of immediately occupying the Kösen defile in significant strength, they halted and set out for Kösen the following morning [21 October, new style]. Bertrand, making the most of this mistake, pushed Graf Gatterburg back to the right bank of the Saale and held the left bank of the river, but could not destroy the bridge under fire from Austrian troops located on the far bank of the Saale.[31]

Seeing himself forestalled at Naumburg by Gyulay's corps, followed by other formations from the main Coalition army, and at Merseburg by the Army of Silesia, Napoleon was forced to head towards Erfurt via Weißenfels and Freyburg, along a very tortuous route. By the evening of 7 (19) October, he had halted at Markranstädt; his main body was stationed in the vicinity of this town, Bertrand's *4e Corps* were pushed forwards to Weißenfels, while Marshal Oudinot, having destroyed the bridges on the branches of the Elster and on the river Luppe behind him, took up positions behind Lindenau with a rearguard composed of the *Jeune Garde*. The Coalition forces, with the exception of those detached to pursue the enemy and those who remained in bivouacs near Leipzig, were deployed on the night after the battle as follows: the Russo-Prussian reserves were at Pegau; Barclay de Tolly's headquarters remained at Audigast. Kreutz's cavalry, having swum across the Pleiße and Elster, forced the enemy artillery, which continued to fire at the city, to cease their bombardment, while 26th Division had crossed the Pleiße via a temporary bridge and had entered bivouacs in the vicinity of Leipzig.[32]

---

31 *Oestereichische Militärische Zeitschrift, 1830*, VIII; Plotho, II, 426-427 & 429; Hofmann, 308-309.
32 Plotho, II, 426-427.

Napoleon, in deciding to give battle at Leipzig, in which the Coalition had managed to concentrate twice as many troops, had been prompted to do so by very important factors. Had he retreated beyond the river Saale, he would not only lose the opportunity to use the resources of Saxony, which would immediately have gone over to the side of the Coalition, but, in all likelihood, he would have found it necessary to retreat beyond the Rhine, and would have resulted in the dissolution of the *Confédération du Rhin*. Moreover, by retreating to the left bank of the Saale, the French army would lose communications with the garrisons of the fortresses on the Elbe: consequently, the Battle of Leipzig was unavoidable for Napoleon. But having lost it, he was not only forced to retreat beyond the Rhine, but also completely disordered his army as well as condemning the fortress garrisons to destruction or imprisonment. Therefore, in deciding on a general battle as the only means of getting out of the dangerous situation in which the successes of the Coalition after the armistice had placed him, Napoleon had to risk everything in the pursuit of a victory: all that remained was for him to add not only Saint-Cyr's corps left in Dresden, but also elements of the garrisons of Torgau, Wittenberg and Magdeburg to the main body. By operating in this manner, on the first day of the battle of Leipzig, he could have opposed the Coalition with almost equal numbers.

Thereafter, having decided to attack the Army of Bohemia first, it was vital to leave only the bare minimum force necessary facing Blücher in order to delay him on the river Parthe and in Leipzig, and to concentrate all the rest at Wachau and Liebertwolkwitz for a decisive offensive against the main Coalition army. The security of the exits at Ranstädt became hugely important, but in this case, a retreat by the French army along the road to Lützen could have been secured even in the event of Blücher successfully taking Leipzig: it would only require the arrangement of several crossings over the Pleiße and Elster upstream of Leipzig.

The advance by a considerable part of Napoleon's forces towards Güldengossa on 4 (16) October did not have a decisive outcome, thanks to the foresight of Emperor Alexander, who had concentrated reserves at the threatened point. Furthermore, as far as can be assessed from the conflicting accounts of this attack, it was carried out in a very incoherent manner. If this were not the case, it would have been very unlikely that a handful of Lifeguard Cossacks could have halted the advance of a cavalry column consisting of several thousand horsemen.

Once Napoleon had failed to defeat the Coalition on 4 (16) October, he had to limit the objective of his further operations to a withdrawal beyond the Elster. It has been claimed that Napoleon did not begin his retreat immediately because not all the units he was expecting had arrived at Leipzig. But this is not in agreement with the evidence: after the fighting on 4 (16) October, only Reynier's corps remained on the march to Leipzig, and even they arrived on the morning of 5 (17) October. Consequently, had Napoleon sent his parks and trains along the Lützen road the previous night, all his formations, including Reynier's corps, would have had chance to retreat in good time without causing congestion in the city and at the crossings over the Pleiße and Elster. As for the negligence with regard to the construction of temporary crossings, the leaving intact of bridges that were subsequently used by the Coalition, and the premature demolition of the masonry bridge on the Elster, all this can be explained only by the customary disorder within the French military administration at that time, despite the fact that they have been praised beyond all measure. The origins of this exaggerated notion of the merits of Napoleon's military logistics lie in his *commissaire des guerres* being highly skilled in the art of extracting the last resources from whichever country served as the theatre of operations; but does not take into account the cost to the population.

Coalition operations generally lacked coherence and coordination. The failure of the offensive on 4 (16) October, as well as the erroneous distribution of forces, must, in all fairness, be attributed to these factors. Indeed, even on 6 (18) October, the Coalition did not take advantage of their enormous superiority in numbers to deliver a decisive blow to the enemy. Instead of attacking the enemy positions simultaneously across the entire sector from Connewitz to Melkau, it would have been better, while awaiting the arrival on the battlefield of the Army of the North and Langéron's Corps, to advance in echelons from the right and conduct a decisive attack from Zweinaundorf to Stötteritz with Bennigsen's forces, supported by strong reserves; the forces under the Erbprinz zu Hessen-Homburg and Count Wittgenstein, avoiding a bitter struggle to take control of Connewitz and Probstheida, could have remained out of cannon range, or limited themselves to a cannonade. Once the Coalition had occupied Stötteritz, the defence of Probstheida, Connewitz and Schönefeld became untenable, and the enemy, in all probability, out of concern at being cut off, would have hastened to retreat to Leipzig. It is also impossible not to notice that the Coalition, not having the opportunity to commit the significant mass of their cavalry into battle on 6 (18) October, could have made full use of them if (as Blücher had proposed) they had sent the majority of them along the line of retreat of the enemy army. It should have been possible to inflict incomparably greater losses on Napoleon by operating in this manner. Considering the Coalition forces' double superiority in numbers, it might have been expected that they would suffer fewer casualties than the enemy; but in reality things turned out differently and the reasons for this were:

1. The skill of the French skirmishers in loose formation.
2. Even more so, the weak pursuit after the battle had been won.

The indecision of Prinz Schwarzenberg frustrated both the bravery of the Coalition troops and the skill of their commanders through his inaction.

43

The Coalition pursuit of Napoleon's army from the Elster to the Main

---

Napoleon's retreat to Weißenfels, and onwards to Freyburg. – Gyulay's move to Naumburg. – Bertrand's movements along the Naumburg road, the return to Weißenfels and on to the Kösen bridge. – Measures taken by the Coalition for the pursuit of the enemy. – 9 (21) October, the actions at Neu-Kösen and Freyburg. – Napoleon's retreat to Erfurt. – 10 (22) October, the action at Weimar. – Russian units sent to the vanguard. – Prince Schwarzenberg pauses the advance by the Army of Bohemia. – Successes of the partisan detachments.

Napoleon at Erfurt. – Reorganisation of the army. – Order of march for the onward retreat. – Emperor Alexander's instructions for the War Department. – *Zentral Verwaltungs Rat* for the administration of conquered territories. – National mobilisation; measures taken for feeding the formations assembled in Saxony. – The onward advance of the Coalition armies. – The situation of the enemy army during the retreat from Erfurt to Mainz. – Misdirection of the Coalition columns.

On the morning of 7 (19) October, having reached Lindenau Napoleon ordered officers left on either side of the Lützen road to meet the disordered units from the army and direct them to assembly areas; while he went to the Lindenauer Mühle himself and, completely exhausted from fatigue, lay down to rest, but soon after the demolition of the masonry bridge he left for Markranstädt, while his troops dragged themselves along in the greatest disorder. Many of the soldiers dispersed along the sides of the road; these marauders, who robbed and devastated the country, received a characteristic nickname from their own brothers-in-arms: *fricoteurs*.

Because the immediate objective of the French army was to reach the fortress of Erfurt quickly, where the troops could draw provisions, cartridges, munitions and footwear, Napoleon set off with the *Garde* at one o'clock in the morning on 8 (20) October, along the Weißenfels road, and upon arrival decided to cross the river Saale there and move onwards towards Erfurt along the indirect, more tortuous route via Freyburg. The reason for this was the news he received regarding the seizure of Naumburg and the defile at Kösen by Coalition forces, from Bertrand who had been sent via Weißenfels with *4e Corps*, along the Erfurt road. Indeed, on the morning of 8 (20) October, Graf Gyulay had positioned himself at Naumburg with the Austrian *III. Korpus*, holding the important defile and crossing at Kösen with five companies commanded by Graf Gatterburg. But Gyulay's force was too weak to hold Bertrand back, neither could it destroy the very sturdy Kösen bridge, and if Bertrand's corps had continued to move towards Naumburg, they would have forced the Austrians to retreat and would have cleared the shortest and most direct route to Erfurt for Napoleon's main body. Instead, Bertrand withdrew to Weißenfels. Napoleon himself, despairing of passing through the Kösen defile within sight of the Austrian force, which he had assessed to be stronger than they actually were, ordered Bertrand to move along the left bank of the Saale towards Kösen, to occupy the high ground there and destroy the bridge in order to shield the movement of the French army towards Freyburg and Eckartsberga. The task force entrusted to Bertrand, in addition to *4e Corps*, consisted of Guilleminot's division (*7e Corps*), Margaron's and Defrance's divisions (*3e corps de cavalerie*) and *5e corps de cavalerie*. Napoleon spent the night of 8 to 9 (20 to 21) October, in Markröhlitz himself, between Weißenfels and Freyburg. Oudinot reached Weißenfels at night with the rearguard consisting of two divisions of the *Jeune Garde* and *1er corps de cavalerie*.[1]

The Coalition forces were issued the following orders for the pursuit of the enemy: the main army were to move towards Erfurt in two columns: the right towards Pegau, Naumburg and Buttelstedt, and the left towards Draschwitz, Zeitz, Crossen [4½ miles east of Eisenberg] and Jena. The Army of Silesia were also to advance in two columns: Yorck's corps from Halle and Merseburg, via Lauchstädt and Frankleben [4½ miles south-west of Merseburg], to Laucha and Freyburg on the Unstrut river, while Langéron's and Sacken's corps went from Schkeuditz to Lützen and on towards Weißenfels;[2] of the formations from the Army of Poland, Kreutz's detachment pursued the enemy from behind and, together with the vanguard of Sacken's corps commanded by Vasilchikov, on 8 (20) October, rounded up some 3,000 prisoners at Lützen and captured parts of the French trains; The main body of Bennigsen's army came under the command of the Crown Prince of Sweden, who remained in Leipzig with the Army of the North until 10 (22) October.

The day before, on 9 (21) October, Bennigsen's force had set out from the vicinity of Leipzig, towards Lützen, following the Army of Silesia, while the Army of the North, in order to avoid difficulties in provisioning the force, departed Leipzig for Artern on 10 and 11 (22 and 23) October, via Merseburg and Querfurt, moving parallel to General Bennigsen. From the formations of the Army of the North, the Prussian *IV. Korps*, under General Graf Tauentzien, was left between the Elbe and the Oder in order to besiege those fortresses still held by the French. Chernyshev's detachment, among other partisans, pursued the enemy all the way to the Rhine, constantly operating against his line of retreat from the northern side. Count Vorontsov's detachment were sent to Kassel and, together with Saint-Priest's corps,

---

1 Vaudoncourt, *Histoire de la guerre soutenue par les Français en Allemagne*, 224; Aster, *Schlachten bei Leipzig*, II, 361-363.
2 For details of the march routes of the Army of Bohemia and Army of Silesia, see Appendix XXXV at the end of this chapter.

sent from the Army of Silesia, occupied this city on 16 (28) October, which resulted in the final dissolution of the Kingdom of Westphalia.[3]

On the morning of 9 (21) October, Gyulay, having advanced with his corps from Naumburg to Kösen, sent forward *1. leichte Division* under Prinz Moritz von Liechtenstein and the brigade under General Salins [Joseph Maria von Lamezan-Salins or Joseph de Lamezan de Salins] in order to support the force defending the defile. The Austrians held the right bank of the Saale; but all their efforts to drive the enemy back and deploy onto the left bank of the river were unsuccessful. Thus, having achieved his objective of shielding the flank of the main body of Napoleon's army retreating towards Freyburg, Bertrand withdrew from the position he had occupied at Neu-Kösen after dark and retreated towards Eckartsberga. The enemy losses amounted to 1,000 men killed or wounded and some 400 taken prisoner; but the Austrian losses were no less significant: some 800 men were lost from Salins' brigade alone. Although the enemy failed to destroy the Kösen bridge, the Austrians were held there for the whole day and only moved on the following morning [22 October, new style].[4]

General Yorck pursued the enemy more tenaciously and caught up with them at Freyburg on the Unstrut. The town of Freyburg lies in a deep bowl surrounded by steep mountains. The roads leading there across gardens and vineyards are so narrow that the troops can barely pass in sub-units; and after reaching Freyburg, the ascent towards Eckartsburga is extremely trying. Moreover, the water level in the Unstrut was very high; the Austrians had burned the bridge in the town two days before, and although the French had built a new one, it was very fragile and almost level with the surface of the water; there was another bridge further up the river, near a mill [Mühle Zeddenbach] a *verst* from the town, and the third, even further upstream, near Laucha. The cannonade at Naumburg, echoing loudly around the mountains, forced the retreating troops to speed up their march; everyone pushed and shoved against each other; many wagons were abandoned at the crossing point. The arrival of Napoleon himself restored order: each arm of service was ordered to cross separately over one of the aforementioned bridges, and thus the congestion was eased somewhat. At three o'clock in the afternoon, when the river valley and the ravines leading to it were still blocked by wagon trains, and Prussian troops appeared, Napoleon crossed the centre bridge onto the right bank. Yorck's corps advanced in two columns: the right, consisting of eight battalions and 16 squadrons with two batteries, commanded by *Oberst* Graf Henckel von Donnersmarck [Wilhelm Ludwig Viktor Henckel von Donnersmarck],[5] moved to Baumersroda [four miles north of Freyburg] and on towards Laucha, while the left, from Horn's and Hünerbein's divisions, which had linked up at seven o'clock in

---

3 For details of the march routes of the Army of Poland and Army of the North, see Appendix XXXVI at the end of this chapter.
4 *Oestereichische Militärische Zeitschrift, 1836*, VIII.
5 Graf Henckel von Donnersmarck's column consisted of: *Schlesisches Grenadiere*, combined fusiliers of *8. Brigade* and *Thüringishe Bataillon*, first battalion of *Leib Infanterie*, two *Landwehr* battalions, three companies of *Ostpreußische Jäger*, two Austrian jäger battalions; *2. Leib Husaren, Brandenburgisches Husaren, Sächsisches Ulanen*; one *Batterie zu Fuß* and one *Reitende Batterie*: for a total of 7¾ battalions, 16 squadrons and 16 guns. Plotho, II, 476.

the morning at Pechkendorf [sic, Lützkendorf], near Mücheln [6½ miles south of Schafstädt], and headed for Schleberoda and on towards Freyburg. Upon reaching Baumersroda, Graf Henckel's detachment received intelligence that a significant convoy of Coalition prisoners, having spent the night there with a small escort of Poles, had just set off for Laucha. Having devolved command of his infantry component to Major Burghoff [Johann Karl Friedrich Christoph von Burghoff], the most senior of his officers, Graf Henckel chased after the enemy with the cavalry. The valiant hussars, having caught up with the French at Gleina [3½ miles north-east of Laucha], cut down some of the escort, took three officers and 400 lower ranks prisoner, and liberated 4,000 Coalition prisoners.[6] Because there were no longer any enemy in the vicinity of Laucha, Henckel's detachment received orders to go to the village of Zscheiplitz, where the French were crossing at a mill [Mühle Zeddenbach] close by; Horn's division moved to the left, Hünerbein's division followed them in reserve, while Jürgaß's reserve cavalry headed for Markröhlitz. The enemy managed to transfer most of their troops, artillery and trains to the right bank of the river and blew up several ammunition caissons; French batteries with infantry protection, located on the high ground to the front, halted Yorck's advance and delayed them until nightfall. The trophies for the Prussian force consisted of 18 guns, with three more captured by Jürgaß; 1,200 prisoners and many wagons fell into the victors hands, whose casualties amounted to 800 men. Many German and Polish soldiers defected to the Coalition side during the retreat from Freyburg. On that same day, at dawn on 9 (21) October, the corps under Langéron and Sacken advanced from Lützen to Weißenfels, where the enemy rearguard had crossed to the left side of the Saale and destroyed the bridges. Blücher, who was with the Russian force at the time, immediately ordered the deployment of strong batteries, which forced the French to clear the opposite (left) bank of the river; then, as soon as the bridge was restored, Vasilchikov's vanguard advanced towards Freyburg. The Cossack detachments under Platov and Ilovaisky 12th were sent to Camburg and on to Weimar in order to destroy the crossings and to delay the enemy on their line of retreat.[7]

Also on the march to Weißenfels, on 9 (21) October, Prinz Wilhelm, having arrived at the headquarters of the Army of Silesia, announced to Blücher his promotion to *Feldmarschall*. The Russian troops, who had long since been referring to him as '*Feldmarschall vorwärts*' were very pleased.[8]

During the night of 9 to 10 (21 to 22) October, the French rearguard withdrew behind the Unstrut and continued to retreat towards Eckartberga, where Bertrand's force rejoined Napoleon's main body. The next day, 10 (22) October, Blücher, having concentrated all his corps in the vicinity of Freyburg, intended to cross the Unstrut immediately; but as the enemy had destroyed all the bridges on this river, the

---

6   Droysen, *Das Leben des Feldmarschalls Grafen Yorck von Wartenburg*, III, 176; Förster, *Geschichte der Befreiungskriege, 1813, 1814, 1815*, II, 393-396.
7   Plotho, II, 431-432 & 476-478; Droysen, III, 176-177; Beitzke, *Geschichte der deutschen Freiheitskriege in den Jahren 1813 und 1814*, II, 463-466; Sporschill, *Die große Chronik*, I, 954-960; Barclay de Tolly's letter No. 736 to Platov dated 8 [20] October; Blücher's report to Emperor Alexander dated 10 (22) October, from Freyburg.
8   Beitzke, II, 670.

Coalition were forced to halt, in anticipation of their reconstruction. *Feldmarschall* Blücher decided to head for Langensalza and on towards Eisenach, to the flank and rear of the enemy army, in order to prevent Napoleon from making a stand at Erfurt.

Despite the losses suffered by French forces in the actions at Kösen and Freyburg, Napoleon had managed to delay the Coalition on the Saale and the Unstrut. Taking advantage of this, he brought his bedraggled army into some kind of order and, on 9 (21) October, halted for the night in Eckartsberga; all night long, the retreating troops trudged past him; he departed himself at ten o'clock in the morning on 10 (22) October. The most convenient route to Erfurt led through Weimar, but the day before, intelligence had been received on the seizure of this city by Coalition troops,[9] and therefore Napoleon preferred to head for Buttelstedt, detaching Lefebvre-Desnouettes to attack Weimar with a large cavalry force, and, as it later emerged, to take the *Herzog* and his family hostage. But this under-handed attempt failed. The city had been occupied by Count Platov's detachment shortly before the French reached it, while another Cossack detachment under Ilovaisky 12th was stationed nearby. Exploiting the thick fog, Lefebvre approached the city unnoticed, from a direction from which he was not at all expected, burst into the streets and raced towards the Residenzschloss, but was driven back by the brave Don Cossacks and pursued for several *versts* along the Buttstädt road.[10]

Napoleon stopped for the night on reaching Ollendorf (eight miles east of Erfurt) but as Cossack patrols had been appearing on the flanks of the French columns continually during the march, Napoleon's *quartier général* departed Ollendorf at midnight and arrived in Erfurt before dawn. The troops, continuing to move almost without a halt, were extremely tired but strained the last of their strength in order to reach Erfurt as quickly as possible. The rearguard, having retreated to Eckartsberga, halted there, while Gyulay, having reached Poppel [3½ miles north of Sulza], went no further. The Russian 3rd Cuirassier Division, which had been sent to reinforce him, also arrived there.[11]

---

9 Weimar was seized by Major General Ilovaisky 12th's detachment, consisting of his own Cossack regiment together with Grekov 1st's and Grekov 8th's Cossacks. As this detachment continued their advance towards Gotha, Count Platov reinforced it with a Cossack regiment under Lieutenant Colonel Kostin.

10 Platov's letter to Her Imperial Highness, Grand Duchess Maria Pavlovna: 'Your Imperial Highness, Most Gracious Empress! Today I arrived in Weimar with my troops, was received and presented with bread and salt by the Herzog and you husband His Highness the Erbrinz, and had the pleasure of seeing your most beloved daughter and kissing her hand.

Just after my arrival in Weimar, at one o'clock in the afternoon, the enemy attacked the city suddenly from an unexpected direction with large forces, had already broken into the city and were approaching the Residenzschloss, with the intention, it is assessed, of plundering the city, but with God's assistance they were ejected and driven off with fearsome losses along the Buttstädt road for more than a *Meile*, with a considerable number being taken prisoner, in addition to those who were killed, and the city was saved from pillage by the enemy.

I have the pleasure to congratulate Your Imperial Highness on this positive outcome, and with the deepest respect for Your Person I shall forever remain...' and so on (Archive of the M.T.D. No. 47,353, document No. 25).

11 Plotho, II, 433 & 478-479; Vaudoncourt, 224-225; Sporschill, I, 961-962.

Without a doubt, had Gyulay managed to forestall the French at the Kösen defile (as he had been ordered) and occupied the crossings over the Unstrut at Freyburg and Laucha before the arrival of Napoleon's main body, then the enemy situation would have been desperate, being engaged by Austrian forces and attacked at the same time from behind by Yorck's corps, but Gyulay, having only reached the village of Poppel, near Eckartsberga, by 10 (22) October, not only failed to carry out the mission assigned to him, but also hindered the forces under Barclay de Tolly and Wittgenstein as they followed him. Count Barclay de Tolly, wishing to speed up the pursuit, on 11 (23) October, ordered Wittgenstein to get ahead of Gyulay with his corps and with the Prussian reserve cavalry under Röder, and pursue the enemy along the axis from Eckartsberga to Buttelstedt. Whereupon, by order of Emperor Alexander, Adjutant General Count Ozharovsky [Adam Petrovich Ozharovsky] was sent to Auerstedt [two miles north-west of Sulza] with two battalions and 12 squadrons from the Lifeguard,[12] in order to shield the left flank of the vanguard of Wittgenstein's force, which consisted of his light cavalry commanded by Count Pahlen, reinforced by 3rd Cuirassier Division and the reserve cavalry under General Röder, with 23rd Horse Artillery Company and the Prussian *7. Reitende Batterie* and *8. Reitende Batterie*.[13] Count Pahlen, having caught up with the enemy that same day between Eckartsberga and Buttelstedt, attacked them with support from Kreutz's detachment and drove the French back. The Russian forces captured some 600 men, mostly *Jeune Garde*.[14]

Prince Schwarzenberg, believing that Napoleon would give battle at Erfurt, halted the advance of the Coalition forces and took steps to concentrate the Army of Bohemia in front of Weimar, while the Army of Silesia, by heading for Tennstedt and Langensalza, was to envelope the enemy left flank, while the Army of the North was to move towards Artern with the same objective; at the same time, the raiding detachments under Ilovaisky 12th, Count Platov and Thielmann were racing into the rear areas of Napoleon's army, in the sector between Erfurt and Gotha.[15] Operations by Russian partisans were quite successful. On 9 (21) October, Colonel Khrapovitsky [Stepan Semënovich Khrapovitsky], with a detachment of 500 men from the Pavlograd Hussars, Volhynia Ulans and Dyachkin's Cossacks, launched a surprise attack on Gotha, captured the French resident at the courts of the Saxon Duchies, Baron Saint-Aignan [Nicolas Auguste Marie Rousseau de Saint-Aignan], 73 officers and 900 lower ranks, and blew up 30 ammunition caissons. Baron Saint-Aignan claimed that under international law, there was no basis for him to be detained; but Colonel Khrapovitsky replied that, 'not being an accredited diplomat,

---

12 Count Ozharovsky's detachment consisted of: the Lifeguard Finland Regiment, Lifeguard Dragoons, Lifeguard Hussars and two squadrons of Lifeguard Ulans with two horse artillery pieces.
13 Count Barclay de Tolly's report to the Tsar, No. 785, dated 11 [23] October; Plotho, II, 432-433; Schulz, *Geschichte der Kriege in Europa seit dem Jahre 1792*, XI, 2. Band, 10.
14 Barclay's report to the Tsar, No. 786, dated 11 [23] October.
15 General Thielmann's detachment, on the occasion of his appointment as commander of all Saxon forces that had defected to the Coalition, came under the command of Adjutant General Count Orlov-Denisov, to whom the detachment under *Oberstleutnant* Graf Mensdorff was also subordinated.

he would be well advised to hurry with packing his things, and that, otherwise, he might be obliged to be assigned valets that he might not like.' Three days later [24 October, new style], Major General Ilovaisky 12th, having caught up with General Fournier's French cavalry division beyond Eisenach, with his detachment, reinforced by Kostin's Cossacks, and Colonel Khrapovitsky, defeated the enemy and captured seven officers and some 400 lower ranks, having lost 40 men killed or wounded, and the next day [25 October, new style], Major General Ilovaisky captured two guns and many wagons between Vacha and Hünfeld. At the same time, beyond Erfurt, two Bavarian battalions surrendered to Platov, who were immediately directed towards the Main in order to join up with Wrede's army, which was moving towards the lines of communications of the French army. The remnants of Franquemont's Württemberg division joined Orlov-Denisov's detachment.[16]

The disarray of the enemy army and its weakening at every step, from straggling units, marauders and deserters, forced Napoleon to bring forward his departure from Erfurt, especially since he received intelligence there on the movements of the Austro-Bavarian army under General Wrede towards Würzburg. During his two-day stay in Erfurt, in the very same office where, five years before, he had decided the fate of Europe together with Emperor Alexander, Napoleon tried to reorganise and put his army in good order, which had barely 80,000 men remaining. Of the 14 infantry corps, only six had reached Erfurt, namely: Victor's *2e Corps*, Ney's *3e Corps*, Bertrand's *4e Corps*, Marmont's *6e Corps*, Augereau's *9e Corps* and Macdonald's *11e Corps*.[17] The artillery received guns and ammunition caissons from the Erfurt arsenal. The troops were supplied with provisions, clothing and footwear wherever possible. Officers and scouts travelled incognito to Marshals Saint-Cyr and Davout with orders to assemble the French garrisons of the fortresses on the Elbe and to head for the Rhine. While preparing for the onward retreat, Napoleon received intelligence about the movements by General Wrede to intercept his retreat with an Austro-Bavarian army. Murat left him at this point… It has been claimed that he was already making plans to betray Napoleon.

On 12 (24) October, the vanguard, consisting of the corps under Victor, Macdonald and the cavalry under General Sébastiani, set off for Gotha; they were followed the next day [25 October, new style] by: two divisions of the *Jeune Garde* commanded by Oudinot, the remaining four infantry corps, the *Vieille Garde* under Friant and Curial, General Bordesoulle's cuirassiers, Nansouty's *cavlerie de la Garde*, the artillery parks under Sorbier [Jean Barthélemot de Sorbier], Neigre [Gabriel Neigre] and Dulauloy, and finally in the rearguard, two divisions of *Jeune Garde* commanded by Mortier.[18]

After the battle of Leipzig, Emperor Alexander remained in this city dealing with military and diplomatic business. The Commander-in-Chief of the Reserve Army,

---

16 Barclay de Tolly's War Diary; Plotho, II, 435; Extract from Stepan Semënovich Khrapovitsky's notes.
17 Of the 14 infantry corps from Napoleon's army, Oudinot's *12eCorps* had been disbanded after the battle of Dennewitz; Lauriston's *5e Corps*, Reynier's *7e Corps* and Poniatowski's *8e Corps* were destroyed during the battle of Leipzig; *1er Corps* and *14e Corps* remained in Dresden under Saint-Cyr; Rapp's *10e Corps* was in Danzig; Davout's *13e Corps* was in Hamburg.
18 Fain *Manuscrit de 1813*, II, 465-470.

Prince Lobanov-Rostovsky, was sent orders to send reserves up to the active corps; and to execute a recruitment of eight men per 500, announced on 21 August [2 September], in order to replenish the Reserve Army. Malorussia Cossacks from the Poltava Governorate and Chernigov Governorate were excluded from this conscription.[19] Hospitals and designated collection points for convalescents were established in Saxony; all the parks echelons were moved forward; orders were issued to form three companies with guns in the Reserve Army for the equipping of the Lifeguard artillery: heavy, light and horse, as well as a Cossack company for the Don artillery. The main depot for repairing guns and reconstituting artillery companies was established in Altenburg; the main laboratory for filling shells and cartridges was relocated to Prague.

The most important of the questions decided by the Coalition monarchs at that time, was the governance of conquered territories and the raising of revenue from them for the benefit of the common cause. A proposed policy on these subjects, drafted by Stein together with Humboldt [Friedrich Wilhelm Christian Carl Ferdinand von Humboldt], was approved on 21 October, new style, by the empowered ministers, Metternich, Hardenberg [Karl August von Hardenberg] and Nesselrode [Karl Vasilievich Nesselrode or Karl Robert von Nesselrode-Ehreshoven]; the Swedes expressed their approval on 22 October, and Great Britain a few days later. It was decided to establish a *Zentral Verwaltungs Rat* to govern all lands whose rulers refused to join the Coalition against the common enemy; while those states whose rulers would come over to the Coalition side were to have agents from the Central Administration. The Coalition monarchs, having appointed Minister Stein as president of the *Zentral Verwaltungs Rat*, entrusted him with the selection of the members of the committee and the organisation of all subordinate offices. The *Zentral Verwaltungs Rat* were to govern the occupied regions through the Governors General. Revenue from these territories was to be divided between the allies, in proportion to the number of troops provided by each of the states, namely: Austria, Russia and Prussia were to receive a pro rata equal share for 150,000 men; Sweden for 30,000 men; Hanover, depending on the strength of their force. One of the policies proposed by Stein and Humboldt, but rejected by the Coalition sovereigns' representatives, was that *Landstände* (regional assemblies) would be established in each region, who would act on public opinion and encourage the people to participate in the common cause.[20] The *Zentral Verwaltungs Rat* began to carry out their assigned duties, establishing the administration for Saxony in Leipzig, due to the occupation of Dresden by French forces. On 9 (21) October, on the same day that the *Zentral Verwaltungs Rat* was established, Lieutenant General Prince Repnin [Nikolai Grigorievich Repnin-Volkonsky], who had previously been the Russian resident in Kassel and was fully acquainted with the culture and laws of Germany, was appointed Governor General of Saxony. The Germans, who are generally not generous with their praise for Russians, nevertheless give full credit to his

---

19 Manifesto on recruitment, 21 August [2 September] 1813, Complete Collection of Laws, No. 25,438.
20 Georg Heinrich Pertz, *Das Leben des Ministers, Freiherrn vom Stein*, III, 444-448.

magnanimity and administrative abilities.[21] The main difficulty was provisioning the units that remained in Saxony. Their numbers, together with the newly formed Saxon corps, with the blockade detachments and with the reserves passing through the country, amounted to 87,000 men, not including 40,000 sick and wounded; their supply of vital provisions required 1,000,000 Thalers monthly; in addition, requisitions were issued for clothing and equipment for the Saxon forces and for Coalition troops discharged from hospital. In order to ease the burden on the country, at Stein's suggestion, grain was brought in from Bohemia and Silesia, as well as requisitions and purchases of grain and livestock in the Duchy of Warsaw and Mecklenburg; The troops besieging Dresden received provisions from magazines in Theresienstadt and Königsgrätz [Hradec Králové], and so on. Armaments were being industriously produced in Saxony. General Thielmann, who was in charge of the Saxon forces, numbering 15,000 men, managed to assemble and arm two-thirds of this number of soldiers in two weeks. At the same time, Saxony called up 20,000 *Landwehr* soldiers to active service and a similar number for the reserve.[22]

Napoleon's two-day halt in Erfurt, where he had been forced to stop in order to reorganise his army, gave Prinz Schwarzenberg the opportunity to attack him with superior strength. But the Coalition Commander-in-Chief, unsure of himself in a decisive encounter with the enemy, lost much time in concentrating his troops and moved forward no earlier than 14 (26) October, the day after Napoleon's departure from Erfurt. The Army of Bohemia set off from the Weimar area in three columns: the right towards Erfurt, of Wittgenstein's and Kleist's forces; the centre towards Arnstadt, of the entire Austrian contingent;[23] the left towards Kranichfeld, of Barclay de Tolly's Russo-Prussian reserve. Count Wittgenstein left Adjutant-General Prince Gorchakov behind for the blockade of the Erfurt citadels [Zitadelle Petersberg and Zitadelle Cyriaksburg], with 14th Division and part of Kleist's corps, while he went around Erfurt to the right himself, with the rest of the force, and moved towards Gotha.[24] His vanguard, commanded by Adjutant General Count Pahlen, consisting of his cavalry, reinforced with Mezentsov's 5th Division and Pirch's Prussian *10. Brigade*, approached Gotha, while Wittgenstein halted at Töttelstädt, a half-stage [ten miles] from Gotha, himself, with Prinz Eugen von Württemberg's II Corps and Zieten's Prussian *11. Brigade*. On that same day, the Army of Silesia headed from Langensalza towards Eisenach, sending cavalry and the vanguard of Langéron's corps towards the Gotha to Eisenach road. General Yorck attacked Bertrand's corps, which was moving as the rearguard, at Hörselberg [four miles west of Reichenbach], before reaching Eisenach, and inflicted heavy losses on them. Langéron's vanguard, commanded by Rudzevich, captured many prisoners during the pursuit from Gotha. The French themselves admit to losing 2,000 men at Gotha. Count Bennigsen's

---

21 Pertz, III, 448.
22 Pertz, III, 454-456.
23 Except Graf Klenau's *IV. Korpus*, which had been sent to Dresden on 10 (22) October in order to reinforce Count Tolstoy (Orders for Lieutenant General Count Tolstoy, dated 11 (23) October, Log of Incoming Documents, No. 132).
24 The Prussians from Kleist's corps, left at Erfurt on 14 (26) October included: Klüx's *9. Brigade*, Prinz August's *12. Brigade*, *1. Schlesisches Husaren*, and *Neumärkisches Dragoner* with the reserve artillery.

Army of Poland received a new mission from 14 (26) October. Emperor Alexander, having learned of the sortie by Saint-Cyr from Dresden towards Torgau, with the aim of freeing the garrisons of the fortresses on the Elbe from blockade, and having concentrated them, to march towards Wesel, ordered General Bennigsen to march with Dokhturov's force in order to assist Count Tolstoy and Tauentzien, and to place the rest of his army at the disposal of the Crown Prince of Sweden. Having received these orders, Bennigsen dispatched Lieutenant General Count Stroganov from Rastenberg [eight miles east of Kölleda] to Oberheldrungen and on towards Heiligenstadt with 12th Division, one brigade of 13th Division, three batteries and two Bashkir regiments,[25] in order to join the Army of the North, while he moved to Nebra and on to Halle himself, with Kreutz's detachment, Chaplits' cavalry, 26th Division and one brigade from 13th Division.[26]

The enemy army, during their onward retreat to Vacha and Fulda, were obliged to make forced marches, leaving the evidence of extreme disorder and chaos at every step. The number of men dying from hunger, exhaustion and typhus increased daily. Corpses and collapsed horses, abandoned weapons and carts were constantly encountered all along the road. The forests and mountains on either side were filled with stragglers and sick soldiers. Just as on the final days of the war of 1812, the French army was surrounded by raiding detachments, which accompanied and forestalled the enemy, destroyed their magazines and demolished the bridges along their line of retreat.[27] Under these circumstances, decisive action by Napoleon against the armies pursuing him was considered highly unlikely, and so Blücher issued orders for the troops to be accommodated in quarters each night. The need to spare the men from forced marches following a hard campaign, obliged the Coalition to slacken the pursuit: only the raiding detachments stayed in contact with the enemy army. The Army of Silesia, on the day of Napoleon's arrival at Hanau, 18 (30) October, was 70 *versts* from him at Fulda, while the Army of Bohemia was more than 100 *versts* away, at Vacha and Meiningen.

Because the intelligence delivered by the raiding detachments was not received at the headquarters in a timely manner, Prinz Schwarzenberg was completely unaware of the movements of the enemy army, and believing that Napoleon might turn towards Koblenz in order to avoid a clash with General Wrede, he suggested to Blücher that he move through the Vogelsgebirge into Hessen and towards Wetzlar [8½ miles west of Giessen]; to that same end, Count Wittgenstein was ordered to advance from Gotha and Eisenach, to Berka and Hersfeld, and on towards Alsfeld with his two corps and some of Kleist's cavalry (Kleist had been left to blockade the Erfurt citadels with his corps, with the exception of three cuirassier regiments and a horse artillery battery, which were attached to Wittgenstein's force). The other

---

25 Count Stroganov's force consisted of: Prince Khovansky's 12th Division – Smolensk Infantry, Narva Infantry, Alexopol Infantry, Novoingermanland Infantry, 6th Jägers and 41st Jägers; the brigade from 13th Division – Saratov Infantry and Penza Infantry; 9th Horse Artillery Company, 48th Light Artillery Company and 53rd Light Artillery Company; 9th Bashkirs and 11th Bashkirs.
26 The Tsar's orders to Count Bennigsen, dated 12 [24] October (Log of Outgoing Documents, No. 138); Plotho, II, 438-439, 480-481 & 499.
27 Marmont, *Mémoires*, V, 189.

formations of the Army of Bohemia, after crossing the Thüringer Gebirge and reaching the environs of Schmalkalden and Meiningen, were given a rest day on 18 (30) October. Thus, the Army of Silesia and the forces under Count Wittgenstein deviated to the right of the enemy army's line of retreat, the majority of the Army of Bohemia went to the left, and only raiding detachments pursued the enemy, which gave Napoleon the opportunity to attack the Austro-Bavarian army under General Wrede with his full strength.[28]

---

28 Plotho, II, 440-444; Beitzke, II, 672-674.

Appendix XXXV

Planned march-routes for the Army of Bohemia and Army of Silesia after Leipzig

Intended movements of the Army of Bohemia and Army of Silesia based on the disposition for 20 to 22 October, new style (Barclay de Tolly's War Diary, Archive of the M.T.D. No. 29,188; War Diaries of Langéron and Sacken; Plotho, II, 475-478)

Right Column, Army of Bohemia:
8 (20) October: Gyulay's *III. Korpus*, Prinz Moritz Liechtenstein's *1. leichte Division* and Nostitz's cavalry to Naumburg; Russo-Prussian reserves to Teichern [8½ miles north-west of Zeitz]; Wittgenstein's and Kleist's corps to Pegau.
9 (21) October: Gyulay, Liechtenstein and Nostitz to Eckartsberga; Russo-Prussian reserves to Hassenhausen [four miles west of Kösen]; Wittgenstein and Kleist to Stößen.
10 (22) October: Gyulay, Liechtenstein and Nostitz to Buttelstedt; Russo-Prussian reserves to Auerstedt; Wittgenstein and Kleist to Eckartsberga.
Left Column, Army of Bohemia:
8 (20) October: Colloredo's I. Korpus, Alois Liechtenstein's 2. leichte Division and Bianchi's reserve infantry to Zeitz; Graf Klenau's IV. Korpus to Draschwitz.
9 (21) October: I. Korpus, II. Korpus and Bianchi to Eisenberg; Klenau to Crossen.
10 (22) October: I. Korpus, II. Korpus and Bianchi to Jena.
The headquarters of Emperor Alexander and the King of Prussia was to remain in Leipzig on 8 to 9 (20 to 21) October, while the Austrian Kaiser's was in Rötha on 8 (20) October and in Zeitz on 9 (21) October.

Yorck's Corps, Army of Silesia:
8 (20) October: Hünerbein's division to Lauchstädt; Horn's division with Yorck's *Hauptquartier* to Frankenleben.
9 (21) October: the entire corps to Freyburg.
Russian Forces, Army of Silesia:
8 (20) October: to Lützen.
9 (21) October: to Weißenfels.

Appendix XXXVI

Movements by the Army of Poland and Army of the North after Leipzig

Movements of the Army of Poland and Army of the North 8 to 18 (20 to 30) October (Plotho, II, 497-498 and 506-508)

Army of Poland:
8 (20) October: Kreutz's detachment and Count Stroganov's vanguard to Lützen; Chaplits' cavalry to Markranstädt, Dokhturov's infantry to Schönau.
9 (21) October: Kreutz to Weißenfels and onto the left bank of the Saale; Stroganov to Merseburg; Chaplits to Göhrenz [two miles south-east of Markranstädt]; Dokhturov to Möglitz [*sic*, Oeglitzsch five miles west of Lützen?].
10 (22) October: Kreutz to Freyburg; Stroganov and Chaplits to Mücheln; Dokhturov to Weißenfels.

Army of the North:
10 to 11 (22 to 23) October, from Leipzig to Merseburg; 12 (24) October, to Querfurt; 13 (25) October, to Artern; 14 (26) October, to Sondershausen; 15 (27) October, to Mühlhausen; 18 (30) October, to Heiligenstadt; 19 October (1 November), to Göttingen.

44

The Battle of Hanau

The breach between Bavaria and France. The composition and troop strength of the Austro-Bavarian army. – The movements by General Wrede from the Inn to the Main. – The investment of the Würzburg citadel; the detachment of Rechberg's division to Frankfurt and the occupation of positions at Hanau by the Coalition. – The movements of Napoleon's army towards Hanau. – Wrede's planning.

The ground around Hanau. – The dispositions of the Austro-Bavarian army in the Hanau position. – The fighting on 18 (30) October. Napoleon's advance. – Macdonald's attempts to debouch from the forest. – The reconnaissances by Drouot and Napoleon. – The French attack on Wrede's position and the retreat of the Coalition beyond the Kinzig. – The bombardment of the town. – Operations on 19 (31) October. The seizure of Hanau by the French. – The movements of Napoleon's main body towards Frankfurt and the deployment of the rearguard. – The Coalition recapture of Hanau. – The retreat of the French rearguard towards Frankfurt. – Operations around Frankfurt. – The casualties on both sides. – Points to note.

The retreat of the French army behind the Rhine. – The arrival of Emperor Alexander and Kaiser Franz in Frankfurt. – The action at Hochheim. – The deployments of both sides. – Blücher reaches the Lahn. – His intention to cross the Rhine. – His advance towards Mülheim and the move towards Frankfurt. – The deployments of the Army of Bohemia and Army of Silesia.

The Coalition's options. – The composition of Coalition forces. – Saint-Aignan's departure for Paris with a proposal for peace. – The accession of the German states to the Coalition. – Their mobilisation and financial contributions.

The provisioning of Russian forces. – The Aschaffenburg tariff. – Outfitting the troops.

The mobilisation of Germany. – The composition of the German corps. – Factors which prevented the Coalition from immediately invading France.

Bavaria broke away from their alliance with Napoleon shortly before the Battle of Leipzig.

The Kingdom of Bavaria owed much to the *Empereur des Français*; it had become apparent that the Bavarians were expected to take his side to the bitter end, just as they had loyally assisted France in earlier times against their natural enemy, the Austrians. But the rise of Bavaria was bought at a high cost: in the war of 1812, the 25,000 Bavarian contingent perished almost to a man in Russia; and in the war of 1813, Bavaria was obligated to send some 10,000 men to the active French army. There were very few families that were not mourning the loss of their closest blood relatives who had fallen in order to satisfy Napoleon. The people hated both the French and their ruler, and although the government still remained on his side, this was partly due to the intrigues of the Bavarian *Außenminister* Montgelas [Maximilian Carl Joseph Franz de Paula Hieronymus von Montgelas], who was loyal to Napoleon, and partly out of fear of losing the territories annexed from Austria. Yet Emperor Alexander and Metternich managed to dispel the doubts of the Munich cabinet,[1] and on 26 September (8 October) a convention was concluded in Ried, on the basis of which the Austrian government vouched for the territorial integrity of Bavaria, or for compensation in the event of regions belonging to Austria being returned, while Bavaria pledged to subordinate their army to Coalition forces operating against Napoleon.[2] On 2 (14) October, the King of Bavaria declared war on France, and the next day his forces commanded by the Bavarian *General der Kavallerie*, Graf Wrede linked up with the Austrian corps under *Feldmarschallleutnant* von Fresnel [Johann Karl Peter Ferdinand Hennequin de Fresnel et Curel], on the Inn at Braunau [122 miles west of Zwettl]. The Austro-Bavarian Coalition army consisted of about 50,000 men with 116 guns, namely:

> Infantry: 30 Bavarian battalions numbering 22,218 men; 18 Austrian battalions numbering 19,800 men, for a total of 48 battalions with 42, 018 infantrymen.
> Cavalry: 31 Bavarian squadrons numbering 3,500 men; 36 Austrian squadrons numbering 4,320 men, for a total of 67 squadrons with 7,820 cavalrymen.
> Artillery: 11 Bavarian batteries with 74 guns, numbering 800 men; seven Austrian batteries with 42 guns, a pioneer company and a medical company, numbering 600 men.

---

1 Münster, *Lebensbilder Aus Dem Befreiungskriege*, II, 25-27. For the text of Emperor Alexander's letter to the King of Bavaria, see Appendix XXXVII at the end of this chapter.
2 The convention concluded in Ried on 8 October, new style, was signed by Prinz Reuss and General Wrede.

Thus: 26,518 Bavarians with 74 guns, and 24,750 Austrians with 42 guns; for a combined total of 51,000 men and 116 guns.[3]

Graf Wrede, having set off from the environs of Braunau with his army on 5 (17) October, moved via Donauwörth [18 miles south-east of Nördlingen] reaching Uffenheim on 11 (23) October; his vanguard, consisting of ten battalions from the Bavarian First Division and ten squadrons from *3. leichte Kavallerie Brigade*, reached Ochsenfurt and crossed to the right bank of the Main; one of the Bavarian divisions with some of the cavalry monitored the 7,000 strong Württemberg division as it withdrew [westwards] behind the Kocher river. Thus, the Austro-Bavarian army covered 40 *Meilen* (280 *versts*) in seven stages, without rest days. This forced march, partly on poor roads in inclement weather, had a very negative impact on the troops, half of whom were new recruits. General Wrede, wishing to give his army a rest, made the most of this enforced inaction in order to capture Würzburg.

On 12 (24) October, both Austrian infantry divisions with the Bavarian Second Division and *2. leichte Kavallerie Brigade* encircled the city. Because the commandant of the fortress, *général de division* Turreau [Louis Marie Turreau de Lignières], refused to surrender to the Coalition force, a bombardment was launched against the city, initially on 12 (24) October, and then, during the night of 13 to 14 (25 to 26) October, from 82 guns, and in total more than 3,000 rounds were fired. The next day, Wrede prepared to storm Würzburg, but the commandant, without waiting for the assault, surrendered the city and retreated [two miles west] into the Festung Marienberg with the garrison. Whereupon, General Graf Spreti [Maximilian von Spreti] was left to occupy the city and blockade the fortress with three Austrian battalions; the remaining Coalition formations marched to Aschaffenburg, where Wrede's entire army was concentrated on 16 (28) October, just as the King of Württemberg [Friedrich I] was joining the Coalition against Napoleon.[4]

General Wrede, having received a proposal from Prinz Schwarzenberg's *Hauptquartier* to head across Napoleon's line of retreat towards Frankfurt or rather, towards Fulda, was misled by Schwarzenberg's intelligence assessment and by reports by the Cossack detachments operating on the flanks of the French army. On the basis of this assessment, he believed that Napoleon would turn towards Bonn or Koblenz, and that all that was moving towards Frankfurt from Fulda was a French corps of some 20,000 men. Wanting to take advantage of this situation, Wrede decided to sever this enemy line of retreat, and he headed towards Hanau with that objective.

At eight o'clock in the morning on 16 (28) October, the Bavarian *1. Cheveauxlegers* burst into the town unexpectedly and took the Italian General Sant'Andrea and many men prisoner. After the capture of Hanau, the Bavarian *1. leichte Kavallerie Brigade* sent from there along the road to Gelnhausen encountered 3,000 men from the French reserves, commanded by General Grouvel [François Grouvel], and were forced to retreat behind Hanau; the Bavarian Third Division under La Motte [Peter

---

3   For details of these forces, see Appendix XXXVIII at the end of this chapter.
4   Plotho, II, 452-454; Vaudoncourt, *Histoire de la guerre soutenue par les Français en Allemagne*, 227; Schulz, XI, *2 Band*, 21-22.

de La Motte] also arrived from Aschaffenburg at eight o'clock in the morning, whereupon the Coalition reoccupied Hanau, capturing 20 officers and 500 lower ranks. On 17 (29) October, another column from the French reserves, 4,000 strong, commanded by General Guérin [Jacques Julien Guérin], in attempting to take the town, was driven back and forced to turn to the right of the main road, with the loss of many prisoners and two guns.[5]

General Wrede reached Hanau with the main body at about midday, having detached Graf Rechberg's Bavarian First Division [Anton von Rechberg] from Aschaffenburg towards Frankfurt; Kaisarov's, Chernyshev's, Count Orlov-Denisov's, Ilovaisky 12th's and Mensdorff's partisan detachments also arrived there. La Motte's division, assigned as the vanguard, occupied Langenselbold [7½ miles north-east of Hanau] and positioned themselves between this town and the forest, setting up two batteries. Volkmann's Austrian brigade [Anton von Volkmann], reinforced by *3. Jäger Bataillon* and the *Schwarzenberg Uhlanen* and *Erzherzog Joseph Husaren*, was sent to the right through the forest, towards Alzenau [7½ miles south-east of Hanau], on the enemy's flank.

At three o'clock in the afternoon, the leading formations of the French army (two divisions of *Jeune Garde*, *11e Corps* and almost all the cavalry) reached Langenselbold, captured this town and pushed the Bavarians back towards Rückingen [four miles north-east of Hanau]; Volkmann's detachment had reached Gelnhausen via minor roads; *Oberst* Mengen's lancers [Carl von Mengen], having engaged Sébastiani's cavalry, launched several successful attacks, while *3. Jäger Bataillon*, having occupied Gelnhausen, defended themselves there for an entire hour and a half. Thereafter, when Volkmann received orders from Graf Wrede not to engage in a committed action with the enemy, the Coalition retreated, under the protection of both cavalry regiments, to Langenselbold, and on to Rückingen.

On the night of 17 to 18 (29 to 30) October, the Coalition army was positioned as follows: La Motte's Bavarian Third Division and Volkmann's brigade in Rückingen; the Bavarian Second Division and Austrian First Division forwards of Hanau, astride the main road; the grenadier brigade of the Austrian Second Division were holding the town; the other brigade from this division was stationed forwards of the Nürnberger Tor, together with the Austrian cavalry, on the Aschaffenburg road. Napoleon, having transferred part of his army across the Kinzig, over three bridges, deployed around the Fürst zu Isenburg und Büdingen's Schloss Langenselbold. On that same day, Rechberg's Bavarian division reached Frankfurt and occupied the city the next morning [30 October, new style].[6]

Graf Wrede was still convinced that only part of the French army was moving against him throughout the period of the actions in the vicinity of Hanau just

---

5   Of the remaining formations of the French reserve formed on the Rhine and sent to reconstitute the active army, 5,000 men, commanded by General Préval [Claude Antoine Hippolyte de Préval], moving from Eschwege to Frankfurt, arrived there without encountering the Coalition army, while General Rigaux had been sent to Kassel with the fourth column and accompanied King Jérôme on his retreat to Cologne.

6   *Oesterreichische Relation über die Ereignisse bei Hanau, vom 29 October bis zum 1 November*; Plotho, II, 454-457.

described. On 17 (29) October, he wrote to Prinz Schwarzenberg: 'it would seem that the strongest enemy column has headed towards Wetzlar.' But by the following morning he was already thinking differently: 'I have the honour to inform Your Highness' he wrote to the Commander-in-Chief, 'that intelligence received last night from the Russian General Count Orlov and *Oberst* Scheibler [Karl Wilhelm von Scheibler] does not agree with the previous assessment of enemy movements toward Wetzlar or Koblenz, and that both of them report the advance of a very significant corps against me.'[7] Thus, Graf Wrede had to accept an unequal battle or retreat. Later, after he had been defeated, he was criticised for his reckless bravery. And indeed, had there been no other army on the Coalition side in this theatre of war except the one commanded by Wrede, then he should not have made a stand on the line of retreat of such a powerful enemy. But the Bavarian commander, on the contrary, knew that there were significant Coalition formations behind Napoleon's army, weakened in the battle of Leipzig, that could, by relentlessly pursuing the enemy, inflict a final defeat on them.

It is true that the last report to General Wrede from Prince Schwarzenberg, dated 15 (27) October, from Elleben (en route from Weimar to Arnstadt), suggested that the main body of the Army of Bohemia could not reach Gelnhausen before 18 (30) October, but since at the same time Wrede had not received any news from the Army of Silesia, did he not have reason to hope for the assistance of the enterprising Blücher? Therefore, General Wrede had to fix the enemy in order to win time for the other Coalition armies to catch up with them. But in order to achieve this objective, the Coalition should have deployed at Gelnhausen, and not in front of Hanau, where the enemy, exploiting their numerical superiority, could push the Austro-Bavarian force back to the Kinzig river.[8]

The city of Hanau, surrounded by moated ramparts, lies within a loop of the Kinzig which encircles it on the northern and western sides to its confluence with the river Main, while its southern side is located near the Main, which is linked to the city by a canal.[9] Communications with Hanau from the opposite bank of the Kinzig are only carried out via the so-called Kinzigbrücke, on the western side of the city. The other bridge, the Lamboy bridge, is located further upstream, about two *versts* east of the city, near the Neuhof manor. The area around the city is completely open for a radius of two *versts*; further out are extensive forests: to the east, the Bulauwald and Lamboywald, and to the north, the Puppenwald and Bruchköbelerwald; the first two are separated from each other by the Kinzig, roads to Gelnhausen run along both banks: the highway along the left bank and the old road along the right. The road to Friedberg passes through the Bruchköbelerwald; the main Frankfurt road passes along the northern side of the city; finally, the Aschaffenburg road, between Kinzig and Main, passes an obelisk [the Ehrensäule] and the Lehrhof manor.

On the morning of 18 (30) October, Wrede's Coalition army, numbering about 40,000 men, was deployed as follows: the right wing, consisting of Becker's

---

7   Sporschill, *Die große Chronik*, I, 1006-1007.
8   Sporschill, I, 1007-1010.
9   See Map No. 16 Plan of the Battle of Hanau.

Legend to Map No 16
Light grey – French forces
Dark grey – initial Austro-Bavarian positions
Light grey straight lines – subsequent Austro-Bavarian positions
Isolated light grey heading towards the French – Russian partisans.

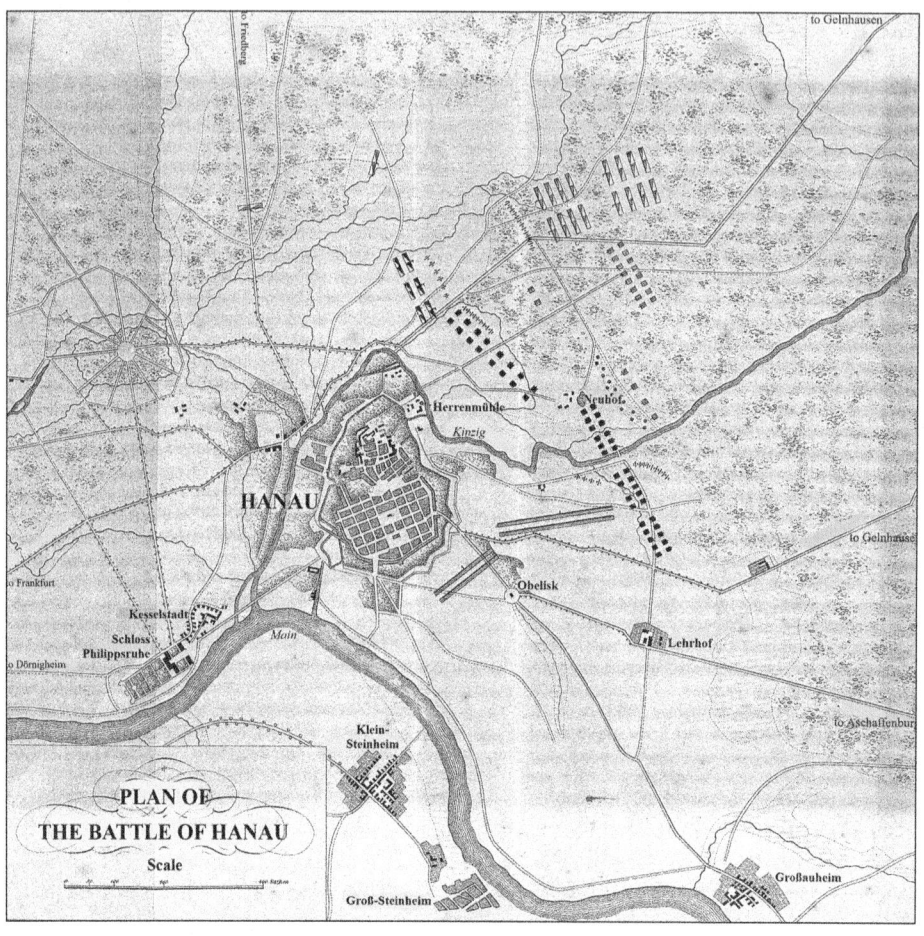

Plan of the Battle of Hanau.

Bavarian Second Division [Karl August von Beckers zu Westerstetten], on both banks of the Kinzig from the Neuhof manor to the highway; Graf Klenau's Austrian grenadier brigade was stationed in reserve behind the Lamboy bridge; the centre consisted of Bach's Austrian division and La Motte's Bavarian Third Division after they had withdrawn into the position from Rückingen; 50 guns were placed to the front, facing the exits from the forest, commanded by Austrian General Stwrtnik [August von Stwrtnik]; the left wing consisted of the Austrian and Bavarian cavalry, formed up in several waves between the old Gelnhausen road and the Bruchköbelerwald; Russian partisans were stationed behind the left wing, on the Friedberg road,. Diemar's Austrian grenadier brigade [Karl von Diemar] held the city.[10]

Napoleon, having decided to move directly against the Coalition army, sent convoys of the wounded, sick and unarmed along the country lanes leading from Langenselbold to Bergen [5½ miles north-east of Frankfurt] and on to Mainz, under the protection of Arrighi's *3e corps de cavalerie*; and at dawn on 18 (30) October, he set off along the highway himself: Macdonald moving in the vanguard with *11e Corps* and Sébastiani's cavalry; they were followed by the *Vieille Garde* and the infantry under Victor, Marmont and Bertrand; Oudinot would be able to reach the battlefield with his divisions before dark, while Mortier's force and *1er corps de cavalerie* would reach Gelnhausen at the same time. Macdonald attacked La Motte's vanguard at Rückingen at eight o'clock in the morning, with 2,000 cavalry and two guns.[11] The vanguard, despite their small numbers, defended themselves stubbornly until ten o'clock. Macdonald was forced to deploy Charpentier's division from his own corps and Exelmans' division [Rémy Joseph Isidore Exelmans] (from General Sébastiani's corps) facing Rückingen, with a large number of guns. Whereupon the Bavarian force retreated in good order to their positions at Hanau. Macdonald quickly followed them through the Lamboywald; his troops appeared at the edge of the forest facing the Coalition positions at about midday, but were held back by the effective fire of the Austro-Bavarian artillery.

Napoleon ordered General Dubreton to debouch from the forest with 2,000 skirmishers from *2e Corps* and some light guns, facing the right wing of the Coalition army. The battle continued here for a long time with varying success; Graf Pappenheim [Karl Theodor Friedrich zu Pappenheim], who was stationed on the left bank of the Kinzig, crossed the Lamboy bridge and attacked the enemy in the forest, but was driven back from there; as a result, the French could not get out of the forest and were forced to limit themselves to firefight.

It was already three o'clock in the afternoon. Napoleon, from the very beginning of the battle, had been at the edge of the forest facing Langenselbold; there he sat, under the trees, on his camp stool, by a campfire lit near two hastily pitched tents. He was constantly receiving reports on the impossibility of debouching from the forest. Deep in thought, Napoleon sent his chief of artillery, Drouot, to the battlefield to see if it might be possible to counter the Coalition with a sufficiently strong battery. Half an hour later, Drouot returned with a report that he had found a crossroad to the right of the main road, in the vicinity of which the forest, right up to the edge facing the enemy, was quite sparse and presented the opportunity to bring up 50 guns with protection from two battalions of the *Garde*. Napoleon quickly mounted his horse and, together with Drouot, Caulaincourt and several officers of his retinue, rode along the indicated minor road. Drouot explained his plan during this reconnaissance under a hail of grapeshot and musket balls: in his opinion, it was necessary to push several guns out of the forest along the main road and in its

---

10 Plotho, II, 457-458; Richter, *Geschichte des Deutschen Freiheitskrieges vom Jahre 1813 bis zum Jahre 1815*, II, 366-367.
11 Graf La Motte's vanguard at Rückingen consisted of: the marksman company of 9. Linieninfanterie, a platoon of *Szekler Husaren* and a half-squadron of *Cheveauxlegers*.

vicinity, and as soon as they had opened fire and drawn the attention of the enemy, to bring up the other batteries to the right of the road.

Napoleon, having approved this course of action, decided to launch a general attack on the Austro-Bavarian position at the same time as the cannonade opened. The *cavalerie de la Garde* approached the edge of the forest along the main road; the artillery, escorted by two battalions of Curial's *Vieille Garde*, moved to the right along the minor road; Sébastiani's cavalry were directed along the main road behind Nansouty, while the *Garde* infantry were directed to the right, in order to support the cavalry attack; Macdonald was tasked with preventing the Coalition right wing from interfering. This excellent concept was executed with complete success. General Curial quickly lined the edge of the forest with two battalions, pelted the crews of the large Coalition battery with bullets and forced the Austro-Bavarian artillery to retreat. Taking advantage of this, Noury [Henri Marie Lenoury] and Desvaux [Jean-Jacques Desvaux de Saint-Maurice] dragged several light guns out of the forest; heavy artillery moved into position behind them.

Having observed the emplacement of the French batteries, Wrede directed his cavalry against them; but the French, allowing the Coalition to approach, engaged them with canister shot, and at the same time the *cavalerie de la Garde* attacked them; Sébastiani followed up with the divisions under Saint-Germain [Antoine Louis Decrest de Saint-Germain] and Exelmans. The French cavalry formed up in three waves with lightning speed, and raced towards the centre of the Austro-Bavarian position under canister fire, cut down the crews of the large battery, drove off the cavalry, and, turning against the infantry, sought to break through the Coalition battle line. Despite the numerical superiority of the enemy horsemen, the Austro-Bavarian cavalry rallied back, and at the same time Chernyshev's detachment struck the French in the flank and forced them to fall back. The Coalition quickly pursued the enemy, but being engaged with canister shot from 50 guns, they retreated with heavy losses.

The large Austro-Bavarian battery, having expended their ammunition and lost most of their crews, were unable to counter the French artillery. General Wrede was forced to pull his army back beyond the Kinzig. The retreat of Coalition centre and right wing across the Lamboy bridge was fraught with great risk. The bridge was narrow, the wooden structure was flimsy. Many men died in the deep river water as the troops crowded at the crossing. The units on the left wing retreated across the Kinzigbrücke and came back through the city. One of the battalions of the Austrian *Jordis Infanterie* and several hundred Bavarians were driven back by the enemy towards the Herrenmühle, some crossed over the weir into the city with the help of the fearless miller, Koch, some drowned. The French chased after them, but all those enemy who broke into the city were taken prisoner. After retreating beyond the Kinzig, Wrede repositioned his army in the vicinity of the Lehrhof, leaving a battery with its escort at the Lamboy bridge and holding the city with three Austrian grenadier batteries [sic, battalions] commanded by General Diemar. The cannonade at the Lamboy bridge continued until midnight.

The population of Hanau awaited their fate in trepidation. At two o'clock in the morning, Napoleon, probably wishing to distract the attention of the Coalition from the Bergen road along which his forces were retreating, ordered the city to be bombarded with explosive shells from howitzers; fires broke out in several locations.

On the morning of 19 (31) October, Marmont was ordered to attack the Lamboy bridge, the weir by the Herrenmühle and the Kinzigbrücke; but he was only successful in taking the latter crossing. Whereupon Graf Wrede, wishing to save the city from complete destruction, ordered it to be evacuated and the enemy occupied Hanau with some of their units, while the rest continued the retreat towards Frankfurt along the highway or along the minor roads towards Bergen.

Napoleon spent almost the entire morning of 19 (31) October in the Puppenwald, from where he summoned a deputation of Hanau residents. The *Empereur des Français* received the deputation with reproaches for having greeted the Coalition with joyful cheering. 'Of course' he said, 'it is not within my powers to make you love the French. But prudence must demand that you remain on the side of France, which is closer to you than Russia, and therefore can more easily come to your defence. I ordered the city to be shelled last night in order to punish you.' Then he asked: 'how much was burned?' Once the deputation had answered that there had been fires in many places and had caused great damage, Napoleon said: 'I wanted to burn half the city.' When the prefect began to remind him of the self-sacrifice of his fellow Bavarians and Marshal Augereau began to praise the diligence of the city administration, Napoleon dismissed the deputies, saying: 'I know that the magistrates are good men, but the bourgeoisie are scum!'[12]

At around 11 o'clock in the morning, a significant part of the French army had already passed Hanau, and the light cavalry was approaching Frankfurt; Napoleon was still in the Puppenwald, but having received word of the seizure of Frankfurt by Coalition forces, he immediately headed there with the *Garde*, entrusting operations at Hanau to Marmont and Bertrand. At around one o'clock in the afternoon, the former set off for Frankfurt with *3e Corps* and *6e Corps*, leaving Bertrand to defend the city and hold the Coalition back with *4e Corps*: Fontanelli's division holding Hanau; Guilleminot's division was stationed at the Lamboy bridge with 14 guns, whose decking had been burned away, while Morand's division remained in reserve.

On the Coalition side, the right wing was about a *verst* from the Lamboy bridge, to the left of which stood a Bavarian 12-pounder battery, which operated all day to great effect; the left wing of the Austro-Bavarian army was located 800 paces from the city. For several hours, the fighting on the Kinzig was limited to a cannonade and skirmishing; while flankers exchanged fire with each other in front of the city, at the Nürnberger Tor.

At two o'clock in the afternoon, having learned of Napoleon's departure and observing that a significant part of the enemy army was heading towards Frankfurt, General Wrede decided to attack the French. Wanting to attack the city from several directions simultaneously, he ordered 32 guns to be sent to the Lamboy bridge in order to provide covering fire for a crossing onto the right bank of the Kinzig by part of the force, while he attacked the city from the direction of the Nürnberger Tor himself with six Austrian battalions supported on the right flank by fire from Danner's battery, being the first to descend into the ditch and scale the walls; while

---

12 *'Je sais que les magistrats sont de braves gens, mais la bourgeoisie est de la canaille.'*

Major Jambein, having opened the gates with one of the battalions of *Erzherzog Rudolph Infanterie*, cleared the way for the rest of the force to enter the city.[13]

The enemy attempted to hold the Coalition back, but all their efforts were in vain; forced to flee across the Kinzigbrücke, they lost two generals and many officers and lower ranks taken prisoner by the Austrians. General Wrede, at the head of the advancing column, raced towards the bridge and was seriously wounded by a bullet. *Feldmarschallleutnant* Fresnel assumed command of the army. The Bavarians, enraged at the loss of their commander, raced towards the bridge in competition with the Austrians. Morand's division, unable to hold them back, retreated from the bridge with heavy losses; generals Lejeune [Louis-François Lejeune] and Hulot [Étienne Hulot] fell [wounded] leading the French *8e légère* and *23e ligne*. Yet the French managed to burn the bridge decking, and so the Coalition were forced to halt on the banks of the Kinzig. Only the Austrian hussars, having galloped up to the river, swam across and took many prisoners. The infantry, remaining in the city, limited themselves to clearing the enemy from houses they had occupied and putting out fires.

The right wing of the Coalition army crossed the Lamboy bridge in the evening. Taking advantage of the darkness, Bertrand's corps retreated along the highway to Frankfurt; the rearguard of the French army, numbering 14,000 men commanded by Marshal Mortier, also headed towards Frankfurt along the Hochstadt road. Platov's Cossack detachment[14] and the partisan detachments under Chernyshev, Ilovaisky 12th, Count Orlov-Denisov and Kaisarov inflicted heavy losses on the enemy and took more than 3,000 men prisoner.[15]

As has already been mentioned, General Rechberg had seized Frankfurt with the Bavarian First Division on 18 (30) October. He sent Major Karvinsky to the Nidda river [north of Frankfurt] with the Bavarian *5. Cheveauxlegers*; this detachment caught up with two squadrons of the French *Chasseurs à cheval de la Garde* at Rödelheim [four miles west of Frankfurt] and defeated them. The next day [31 October, new style], the movements of the main body of the French army from Hanau towards Frankfurt forced Rechberg to retreat to the left bank of the Main, into Sachsenhausen [one mile south of Frankfurt], and to remove the decking and crossbeams from the bridges. The French attempted to cross the river, but were repelled by the Bavarians and the fighting was limited to a cannonade and firefight that continued until nightfall.[16]

On the evening of 19 (31) October, Napoleon's army was deployed as follows: the *Garde, 11e Corps* and *2e Corps* were in Frankfurt; Sébastiani's cavalry were on

---

13 Graf Wrede assaulted the city of Hanau with Frisch's, Gromadi's (*sic*) and Posmann's grenadier battalions, two battalions of *Erzherzog Rudolph Infanterie* and *3. Jäger Bataillon*.
14 Count Platov's detachment consisted of: the Ataman's Cossacks, Black Sea Cossacks, elements of: Grekov's, Ilovaisky 10th's and Teptyar Cossacks, Olviopol Hussars, a squadron of Austrian *Klenau Cheveauxleger*, Major Baltenstern's Prussian partisan detachment and Tatsyn's Don Cossack artillery half-company.
15 Count Platov's report No. 76 to Count Barclay de Tolly, dated 19 [31] October.
16 The description of the battle of Hanau was extracted from: Plotho, II, 458-462; Richter, II, 370-389; Vaudoncourt, 230-234; Völderndorf, IV, 271-289 & 369-379; *Oestereichische Militärische Zeitschrift, 1835*, IX, 275-278; *Spectateur militaire*, III, 573-584.

the river Nidda; *3e Corps* and *6e Corps* were approaching Frankfurt; *4e Corps* and Mortier's rearguard were on the march from Hanau towards Frankfurt.[17]

The casualties in the French army at the battle of Hanau amounted to 15,000 men killed or wounded. Prisoners taken by the Coalition included four generals (Sant'Andrea, Moroni [Ange-Pierre Moroni], Avezzano and Martel [Philippe André Martel]), 280 officers and 10,000 lower ranks (including sick and stragglers, as well as those taken by partisans); two guns were captured. The Coalition lost more than 9,000 men in total, namely:

	Killed		Wounded		Missing	
	Officers	Other Ranks	Officers	Other Ranks	Officers	Other Ranks
Bavarian Forces	21	324	58	1,014	15	2,709
Austrian Forces	14	1,400	50	1,961	16	1,655
Total:	35	1,724	108	2,975	31	4,364

Those wounded included: in addition to Graf Wrede, the Bavarian generals: Graf Pappenheim and Janson von der Stock, the latter mortally; the Austrians: *Feldmarschallleutnant* Baron Trautenberg and *Generalmajor* Graf Klenau.[18]

Both sides claimed victory: the Coalition because they had taken the city of Hanau in battle, and the French considered themselves victors because they had cleared their way to the Rhine through force of arms. Because the objective of Graf Wrede's operations was to block this route to the enemy, and Napoleon's objective was to preserve the remnants of his army, it is clear that the glory of the victory belongs to the latter. The French lost more men than the Coalition, but this, in all fairness, should be attributed not to the tactical superiority of the Austro-Bavarian troops, against whom Napoleon's elite force, the *Vieille Garde* and *Jeune Garde*, fought for the most part, but to the general disorder in the French army, which lost more men from exhaustion and marauding than in action against the enemy. Here, as also on the Berezina, Napoleon was able to lead his army out of a very dangerous situation; but one cannot deny that in both cases he owed much to the errors of his opponents. Had the Coalition relentlessly pursued the French after the battle of Leipzig, then Napoleon's army, constrained from all sides at Hanau, would have suffered a total defeat. Graf Wrede is rightly criticised for having spent three whole days at Würzburg, held by an enemy force of just 2,000 men. Had he reached Gelnhausen on 14 (26) October, he would have had time to deploy at the Wirthheim defile [4½ miles east of Gelnhausen], where the Kinzig river flows through a deep valley, bordered on both sides by steep mountains. By occupying this position and strengthening it with additional obstacles, Wrede could have checked the enemy and, despite the slowness of Prince Schwarzenberg, would have given him the opportunity to catch up with Napoleon.[19]

---

17 Vaudoncourt, 234.
18 Plotho, II, 462.
19 Plotho, II, 463.

On the morning of 20 October (1 November), the French army set off from the vicinity of Frankfurt along the Mainz road; Napoleon departed at two o'clock in the afternoon; the rearguard units left the city the following morning [2 November, new style]. Orlov-Denisov's detachment caught up with the enemy near Bergen, captured two guns and 15 ammunition caissons, and took 1,300 men prisoner. General Fresnel advanced from Hanau along the Frankfurt highway with the Austro-Bavarian army, camping overnight, 20 to 21 October (1 to 2 November), at Dörnigheim [4½ miles west of Hanau], and moved to Frankfurt that day; ahead of them moved Platov with the Cossacks and the partisan detachments under Count Orlov-Denisov, Kaisarov and Chernyshev, who the day before [1 November], in pursuing the French from Hanau to Frankfurt, took more than 3,000 men prisoner.[20] On that same day, 21 October (2 November), the French army crossed into Mainz on the left bank of the Rhine, with the exception of the divisions under Morand and Guilleminot, left under Bertrand's command in the fortifications at Hochheim [11 miles south-west of Höchst] and Kastel [five miles south of Wiesbaden]. Platov's Cossack detachment attacked the enemy between the village of Wicker [8½ miles south-west of Höchst] and Hochheim and 'fought with them until nightfall, but due to the overwhelming strength of their infantry and cavalry and the large number of cannon, were unable to defeat them.'[21] The Austro-Bavarian army, having sent their leading elements in the direction of Höchst, took up quarters in the vicinity of Frankfurt.[22]

During the period of Graf Wrede's operations just described, the other Coalition armies were also approaching the Rhine. The advance by the Army of Bohemia had been planned by Prinz Schwarzenberg's general staff such that Austrian forces would reach Frankfurt before the other Coalition formations, and so that Kaiser Franz could make a ceremonial entrance to this city three days before Emperor Alexander (the King of Prussia had left for Berlin by this time). Austrian diplomats hoped that by appearing in the ancient imperial city at the head of a Coalition force, Kaiser Franz would present himself as being the leader of the Coalition mobilised against Napoleon. To that end, the Russo-Prussian troops under Barclay de Tolly, which from the very beginning of the campaign had been constantly operating on the right wing of the Army of Bohemia, were transferred to the left wing. Austrian forces advanced from Schmalkalden to Fulda, along the shortest route to Frankfurt; the forces under Barclay de Tolly were sent to this city via an indirect route, from Meiningen, to Mellrichstadt, Münnerstadt, Veitshöchheim, Homburg and Aschaffenburg. According to the march-routes drafted by the Austrian staff officers, Kaiser Franz was to enter Frankfurt on 25 October (6 November), while Emperor Alexander would arrive on 28 October (9 November). The Emperor initially paid no attention to this 'politicised' route; but then, having become convinced of Austrian intentions, with his characteristic dexterity, he would not allow himself to be outmanoeuvred. Because the Russian infantry were lagging far behind the Austrians, the entire Russo-Prussian cavalry, having received revised march-routes, advanced via

---

20 Count Platov's dispatch to Adjutant General Volkonsky, from Frankfurt am Main, dated 21 October [2 November].
21 Count Platov's note to Adjutant General Chernyshev, dated 23 October [5 November].
22 Plotho, II, 465.

forced marches, seven *Meilen* (50 *versts*) per day, and arrived in Frankfurt, together with Emperor Alexander's headquarters, on the eve of the day appointed for the Austrian Kaiser's ceremonial entrance into the city. The Russian Monarch suddenly appeared in Frankfurt on 24 October (5 November), and at one o'clock in the afternoon, the Lifeguard Light Cavalry Division, 12 Russian cuirassier regiments, and the Prussian Guard Cavalry, numbering more than 7,500 horsemen, marched past him through the city in full dress. The population greeted their liberators with joyful cheering. The next day [6 November, new style], Kaiser Franz entered just as ceremonially, but the majority of the troops lining the streets along which he rode from the city gates to the cathedral were not Austrians, but Russian cuirassiers, and, moreover, Emperor Alexander greeted his ally as a host, meeting him at the gates and escorting him from there to the cathedral.[23]

On that same day, 25 October (6 November), in accordance with the disposition issued by Prinz Schwarzenberg, a vanguard under Graf Bubna, reinforced by the leading elements of the Austrian *II. Korpus*, relieved the vanguard of the Austro-Bavarian army at Wicker, facing Hochheim, which then moved to the Darmstadt area; the Austrian contingent of the Army of Bohemia were stationed on the right bank of the Main, around Frankfurt and Hanau; the Russo-Prussian reserves under Barclay de Tolly were in Frankfurt and along the left bank of the Main, from Offenbach [five miles south-east of Frankfurt] to Obernburg; Wittgenstein's force was in the vicinity of Friedberg, along the Nidda river. Because the enemy were still holding Hochheim with 2,000 men and 20 guns, Prinz Schwarzenberg ordered Gyulay to attack the French on 28 October (9 November), with Graf Bubna's vanguard and the Austrian *II. Korpus* and *III. Korpus*. This attack was a complete success: the enemy were driven out of Hochheim, with the loss of one banner, four guns and 30 officers and 1,000 lower ranks taken prisoner. As a result of this, the French were cleared from the right bank of the Rhine, except for the bridgeheads at Kastel opposite Mainz, and at Kehl opposite Strasbourg. Graf Bubna's vanguard were stationed around Kastel; Platov's Cossack detachment was at Wiesbaden and Biebrich [seven miles south-west of Diez]. The headquarters of Emperor Alexander, Kaiser Franz, King Friedrich Wilhelm, who had returned to the active army on 1 (13) November, Prinz Schwarzenberg, Grand Duke Konstantin Pavlovich and Counts Barclay de Tolly and Miloradovich were in Frankfurt, while the headquarters of the Austro-Bavarian army were in Groß-Gerau, near Darmstadt.[24]

On 18 (30) October, just as the formations of the Army of Bohemia were reaching Schmalkalden and Meiningen on the Werra river, Blücher arrived at Fulda and Hünfeld with his army. Because Graf Wrede's advance from the Danube to the Main, in order to sever the line of retreat of the French army, was already known about at that time, it was assumed that Napoleon, wishing to mitigate the danger of being surrounded by the Coalition, would move to the right across the Vogelsberg Mountains towards Koblenz rather than towards Mainz. Blücher, by agreement with Prinz Schwarzenberg, headed for Giessen and Wetzlar in order to deny this route

---

23 Alexander Andreevich Shcherbinin's notes; Bernhardi, *Denkwürdigkeiten des Grafen von Toll*, III, 478-479.
24 Plotho, II, 469-473.

to the enemy, and having arrived at these locations on 21 October (2 November), he placed his troops in quarters and granted a rest day to his army, fatigued from incessant marching. But Blücher's inaction did not last long; he decided to exploit the enemy's disorder, by invading France by force of arms.

According to the plan of operations drawn up at his *Hauptquartier*, the Army of Silesia was to cross the Rhine at Mülheim, near Cologne [Köln], on 2 and 3 (14 and 15) November; the Army of the North, already approaching Hanover at the time, would move through the Netherlands into Belgium, while the Army of Bohemia would cross the middle Rhine; thereafter, all three armies would march on Paris. The Coalition hoped for a Dutch uprising, for assistance from the Anglo-Spanish army and, in all likelihood, for Murat to break with France. Napoleon had no more than 60,000 or 70,000 exhausted troops left; the people were impatient for peace. All these factors caused Blücher to undertake a quick, decisive offensive. He sent General Gneisenau to a conference at the headquarters of the Coalition monarchs with the intention of inducing Prince Schwarzenberg to do the same, but in order to lose no time waiting for an answer, he immediately moved towards the Rhine. On 26 October (7 November), the Army of Silesia set off from their quarters in two columns: the left, consisting of Sacken's and Yorck's corps, accompanied by the *Hauptquartier*, was directed towards Weilburg, Altenkirchen and Siegburg, while Langéron's corps formed the right hand column advancing from Dillenburg and Siegen, where he was to be joined by the forces under comte Saint-Priest and Prince Shcherbatov.[25]

Once all the corps had assembled at Mülheim on 2 (14) November, it was planned to build a bridge from boats collected along the Rhine on the following day [15 November, new style], cross this river and swiftly invade the Netherlands in the direction of Aachen and Lüttich [Liège]. Intelligence received at Blücher's *Hauptquartier* confirmed that the enemy were unable to offer decisive resistance anywhere, that their fortresses had not been placed on a war footing, and that the population of France were not hostile to the Coalition. As a tireless supporter of Blücher, Gneisenau was convinced of the need to act quickly and without delay. 'One must strike while the iron is hot, giving the defeated enemy neither rest nor repose' he wrote to Sir Charles Stewart.[26] But on 30 October (11 November), Blücher received orders from the headquarters of the Coalition monarchs to return to Frankfurt and besiege the bridgehead opposite Mainz. Upon arrival there, on 3 (15) November, the Army of Silesia, having relieved the Austrian force at Kastel, settled into quarters in the vicinity of this location and occupied outposts along the right bank of the Rhine from the confluence of the Main to Düsseldorf. Blücher's *Hauptquartier* was located in Höchst.[27] The Army of Bohemia was positioned along the left bank of the Main as far [south] as the Kocher river.[28]

---

25 Disposition for the advance by the Army of Silesia, dated 6 November, new style, signed by Blücher.
26 Varnhagen von Ense, *Leben des Fürsten Blücher von Wahlstadt*, 257-258; Droysen, *Yorcks Leben*, III, 194; Bernhardi, IV, 16-17; Förster, *Befreiungskriege 1813, 1814, 1815*, II, 483-484.
27 Varnhagen von Ense, 258-259.
28 Dispositions of the main army, dated 18 November, new style, signed by Prinz Schwarzenberg.

The Coalition, upon reaching the Rhine, could have immediately crossed this river (as Gneisenau proposed) and ended the war with a decisive blow by marching on Paris. It is true that their armies were tired and in disarray, but the pitiful state of the enemy forces prevented them from even thinking about resisting the Coalition. Nevertheless, the draft proposals from the headquarters of the Army of Silesia, having been subjected to discussion on 26 October (7 November) by a Council of War, in the presence of Emperor Alexander, were rejected by the 'peace party.' Even at the beginning of the war of 1813, many of the Russian generals, including Kutuzov himself, believed that after driving the enemy from Russian territory, it would be more profitable for Russia to conclude a peace than to continue the fight with Napoleon for an 'alien' cause, the liberation of Germany. The concerns of the peace advocates were not justified: Emperor Alexander appeared as the leader of the nations rising up against France; thanks to his ability to maintain the cooperation of the Coalition governments, Napoleon's armies were destroyed and the oppressed nations breathed freely. All this notwithstanding, however, the Russians believed that, after such a difficult, albeit glorious campaign, the time had finally come to conclude peace and that further continuation of the war would be a gross mistake in political terms as it offered Russia no benefits. Emperor Alexander alone did not believe in the possibility of a lasting peace with Napoleon and wanted to fight to the bitter end.

In contrast, the 'war party' were predominant in the Prussian army. Blücher, Gneisenau and many others were convinced of the need to continue decisive operations against Napoleon. But even in the Prussian camp, voices were heard in favour of peace. The King himself considered an invasion of France to be risky. General Knesebeck also believed that it was impossible to hope for unending successes, and therefore it was necessary to take advantage of this favourable opportunity to conclude an advantageous peace. The removal of Napoleon from the throne was considered by General Knesebeck's circle to be 'the romantic ideal of the mavericks in Blücher's *Hauptquartier*.' Memories of the ill-fated campaign of 1792 led him to predict a most desperate resistance as soon as the Coalition crossed the ancient borders of France.[29]

General Knesebeck's doubts found support in a letter to him from General Yorck, describing the situation in his corps in a most gloomy fashion. According to his returns, the Army of Silesia numbered no more than 36,000 men in its ranks overall, with whom it would be necessary to begin a difficult winter campaign by making their way through several lines of enemy fortresses. The Prussian corps, which had possessed more than 100 guns in August, retained only 42 of them, most of them with lashed-up axles and poor quality wheels. The resupply of projectiles received before the battle of Möckern had been depleted and had only been partially replenished from parks captured from the enemy. The weapons had become unserviceable due to damp and many Prussian soldiers did not even have muskets. Their uniforms were in a pitiful state; the troops that had taken part in the campaign of 1812 still wore the uniforms they had been issued in 1811. The *Litevka* coats of the

---

29 Müffling, *Aus meinem Leben*, 78-79; Bernhardi, IV, 11-15.

Schlesisches Landwehr, made of poor quality, uncompacted cloth, had shrunk and become extremely short and tight. The soldiers did not have woollen trousers in preparation for a winter campaign. Most of them were barefoot and especially the *Landwehr* and *Freiwillige*. Only those who managed to obtain them from prisoners had greatcoats. The trains lagged behind their formations; many of the horses in the cavalry and artillery had become unfit for service.[30] This sorry depiction of the state of the Prussian forces left an impression on many, and especially on the cautious Knesebeck.

There was even more inclination towards peace on the Austrian side. Here, Metternich's influence prevailed. Once concerns at Napoleon's dominance began to dissipate, doubts about Emperor Alexander's intentions arose in the minds of Austrian statesmen: believing, not without reason, that Russian annexation of the Duchy of Warsaw to its territories was the only way to compensate Russia for its sacrifices and losses, the Austrians feared the loss of Galicia in this new partition of Europe. The Austrian government was no less anxious of the national mobilisations inspired by the Coalition struggles against Napoleon. Under these circumstances, Metternich turned his full attention to a complete suspension of hostilities, the opening of peace negotiations, and turning them to Austria's advantage. The opinions of this Austrian diplomat gained ground due to the absence of Stein, who considered the overthrow of Napoleon to be vital to the peace of Europe.[31]

As early as 14 (26) October, during the presence of the headquarters of the Coalition monarchs in Weimar, a suggestion was made to the captured French diplomat, Baron Saint-Aignan, about the readiness of the Coalition to make peace if Napoleon really wanted it. Upon the arrival of the headquarters in Frankfurt, on 27 October (8 November), Metternich spoke about the rousing of German thought, the need to make peace, and so on, at a meeting with Saint-Aignan. The next day, he handed Saint-Aignan a letter from his sovereign to Marie-Louise, and informed him of the conditions under which the Coalition proposed to conclude peace with Napoleon. Count Nesselrode, who had arrived in the meantime, announced that everything proposed in the current meeting had been agreed with Hardenberg. From the initial speech by Prinz Metternich, the French diplomat would conclude that the Coalition, not limiting themselves to the continental peace that had been under negotiation in Prague, desired a global settlement with the participation of Britain.

As to their terms, Metternich told Saint-Aignan that the Coalition sovereigns were agreed among themselves to preserve French power and *prépondérance* inviolably, restrained by their natural boundaries, the Rhine, the Alps and the Pyrenees. The independence of Germany was an essential condition for peace, and therefore, while maintaining the influence inevitable to every powerful state over its weaker neighbours (*sine qua non*), France must renounce dominion over German lands, especially since Emperor Napoleon himself recognised the benefit of dismantling large states into smaller ones. The independence of Spain and the restoration of its ancient dynasty were equally vital conditions of peace. In Italy the borders of

---

30 Droysen, III, 195-196.
31 Pertz, Das Leben des Ministers, Freiherrn vom Stein, III, 462-463.

Austrian territories would be determined in agreement with Piedmont; both this question and the state of Italy in general would be subject to negotiations, the basis of which was that this country, like Germany, would be completely independent of the influence of France and other dominant powers. The status of the Netherlands would also be determined by negotiations, on the basis of recognition of their independence. A willingness was expressed on Britain's behalf, to make significant concessions in order to make peace on the stated terms and for an agreement on freedom of navigation and trade.

Having thus explained the Coalition demands, should Emperor Napoleon accept them, Metternich proposed to recognise the neutrality of any city on the right bank of the Rhine and to invite the representatives of all the belligerent powers there in order to conduct negotiations, while continuing military operations. Baron Saint-Aignan, having heard these proposals, expressed a desire to write notes on everything he had been told and, being invited by Prinz Metternich into his office, he transcribed the required conditions on paper. Then, upon re-entering the room where Prinz Metternich and Count Nesselrode were waiting, he found them together with the British ambassador to Vienna, Lord Aberdeen [George Hamilton-Gordon, 4th Earl of Aberdeen]. At Metternich's request, Saint-Aignan read out his notes, and when it came to that which concerned Britain, Aberdeen renewed his assurances of his government's willingness to make the greatest concessions. At the same time, the Coalition diplomats made it clear to Saint-Aignan that they would be more comfortable negotiating with Caulaincourt than with Maret. Prinz Schwarzenberg arrived as the meeting was ending, and having agreed all the conditions set out, gave Saint-Aignan a letter addressed to Marshal Berthier. On the night of 29 to 30 October (10 to 11 November), Saint-Aignan set off for Paris via Mainz.[32]

The Coalition headquarters, during the involuntary inactivity of the army on the Rhine, presented a spectacle of extraordinary diplomatic activity. The rulers of the *Confédération du Rhin*, hitherto obedient executors of Napoleon's orders, vied with each other to erase the memory of their betrayal of their common fatherland – Germany. The Herzog von Nassau [Friedrich August von Nassau-Usingen] hastened to lift the sequestration on Stein's estates imposed on Napoleon's orders; the King of Württemberg, following the example of Bavaria, on 3 November, new style, ratified a treaty in Fulda, pledging to add a corps of 12,000 men to the Austrian army; the Austrian government vouched for the inviolability of the territories that had belonged to the House of Württemberg since antiquity, and for compensation in the event that any of the lands newly annexed to the Kingdom had to be expropriated in favour of other German rulers.

Although the members of the *Confédération du Rhin* did not all come over to the Coalition side simultaneously, and many of them even decided to do so against their own convictions, nevertheless, on Metternich's insistence, they were guaranteed full and unlimited retention of all the lands granted to them by Napoleon. The reasons for such leniency might have been the intention of the Austrian government to form a grouping of Rhine princes in their favour, or more likely, indifference regarding

---

32 *Rapport de M. le baron de St-Aignan*; *Note écrite à Francfort le 9 Novembre par le baron de St-Aignan*; Fain, *Manuscrit de 1814*, 49-56; Pertz, III, 463-465.

the future fate of the *Deutscher Bund*. It was common for Prinz Metternich, while denying the very existence of Germany, to refer to it as 'a geographical concept.' The conclusion of bilateral treaties between Austria and the German princes freed them from subordination to the Central Administration. Thus Stein's proposal that the Coalition should administer conquered territories and exploit their resources to wage war against the common foe until peace was concluded was rejected.

Only a few German princes, the *Großherzog* of Frankfurt [Dalberg] and the Fürst zu Isenburg [Carl Friedrich Ludwig Moritz zu Isenburg] and Fürst von der Leyen [Philipp Franz Wilhelm Ignaz von der Leyen], were excluded from the general amnesty: the former had been the *Reichserzkanzler* [Grand Chancellor] of the Holy Roman Empire, the *Président du collège des princes* of the *Confédération du Rhin* and the *Fürstprimas* [Prince-Primate] of the Catholic Church in Germany, and had fled Frankfurt, which resulted in the transfer of his territories to the control of the *Zentral Verwaltungs Rat*. The Fürst zu Isenburg had served as a general in the French army in the war of 1806 against Prussia, and the Fürst von der Leyen had sworn allegiance to the French government, so neither could remain members of the *Deutscher Bund*.

The King of Westphalia had fled beyond the Rhine; administrations were formed (as was done with Saxony) for his lands, together with the Großherzogtum Berg and the German regions belonging to the House of Orange [Huis Oranje-Nassau], both subordinate to the *Zentral Verwaltungs Rat*; The Austrian general, Prinz Philipp zu Hessen-Homburg was initially appointed Governor-General of Frankfurt, thereafter, the Prinz zu Reuss [Heinrich XIII. Reuss-Greiz], while the Governor-General of Berg, on Stein's orders, was initially the Prussian *Geheimer Staatsrat* [privy councilor], Gruner [Karl Justus Gruner], and later General Prinz Solms [Friedrich Alexander zu Solms-Hohensolms-Lich].

The *Zentral Verwaltungs Rat* immediately took care to rouse the spirits of the people in the territories under its jurisdiction, to form local authorities from the most capable officials, to raise active troops and a landwehr as a priority, and to conscientiously collect and spend revenue.[33] The provision of supplies in kind and the sums contributed by the ruling princes were under the jurisdiction of a special commission, consisting of state dignitaries and generals, under the chairmanship of Prinz Metternich. A contribution of 17,000,000 Guilders (about 10,000,000 silver Roubles) was levied from former members of the *Confédération du Rhin* for the year's military expenses. This sum was to be paid in 24 quarterly installments from the income of their estates, while six-percent bonds were issued as collateral for this. Russia, Austria and Prussia would received 5/16 of the total value of the bonds, and Sweden 1/16. Every quarter, 1/24 of the bonds had to be redeemed and thus the entire debt would be paid off in three years.[34]

The provision of rations for the troops was secured through the following orders: each member of the Coalition was obliged to prepare the necessary supplies in kind and deliver them free of charge in the required quantities for a year's subsistence for

---

33 The administrations for Frankfurt and Berg were directed to assemble 17,000 line troops and a similar number of *Landwehr*.
34 Pertz, III, 465-470.

their deployed contingent. They were also responsible for the delivery of their own supplies and for those crossing their territory, and the allocation of pasture for horse grazing. The Coalition powers, Russia, Austria and Prussia, were obliged to deliver a six-month supply of provisions and forage for their troops by boat or overland, but had the right to collect provisions from the country at the request of the intendant-general or corps commanders, paying for it by drawing on bonds.[35]

Upon the arrival of the Coalition armies on the Rhine, Russian forces were supplied with provisions on the basis of the so-called Aschaffenburg Tariff, issued on Count Barclay de Tolly's orders. This same tariff was subsequently introduced into every Coalition army. According to the Aschaffenburg Tariff, the following daily rations were assigned to the lower ranks:

Rye or white bread	2 pounds[36]
Cereals, either rice, beans, peas, lentils	¼ pound[37]
Beef	½ pound
Vodka ration	¹¹⁄₁₆ *Mass*[38]
Salt (per month)	1 pound

The daily ration for officers was:

Bread	2 pounds
Beef	1 pound
Rice or cereals	¼ pound
Vodka, beer or wine	one ration

Forage was supplied in Austrian quantities, a ration of ⅛ *Metze* of oats and ten pounds of hay;[39] cuirassiers, officers' riding horses and artillery horses received 1½ rations of oats, ten pounds of hay and two pounds of straw.

As far as uniforms for the troops were concerned, important preparations were begun as soon as the headquarters moved to Frankfurt: firstly, a depot was established for the parks in Nuremberg [Nürnberg] for finished items; secondly, at the request of General Count Wittgenstein, his force Intendant 5th Class, Zhukovsky [Mikhail Stepanovich Zhukovsky], was given a sum for the purchase of cloth and other items in Swabia. But in the case of the campaign in France, the purchased

---

35 Pertz, III, 465-470.
36 Or 1⅙ pounds of hard-tack, or one pound of flour; if there was a shortage of bread, one pound could be replaced with ¼ pound of beef [the Russian pound was just under 14½ imperial ounces].
37 Or one pound of potatoes and other fresh vegetables.
38 The vodka ration was about 0.08 of a Russian *Vedra*, or 0.06 of a Russian *Vedra* of beer [one *Vedra* equals 2.7 imperial gallons or 12.3 litres].
39 About 2⅓ Russian *Garnets* [one *Garnets* equals 5¾ pints or 3.28 litres]. Four measures of oats could be replaced by three measures of barley or rye. Half the oats ration could be replaced with five pounds of hay. Five pounds of hay could be replaced by five pounds of straw, and one pound of flour.

materials arrived at the regiments so late that the uniforms were not made up until after the conclusion of peace, and some were even delivered to the troops in Thorn on their return march. The sheepskin coats sent to Prague also did not reach the army before the onset of spring, that is, at a time of year when they were no longer needed, and therefore it was permitted to sell them in Bohemia (at a rather significant loss) for 500,000 Guilders.

On arrival at the Rhine, the hospitals were maintained partly through bonds, partly by requisitioning from the local population, whose enthusiasm for the common cause and compassion for the sick and wounded brought great benefits.[40]

With regard to the mobilisation of Germany, it was decided that in each of the territories, following the example of Prussia, in addition to line units, *Freiwillige* groups, *Landwehr* and, where necessary, *Landsturm*, should be raised. Every former member of the *Confédération du Rhin* was to furnish a similar contingent of line troops as they had furnished for Napoleon, and a similar number of *Landwehr*, with sufficient reserves to replenish them. A dedicated commission, composed of Prinz Schwarzenberg, Stein, Adjutant General Prince Volkonsky, Radetzky and Gneisenau, decided, on 24 November, new style, that the German rulers should raise 145,000 men for the line forces and a similar number of *Landwehr* soldiers. It was decided to divide this mobilised force into six corps, which included: Bavarians, Hanovarians, Saxons, Württembergers, Hessians and Badenese, with additional contingents from the smaller territories. In order to encourage the German princes to raise forces as quickly as possible, it was decided not to approve treaties of alliance with them until after the complete formation of their contingents, and the following deadlines were set: 31 December, new style, for line units, and 12 January 1814, new style, for *Landwehr*.

At a meeting of the commission on 26 November, new style, which, in addition to Schwarzenberg and Stein, included the following: Metternich, Nesselrode, Hardenberg, General Knesebeck and the Prussian Intendant-General, Graf Lottum [Carl Friedrich Heinrich von Wylich und Lottum], appointed the following as commanders of the newly reorganised corps: General Wrede to *I Armeekorps*, General Wallmoden to *II Armeekorps*, the Herzog von Weimar [Carl August von Sachsen-Weimar-Eisenach] to *III Armeekorps*, the Herzog von Coburg [Ernst I. Anton Carl Ludwig von Sachsen-Coburg-Gotha] to *IV Armeekorps*, Prinz Philipp zu Hessen-Homburg to *V Armeekorps*, the Kronprinz von Württemberg [Wilhelm Friedrich Karl von Württemberg] to *VI Armeekorps*. *I*, *V* and *VI Armeekorps* were assigned to the Coalition Main Army, *III* and *IV Armeekorps* came under Blücher's command, while *II Armeekorps* became part of the Army of the North.

That the execution of the *Zentral Verwaltungs Rat* plans related to the general mobilisation of Germany met with much enthusiasm and achieved the desired objective was largely thanks to the energy and activity of Stein and his associates. Almost every German ruler restored or spared by the Coalition powers tried to evade the responsibilities assigned to them. These same princes who had shamefully humbled

---

40 Account of the activities of the Quartermaster's Department in the war against the French in 1812, 1813 and 1814, submitted to Emperor Alexander I by General Barclay de Tolly (manuscript).

themselves before Napoleon and meekly sacrificed the blood and treasure of their subjects to him, turning instantly from wretched slaves into arrogant rulers, refused to fulfil the demands of Emperor Alexander, which were aimed at strengthening the independence of Germany. Many of these princes did not inspire any loyalty from their subjects and did not trust them, they feared the *Landwehr* and *Landsturm* and considered it necessary to hinder the national mobilisation in every possible way for their own security.

No less harmful to the common cause of Germany was the sympathy of some rulers for Napoleon, the conviction of his invincibility and the fear of his vengeance. The King of Württemberg, in dismissing the French ambassador from his Court, expressed his sincere regret regarding the current situation and the grave necessity of breaking with Napoleon. Refusing to acknowledge his sacred duty to stand in defence of the common fatherland – Germany, he disbanded those cavalry regiments which had gone over to the Coalition at Leipzig, and dismissed the officers of this cavalry brigade from service; their commander, General Normann, not only suffered the same fate, but, being persecuted and exiled, was not accepted into Austrian service (unlike Westphalian General Hammerstein [William Friedrich von Hammerstein-Equord] who had managed so to do). The king, wishing to prevent the people from arming themselves, ordered the confiscation of firearms in his dominions; at the same time, he tried by every means to break off relations with the *Zentral Verwaltungs Rat* and even wanted to arrest Colonel Rühle von Lilienstern in Karlsruhe, who was entrusted with organising the national mobilisation in the territories of the former *Confédération du Rhin*.

The Großherzog von Baden [Karl Ludwig Friedrich von Baden], when parting with Bignon [Louis Pierre Édouard Bignon], felt obliged to express his feelings of deep regret about the state of affairs which had forced him, against his will, to take the side of the enemies of France. In Bavaria, the Montgelas ministry tried to stymie the orders of the *Zentral Verwaltungs Rat*. The Kronprinz [later King Ludwig I], devoted to the common cause of Germany, was deprived of influence over the actions of the government. In Hanover, national mobilisation was slowed down by the incompetence of the Duke of Cumberland and Teviotdale [Ernest Augustus, later King of Hanover]: young men who had travelled from Göttingen in order to join the *Freiwillige* units were leaving after several weeks of waiting in vain. The Duke's entire contribution was limited to the raising of a cavalry regiment in which the officers were exclusively of noble birth. In the territories of Baden and Darmstadt the national mobilisation was slow, the Hesse-Kassel contingent arrived just at the end of the war, while the Hanoverians were not in time to take part in operations at all. Of all the German princes, only the Herzog von Anhalt [Leopold III. Friedrich Franz von Anhalt-Dessau], the Saxon dukes, the Schwarzburg princes and the Fürst von Lippe-Bückeburg [Georg Wilhelm zu Schaumburg-Lippe], and the cities of Bremen and Lübeck fulfilled their duties exactly.[41]

Many military historians have criticised the Coalition for not taking advantage of the disorder in Napoleon's army and for not crossing the Rhine after them. Yet these

---

41 Pertz, III, 471-477; Bernhardi, IV, 5-6.

harsh judgements overlook the fact that the Coalition forces were also in dire need of rest after a difficult campaign, needed reconstituting and a resupply of clothing, footwear, weapons and ammunition. It was necessary to establish magazines and hospitals at the expense of the Rhineland regions, whose rulers were hostile or indifferent to the common cause of Germany. Had they decided to cross to the left bank of the Rhine immediately, with an army that numbered no more than 150,000 men, it would have been necessary to leave some of them on the right bank of this river in order to monitor the fortresses that were in the hands of the French, and to stiffen the shaky allies; thereafter, during the advance towards Paris, it would be necessary to further weaken the army by detaching blockading corps and other detachments to guard lines of communications back to the Rhine. Having reached the capital of France in insufficient strength, the Coalition could have been subjected to a defeat, and in such an event a guerilla war could flare up to their rear. During the two-month pause on the Rhine, they managed to significantly replenish their army with recovered men, to bring up several corps that had remained behind or had been raised by German rulers, and to bring the reserves and parks up closer. Napoleon, for all his amazing activity, could not assemble sufficient forces during this period and only the disagreements and errors of the Coalition gave him the chance to continue the unequal struggle, the outcome of which was already fated to be inevitable.

Appendix XXXVII

Emperor Alexander's letter to the King of Bavaria, dated 11 (23) September 1813

Emperor Alexander's letter to King Maximilian Joseph of Bavaria:

Sir, my brother! Your Majesty's reply has just been presented to me. The provisions that You have announced to me, the precious confidence that You show, have touched me deeply. Your Majesty will never regret having given yourself over to the feelings that I have for you with such abandon. United with the Austrian Kaiser by the most indissoluble bonds, I do not hesitate to accede to all the proposals that he will make to Your Majesty and to give my guarantee to the resultant exchanges. The objective towards which all our efforts tend is the return to an order of affairs which will assure Europe of a long period of peace and happiness. I regard the strength and independence of the intermediate powers as the first means of attaining this. This important consideration makes it essential that the borders of Austria be better established, from a military point of view, which can only be achieved by arrangements to be made with Your Majesty. You doubtless view the current state of affairs from such an elevated point of view not to be unconvinced of this; and I am too frank not to explain myself to You on such a delicate subject without the slightest reserve. But the most complete compensation calculated on the geographical, statistical and financial proportions of the ceded lands, will be formally guaranteed to Your Majesty such that an exchange can only be to Your advantage, because You would only be rid of those provinces which cannot assimilate with the other parts of Your States and where the wish to return to their former masters is too strongly nourished in the hearts of every inhabitant for the spirit of insurrection not to cause continual troubles for the government.

Far from wanting the power of Bavaria to experience the slightest diminution in this way, my attachment to Your Majesty will rather be a means of enlargement for You, in the changes that circumstances might require. It would be difficult for me to furnish you, at this moment, with more pronounced proofs of how much I have your interests at heart, and as soon as the preliminary arrangements with Austria have been signed, I shall be ready to conclude engagements based on the principles which I have just elucidated with any person you wish to send to my headquarters. On the other hand, I expect active and immediate cooperation from Your Majesty. Every moment is precious. The very positive assurances that You have given me permit me to rely on Your eagerness to seize them. Otherwise, and if the finest chance for the deliverance of Europe were to be lost, His Majesty should feel that I would no longer be able to realise the views dictated by friendship and confirmed by the policy of all my allies with regard to him. The military arrangements which are going to be proposed to Your Majesty must inspire him with every confidence and add new evidence in favour of the principles which guide us.

Alexander

Teplitz, 11 (23) September 1813.

M. mon frère! La réponse de V.M. vient de m'être remise. Les dispositions qu'Elle m'annonce, la confiance précieuse qu'Elle témoigne, m'ont vivement touché. V.M. ne regrettera jamais de s'être livrée, avec un tel abandon, aux sentiments que je lui porte. Uni avec l'empereur d'Autriche par les liens les plus indissolubles, je n'hésite pas à acceder à toutes les propositions qu'il va faire à V.M. et à donner ma garantie aux transactions qui en seront le résultat. Le retour d'un ordre de choses qui assure à l'Europe un long intervalle de paix et de bonheur, forme le but vers le quel tendent tous nos efforts. Je regarde la force et l'indépendance des puissances intermédiaires comme le premier moyen de l'atteindre. Cette importante considération rend indispensable que les froutières de l'Autriche soient mieux établies, sous le rapport militaire, ce qui ne saurait être obtenu que par des arrangements à prendre avec V.M. Elle envisage, sans doute, l'état actuel des choses d'un point de vue trop élevé, pour ne pas en être convaincu; et moi, je suis trop franc, pour ne pas m'expliquer envers Elle sans la moindre réserve, sur un objet aussi délicat. Mais l'indemnisation la plus complète calculée sur les proportions géographiques, statistiques et financières du pays cédé, sera formellement garantie à V.M. afin qu'un pareil échange ne puisse même qu tourner à son avantage, car Elle ne se déferait que de celle de ces provinces qui ne s'amalgame guère avec les autres parties de ses Etats, et où le voeu de retourner à leurs anciens maîtres est trop fortement mourri dans le coeur de chaque habitant, pour que l'esprit d'insurrection ne suscite des embarras continuels au gouvernement.

  Loin de vouloir que par là la puissance de la Bavière éprouve la moindre diminution, mon attachement pour V.M. me fera plutot un moyen d'agrandissement pour Elle, dans les changements que les circonstances pourraient réclamer. Il serait difficile qu je lui fournisse, dans ce moment, des preuves plus prononcées combien j'ai ses intérêts à coeur, et aussitôt que les arrangements préliminaires avec l'Autriche auront été signés, je serai prêt à faire conclure, avec toute personne qu'Elle voudra envoyer à mon quartier-général, des engagements basés sur les principes que je viens de developper. J'attends, en revanche, une coopération active et immédiate de la part de V.M. Les moments sont précieux. Les assurances si positives qu'Elle m'a données m'autorisent à compter sur Son empressement à les saisir. Dans le cas contraire, et si la plus belle chance pour la délivrance de l'Europe devait être perdue, S.M. sentirait que je ne serais plus le maître de réaliser à son égard des vues dictées par l'amitié et confirmées par la politique de tous mes alliés. Les arrangements militaires qui vont être proposés à V.M. doivent lui inspirer toute confiance et ajouter une nouvelle preuve en faveur des principes qui nous guident.

Alexandre.

Teplitz, le 11 (23) Septembre, 1813.'

Appendix XXXVIII

Composition of Graf Wrede's Austro-Bavarian army

Listing of the composition of the Austro-Bavarian army of *General der Kavallerie* Graf Wrede:

Bavarian Contingent:

First Division, *Generalleutnant* Graf Rechberg: *Generalmajor* Prinz Karl von Bayern's brigade of two battalions from *1. Linieninfanterie König*, one battalion from *3. Linieninfanterie Prinz Karl*, *3. Leichte Bataillon* and *10. National Bataillon Augsburg*; *Generalmajor* Maillot's brigade of one battalion each from *2. Linieninfanterie Kronprinz* and *10. Linieninfanterie Juncker, 2. Leichte Bataillon, 11. National Bataillon Ingolstadt* and *15. National Bataillon Bayreuth*; two six-pounder batteries under *Oberstleutnant* Göschl: for a total of seven line battalions, three *Landwehr* battalions, and 14 guns.

Second Division, *Generalleutnant* Graf Becker: *Generalmajor* Graf Pappenheim's brigade of two battalions from 4. Linieninfanterie Herzog von Sachsen-Hildburghausen, *4. Leichte Bataillon, 4. National Bataillon Salzburg, 9. National Bataillon Regensburg*; *Generalmajor* Baron Zollern's brigade of two battalions from *6. Linieninfanterie Herzog Wilhelm, 1. Leichte Bataillon, 13. National Bataillon Innsbruck, 14. National Bataillon Ansbach*; one six-pounder horse artillery battery and one six-pounder foot battery under Major Casper: for a total of six line battalions, four *Landwehr* battalions, and 14 guns.

Third Division, *Generalmajor* La Motte: *Generalmajor* Habermann's brigade of two battalions from *11. Linieninfanterie Kinkel*, one battalion from *7. Linieninfanterie Fürst Löwenstein*, one battalion each from *mobilen Legion Unter-Donau* and *mobilen Legion Iller*; *Generalmajor* Deroy's brigade of one battalion each from *5. Linieninfanterie, 8. Linieninfanterie Herzog Pius* and *9. Linieninfanterie Fürst Isenburg, 5. National Bataillon München, 6. National Bataillon Lindau*; one six-pounder horse artillery battery and one six-pounder foot battery under Major Wagener: for a total of six line battalions, four *Landwehr* battalions and 14 guns.

Cavalry Division – 31 squadrons:
1. *leichte Kavallerie Brigade*, *Generalmajor* Baron Vieregg: four squadrons each from *1. Cheveauxlegers* and *2. Cheveauxlegers Fürst Taxis*, six squadrons from *7. Cheveauxlegers Prinz Karl*.
2. *leichte Kavallerie Brigade*, *Generalmajor* Ellbracht: four squadrons each from *3. Cheveauxlegers Kronprinz*, and *6. Cheveauxlegers Bubenhofen*.
3. *leichte Kavallerie Brigade*, *Oberst* Dietz: four squadrons each from *4. Cheveauxlegers König* and *5. Cheveauxlegers Leiningen*, and one squadron of *Gensd'armerie*.

Reserve artillery, commanded by *Generalmajor* Baron Colonge: one six-pounder horse artillery battery, one six-pounder foot battery and three 12-pounder foot batteries, for a total of 32 guns.

Total for the Bavarian contingent: 30 battalions, 31 squadrons and 11 batteries, numbering 26,518 men with 74 guns.

Austrian Contingent:

Commanded by *Feldmarschallleutnant* Baron von Fresnel:

First Division, *Feldmarschallleutnant* Baron Bach: *Generalmajor* Graf Hardegg's brigade of *3. Jäger Bataillon*, two battalions from *1. Szekler Infanterie*, one six-pounder battery; *Generalmajor* Volkmann's brigade of four battalions each from *Erzherzog Rudolph Infanterie* and *Jordis Infanterie*, one six-pounder battery, for a total of 11 battalions with 12 guns.

Second Division, *Feldmarschallleutnant* Baron Trautenberg: *Generalmajor* Diemar's brigade of Kramer's, de Pest's and Frisch's grenadier battalions with one six-pounder battery; *Generalmajor* Graf Klenau's brigade of Mössel's, Puteany's, Posmann's and Lany's grenadier battalions with one six-pounder battery, for a total of seven battalions with 12 guns.

Cavalry Division, *Feldmarschallleutnant* Freiherr Ignaz Spleny: *Generalmajor* Minutillo's brigade of six squadrons each from *Erzherzog Joseph Husaren*, *Frimont Husaren* and *Szekler Husaren*; Generalmajor Graf Spreti's brigade of six squadrons of *Knesevich Dragoner*, eight squadrons of *Schwarzenberg Uhlanen* and four squadrons of *Fürst Liechtenstein Kürassier*, one horse artillery battery, for a total of 36 squadrons with six guns.

Reserve artillery, under *Generalmajor* Baron Strotnick: one 12-pounder battery, one six-pounder battery, one pioneer company.

Headquarters troops: one infantry company, a half-squadron of dragoons one *Sanitäts infanterie* [medical] company.

Total for the Austrian contingent: 18 battalions, 36 squadrons and seven batteries, numbering 24,750 men with 42 guns.

Eduard Von Völderndorff Und Waradein, *Kriegsgeschichte von Bayern unter König Maximilian Joseph I*, IV, Book 7, 331-334 & 357-358; Plotho, *Der Krieg in Deutschland und Frankreich in den Jahren 1813 und 1814*, 447-452; Schulz, *Geschichte der Kriege in Europa seit dem Jahre 1792*, XI, 2 Band, 189.

45

Operations against the Danes and the liberation of the Netherlands

The advance to the Göttingen area by the Army of the North. – The advance towards Hanover by the Crown Prince of Sweden. – His offensive against the Danes. – The Coalition occupation of Lübeck and the retreat of Prinz Friedrich von Hessen to Kiel. – The Coalition advance towards the Eider. – The situation of the Danish force. – The crossing of the Eider by the Coalition. – The action at Sehestedt. The Coalition victory. – The armistice of Kiel. – The peace treaty of 2 (14) January, 1814. – The advance towards the lower Rhine by the corps under Bülow and Wintzingerode. – The revolt in the Netherlands. – Benckendorff's advance on Amsterdam. – Bülow's advance. – The capture of Arnhem. – Molitor's retreat beyond the Waal. – Benckendorff's seizure of Breda. – The arrival of the Prince of Orange in Amsterdam. – Napoleon's orders for the defence of Belgium. – Roguet's advance on Breda. – The Coalition defence of Breda. – Dispositions of both sides at the end of 1813.

At the end of October, new style, the Army of the North moved from Merseburg, via Sonderhausen, Mühlhausen and Heiligenstadt, to the Göttingen area, in order to encourage Davout to retreat beyond the Rhine as quickly as possible. But because Davout remained in the positions he held on the river Stecknitz facing Graf Wallmoden, the Crown Prince of Sweden, having directed the corps under Bülow and Wintzingerode towards the lower Rhine, moved with the Swedish corps, Count Vorontsov's corps and the force under Count Stroganov detached from Bennigsen's army, towards Hamburg in order to take possession of this city and to mount operations against the Danes, with the objective of securing the Swedish government's state interests.

On 25 (6 November), the prince's headquarters were relocated to Hanover; Swedish troops were stationed in Hanover, Braunschweig and Hildesheim, while Vorontsov's and Stroganov's Russians were in the vicinity of Lüneburg. A few days later, Davout received a dispatch from General Carra-Saint-Cyr [Claude Carra de Saint-Cyr] in Mainz, containing Napoleon's orders to hold Mainz [*sic*, Hamburg] with a sufficient garrison, and to march to the Netherlands with the remaining troops. Being cut off from the Rhine, Davout could no longer carry out these order, but considering it necessary to concentrate his forces, evacuated Ratzeburg and stationed his corps on the Stecknitz between Lauenburg and Mölln; the Danish forces under his command were stationed downstream to its mouth at Lübeck.[1]

On 4 (16) November, the Crown Prince set off from the vicinity of Hanover with the Swedish corps, to Celle and on to Boizenburg, and crossed to the right bank of the Elbe on 12 (24) November: at the same time, the Russian corps under Vorontsov and Stroganov relocated to the sector from Winsen to Stade and blockaded Harburg. The Coalition forces on the lower Elbe amounted to 60,000 men overall.[2]

Having been assigned to tighten the blockade, on 15 (27) November, General Stroganov led an attack on Stade, a strongly fortified town held by 3,000 men. The commandant issued orders for all the causeways leading to the town to be cratered except one and, by means of sluices, he turned the surrounding area into a vast lake. In spite of all this, however, the brave Saratov Infantry and Penza Infantry, under crossfire from French batteries, raced up the only causeway left for communications with the town, but upon reaching its end they found that the bridge over the deep ditch had been dismantled. The commander of the Saratov Infantry, Colonel comte Rastignac [Anne Charles Parfait Chapt de Rastignac] went down into the ditch with his officers and attempted to climb the ramparts; assault columns dashed after them, but since many of the officers and more than 300 soldiers were killed or wounded, Count Stroganov ordered them to fall back. Nevertheless, the garrison, that very night, crossed the Elbe in boats, leaving three guns and several hundred sick and wounded in the town.

After the Russian troops had taken Stade, Cuxhaven and other locations on the left bank of the Elbe, in which more than 1,000 men and 30 guns were captured, Count Stroganov blockaded Harburg, held by 5,000 men commanded by General Pécheux, while on 17 (29) November, Count Vorontsov moved to Boizenburg via Lüneburg in order to link up with the Swedes. The Crown Prince, having assembled more than 50,000 men on the right bank of the Elbe, had the intention of attacking Marshal Davout together with the corps under Wallmoden, but the French voluntarily abandoned the very advantageous position on the Stecknitz and on 20 November (2 December), retreated behind the river Bille [flowing through Bergedorf], while the Danish troops, separated from their allies, deployed behind the Trave river, between Oldesloe and Lübeck.

Davout's retreat made it easier for the Crown Prince to carry out his intention of turning on the Danes. To that end, he issued the following orders: General Vorontsov's detachment (numbering 8,000 men with 56 guns) and Lützow's detachment (of 1,900 men) were to advance towards Bergedorf and Hamburg in order to monitor Davout's force; Tettenborn's detachment (of 1,600 men with two guns) was to head between Bergedorf and Mölln in order to sever communications between Davout and the Danish forces; Graf Wallmoden's corps (numbering 10,400 with 52 guns) were directed towards Oldesloe, to envelope the Danes' right flank and

---

1 Plotho, *Der Krieg in Deutschland und Frankreich in den Jahren 1813 und 1814*, II, 508-510; Vaudoncourt, *Histoire de la guerre soutenue par les Français en Allemagne*, 238; Schulz, *Geschichte der Kriege in Europa seit dem Jahre 1792*, XI, 2 Band, 38.
2 Plotho, II, 510-511; Schulz, XI, *2 Band*, 93.

cut their line of retreat to Rendsburg. The Crown Prince was to advance on Lübeck himself, with the Swedish corps and Vegesack's brigade (from Wallmoden's corps), numbering 31,500 men with 68 guns, in order to seize this city and to envelope the enemy position on their left flank.[3]

General Wallmoden, heading between Mölln and Ratzeburg, crossed the Stecknitz on 22 November (4 December); his vanguard, commanded by Dörnberg, forced the leading elements of the Danish corps to retreat beyond the Trave. But the Coalition remained static at Siebenbäumen, between Ratzeburg and Oldesloe, the whole of the next day awaiting the Prince's promised assistance from Vegesack's division. On that same day [5 December, new style], the main body under the Crown Prince, approaching Lübeck, prepared for an assault, but General Lallemand [François Antoine 'Charles' Lallemand], surrendered the city without waiting for this, and set off for Segeberg, which forced Prinz Friedrich von Hessen-Kassel to abandon the Oldesloe position and move to Segeberg with the Danish corps and on towards Kiel. General Tettenborn, having learned of the enemy retreat, quickly raced around their flank and at dawn on 24 November (6 December) caught up with one of the Danish columns at Bramstedt and took many prisoners, while Graf Wallmoden, having detached General Dörnberg to Segeberg with four battalions and eight squadrons, advanced towards Neumünster.

The next day [7 December, new style], the Crown Prince, having moved his headquarters to Lübeck, ordered Wallmoden to pursue the enemy vigorously in order to cut them off from Rendsburg, and sent not only Vegesack's brigade to assist the Coalition corps but also 14 Swedish squadrons commanded by General Skjöldebrand [Anders Fredrik Skjöldebrand].[4] Thereafter, having expressed his intention to follow Graf Wallmoden to the Eider with all the remaining troops, the Crown Prince instructed him:

> The Danish force is unable to call upon any reinforcements. In Rendsburg there is no artillery, no provisions, no garrison. Glückstadt has no garrison and will surrender. There is nothing to fear from the direction of Hamburg; General Vorontsov will keep Davout from interfering. The Danish army, numbering no more than 12,000 men, is completely demoralised; Tettenborn's Cossacks are outflanking them on their right, and

---

3   The Crown Prince of Sweden's forces on the lower Elbe consisted of: *Fältmarskalk* Stedingk's corps – 45 battalions and 38 squadrons, numbering 27,400 men (including four battalions and four squadrons from Mecklenburg and two Prussian squadrons, numbering 3,600 men); Count Vorontsov's corps – eight battalions, 24 squadrons and four Cossack regiments with the *Lützowsches Freicorps* of three battalions and fours squadrons and Tettenborn's detachment of four Cossack regiments attached, giving Vorontsov a total of 11 battalions, 28 squadrons and eight Cossack regiments, numbering 12,300 men (including 2,700 Prussians); Count Stroganov's corps – 16 battalions, numbering 8,000 men; Graf Wallmoden's corps – Dörnberg's vanguard of two battalions and 14 squadrons, Arentschildt's and Lyon's divisions of 14 battalions and ten squadrons of reserve cavalry, for a total of 16 battalions and 24 squadrons, numbering 10,400 men, giving a grand total of 88 battalions, 90 squadrons and eight Cossack regiments, numbering 59,100 men. Schulz, XI, *2 Band*, 197-198.
4   *Oestereichische Militärische Zeitschrift, 1827*; Schulz, XI, *2 Band*, 95.

Skjöldebrand's cavalry are enveloping their left flank. The corps entrusted to you is superior to the enemy in numbers.[5]

Indeed, the Danish government, probably in the belief that their powerful ally was invincible, had not bothered to fortify Holstein and Schleswig: their forces were scattered; the fortresses could withstand neither an open assault nor a prolonged blockade. The King sent orders to the Prinz von Hessen to retreat to Kolding [70 miles north of Schleswig], in order to protect Jutland and [the island of] Funen, and to try to negotiate a truce if possible. A copy of this dispatch was intercepted by the Coalition, which strengthened the Crown Prince in his resolve to refuse a truce to the enemy and to pursue them doggedly.[6]

Unfortunately, the Coalition forces encountered extreme terrain obstacles on the march. One particularly important obstacle for them was the Eider Canal, which links the North Sea with the Baltic Sea and, together with the Eider river, formed an advantageous defensive line, reinforced by fortresses: Friedrichsort on the Kiel Fjord, Rendsburg almost in the centre of the line, and the Vollerwiek fieldworks [three miles south of Garding], with 28 guns, at the mouth of the Eider. The area south of this river to the Trave and the Elbe is intersected by lakes, rivers, swamps and forests; the roads were bad, especially at that time of year; the main ones were: from Lübeck to Preetz and Kiel; from Oldesloe to Segeberg and Neumünster; from Hamburg to Itzehoe, with the hub at Rendsburg.[7]

Throughout the retreat from Segeberg to Kiel by the Prinz von Hessen on 26 November (8 December) had lost six guns and 300 men taken prisoner, his rearguard, having been caught the day before [7 December, new style] at Bornhöved by Swedish cavalry. The Cossack detachment under Tettenborn, leading Wallmoden's force, advanced to Neumünster and Nortorf in the vicinity of Rendsburg, along roads where the horses often sank up to their bellies in the mud and swamps, crossing deep ditches and making their way, for several hours, through freezing cold floodwater; having said that, Cossack patrols sent in the directions of Itzehoe and Kiel, captured many officers with important dispatches, transport, several ammunition caissons and a remount depot. On 27 November (9 December), Tettenborn's Cossacks, having crossed the Eider near Friedrichstadt, seized this town, as well as Tönning [seven miles east of Garding] and Husum [9½ miles north of Friedrichstadt], captured ten guns, disarmed the *Landsturm* in all these locations, sent patrols out in all directions and blockaded Vollerwiek.

On 27 November (9 December), having delegated the pursuit of the enemy along the road to Kiel to General Skjöldebrand and having sent detachments to Rendsburg and Achterwehr [7½ miles west of Kiel] in order to secure both his flanks, Graf Wallmoden sent General Dörnberg onto the right bank of the Eider at Kluvensiek [8½ miles east of Rendsburg] with five battalions and ten squadrons, and followed them himself with nine battalions, four squadrons and 24 guns, numbering 4,000

---

5   The Crown Prince's letter to Graf Wallmoden, from Lübeck, dated 25 November (7 December); *Oesterreichische Militärische Zeitschrift, 1827*, VI, 234-239; Plotho, II, 512-514.
6   *Oesterreichische Militärische Zeitschrift, 1827*, VI, 242.
7   *Oesterreichische Militärische Zeitschrift, 1827*, VI, 240.

men. General Dörnberg, having received orders to move to sever the enemy line of retreat, and believing that the Danish corps would retreat from Kiel towards Eckernförde, headed for the Wittensee [nine miles north-east of Rendsburg] and, having driven off part of the enemy force, captured seven guns; but at the same time, the main body of the Danish corps, numbering 10,000 men, after reaching Gettorf [eight miles south-east of Eckernförde], were sent from there towards Rendsburg. They unexpectedly encountered Wallmoden's force at Sehestedt, drove them back and captured two guns. The Coalition losses amounted to over 1,000 men; among the wounded was Major Prinz Gustav zu Mecklenburg-Schwerin [Gustav Wilhelm zu Mecklenburg-Schwerin]. Wallmoden himself was exposed to the greatest danger. On the Danish side, 17 officers and 530 lower ranks were *hors de combat*.

The Crown Prince, primarily concerned with preserving the Swedish corps, ordered Stedingk not to cross the Eider, while Tettenborn and Dörnberg were to join forces at Kropp [nine miles south of Schleswig] and, in the event of an encounter with superior enemy forces, were to retreat to the left bank of the Eider via Friedrichstadt. But, in the meantime, Coalition operations had taken a very favourable turn: Tettenborn had managed to capture another 400 prisoners and eight guns; then, having formed crews for the captured artillery, he went to Fort Vollerwiek, opened an intense cannonade on its defenders and forced the garrison to surrender, under terms of safe passage from the fortification. Eighteen cannon, ten mortars and a considerable quantity of military supplies fell into the hands of the victors; in all, since the invasion of the Danish duchies, Tettenborn had taken 38 cannon.[8]

After the action at Sehestedt, Graf Wallmoden, having restored communications with Dörnberg's vanguard, granted his force a rest day. His corps took up quarters on the left bank of the Eider, in the vicinity of Westensee [12 miles west of Kiel] and Nortorf; the *Hanseatische Brigade*, having occupied Kluvensiek, maintained communications with Dörnberg's detachment, stationed at Wittensee. Tettenborn's detachment was in Tönning. The headquarters of the Crown Prince moved to Kiel on 2 (14) December, while the Swedish corps took up quarters to the south of this city; general measures were taken to concentrate some 35,000 men on the right bank of the Eider within three days, if need be. The investment of the fortresses of Friedrichsort and Glückstadt was entrusted to generals Posse [Carl Henric Posse] and Boije [Gustaf Reinhold Boije af Gennäs].[9]

Upon the arrival of the Crown Prince in Kiel, he concluded an armistice with the Commander-in-Chief of the Danish force, Prinz Friedrich von Hessen-Kassel, on the following terms:

1. Military operations were to cease from 15 to 29 December (new style), with the exclusion of the fortresses of Glückstadt and Friedrichsort.
2. Coalition forces were to evacuate the Duchy of Schleswig and be stationed to the south of a line running from Eckernförde, through

---

8 Plotho, II 514-516; *Oestereichische Militärische Zeitschrift, 1827*, VI, 243-252 & VII, 3-4; Sporschill, Die große Chronik, I, 1098 & 1109.
9 Plotho, II, 517; *Oestereichische Militärische Zeitschrift, 1827*, VI, 255 & VII, 4-5.

Götheby [6½ miles south-east of Schleswig] and Hollingstedt [14 miles east of Friedrichstadt], to Husum.
3. The main road from Rendsburg to Schleswig would be opened for the passage of dispatches and for the delivery of provisions to the force occupying Rendsburg, in the amount of 10,000 to 12,000 rations per day.
4. During the armistice, reinforcement of the Rendsburg garrison and munitions resupply was prohibited. The Commander-in-Chief of Danish forces undertook not to construct any new fortifications, and the Coalition undertook not to conduct siege works against Rendsburg; the area around the fortress [to a radius of between five to seven miles], along a line passing through Jeventedt, Ostenfeld, Bünsdorf, Hohn and Elsdorf, was recognised as neutral and could be occupied by outposts from the garrison.
5. The garrison of the city of Schleswig was not to exceed 1,000 men; troops arriving from the interior of the state could not move beyond Flensburg [22 miles north of Schleswig].

The Coalition, for their part, pledged not to reinforce the units stationed in the Duchy of Schleswig during the armistice.[10]

Swedish forces captured the fortresses of Friedrichsort and Glückstadt during the period of the armistice, which was extended until 5 January 1814, new style: 110 guns, 600 barrels of gunpowder and a significant amount of other military stores were found in the former, while 325 guns were found in the latter. In addition, the Coalition army had captured 470 guns since the invasion of Holstein. The garrisons of both fortresses were released: those from Friedrichsort, on condition of being exchanged for Coalition prisoners taken during the action at Segestedt, while those from Glückstadt pledged not to serve against the Coalition for one year.[11]

Peace negotiations in Kiel were not making any progress. The Danish government, hoping that the situation might take an unexpected turn, tried to buy time, and to that end, although they expressed their consent to the cession of Norway, would not do so unless they received the Hanseatic cities, part of Hanover and the entire North Sea coast as far as Friesland as compensation. The Crown Prince of Sweden, having no right to accept such proposals, laid out to the Danish commissioner who had arrived in Kiel, in the presence of the representatives of the Coalition powers, all the hostile actions of his government to the common cause and concluded his speech with the following words:

> nevertheless, no matter what turn the situation might take, I solemnly declare and give my word of honour that Napoleon shall remain neither the ruler of France nor the King of Rome; perhaps it is perceived that I am

---

10 Extracted from the convention concluded on 15 December, new style, at Rendsburg, signed by the Swedish *Generalmajor* Graf Löwenhielm and the Danish Major von Bardenfleth [Jens Carl Bardenfleth].
11 *Oestereichische Militärische Zeitschrift, 1827*, VII, 7-9.

seeking to take his place, but my vision is restricted to another objective; let the people themselves make a choice and entrust their fate to the most worthy.

When the Crown Prince agreed to extend the truce for another week, until 5 January, new style, the Danes hoped that the bulk of the Army of the North would, at the request of the Coalition powers, head for the Rhine. Indeed, Sir Charles Stewart, having arrived at the Crown Prince's headquarters, urged him to march on the Netherlands. But the prince rejected this proposal and, when the armistice expired, immediately resumed military operations.

General Tettenborn marched into Schleswig without resistance, while Skjöldebrand took Flensburg with the Swedish cavalry, from where the enemy quickly retreated to Kolding. The army of the Crown Prince, incomparably more numerous than the Danish, was further reinforced by the corps under Count Vorontsov, who had set off from Hamburg for Holstein as soon as he was relieved by Bennigsen's troops. This new situation led to the conclusion of peace. By way of treaties concluded in Kiel on 2 (14) January, 1814, the Danish government ceded the Kingdom of Norway to Sweden, with the exclusion of the Faroe Islands and Iceland, receiving in exchange the island of Rügen and Swedish Pomerania;[12] in accordance with these same treaties, Denmark broke with France and pledged to send a 10,000-strong combat corps against Napoleon, receiving 33,333 Pounds Sterling (about 225,000 silver Roubles) in monthly subsidies as a reward from Britain.[13]

As has already been stated above that at the beginning of November, new style, the Army of the North arrived in the vicinity of Göttingen, and that following this the corps under Stedingk and Vorontsov, reinforced by Stroganov's corps detached from Bennigsen's army, moved towards Hanover and against Marshal Davout and the Danes under the personal command of the Crown Prince of Sweden. In order to liberate the Prussian regions of Westphalia, Bülow's Prussian corps moved towards the lower Rhine, reinforced by Thümen's brigade, and the Russian corps under Wintzingerode.

General Bülow, having received orders from the Crown Prince to seize whichever of the fortresses on the Ijssel [flowing through Zutphen, Deventer and Zwolle] was weakest, decided not to restrict himself to such an insignificant objective, rather to liberate the Netherlands. Bülow hoped for assistance from Wintzingerode's corps and for an uprising by the population, who hated Napoleon, during his invasion of a country where the enemy could check the advancing force at every step using natural and artificial obstacles.

The enemy corps occupying the Netherlands, commanded by General Molitor [Gabriel-Jean-Joseph Molitor], counted only 14,000 men in its ranks, very poor quality troops, of whom no more than 5,000 were concentrated at Utrecht, and the rest were

---

12 Subsequently, in exchange for Swedish Pomerania, ceded to Prussia, Denmark received the Duchy of Lauenburg [Herzogtum Sachsen-Lauenburg].
13 Treaties concluded in Kiel on 2 (14) January 1814, between Denmark and Sweden, and between Denmark and Britain. Christophe Guillaume Koch, *Tableau des révolutions de l'Europe*, II, 397; Sporschill, I, 1111-1114.

divided among the fortresses. Another French corps, numbering 15,000 infantry and 7,000 cavalry, guarded the course of the lower Rhine; Marshal Macdonald, who commanded this force, had sent General Amey [François Pierre Joseph Amey] to Deventer with 2,000 men, who, together with the *douaniers* [customs guards] and *gendarmes* assembled by General Lauberdière [Louis-François-Bertrand du Pont d'Aubevoye de Lauberdière], constituted the only detachment assigned to defend the course of the Ijssel.[14]

General Bülow, having set off from the vicinity of Göttingen with his corps on 22 October (3 November), arrived in Minden on 26 October (7 November), where he was greeted by the population with the ringing of bells and joyful cheers. Following a rest day in Minden, Bülow moved from there on 1 (13) November to Herford, Bielefeld, Münster and on to Dülmen, and upon reaching this location on 7 (19) November, he sent the vanguard, commanded by General Oppen, to the river Ijssel via Borken, while Borstell's brigade went to Wesel in order to blockade this fortress.[15]

Wintzingerode's leading elements, having advanced to Kassel from the vicinity of Göttingen at the beginning of November, new style, together with the vanguard of comte Saint-Priest's corps, pursued Rigaux's division [Antoine Rigaux] (which had set out from Kassel for the Rhine) and, on 31 October (12 November) took Düsseldorf; Major General Yuzefovich's detachment cleared the Großherzogtum Berg, while Wintzingerode, having moved into Bremen himself, stationed his corps in Oldenburg and Friesland, sending detachments under Major General Benckendorff, Adjutant General Chernyshev and Colonel Naryshkin up to the Dutch border.

As soon as Molitor learned of the Coalition offensive, he evacuated Amsterdam and other coastal locations and began to concentrate his force around Utrecht. The French withdrawal served as a signal for an uprising by the inhabitants of Amsterdam. On 4 (16) November, they destroyed the customs house, expelled the French *Préfet*, established a *Nationale Garde* and set up a provisional government, under the chairmanship of van der Goop [sic, Gijsbert Karel van Hogendorp]. The entire city rang to shouts of: *Oranje boven!* The country's independence was proclaimed in Den Haag, Rotterdam, Dordrecht, Haarlem, Leiden, and elsewhere. A deputation of the most distinguished citizens went to the Prince of Orange [Willem Frederik van Oranje-Nassau] in London to invite him to accept the government of the Netherlands, as *soeverein vorst* [sovereign prince].

On 2 (14) November, General Benckendorff was sent from Bremen to the Dutch border by General Wintzingerode in order to exploit the favourable situation and clear the country of any enemy forces remaining there. His detachment consisted of 1,100 infantry, 800 cavalry and 1,600 Cossacks, with four horse artillery pieces;[16] he also had two additional detachments under his command: Adjutant General

---

14 Plotho, II, 509-510 & 520; Jean Baptiste Frédéric Koch, *Mémoires pour servir à l'histoire de la campagne de 1814*, I, 54; Schulz, XI, *2 Band*, 39.
15 Plotho, II, 510-513 & 520; Schulz, XI, *2 Band*, 39.
16 Major General Benckendorff's detachment consisted of: the Tula Infantry, one battalion of 2nd Jägers (1,100 men); the Pavlograd Hussars (800 men); five Cossack regiments and four horse artillery pieces (1,600 men), for a total of 3,500 men.

Chernyshev's, commanded in his absence by Colonel Balabin [Stepan Fëdorovich Balabin], of five Cossack regiments, and Colonel Naryshkin's, of three Cossack regiments. General Benckendorff, having sent one detachment towards Doesburg, and a second towards Harderwijk via Kampen, advanced to Zwolle with his main body and crossed the Ijssel, some at this city, some between Deventer and Zutphen.

On 10 (22) November, Major Prince Gagarin [Fëdor Fëdorovich Gagarin] attacked the enemy occupying Deventer with 300 dismounted Cossacks and Bashkirs and ejected them from there, taking 60 men prisoner;[17] on 12 (24) November, one of his leading detachments, including 200 Cossacks commanded by Major Marklay, made its way to Amsterdam across territory still occupied by the enemy, where they were joyfully welcomed by the population. Benckendorff quickly followed him up, sending General Staal [Yegor Fëdorovich Shtal or Georg Johann von Staal] to Amersfoort with some of the cavalry for a show of force against Molitor, who was stationed near Utrecht, while upon reaching Harderwijk himself, loaded 600 infantry aboard ships and on the night of 19 November (1 December) sailed with them to Amsterdam. Although a large enemy flotilla was cruising on the waters of the Zuiderzee [Ijsselmeer], the Russians nevertheless arrived safely in the capital of the Netherlands and, having roused the delight of the population, supported the national uprising. The local militia immediately marched on Muiden [4½ miles west of Naarden] and Halfweg [halfway between Amsterdam and Haarlem] together with their liberators, captured these forts and took 20 guns and more than 1,000 prisoners. Colonel Naryshkin's detachment had taken Amersfoort on 16 (28) November.[18]

Bülow's force also achieved important successes. General Oppen advanced towards Doesburg with the vanguard of the Prussian corps on 11 (23) November, captured this fortified city by assault, and, having defeated some of its defenders, took two guns and more than 100 men prisoner; the following day [24 November, new style], Major Sandrart, having been sent to Zutphen with *1. Leib Husaren* and a single battalion, seized the city and took 300 men prisoner. General Bülow, moving up behind his vanguard, reached the fortified camp in front of Arnhem, occupied by 4,000 men commanded by General Charpentier, attacked it on 18 (30) November, and, having captured both the camp and the town, took 14 guns and 1,000 prisoners (including General Saint-Maurice [Desvaux?] and 24 officers); Charpentier himself was wounded. The victors' casualties amounted to 700 men. General Oppen's vanguard crossed the Lek [flowing from Arnhem to Rotterdam] and pursued the French along the road to Nijmegen; Bülow moved towards Utrecht himself, the rendezvous point for enemy forces; but General Molitor, having received word of the capture of Arnhem by the Coalition and the crossing of the Lek by their vanguard, considering it impossible to hold his defensive line, retreated beyond the Waal [flowing through Nijmegen] and took post in Gorinchem [14 miles east of Dordrecht].

---

17 [The Cossack attack failed to capture the city, and Deventer would remain under blockade until April 1814].
18 Benckendorff's notes (manuscript held in the archive of the M.T.D.); Plotho, II, 519-520; Schulz, XI, *2 Band*, 41.

The uprising in the Netherlands and the Coalition appearance on the Ijssel forced Napoleon to send General Roguet to Holland with one of the *Jeune Garde* divisions. Dissatisfied with Molitor's dispositions, Napoleon replaced him with comte Decaen [Charles-Mathieu-Isidore Decaen] and entrusted him with the defence of Belgium, where the French hoped to concentrate between 16,000 and 18,000 men. Molitor's withdrawal facilitated the Coalition forces' success: General Bülow, having occupied Utrecht, stationed his corps in the vicinity of this city; while General Benckendorff, despite the concentration of enemy forces at Gorinchem, decided to invade the territory lying beyond the Waal. To that end, having concentrated his force at Rotterdam, and having followed orders from General Wintzingerode to send the detachments under Balabin and Naryshkin to Düsseldorf, Benckendorff crossed the Merwede channel towards Dordrecht on 25 November (7 December), seized this city and, having sent patrols to monitor Willemstad and Geertruidenberg [12 miles north-east of Breda], closed in on Breda. At the same time, General Oppen received orders from Bülow to hold the Bommelerwaard (the island between the Waal and the Maas). General Ambert [Jean-Jacques Ambert], who was holding the fortified city of Breda with 800 recruits and three guns, evacuated it on the orders of Decaen, who had turned his attention exclusively to the defence of Antwerp. Making the most of this, Benckendorff seized Breda on 27 November (9 December); while Major General Staal captured Willemstad and Geertruidenberg with a Cossack detachment, where huge military stores were found.[19]

While the Coalition were rapidly gaining success after success, a delegation from the Netherlands arrived in London to see the Prince of Orange, Willem Frederik, inviting him to take over the government of the liberated country. Having received a favourable response, the deputies immediately sent news of this to Den Haag. At the same time, 6,000 British troops commanded by Lieutenant General Graham [Thomas Graham], landed at Scheveningen [three miles north of Den Haag] to assist the common cause. Not satisfied with this, the British government delivered arms and equipment for 25,000 men to the Dutch. On 2 December, new style, the Prince of Orange arrived in Amsterdam.[20]

Napoleon, having received news of Decaen's retreat to Antwerp, delegated command of the troops in Belgium to General Maison and entrusted the administration of this country to Lebrun [Anne-Charles Lebrun]; General Rampon [Antoine-Guillaume Rampon] received orders to defend Gorinchem to the last man; General Roguet was ordered to take Breda and restore communications with Rampon; while Macdonald, who had managed to assemble a fairly significant corps near Nijmegen, was to push Bülow back beyond the Waal. General Roguet, setting off on 7 (19) December from Antwerp with 6,000 infantry, 800 cavalry and 30 guns, closed up to Breda the following day. Benckendorff's detachment had just four light guns. The enemy lobbed a great many shells into the city on 9 (21) December, yet by nightfall, 18 12-pounder guns, without crews, reached the besieged city by water from Willemstad. General Benckendorff, with the assistance of the Prussian Major

---

19 Benckendorff's notes; Plotho, II, 520-523; Koch, I, 56-58 & 62-64.
20 Plotho, II, 525; Richter, *Geschichte des Deutschen Freiheitskrieges vom Jahre 1813 bis zum Jahre 1815*, II, 456.

Steinaecker [Christian Karl Anton Friedrich von Steinaecker], formed gun crews from Dutch volunteers, Cossacks and Major Colomb's jägers (who was in Breda at the time with his partisan detachment and took part in the defence of the city). According to Colomb's account, the Dutch, Prussians and Russians diligently helped each other, but were hampered by the fact that they could not understand each other; despite the fact that the defence of Breda resembled the Tower of Babel, at dawn on 10 (22) December, ten heavy guns had been emplaced on the city ramparts and opened fire on the enemy encamped on the glacis and forced them to retreat. Thereafter, Krafft's Prussian brigade were on their way to assist Benckendorff from one direction, while elements of Graham's British force were coming from another. General Lefebvre-Desnouettes, who had taken command of the blockading detachment, did not dare to await the arrival of these forces and retreated to Hoogstraten [13 miles south of Breda].[21]

Since the enemy force occupying Belgium, together with Macdonald's formation at Nijmegen, numbered some 30,000 men, Bülow, whose command had no more than 12,000 men after the detachment of units for the occupation of conquered territory, brought in Borstell's brigade to his main body, which had been relieved in Wesel by the vanguard of Wintzingerode's corps. General Bülow, unable to conduct decisive operations, limited himself to guerilla warfare until the end of the year and stationed his corps close to Breda. Thus the entire northern part of the Netherlands had been cleared of the enemy, and the Coalition, having established themselves in this country, were able to make use of its rich resources.[22]

---

21 Richter, II, 479; Colomb, *Aus dem Tagebuche*, 152-155; F. Koch, I, 67-69; Schulz, XI, *2 Band*, 53-54.
22 Richter, II, 480.

46

Sieges of the fortresses to the rear of the Coalition Army

Fortresses occupied by the enemy on Napoleon's retreat beyond the Rhine. – Numbers of troops in these fortresses. – Condition of the garrisons. – Blockade of Dresden. Operations by Count Tolstoy. – Arrival of reinforcements with him and Graf Klenau's assumption of command over Coalition forces around Dresden. – Surrender of Dresden. – Deployment by Count Bennigsen along the Elbe and his movements toward Hamburg. – Siege and surrender of Stettin. – Siege and surrender of Zamość. – Siege and surrender of Modlin. – Siege and surrender of Torgau. – Siege and capture of Wittenberg by storm. – Siege and surrender of Danzig. – Siege and surrender of Erfurt. – Numbers of prisoners and guns taken by the Coalition in the conquered fortresses. – German fortresses remaining in French hands in 1814.

The French still held many fortresses in the Duchy of Warsaw and Germany following Napoleon's retreat across the Rhine. Enemy garrisons occupied: Zamość on the right bank of the Vistula, Modlin and Danzig, also on the Vistula; Glogau, Küstrin and Stettin on the Oder; the fortress of Dresden, Torgau, Wittenberg, Magdeburg and the fortress of Hamburg, on the Elbe; Erfurt and Festung Marienberg (citadel of Würzburg), between the Elbe and Rhine; finally, Kehl, Kastel opposite Mainz and Wesel on the Rhine. There were some 140,000 men in all these fortresses and fortified cities, mostly French troops, and therefore their blockade and siege, having deprived Napoleon of the opportunity to reinforce himself from the significant army scattered throughout the fortresses, had a great influence on the course of the subsequent campaign of 1814.[1] Almost all the fortresses in Germany and the Duchy of Warsaw fell to Coalition forces during the campaign of 1813, and only a few remained in French hands until the end of the war. In setting out the sieges in

---

1 The number of enemy troops in the fortresses and fortified cities in the Duchy of Warsaw and Germany were: 30,000 in Danzig; 7,000 in Zamość and Modlin, mostly Poles and Lithuanians; 6,000 in Glogau; 4,000 in Küstrin; 10,000 in Stettin; more than 30,000 in Dresden; more than 10,000 in Torgau; 3,000 in Wittenberg; 10,000 in Magdeburg; some 30,000 in Hamburg; 2,000 in Erfurt and Festung Marienberg, for a total of 140,000 men. Plotho, II, *Beilagen*, 90; Schulz, *Geschichte der Kriege in Europa seit dem Jahre 1792*, XI, *2 Band*, 112-139; Sporschill, Die große Chronik.

the order in which they ended with the capture of the fortresses by the Coalition, I consider it essential to take a general look at the condition of their garrisons.

The population were hostile to the French in every German fortress and were anticipating the Coalition as liberators from the hated yoke. This factor greatly increased the misery – both of the defenders and the population within the fortresses. The French, besieged from the outside, encountering the unconcealed hostility of the inhabitants in the cities they were defending, at every stage considered themselves entitled to show no mercy. Not only food supplies, but also money and possessions belonging to the residents were taken by force, as if it were lawful booty. The poorest of the townspeople were driven out of the fortresses and fortified towns: in October and November 1813, 3,000 households were driven out of Glogau, and the French showed no distinction for either gender or age. The residents who remained in the besieged cities and fortresses suffered all the horrors of starvation: horse meat served as the staple diet; both the troops and the population ate dogs, cats, and it is even claimed that in Danzig it got to the point that the besieged tried resorting to cannibalism. The oppression and misery to which the peaceful townsfolk were subjected were increased by the thoughtless actions of the French, who did not consider it a crime to disturb the domestic peace of their hosts, or to bring shame and dishonour into their homes, and to abuse the women. The French showed the same disrespect to the houses of God and those serving at the altar, robbing them and turning the churches into magazines and stables.

Sick soldiers, who filled the hospitals in the fortresses after the campaign in Russia, were left without supervision and suffered extreme shortages for everything, spreading contagious and lethal diseases among the population; the dead were taken away in large wagons and buried in heaps in pits; these unfortunates, who often still retained a spark of life, shared the fate of their dead comrades and became living victims of the haste of the hospital orderlies. It goes without saying that these French, who showed such criminal indifference to their fellow countrymen and brothers-in-arms, did not win the sympathy of any of the population of these lands, except for those despicable people who collaborated with the enemy for money as informants and spies.

Not only was all private correspondence delivered to the fortresses opened and their recipients subjected to suspicion, but sometimes even a word spoken carelessly within the family circle gave rise to reprisals; rumours alone or even a suspicion of hatred towards the French were sufficient proofs of guilt. The accused were punished through confiscation of property, imprisonment, exile, or were often sentenced to death by firing squad or were sent to the gallows.[2]

The Blockade of Dresden

Of all the fortified locations blockaded by the Coalition, Dresden was the first to fall. Upon leaving Dresden on 25 September (7 October), Napoleon left Marshal Saint-Cyr there, with *1er Corps* and *14e Corps* and a small cavalry detachment,

---

2   Richter, *Geschichte des Deutschen Freiheitskrieges vom Jahre 1813 bis zum Jahre 1815*, II, 481-496.

which included one Polish and one Italian regiment, in all, more than 35,000 men together with the sick. General comte Durosnel, in the appointment of commandant, *Intendant de la Grande Armée* comte Dumas [Mathieu Dumas] and many officials from his administration were also in the capital of Saxony.

Following Bennigsen's departure for Leipzig with the main body of his army, General Count Tolstoy faced the city on the left bank of the Elbe, from Räcknitz to Plauen, with 24,000 men, consisting mostly of *Opolchenie*, and with 64 guns;[3] The Austrian brigade under *Generalmajor* Seethal [Johann Baptist Peter von Seethal] was located on the right bank.[4] The bridgehead opposite Pirna was taken by storm on 26 September (8 October) by the force under Graf Bubna. Some of the Coalition troops monitored the strongly fortified Schloss Sonnenstein; while Festung Königstein, occupied solely by Saxon troops, was treated as neutral.[5]

A total lack of provisions prompted Saint-Cyr to launch a strong sortie, with the objective of pushing back the force under Count Tolstoy and exploiting the resources of the surrounding country. On 5 (17) October, the French mounted their strike in several columns, both from the front and enveloping the left flank of Count Tolstoy's position, through Potschappel and Gittersee. The Russians fought very bravely despite the numerical superiority of the enemy force, but the inexperienced, poorly armed and almost completely untrained warriors could not stand up to their veteran soldiers and were thrown back to Zehista, with the loss of several hundred men and seven guns. According to one impartial historian:

> the Russians could have held their positions had the troops been more experienced and more skilled at manoeuvring. The infantry, which had arrived from the edge of Asia, and the cavalry, which consisted mostly of Cossacks and Bashkirs, having demonstrated their innate bravery, fought stubbornly, but, being inferior to the enemy in speed of movement, they were unable to oppose them in sufficient strength at every point.[6]

However, the main consequence of the action on 5 (17) October was the plundering of the Dresden area by the French. Every barn stocked with grain or hay was devastated, the last of the livestock remaining among the population was herded away, garden vegetables, cabbages and potatoes were taken away, vineyards and beehives were completely destroyed, and many buildings were burned even as the bees were being smoked out of the hives.[7]

---

3   The composition of Count Tolstoy's force is shown in Footnote 68 in Chapter 38 and in Appendix XXVI at the end of Chapter 33.
4   The composition of Seethal's Austrian brigade (from Chasteler's corps stationed in Bohemia) was four battalions from: the *Kaiser Infanterie, Vogelsang Infanterie, Czartoryski Infanterie* and *Kolowrat Infanterie*.
5   Richter, II, 541-542.
6   Plotho, II, 529.
7   Sporschill, I, 1153-1154.

A few days later, Marquis Chasteler arrived from Theresienstadt to assist the Russian corps with the remainder of his corps, numbering some 10,000 men.[8] On 10 (22) October, the Coalition marched against the enemy and pushed them back into Dresden once more;[9] while on 14 (26) October, *General der Kavallerie* Graf Klenau arrived from Leipzig with the Austrian *IV. Korpus*, who took command of the entire Coalition force assembled around Dresden, numbering more than 45,000 men. One of the Austrian divisions, commanded by the Prinz zu Wied-Runkel [Friedrich Ludwig zu Wied-Runkel], was stationed on the right bank of the Elbe in order to cut off Saint-Cyr's communications with Torgau; the other Coalition units tightened the blockade of Dresden on the left bank of the river.

The city was experiencing a shortage of vital necessities: flour, salt (using gunpowder as a substitute), and firewood. Initially they had wanted to drive the poorest residents out of the city, but later abandoned this plan, concerned that these refugees, deprived of shelter, might join the blockading forces. Moreover, the Coalition, wanting to push those blockaded to their limits, would not allow anyone to leave Dresden. The French confiscated all remaining food supplies from the population. *Intendant de la Grande Armée* Dumas ordered the *gendarmes* to carry out the most rigorous searches in order to root out supplies, saying: 'let every Dresden resident perish before even one French soldier dies of hunger.'

The news of Napoleon's defeat at Leipzig and the advance by Klenau's corps towards Dresden forced Saint-Cyr to take precautions to strengthen the city's defences in the event of a formal siege: orders were issued to block all the main streets in the suburbs with abatis, palisades, barricades of barrels, chests, and so on. Many buildings, especially those near the Wilsdruffer Schlag and Pirnaische Schlag, were converted into blockhouses. Finally, the Saxon and Westphalian units, in whom the French had no confidence, were disarmed and disbanded.[10] The shortage of food supplies, which was becoming more and more severe, prompted Marshal Saint-Cyr to attempt to break out towards Torgau with his force, with the objective, together with the garrisons from this fortress and Wittenberg, of marching to Magdeburg and Hamburg in order to link up with Marshal Davout. There is no doubt that had Saint-Cyr decided on such an operation on the occasion of his successful sortie against Count Tolstoy, he could have succeeded in this enterprise; but the favourable opportunity had passed irretrievably.

In preparation for a campaign through devastated country, Saint-Cyr ordered that a third of the remaining supplies be taken from the wealthiest residents of Dresden. At dawn on 25 October (6 November), the French force, 14,000 strong, commanded by Mouton, set out along the Großenhain road; 200 wagons loaded with provisions and a variety of baggage went with them. The forward outposts of Wied-Runkel's division were overrun, but once reinforcements had arrived by ferry from the left bank of the Elbe, the French were unable to make any further progress

---

8   Chasteler's Austrian corps consisted of: 12 battalions, two squadrons, two field artillery companies and another of garrison artillery, 2¼ companies of miners and another of sappers.
9   Count Tolstoy's letter No. 16 to the Chief of the General Staff, Prince Volkonsky, dated 10 [22] October (Log of Incoming Documents, No. 1,720).
10 Richter, II, 542-544.

and returned to Dresden at about four o'clock in the afternoon. After this unsuccessful attempt, there was nothing left but to surrender the city: the last supplies had been exhausted; horse meat was considered a delicacy; between 200 and 300 men and a similar number of civilians were dying every day in the military hospitals. A delegation of Dresden residents went to General Klenau with a letter from [Maria Theresia Josepha Charlotte Johanna von Österreich] the wife of Prinz Anton von Sachsen, and sister of Kaiser Franz; at the same time, colonels Rothkirch and Marion arrived, having been sent to Saint-Cyr in order to negotiate the surrender of the city.[11]

On 30 October (11 November), a capitulation was signed, on the basis of which: 'the garrison were granted free passage to France, on the condition that they would not serve against the Coalition until prisoners were exchanged.' Graf Klenau, however, warned Saint-Cyr in writing that, not having the authority to agree to such favourable terms for the garrison, he might be held accountable for it; but Saint-Cyr paid no attention to this warning, wishing to leave Dresden as quickly as possible, while Klenau exceeded the rights granted to him, being unwilling to expose the civilian population to inevitable destruction. From 12 to 17 November, new style, the French force, having departed the city in several echelons, and having laid down their arms, moved through Saxony, in the direction of Bavaria, but as soon as the first echelon reached Coburg, news arrived that Prinz Schwarzenberg, by the will of the Coalition sovereigns, had not ratified the capitulation, and that the garrison was given a choice – to surrender, or to return to Dresden and continue their defence of this city. Saint-Cyr protested against the violation of the capitulation, but did not dare to expose his troops to the misery of starvation and preferred to surrender as prisoners of war. The garrison, numbering 1,759 officers and 33,744 enlisted men, was escorted to Moravia and Hungary.[12] The prisoners included the corps commanders, Marshal Saint-Cyr and Mouton (comte de Lobau); *généraux de division*, Durosnel, Dumas, Claparède, Bonet, Mouton-Duvernet, Berthezène, Razout, Dumonceau, Gérard [François Joseph Gérard], Cassagne [Louis Victorin Cassagne], Freire [Gomes Freire de Andrade], and 20 *généraux de brigade*. 94 French and 150 Saxon guns were found in the city, while the overall value of the military trophies amounted to 5,000,000 thalers (about 5,000,000 roubles).

Napoleon criticised the Coalition for treacherously violating the capitulation, but if anyone was to blame for this matter it was Graf Klenau alone, who inopportunely and hastily signed terms that were inconsistent with the orders issued to him. Count Tolstoy commented to Prince Volkonsky that 'Saint-Cyr was ready to surrender the city if he were allowed to go to another fortress on the Elbe with his force.'[13] This elicited the following response: 'The Sovereign Emperor has ordered that you be informed that the enemy must not be allowed to leave Dresden for any other

---

11 Saint-Cyr, *Mémoires, Campagne de 1813 en Saxe*, 247-254.
12 The Dresden garrison consisted of: 425 officers and 6,507 lower ranks in *1er Corps*; 947 officers and 17,129 lower ranks in *14e Corps*; 360 officers and 4,077 lower ranks from the original garrison; 6,031 hospitalised, for a total of 1,759 officers and 33,744 lower ranks.
13 Count Tolstoy's letter to Prince Volkonsky, dated 19 (31) October, from Nöthnitz (Log of Incoming Documents, No. 1,824).

fortress; but knowing of his lack of provisions, we must strive to have them capitulate as prisoners of war.'[14] Moreover, no one had less right to insist on the absolute observance of agreements than Napoleon, who himself would not hesitate to violate them at any opportunity.

Following the surrender of Dresden, the Russian force under Count Tolstoy moved towards Magdeburg and Hamburg; one of the divisions from Klenau's corps was sent to join the Army of Bohemia, while the other two went to Italy; the force under Chasteler returned to Bohemia.[15]

General Bennigsen, having received orders from Emperor Alexander on 14 (26) October to detach elements of the army entrusted to him in order to reinforce the Crown Prince of Sweden, while he was to deploy between Dresden and Magdeburg with the remainder of the force, in order to interrupt their mutual communications, sent Lieutenant General Count Stroganov to Heiligenstadt, with 18 battalions [sic], three artillery companies and two Bashkir regiments,[16] while he moved to Halle himself with the rest of the force.[17] Thereafter, having received orders on 19 November (1 December) to reinforce the Prussian blockade corps under *Generalleutnant* Hirschfeld at Magdeburg and to go on to Hamburg, Bennigsen sent Major General de Rossi [Ignaty Petrovich de Rossi] to Magdeburg on temporary detachment with six battalions, one Cossack and one Bashkir regiment and 18 guns,[18] and, having moved to Hamburg with the remaining formations of the Army of Poland,[19] blockaded this city from the right bank of the Elbe together with the corps under Count Wallmoden (blockading Harburg), on 12 (24) December.[20]

The Siege of Stettin

At the end of the armistice, the blockade of Stettin was entrusted to *Generalmajor* von Ploetz [Christian Friedrich Wilhelm von Ploetz], under whose command there were 19 battalions, four squadrons, three batteries and one pioneer company, numbering 14,600 men.[21] The garrison, numbering 8,000 men (10,000 according to other sources), was commanded by général de division Grandeau [Louis Joseph

---

14 Prince Volkonsky's dispatch to Count Tolstoy, dated 25 October [6 November] (Log of Outgoing Documents, No. 209).
15 Plotho, II, 533.
16 Count Stroganov's force consisted of: Prince Khovansky's 12th Division with 12 battalions; Penza Infantry and Saratov Infantry from 13th Division (five battalions); 9th Horse Artillery Company, 48th Light and 53rd Light artillery companies; 9th Bashkirs and 11th Bashkirs.
17 During the move from Freyburg to Halle, Count Bennigsen's force consisted of: General Kreutz's vanguard; 26th Division; Velikiye Luki Infantry and Galits Infantry from 13th Division; a cavalry division, for a total of 26,000 men.
18 General de Rossi's infantry consisted of: two battalions each of Velikiye Luki Infantry and Galits Infantry, and two replacement battalions from 12th Division.
19 Upon arrival at Hamburg, Count Bennigsen's force consisted of: 26th Division, 27 squadrons, three weak Cossack regiments and six artillery companies. General Count Bennigsen's report to the Tsar, dated 24 November [6 December].
20 Plotho, II, 502-506.
21 Plotho, II, *Beilagen*, 78.

Grandeau]. The troops and population suffered a great shortage of provisions; the disease and mortality that prevailed in the city may be assessed from the fact that of the 22,000 residents counted in the census in February, only 6,000 remained in November; the missing 16,000 had either fled the city or died. The large numbers of deserters prompted the French *Gendarmerie* to announce that homeowners sheltering military deserters would be fined 600 thalers; in the event of homeowners being insolvent, the city treasury was to pay a fine of 6,000 thalers.[22]

General Ploetz, wishing to keep the garrison in a constant state of alarm, continually bombarded the city, and even undertook some entrenching works, as if intending to begin a formal siege. Such demonstrations were especially necessary after the departure of the *8. Reserve Infanterie* to the Elbe in October, after which only *Landwehr* remained at Stettin. However, the bombardment was less harmful to the garrison than starvation, which resulted in a complete breakdown of discipline. The incessant complaints of abuses suffered by the population eventually forced General Grandeau to begin negotiations on 3 (15) November; but since the terms of the capitulation concluded by Ploetz were rejected by Tauentzien, negotiations on a new agreement began a few days later on 18 (30) November, on the basis of which the garrison would withdraw to the right bank of the Vistula, having surrendered the city on 23 November (5 December), with all military supplies contained therein. Among the seven generals, 250 officers and 7,280 lower ranks in the troops, there were some 1,400 Dutchmen, who were immediately repatriated to their homeland. 350 guns and a large amount of military stores were found in the city. The victors entered Stettin ceremonially, to the ringing of bells.[23]

The Siege of Zamość

This fortress remained under blockade by 21 *opolchenie* battalions, five squadrons and three Cossack regiments, with three artillery companies, numbering about 15,000 men with 36 guns, under the command of General Rath.[24] These troops were partly armed with pikes and completed their tactical training during the blockade of the fortress. The news of Napoleon's retreat across the Rhine forced the commandant of Zamość, General Hauke [Hans Johann Moritz Hauke], to surrender on 10 (22) November. The garrison, made up of 4,000 Polish troops, were released to their homes. 130 guns were found in the fortress.[25]

---

22 Richter, II, 556 & 558.
23 Richter, II, 558-560.
24 Rath's corps blockading Zamość consisted of: nine battalions of Poltava *Opolchenie*, six of Chernigov *Opolchenie*, three of Nizhegorod *Opolchenie* and three of Simbirsk *Opolchenie*; two squadrons of Pereyaslavl Mounted Jägers and three squadrons of Tiraspol Mounted Jägers; 2nd Teptyar Cossacks, the Atamans regiment of Orenburg Cossacks and 7th Bashkirs; 11th Battery, 22nd Battery and 30th Light artillery companies. For a total of 12,600 infantrymen, 500 cavalrymen, 1,200 Cossacks and 450 artillerymen. Plotho, II, *Beilagen*, 75.
25 Schulz, XI, 2 Band, 133; Convention on the surrender of Zamość (Log of Incoming Documents, No. 1,924).

The Siege of Modlin

During the armistice, the garrison had been strengthened by convalescents discharged from hospital to 6,500 men, mostly newly recruited Lithuanian troops. The fortress contained a significant amount of essential supplies collected before the war of 1812, which, however, due to negligent storage, had partly become unusable. A lack of accommodation to house the troops gave rise to the development of an epidemic in the autumn. Following the departure to Bohemia of Paskevich's blockade corps, together with the rest of Bennigsen's force, Modlin was blockaded by 9,000 *opolchenie*, commanded by Lieutenant General Kleinmikhel [Andrei Andreevich Kleinmikhel], who, unable to begin a formal siege of the fortress, proposed to allow the garrison to leave under free passage. But Emperor Alexander would not consent to approve such terms, and therefore the commandant of Modlin, général de division Daendels [Herman Willem Daendels], was forced to surrender with the troops entrusted to him as prisoners of war, on 1 December, new style. Of the 3,000 men in the Modlin garrison, the French were escorted to Grodno, the Poles and Lithuanians were sent home, while the Saxons and Würzburgers were allowed to keep their weapons and return to Germany. 120 guns were found in the fortress.[26]

The Siege of Torgau

This fortress consists of eight bastions, connected to each other by a curtain wall, in the form of a semicircle on the left bank of the Elbe; forwards of the fortress [to the north-west] lies the strong Fort Zinna – it is impossible to approach the main rampart without taking this place, as well as Fort Mahla [north of Torgau]; on the right bank of the Elbe a significant bridgehead had been built, and lunettes were installed on its flanks: Elblünette Zwetau and Elblünette Werdau. By the end of the armistice the garrison consisted of 20,000 men, among whom, however, there were many sick. On 2 (14) September, a new governor arrived in Torgau, comte Narbonne [Louis-Marie-Jacques-Amalric de Narbonne-Lara], formerly Napoleon's ambassador to the Court of Vienna, an amiable, just man, but of firm character and strict in the performance of the duties assigned to him.

As the battle of Leizig was underway, *Generalleutnant* Wobeser invested Torgau from the right bank of the Elbe with his brigade; the blockade from the left bank, following the aforementioned battle, was entrusted to Saxon forces under General [Gustav] Ryssel. On 8 (20) October, General Graf Tauentzien, having set out from Berlin for Zerbst with the rest of his force, dispatched *Generalmajor* Dobschütz's brigade and *1. Reserve Infanterie* (from General Hirschfeld's corps) to besiege Wittenberg, while he crossed the Elbe at Coswig himself, with *Generalmajor*

---

26 Lieutenant General Kleinmikhel's report No. 249 to General Bennigsen, dated 22 October [3 November], with a draft capitulation for Modlin (Log of Incoming Documents, No. 1,947); Orders for Prince Lobanov-Rostovsky, dated 5 [17] November (Log of Outgoing Documents, No. 236); Plotho, II, 533; Schulz, XI, *2 Band*, 133-134.

Lindenau's brigade, and on 21 October (2 November) blockaded the city from the left bank. In mid-November, new style, the Saxon forces blockading Torgau together with Lindenau's brigade, went to Leipzig in order to be reorganised there by General Thielmann. On 5 (17) November, comte Narbonne died from a severe contusion after a fall from a horse; his place was taken by *général de division* comte Dutaillis [Adrien Jean-Baptiste Aimable Ramon du Bosc Dutaillis].

At the beginning of the siege, Tauentzien had limited himself to shelling the fortress; on 10 (22) November, he began the formal attack. On the night of 14 to 15 (26 to 27) November, the first parallel was opened facing Fort Zinna and the next day, at dawn, two batteries opened heavy fire; on 16 (28) November, the enemy launched a strong sortie, but were repelled with losses. Despite the frost, which made digging difficult, several more batteries were constructed on both banks of the Elbe. Graf Tauentzien demanded that the commandant surrender the fortress; the outcome of the negotiations conducted on this subject was a truce, but as Dutaillis would not agree to the terms offered to him, the bombardment was resumed on 24 November (6 December), and forced the enemy to abandon the crucial Fort Zinna during the night of 28 to 29 November (10 to 11 December). The fall of this key point and great loss of life from an epidemic prompted the commandant to agree to a capitulation on 14 (26) December. The garrison, numbering 10,000 men (along with 4,000 sick), were surrendered as prisoners of war and were escorted to Silesia. 250 guns and significant military supplies were found in the fortress. The King of Prussia appointed *Generalmajor* Schuler von Senden as commandant of Torgau. Since every barracks, casemate and hospital was a nest of contagious diseases, those assigned to the garrison there (namely *17. Schlesisches Landwehr* and one battalion of *11. Schlesisches Landwehr*) would only enter the city on 29 December (10 January, 1814) after it had been completely evacuated. Due to the spread of a rumour across Germany that Napoleon's treasure had been in Torgau, a commission was appointed to find it, but all these rumours turned out to be false.[27]

The Siege of Wittenberg

The Wittenberg fortress, which held a garrison of more than 3,000 men within its walls, was supplied with food and munitions in abundance, and therefore, a formal siege was necessary in order to take control of it. On 11 (23) October, General Dobschütz encircled the fortress with his brigade and proceeded to bombard the garrison from his field howitzers for a period of two months. After the surrender of Torgau, the siege artillery was sent to Wittenberg from there, together with the associated military stores, while Tauentzien himself arrived in Coswig on 16 (28) December. The first parallel was opened that night; the enemy, lulled by previous false alarms, paid no attention to the siege works, which allowed the first parallel to be dug in the role of a second parallel, at a range of 400-500 paces from the main rampart and no more than 200 from the outworks built in the intervals between the

---

27 Plotho, II, 540-545; Schulz, XI, *2 Band*, 119-122; Förster, *Befreiungskriege*, II, 1094-1097.

bastions. The siege works, under the direction of the engineer *Oberst* Ploosen [Jean-Nicolas-Julien Chulliot de Ploosen] and artillery *Hauptmann* Bardeleben [Karl Moritz Ferdinand von Bardeleben], progressed rapidly. During the night of 26 to 27 December (7 to 8 January, 1814), the majority of the glacis crown was completed and construction of the breaching battery began, which, having opened fire on 30 December (11 January), continued throughout the following day, together with indirect fire from four mortars. Since the commandant of the fortress, général de division La Poype [Jean François de La Poype], refused several times to surrender the fortress, Graf Tauentzien decided to storm it in the early hours of 1 (13) January. Prinz August von Preußen, who was 20 *Meilen* (140 *versts*) from Wittenberg, was invited to take part in the assault and arrived in time. Because the besiegers had failed to make a viable breach, Prussian pioneers, taking advantage of the ensuing darkness, constructed ramps from fascines.

The troops tasked with the assault were under the direct command of General Dobschütz.[28] By about one o'clock in the afternoon, the assault columns had managed to take control of all the outworks and the main rampart. General La Poype, having put the Schloss, Rathaus [town hall] and other buildings into a defensive state in advance, defended them for quite some time, but was eventually forced to surrender. In total, more than 1,500 men were taken prisoner; two Eagles were captured. 96 guns were found in the fortress. The losses in the Prussian force during the assault amounted to eight officers and 259 lower ranks; overall, throughout the siege of Wittenberg, the losses amounted to 13 officers and 632 lower ranks; *Generalmajor* von Elsner [Karl Christian von Elsner] was appointed commandant. The *11. Schlesisches Landwehr* were left in the fortress; three battalions and three squadrons were sent to Magdeburg, while the remaining units went to Erfurt and on to the Rhine.

General der Infanterie Graf Tauentzien, as a reward for the capture of Wittenberg, received the *Großkreuz des Eisernen Kreuzes* and the title of Graf von Wittenberg.[29]

Shortly before the capture of Wittenberg, the powerful fortress of Danzig fell to Coalition forces.

The Siege of Danzig

In *le Moniteur* of 26 January, 1813, new style, it stated:

> Danzig, at present is an invincible fortress, it is defended by 30,000 of the best troops, under the command of good generals; the governor of the city, General Rapp [Jean Rapp], is an intrepid warrior. The garrison includes many artillery and engineering officers; the fortress has been stocked with every necessity for two years.

---

28 Plotho, III, 507.
29 Plotho, III, 505; Schulz, XI, *2 Band*, 123-125. [Although Tauentzien was given the title 'von Wittenberg' he was actually eight miles away in Kemberg throughout the storming of the town].

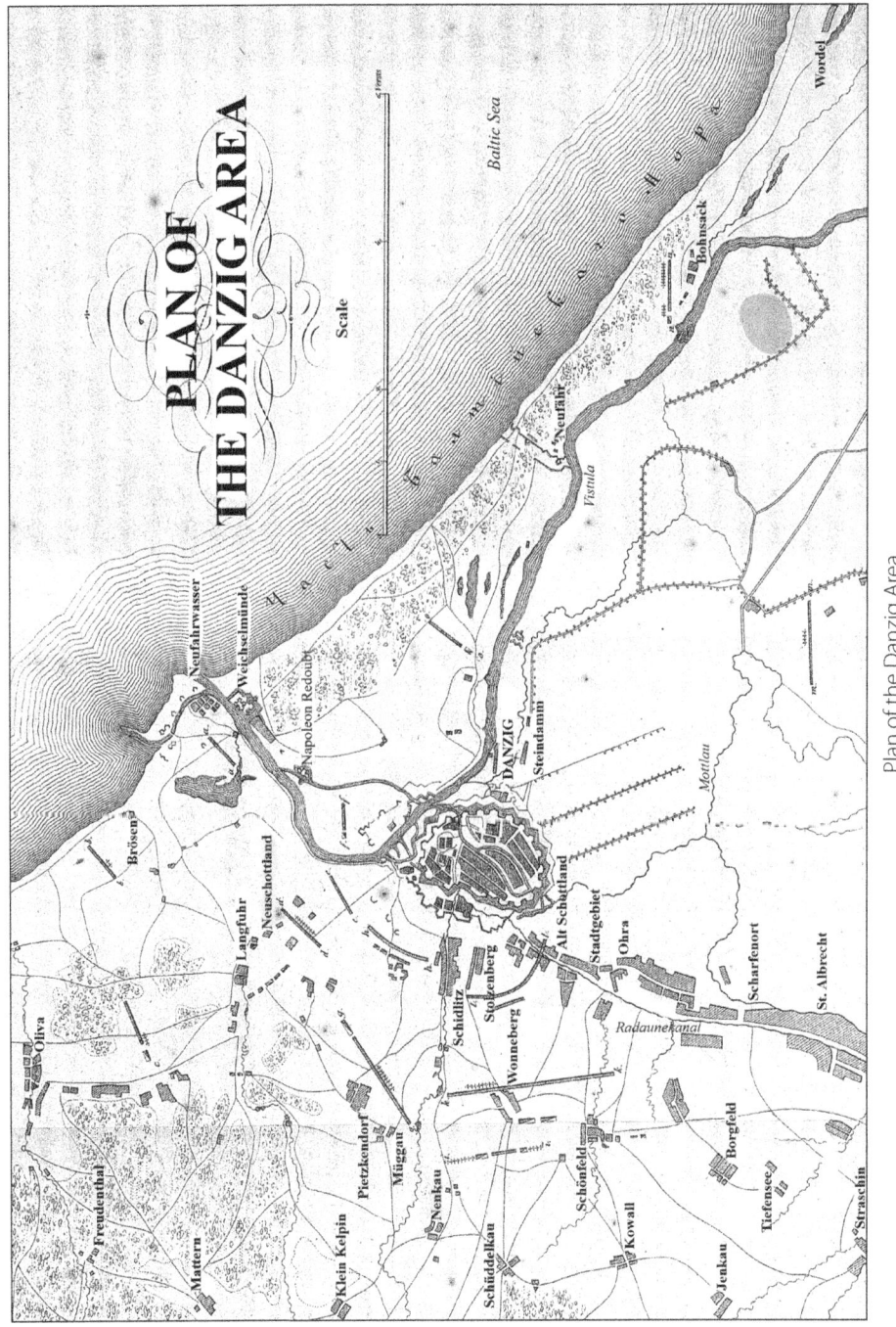

Plan of the Danzig Area.

During the armistice, the blockade corps under Herzog Alexander von Württemberg was increased to 35,000 men. These included ten battalions and six squadrons of *Ostpreußisches Landwehr*, with one six-pounder battery, commanded by *Oberst* Dohna [Ludwig zu Dohna-Schlobitten].[30] During the armistice, active digging works were carried out by both sides, and although, on the basis of the armistice convention, a certain amount of essential provisions were to have been allowed into the fortress every five days, this condition was not fulfilled (probably in retaliation for the treacherous attack on Lützow's detachment). As a consequence of this there was a shortage of many vital necessities and the spread of contagious diseases in the city. General Rapp, unable to satisfy the needs of the force entrusted to him, imposed a contribution of 3,000,000 francs on the city, and in order to induce them to pay up promptly, he placed many wealthy residents under guard, threatening to shoot one in ten of them.

When military operations resumed after the armistice, orders were issued to expel 400 orphans (who had been taken into care in shelters) from the city as well as several thousand poor people, mostly elderly residents. These unfortunates, doomed to die, owed their salvation solely to the generosity of Herzog Alexander von Württemberg, who took the care of their subsistence upon himself. The extortion of the population did not, however, improve the situation of the troops in any way; sickness and mortality increased every day: there were many officers who, having lost the lower ranks subordinate to them, remained surplus to manning, the so-called régiment du roi de Rome was formed, numbering 1,600 men, in which the officers served as privates; many of them, commanded by Captain Chambure [Laurent Augustin Pelletier de Chambure], who had lost an arm, formed a special squad, assigned for sorties and other dangerous missions and referred to under the nickname 'the devil's brothers' or *l'Infernale*.[31]

Once the armistice had expired, on 12 (24) August, the Herzog von Württemberg, having received a considerable number of guns and Congreve rockets sent from Britain, decided to begin a formal siege of Danzig immediately, and, in the meantime, following his previous modus operandi, he harassed and wearied the enemy with incessant attacks. The main director of the siege works was the Prussian Major Pullet [Samuel Pullet], who had taken an active part in the fitting out of the defences at Danzig in 1807.

On 17 (29) August, the besiegers seized two enemy redoubts near Ohra [Orunia], and that night occupied the forest near the suburb of Langfuhr [Wrzeszcz].[32] General Rapp, for his part, launched a major sortie and attacked the Coalition at Pietzkendorf [Piecki], but were rebuffed with losses. Colonel Treskin [Mikhail Lvovich Treskin] and the Azov Infantry particularly distinguished themselves; after that the enemy turned on the Langfuhr forest, but had no success there either. Their losses amounted to over 1,600 men overall, while on the Coalition side no more than

---

30 For details of Herzog Alexander von Württemberg's blockade corps, see Appendix XXXIX at the end of this chapter.
31 Sporschill, I, 1145.
32 See Map No. 17, Plan of the Danzig Area.

600 men were *hors de combat*, and in spite of everything, the artillery of the siege corps fired more than 10,000 rounds.[33]

On 21 August (2 September), the Herzog von Württemberg attacked the enemy once more, wanting to drive them out of Langfuhr and the Schellmühl [Młyniska] manor. 'Knowing that General Rapp takes a very long time over his meals,' the Herzog wrote in his report on this matter, 'I ordered a surprise attack on him at five o'clock in the afternoon.' The enemy, having been taken completely by surprise, were driven off; while Colonel Prince Balatukov [Kirill Matveevich Balatukov or Kaya-Bey Balatukov], in order to cut them off from the fortress, had moved towards the Langfuhr to Danzig road with two Tatar regiments, supported by one battalion of 2nd Jägers and two battalions of Nizov Infantry. Within half an hour the besiegers had captured Langfuhr and almost all the nearby outer fieldworks. When the enemy began to retreat to the fortress, having been driven out of the last two blockhouses in the evening, the Tatar regiments rushed to engage them and cut down many men. General Rapp sortied against the Coalition with three columns each containing at least 2,000 men and gave them supporting fire from their field artillery and 50 24-pounder guns but, being engaged with fixed bayonets, they retired back to the fortress with losses of over 1,500 men; the casualties in the Coalition force amounted to over 500 men.[34]

In this manner, the besiegers had managed to close up to the fortress to a range that allowed them to attack the main ramparts. The gunboat flotilla, commanded by Rear Admiral Greig [Alexei Samuilovich Greig], entered the mouth of the Vistula several times and bombarded Weichselmünde [Twierdza Wisłoujście] and Neufahrwasser [Nowy Port].[35]

The Herzog von Württemberg, intending to begin opening the first parallel, proceeded to protect its flanks and take possession of the village of Schottenhäuser [Neuschottland, Nowe Szkoty] together with three redoubts built in front of it, and in order to distract the attention of the French, he also launched a feint attack from Langfuhr towards the Olivaer Tor [northern outer gates]. After dark from 28 to 29 September (10 to 11 October), the action began with a cannonade, bombardment and the use of Congreve rockets in the direction of the Olivaer Tor. The town caught fire in several places, which forced Rapp to bring the greater part of the garrison closer to Langfuhr; meanwhile, Coalition troops quickly moved towards Schottenhäuser,[36]

---

33 Herzog Alexander von Württemberg's report No. 1,424 to the Tsar, dated 31 August [new style?]; Plotho, II, 533-534; Schulz, XI, *2 Band*, 134-135.
34 The Herzog von Württemberg's dispatch No. 1,431 to the Chief of the General Staff, Prince Volkonsky, dated 31 August [12 September]; Plotho, II, 534.
35 Herzog von Württemberg's report No. 1,739 to the Tsar, dated 17 [29?] September.
36 The Coalition columns for this night attack consisted of: Prussian Major Graf von Eulenburg's First Column – Major Grinkevich's battalion of Volhynia Infantry, 200 labourers from the *9. 14.* and *16. Preußisches Landwehr* and 1st Battalion of St. Petersburg *Opolchenie* with 50 labourers and 12 carts with timber, ladders, straw, etcetera; Russian Major Yulius' Second Column – two battalions of Bryansk Infantry, two squadrons of Kazan Dragoons, one squadron of *5. Ostpreußisches Landwehr Kavallerie*, and Russian Lieutenant Colonel Härbel's 19th Horse Artillery Company; Major General Kolyubakin's Third Column – four squadrons of *4.* and *5. Ostpreußisches Landwehr Kavallerie*, four squadrons of Kazan Dragoons, one Russian and one Prussian light battery, *19. Ostpreußisches Landwehr Bataillon*, three battalions of St. Petersburg *Opolchenie* and one battalion each of 3rd Jägers and 1st Marines.

seized this village and took the redoubts in front by storm. General Rapp, having eventually realised the besiegers' real intent, turned on Schottenhäuser and retook the lost fortifications, but the Coalition drove the enemy out of the village and redoubts once more, as well as from several blockhouses. This action lasted for ten whole hours and cost the French some 1,000 men, including as many as 400 brave men from Chambure's group; on the side of the Coalition the losses amounted to 680 men (430 Russians and 246 Prussians); Colonel Bugaevsky of the 3rd Jägers was among those killed. The following particularly distinguished themselves: Prussian *Oberst* Graf Dohna, Major Yulius [Alexander Bogdanovich Yulius] of the Bryansk Infantry, Major Grinkevich of the Volhynia Infantry, Staff-Captain [O.I.] Korff of 19th Horse Artillery Company, British Colonel Campbell and Lieutenant Gelbel [*sic*] of the British Rocket Battery.[37]

The occupation of Schottenhäuser enabled the Herzog von Württemberg to place mortar batteries close to the fortress and to direct plunging fire into the central part of the city (Speicherinsel [Wyspa Spichrzów]), where the majority of the enemy magazines were located; on the night of 20 to 21 October (1 to 2 November), more than 100 stores containing flour, hard-tack and other provisions were burned down. The following night the Coalition captured the suburbs of Schidlitz [Siedlce] and Stolzenberg [Chełm] and laid the first parallel facing Bischofsberg [Biskupia Górka], the weakest point of the fortress;[38] and on the night of 24 to 25 October (5 to 6 November), the redoubt on the Zigankenberg [Suchanino] was taken by storm, which was essential in order to secure the trenches on the left flank. The losses suffered by the Coalition in these actions did not exceed 500 men.[39]

On 5 (17) November, fire was opened from every battery in the first parallel (130 guns in total). Their operations soon gained them superiority over the enemy artillery; many of the fortress outworks, including the Frioul redoubt and the Clarke lunette, were destroyed, which forced the French to abandon them. The besiegers immediately occupied the former of these fortifications and thus gained security for the right flank of their trenches. On the night of 9 to 10 (21 to 22) November, the enemy voluntarily abandoned the redoubts near the Bischofsberg (Jesuit Redoubt and Jewish Redoubt) and set the remaining houses of Alt Schottland and the Jesuit monastery on fire. One of the mortar bombs lobbed by the besiegers blew up a powder magazine on the Bischofsberg, which, by spreading confusion among the garrison, facilitated the completion of the siege works. The besiegers, having constructed six new batteries, closed up to the Petershager Tor and caused so much destruction to the Bischofsberg that even an assault attempt was possible in the very near future. All these factors forced Rapp to begin negotiations.[40]

---

37 Herzog von Württemberg's report No. 2,100 to Prince Volkonsky, dated 7 [19] October.
38 See Map No. 18, Plan of the Siege of Danzig. This plan shows the lines of: A-A Major General Turchaninov's detachment; B-B Major General Treskin's detachment; C-C Lieutenant General Löwis' detachment; D-D Major General Yurlov's reserves (Major General Chernysh's detachment were between Alt Schottland and Ohra, off the southern edge of the map).
39 Herzog von Württemberg's report No. 2,373 to Prince Volkonsky, dated 29 October [10 November].
40 The Herzog von Württemberg's report No. 2,506 to the Tsar, dated 19 November [1 December].

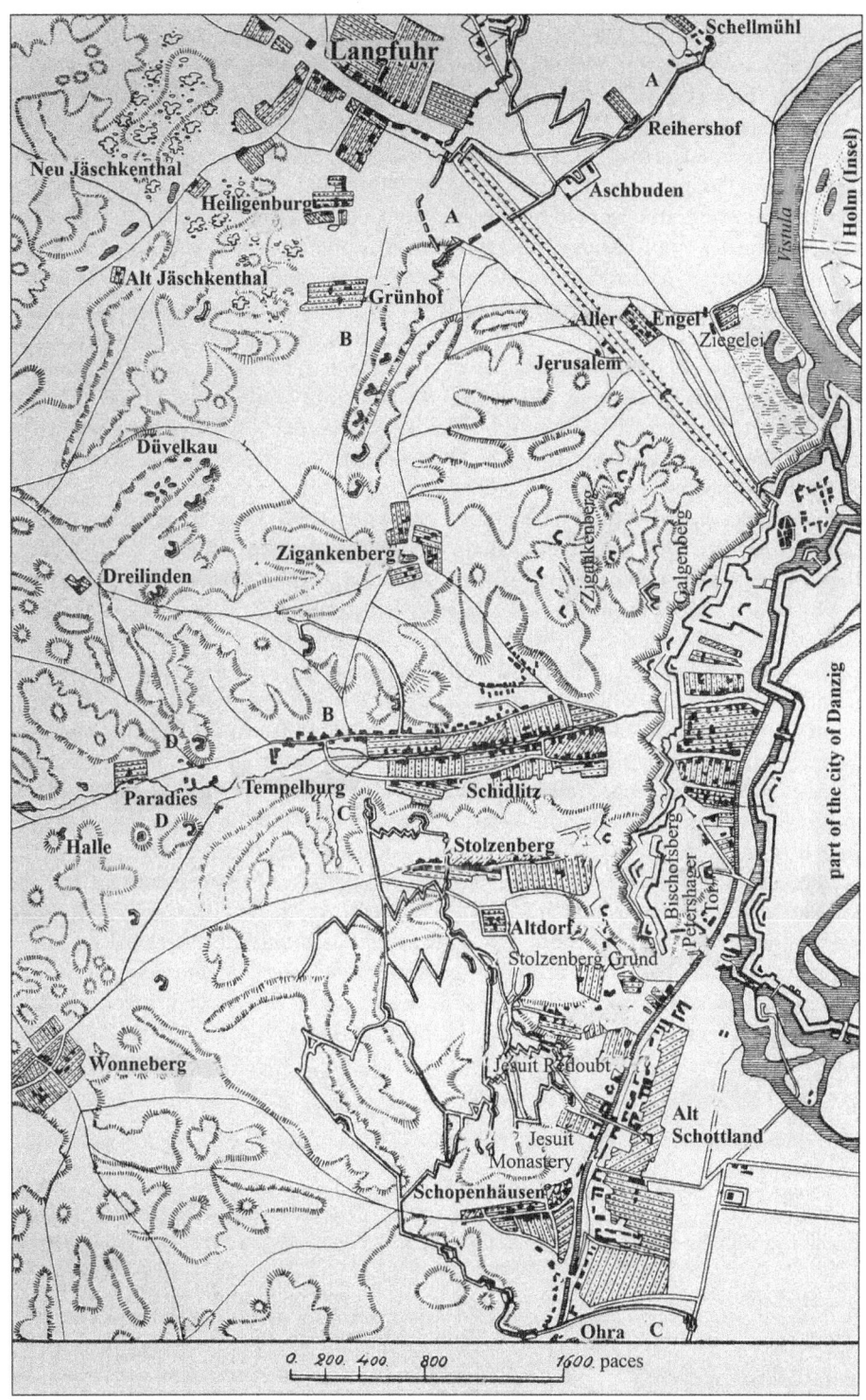

Plan of the Siege of Danzig.

On 15 (27) November, a truce was concluded, and two days later [29 November, new style] a capitulation was signed for the surrender of Danzig, under the terms of which the garrison of the fortress were obliged to vacate the fortress on 20 December (1 January, 1814); the fortifications at Weichselmünde and on the island of Holm [Wyspa Ostrów], as well as the keys to the Olivaer Tor, were to be surrendered to the Coalition on 12 (24) December. The garrison, having left the fortress with military honours, were to be released to France, on their word of honour – not to serve against the Coalition for one year and one day from the exchange, and so on.[41] Emperor Alexander would not ratify this capitulation, demanding that General Rapp and all his troops surrender as prisoners of war. When the Herzog von Württemberg presented the thoughts of the Council of War he had convened to the Emperor – regarding the impossibility of continuing the siege and about the danger to which the besieging force, and especially the siege artillery, had been exposed during the transition from siege to blockade – Emperor Alexander insisted on the strict observance of the regulations he had implemented regarding the surrender of enemy fortresses.[42]

Meanwhile, in early (mid) December, three battalions and an artillery unit of *Confédération du Rhin* troops left Danzig.[43] As a consequence of the persistence of the Russian monarch, a new capitulation was concluded on 17 (29) December, on the basis of which General Rapp, having evacuated the fortress on 21 December (2 January, 1814), would surrender with the entire garrison as prisoners of war.[44] Thus ended the blockade of Danzig, which lasted 11½ months. The following were taken prisoner: *généraux de division* comte Rapp, Grandjean [Charles Louis Dieudonné Grandjean], Heudelet [Étienne Heudelet de Bierre], Franczeski, Bachelier, Cavaignac [Jacques-Marie Cavaignac de Baragne], Lepin [Pierre Henri Lepin] and Campredon [Jacques David Martin de Campredon], six *généraux de brigade*, over 1,000 officers and 9,000 lower ranks from the French forces; some 6,000 Poles were released to their homes. More than 1,300 guns were found in the fortress. Only 13,000 of the city's 60,000 population remained; 970 of the 4,000 houses had been damaged by the bombardment. After the surrender of the fortress, which was immediately handed over to the Prussian government, *Generalleutnant* Massenbach [Eberhard Friedrich Fabian von Massenbach] was appointed governor; the Prussian Landwehr garrisoned the city, the Russian *opolchenie* were sent home, while the Russian regular troops joined the reserve army located in the Duchy of Warsaw.[45]

---

41 From the copy of the capitulation of the fortress of Danzig, signed by Herzog Alexander von Württemberg.
42 Report by the Herzog von Württemberg's Chief of Staff, Major General Velyaminov, to Prince Volkonsky, dated 29 November [11 December]; the Herzog von Württemberg's letter to the Tsar with the submitted thoughts of the Council of War, held on 2 (14) December; the Tsar's letter to the Herzog von Württemberg's, dated 15 [27] December (Log of Outgoing Documents, No. 324).
43 The Herzog von Württemberg's dispatch to Prince Volkonsky, dated 11 [23] December.
44 The Herzog von Württemberg's letter to Prince Volkonsky, dated 18 [30] December, with a draft copy of the capitulation of Danzig attached.
45 Plotho, II, 538-539. Interesting details regarding the surrender of Danzig may be found in Steinheil's work: Notes on the St. Petersburg *Opolchenie*.

The Siege of Erfurt

This city and its citadels (ancient monasteries) Petersburg and Cyriaksburg, had been carefully fortified on Napoleon's orders, and during his retreat were provided with a garrison of 5,000 men, of whom, however, only 2,000 were fit to fight, under the command of General d'Alton [Alexandre d'Alton]. At the end of October, new style, Kleist's Prussian *2. Korps* had blockaded the city, but due to having no siege park, they could not immediately begin a formal attack. Once the Austrian siege guns arrived, General Kleist, having built several batteries, bombarded the city on 25 October (6 November) and reduced more than 100 building to rubble. The result of this was the conclusion of a truce, to which Kleist had agreed in the hope of inducing the enemy to surrender; this lasted until 8 (20) November and gave the besiegers the opportunity to bring up artillery and munitions from Theresienstadt and Bavaria, while General d'Alton at the same time extracted a significant contribution from the population of Erfurt and forced them to supply the troops with large quantities of firewood, cloth, and such like. On 20 November [new style], the siege works were resumed and continued very actively. General d'Alton, convinced that it would be impossible to repel an assault on the city, concluded a convention on 8 (20) December, according to the terms of which he was obliged to vacate Erfurt and withdraw into the citadels on 25 December (6 January, 1814), and a truce was agreed until that time. Following the surrender of Erfurt to Prussian forces, Kleist's corps moved to the Rhine to rejoin the main body of Blucher's army, leaving *Generalmajor* Jagow surrounding the enemy held citadels with six battalions of the *6. Reserve Infanterie* and *10. Reserve Infanterie* and four *Schlesisches Landwehr* regiments (*7. 8. 9.* and *10.* each of which consisted of a single weak battalion), *1. Schlesisches Landwehr Kavallerie*, *2. Schlesisches Landwehr Kavallerie*, the six-pounder *14. Batterie* and *7. Pionier Kompagnie*.[46]

Thus, by the beginning of 1814, eight fortified cities and fortresses occupied by the enemy in Germany and the Duchy of Warsaw had been taken by the Coalition. About 80,000 men had laid down their arms; the number of guns captured in the fortresses amounted to 2,500. To the rear of the Coalition armies, enemy flags fluttered only on the walls of Glogau, Küstrin, Magdeburg, Hamburg, and the citadels of Erfurt and Würzburg. A description of the sieges of these fortified points, which surrendered after the end of the war, belongs to the account of the operations that took place in 1814.

---

46 Plotho, II, 550-554 & III, 500.

Appendix XXXIX

Composition of the Coalition blockade corps at Danzig

The Russian contingent of Herzog Alexander von Württemberg's blockade corps at Danzig consisted of:

General Löwis' corps: 6th Division – Azov Infantry, Nizov Infantry, Koporsk Infantry, Bryansk Infantry, 3rd Jägers, 18th Jägers; 25th Division – Voronezh Infantry, 1st Marines, 2nd Marines, 31st Jägers, 47th Jägers.

Replacement battalions: Reval Infantry, 20th Jägers, 21st Jägers (from 3rd Division); Volhynia Infantry, Tobolsk Infantry, Minsk Infantry, 4th Jägers, 34th Jägers (4th Division); Ryazan Infantry, Belozersk Infantry, Brest Infantry, 30th Jägers (17th Division); 2nd Jägers (21st Division).

Four squadrons each of Kazan Dragoons and Yamburg Ulans; one replacement squadron each from the Moscow Dragoons, Ingermanland Dragoons and Kargopol Dragoons.

Don Cossack regiments: Grekov 5th's, Grekov 17th's, Chernozubov 8th's, Suchilin 2nd's, Kharitonov 7th's; 2nd Teptyar Cossacks; Perekop Tatars, Simferopol Tatars; Ataman's Orenburg Cossacks; 7th Bashkirs; Schmitt's *Freikorps*.

12 guns each from 6th Battery Company, 10th Light Company, 40th Light Company, 19th Horse Artillery Company; 11 guns from 11th Light Company; 25th Garrison Artillery Company.

11th Pontoon Company; Major General Count Siever's and Captain Savich's sapper companies; Lieutenant Colonel Orlov's pioneer company.

Five combined infantry groups of Saint Petersburg *Opolchenie*; four combined infantry groups of Novgorod *Opolchenie*; one mounted group, four infantry groups and one jäger regiment of Tula *Opolchenie*; two infantry regiments of Yaroslavl *Opolchenie*; one mounted regiment, five infantry groups and one jäger group of Kaluga *Opolchenie*.

Extracted from the Army Listings, dated 9 (21) November, signed by General Sabaneev (Log of Incoming Documents, No. 1,895).

The Prussian contingent of Herzog Alexander von Württemberg's blockade corps at Danzig consisted of:
One battalion each of *7. Ostpreußisches Landwehr* and *13. Ostpreußisches Landwehr*; *4. Ostpreußisches Landwehr, 5. Ostpreußisches Landwehr.*
4. Ostpreußisches Landwehr Kavallerie, 5. Ostpreußisches Landwehr Kavallerie.
Hauptmann Sommer's six-pounder foot battery.
(Plotho, II, *Beilagen*, 74).

47

Conclusions

The war of 1813 for German independence ended with the retreat of the pitiful remnants of the army that Napoleon had raised during the armistice with astonishing speed. Considering that he had assembled two armies that year, it is apparent that the losses suffered by the French during the struggle in Germany were only slightly fewer than those suffered during the invasion of Russia in 1812. Of the force assembled by Napoleon in April 1813, the losses before the armistice amounted to 40,000 men overall; in the second campaign, of the 400,000 men raised by the time of the resumption of hostilities, some 70,000 men remained at the crossing of the Rhine (many of whom subsequently died during disease epidemics): consequently, Napoleon lost some 330,000 men in this campaign. In addition, by the end of 1813 and the beginning of 1814, no less than 80,000 men from the French garrisons in the fortresses of Germany and the Duchy of Warsaw had been killed or taken prisoner, thus some 450,000 men were lost in total in the war of 1813.

No matter how disastrous the situation was for the *Grande Armée*, upon Napoleon's return to Paris [in January 1813], France could still, with the help of their vassals, wage war with success against Russia and Prussia. The victories at Lützen and Bautzen, despite the lack of a decisive outcome, gave Napoleon the opportunity to push the Russians back beyond the Oder and neutralise the Prussian army before it could receive reinforcements. But Napoleon had neither accurate intelligence on the weakness of the Russo-Prussian forces, nor of the disagreements between the allies – a natural consequence of their unsuccessful operations. All he knew for certain was that his own forces, consisting of foreigners who had not had time to be tempered by combat and campaigning, were very much exhausted and disordered, and therefore, failing to take into account that his adversaries were not in the best condition, he agreed to conclude an armistice. During the two-month suspension of hostilities, he managed to assemble a huge army. The Coalition were aware of this and, although they hoped for the assistance promised to them by Austria, they nevertheless offered Napoleon peace terms that would have given him the opportunity to draw strength and, within a few years, acquire hegemony over Europe once more. But he did not fully appreciate the situation he was in and decided to use his sword to cut the Gordian knot of Austrian foreign policy in which he was entangled.

Despite the disproportionate strength of Napoleon's forces compared with those of the Coalition, at the beginning of the second campaign, Victory remained true to its favourite. But having achieved a brilliant and well-deserved success at the battle of Dresden, he did not fully exploit it, and one consequence of the hesitant measures taken was the destruction of Vandamme's corps at Kulm. Meanwhile, even Napoleon's most worthy companions could not live up to his expectations: the cautious Macdonald recklessly ran into a stronger enemy and was defeated at Katzbach; the fearless Oudinot, *le brave des braves* Ney, operated sluggishly, indecisively, and suffered defeat at Großbeeren and Dennewitz; Davout himself more than once missed the opportunity to destroy the weak corps facing him under Wallmoden. Indeed, all in all it emerged that Napoleon, after 20 years spent in administrative work and military concerns, still retained the energy necessary to accomplish great feats, but this could not be said of his marshals, satiated with glory and honours yet thirsting for peace and quiet.

Eventually, after many bloody encounters, the Coalition were pressing Napoleon from several directions. The Battle of Nations at Leipzig began! Here, for the last time, despite the numerical superiority of the Coalition hordes, the military genius had the opportunity to tilt the balance in his favour. He struck a terrific blow at Güldengossa, but could not sustain it with renewed strength and passed the opportunity to gather sufficient reserves at the threatened location and avert the danger to his rivals in the fight for the freedom of Germany and Europe. Napoleon, having failed to break through the centre of the Coalition Main Army, was forced to retreat immediately, and while he once again broke contact with his enemies, the results were enormous losses from his force and their disastrous retreat beyond the Rhine.

The Coalition began their first campaign in Germany commanded by Count Wittgenstein, who had gained great renown in the Patriotic War of 1812. But in operations in Germany, he found himself in a completely different situation than in Russia: instead of the friendly assistance of the generals subordinated to him and the local authorities, he was forced to fight at every step, not only with the administration of a foreign country ruined by Napoleon and possessing very meagre resources, but also with the resistance that Wittgenstein encountered in his relations with the senior generals subordinated to him: Barclay, Miloradovich and Blücher. Following the battle of Bautzen, supreme command of the Coalition armies passed from Count Wittgenstein to Barclay de Tolly, but the latter's short-lived command left no trace, except for the very prudent precautions he took regarding the logistics of the Russian forces. At the end of the armistice, none of the Russian military commanders were appointed commander-in-chief of any of the Coalition armies, which gave foreign military historians reason to conclude that this was due to the Coalition monarchs acknowledging the incompetence of senior Russian generals. But this matter had been resolved quite differently: Emperor Alexander, caring more about the success of the cause undertaken than in basking in its ephemeral brilliance, proposed entrusting command of the armies to foreign commanders himself: to Schwarzenberg – an army only half of which consisted of Austrian troops and protected Bohemia; to Blucher – the army defending Silesia; to the Crown Prince of Sweden – the army that was closest to his base of operations.

The Emperor, in making this concession, granted himself the right to control the operations not only of his own troops, but also of those that belonged to his constant ally, Friedrich Wilhelm. The involvement of the Russian Emperor had very beneficial consequences in the battle of Kulm, and especially in the battle of Leipzig. Operating under the orders of foreign commanders, the Russians covered themselves with glory wherever they had to fight. At Kulm, they – and they alone – saved the Main Army from defeat. They were decisive in the victory on the Katzbach. At Leipzig, they checked the enemy who had broken through the centre of the Main Army and captured one of the strongest points of the enemy position – Schönefeld; the losses suffered by Russian forces in this battle indicates the extent of their participation in the liberation of Germany. Lüneburg, Halberstadt, Göhrde, Altenburg, Kassel, are a testament to the skill and courage of the Russian partisans.

Half a century has passed; the memory of the great deeds accomplished by Emperor Alexander have not yet had time to fade from living memory in the nations that owe their independence to his bright mind, his generosity, and yet just a few military historians, considering gratitude too heavy a burden, have tried to eclipse the glory of the Russian Tsar and Russian soldiers. We must refute biased testimony. Let the reliable facts conveyed by their witnesses and participants serve to clarify the truth!

Sources For The History of the War Of 1813

No recent war bears comparison with the war of 1813 for the abundance of books and resources. For ease of access, I have allocated each of the sources relating to this war into one of two categories:

1. Official documents.
2. Memoirs and published works, subdivided into:
    a) Books containing a complete description of the war of 1813.
    b) Monographs.

Let us consider each of these sections in detail.

Unpublished Manuscripts

Official Documents

1. War Diary, signed by Prince Kutuzov (*Журнал военных действий, за подписью князя Кутузова*).
2. Logs of Outgoing Documents of 1813 (*Журналы исходящим бумагам 1813 года*) – Archive of the M.T.D. No. 29,181 and No. 29,190.
3. Logs of Incoming Documents of 1813 (*Журналы входящим бумагам 1813 года*) – Archive of the M.T.D. No. 29,182.
4. War Diary of Lieutenant General Sacken's corps (*Журнал действий корпуса генерал-лейтенанта Сакена*) – Archive of the M.T.D. No. 16,643.
5. Outgoing Log for the former located in the Archive of the M.T. Depot, No. 44, 585, folio 35 (*Исходащий Журнал его-же находится в Архиве В.Т.Депо*).
6. Siege Diary for Thorn (*Журнал осады Торна*) – Archive of the Engineering Department.
7. War Diary of Miloradovich's rearguard (*Журнал действий арриергарда Милорадовича*).
8. War Diary, signed by Prince Volkonsky (*Журнал военных действий, за подписью князя Волконского*).
9. *Journal der Kriegs-Operationen der Kaiserlich-Russischen und Verbündeten Armeen von der Eroberung Thorns bis zur Einnahme von Paris.*
10. Siege Diary for Glogau (*Журнал осады Глогау*) – Log of Incoming Documents, No. 636 and No. 767.

11. War Diary of Prince Shcherbatov's VI Corps (*Журнал (Военныя дневныя записки) 6-го пехотного корпуса, князя Щербатова*).
12. War Diary of Adjutant-General Baron Korff's corps (*Журнал движениям корпуса генерал-адъютанта барона Корфа*).
13. Comte Langéron's diary (military memoirs) (*Журнал (Военныя записки) графа Ланжерона*).
14. War Diary (memoirs) of Count Vorontsov (*Журнал (Записки) действий графа Воронцова в 1813-мъ году*) – Archive of the M.T.D. No. 16,642.
15. War Diary signed by Barclay de Tolly (*Журнал военных действий за подписью Барклая де Толли*) – Archive of the M.T.D. No. 29,188.
16. War Diary of General Bennigsen's Army of Poland, signed by General Opperman (*Журнал действий Польской армии, генерала Беннигсена, за подписью генерала Оппермана*) – Log of Incoming Documents, No. 1,822.
17. War Diary of General Essen's corps (*Журнал военных действий корпуса генерала Эссена*) – Archive of the M.T.D. No. 16,646.
18. Siege Diary for Danzig (*Журнал осады Данцига*) – Archive of the M.T.D. No. 15,393.

Of all these war diaries, the most noteworthy are: the logs of outgoing and incoming documents, the war diaries by Bennigsen, Langéron, Miloradovich and Sacken, the diaries signed by Kutuzov, Barclay de Tolly and Adjutant-General Prince Volkonsky.

19. General summary of the movements and operations by the Imperial Russian and Coalition forces in the war against the French, 1812, 1813 and 1814 (*Общий свод движений и действий Императорских Российских и Союзных с ними войск в войну против Французов, 1812, 1813 и 1814*) – Archive of the M.T.D. No. 37,640.
20. Emperor Alexander's correspondence with: King Maximilian Joseph of Bavaria, King Friedrich August of Saxony, the Crown Prince of Sweden, Prince Kutuzov-Smolensky, Count Wittgenstein, Blücher and Moreau's widow, located in the Archives of the M.T.D. and the Ministry of Foreign Affairs [M.F.A.], as indicated in the footnotes and appendices.
21. Letters and dispatches by: Napoleon, King Friedrich August of Saxony, the Crown Prince of Sweden, Herzog Alexander von Württemberg, Prince Kutuzov, Barclay de Tolly, Count Wittgenstein, Bennigsen, Prince Volkonsky, Gneisenau, Toll, Opperman, Berthier, Yermolov, Count Platov, Yorck, Bülow, Dovré, Sacken, Scharnhorst, Moreau, comte Lauriston, Thielmann, Dörnberg, Wintzingerode, Reynier, Neverovsky, Rath, Kaptsevich, Stein, Graf Stackelberg, Pozzo di Borgo, Anstett, Count Nesselrode, Metternich, comte Otto, Baron Theil, and Caulaincourt.
22. Reports by unit commanders, for the most part located in the Log of Incoming Documents.
23. Dispositions: Blücher's prior to the battle on the Katzbach; Schwartzenberg's prior to the battle of Dresden on 14 (26) August; Barclay de Tolly's prior to the battle of Kulm on 18 (30) August; the Crown Prince of Sweden's prior to the

battle of Dennewitz; General Yorck's prior to the battle of Wartenburg; Prinz Schwartzenberg's prior to the battle of Leipzig.
24. The original instructions to Count Anstett and other documents relating to the Prague Congress held in the M.F.A.
25. Account of the activities of the Quartermaster's Department in the war against the French in 1812, 1813 and 1814, submitted to Emperor Alexander I by General Barclay de Tolly, dated 24 March [5 April], 1815.
26. Force strength returns (included in the minutes of the Archive of the M.T.D. No. 46,692).

Memoirs

1. *Extrait de mon journal militaire des campagnes 1812, 1813 et 1814. Par le prince Eugéne de Würtemberg*. War Diary of II Corps (manuscript) (*Журнал 2-го пехотного корпуса*) – Archive of the M.T.D. No. 47,344.
2. General Benckendorff's notes on the war of 1812 and 1813 (*Записки генерала Бенкендорфа о войне 1812 и 1813 годов*) – Archive of the M.T.D. No. 47,352.
3. Alexander Andreevich Shcherbinin's notes, who served in His Majesty's Suite in the Quartermaster's Department (General Staff) and served with General Toll.
4. Notes on operations by the Lifeguard Artillery in 1813, by V.F. Ratch.
5. *Anmerkungen*, most likely compiled in Barclay de Tolly's headquarters (manuscript) – Archive of the M.T.D. No. 47,353.
6. I.O. Sukhozanet's notes.
7. Balmain's notes, who served in Adjutant General Chernyshev's detachment during his expedition to Kassel.
8. Lishin's notes, commander of the guns in Chernyshev's detachment during his expedition to Kassel.
9. Wachten's notes on the retreat by Count Osterman's detachment to Kulm.
10. General Nikitin's notes.
11. Count Orlov-Denisov's notes on the fighting at Leipzig on 4 (16) October.
12. Yaroshevitsky's notes on the fighting at Leipzig.
13. Notes on operations by Markov's 23rd Horse Artillery Company.

Published Works

Books Containing A Complete Description Of The War Of 1813

It is quite remarkable that there is not a single good work about this war in French.

1. General Vaudoncourt, *Histoire de la guerre soutenue par les Français en Allemagne en 1813*, extremely biased.
2. Fain, *Manuscrit de 1813*, contains many fascinating details relating to Napoleon, but, unfortunately, all the facts set out in it are more or less dubious.

3. Compiled by Norvins, *Portefeuille de 1813*, is remarkable for the abundance of information extracted from official sources, but since this information itself is partly incorrect or incomplete, it is not entirely reliable.
4. Thiers, *Histoire du Consulat et de l'Empire*, volumes XV and XVI, there are many interesting facts relating to the war of 1813, but the description of this war is incomplete and incorrect.

The war of 1813 has been described by many German historians.

5. Bernhardi, *Denkwürdigkeiten des Grafen von Toll*, this is one of the best works, part of which relates to the war of 1813. It contains valuable details about the commanders of the Coalition armies, but the description of operations contained therein is very incomplete.
6. Beitzke, *Geschichte der deutschen Freiheitskriege in den Jahren 1813 und 1814*, the author has painted a picture of operations from this period with great skill and knowledge of the subject matter. Unfortunately, however, he is not always impartial, and an example of his erroneous assessments may be found in the conclusions of Volume 3, where he, forgetting about the services rendered to his fatherland by Emperor Alexander and the Russians, rants about the danger threatening Germany from Russia.
7. Plotho, *Der Krieg in Deutschland und Frankreich in den Jahren 1813 und 1814*, the author references a lot of official sources and presents events in a very detailed and impartial manner. His book is one of the best references for studying this period.
8. Schulz, *Geschichte der Kriege in Europa seit dem Jahre 1792*, volumes 10 and 11, based on the best available sources from the past 20 years, these volumes include a history of the war of 1813.

The works by Plotho and Schulz contain a wealth of data on force composition and strengths.

9. Richter, *Geschichte des deutschen Freiheitskrieges vom Jahre 1813 bis zum Jahre 1815*, this work, which was one of the first to appear, has a wealth of interesting details.
10. Sporschill, *Die grosse Chronik*, this work presents a very detailed description of the wars of 1813, 1814 and 1815, with sources indicated. In general, this work is remarkable, and if the author can be criticised for anything, it would be for his bias in favour of Schwarzenberg and the Austrians in general.
11. Förster, *Befreiungskriege, 1813, 1814, 1815*, contains interesting details about the main figures of this period and the participation of the German peoples in the war of 1813. Yet much of the information offered by the author is not worthy of attention and is subject to doubt, and in general his book may be considered more of a narrative than a history.

In addition, the following complete descriptions of the war of 1813 have been published.

12. Olvenstedt, *Geschichte deutschen Freiheitskampfes in den Jahren 1813, 1814 und 1815.*
13. W. Zimmermann, *Die Befreiungskämpfe der Deutschen gegen Napoleon.*

Both of them contain some interesting details about Europe's struggle with Napoleon.

14. Hofmann, *Zur Geschichte des Feldzuges von 1813*, one of the best descriptions of this war, written with impartiality and knowledge of the subject matter by one of its participants.
15. General Mikhailovsky-Danilevsky published two works on the same subject: Notes On The War Of 1813 and Description Of The War Of 1813 (*Записки о войне 1813 года* and *Описание войны 1813 года*). The former, as a contemporary account of the events described, has relatively greater merit than the second, which is very incomplete and often inconsistent with the facts. It may be said with certainty that General Danilevsky, having exaggerated the merits of some of the Russian personalities in this war beyond all measure, has given foreign historians grounds to deny undoubted feats of valour by our compatriots; moreover, the author omitted much that was accomplished by the Russians, probably due to a lack of resources that have more recently been unearthed.

Monographs

Of the many books, pamphlets and articles relating to the war of 1813, the most important ones are:

1. Carl von Weiß (Müffling). This author, one of the noteworthy personalities of the war of 1813, published:
a) *Betrachtungen über die grossen Operationen und Schlachten der Feldzüge von 1813 und 1814.*
b) *Zur Kriegsgeschichte der Jahre 1813 und 1814: Die Feldzüge der schlesischen Armee unter dem Felmarschall Blücher.*
c) *Napoleons Strategie im Jahr 1813.*
d) *Aus meinem Leben.*

Particularly important is the latter work, in which Müffling tries to present and explain many of the events of this war in a new light. As quartermaster general in Blücher's army, he together with the chief of staff, General Gneisenau, had a primary influence on operations by the Army of Silesia, and therefore had a great deal of knowledge and could identify the factors behind the most important events.

2. Lord Burghersh (11th Earl of Westmorland). Memoir of the Operations of the Allied Armies: Under Prince Schwarzenberg, and Marshal Blucher, During the Latter End of 1813, and the Year 1814. The author was posted as an attaché to the headquarters of the Coalition armies. The first two chapters of his book contain a brief overview of the later events of the war of 1813.
3. Gouvion Saint-Cyr, *Mémoires: Campagne de 1813 en Saxe*. An outstanding, though incomplete and somewhat biased account of operations by the French against the formations of the Army of Bohemia and Army of Poland.
4. Maréchal Marmont, *Mémoires*. Parts of these memoirs are devoted to describing the war of 1813.
5. Odeleben, *Relation circonstanciée de la campagne de 1813 en Saxe*.

The latter three works contain many details about Napoleon himself, his headquarters and the logistics elements of the French forces.

6. Wolzogen, *Memoiren*. These memoirs by one of the participants in the war of 1813 present some fascinating facts, but, according to contemporaries of that period, are not distinguished either by impartiality or honesty.
7. Friccius, *Geschichte des Krieges in den Jahren 1813 und 1814*. Eyewitness accounts of operations by the Prussian *Landwehr* and the Coalition Army of the North.
8. Wagner, *Plane der Schlachten und Treffen, welche von der preussischen Armee in den Feldzügen der Jahre 1813, 14 und 15 geliefert worden*. Very good maps with descriptions of the battles in which Prussian forces took part.
9. Weinhold, *Dresden und seine Schicksale, im Jahr 1813*. A work by the physician Weinhold, published in 1814 and dedicated to the Governor-General of the Kingdom of Saxony, Prince Repnin, contains many details about the occupation of Dresden by Napoleon and his troops, as well as operations by both sides in the vicinity of this city.
10. Franz von Dressler von Scharfenstein, *Napoleon in Dresden* and *Tagebuch der Begebenheiten in Dresden vom 13-ten bis 27-ten März 1813*. These pamphlets, published in 1814, are not distinguished by impartiality, but may give an approximate idea of the disorderly state of the logistics elements of the French forces.
11. Various, *Actenstücke und Materialen zu der Geschichte des grossen Kampfes um die Freiheit Europa's in den Jahren 1812 und 1813*. This anthology, which appeared in 1813 and 1814, contains official and personal accounts of some of the military events of 1813.
12. General D.P. Buturlin, Depiction of the Autumn Campaign of 1813 in Germany, after the armistice (*Картина осенняго похода 1813 года в Германии, после перемирия*). Contains a very brief description of events from the resumption of hostilities in August 1813 to the Coalition arrival on the Rhine.
13. Aster, *Schilderung der Kriegsereignisse in und vor Dresden, vom 7 März bis 28 August 1813*.
14. Aster, *Die Kriegsereignisse zwischen Peterswalde, Pirna, Königstein und Priesten, im August 1813, und die Schlacht bei Kulm*.
15. Aster, *Die Gefechte und Schlachten bei Leipzig im Oktober 1813*.

All three of these works by Aster are distinguished by their completeness and thorough discussion of the facts. In addition, very good maps are included with them.

16. Helldorff, *Zur Geschichte der Schlacht bei Kulm*. A very good description of the events leading up to the Battle of Kulm and of the battle itself.
17. Berneck, *Die Schlachten bei Leipzig*. A brief but fairly clear and distinct description of the battle of Leipzig.
18. Pelet, *Des principales opérations de la campagne de 1813*. Published in the *Spectateur militaire* and containing a description of the most important battles, in relation to operations by French forces.
19. *Die Feldzüge der Sachsen* [Cerrini?].
20. Von Völderndorff and Waradein, *Kriegsgeschichte von Bayern*.
21. [Kösterus], *Die Grossherzoglich Hessischen Truppen in dem Feldzuge von 1813*.
22. [an eyewitness], *Mémoire sur les opérations de l'avantgarde du huitième corps* and *Journal historique de la 7-me division de cavalerie légère polonaise*.

These last two works are somewhat biased.

23. *Geschichte des Corps von Walmoden*. Description of operations by Wallmoden's corps, published in several issues of the periodical: *Oestereichische Militärische Zeitschrift, 1827*.

In addition, one can find descriptions of battles and other episodes from the war of 1813, both in the above-mentioned journal and in the following: *Militair Wochenblatt*; *Zeitschrift für Kunst und Geschichte des Krieges*, also even in the periodicals: *Denkwürdigkeiten für die Kriegskunst* and in the Russian Military Journal published by the headquarters of the Lifeguard Corps (*Военном Журнале издававшемся при штабе Гвардейского Корпуса*).

24. Specht, *Das Königreich Westphalen und seine Armee im Jahr 1813*. This work contains:
    a) A description of the kingdom and Westphalian forces.
    b) A detailed description of the expedition by Adjutant General Chernyshev to Kassel and the dissolution of the Kingdom of Westphalia.
25. Colomb, *Aus dem Tagebuche des Rittmeisters von Colomb*. A description of the expeditions by this famous partisan, compiled by the man himself.
26. Löwenstern, *Denkwürdigkeiten eines Livländers*. Diary of the partisan Löwenstern.
27. The occupation of Dresden in 1813 by Russian forces (*Занятие Дрездена в 1813 году русскими войсками*). This article was published in Part 1 of the works of D.V. Davydov.
28. Varnhagen von Ense, *Biographische Denkmale*. Very well compiled biographies of Blücher and other Prussian military commanders.
29. Droysen, *Das Leben des Feldmarschalls Grafen Yorck von Wartenburg*. A biography of Yorck, which contains, in addition to facts relating to his activities, a very clear account of the political and military events in which he took part.

30. [Helldorff?], *Memoiren des Herzogs Eugen von Württemberg*. The biography of this remarkable commander contains a brief description of the campaigns in which he participated.
31. Lecomte, *Le général Jomini: sa vie et ses écrits*. This work, in addition to details relating to General Jomini and his military-scientific activities, contains many interesting observations on operations during 1813.
32. Minutoli, *Beiträge zu einer künftigen Biographie Friedrich Wilhelms III*. An account of the character and achievements of King Friedrich Wilhelm III and the main Prussian military commanders and statesmen of his time.
33. [Mikhailovsky-Danilevsky], Emperor Alexander I and his associates in 1812, 1813, 1814 and 1815 (*Император Александр I и Его сподвижники в 1812, 1813, 1814 и 1815 годах*).
34. Comte de Garden, *Histoire générale des traités de paix*. The final published volume of this work, XIV, contains an explanation of diplomatic relations in 1813 until the armistice concluded in Pläswitz.
35. Allonville, *Mémoires Tirés des Papiers d'un Homme d'état*. Volume XII contains the history of diplomatic relations in 1813 and 1814.
36. [Hormayr], *Lebensbilder aus dem Befreiungskriege*. A collection of documents relating to the period of Napoleon's dominance of Europe.
37. Pertz, *Das Leben des Ministers, Freiherrn vom Stein*. An account of the achievements of this famous man, enriched with a multitude of documents relating to his political activities.
38. Baron Steinheil, notes concerning the preparations and campaigns of the St. Petersburg *Opolchenie* against the enemies of the fatherland in 1812 and 1813 (*Записки касательно составления и самого похода Св Петербургского Ополчения против врагов отечества, в 1812 и 1813 годах*), and so on, with a detailed description of the siege and capture of Danzig.

Index

Abele von und zu Lilienberg, Franz; 198, 205-206, 210, 266, 411, 416.
Aberdeen, George Hamilton-Gordon, Earl of; 479.
Adelsdorf [Zagrodno]; 26-27, 37.
Adlercreutz, Carl Johan; 75, 322, 407.
Agerbach river; 226, 228-229, 231, 233-234.
Ahrensdorf; 80, 85.
Aken; 262, 293, 312-313, 321, 323, 332-333, 337, 360.
Allix de Vaux, Jacques-Alexandre; 295-299.
Altenberg; 108, 110, 169-170, 172, 176-177, 182, 190, 214, 216, 242, 247-248, 250, 278, 284.
Altenburg; 14, 286-288, 339-342, 344, 348, 350, 368, 457, 522.
Altona (Dresden); 124, 133, 135.
Amsterdam; 497-499.
Annaberg; 338.
Anstett, Ivan Osipovich; 443, 524-525.
Antwerp; 499.
Arbesau [Varvažov]; 206-211, 213, 215, 256.
Arentschildt, Wilhelm Daniel von; 97.
Arnoldi, Ivan Karlovich; 234, 421, 445.
Arrighi, Jean-Thomas (duc de Padoue); 74, 77, 80, 82, 86, 222, 229, 235, 312, 321, 334, 377, 388, 402, 422, 437, 469.
Artern; 451, 455, 462.
Aschaffenburg; 300, 465-467, 474.
Audigast; 348, 366, 368, 447.
Auenhain; 345, 376, 378-381, 383-386.
Augereau, Charles-Pierre; 335-336, 339-340, 342, 344, 355, 365, 372, 376-378, 382, 386, 388, 411, 413, 426, 436, 440, 456, 471.
Auschina [Úžín]; 206-207, 209.
Aussig [Ústí nad Labem]; 108, 169, 177-178, 182, 188, 215, 217, 242, 247, 254, 256, 261, 276, 337, 350-351.

Austrian Corps;
  I. Korpus; 256, 263, 341, 350, 368, 418, 461; *II. Korpus*; 256, 264, 337, 342, 344, 348, 367-369, 385, 389, 461, 475; *III. Korpus*; 256, 265, 339, 342, 344, 348, 367, 369, 389, 446, 451, 461, 475; *IV. Korpus*; 265, 339, 345, 347, 369, 389, 461, 504.
Austrian Divisions;
  1. leichte Division; 119, 121, 123, 168, 170, 216, 248, 263, 348, 367, 369, 385, 389, 430, 446-447, 452, 461; *2. leichte Division*; 24, 263, 277, 351-352, 411, 424, 431, 436, 446, 461; *3. leichte Division*; 109, 124, 129, 411.

Baalsdorf; 373, 413-416.
Baden Armed Forces; 114, 403, 416, 437, 440, 445, 482-483.
Baden, Karl Ludwig von; 483.
Baden, Wilhelm Ludwig von; 440, 445.
Bagration, Roman Ivanovich; 268, 350.
Baikov, Ivan Ivanovich; 184, 186-187, 197.
Balabin, Stepan Fëdorovich; 498-499.
Balmain, Alexander Antonovich de; 293, 297-298, 525.
Barclay de Tolly, Michael Andreas or Mikhail Bogdanovich; 9-12, 17, 24, 108, 113, 115, 134, 141-142, 152-153, 157, 167-168, 171, 176, 187-188, 201-202, 204-206, 213, 216, 219, 247, 250, 252, 254, 277, 280, 348, 367-369, 380, 390, 414, 417-418, 437, 446-447, 455, 458, 461, 474-475, 481, 521, 524-525.
Barrois, Pierre; 123, 127, 133-135, 146, 148, 150, 216.
Baruth; 75-76, 86.
Bastineller, Westphalian general; 292-295, 297.

531

Bautzen; 24, 116, 118-119, 121, 123, 128, 244, 247, 252-253, 259-261, 274, 277-278, 308-311, 313; Battle of; 13, 75, 520-521.
Bavarian Armed Forces; 233, 333, 337, 445, 456, 460, 464-475, 482, 488-489.
Baykov, Ivan Ivanovich; 140-141.
Beaumont, Marc-Antoine de; 315, 317.
Beck, August von; 411, 426.
Bedryaga, Yegor Ivanovich; 294, 299.
Beelitz; 76, 78, 86.
Belgium; 476, 499-500.
Bellwitzhof Manor; 45, 47, 51.
Belzig; 71, 92-96, 100.
Benckendorff, Konstantin Alexander von; 70, 497-500, 525.
Benckendorff, Konstantin Friedrich von; 292, 294-295, 297-298, 445.
Benken; 92-93, 103.
Bennnigsen, Levin von; 34, 163, 241, 243, 250, 258-259, 261, 268, 272, 275-276, 278-279, 281-285, 308, 332, 337, 341, 350-352, 368-369, 386, 403, 414-417, 422-425, 428-429, 438, 440-441, 446, 449, 451, 458-459, 490, 496, 503, 506, 508, 524.
Berckheim, Sigismond-Frédéric de; 245, 379.
Bergen; 469-471, 474.
Berggießhübel; 110-111, 117, 140-141, 159, 168-169, 171-175, 187, 196, 251, 254, 258, 350.
Berlin; 70-71, 74, 76-78, 80-81, 83, 87-88, 91, 97, 161, 169, 216, 223-225, 244, 262, 276, 298, 302, 312, 323, 331-333, 349, 351, 357, 360-361, 443, 474, 508.
Bernadotte, Jean-Baptiste Jules, Crown Prince of Sweden; 17, 69-71, 74-76, 78, 81, 83, 86, 97, 115, 163, 212, 216, 224-226, 228, 232-234, 236, 242-243, 247, 257, 259, 262, 274-279, 281-283, 285, 287, 292, 299-300, 309-313, 320-324, 328-331, 333, 335, 339, 341, 348-349, 352, 360, 366, 401, 403, 407, 414, 416, 419-422, 425, 427, 429, 439, 441, 451, 459, 490-496, 506, 521, 524.
Bernburg; 262, 293, 300, 323.
Berthezène, Pierre; 114, 133, 135, 505.
Berthier, Louis-Alexandre (prince de Neuchâtel et de Wagram); 41, 160, 177, 216, 257, 334, 337, 353, 357, 407, 419, 431, 441-442, 479, 524.
Bertrand, Antoine-Joseph; 445.
Bertrand, Henri-Gatien; 74-77, 80-81, 136, 222, 224-230, 233, 235, 312-313, 316, 329,
336-337, 365, 377, 384, 386, 388, 407, 413, 418, 431, 447, 450-453, 456, 458, 469, 471-472, 474.
Bianchi, (Vincenz Ferrer) Friedrich von; 109, 115, 119, 123, 124, 129, 133, 136, 138, 146, 148, 157, 183, 190, 198, 203-205, 210, 215, 218-219, 266, 368, 382-383, 389, 411, 418, 426, 461.
Bischofswerda; 244, 259-260.
Bismarck, Friedrich Adolf von; 93-94, 102-103.
Bistrom 1st, Karl Ivanovich; 174, 184-185, 196, 200.
Bistrom 2nd, Adam Ivanovich; 400, 440.
Bistrom, Anton Antonovich; 184, 186-187, 197, 390.
Blankenfelde; 78, 80-81.
Blasewitz; 119-120, 129, 147, 149, 151.
Bleddin; 313, 315-317, 319, 321.
Blücher, Franz Ferdinand Joachim von; 190, 204, 206, 218, 255.
Blücher, Gebhard Leberecht von; 16-19, 22-29, 32-38, 40-43, 45, 47, 49-53, 55-57, 59, 61-63, 65-67, 76, 110, 115, 163, 212, 241-244, 246-248, 252-253, 257-261, 274-286, 308-313, 316, 318, 320-324, 328-333, 335-336, 338, 341, 344, 348-349, 351, 353-355, 360-361, 366, 369, 375, 384-386, 393-395, 400-403, 407, 414, 420, 422, 427, 439, 441, 446, 448-449, 453-454, 459, 467, 475-477, 482, 517, 521, 524, 527-529.
Bober river [Bóbr]; 19, 22-26, 29, 56, 59-61, 68, 116, 261, 275.
Boguslawski, Carl Anton von; 93-94, 102-103.
Böhmisch Kamnitz [Česká Kamenice]; 247-248, 275, 277.
Böhmisch Leipa [Česká Lípa]; 248, 274, 277, 283, 309.
Böhmisch Mittelgebirge [České středohoří]; 251, 254, 258, 338.
Böhmisch-Neudörfel [Český Újezd]; 183, 204-206.
Boizenburg; 98, 302-304, 306, 491.
Bonet, Jean-Pierre; 350, 505.
Borcke, Karl August von; 48, 51.
Bordesoulle, Étienne Tardif de Pommeroux de; 154, 378, 380-381, 426, 456.
Borna; 110, 174, 247-248, 251, 258, 340-342, 344, 350-351, 368, 375, 386.
Bornstädt, Prussian Major; 94, 102-104.

INDEX 533

Borstell, Karl Leopold von; 71, 76, 81, 83-85, 89, 222, 224-226, 232-235, 411, 422, 428, 438-439, 497, 500.
Bose, Karl August von; 82, 445.
Brandenburg; 71, 75-76, 78, 91-92, 323.
Braunschweig; 249, 289-290, 296, 300, 490.
Braunschweig, Friedrich Wilhelm von; 287.
Brause, Friedrich August von; 85, 230, 421, 424.
Brechelshof [Brachów]; 43, 45, 47, 55, 65.
Breda; 499-500.
Breitenau; 108, 251, 254, 350.
Breitenfeld; 354, 365, 392, 394-396, 403, 407, 414, 421.
Bremen; 220, 306-307, 483, 497.
Breslau [Wrocław]; 8, 18-19, 56, 163, 243, 261.
Broglie-Revel, Charles-François-Ladislas de; 174.
Bromberg [Bydgoszcz]; 8.
Bruchköbelerwald; 467-468.
Brüx [Most]; 108-109, 111, 152, 170, 250, 254, 258, 338.
Bubna und Littitz, Ferdinand von; 24, 74, 242-243, 252-253, 256, 259, 263, 274, 277, 283, 309, 313, 341, 351-352, 369, 403, 411, 415, 417, 423-424, 428-429, 431, 436, 475, 503.
Budin [Budyně nad Ohří]; 16, 108, 110, 170, 274, 284.
Bulatov, Mikhail Leontievich; 268, 351.
Bülow, Friedrich Wilhelm von; 70-71, 74-78, 81, 83-86, 89, 225-234, 236, 239, 262, 311-313, 321-322, 331, 411, 421, 423, 428-430, 438-440, 442, 490, 496-500, 524.
Bunzlau [Bolesławiec]; 19, 22-26, 42, 45, 58-61, 243.
Burgstädtel; 124, 148, 155.
Buschmühle [Bogaczów]; 45, 53.
Buttelstedt; 451, 454-455, 461.
Bykhalov, Vasily Andreevich; 236, 239.

Cancrin, Georg Ludwig Daniel; 9.
Cardell, Carl von; 84, 234, 429.
Caulaincourt, Armand-Augustin de; 329-330, 353, 469, 479, 524.
Chambure, Laurent-Augustin de; 512, 514.
Chaplits [Czaplic], Yefim Ignatievich ; 415-416, 424-425, 459, 462.
Charpentier, Henri; 46, 373, 386, 416, 445, 469, 498.

Chasteler de Courcelles, (Johann) Gabriel; 109, 112, 115, 119, 121, 123-124, 129-130, 132-133, 138, 146, 148, 157, 190, 215, 504, 506.
Chemnitz; 108-109, 277, 279-280, 282, 286-288, 339-341, 368.
Cheremisinov, Yakov Yakovlevich; 184, 186-187.
Chernyshev, Alexander Ivanovich; 70-71, 78, 92, 94-96, 105, 225, 262, 289, 292-298, 300-301, 306, 446, 451, 466, 470, 472, 474, 497-498, 525, 529.
Chiesa, Franz von; 209-210, 212.
Christiani, Charles-Joseph; 424, 427.
Christianshöhe Manor; 47, 49-50.
Civalart d'Happoncourt, Karl Leopold; 109, 115, 118, 138, 146, 148, 157, 216, 267.
Claparède, Michel-Marie; 110, 114, 505.
Coehorn, Louis-Jacques de; 393, 430.
Colloredo-Mansfeld, Hieronymus Karl von; 109, 112, 115, 119, 120-121, 123, 129-130, 132, 135, 138, 146, 148, 157, 183, 190, 198, 203-206, 209, 215, 218-219, 242, 248, 254, 256, 263, 341, 350-352, 368-369, 386, 403, 414, 418, 427, 431, 437-438, 461.
Colmberg; 373-374, 378, 382, 384, 386, 403, 416.
Colomb, Friedrich August von; 258, 288, 500, 529.
Compans, Jean-Dominique; 216, 390, 396-397, 400, 430, 445.
Confédération du Rhin; 74, 249, 290, 405, 407, 426, 448, 479-480, 482-483, 516.
Connewitz; 343, 365, 366, 368-370, 374-376, 380, 385-386, 389, 413, 426-427, 431, 449.
Corbineau, Jean-Baptiste; 125, 176-177, 180, 185, 198, 202, 206, 208-210, 216.
Cotta; 111, 113, 124, 129, 133, 136, 139, 141, 159, 172-173, 196, 251.
Crenneville-Poutet, Ludwig Karl de; 109, 115, 124, 129, 133, 157, 176, 265, 385, 389.
Creutzer, Charles-Auguste; 188, 202, 215, 256-257.
Cröbern; 344-345, 347, 369, 372, 375-376, 378-379, 382-383, 385, 418.
Crottendorf; 424, 429, 431.
Csollich, Markus; 135-136, 265, 385.
Curial, Philibert-Jean-Baptiste; 127, 216, 365, 377, 386, 456, 470.

Dąbrowski, Jan Henryk; 223, 321, 329, 337, 365, 388, 390, 393-394, 396, 399-400, 402, 413-414, 422, 435.
Dahme; 76, 226, 235.
Dalberg, Karl Theodor von und zu; 300, 480.
Dalichow; 225, 232.
Danish Armed Forces; 69, 97, 100, 106, 302, 311, 490-492, 494-496.
Dannenberg; 303, 306.
Danzig [Gdańsk]; 10-11, 404, 501-502, 510-513, 516, 518-519, 524, 530.
Darmstadt; 475, 483.
Davout, Louis-Nicholas (duc d'Auerstaedt, prince d'Eckmühl); 70, 74, 97-100, 106, 241, 302-304, 306, 311, 333, 336, 456, 490-492, 496, 504, 521.
Davydov, Yevgraf Vladimirovich; 379.
Decaen, Charles-Mathieu; 499.
Decouz, Pierre; 123, 126, 130, 133-134, 146, 148-150, 426.
Defrance, Jean-Marie; 227, 230, 329, 365, 377, 411, 451.
Delitzsch; 321-322, 336-337, 349, 354.
Delmas, Antoine-Guillaume; 354, 366, 390, 393, 399, 429, 445.
Den Haag (the Hague); 497, 499.
Dennewitz; 70, 222, 224-230, 233, 235-236, 238-239, 241-242, 248, 251-252, 278-279, 281, 289, 311, 316, 419, 521, 525.
Depreradovich, Nikolai Ivanovich; 203, 390.
Dessau; 312-313, 321-322, 332, 337, 360-361.
Deutsch-Neudörfel [Děलouš]; 205-206.
Deventer; 496-498.
Diebitsch und Narten, Hans Karl Friedrich Anton von; 17, 149, 187, 213, 345, 367, 446.
Diemar, Karl von; 469-470, 489.
Dietrich, Andrey Bogdanovich; 60.
Dietrichs, Russian artillery colonel; 84, 89, 222, 229, 233, 236, 239, 371, 411, 428-429, 445.
Dippoldiswalde; 108, 110, 112-113, 115-116, 118, 123, 128, 138, 148, 153, 156-157, 168-169, 176, 190, 242, 338, 341, 350-351.
Dippoldiswalder Schlag (Dresden); 127, 132-133, 137.
Dobritz; 115, 150-151.
Dobschütz, Leopold Wilhelm von; 70-71, 76, 224, 262, 508-510.
Dohna; 108, 110-111, 129, 138, 150, 157, 169, 172, 196, 248, 250, 351.

Dohnaer Schlag (Dresden); 114, 131-132, 135, 137.
Dohnau [Dunino]; 28, 52, 65.
Dokhturov, Dmitry Sergeevich; 269, 350, 352, 386, 416, 424, 459, 462.
Dölitz; 355, 376, 382-384, 386, 413-414, 418, 426-427, 431, 437.
Dölzschen; 124, 148, 155.
Dömitz; 98, 100, 300, 303, 306.
Dordrecht; 497-499.
Dörnberg, partisan major; 293, 298-299.
Dörnberg, Wilhelm Caspar von; 70, 97-99, 304-305, 492-494, 524.
Dösen; 365, 376, 386, 414, 418, 426-427, 431.
Doucet, Pierre; 188, 198, 202, 207.
Doumerc, Jean-Pierre; 123, 134, 154.
Drescherhäuser; 136, 154.
Dresden Altstadt; 113, 127, 133, 137, 148.
Drouot, Antoine; 251, 378, 381, 469.
Düben; 318, 321-322, 329-330, 332-333, 335-337, 341, 349, 353-354, 357, 393, 395, 399.
Dubreton, Jean-Louis; 154-155, 469.
Duka, Ilya Mikhailovich; 203, 376, 379, 390, 445.
Dulauloy, Charles-François; 160, 442, 456.
Dumas, Mathieu; 503-505.
Dumonceau de Bergendal, Jean-Baptiste; 125, 188, 209, 254, 505.
Dumoustier, Pierre; 123, 127, 133, 135-136, 146, 148, 150, 216.
Dunesme, Martin-François; 188, 198, 202, 205-209, 212.
Durosnel, Antoine-Jean-Auguste; 116, 503, 505.
Dürrenberg; 173-175.
Durutte, Pierre; 77, 82, 85, 222, 228-230, 233, 237, 411, 413, 417, 423-424, 428, 435, 440.
Düsseldorf; 476, 497, 499.
Dutch Armed Forces; 98, 114, 499-500, 507
Dux [Duchcov]; 108, 153, 168, 182-183, 190, 205, 215, 219, 254, 256, 258.

Ebersdorf [Habartice]; 250, 254-255.
Eckartsberga; 451-452, 454-455, 461.
Eckmannsdorf; 225, 228, 232.
Eger [Cheb]; 109, 275.
Eger river [Ohře]; 24, 108, 110-111, 161, 170-171, 183, 258, 273-274, 276, 282, 284, 328, 338.

INDEX 535

Eichholz [Warmątowice Sienkiewiczowskie]; 45, 47-48, 52, 62, 66-67.
Eichwald; 157, 215-216.
Eider river/canal; 492-494.
Eilenburg; 312, 321-322, 329, 336-337, 353, 415, 419.
Einsiedel, Detlev von; 436-437.
Eisenach; 454, 456, 458-459.
Eisernes Kreuz [Iron Cross]; 62, 189.
Elster river; 311, 337, 344, 348, 355, 364, 366, 369, 374-376, 378, 385, 394-395, 400-402, 407, 414, 430-431, 435-436, 441-443, 445-448
Elster (village); 262, 310-313, 332-333, 351
Elsterwerda; 259, 278, 310.
Emmanuel, Georgi (Yegor) Arsenievich; 19, 23, 32, 54, 58, 60, 245, 260, 320, 390, 396, 400, 411, 415, 420-421, 442.
Engelhardt manor (Dresden); 121, 130, 133-134.
Erfurt; 334, 349, 447, 450-451, 454-456, 458-459, 501, 510, 517.
Espenhain; 342-343, 347.
Eutritzsch; 354, 365, 393, 396, 400-402, 408, 414, 422, 427.
Exelmans, Rémy-Joseph; 469-470.

Fain, Agathon-Jean-François; 169, 216, 525.
Falkenhain; 108, 247.
Falkenschlag (Dresden); 114, 127, 133, 135, 148.
Feldschlößchen; 124, 135.
Ferchland; 289, 300, 323.
Figner, Alexander Samoilovich; 252, 301.
Flensberg (Silesia); 27, 29, 32.
Flöha river; 170, 216, 339.
Fontanelli, Achille; 77, 227, 313, 319, 471.
Fournier-Sarlovèze, François-Louis; 85, 227, 329, 354, 365, 411, 456.
Frankfurt am Main; 465-466, 471-476, 478, 480-481.
Frankfurt an der Oder; 163.
Franquemont, Frédéric de; 227, 313, 316-318, 456.
Franz I, Austrian Kaiser; 62, 111, 113, 115, 190, 236, 348, 375, 381, 386, 406, 441, 443, 446, 461, 474-475, 485, 505.
Frauenstein; 108, 258, 284.
Freiberg; 108-109, 111-113, 115, 120, 124, 138, 155-157, 168-169, 176, 216, 248, 253, 258, 274-275, 282-284, 292, 329, 338-339, 341, 351.

Freiberger Schlag (Dresden); 114, 118, 127, 133, 154.
French Corps;
 1er corps de cavalerie; 25, 28, 127, 154, 176, 321, 329, 354, 365, 376-378, 386, 388, 411, 413, 431, 451, 469; *2e Corps*; 118, 125, 137, 146, 148, 154, 176, 244, 248, 250, 257, 329, 338, 343, 359, 365, 377-378, 383, 386, 388, 411, 413, 425, 456, 469, 472; *2e corps de cavalerie*; 28, 64, 329, 354, 365, 377-378, 388, 411, 413, 424-425; *3e Corps*; 25, 28, 34, 43, 45-47, 52-53, 58, 64, 247, 329, 332, 354, 365-366, 377, 388, 390, 393, 399, 411, 413, 420, 429, 435, 456, 471, 473; *3e corps de cavalerie*; 74, 329, 377, 388, 402, 413, 431, 451, 469; *4e Corps*; 71-74, 76-77, 222, 225-226, 235, 237, 242, 329, 354, 365, 377, 384, 386, 388, 413, 431, 447, 451, 456, 471, 473; *4e corps de cavalerie*; 339, 344, 359, 365, 372, 386, 388, 411, 413; *5e Corps*; 25, 28, 30, 34, 43, 45-47, 64, 247, 321, 329, 338, 359, 365, 378, 386, 388, 411, 413, 425; *5e corps de cavalerie*; 321, 339, 344, 346, 359, 365, 377-378, 386, 388, 411, 413, 431, 451; *6e Corps*; 25, 28, 137, 146, 148, 176, 215, 250, 321, 329, 344, 354, 365, 377, 388, 390, 392-393, 400, 411, 413, 428, 430, 435, 456, 471, 473; *7e Corps*; 71, 76-77, 82, 86, 222, 225-226, 228, 230, 235, 237, 242, 329, 332, 354, 366, 387, 402, 407, 411, 413, 417, 419, 451; *8e Corps*; 247, 329, 338, 343, 359, 365, 376, 386, 388, 411, 413, 435; *9e Corps*; 456; *11e Corps*; 22, 25, 28, 30, 34, 43, 45-47, 52, 59, 64, 247, 329, 354, 365, 378, 386, 388, 411, 413, 435, 443, 456, 466, 469, 472; *12e Corps*; 71, 76-77, 80, 82, 222, 225-226, 229, 231-233, 235, 237; *13e Corps*; 97; *14e Corps*; 110, 125, 136-137, 146, 148, 190, 244, 248, 250, 329, 338, 350, 502; *Garde impériale*; 24-26, 28, 117, 126-128, 130, 133-137, 146, 148-150, 153, 157, 160, 169-170, 172, 176, 216, 223, 242, 244, 247-248, 250-251, 255-256, 260, 287, 329, 332, 336, 353-354, 357, 360-361, 365, 376-378, 381-384, 386-388, 396, 411, 413-414, 417-419, 422, 424, 426-427, 432, 447, 450-451, 455-456, 466, 469-473, 499.

French Divisions;
- *42e Division*; 110-111, 125, 177, 185, 188, 350, 352; *43e Division*; 110, 114, 350; *44e Division*; 110, 114, 126, 135, 350; *45e Division*; 110, 114, 350, 352;

Fresnel et Curel, Johann Karl de; 464, 472, 474, 489.
Freyburg; 407, 430, 447, 450-455, 461-462.
Friant, Louis; 127, 365, 377, 386, 456.
Friedberg; 467, 469, 475.
Friederichs, Jean-Parfait; 390, 400, 430, 445.
Friedrich I, King of Württemberg; 465, 479, 483.
Friedrich August, King of Saxony; 117-118, 238, 329, 353, 382, 423, 432, 435-437, 441, 443, 524.
Friedrichstadt (Dresden); 114, 119, 127, 133-134, 136, 137, 148.
Friedrichstadt (Schleswig); 493-495.
Friedrichsort; 493-495.
Frohburg; 338, 340, 342.
Fuchshain; 343, 347-348, 374, 386, 403.
Fulda; 459, 465, 474-475, 479; river; 294-297.
Fürstenwalde; 108, 183, 190-191, 250-251, 257.

Gabel [Jablonné v Podještědí]; 24, 245, 248, 275, 277, 281, 284, 309.
Gablenz, Heinrich Adolf von; 82.
Gadebusch; 71, 100, 303.
Gaschwitz; 375-376.
Gatterburg, Karl Josef von; 447, 451.
Gaudi, Friedrich von; 26, 34.
Gautzsch; 348, 375, 382, 419, 438.
Geiersburg [Kyšperk]; 108, 110, 157, 168, 182, 191-192, 202, 204, 250, 252, 254-255, 257.
Gelnhausen; 465-469, 473.
Gérard, Étienne; 30, 46, 386, 416.
Gérard, François; 505.
Gerbertor (Leipzig); 435-436, 439.
Gersdorff, Karl Friedrich von; 116, 128, 160-161, 445.
Girard, Jean-Baptiste; 74, 77, 91-97, 100, 105, 302.
Gittersee; 138, 148, 155, 503.
Glashütte; 118, 190-191, 215-216.
Glien; 93, 95-96, 103-104.
Globig; 313, 315, 317-319.
Glogau [Głogów]; 65, 70, 501-502, 517, 523.
Glückstadt; 492, 494-495.

Gneisenau, August Wilhelm Anton Neidhardt von; 18, 42, 55-56, 281-282, 323, 446, 476-477, 482, 524, 527.
Gobrecht, Martin Charles; 125, 176, 185, 187, 198, 202, 206.
Gohlis; 400-402, 414, 422, 427, 431, 435.
Göhrde; 303-304, 306, 522.
Göhren; 345, 375, 378-379.
Goldberg [Złotoryja]; 19, 22, 27-34, 37, 42-43, 46-47, 54, 56-58, 65.
Golenishchev-Kutuzov, Mikhail Illarionovich; 477, 523-524.
Golitsyn 5th, Dmitry Vladimirovich; 151-152, 203, 369.
Gölsdorf; 226, 229-234, 237.
Goltz, Alexander von der; 305, 322, 324, 400.
Goltz, Ferdinand von der; 27-29, 31-33.
Göppersdorf; 108, 110, 174-175, 350.
Gorbitz; 133, 148, 154-155.
Gorchakov, Andrei Ivanovich; 147, 247, 254, 343, 345, 347, 369, 372, 374, 376, 378, 384, 389, 411, 417, 446, 458.
Gorinchem; 498-499.
Görlitz; 24, 29, 41, 115-116, 242-246, 252-253, 276, 325.
Göselbach stream; 342, 345, 382.
Gossa [Güldengossa]; 342-345, 347-348, 369-371, 375-382, 384-386, 407, 417, 448, 521.
Gostritz; 147, 170, 352.
Gotha; 455-456, 458-459.
Göttingen; 292, 296, 300, 462, 483, 490, 496-497.
Gottleuba river; 140, 142, 158-159, 173.
Gourgaud, Gaspard; 116-117, 343.
Graham, Thomas; 499-500.
Grandeau, Louis-Joseph; 506-507.
Grassdorf; 414, 421-422.
Graupen [Krupka]; 182, 190-191, 250, 257.
Greiffenberg [Gryfów Śląski]; 56.
Greth, Carl Joseph von; 123-124, 129, 264, 411, 427.
Grevesmühlen; 98-100.
Grimma; 336, 368, 386, 434-435.
Grimmaisches Tor (Leipzig); 353-354, 434-436, 438, 440-441.
Grimmer von Risenburg, Anton; 136, 265.
Gröditzberg [Burg Grodziec]; 22-23, 26, 37.
Grodno; 12, 508.
Grolman, Karl Wilhelm; 168, 191, 208.

Grolman, Wilhelm Heinrich von; 96.
Gros, Jean-Louis; 123, 135.
Großbeeren; 57, 70, 78-85, 87, 91, 100, 103, 105, 116, 212, 216, 223-224, 242, 287, 311, 521.
Großenhain; 251, 259-260, 262, 310, 504.
Großer Garten (Dresden); 112, 114, 117, 119-121, 129-132, 134-135, 137, 148-150.
Großpösna; 343, 369, 373-374, 386.
Gruna (Dresden); 115, 117, 129, 134, 138, 147, 149-150, 152, 351.
Gruna [Gronów]; 246.
Gruna (Leipzig); 375.
Grünewiese; 129, 134-135, 147, 149-150.
Guilleminot, Armand-Charles; 85, 231-232, 407, 451, 471, 474.
Güldengossa, See Gossa.
Gyulay von Maros-Németh und Nádaska, Ignác (Ignaz); 109, 124, 129-130, 133, 136, 138, 242, 248, 256, 265, 338-339, 341, 342, 344, 348-349, 367, 377, 384-385, 389, 414-415, 418, 422, 430-431, 446-447, 451-452, 454-455, 461, 475.

Hagelberg; 91, 94-96, 302.
Hagenow; 98-99.
Halle; 70, 300, 331, 340, 344, 349, 356, 360-361, 377, 392-393, 401, 427, 435, 446, 451, 459, 506.
Hallisches Tor (Leipzig); 353, 402, 404, 422, 427, 434-436, 439.
Hamburg; 69-70, 74, 97, 106, 220, 304, 490-493, 496, 501, 504, 506, 517.
Hanau; 459, 465-475.
Hanover; 289, 300, 405, 476, 490-491, 495-496.
Hanoverian Armed Forces; 97-98, 296, 305, 457, 483.
Hanseatische Legion; 97-98, 302, 494.
Harburg; 306, 491, 506.
Hardegg, Ignaz; 267, 350-351, 411, 446.
Hardenberg, Karl August von; 457, 478, 482.
Hausdorf; 176, 183, 190, 243.
Haxo, François-Nicolas; 117, 212.
Haynau [Chojnów]; 19, 22, 43, 47, 56-58, 65.
Heidenau; 248, 351.
Heiligenstadt; 292-294, 459, 462, 490, 506.
Heimrod, Friedrich von; 206, 212.
Heinersdorf; 77, 81-82, 86-87, 89.
Heiterblick; 402, 413, 419-421.

Helffreich 1st, Gotthard August von; 111-113, 139-142, 159, 172, 174-175, 177-179, 181, 184-185, 189, 196, 202, 218, 345, 347, 371-372, 382, 389.
Hellendorf; 168, 172-177, 197, 204, 247, 250-251, 254-255, 350.
Henckel von Donnersmarck, Wilhelm Ludwig; 452-453.
Hennersdorf [Chroślice]; 32-33, 42-43, 45-48, 53-55.
Hennersdorf (Dippoldiswalde); 111.
Herrmannsdorf [Męcinka]; 48, 53-54.
Herzberg; 76, 235, 312.
Herzogenberg, August von; 136, 265.
Hessen-Homburg, Friedrich Joseph zu; 109, 242, 248, 266, 341-342, 368-369, 376, 389, 414, 417, 446, 449.
Hessen-Homburg, Gustav Adolf zu; 263.
Hessen-Homburg, Ludwig Wilhelm von; 81, 83, 85, 89, 222, 224-225, 228-230, 235, 411, 421, 428-429, 438-439, 445.
Hessen-Homburg, Philipp August von; 135-136, 198, 202, 205, 210, 266, 385, 389, 418, 480, 482.
Hiller von Gaertringen, Johann August von; 45, 49, 51, 245, 325, 390, 394-395.
Hiller von Gaertringen, Johann Rudolph von; 234.
Hintertor (Leipzig); 435-436, 438-439
Hirschberg [Jelenia Góra]; 18-19, 22, 27, 46-47, 59-60, 64, 110.
Hirschfeld (Leipzig); 373.
Hirschfeld, Karl Friedrich von; 71, 76, 78, 89, 91-96, 101-102, 105, 225, 235, 262, 321, 332, 506, 508.
Hochheim; 474-475.
Hochkirch [Babin-Kościelec]; 33.
Hochkirch (Bautzen); 244-245.
Höchst; 474, 476.
Hof; 110, 280, 287.
Höfel [Dworek]; 25-26.
Hofmann, Georg Wilhelm von; 141-142, 174, 186, 219, 527.
Hohberg [Wysok]; 29, 31.
Hohendorf [Wysocko]; 43, 65.
Hohenlohe-Bartenstein, Ludwig Alois zu; 109, 266, 373-374, 389, 411.
Hohenossig; 354, 399, 401.
Hohkirch [Przesieczany]; 243, 246.
Holstein; 493, 495-496.

Holtzendorff, Karl Friedrich; 83-84, 428.
Holzhausen; 354, 365-366, 373, 377, 413-414, 416, 418, 431.
Hopfgarten manor (Dresden); 114, 121, 130.
Horn, Heinrich Wilhelm von; 33, 48, 51, 56-58, 61, 243, 315-320, 325, 390, 395, 398-399, 401, 422, 452-453, 461.
Hospitaltor (Leipzig); 435-436, 438-439.
Hoyningen-Huene [Gine], Jakob von; 422, 445.
Hünerbein, Friedrich von; 33, 48, 53, 315-316, 318, 326, 390, 395, 398, 401, 406-407, 452-453, 461.

Iashvili, Levan Mikhailovich, Prince; 14, 176, 234.
Ijssel river; 496-499.
Ilovaisky 3rd, Alexei Vasilievich; 224.
Ilovaisky 4th, Ivan Dmitrievich; 234, 262.
Ilovaisky 12th, Vasily Dmitrievich; 111, 140-143, 159, 203, 344-345, 347, 453-456, 466, 472.
Italy, Kingdom of, contingent of the Grande Armée; 22, 74, 77, 136, 227, 312-313, 319, 336, 465, 503.

Jagow, Friedrich Wilhelm von; 123, 129, 131, 135, 146-147, 208, 213, 517.
Jauer [Jawor]; 19, 27, 32-34, 37-38, 40-43, 45-47, 53-55, 57.
Jérôme, King of Westphalia; 290, 292, 294-296, 299-300.
Jeßnitz; 322, 330-331.
Johnsdorf [Janov u Litvínova]; 108-109, 250, 254, 256, 350.
Jomini, Antoine-Henri de; 41, 112-113, 123-124, 152, 156-158, 183, 192, 274, 366, 375-376, 530.
Jühnsdorf; 77, 80-81.
Jürgaß, See Wahlen-Jürgaß.
Jüterbog; 76, 78, 222, 224-228, 235, 242, 351.

Kaisarov, Paisy Sergeevich; 22, 247-248, 254-255, 342, 466, 472, 474.
Kaiserswaldau [Okmiany], action at; 22.
Kaitz; 119, 168, 352.
Kaitzbach stream; 132, 149.
Kalisz, Convention of; 11, 13.
Kapellenberg [Horka]; 182, 207, 211.

Kaptsevich, Pëtr Mikhailovich; 26-27, 29, 31, 54, 57, 253, 390, 396, 399, 402, 411, 420, 439-440, 524.
Karbitz [Chabařovice]; 178, 183-184, 203-206, 256, 276.
Karpov 2nd, Akim Akimovich; 48, 51-52, 57, 67.
Kassel; 289-301, 306, 451, 457, 497, 522, 525, 529.
Kastel; 474-476, 501.
Katzbach river [Kaczawa]; 19, 22, 27-31, 34, 37, 42-47, 49-50, 52-53, 56-59, 65, 67-68, 275.
Katzler, Andreas von; 27-28, 31, 33, 47, 51, 57-58, 61, 243, 245-246, 252-253, 260, 313, 320, 325, 330, 390, 394-395, 409, 445.
Kellermann, François-Étienne; 118, 245, 247, 260, 329, 365, 376, 378, 382, 386, 388, 413.
Kemberg; 320, 324, 354.
Kern, Yermolai Fëdorovich; 318, 420.
Kiel; 492-496.
King's German Legion - See Hanovarian Armed Forces.
Kinzig river; 466-473.
Khrapovitsky, Matvei Yevgrafovich; 179, 186, 197, 200.
Khrapovitsky, Stepan Semënovich; 455-456.
Kleinbeeren; 82-84.
Klein Hamburg (Dresden); 124, 133, 135.
Kleinpösna; 374, 384, 386, 415-416.
Klein-Schweinitz; 52-53.
Kleinzschocher; 369, 385.
Kleist, Friedrich Emil von; 109, 111-112, 115, 119-120, 129-132, 135, 138, 152, 168, 176, 178, 183, 188, 190-192, 198, 201, 203-209, 211-215, 218, 227, 247-248, 250, 254-257, 337-345, 347, 368-372, 374, 376, 378, 382, 384-385, 389-390, 411, 417-418, 425, 431, 437-438, 440, 446, 458-459, 461, 517.
Klenau und Janowitz, Johann Joseph von; 109, 112, 115, 117-118, 120, 138, 155-157, 168, 216, 242, 248, 250, 256, 258, 265, 277, 338-343, 345-348, 350, 368-370, 372-374, 378, 386, 389, 416, 425, 461, 468, 473, 489, 504-506.
Klüx, Joseph Friedrich; 123, 129, 134, 146-147, 168, 176, 215, 255, 371, 379, 381, 385, 389, 395.
Knesebeck, Karl Friedrich von dem; 279, 477-478, 482.
Knobloch, Sigismund Erhard von; 84, 245.

Knorring, Karl von; 159, 172, 174-175, 179, 181-182, 204-207, 210.
Koblenz; 459, 465, 467, 475.
Kohlberg; 141, 159, 172-175, 196.
Komotau [Chomutov]; 108-109, 112, 170, 262, 287, 337-338, 350.
Konstantin Pavlovich, Grand Duke; 118, 139, 203, 210, 367, 369, 390, 425, 429, 446, 475.
Königsberg [Kaliningrad]; 11-12.
Königstein; 24, 108-113, 115-117, 125, 138-139, 141-142, 168, 203, 215, 254, 278, 338, 341, 350-351, 503, 528.
Konradswaldau [Kondratów]; 42, 53, 55, 65.
Korff, Friedrich von; 29, 32, 60, 390, 396, 420, 524.
Korff, O.I. (Staff-Captain); 514.
Körner, Theodor; 98, 100.
Kornilov, Pëtr Yakovlevich; 32.
Kösen; 446-447, 450-452, 454-455, 461.
Köthen; 333, 349, 360.
Krafft, Karl August von; 81, 83-84, 89, 222, 224-225, 228, 230-231, 235, 411, 422, 428-429, 438, 500.
Krakau [Kraków]; 8.
Krayn [Krajów]; 28, 43, 45, 47, 49, 52.
Kreibau [Krzelów], action at; 22.
Kretov, Nikolai Vasilievich; 203, 445.
Kreutz, Kiprian Antonovich; 350, 411, 415-416, 425, 445-447, 451, 455, 459, 462.
Krietzschwitz; 111, 139-141, 172-175.
Kroitsch [Krotoszyce]; 42 43, 45, 47, 49, 52, 56-57, 65.
Kropstädt; 224-226, 232.
Krosigk; 331.
Korsigk, Heinrich Ferdinand von; 400, 445.
Kudashev, Nikolai Danilovich; 115, 258, 288, 343, 445.
Kulm [Chlumec]; 62, 115, 169, 171, 175, 178-179, 181-190, 192-197, 202, 206-208, 210-217, 219, 223, 250, 252, 254, 256-257, 273, 277, 284, 286-287, 521-522, 524-525, 528-529.
Küstrin [Kostrzyn]; 70-71, 501, 517.
Kutuzov - See Golenishchev-Kutuzov.

Lagrange, Joseph; 390, 396, 428.
Lähn [Wleń]; 22-23, 60.
La Motte, Peter de; 465-466, 468-469, 488.
Landeshut [Kamienna Góra]; 18-19, 32.
Landgraben drain (Dresden); 130, 135, 150.

Landsberg; 337, 349, 377, 392, 401, 403.
Landsturm; 34, 59, 87, 482-483, 493.
Langenau, Friedrich Karl von; 128-129, 219, 366-367.
Langenhennersdorf; 173-174, 255.
Langensalza; 454-455, 458.
Langenselbold; 466, 469.
Langéron, Louis-Alexandre de; 17-19, 22-27, 30, 32-34, 37, 42, 45-46, 48, 53-65, 110, 243, 245-247, 252-253, 259, 318, 320-322, 330-331, 369, 390, 393-396, 399-402, 408, 411, 414-415, 419-422, 427, 429, 439-440, 446, 449, 451, 453, 458, 461, 476, 524.
Langfuhr [Wrzeszcz]; 512-513.
Lanskoy, Sergei Nikolaevich; 52, 67, 245.
Latour-Maubourg, Marie-Victor; 24-25, 28, 118, 123, 127, 133, 135-137, 146, 148, 154-155, 162, 169, 176, 244-247, 250, 255, 260, 262, 321, 329, 336-337, 365, 376-378, 388, 445.
Lauban [Lubań]; 25, 61, 243, 246, 252.
Lauberdière, Louis-François; 307, 497.
Laucha; 451-453, 455.
Lauenburg; 97-99, 491.
Laun [Louny]; 153, 170, 274, 282, 284.
Lauriston, Jacques-Jean de; 19, 23, 25-26, 30-32, 34, 43, 45, 47, 53-55, 57, 253, 260, 278, 335, 338, 344, 359, 365, 376-378, 386, 388, 411, 413, 425, 442, 445, 524.
Lausick; 340, 342.
Lauterseiffen [Bielanka]; 23, 60.
Lebrun, Anne-Charles; 248, 499.
Le Coq, Karl Christian von; 77, 82, 85, 230.
Lederer, Ignaz Ludwig von; 109, 115, 119, 138, 146, 148, 157, 190, 215, 264, 389, 414, 431, 447.
Ledru des Essarts, François; 46, 59-60, 373, 386.
Lefebvre-Desnouettes, Charles; 25, 117, 250, 287-288, 300, 312, 411, 454, 500.
Leitmeritz [Litoměřice]; 108, 248, 261, 274, 276-281, 283-284, 309.
Leubnitz; 115, 134-135, 147, 149.
Leutzsch; 385.
Levashov, Vasily Vasilievich; 372, 445.
Lhéritier de Chézelles, Samuel François; 110, 112.
Liebenau; 190, 204, 210, 214-216.
Liebertwolkwitz; 343-348, 354-355, 364-366, 370-378, 380, 384, 386, 403, 414, 417, 426, 431, 448.

Liechtenstein, Alois Gozaga von und zu; 109, 115, 138, 146, 148, 154-155, 157, 168, 216, 264, 383, 385, 389, 411, 418, 426, 461.
Liechtenstein, Moritz Joseph von und zu; 109, 112, 115, 121, 123, 129, 138, 146, 148, 157, 168, 170, 176, 216, 242, 248, 263, 277, 338, 340, 342, 344, 348, 367, 369, 385, 389, 395, 430, 452, 461.
Liechtenstein, Joseph Wenzel von und zu; 243, 274.
Liegnitz [Legnica]; 19, 28, 34, 37, 42-43, 46-47, 56-58, 65, 67, 261, 353.
Lieven 3rd, Johann Georg von; 47, 52, 66-67, 445.
Lilienstein; 110-111, 115, 177, 248, 253, 350.
Lindenau; 348-349, 364, 366, 369-370, 377, 384-386, 413, 415, 418, 431, 435, 441-443, 447, 450.
Lindenthal; 377, 392-395, 401.
Lishin, Russian artillery captain; 292, 294-295, 525.
Lobanov-Rostovsky, Dmitry Ivanovich; 261, 457.
Lobbese; 225, 228.
Lobenthal, Karl Friedrich Ludwig von; 22-23, 25, 31, 317, 396-397.
Löbtau; 115, 118-119, 124, 129, 133, 135-136, 154.
Lockwitz; 108, 112, 148, 152, 168.
Loison, Louis-Henri; 99-100.
Looting; 14, 28, 63, 170, 212, 259
Lorge, Jean-Thomas; 226-227, 329, 365, 390, 398, 400.
Lößnig; 375, 413, 418, 426-427, 431.
Lottum, Carl Friedrich von Wylich und; 482.
Lottum, Heinrich Cristoph von Wylich und; 235.
Löwenberg [Lwówek Śląski]; 19, 22-23, 25-26, 28, 58-59, 61, 243.
Löwenhielm, Gustaf Carl; 75, 83.
Löwenstern, Woldemar Hermann von; 75-76, 529.
Lübeck; 69, 97-98, 100, 220, 302, 483, 491-493.
Lübnitz; 92-94, 96.
Lukau; 70, 76.
Lukov, Fëdor Alexeevich; 123, 130.
Lüneburg; 303-306, 490-491, 522.
Luppe river; 385, 430, 447.
Lusatia [Lausitz]; 24, 41, 43, 109-111, 115, 124, 243, 247-248, 250, 252, 258, 261, 277, 309-310.

Lützen; 340, 342, 344, 348, 364, 366, 407, 431-432, 436, 439, 441, 443, 446, 448, 450-451, 453, 461-462; Battle of; 13, 443, 520.
Lützow, Ludwig Adolf von; 97-100, 302, 304-307, 491, 512.
Lyon, James Frederick; 305.

Macdonald, Étienne (duc de Tarente); 19, 22-26, 28, 30, 41, 43, 45-47, 49, 52, 57, 59, 63-64, 115, 161, 244-245, 247, 252-253, 258-261, 301, 329, 336, 365, 373, 377-378, 381, 384, 386, 388, 411, 413, 425, 435, 443, 445, 456, 469-470, 497, 499-500, 521.
Madatov, Valerian Grigorievich; 244, 301.
Magdeborn; 342, 344-345, 347, 369, 375-376, 378, 380, 386, 403.
Magdeburg; 16, 69, 71, 74, 91, 96, 105, 278, 331, 333-334, 336, 401, 448, 501, 504, 506, 510, 517.
Magdenko, Mikhail Semënovich; 400, 420.
Main river; 11, 344, 456, 465, 467, 472, 475-476.
Mainz; 164, 334, 336, 469, 474-476, 479, 490, 501.
Maison, Nicolas-Joseph; 26, 344, 445, 499.
Malitsch [Małuszów]; 28, 33, 42-43, 46, 66.
Manteuffel, Gotthard Johann von; 411, 429, 445.
Marauding; 13, 15, 450, 456, 473.
Marchand, Jean-Gabriel; 373, 386, 416, 440.
Markov 1st, Yevgeny Ivanovich; 243, 268, 350, 352.
Markov, Alexander Ivanovich; 380, 525.
Markranstädt; 348, 367, 369, 377, 384-385, 418, 435, 443, 447, 450, 462.
Marzahna; 224-225.
Maret, Hugues-Bernard (duc de Bassano); 116-117, 249, 334, 432, 479.
Margaron, Pierre; 287, 451.
Maria-Theresien-Orden; 62, 190, 213, 236, 381, 446.
Mariássy von Markus und Batisfalva, Andreas; 135-136.
Marienberg; 108-110, 216, 248, 254, 256, 258, 285, 338, 341, 465.
Marienberg Festung (Würzburg); 501.
Markkleeberg; 343, 345, 355, 365, 370-372, 375-376, 382-386, 418, 432.
Marmont, Auguste Frédéric Louis Viesse (duc de Raguse); 15, 19, 22-23, 25, 28, 115, 118, 137, 169, 176, 214-216, 242, 244, 247,

250-251, 259-260, 321, 329, 336, 344, 353, 357, 365, 377, 387-388, 390, 392-397, 400, 402, 411, 413, 420, 428, 430, 435, 445, 456, 469, 471, 528.
Marwitz, Friedrich August von der; 93-96, 102-104, 289.
Maxen; 108, 112, 115, 118, 168-169, 171-172, 176, 190, 214.
Maximilian Joseph, King of Bavaria; 464, 485, 524.
Mayer von Heldensfeld, Anton; 109, 266, 373, 389, 411.
Mecklenburg-Schwerin, Friedrich zu; 97.
Mecklenburg-Schwerin, Gustav zu; 494.
Mecklenburg-Strelitz, Karl zu; 25, 29-31, 48, 51-52, 315-317, 319, 325, 390, 395-396, 445.
Meiningen; 459-460, 474-475.
Meißen; 133, 261, 310, 313, 322, 353.
Melissino, Alexey Petrovich; 113, 121, 123, 129-130, 151.
Melnik [Mělník]; 108, 110, 275, 283-284.
Mellnitz; 224-225.
Melsungen; 295-297.
Mensdorff-Pouilly, Emmanuel von; 109, 258, 276, 287-288, 340, 344, 348, 369, 385, 389, 430, 447, 466.
Merseburg; 287, 300, 323, 331, 340, 344, 348-349, 393, 427, 430, 446-447, 451, 462, 490.
Merveldt, Maximilian von; 242, 248, 256, 264, 337, 341-342, 367-369, 374-376, 383-384, 387, 404-406.
Meshcherinov, Vasily Dmitrievich; 54, 60.
Mesko von Felsö-Kubiny, Joseph; 109, 112, 115, 123-124, 129, 133, 136, 138, 146, 148, 155-156.
Metternich, Klemens Wenzel von; 156, 183, 190, 457, 464, 478-480, 482, 524.
Meusdorf; 365, 376-377, 386-387, 417.
Mezentsov, Vladimir Petrovich; 113, 121, 255, 389, 458.
Milhaud, Jean-Baptiste; 365, 377-378, 388.
Miloradovich, Mikhail Andreevich; 11, 118, 176, 188-189, 194, 203, 369, 381, 446, 475, 521, 523-524.
Mittelsaida; 111-112, 116.
Mobile magazines; 8-10, 168, 170, 335.
Mockau; 365, 377, 420, 427.
Möckern; 364-365, 370, 377, 385, 391-398, 400-401, 403, 407, 409, 477.

Mockrehna; 321-322, 329.
Modlin; 501, 508.
Mohr, Johann Friedrich von; 339, 342-343, 345, 373, 389, 446, 465.
Mokau; 354, 414, 420, 422.
Molitor, Gabriel-Jean; 496-498.
Mölkau; 415, 429, 431.
Mölln; 98, 491-492.
Monarchenhügel; 414, 417, 430.
Mönchswald [Pogórze Kaczawskie]; 46, 53.
Moniteur, le; 212, 296, 510.
Montgelas, Maximilian Carl von; 464, 483.
Montmarie, Aimé Sulpice de; 209, 347, 445.
Morand, Charles-Antoine; 227, 237, 313, 319, 471-472, 474.
Moreau, Jean-Victor-Marie; 112-113, 152-153, 158, 162, 165, 524.
Mortier, Adolphe-Édouard; 127, 130, 133-135, 137, 148, 151-152, 160, 172, 176-177, 214, 216, 250, 337, 365, 377-378, 384, 386, 413, 418, 456, 469, 472-473.
Mosczinski Garten (Dresden); 132-133, 135, 153.
Mouton-Duvernet, Régis Barthélemy; 111, 180, 185, 189, 198, 207-208, 210, 505.
Müffling, Philipp Friedrich Carl Ferdinand von; 18, 46, 55-56, 322, 527.
Mühlberg; 262, 309-311, 313.
Mühlhausen; 293-294, 462, 490.
Mulde river; 321-322, 329-330, 333-337, 339, 354, 357-358, 360.
Mumb, Franz; 123, 129, 146, 148, 155, 264.
Münden; 292, 296.
Münster; 497.
Münster, Ernst Friedrich zu; 156, 282.
Murat, Joachim (king of Naples); 28, 112, 116, 133-137, 148-149, 154-156, 169, 176, 216, 246, 248, 251, 259-261, 329, 334-336, 338-347, 353-354, 357, 359, 375, 378-379, 381-382, 413, 419, 456, 476.
Nansouty, Étienne de; 134, 137, 146, 148, 150-152, 160, 256, 365, 377, 411, 413, 424, 429, 456, 470.
Narbonne-Lara, Louis-Marie de; 508-509.
Naryshkin, Lev Aleksandrovich; 234, 497-499.
Natzmer, Oldwig Anton von; 436-437.
Naumburg [Nowogrodziec]; 61, 242-243, 246.
Naumburg (Saxony); 287, 340, 355, 367, 446-447, 450-452, 461.

Naunhof; 342, 403.
Naußlitz; 133, 136, 154-155.
Neindorff, Friedrich Ludwig von; 84, 230.
Neipperg, Adam Albert von; 111, 243, 263.
Neiße [Nysa]; 26.
Neisse river; 245-247, 252, 261, 278, 281.
Nesselrode, Karl Vasilievich; 457, 478-479, 482, 524.
Neubeeren; 82, 85.
Neudorf [Nowa Wieś Legnicka]; 43.
Neudorf [Nowa Wieś Złotoryjska]; 37.
Neuhausen (Erzgebirge); 111, 170, 216.
Neumünster; 492-493.
Neverovsky, Dmitry Petrovich; 22, 47, 52, 66-67, 422, 445, 524.
Ney, Michel (duc d'Elchingen, prince de la Moskawa); 19, 22-26, 28, 34, 43, 88, 127, 133, 135, 137, 148, 162, 223-229, 233, 235-238, 242, 244, 248, 250-251, 257, 259, 261, 278, 281, 311-313, 321, 329, 332, 337, 365, 377, 393, 402-403, 407, 411, 413, 424, 428-429, 445, 456, 521.
Nidda river; 472-473, 475.
Niederau; 29, 43.
Niedergörsdorf; 226, 228-230.
Nijmegen; 498-500.
Nikitin, Alexey Petrovich; 344-346, 525.
Nollendorf [Nakléřov]; 110, 141, 175, 177-179, 181-182, 191, 197, 201, 203-206, 209, 213-214, 218, 247, 250-251, 253-257, 282, 284, 350.
Normann-Ehrenfels, Karl Friedrich von; 146, 148, 390, 393-394, 398, 421, 483.
Nostitz-Rieneck, Johann Nepmuk; 109, 115, 119, 138, 146, 148, 157, 190, 215, 266, 367-368, 382, 389, 418, 426-427, 446-447, 461.
Nöthnitz; 113, 115, 120-121, 138, 148, 153.
Notte river; 71, 76.
Nürnberger Tor (Hanau); 466, 471.
Nuthe river; 71, 76, 226.

Oder river; 8, 10, 70, 163, 261, 333, 404, 451, 501, 520.
Oehna; 76, 226-227, 234-235.
Oelsen; 247, 254-255.
Oldesloe; 491-493.
Olivaer Tor (Danzig); 513, 516.
Olsufiev 1st, Zakhar Dmitrievich; 29, 32, 45, 48, 54, 390, 396, 399, 420-421, 428.
Opolchenie; 261-262, 268-269, 271-272, 283, 350-351, 416, 425, 503, 507-508, 516, 518, 530.
Oppen, Adolf Friedrich von; 77, 81, 89, 222, 224, 228, 233-234, 411, 422, 428, 497-499.
Opperman, Karl Ivanovich; 353, 524.
Oranje-Nassau, Willem Frederik van; 192, 497.
Order of St. Alexander Nevsky; 213, 446.
Order of St. Andrew the First-Called; 63, 446.
Order of St. George; 63, 189, 213, 236, 446.
Order of St. Vladimir; 301, 446.
Ore Mountains [Erzgebirge]; 9, 16, 108, 124, 128, 182-183, 216, 242, 253, 258, 277, 350.
Orlov-Denisov, Vasily Vasilievich; 375, 380, 456, 466, 472, 474, 525.
O'Rourke, Joseph Cornelius; 71, 76, 235, 411, 429.
Osten-Sacken, Fabian Gottlieb von der; 17-19, 22-23, 26, 28, 33-34, 36-37, 42, 45, 47-53, 55-58, 61-66, 243, 245-246, 252-253, 261, 310, 312-313, 315, 320-322, 330-331, 369, 393-395, 398, 401-402, 411, 414, 422, 427, 439-440, 442, 446, 451, 453, 461, 476, 523-524.
Osterman-Tolstoy, Alexander Ivanovich; 139-140, 142, 144, 158, 167-168, 171-174, 178-179, 182-191, 193-194, 196, 204, 213-214, 525.
Oudinot, Nicolas Charles (duc de Reggio); 71, 74-77, 80, 82-83, 86-88, 91-92, 100, 116, 169, 222-223, 225, 227, 229, 232-233, 235, 242, 302, 337, 365, 377, 386, 413, 418, 427, 447, 451, 456, 469, 521.

Pahlen 1st, Peter von der; 247-248, 253-256, 339-340, 342-347, 372, 374, 378, 381, 386, 389, 411, 417-418, 431, 446, 455.
Pahlen 2nd, Paul von der; 19, 22, 27, 32, 42, 46, 53, 55, 64, 396, 421, 428, 445, 458.
Pahlen 3rd, Carl von der; 234.
Pajol, Pierre-Claude; 123, 127, 133, 135, 137, 146, 148, 154, 347, 445.
Panchulidzev 1st, Ivan Davydovich; 58.
Pappenheim, Karl Theodor zu; 469, 473, 488.
Parlementaire; 58, 297, 306.
Paris; 195, 476-477, 479, 484, 520, 523.
Parthe river; 337, 343, 354-355, 364-365, 400-402, 407-408, 413-415, 419-422, 427, 431, 435, 439, 448.

INDEX   543

Paskevich, Ivan Fëdorovich; 269, 350-351, 411, 416, 425, 438, 446, 508.
Paunsdorf; 411, 413, 415, 417, 419, 421-423, 428, 438.
Pécheux, Marc-Nicolas; 302-305, 491.
Pegau; 340, 342, 344, 348, 356, 368, 375, 386, 430-431, 434, 436, 438, 447, 451, 461.
Pelet-Clozeau, Jean-Jacques; 136, 150, 432, 529.
Penig; 288, 329, 339-341, 352, 368.
Pesterwitz; 148, 155.
Petersberg; 331, 349, 360-361.
Petersberg (Erfurt citadel); 458.
Peterstor (Leipzig); 434, 436, 438, 440-441.
Peterswald [Petrovice u Chabařovic]; 115, 117, 157, 169, 171-172, 175, 177-179, 182, 191, 196-197, 202, 204, 209, 214-215, 217, 247-248, 250-251, 254-255, 274-275, 284, 350, 528.
Peterwitz [Piotrowice]; 49, 54.
Pfaffendorf; 337, 402, 414-415, 422, 427, 435, 439.
Pfuel, Ernst Heinrich von; 304-305.
Philippon, Armand; 125, 180, 185, 189, 198, 202, 207-210.
Pilgramsdorf [Pielgrzymka]; 26-27, 37, 56-58, 60.
Pillnitz road; 118, 121, 126, 134, 147, 149-150.
Pirch, Georg Dubislav von; 121, 123, 129, 131-132, 146-147, 207-208, 256, 372, 380-381, 385, 389, 458.
Pirna; 108-112, 116-117, 124, 130, 138-142, 147, 149-150, 152-153, 157-159, 167, 169-172, 176-178, 196, 214, 216, 248, 250, 253, 257, 259, 276-278, 280-283, 350-351, 353, 503, 528.
Pirnaischer Schlag/Vorstadt (Dresden); 114, 121, 126-127, 131, 133-134, 137, 504.
Plagwitz (Leipzig); 385.
Plagwitz [Płakowice]; 23, 25-26, 60.
Platov, Matvey Ivanovich; 258, 288-289, 340, 342-343, 348, 369, 374, 386, 403, 411, 415, 421, 431, 436, 446, 453-456, 472, 474-475, 524.
Plauen; 109, 113, 115, 117, 119-121, 124, 129, 133, 148, 276, 352, 503.
Plauenscher Grund (Weißeritz ravine); 120, 124, 127, 129, 133, 138, 148, 154-155.
Plaußig; 411, 414, 422.

Pleiße river; 288, 343-344, 348, 355, 364, 366-369, 374-376, 378, 382-386, 395, 403, 413-414, 417-418, 422, 427, 431, 435-436, 441-443, 447-448.
Plinsa river [Błotnica]; 46, 48-49, 54.
Ploetz, Christian Friedrich von; 506-507.
Plösen; 400, 414, 420.
Podelwitz; 354, 394-395, 399, 401.
Pomßen; 342-343, 347.
Poniatowski, Józef Antoni; 24-25, 111, 244-245, 247, 253, 260, 278, 338-340, 343, 355, 359, 365, 372, 376, 378, 382, 386-388, 411, 413, 418-419, 426-427, 435-436, 443, 445.
Potemkin, Yakov Alekseevich; 174, 197-198, 200.
Potschappel; 155, 503.
Potsdam; 71, 76, 224, 332.
Pozzo di Borgo, Charles André; 349, 524.
Prague; 41, 161, 170, 178, 275, 282, 284, 404, 457, 478, 482, 525.
Prausnitz [Prusice]; 32, 34, 43, 47, 58.
Pretzschendorf; 168, 176.
Preußen, Friedrich Wilhelm Heinrich August von; 129, 208-209, 510.
Preußen, Friedrich Wilhelm Karl von; 322.
Priesten [Přestanov]; 181-187, 202-205, 207, 210, 528.
Prinz Antons Garten (Dresden); 114, 131-132.
Probstheida; 347, 365, 413-415, 417-419, 425-426, 431, 434, 437, 449.
Prochaska, Marie Christiane Elenore; 305-306.
Prohlis; 150-152, 168.
Prussian Brigades;
    1. Brigade; 33, 45, 48, 316, 319, 390, 395-398, 401, 409; *2. Brigade*; 25, 29, 45, 48, 51, 316, 390, 395-397, 401, 409; *3. Brigade*; 76, 81, 83, 85, 89, 222, 224, 228-230; *4. Brigade*; 76, 81, 83, 85, 89, 222, 224, 228, 230; *5. Brigade*; 76, 81, 83-84, 89, 222, 224-225, 232; *6. Brigade*; 76, 81, 83, 89, 222, 224, 228, 230-231; *7. Brigade*; 33, 45, 48, 51, 56, 315-319, 390, 395, 401, 409; *8. Brigade*; 33, 45, 48, 50-51, 168, 315-316, 390, 395, 399, 401, 409; *9. Brigade*; 121, 123, 129, 131, 134, 146-147, 209, 215, 218, 340, 347, 369, 389, 425; *10. Brigade*; 121, 123, 129, 131, 135, 146, 147, 149, 207-209, 218, 340, 343, 347, 369, 372, 389, 425,

458; *11. Brigade*; 123, 129, 131-132, 135, 146-147, 208-209, 218, 340, 343, 347, 369, 373, 384, 389, 411, 425, 458; *12. Brigade*; 121, 123, 129, 135, 146-147, 208-209, 218, 255, 340, 347, 369, 371, 389, 425;
Prussian Corps;
   III. Korps; 71, 222, 225-226, 232, 256; *IV. Korps*; 71, 222, 224, 451; *V. Korps*; 224.
Pückler-Groditz, Wilhelm Erdmann von; 258, 288.
Puppenwald; 467, 471.
Puthod, Jacques; 43, 46, 59-60, 64.
Putlitz, Friedrich Ludwig zu; 91-95, 101-102.
Pyshnitsky, Dmitry Ilyich; 140-142, 158, 173-175, 188, 202, 218, 254, 371, 389.

Queis river [Kwisa]; 41, 61, 242-244, 246.
Querfurt; 293, 451, 462.
Quiot du Passage, Joachim; 125, 188, 198, 202, 206-208, 212.

Rabenstein; 86, 224, 228.
Räcknitz; 112, 115, 119-121, 129, 132, 148, 152-153, 168, 351-352, 503.
Radefeld; 365, 393-394.
Radegast; 322, 324, 331, 341.
Radetzky von Radets, Johann Josef; 128-129, 141-142, 157, 219, 367, 375, 446, 482.
Raevsky, Nikolai Nikolaevich; 188, 198, 202, 210, 250, 369, 376, 383, 390, 445-446.
Rakhmanov, Pëtr Alexandrovich; 402, 422.
Rampischer Schlag (Dresden); 118, 126, 130, 133.
Ranstädter Tor (Leipzig); 434-435, 440-441.
Rapp, Jean; 510, 512-514, 516.
Ration tariffs; Kutuzov Tariff; 11.
   Aschaffenburg Tariff; 481.
Ratzeburg; 302, 491-492.
Rauch, Johann Justus von; 309, 321, 333, 427.
Razout, Louis-Nicolas de; 114, 505.
Rechberg, Anton von; 466, 472, 488.
Rechenberg; 108, 111, 251.
Reibnitz, Karl Pavlovich; 254, 326, 370-371.
Reiche, Ludwig von; 97, 306.
Reichenbach [Dzierżoniów]; 17.
Reichenbach-Goschütz, Christoph Joachim Heinrich von; 325, 399.
Reichenbach (Saxony); 245, 247, 252-253.
Reichenbach (Thüringen); 458.
Reichenberg [Liberec]; 24, 111, 292.

Reick; 112, 150-152.
Rendsburg; 492-495.
Repnin-Volkonsky, Nikolai Grigorievich; 457, 528.
Residenzschloss (Dresden); 127, 137, 157.
Residenzschloss (Erfurt); 454.
Reudnitz; 354-355, 413, 427, 429, 431, 439, 441.
Reuss-Greiz, Heinrich zu; 480.
Reuss, Prussian *Oberstleutnant*; 93-94, 102-104.
Reuß zu Köstritz, Heinrich; 125, 176-177, 180, 185, 189, 198, 202, 207-208, 212.
Reynier, Jean-Louis; 71, 75-77, 80, 82, 84-86, 222, 225, 227-229, 233, 235, 237, 312-313, 321, 329, 332, 336-337, 366, 387, 403-404, 411, 413, 419, 423-424, 442, 445, 448, 524.
Ricard, Étienne-Pierre-Sylvestre; 365, 411, 429-430.
Richemont, Christophe-François de; 430, 445.
Ried im Innkreis, Treaty of; 333, 464.
Rietzschke stream; 393-394, 399-400, 402.
Rimberg [Rzymówka]; 43, 49.
Rochambeau, Donatien de Vimeur de; 32, 426, 445.
Röchlitz [Rokitnica]; 29, 43, 46, 58, 65.
Rochlitz (Saxony); 340-341, 434.
Rockets (Congreve); 262, 305, 356, 411, 424, 428, 512-514.
Röder, Friedrich Erhard von; 123, 129, 146-147, 150-151, 256, 344, 384, 389, 455.
Roguet, François; 123, 127, 130, 133-134, 146, 148-151, 499.
Rohrbeck; 222, 226-227, 229-230, 233.
Rosen, Georg Andreas von; 174, 197, 200, 390.
Rosenhagen; 100.
Rosental; 414, 422, 427, 431, 435, 440, 442.
Roßla; 293.
Roßlau; 262, 312, 321, 323, 332-333, 351, 354, 360.
Roßthal; 124, 129, 154-155.
Roth, Loggin Osipovich; 111, 121, 123, 129-131, 134, 138-139, 146-147, 149-152, 168, 176.
Rötha; 342, 345, 368, 386, 441, 461.
Rothenburg; 331-332, 360.
Rothen Haus (Dresden); 129, 131-132.
Rothkirch, *Oberst* (Klenau's *Chef des Stabes*); 156, 168, 373, 505.
Rothkirch [Czerwony Kościół]; 28, 34, 43, 47, 52, 65.

INDEX 545

Rottembourg, Henri; 383, 427.
Rotterdam; 497-499.
Rückingen; 466, 468-469.
Rüdiger, Friedrich Alexander von; 216, 253-254, 340, 345.
Rudzevich, Alexander Yakovlevich; 23-24, 29, 32, 53-54, 56-58, 60, 313, 330, 390, 396, 400, 411, 420, 428-430, 458.
Rühle von Lilienstern, Johann Jakob; 259, 281-282, 311, 322-323, 348, 483.
Rumburg [Rumburk]; 24-25, 244, 248, 261, 274, 276-278, 280-281, 283, 310.
Russian Armies;
  Army of Moldavia; 8. Army of Poland (Reserve Army); 34, 262, 268, 272, 337, 341, 350-352, 355, 369-370, 386, 415, 419, 424-425, 431, 436-438, 446, 451, 459, 462, 506, 524, 528.
Russian Artillery units;
  6th Horse Artillery Company; 129, 149, 151, 372; 7th Horse Artillery Company; 344, 347, 372; 10th Horse Artillery Company; 268, 380, 416; 13th Battery Company; 50, 422; 14th Battery Company; 184; 14th Light Company; 140, 143; 15th Battery Company; 32; 23rd Horse Artillery Company; 380, 455, 525; 27th Light Company; 140, 184; 34th Battery Company; 400; 34th Light Company; 55, 60; Lifeguard Battery Company; 378-379.
Russian Corps;
  I Corps; 109, 111, 113, 138, 143, 247, 254, 342, 343, 411, 417; II Corps; 109, 111-113, 138-144, 154, 158-159, 172-176, 178-179, 181, 184-186, 188-189, 193, 196-197, 202, 210, 218, 247, 256, 342-343, 345, 369, 372, 378-379, 381, 384-385, 389, 411, 417, 426, 458, 525; VI Corps; 29, 48, 54, 60, 310, 524; VIII Corps; 19, 110, 315, 420; IX Corps; 29, 32, 48, 396, 420; X Corps; 26, 29, 31, 48-49, 54-55, 57, 315, 396, 411, 420; Grenadier Corps; 11, 109, 250, 337, 347, 369, 383, 390.
Russian Divisions;
  1st Cuirassier Division; 118, 180, 187, 198, 203, 210, 369, 376, 386, 390, 411; 1st Grenadier Division; 111, 115, 118, 146, 148, 188, 198, 202, 205, 218, 380-381, 385-386, 431; 1st Lifeguard Division; 111, 142, 154, 159, 172-173, 175, 180-182, 188-189, 193, 196-197-198, 200, 203, 218; 2nd Cuirassier Division; 118, 180, 187, 198, 203, 369, 376, 386, 390, 411, 417, 431; 2nd Grenadier Division; 110, 198, 248, 380-381, 383, 385, 411, 419, 431; 2nd Hussar Division; 48, 51, 402; 2nd Lifeguard Division; 111, 115, 118, 147, 188, 203, 218; 3rd Cuirassier Division; 118, 198, 203, 341, 344-345, 347, 369, 379, 385, 390, 411, 419, 431, 454-455; 3rd Division; 255, 340, 379, 426, 518; 4th Division; 340, 379, 389, 518; 5th Division; 113, 121, 129-130, 147, 168, 215, 254-255, 340, 345, 347, 369, 372, 386, 389, 458; 7th Division; 48; 9th Division; 48, 396, 399; 10th Division; 47, 52; 12th Division; 269, 353, 411, 416, 438, 459; 13th Division; 268, 270, 353, 416, 438, 459; 14th Division; 113, 345, 347, 369, 389, 458; 15th Division; 32, 48; 16th Division; 268, 351; 18th Division; 48; 26th Division; 269, 350-351, 353, 411, 416, 424-425, 438, 446-447, 459; 27th Division; 22, 47, 52, 422; Lifeguard Light Cavalry Division; 115, 118, 180, 198, 203, 210, 218, 379, 411, 431, 475;
Russian Regiments, Cavalry;
  Akhtyrka Hussars; 52, 63, 402; Alexandria Hussars; 52, 63, 245, 402; Belorussia Hussars; 52, 63, 402; Chernigov Mounted Jägers; 58; Chevalier Garde; 210; Chuguev Ulans; 110, 255-256, 344-345; Courland Dragoons; 26, 47; Dorpat Mounted Jägers; 396; Finland Dragoons; 234; Grodno Hussars; 112, 129, 149, 248, 344-345, 347, 418; Her Majesty's Leib Cuirassiers; 139, 159, 177, 179-180, 184, 203, 205, 207, 218; Izyum Hussars; 234, 294-295; Kiev Dragoons; 23, 32, 48, 54, 58, 60, 245, 320, 396; Kharkov Dragoons; 58, 60, 320, 396; Lifeguard Cossacks; 375, 380-382, 448; Lifeguard Dragoons; 187, 198, 203, 379; Lifeguard Hussars; 142, 159, 180, 184, 203, 210-211, 379; Lifeguard Ulans; 187, 198, 203, 379; Livland Mounted Jägers; 23, 32, 48, 54, 396; Lubny Hussars; 111, 113, 121, 129, 139, 143, 149-150, 218, 254, 344-345, 369, 371, 378, 389, 411;

Malorussia Cuirassiers; 378; Mariupol Hussars; 52, 63, 402; Novgorod Cuirassiers; 378; Pavlograd Hussars; 311, 455; Riga Dragoons; 234, 294; Seversk Mounted Jägers; 26, 58; Siberia Ulans; 270, 350; Smolensk Dragoons; 26, 47; Sumy Hussars; 112, 121, 129, 149, 254-256, 344-345; Taganrog Ulans; 270, 350; Tatar Ulans; 142, 159, 172, 174-175, 177, 179, 180-181, 184, 203, 205, 207, 218; Tver Dragoons; 58;

Russian Regiments, Cossacks;
Bashkirs; 269, 289, 459, 498, 503, 506, 518; Black Sea Cossacks; 288; Don Cossacks; 9, 19, 23, 30-31, 45, 48, 52, 57-58, 60, 64, 75-76, 92, 95-100, 105, 111, 113, 119, 138, 140, 143, 147, 149, 153, 163, 178, 203, 211, 224, 226-227, 230, 234, 236, 239, 250, 253, 258, 262, 268-269, 274-276, 286-288, 292-296, 298, 300-301, 303-304, 306-307, 310, 320, 340, 342, 344-348, 350, 369, 374, 385-386, 390, 400, 402-403, 411, 415, 421, 427, 431, 436, 447, 453-457, 465, 472, 474-475, 492-493, 497-500, 503, 506, 518; Kalmyks; 320; Orenburg Cossacks; 289, 518; Ukrainian Cossacks; 26, 29, 32, 48, 54, 245, 310, 320, 396; Ural Cossacks; 269, 271.

Russian Regiments, Infantry;
2nd Jägers; 513, 518; 3rd Jägers; 514, 518; 4th Jägers; 140-141, 143, 158, 172, 174, 179, 181, 184, 186, 211, 371-372, 399, 518; 5th Jägers; 269, 350, 352, 438; 6th Jägers; 269, 425; 7th Jägers; 26-27, 31; 8th Jägers; 22, 47, 66, 402, 440; 9th Jägers; 22; 10th Jägers; 48, 54, 399; 11th Jägers; 48, 60; 12th Jägers; 48, 54; 20th Jägers; 130, 378, 381, 518; 21st Jägers; 130, 378, 381, 518; 22nd Jägers; 48; 23rd Jägers; 130; 24th Jägers; 130; 25th Jägers; 121, 130; 26th Jägers; 121, 130; 28th Jägers; 48, 54, 60; 29th Jägers; 48, 420; 32nd Jägers; 48, 54, 60; 34th Jägers; 130, 518; 36th Jägers; 48, 60; 37th Jägers; 26-27, 31, 420; 38th Jägers; 48, 54, 399; 39th Jägers; 47, 66, 440; 41st Jägers; 269, 352, 425; 42nd Jägers; 269, 350, 352; 44th Jägers; 234; 45th Jägers; 48, 420; Arkhangelogorod Infantry; 48, 399-400, 439; Azov Infantry; 512, 518; Bryansk Infantry; 514, 518; Chernigov Infantry; 139-140, 143, 172, 174-175, 185, 371; Galits Infantry; 270; Kaluga Infantry; 130; Kamchatka Infantry; 47, 61, 66, 402, 422; Kremenchug Infantry; 140-141, 143, 173-175, 202, 205, 254, 256, 378-379, 381; Ladoga Infantry; 269, 350, 438; Lifeguard Finland; 381, 386; Lifeguard Jägers; 172-175, 180-181, 184-185, 189, 197, 381, 385; Lifeguard Preobrazhensky; 173-174, 184-185, 187, 189, 196-198; Lifeguard Semenovsky; 172-174, 184-185, 189, 196-198; Minsk Infantry; 140, 143, 174-175, 186, 254, 371, 518; Mogilev Infantry; 130, 149; Murom Infantry; 139-140, 143, 172, 174-175, 179-180, 184, 381; Narva Infantry; 269, 416, 438; Nasheburg Infantry; 54, 399, 420; Nizhegorod Infantry; 269, 352; Nizov Infantry; 513, 518; Okhotsk Infantry; 47, 61, 66, 402, 422; Orël Infantry; 269, 352, 438; Pavlovsk Grenadiers; 381,386; Penza Infantry; 268, 491; Perm Infantry; 130; Poltava Infantry; 269, 350, 438; Reval Infantry; 139, 143, 158-159, 172, 174, 179, 181, 184, 186, 381, 518; Ryazhsk Infantry; 54, 399; Saratov Infantry; 268, 491; Sevsk Infantry; 130; Smolensk Infantry; 269, 416; Staro Ingermanland Infantry; 48, 420, 439; Staroskol Infantry; 399, 420; Tobolsk Infantry; 140, 143, 174-175, 179, 185, 210, 254, 371, 518; Velikiye Luki Infantry; 270; Volhynia Infantry; 140-141, 143, 173-175, 202, 205, 254, 256, 514, 518; Vyatka Infantry; 400, 420; Wilmanstrand Infantry; 399, 420; Yakutsk Infantry; 54, 399, 420;

Russo-German Legion; 97-99, 303-305.
Ryssel, Anton Friedrich von; 436-437.
Ryssel, Gustav Xaver von; 82, 421, 424, 508.

Saale river; 262, 292, 323, 330-333, 335-336, 360-361, 406, 447-448, 450-454, 462.
Saarmund; 76, 78, 86, 89, 91.
Sachsen-Coburg-Gotha, Ernst I. von; 482.
Sachsen-Coburg-Saalfeld, Ferdinand Georg von - See Sorbenberg.
Sachsen-Coburg-Saalfeld, Leopold Georg von; 139, 159, 203.

Sacken - See Osten-Sacken.
Sahr, Otto Sahrer von; 77, 82, 85, 230.
Saint-Aignan, Nicolas-Auguste de; 455, 478-479.
Saint-Cyr, Claude Carra de; 490.
Saint-Cyr, Laurent de Gouvion; 108, 110-112, 114, 116-118, 136-137, 148-149, 169, 172, 176, 190-191, 214-216, 244, 247-251, 255, 257-259, 328-329, 334, 336, 338, 350-352, 448, 456, 459, 502-505, 528.
Saint-Priest, Guillaume-Emmanuel de; 19, 32, 42, 46, 56, 62, 64, 110, 246, 252-253, 259-261, 275, 331, 349, 367, 390, 393-395, 399-400, 402, 414, 420, 428-429, 439, 451, 476, 497.
Sandrart, Karl Wilhelm von; 81, 85, 498.
Sandtor (Leipzig); 435-436, 438.
Saxon Armed Forces; 77, 82, 84-87, 114, 136, 155, 222, 230-235, 237-238, 312, 329-330, 353, 355, 379, 403, 411, 413, 415, 419, 421, 423-424, 426-427, 432, 435-437, 458, 482, 503-505, 508-509.
Sayda; 108-109, 111.
Schanda [Žandov]; 207-208, 210-211.
Schkeuditz; 348-349, 365, 369, 393-394, 400, 436, 446, 451.
Schlaup [Słup]; 43, 48, 53-55.
Schleswig, Duchy of; 494-495.
Schmalkalden; 460, 474-475.
Schmiedeberg [Kowary]; 19, 27, 32.
Schmochwitz [Smokowice]; 28, 33, 37, 43, 53, 56-57.
Schmiedeberg (Saxony); 320.
Schneeberg [Sněžník]; 108, 210, 215.
Schnelle Deichsa river [Skorą]; 26-27, 56-57, 65.
Schneller, Andreas von; 109, 115, 119, 123-124, 129, 133, 136, 138, 146, 148, 157, 168, 215, 263.
Schöler, *Oberst*; 183, 191-192, 201.
Schönau (Katzbach) [Świerzawa]; 19, 22, 42-43, 46-47, 49, 54, 59, 64-65.
Schönau (Leipzig); 385, 462.
Schönefeld; 377, 400, 413, 415, 420-421, 427-431, 435, 449, 522.
Schönwald; 175, 179, 255, 350.
Schottenhäuser [Nowe Szkoty]; 513-514.
Schusterhaus; 118-119, 124, 133, 154.
Schwarze Elster river; 235, 309-313.

Schwarzenberg, Karl Philipp zu; 107, 109, 111-113, 115, 117, 120, 123, 128-129, 138, 141, 148, 152, 154, 156, 158, 167-168, 170, 176, 183, 188, 191, 201, 216, 219, 242-243, 247-248, 250, 254, 257, 273-277, 279-281, 283, 309, 332, 338-342, 344, 347, 348-349, 355, 366-367, 375-376, 380-381, 383, 386, 403, 418, 431, 441, 446, 449, 455, 458-459, 465-467, 473-476, 479, 482, 505, 521, 526, 528.
Schwarzer Adlerorden [Order of the Black Eagle]; 63, 213, 446.
Schweidnitz [Świdnica]; 8, 18.
Schweinitz; 76, 242, 311.
Schwerin; 71, 98-100, 102-103.
Sébastiani, Horace; 19, 25, 30, 32, 34, 43, 45, 49, 51, 58, 62, 244-245, 247, 260, 278, 329, 336, 359, 365, 373-374, 377, 388, 416, 423, 425, 445, 456, 466, 469-470, 472.
Sebastiansberg [Hora Svatého Šebestiána]; 248, 279, 338.
Seehausen; 337, 396, 400.
Segeberg; 492-493.
Seichau [Sichów]; 27, 42-43, 46.
Seifertshain; 348, 369, 373, 377-378, 384, 386, 416.
Sellerhausen; 423, 428-431.
Shakhovskoy, Ivan Leontievich; 139-141, 173-175, 177-179, 181-182, 184-186, 251, 254, 371, 426.
Shcherbatov, Alexei Grigorievich; 29, 45, 48, 54-55, 60, 310, 313, 332, 341, 351, 476, 524.
Shenshin, Vasily Nikanorovich; 399, 439.
Shevich, Ivan Yegorovich; 198, 379, 390, 445.
Siegersdorf [Zebrzydowa]; 61, 243, 246.
Sievers, Carl Gustav von; 11-12.
Sjöholm, Ferdinand Ludwig von; 230-231.
Sjöholm, Friedrich Wilhelm von; 396.
Skjöldebrand, Anders Fredrik; 492-493, 496.
Sobochleben [Soběchleby]; 203-205, 250, 256.
Sondershausen; 293, 462, 490.
Sorbenberg; 183, 205-206, 264, 342.
Souham, Joseph; 28, 34, 43, 45, 47, 52, 58, 260, 329, 365, 388, 413, 420, 429, 435, 445.
Spandau; 71, 262.
Spree river; 71, 76, 78, 244, 253.
Spreti, Maximilian von; 465, 489.
Sputendorf; 76, 80.
Staal; Georg Johann von; 498-499.
Stahmeln; 385, 394-395.

Stecknitz river; 97-99, 302, 311, 490-492.
Stedingk, Curt Bogislaw von; 71, 411, 494, 496.
Stein, Heinrich Friedrich vom und zum; 156, 457-458, 478-480, 482, 524, 530.
Steinberg (Saxony); 416-417.
Steinberg (Silesia); 25, 45, 54.
Steinmetz, Karl Friedrich von; 33, 48, 55, 315-316, 319, 325, 390, 395-397, 445.
Stettin [Szczecin]; 70-71, 89, 501, 506-507.
Stewart, Charles William; 70, 331, 349, 401, 476, 496.
Stolpen; 116-117, 253, 258, 260, 309, 313.
Stössel, Johann Otto von; 318-319, 398.
Stötteritz; 354, 386, 413-415, 417-418, 422, 425-427, 431, 438, 449.
Straden; 185-186, 202.
Stralsund; 97, 333.
Streckenwald [Větrov]; 191, 204.
Strehlen; 112, 119, 121, 129, 132, 135, 148-149.
Striesen; 115, 119, 129, 134-135, 148-149.
Strisowitz [Střížovice]; 183, 205-206, 256.
Stroganov, Pavel Alexandrovich; 352, 415-417, 425, 429, 446, 459, 462, 490-491, 496, 506.
Struppen; 139-141.
Stünz; 424, 428-430.
Sukhozanet, Ivan Onufrievich; 14, 176, 380-381, 525.
Swedish Armed Forces; 70-71, 76, 78, 86, 97-98, 222, 225, 228, 231-232, 234-235, 262, 302, 311-312, 321, 331, 370, 411, 422, 429, 439, 441, 444, 490-496.
Swiss Armed Forces; 306-307.
Sylbitz; 331, 349, 361.

Tabaksmühle (Quandtsche); 418-419, 427, 431.
Taube, Maxim Maximovich; 417, 425, 429.
Taucha; 329, 354, 360-361, 401-403, 414, 419-423, 428-429.
Tauentzien, Bogislav Friedrich von; 70-71, 74, 76, 78, 80-81, 83, 86, 224-230, 233, 235-236, 259, 262, 310-311, 321-322, 331-332, 351, 360-361, 451, 459, 507-510.
Tellnitz [Telnice]; 181-182, 201, 206-207, 210-211, 213, 215, 251, 253, 256-257.
Teplitz [Teplice]; 9, 12, 108-111, 113, 115, 128, 157, 168-172, 174-177, 179, 182-183, 185, 190-191, 192, 196, 200, 201-202, 211, 213-217, 219, 242, 247, 249-250, 255, 258, 262, 274, 276, 279, 281-282, 284-285, 309, 350, 352.

Teste, François-Antoine; 117, 123, 127, 133, 135-136, 146, 148, 154-155, 244.
Tetschen [Děčín]; 169, 177, 217, 283.
Tettenborn, Friedrich Karl von; 70, 97-100, 302-304, 306-307, 491-494, 496.
Tharandt; 115, 118, 120, 155-157, 168.
Theresienstadt [Terezín]; 112, 215, 243, 274, 284, 458, 504, 517.
Thielmann, Johann Adolf von; 258, 276, 287-288, 300, 340, 342, 344, 348, 367, 369, 385, 389, 426, 430, 447, 455, 458, 509, 524.
Thonberg; 418-419, 427, 435-436.
Thomaswaldau [Tomaszów Bolesławiecki]; 22-23.
Thorn [Toruń]; 8, 11, 482.
Thümen, Heinrich Ludwig von; 71, 76-77, 81, 83-85, 89, 222, 224-225, 228-230, 233, 235, 321, 332, 360-361, 496.
Thyrow; 76-77, 86.
Tolkewitz; 134, 147, 149-151.
Toll, Karl Wilhelm von; 113, 157, 194, 205-206, 286, 344, 366-367, 373, 436-437, 524-526.
Tolstoy, Pëtr Alexandrovich; 261, 271, 341, 350-352, 459, 503-506.
Torgau; 16, 69, 88, 234-235, 252, 259, 262, 278-279, 281, 310, 321, 332, 334, 351, 419, 448, 459, 501, 504, 508-509.
Torna; 115, 129, 135, 147, 150-151.
Trachenberg [Żmigród]; 69; Plan; 16, 24, 69, 107, 123, 128, 247, 249, 273, 339.
Trave river; 97, 491-493.
Trebbin; 76, 78, 80, 82, 86.
Treuenbrietzen; 69, 78.
Turchaninov, Pavel Petrovich; 420.
Tuyll van Serooskerken, Diederik Jakob van; 309.

Udom 1st, Ivan Fëdorovich; 188, 203, 390.
Udom 2nd, Yevstafy Yevstafievich; 54, 390, 399, 428.
Ulbersdorf [Wojcieszyn]; 37, 56.
Universitäts Waldungung; 342, 345, 364, 372, 374, 378, 384, 386, 417.
Unstrut river; 451-455.
Ushakov 2nd, Sergei Nikolaevich; 26, 47, 66.
Utrecht; 496-499.

Vacha; 456, 459.
Vandamme, Dominique; 25, 62, 116-117, 125, 137-139, 141, 157-160, 168-173, 176-177,

179, 182-186, 188-192, 198, 202, 204-208, 211-220, 273-274, 521.
Vasilchikov 2nd, Dmitry Vasilievich; 57, 67, 313, 402, 446, 451.
Vasilchikov 1st, Illarion Vasilievich; 22, 45, 47, 51, 56, 66-67, 244-246, 390, 402, 446, 453.
Vasilchikov 3rd, Nikolay Vasilievich; 390, 400, 420.
Vegesack, Eberhard Ernst von; 97, 99-100, 302, 492.
Vellahn; 99, 303.
Verden; 306-307.
Vial, Honoré; 154, 426, 445.
Victor Perrin, Claude (duc de Bellune); 25, 116, 118, 137, 148, 154-155, 169, 176, 216, 244, 248, 250-251, 255, 258-259, 338-339, 343, 359, 365, 376-378, 383, 386, 388, 411, 413, 425, 436, 443, 456, 469.
Vistula river; 8, 10, 353, 501, 507, 513.
Vlastov, Yegor Ivanovich; 123, 130, 216, 248.
Volkmann, Anton von; 466, 489.
Volkonsky, Pëtr Mikhailovich; 66, 141, 352, 446, 482, 505, 523-524.
Vollerwiek; 493-494.
Vorontsov, Mikhail Semënovich; 70, 225, 411, 429-430, 439, 446, 451, 490-492, 496, 524.

Waal river; 498-499.
Wachau; 343-346, 348-349, 353, 364-365, 370-372, 375-378, 382-386, 389, 401, 403, 407, 414, 417-418, 431, 448.
Wachten, Hans Otto von; 139, 144, 186, 378, 525.
Wahlen-Jürgaß, Georg Ludwig Alexander von; 22, 34, 48-51, 56-57, 326, 390, 395, 409, 446, 453.
Waldheim; 338, 341, 352.
Wallmoden-Gimborn, Ludwig Georg von; 71, 97-100, 241, 302-304, 306, 311, 482, 490-494, 506, 521, 529.
Walther, Frédéric-Henri; 148, 417, 423.
Warburg, Ernst Wilhelm von; 317, 319, 398.
Warsaw, Duchy of; 8, 10-13, 34, 249, 261, 353, 406, 458, 478, 501, 516-517, 520; Armed Forces; 114, 222-223, 226, 229, 255, 258, 321, 329, 345, 347, 353, 372, 382, 396, 440, 443, 453, 503, 507.
Wartenburg; 261, 310-321, 323, 330, 336, 525, 529.
Weimar; 339, 453-455, 458, 467, 478, 482.

Weinberg (Kassel); 297.
Weinberg [Winna Góra]; 25-26.
Weinberg [Winnica]; 43, 45, 48-52, 54, 65.
Weißenfels; 287, 340, 344, 367, 407, 413, 447, 450-451, 453, 461-462.
Weissenwolf, Nikolaus Joseph von; 109, 115, 123-124, 129, 133, 135-136, 138, 146, 148, 157, 168, 216, 266, 368, 383, 389, 411, 418.
Weißeritz river; 120, 124, 129, 133, 148, 155-156.
Weltzien, Heinrich Wilhelm von; 318-319.
Wesel; 336, 459, 497, 500-501.
Westphalian Armed Forces; 111, 114, 126, 260, 289-290, 292, 294, 296-299, 312-313, 317, 419, 427, 504, 529.
Wettin; 322, 331.
Wetzlar; 459, 467, 475.
Wiederitzsch; 337, 354, 377, 394, 396, 400-402.
Wietstock; 76-77, 80, 82, 85-86.
Wildschütz [Wilczyce]; 49, 56.
Wilmersdorf; 76-77.
Wilsdruff; 352.
Wilsdruffer Schlag/Vorstadt (Dresden); 126, 504.
Wimpffen, Maximilian Alexander von; 264, 411, 426.
Windischleuba; 288, 340.
Wintzingerode, Ferdinand von; 11, 70-71, 75-76, 78, 86, 225, 299-300, 321, 331, 401, 403, 411, 421, 429-430, 446, 490, 496-497, 499 500, 524.
Wismar; 99.
Witt, Ivan Osipovich de; 54, 260, 396.
Wittenberg; 86-87, 96, 163, 224, 234, 262, 278, 281, 319-321, 332-334, 336, 351, 354, 359-361, 448, 501, 504, 508-510.
Wittenburg; 98-99.
Wittgenstein, Ludwig Adolf; 11, 74, 109-113, 115, 119, 121, 123, 129-130, 134, 136, 138-139, 141, 143, 147, 150, 152, 168, 170, 176, 215, 218, 242, 247-248, 250, 253-257, 337-342, 344-345, 347-348, 368-369, 371, 374, 381, 384, 417, 431, 437, 440, 446, 449, 455, 458-461, 475, 481, 521, 524.
Wobeser; Karl Georg von; 76, 78, 86, 224, 235, 321, 332, 508.
Wolfe, Ivan Pavlovich; 139-140, 172, 174-175, 188.
Wölfnitz; 124, 154-155.
Wolfsberg [Wilcza Góra]; 27-32, 58.

Wolfsdorf [Wilków]; 28-29, 31-32.
Wölmsdorf; 226, 228, 230, 234, 237.
Wolzogen, Justus Philipp von; 153, 159, 171-172, 192, 375, 383, 528.
Wrede, Carl Philipp von; 456, 459-460, 464-467, 470-475, 482, 488.
Württemberg, Alexander von; 512-514, 516, 518-519, 524.
Württemberg Armed Forces; 227, 312-313, 316-317, 393-394, 398, 403, 421, 426, 445, 456, 465, 482.
Württemberg, Friedrich Eugen von; 113, 139-143, 153-154, 159, 169, 171-172, 174-175, 177-178, 181, 184-186, 188, 193-194, 196-197, 203, 210, 21, 215, 247, 253-256, 340, 343, 345, 347, 369-372, 376, 378-379, 381-384, 389, 411, 417, 425, 446, 458, 530.
Württemberg, Wilhelm Friedrich (Kronprinz) von; 482.
Wütende Neiße river [Nysa Szalona]; 33, 43, 45-50, 52-53, 55, 57, 67.
Würzburg; 333, 456, 465, 473, 501, 517.
Wurzen; 283, 322, 329, 336, 339, 353-354, 357, 368, 415, 419, 434.

Yaroshevitsky, Russian artillery lieutenant; 379, 525.
Yermolov, Alexei Petrovich; 142, 159, 171-174, 179, 181, 183, 185-187, 189, 193-194, 196, 213, 369, 390, 524.
Yorck, Johann David Ludwig von; 17-19, 22-23, 25, 27-29, 31, 33-35, 37-38, 42, 45, 47-53, 55-59, 61-65, 243, 245-246, 252-253, 259-260, 312, 315-316, 318-322, 325, 330-331, 369, 393-402, 406-407, 411, 414, 422, 424, 427, 430, 446, 451-453, 455, 458, 461, 476-477, 524-525, 529.
Yuzefovich, Dmitry Mikhailovich; 54, 59, 320, 330, 497.

Zahna; 224-225.
Zallmsdorf; 224-226.
Zakharzhevsky, Yakov Vasilievich; 149, 372.
Zamość; 501, 507.
Zandt, Westphalian general; 292, 296.
Zehista; 110-111, 113, 115, 139, 141-142, 157-159, 171, 173-174, 196, 248, 351, 503.
Zeitz; 288, 340, 342, 344, 367-368, 451, 461.
Zentral Verwaltungs Rat; 14, 457, 480, 482-483.
Zerbst; 242, 262, 311, 332, 508.
Zeschau, Heinrich Wilhelm von; 421, 423, 437, 443, 445.
Ziegelschlag (Dresden); 114, 121, 127, 130, 133-134.
Ziesar; 77, 92, 103.
Zieten, Hans Ernst von; 121, 123, 129-132, 146-147, 203, 209-210, 213, 215, 247-248, 256, 340, 342, 373-374, 384, 386, 389, 411, 416, 425, 431, 458.
Zinnwald; 108, 168, 250, 254, 284.
Zittau; 24-25, 41, 110, 116, 244, 261, 274, 276-278, 281, 284, 309.
Zobten [Sobota]; 22-24, 26, 59-61.
Zörbig; 322, 329-330, 360-361.
Zschertnitz; 129, 148.
Zuckelhausen; 365, 372, 376, 416, 425, 431.
Zutphen; 496, 498.
Zweinaundorf; 414-415, 417, 425, 431, 449.
Zwenkau; 343, 348, 368-369.
Zwickau; 14, 275-276, 287, 339.

From Reason to Revolution – Warfare 1721-1815

http://www.helion.co.uk/series/from-reason-to-revolution-1721-1815.php

The 'From Reason to Revolution' series covers the period of military history 1721–1815, an era in which fortress-based strategy and linear battles gave way to the nation-in-arms and the beginnings of total war.

This era saw the evolution and growth of light troops of all arms, and of increasingly flexible command systems to cope with the growing armies fielded by nations able to mobilise far greater proportions of their manpower than ever before. Many of these developments were fired by the great political upheavals of the era, with revolutions in America and France bringing about social change which in turn fed back into the military sphere as whole nations readied themselves for war. Only in the closing years of the period, as the reactionary powers began to regain the upper hand, did a military synthesis of the best of the old and the new become possible.

The series examines the military and naval history of the period in a greater degree of detail than has hitherto been attempted, and has a very wide brief, with the intention of covering all aspects from the battles, campaigns, logistics, and tactics, to the personalities, armies, uniforms, and equipment.

Submissions

The publishers would be pleased to receive submissions for this series. Please email reasontorevolution@helion.co.uk, or write to Helion & Company Limited, Unit 8 Amherst Business Centre, Budbrooke Road, Warwick, CV34 5WE

You may also be interested in:

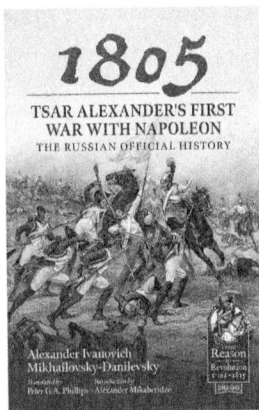
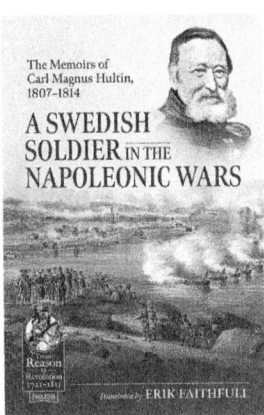
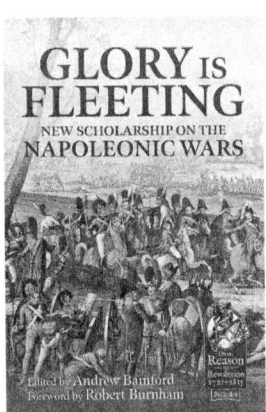
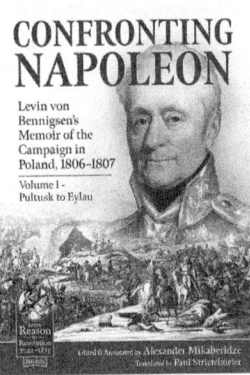
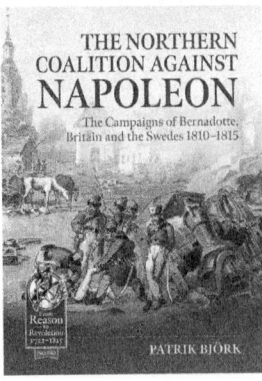